bauhaus
art as life

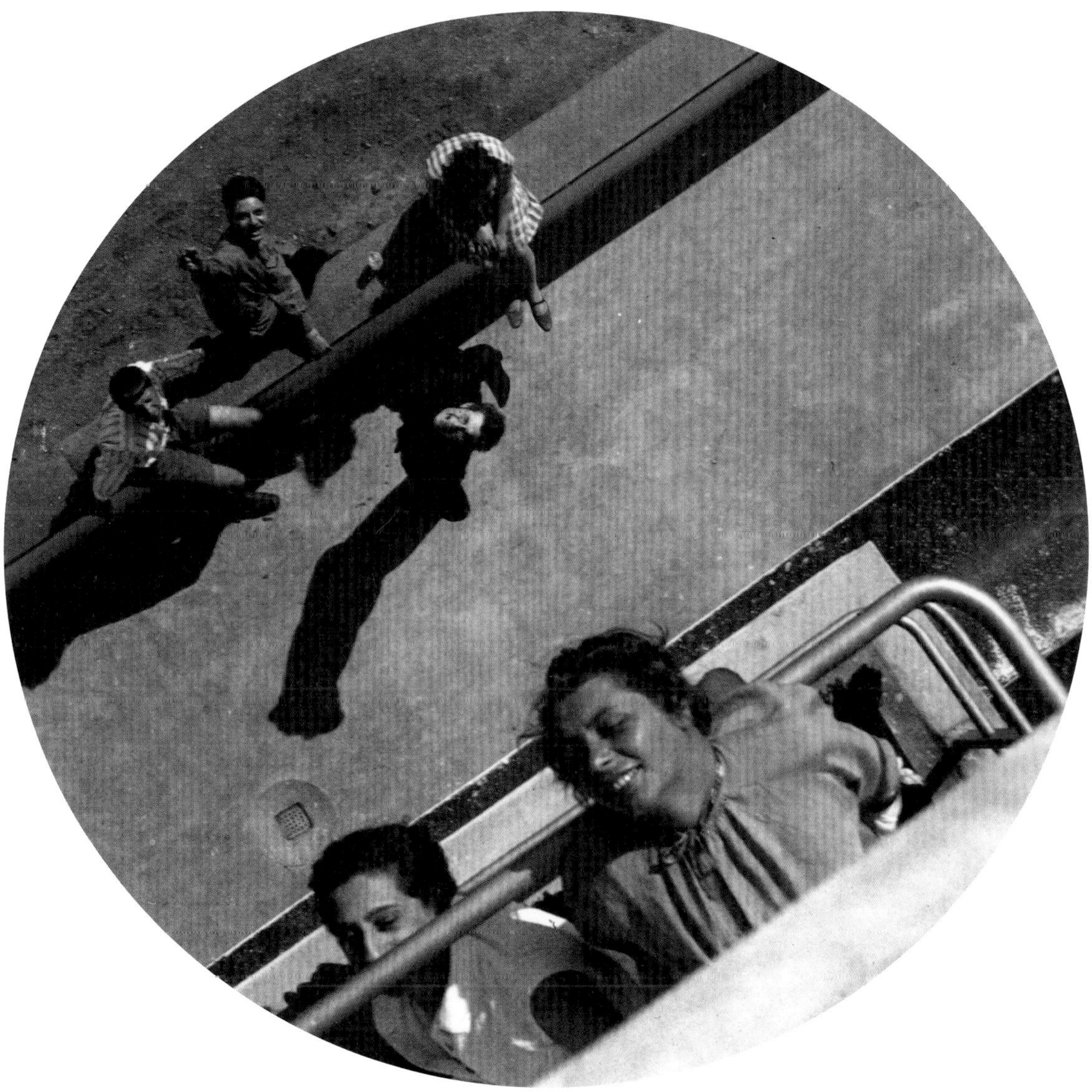

catalogue supported by
ernst von siemens art foundation

bauhaus
art as life

barbican art gallery

koenig books

contents

• reprinted texts

foreword and acknowledgements

The world's most famous art school, the Bauhaus was also a crucible of modernism: an inescapable force in the development of modern visual culture, whose impact was to be felt around the world from Tel Aviv to Tokyo, Moscow to Chicago. The Bauhaus was inspiring not just because of the extraordinary group of brilliant, visionary people who worked and made art there, but because it was fuelled by idealism and a commitment to creativity and experiment that remains, in our market-driven times, ever more relevant.

Bauhaus: Art as Life traces the turbulent, fourteen-year history of the school from its founding by Walter Gropius in Weimar in 1919, and its Expressionist-influenced roots, to the embrace of art and industry and subsequent move to a purpose-built campus in Dessau in 1925 under the direction of Gropius and then Hannes Meyer. Finally, it looks at the Bauhaus's brief period in Berlin, led by Ludwig Mies van der Rohe and its dramatic closure in 1933, under pressure from the National Socialists.

The Bauhaus pioneered a new educational approach. Its founding tenets were indebted to the nineteenth-century Arts and Crafts movement in Britain; Gropius drew inspiration from the social and economic reforms and the emphasis on craftsmanship and unity of the arts that John Ruskin and William Morris espoused a half century earlier. The Bauhaus, however, soon evolved to embrace industrial production and new technologies.

At the Bauhaus, the greatest avant-garde artists and designers from across Europe gathered together to form a school that was built on utopian principles: the belief that art could change and improve the quality of people's lives everywhere, not just the privileged few. The school taught not one thing, but many things: it was multidisciplinary. Students could explore diverse art forms – painting, architecture, textiles, theatre design, film, photography, furniture, graphics – under the tutelage of 'masters' such as Wassily Kandinsky, László Moholy-Nagy and Gropius, who encouraged an experimental, often collaborative approach.

Bauhaus: Art as Life is the biggest and most comprehensive Bauhaus exhibition in the UK for more than forty years – and it is apposite that its home is the Barbican Art Gallery. The Barbican, like the Bauhaus, is committed to producing and presenting not one art form, but many. We are a multidisciplinary venue in which the visual arts, dance, film, music and theatre take place under one roof, sometimes interacting, sometimes colliding and sometimes directly complementing one another. Each art form at the Barbican unfolds in a context designed to encourage learning and access through creativity: again, like the Bauhaus, education is fundamental to our mission.

The Bauhaus also stood for an international spirit in art and life, a spirit shining in the last years before Europe was engulfed by a dark and destructive nationalism. After the National Socialists seized power in Germany, a number of important Bauhauslers took refuge in the UK, including Gropius, Marcel Breuer and Moholy-Nagy. All three were part of the community of artists and intellectuals at Lawn Road Flats in Hampstead and made significant contributions to British culture during their relatively short time here. Gropius, with Maxwell Fry, designed Impington Village College in Cambridgeshire; Breuer's influential plywood furniture for Isokon is still in production today and Moholy-Nagy produced several documentary photographic and film works. But it was Naum Slutzky, a student in the metal workshop in Weimar, who best exemplified the Bauhaus spirit in the UK, teaching at and shaping a number of influential schools, including Dartington Hall in Devon, the Royal College of Art in London and the Birmingham School of Arts and Crafts.

We are delighted to be presenting this exhibition as a key cultural event in the UK this year. As the world gathers in London for the 2012 Olympic Games, *Bauhaus: Art as Life* signals the indelible values of idealism, internationalism, creativity and collaboration. This exhibition would not have been possible without the close cooperation of our partners in

Germany: Bauhaus-Archiv Berlin/Museum für Gestaltung, Stiftung Bauhaus Dessau, and Klassik Stiftung Weimar. We are most grateful to Annemarie Jaeggi, Director, Bauhaus-Archiv Berlin; Philipp Oswalt, Director, Stiftung Bauhaus Dessau and Wolfgang Holler, Director, Klassik Stiftung Weimar for their willingness to share their unparalleled collections. Loans from these institutions account for more than two-thirds of the works in the exhibition and many are presented for the first time in the UK.

Bauhaus: Art as Life is the product of the creativity, scholarship and imagination of a group of talented people at the Barbican and at the Bauhaus institutions. It is co-curated by Barbican curators Catherine Ince and Lydia Yee, who were assisted by a highly dedicated curatorial team, including Leila Hasham, Corinna Gardner and Juliette Desorgues. Jane Alison provided advice and guidance throughout the project. We have been most fortunate to work with colleagues at the Bauhaus institutions who generously shared their expertise, knowledge and time with us. We thank Klaus Weber, Christian Wolsdorff, Antje Möller-Holzhauser, Sibylle Hoiman, Ulrich Weigand, Dina Blauhorn, Sabine Hartmann and Randy Kaufman in Berlin; Torsten Blume, Wolfgang Thöner, Rüdiger Messerschmidt, Ingolf Kern, Andreas Kühnlein, Rhoda Riccius and Dorothea Bethke in Dessau; Ulrike Bestgen, Michael Siebenbrodt, Konrad Katzer, Laura Petzold, Anne Levin, Sabine Breuer and Nicole Mende in Weimar.

The exhibition has been enriched by the incredible generosity of public and private collections in Europe and the US. Our sincere thanks are due to: Nicholas Fox Weber, Brenda Danilowitz and Oliver Barker, The Josef and Anni Albers Foundation, Bethany, Connecticut; Hendrik Berinson and Natalia Kazmierczak, Galerie Berinson, Berlin; Angela Thomas Schmid, Max Bill, Georges Vantongerloo Stiftung, Zumikon, Switzerland; Jonathan Riddale, British Architectural Library, Royal Institute of British Architects, London; Neil MacGregor, Jill Cook, Judy Rudoe and Helen Parkin, British Museum, London; Alfred Pacquement, Quentin Bajac, Françoise Guichon, Angela Lampe, Brigitte Leal, Jonas Storsve and Olga Makhroff, Centre National d'Art et de Culture Georges Pompidou, Paris; Gustavo Grandal Montero, Chelsea College of Art and Design, London; Anke Hahn and Anna Schierse, Deutsche Kinemathek, Museum für Film und Fernsehen, Berlin; Thomas Lenz and Lynette Roth, Harvard Art Museum, Busch-Reisinger Museum, Cambridge, Massachusetts; Rudolf Kicken and Ina Schmidt-Runke, Kicken Gallery, Berlin; Christoph Grunenberg, Anne Buschhoff and Jutta Putschew, Kunsthalle Bremen; Carl-Heinz Heuer and Nicolai von Cube for the Viktor and Marianne Langen Collection; Raimund Stecker, Marion Bornscheuer and Elke Kubisz, Lehmbruck Museum Duisburg; K.F.K. De Belder, Maartje van den Heuvel and Joke Pronk, Prentenkabinet Universiteit Leiden; Thorsten Rodiek, Museen für Kunst und Kulturgeschichte der Hansestadt Lübeck; Cathrin Klingsöhr-Leroy, Franz Marc Museum, Kochel am See, Germany; Arie Hartog and Yvette Deseyve, Gerhard-Marcks-Haus – das Bildhauermuseum im Norden, Bremen; Claude Miglietti and Isabelle Revoire, Musée Cantini, Marseilles; Glenn Lowry, Barry Bergdoll, Paul Galloway, Ann Temkin, Anne Umland, Cora Rosevear, Starr Figura, Katherine Alcauskas, Eva Respini and Dan Leers, The Museum of Modern Art, New York; Florian Hufnagl, Corinna Rösner and Josef Strasser, Die Neue Sammlung – The International Design Museum, Munich; Timothy Rub, Carlos Basualdo, Innis Howe Shoemaker and Shelley Langdale, Philadelphia Museum of Art; Igor Jenzen, Katrin Bäsig and Ines Handel, Staatliche Kunstsammlungen Dresden, Puppentheatersammlung; Anita Hopmans and Wietse Coppes, Rijksbureau voor Kunsthistorische Documentatie, The Hague; C. Raman Schlemmer and Mariah Mazur, Bühnen Archiv Oskar Schlemmer, The Oskar Schlemmer Theatre Estate and Archive, Oggebbio, Italy; Nicholas Serota, Chris Dercon, Caroline Collier, Matthew Gale and Simon Baker, Tate, London; Gerald Köhler, Theaterwissenschaftliche Sammlung Universität zu Köln; Bernhard Post and Dagmar Blaha, Thüringisches Hauptstaatsarchiv Weimar; Martin Roth, Christopher Wilk, Martin Barnes and Abraham Thomas, Victoria and Albert Museum, London; Michael Baumgartner and Edith Heinimann, Zentrum Paul Klee, Bern; and to the following individuals: Paul Sommerfeld, Wulf Herzogenrath and an anonymous private collector.

In addition to our lenders, we thank the following estates and descendants of Bauhaus artists for their advice and enthusiasm: Stephan Consemüller, Estate of Erich Consemüller; Conrad Feininger, Estate of T. Lux Feininger; Ursula Graeff-Hirsch and Bernd Eichhorn, Estate of Werner Graeff; Hattula Moholy-Nagy, The Moholy-Nagy Foundation and Yael Aloni and Monika Stadler, the daughters of Gunta Stölzl.

The exhibition benefited from the knowledge and guidance of a group of scholars: Professor Jeremy Aynsley, Director of Research at the Royal College of Art, London; Anja Baumhoff, Lecturer in the History of Art and Design, Loughborough University; Melissa Trimingham, Senior Lecturer in Drama, University of Kent, and Christopher Wilk, Keeper of Furniture, Textiles and Fashion at the Victoria and Albert Museum, London. A number of other individuals have provided invaluable advice and counsel to the curators:

Achim Borchardt-Hume, Lilly Dubowitz, Cindy Keefer, Emma Lavigne and Achim Moeller.

An undertaking as ambitious as this requires a huge collective effort. We thank Katrina Crookall, Priya Saujani and Hannah Lunt in the art gallery team; Ann Berni and Jess Hookway in media relations; Kate Davis and Rachel Taylor in marketing; Lynette Brooks, Barbara Jobmann, Dan Maggs and Praveen Riat in development; Peter Sutton, Margaret Lily and Bruce Stracy in the production team; Emma Ridgway in creative learning, and Robert Rider and Erica Rodrigues in cinema. A terrific group of interns assisted the curatorial team: Lauren Barnes, Ruth Geddie, Sylwia Krason, Maria Merseburger, Petra Schtirba, Lea Schleiffenbaum and Rachel Walker.

The bold and elegant design for the exhibition, which draws inspiration from the Bauhaus's print and wall-painting workshops, is the work of the architects Carmody Groarke in collaboration with graphic designers A Practice for Everyday Life who also designed this book. The scholars and historians who contributed essays to this publication offer illuminating insight into the Bauhaus and the work and life of the school. We thank Anja Baumhoff, Torsten Blume, Éva Forgács, Kathleen James-Chakraborty, Philipp Oswalt, Michael Siebenbrodt, Wolfgang Thöner, Melissa Trimingham, Philip Ursprung, Klaus Weber and Nicholas Fox Weber. Elizabeth Volk translated the essays from the German Bauhaus institutions into English and Melissa Larner has done a terrific job editing the texts of this diverse group of authors. This publication would not have been possible without the generous support of the Ernst von Siemens Art Foundation. Our special thanks to Professor Dr Joachim Fischer, Ernst von Siemens Kunststiftung.

Key supporters have helped make this exhibition possible. We are enormously grateful to the following funders: tp bennett, The Swiss Arts Council Pro Helvetia, The Stanley Thomas Johnson Foundation and The Henry Moore Foundation and to our media partner Wallpaper*. Government indemnity cover for the exhibition has been provided by the Department of Culture, Media and Sport and administered by the Arts Council England.

Lastly, we acknowledge the tremendous achievement of all the Bauhauslers. Their work and ongoing legacy continue to shape the way in which we experience art and life today.

kate bush
head of art galleries
barbican centre

preface

Despite its relatively short lifetime, the Bauhaus has come to stand for classical modernism like no other institution. Founded by the architect Walter Gropius in Weimar in 1919, moving from there to Dessau in 1925 and then to Berlin in 1932, where it was ultimately closed in 1933, it is regarded today as the most important and influential art school of the twentieth century. The Bauhaus was an eminently international project, a nodal point in the worldwide network of the avant garde. It gathered together protagonists from extremely diverse backgrounds, with the goal of jointly striking out on new paths in the fields of art, design and architecture, but above all, in order to educate and train a new type of artist who could bring about changes in society by shaping his or her living environment. Prominent foreign Bauhaus masters include the Swiss citizens Johannes Itten, Paul Klee and Hannes Meyer, the Russian Wassily Kandinsky, the Austrian Herbert Bayer, the Hungarians Marcel Breuer and László Moholy-Nagy and the Dutchman Mart Stam. But Bauhaus internationalism also manifested itself in the composition of the student body. The proportion of twenty percent foreign students was considerably higher than at other German art schools. Young people came from all over Europe, some of them even from faraway countries such as Japan or the US, to be a part of the social and artistic experiment of the Bauhaus. In a reaction to the traumatic experiences of World War I, it was a founding principle of the Bauhaus to overcome nationalism and establish an interconnected world society. In keeping with the ideas of the Enlightenment, a principle of equality was to prevail that was based on the idea of the New Man. In order to gain worldwide acceptance for this claim, the Bauhaus searched for universally valid principles and means of communication. Global languages and forms of typography were conceived, which could be applied internationally.

London in the summer of 2012 is an ideal time and place to stage a Bauhaus exhibition. It coincides with the Olympic Games, which, like no other global event, strives to pool the synergetic forces of the world community. In accordance with the ideal of promoting international understanding, in 1880 the Frenchman Pierre de Coubertin proposed the idea of reviving the antique Olympic spirit by bringing together athletes from all over the world. In 2012, for the third time, London will be holding the summer Olympic Games, bringing together the youth of the world for a peaceful sports competition with 302 events in twenty-six different disciplines.

The first major Bauhaus exhibition in the UK took place in 1968 at the Royal Academy in London. This was the second venue for the touring exhibition, *50 years Bauhaus*, which began in Stuttgart before it came to London, and continued on to Amsterdam, Paris, Chicago, Toronto, Los Angeles, Buenos Aires and Tokyo. This show, which established the Bauhaus's reputation on an international level, was initiated by the art historian Ludwig Grote and organised by the Württembergischer Kunstverein in collaboration with the Bauhaus-Archiv. Initially founded in Darmstadt only a few years earlier in 1960 at the suggestion of Gropius, the Bauhaus-Archiv viewed it as its task to establish contact with as many former masters and students as possible, and to function as a central institution for Bauhaus research. Owing to the generous support of many Bauhauslers, who responded positively to Gropius's appeal, with Gropius himself setting an example, a comprehensive collection was built up. It was also the former Bauhauslers – again Gropius, but above all, Herbert Bayer – who played a major role in the anniversary exhibition of 1968.

Due to the division of Germany, as well as the Cold War, which also created an icy climate in terms of cultural politics back in 1968, a joint organisation of *50 years Bauhaus* with the museums in East Germany was inconceivable – although in the GDR during the course of the 1960s, there had been a change in the way in which the Bauhaus was viewed. Whereas initially a hostile attitude prevailed at the official level, with the Bauhaus being branded as formalistic and bourgeois, later there was an increasing appreciation of the school in the GDR, which then declared it as part of the national heritage. The first exhibitions took place both in Weimar and in Dessau, beginning in 1963. Weimar had already begun, during the Bauhaus period, a Gropius-initiated collection of works from the school. This was plundered during the Nazi 'degenerate art' actions, however, and painful losses were suffered, above all with respect to the collection of paintings – works by Klee, Kandinsky, Moholy-Nagy, Lyonel Feininger and Oskar Schlemmer. In Dessau too, a collection of, for the most part, visual arts had begun in 1927, under Ludwig Grote, the Director of the Anhaltische Gemäldegalerie in Dessau, but this was almost completely liquidated in 1932 after the Nazi election victory. It was not until 1976, when the Bauhaus building, heavily damaged during the war, was restored to its original state to mark its fiftieth anniversary, which also coincided with the founding of the Wissenschaftlich-Kulturelles Zentrum Bauhaus (Bauhaus Centre for Science and Culture), that Dessau was again in a position to begin collecting systematically.

Whereas the first major Bauhaus exhibition in England in 1968 was based in large part on the collections of the Bauhaus-Archiv, the situation in 2012 is completely different. German Reunification in 1990 afforded the three Bauhaus institutions – the Bauhaus-Archiv/Museum für Gestaltung Berlin, the Stiftung Bauhaus Dessau and the Klassik Stiftung Weimar – the possibility to organise projects together. But even before the turn of political events in 1989, a remarkable cooperation between East and West had already begun that demonstrated at the political level the significance of the Bauhaus for the two Germanys: in 1988, as part of the agreement on cultural exchange between East and West, the Bauhaus-Archiv was invited to show an exhibition at the Bauhaus in Dessau called *Experiment Bauhaus*. In 2000, the Design Museum, London, and the Stiftung Bauhaus Dessau, with the support of the Bauhaus-Archiv Berlin, presented the important exhibition *bauhaus dessau* in London. Today, the cooperation between these independently operating institutions is an everyday occurrence, laid down and regulated in a contract agreement. For this exhibition, *Bauhaus: Art as Life*, we have joined forces to loan around seventy percent of the works on display.

Curated and organised by the Barbican Art Gallery in London, this exhibition breaks with the widespread notion that confines the Bauhaus to a functional style in architecture and design. By contrast, it emphasises the social aspirations and plurality of the Bauhaus and the Bauhauslers by highlighting the diversity of their design creations and the significance of their living and working together. Three of the most prominent – Gropius, architect and designer Marcel Breuer, whose furniture designs became the epitome of functional design, as well as the versatile Constructivist and later founding director of the New Bauhaus in Chicago, Moholy-Nagy – left Nazi Germany for London. Lesser-known Bauhauslers at the time, such as George A. Adams-Teltscher, Werner Jackson, Margaret Leischner, Heinz Loew, Lucia Moholy, Franz Singer and Naum Slutzky, also found refuge in the UK.

As was the case with the Bauhaus, the success of the exhibition *Bauhaus: Art as Life* is founded on international exchange and cooperation. The three German Bauhaus institutions express their gratitude to the Barbican Art Gallery for showing such dedication to and enthusiasm for the Bauhaus theme, as well as for making the exhibition possible. As a result, during the Olympic summer 2012, the interest not only of the British public, but also of a global audience, will be directed towards this visionary school of art.

dr annemarie jaeggi
bauhaus-archiv berlin

prof. philipp oswalt
stiftung bauhaus dessau

prof. dr wolfgang holler
klassik stiftung weimar

1
Hannes Meyer
Back cover of the brochure *Bauhaus*, 1929
Photograph by Andreas Feininger
Letterpress on paper
14.8 × 21 cm
Bauhaus-Archiv Berlin

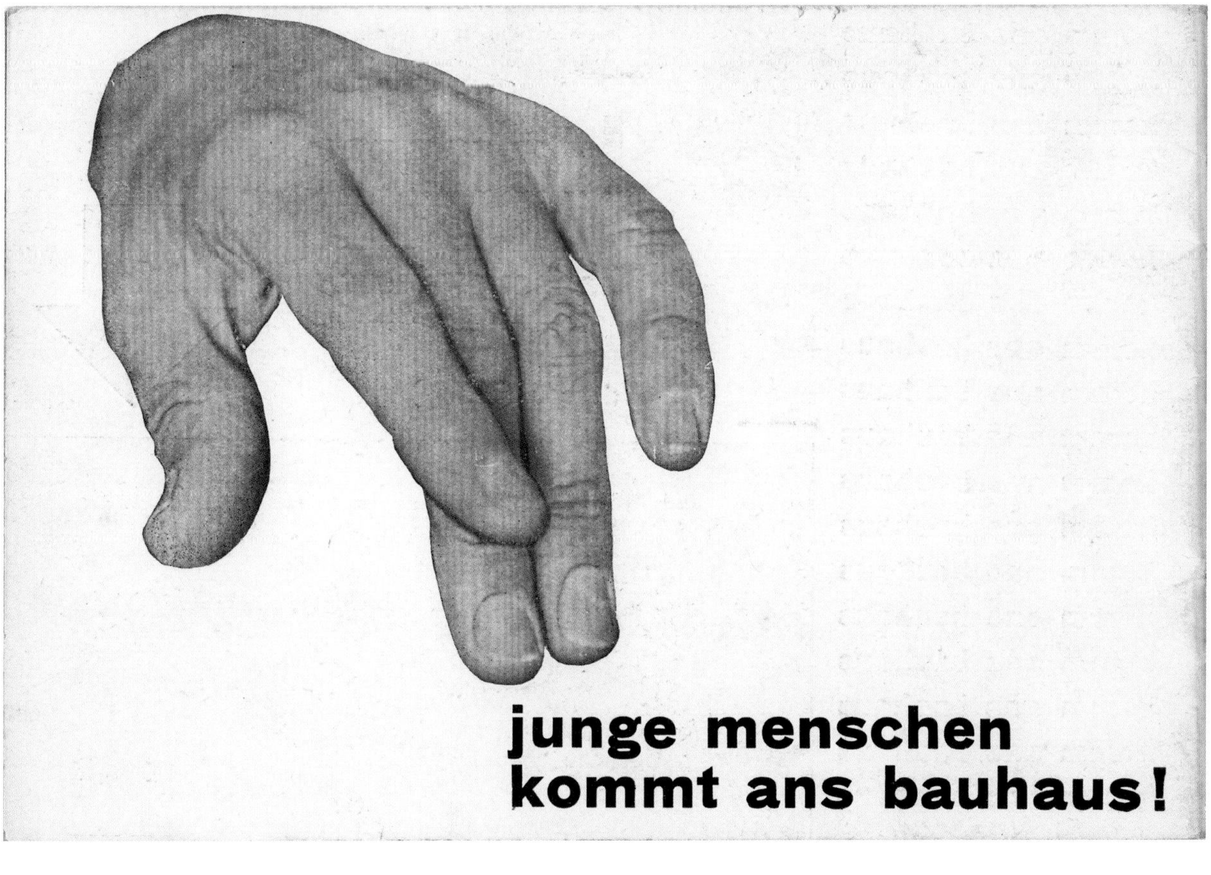

new beginnings

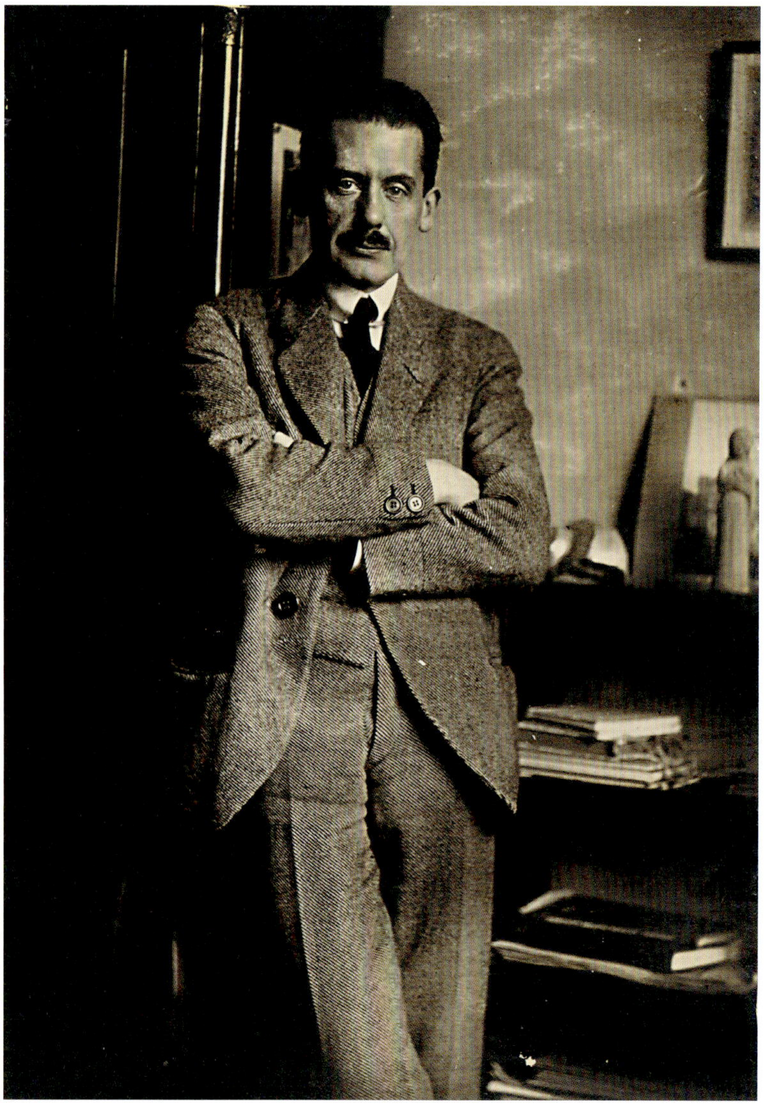

In 1919, architect Walter Gropius was appointed to head a new art school formed from the merger of the Grand-Ducal Saxon Academy of Fine Arts and the Grand-Ducal Saxon School of Arts and Crafts in the city of Weimar. Germany was in the midst of a period of political turmoil and social upheaval as it emerged from World War I and a new parliamentary democracy, known as the Weimar Republic, replaced the old imperial government. The new institution was founded with a mix of romantic socialist and utopian aspirations. Gropius's approach to arts and crafts teaching grew out of late nineteenth- and early twentieth-century efforts to reform art school education in the wake of industrialisation and was directly influenced by the writings of architects Bruno Taut and Otto Bartning, who along with Gropius were part of the Arbeitsrat für Kunst, a union of artists and intellectuals that sought to dissolve the barriers between art and the people.

Gropius called the school Staatliches Bauhaus Weimar. Although its name State Bauhaus signified a break with the past, the school inherited much from its more conventional predecessors. The Bauhaus moved into the adjacent buildings of the Academy of Fine Arts and School of Arts and Crafts, designed by Henry van de Velde, who had been director of the latter until it closed in 1915. Gropius employed former faculty from both schools, made use of their facilities and equipment, adopted aspects of the School of Arts and Crafts' workshop structure and made training in the crafts central to the Bauhaus curriculum.

Gropius's first new appointments to the faculty – Lyonel Feininger, Johannes Itten and Gerhard Marcks – were drawn from German Expressionist circles and the Deutscher Werkbund, a German federation of architects, artists, designers and industrialists. In order to attract new students, he published the pamphlet *Programme of the Staatliche Bauhaus in Weimar*. Written in the urgent language of a manifesto, it called for artists to return to crafts and work together towards the aim of building, as in the medieval guilds. It also sought to give equal status to artist and craftsman and advocated contacts between craft and industry. Feininger's Expressionist woodcut, *Cathedral* – depicting a cathedral with three steeples, each topped by a radiating star – served as the cover design.

By the 1919–20 winter semester, the Bauhaus increased enrolment by fifty percent to 245 students from across Germany. Hinnerk Scheper and Gunta Stölzl were among the new recruits.

2
Portrait of Walter Gropius at the Staatliches Bauhaus Weimar, 1921
Bauhaus-Archiv Berlin
Photographer unknown

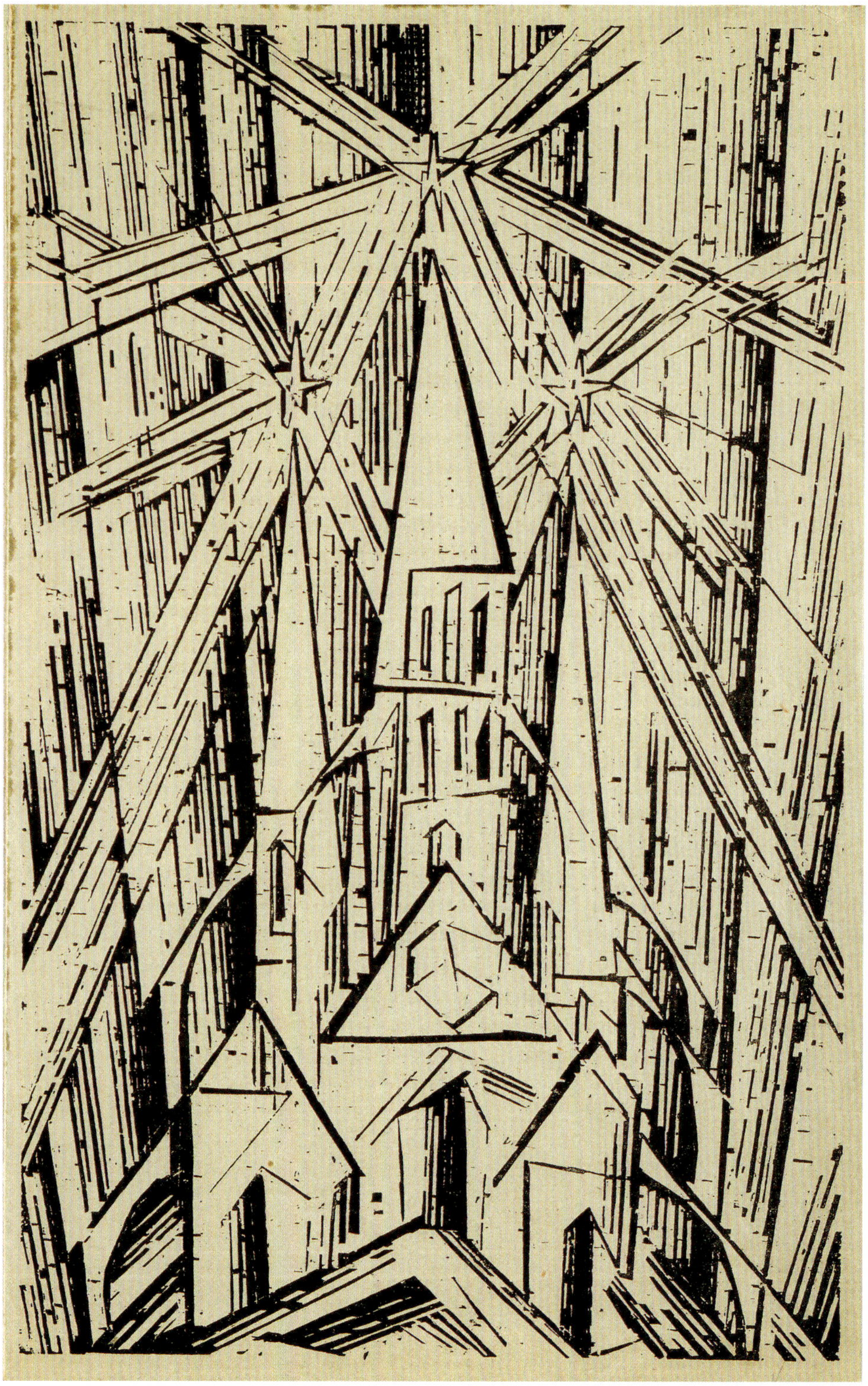

3
Lyonel Feininger
Cathedral for the *Programme of the Staatliche Bauhaus in Weimar*, 1919
Letterpress printing on paper, zinc etching after original woodcut for the cover illustration
31.8 × 19.7 cm
Bauhaus-Archiv Berlin

walter gropius
programme of the staatliche bauhaus in weimar

The ultimate aim of all visual arts is the complete building! To embellish buildings was once the noblest function of the fine arts; they were the indispensable components of great architecture. Today the arts exist in isolation, from which they can be rescued only through the conscious, cooperative effort of all craftsman. Architects, painters, and sculptors must recognise anew and learn to grasp the composite character of a building both as an entity and in its separate parts. Only then will their work be imbued with the architectonic spirit which it has lost as 'salon art.'

The old schools of art were unable to produce this unity; how could they, since art cannot be taught. They must be merged once more with the workshop. The mere drawing and painting world of the pattern designer and the applied artist must become a world that builds again. When young people who take a joy in artistic creation once more begin their life's work by learning a trade, then the unproductive 'artist' will no longer be condemned to deficient artistry, for their skill will now be preserved for the crafts, in which they will be able to achieve excellence.

Architects, sculptors, painters, we all must return to the crafts! For art is not a 'profession.' There is no essential difference between the artist and the craftsman. The artist is an exalted craftsman. In rare moments of inspiration, transcending the consciousness of his will, the grace of heaven may cause his work to blossom into art. But proficiency in a craft is essential to every artist. Therein lies the prime source of creative imagination. Let us then create a new guild of craftsman without the class distinctions that raise an arrogant barrier between craftsman and artist! Together let us desire, conceive, and create the new structure of the future, which will embrace architecture and sculpture and painting in one unity and which will one day rise toward heaven from the hands of a million workers like the crystal symbol of a new faith.

walter gropius

programme of the staatliche bauhaus in weimar

The Staatliche Bauhaus resulted from the merger of the former Grand-Ducal Saxon Academy of Fine Arts with the former Grand-Ducal Saxon School of Arts and Crafts in conjunction with a newly affiliated department of architecture.

aims of the bauhaus

The Bauhaus strives to bring together all creative effort into one whole, to reunify all the disciplines of practical art – sculpture, painting, handcrafts, and the crafts – as inseparable components of a new architecture. The ultimate, if distant, aim of the Bauhaus is the unified work of art – the great structure – in which there is no distinction between monumental and decorative art.

The Bauhaus wants to educate architects, painters, and sculptors of all levels, according to their capabilities, to become competent craftsmen or independent creative artists and to form a working community of leading and future artist-craftsmen. These men, of kindred spirit, will know how to design buildings harmoniously in their entirety – structure, finishing, ornamentation, and furnishing.

principles of the bauhaus

Art rises above all methods; in itself it cannot be taught, but the crafts certainly can be. Architects, painters, and sculptors are craftsmen in the true sense of the word; hence, a thorough training in the crafts, acquired in workshops and in experimental and practical sites, is required of all students as the indispensable basis for all artistic production. Our own workshops are to be gradually built up, and apprenticeship agreements with outside workshops will be concluded.

• The school is the servant of the workshop, and will one day be absorbed in it.
• Therefore there will be no teachers or pupils in the Bauhaus but masters, journeymen, and apprentices.
• The manner of teaching arises from the character of the workshop:
• Organic forms developed from manual skills.
• Avoidance of all rigidity; priority of creativity; freedom of individuality, but strict study discipline.
• Master and journeymen examinations, according to the Guild Statutes, held before the Council of Masters of the Bauhaus or before outside masters.
• Collaboration by the students in the work of the masters.
• Securing of commissions, also for students.
• Mutual planning of extensive, Utopian structural designs – public buildings and buildings for worship – aimed at the future. Collaboration of all masters and students – architects, painters, sculptors – on these designs with the object of gradually achieving a harmony of all the component elements and parts that make up architecture.
• Constant contact with the leaders of the crafts and industries of the country.
• Contact with public life, with the people, through exhibitions, to solve the problem of displaying visual work and sculpture within the framework of architecture.
• Encouragement of friendly relations between masters and students outside of work; therefore plays, lectures, poetry, music, costume parties. Establishment of a cheerful ceremonial at these gatherings.

range of instruction

Instruction at the Bauhaus includes all practical and scientific areas of creative work.
a. architecture,
b. painting,
c. sculpture
including all branches of the crafts.
Students are trained in craft (**1**) as well as in drawing and painting (**2**) and science and theory (**3**).

1 Craft training – either in our own, gradually enlarging workshops or in outside workshops to which the student is bound by apprenticeship agreement – includes:
a) sculptors, stonemasons, stucco workers, woodcarvers, ceramic workers, plaster casters,
b) blacksmiths, locksmiths, founders, metal turners,
c) cabinetmakers,
d) painter and decorators, glass painters, mosaic workers, enamelers,
e) etchers, wood engravers, lithographers, art printers, enchasers,
f) weavers.
Craft training forms the basis of all teaching at the Bauhaus. Every student must learn a craft.

2 Training in drawing and painting includes:
a) free-hand sketching from memory and imagination,
b) drawing and painting of heads, live models, and animals,
c) drawing and painting of landscapes, figures, plants, and still lifes,
d) composition,
e) execution of murals, panel pictures, and religious shrines,
f) design of ornaments,
g) lettering,
h) construction and projection drawing,
i) design of exteriors, gardens, and interiors,
j) design of furniture and practical articles.

3 Training in science and theory includes:
a) art history – not presented in the sense of a history of styles, but rather to further active understanding of historical working methods and techniques,
b) science of materials,
c) anatomy – from the living model,
d) physical and chemical theory of colour,
e) rational painting methods,
f) basic concepts of bookkeeping, contract negotiations, personnel,
g) individual lectures on subjects of general interest in all areas of art and science.

divisions of instruction

The training is divided into three courses of instruction:
i. course for apprentices,
ii. course for journeymen,
iii. course for junior masters.
The instruction of the individual is left to the discretion of each master within the framework of the general programme and the work schedule, which is revised every semester. In order to give the students as versatile and comprehensive a technical and artistic training as possible, the work schedule will be so arranged that every architect, painter and sculptor-to-be is able to participate in part of the other courses.

admission

Any person of good repute, without regard to age or sex, whose previous education is deemed adequate by the Council of Masters, will be admitted, as far as space permits. The tuition fee is 180 marks per year (It will gradually disappear entirely with increasing earnings of the Bauhaus). A nonrecurring admission fee of 20 marks is also to be paid. Foreign students pay double fees. Address inquiries to the Secretariat of the Staatliche Bauhaus in Weimar.

Published by the Staatliche Bauhaus Weimar, April 1919

between revolution and reform: the bauhaus in context 1919–23

kathleen james-chakraborty

The Bauhaus was officially founded on 1 April 1919, less than five months after the November Revolution toppled Germany's emperor, kings, and all its other hereditary rulers, and just over two months after the Sparticist uprising, a final attempt to impose Communism, was quelled in Berlin. The school was established in Weimar, where the constitution of the new republic was being drafted. Both of these fragile experiments collapsed within weeks of one another in 1933 as National Socialism suppressed most experimental art and all democratic politics. The Bauhaus would come to be associated with an apparently objective approach to art, an abstraction intended to be as rational as the assembly lines that produced Model T Fords, but it began in the kind of emotional ferment common to all revolutions. In consequence, the twentieth century's most innovative and influential school of art and design has always been linked with substantive political and social change.

The relentless focus on the break that the First World War and the November Revolution made with the immediate past has overshadowed the degree to which Walter Gropius, the Bauhaus's founding director, located a middle ground between the reforms underway since the first years of the new century and more comprehensive challenges to the artistic and architectural status quo. During the school's first four years, the fledgling institution built upon the precedents established by Henry van de Velde, the Deutscher Werkbund and Expressionism, while avoiding the extremes represented by Dada and Surrealism.

The ties to revolutionary politics were real, if often exaggerated. Gropius was, with fellow architect Bruno Taut and architectural critic Adolf Behne, one of the founders of the Arbeitsrat für Kunst. A workers' council established in November 1918 along the lines adopted by many trade unions but intended for artists, it unsuccessfully lobbied the new Social Democratic president Friedrich Ebert, who was pre-occupied with establishing political control in the face of often violent opposition from both the far left and the far right. In declaring that 'art and people must form a unity', its initial manifesto set the tone that Gropius would take less than six months later in the Bauhaus manifesto, when he concluded with a vision of 'the new structure of the future, which will embrace architecture and sculpture and painting in one unity and which will one day rise towards heaven from the hands of a million workers like the crystal symbol of a new faith'.[1] In late 1919 and throughout 1920, Gropius was also active in the Crystal Chain, a group of architects who corresponded with regard to their aspirations for a utopian architecture. Nonetheless, Gropius, like many German intellectuals, remained wary of party politics. He wrote to Behne in 1920, 'We must destroy the [political] parties. I want to found an unpolitical community here.'[2]

Gropius's engagement in the Arbeitsrat and the Crystal Chain helped tie the early Bauhaus to Expressionism, a movement in German art and literature launched in the last years before the war. Expressionism's capacity to capture emotional anguish and depict violently altered forms, as well as the emphasis that many of its practitioners – who included poets and playwrights in addition to painters and architects – placed on spiritual renewal, proved particularly suited to post-war conditions in a defeated country wracked by political strife and economic uncertainty. Gropius only became an adherent after fighting at the front, an experience that encouraged many members of his generation to espouse new forms of cultural expression. A number of the early Bauhaus faculty were Expressionist painters. With Lyonel Feininger, hired in 1919, Georg Muche in 1920, Paul Klee in 1920, and Wassily Kandinsky in 1922, the school acquired an increasingly impressive array of artists. By far the most celebrated at the time was Kandinsky. A Russian who returned to his native country from 1914 to 1921 because of the war, he had trained in Munich, where he belonged to the Expressionist group *Der Blau Reiter* (The Blue Rider), authored *Concerning the Spiritual in Art* (1911), a major theoretical treatise that was quickly translated into English, and painted some of the first entirely abstract works. By the time he arrived in Weimar, however, Kandinsky's work had changed dramatically. His sojourn in Moscow brought him into contact with the Constructivists and thus with the geometrical abstraction that he would espouse for the rest of his career.

Although the Weimar bourgeoisie, who scoffed at the eccentric wardrobes of early Bauhaus students, would never have wanted to concede the point, Expressionism was hardly the most controversial choice available to them. Indeed, by the mid-1920s, when the Bauhaus had moved on to the crisp, machine-edged geometry for which it remains best known, expressionist-tinged office buildings and churches would be seen as the conventional alternative to it. That Surrealism remained outside the Bauhaus's cone of vision is hardly surprising considering its French origins. The disruptive activities of Dada, however, which challenged conventional definitions of the work of art, were enlivening the Berlin gallery scene. Rather than focusing on unity between art and the people or between the arts, Raoul Hausmann, the Dada provacateur, simply declared, 'Art no longer exists! It is dead!'[3] The distance maintained by the early Bauhaus from Dada indicates the limits of its adventurousness.

Even in 1919, Gropius oscillated between advocating pragmatic ties to industry and utopian Expressionist visions. In a speech to the industrialists that he hoped would help fund the school, he struck several different notes. First, he emphasised the importance of an economic use of raw materials and the quality of handwork, and yet he also conveyed a utopian vision. In language tinged with Expressionist ardour, he next established the status of art, which he distinguished from the purpose of the Bauhaus. 'Art is holy', he declared. 'It is seldom without a function, but it strays far from the simplest path, and is born and understood in the highest state of ecstasy.'[4] He contrasted this with the importance of well-made, simple and useful objects in daily life.

Indeed, the Bauhaus was more tightly bound to late Wilhelmine reform efforts than either its early proponents or its detractors usually cared to admit.[5] While Gropius's post-war adoption of Expressionism marked a break with his earlier focus on industrial architecture, it chimed with the work of fellow Arbeitsrat founder Taut. Taut's Glass House at the Werkbund Exhibition held in Cologne in 1914 incorporated stained glass by leading Expressionist painters, as well as displaying a faith in the redemptive power of crystalline forms already espoused in the first years of the century by Peter Behrens, the artist and architect who was in the early years of the twentieth century Germany's leading industrial designer and for whom Gropius worked from 1908 to 1910. Founded in 1906, the Werkbund brought together designers, architects, critics and industrialists in an effort to make industrialisation less corrosive of culture and at the same time ensure that German goods were more competitive internationally. Both goals were to be achieved by paying more attention to the design of manufactured goods, their advertising, and the environments in which they were produced and sold.

The concerns that prompted the founding of the Werkbund also underlay early twentieth-century changes in German design pedagogy. Many of these were encouraged, if not always instigated, by Hermann Muthesius, an architect and former German cultural attaché in London, who upheld British Arts and Crafts architecture as a model. From his position in the Prussian Trade Ministry, he encouraged fellow Werkbund leaders such as Behrens and Van de Velde in their efforts to develop new means of training designers.

The workshop instruction that was a hallmark of Bauhaus education was an approach originally championed by Muthesius and adopted by Van de Velde at the Grand-Ducal Saxon School of Arts and Crafts, the predecessor to the Bauhaus. Although the Bauhaus inherited several crafts masters, along with workshops, from the School of Arts and Crafts, neither Van de Velde nor Muthesius anticipated that the workshops would be paired with instruction by the likes of Feininger, Klee and Kandinsky. These artists proved able from the beginning to challenge students to think about form and colour in far more adventurous ways than had any of their Wilhelmine predecessors. Even though one of the original impetuses for Kandinsky's abstraction had been Jugendstil, the German term for Art Nouveau, Van de Velde never envisioned the transfer of decorative patterns to easel paintings.

Van de Velde, who laid much of the groundwork for his successor, recommended Gropius as a possible candidate for the position. His contribution radiated out from the modestly successful Grand-Ducal Saxon School of Arts and Crafts, founded in 1908, whose buildings (along with those of the neighbouring Grand-Ducal Saxon Academy of Fine Arts (fig. 4), which would also be occupied by the Bauhaus), he designed in an understated style that definitively broke with the academic classicism customarily employed for such commissions. The court of Wilhelm Ernst, Grand Duke of Saxe-Weimar-Eisenach, who ruled from 1901 to 1918, was relatively stuffy, and the Grand Duke did not consistently support new directions in art and architecture. Nonetheless, during his reign,

Weimar retained much of the reputation for cultural accomplishment and experimentation established in the late eighteenth and early nineteenth centuries. At this time, it had been the home of both the poet Johann Wolfgang von Goethe, who moved there in 1775, and the playwright Friedrich Schiller, who joined him there in 1787. Van de Velde's design of the interior of the Nietzsche Archive in Weimar as well as of a number of suburban residences, including his own 'Hohe Pappeln', ensured that Weimar was a showcase for the architectural reforms that flourished across Germany in the early twentieth century. This was the case even though his most ambitious projects, including that for a theatre for Louise Dumont and a Nietzsche Memorial, remained unbuilt.

The biggest challenge facing the school was funding. Gropius struggled, not always successfully, to secure an adequate budget from the government of Thuringia, a state much bigger and more democratically governed than the former Grand Duchy of Saxe-Weimar-Eisenach, and – with far fewer results – from local and national industrialists. This effort required him to balance bold new artistic directions shrewdly, with respectful nods towards the pre-war establishment. He was able to reach out for support to national luminaries, such as Wilhelm von Bode, the eminently respectable director of the Berlin museums, in order to deflect criticism from local dignitaries like Elisabeth Förster-Nietzsche, the philosopher's sister, who commented in a letter to Van de Velde , 'Everyone looks back on the years that you were here as a golden time, and all of the craftspeople', before concluding that Gropius had destroyed everything Van de Velde had accomplished.[6] He lobbied extensively when, in a controversy widely reported in the national press, the faculty of the former Academy of Fine Arts, whom he described as 'a small clique of old established art mummies' successfully seceded from the new school.[7] Launching Germany's first combined school of fine arts and design in the teeth of enormous economic and political challenges required tact as well as vision. Especially before 1923, but even afterwards, the Bauhaus was Janus-faced, building upon substantial pre-war achievements as well as forging its own independent way.

1 As published in translation in Rose-Carol Washton Long (ed.), *German Expressionism: Documents from the End of the Wilhelmine Era to the Rise of National Socialism*, University of California Press, Berkeley, 1993, pp.193, 248.

2 Walter Gropius, letter to Adolf Behne, 31 January 1920, in Volker Wahl (ed.), *Das Staatliche Bauhaus in Weimar: Dokumente zur Geschichte des Instituts 1919–1926*, Böhlau Verlag, Cologne, 2009, p.514.

3 Raoul Hausmann, 'The German Philistine Gets Upset', published in translation in Anton Kaes, Martin Jay and Edward Dimendberg (eds), *The Weimar Republic Sourcebook*, University of California Press, Berkeley, 1994, p.482.

4 Walter Gropius, speech to industrialists and handworkers, 28 June 1919, in Wahl, *Das Staatliche Bauhaus in Weimar*, op, cit., p.246.

5 John Maciuika, *Before the Bauhaus: Architecture, Politics and the German State, 1890–1920*, Cambridge University Press, Cambridge, 2005, and Frederic J. Schwarz, *The Werkbund: Design Theory and Mass Culture before the First World War*, Yale University Press, New Haven, 1996.

6 Elisabeth Förster-Nietzsche, letter to Henry van de Velde, 6 July 1921, FSX 403/34, Henry van de Velde Archives, Archives & Musée de la Littérature, Bibliothèque Royale Albert Premier, Brussels.

7 Walter Gropius, letter to Walter Müller-Wulckow, 15 January 1920, in Wahl, *Das Staatliche Bauhaus in Weimar*, op, cit., p.518.

4
Louis Held
Grand-Ducal Saxon Academy of Fine Arts
by Henry van de Velde, c. 1909
Bauhaus-Archiv Berlin

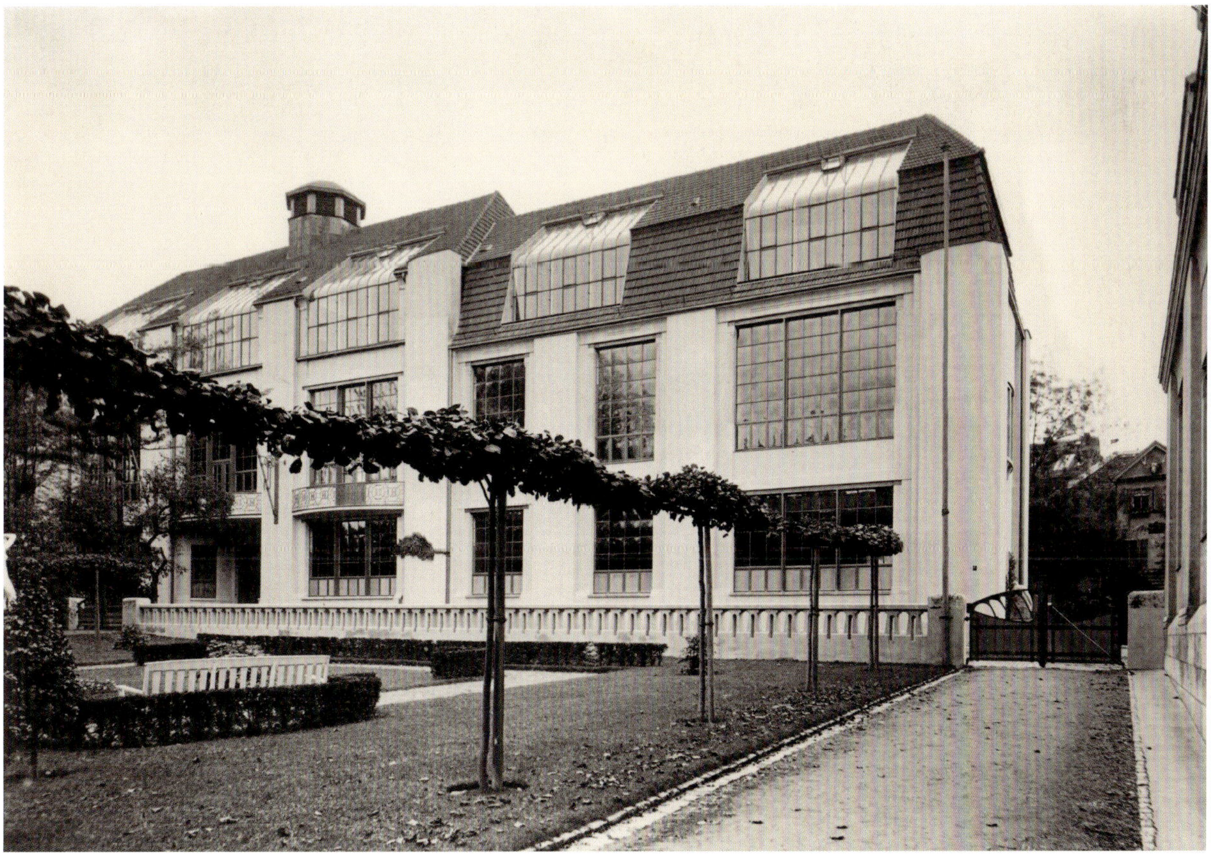

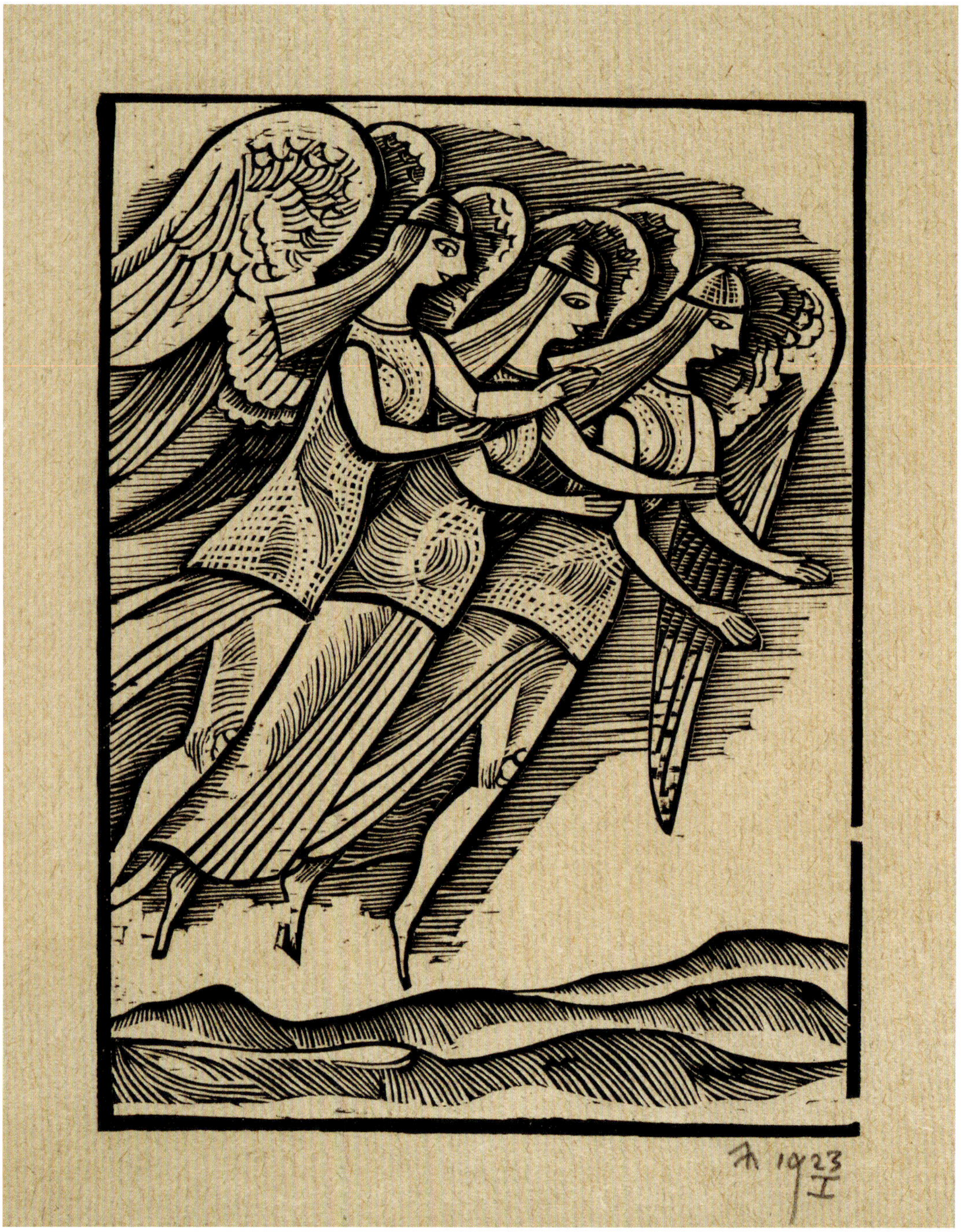
1923
I

5
Gerhard Marcks
The Three Valkyries, plate I of *Das Wielandslied der älteren Edda* (*The Wieland Saga of the Elder Edda*), 1923
Portfolio of ten prints, woodcut on brown paper
19.8 × 14.3 cm
Stiftung Bauhaus Dessau

6
Gerhard Marcks, with painting by Alfred Partikel
Small Altar, 1920
Paint and gold leaf on wood
40.5 × 42.5 × 8 cm
Gerhard-Marcks-Stiftung, Bremen

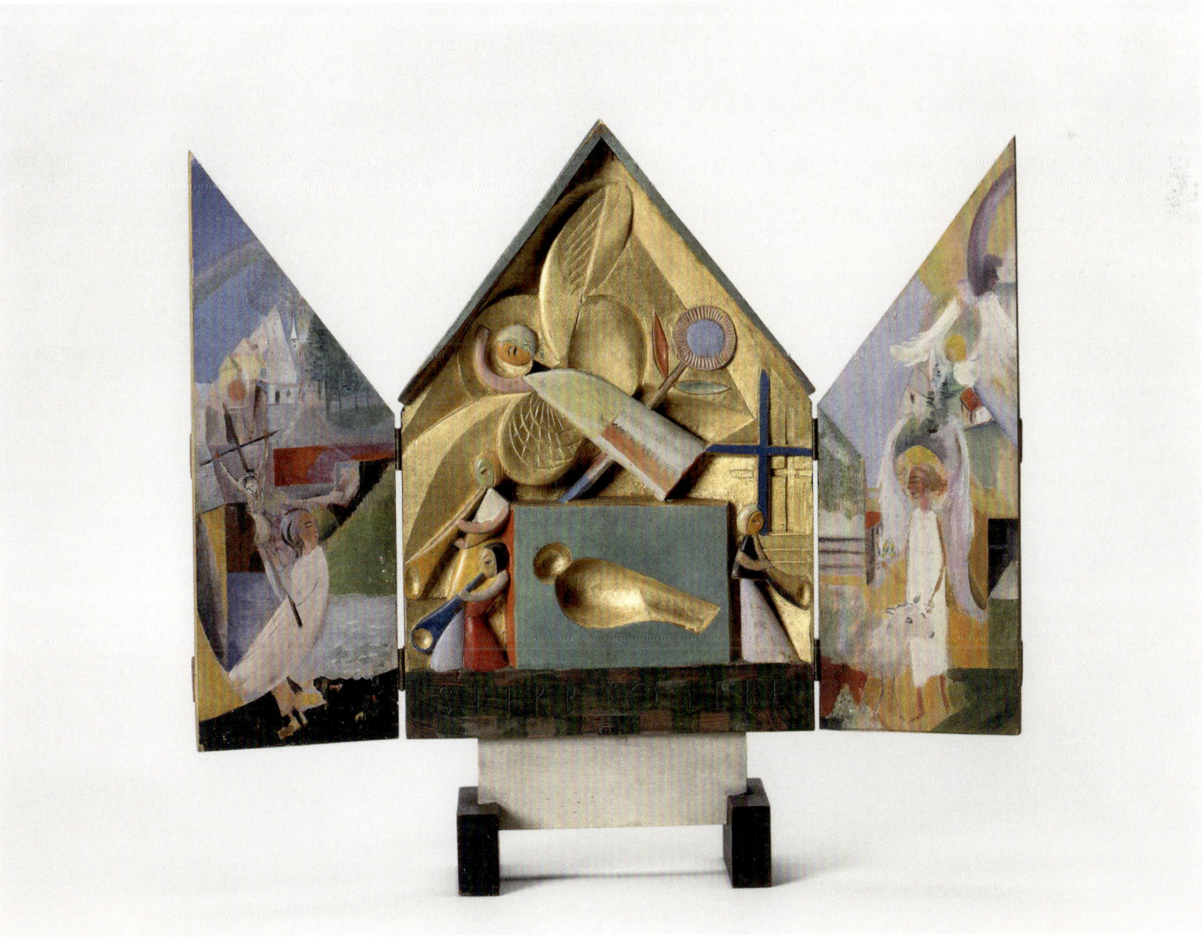

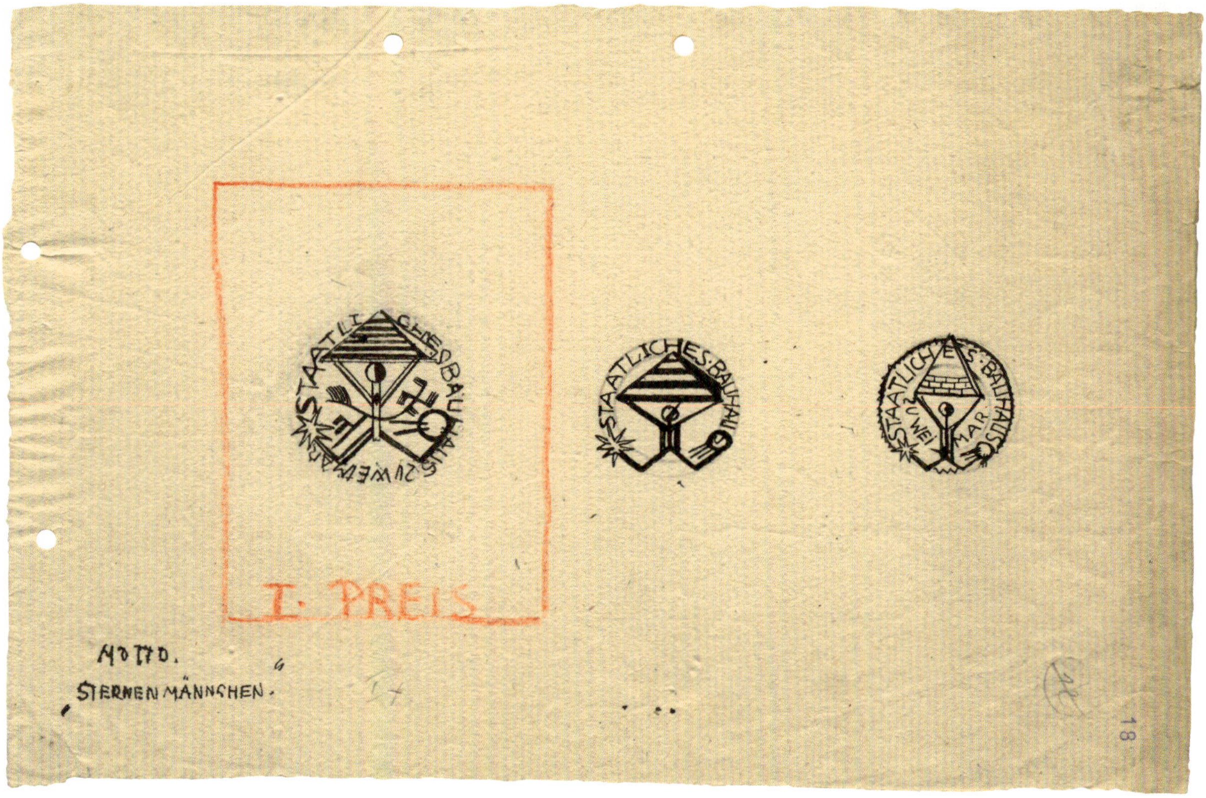

7
Karl Peter Röhl
Three designs for the Bauhaus seal, 1919
Ink and pencil on paper
21.5 × 32.5 cm
Thüringisches Hauptstaatsarchiv Weimar,
Staatliches Bauhaus Weimar, 78

In 1919, when Walter Gropius announced a student competition for a Bauhaus seal, Karl Peter Röhl's design, *Little Star Man*, won first prize. It became the official Bauhaus seal until 1921, when it was replaced by Oskar Schlemmer's simpler design, reflecting the changing spirit of the school. With its complex pictorial message, Röhl's seal clearly articulates the school's early utopian vision. A stick figure with arms and legs extended like the points of a star is crowned by a pyramid, symbolising the 'Great Building'. The head, divided equally into black and white, incorporates the Chinese symbols for yin and yang. The signs of the sun, star and swastika (not yet associated with Fascism) are integrated into a cosmic whole, proclaiming the school's early Expressionist spiritual ideals.

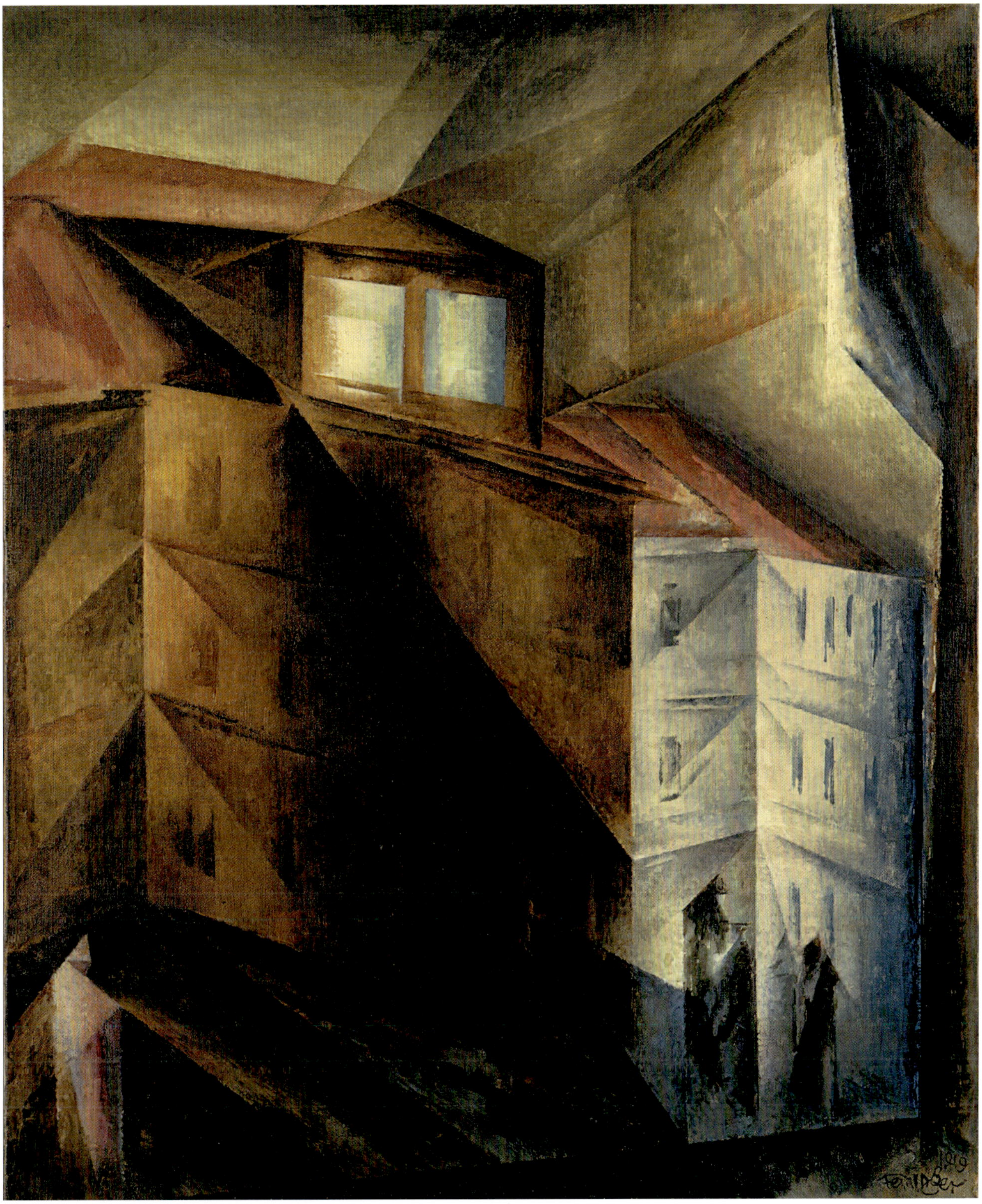

8
Lyonel Feininger
The Studio Window, 1919
Oil on canvas
100 × 80 cm
Lehmbruck Museum Duisburg

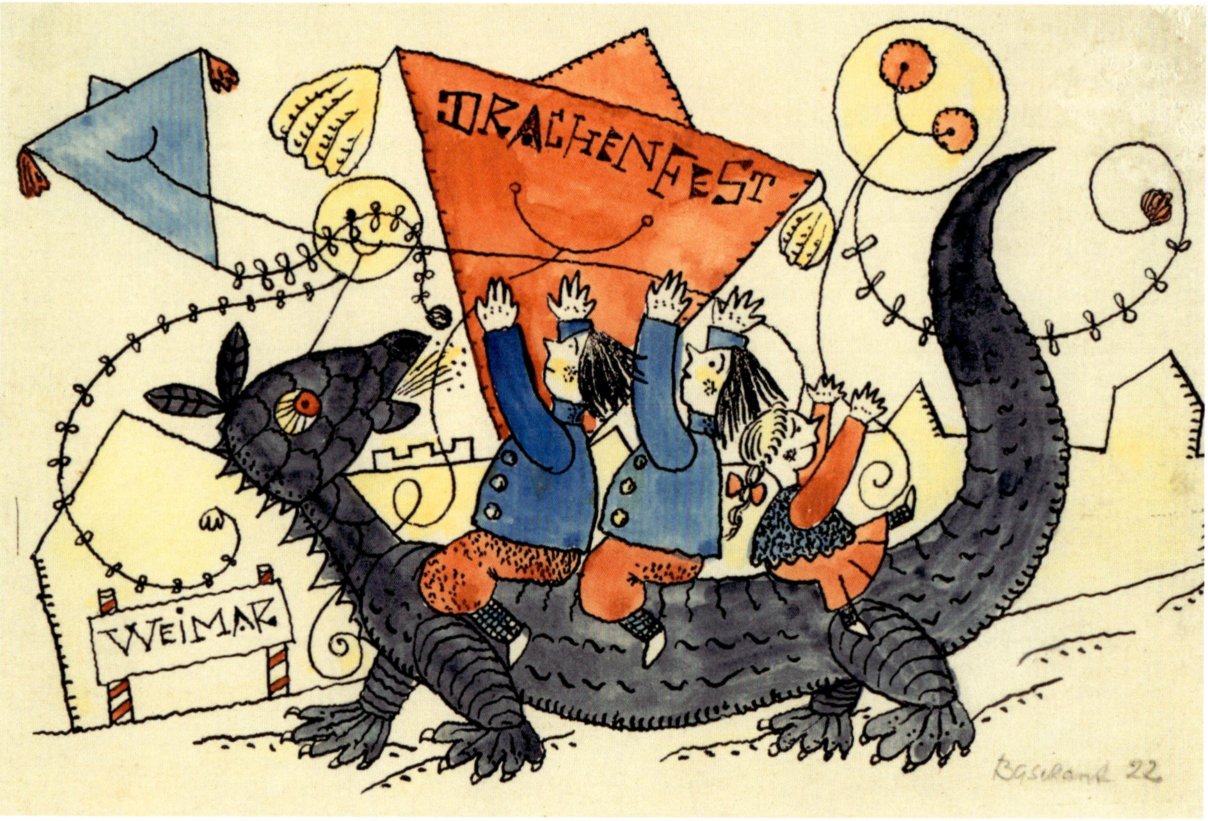

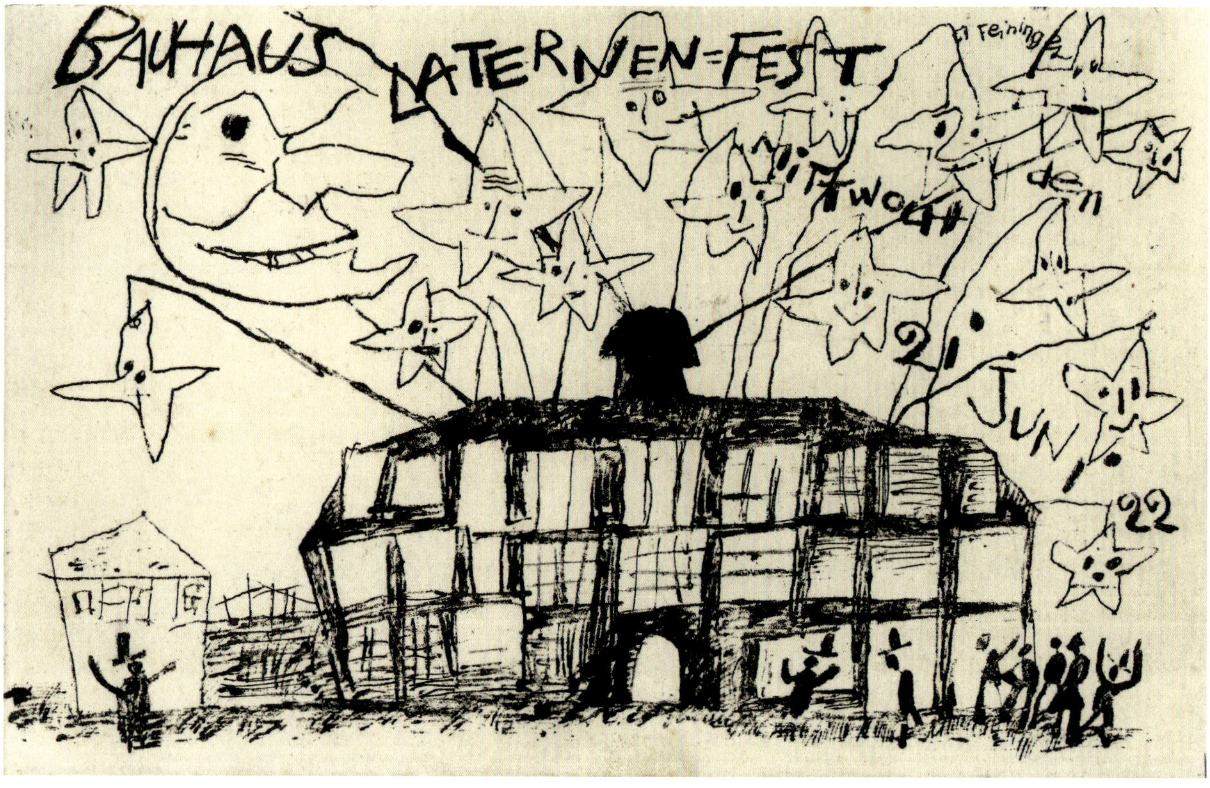

9
Rudolf Baschant
Postcard for the Kite Festival, 1922
Watercolour and lithograph on card
11.1 × 15.6 cm
Bauhaus-Archiv Berlin

10
Lyonel Feininger
Postcard for the Lantern Festival, 1922
Lithograph on card
9.3 × 14.7 cm
Bauhaus-Archiv Berlin

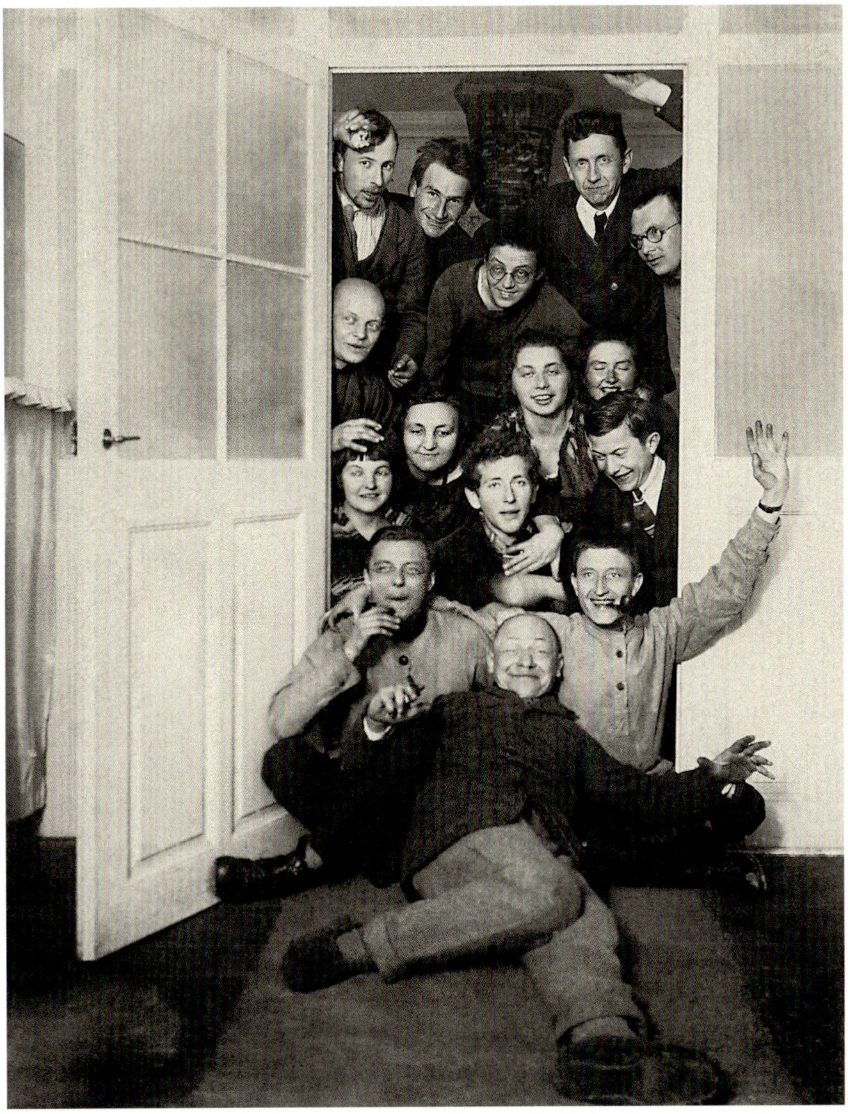

11
Bauhauslers in Weimar, c.1922
Bauhaus-Archiv Berlin
Photographer unknown

From the beginning, parties, festivals and gatherings were an integral part of the Bauhaus. The school's predecessor, the Academy of Fine Arts in Weimar, had initiated the tradition of holding masked balls. Gropius saw the value in continuing these festivities as occasions to foster communal relations between masters and students, to provide a creative outlet for their inspirations and to serve as a kind of catharsis to ease social conflicts. Four times a year, Bauhauslers celebrated the seasons. In late spring, homemade lanterns were lit and carried through the park at night to the houses of various masters and students. The solstice was commemorated in the summer, the beginning of the semester was marked by the Kite Festival, and a Christmas party rounded out the year. These events were sometimes the impetus for new work, as in Kurt Schwerdtfeger's *Reflecting Colour-Light-Play*, which he developed after working on a shadow play for a lantern festival.

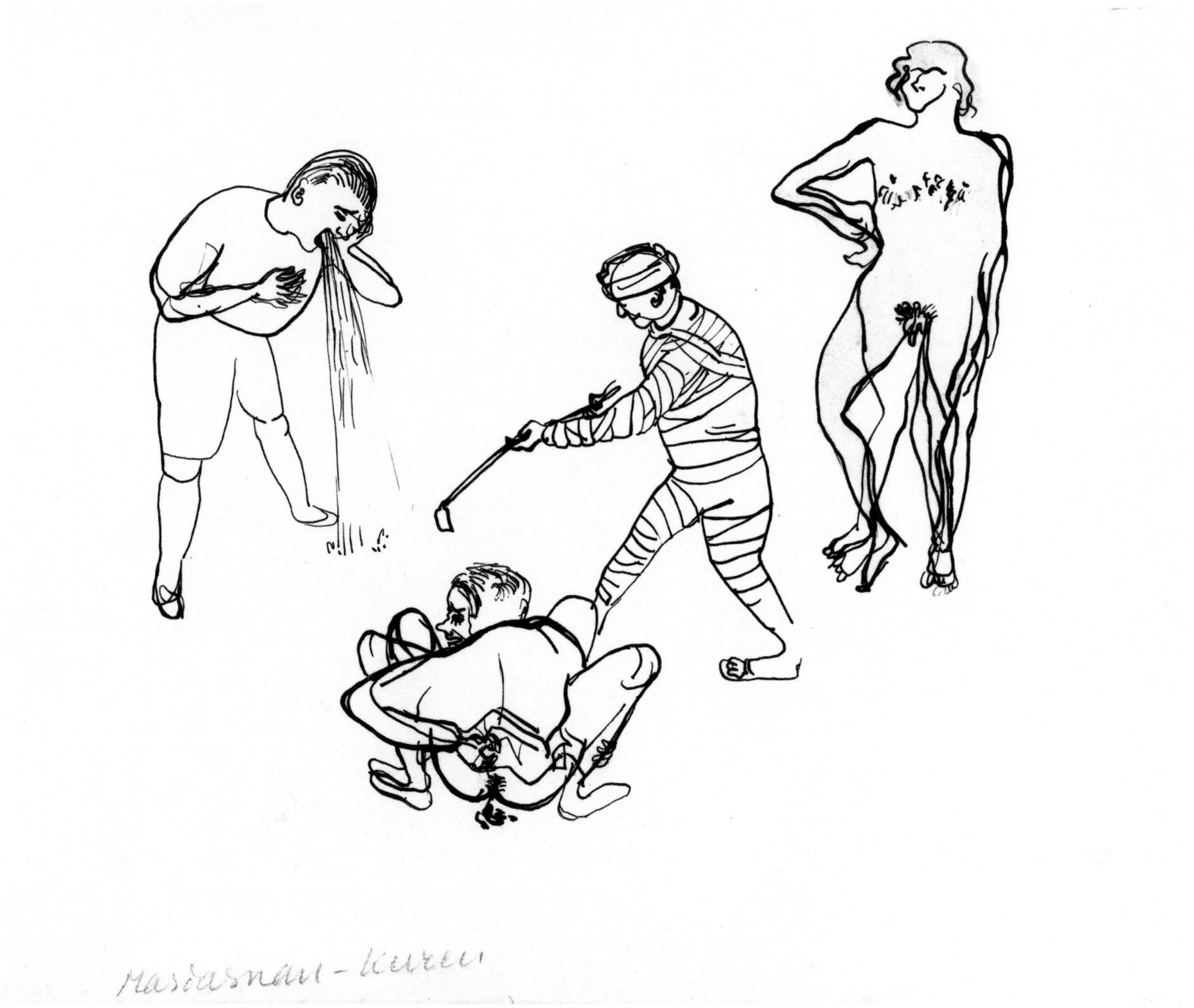

12
Paul Citroën
Mazdaznan Cures, c.1922
Pen, ink and watercolour on tracing paper
24.5 × 30.5 cm
Bauhaus-Archiv Berlin

Citroën's crude depiction of figures defecating, vomiting and puncturing their skin, suggests the strong impression that Mazdaznan practices would have made on young Bauhaus students such as himself. Mazdaznan syncretic philosophy, which combined core Hinduistic and Christian beliefs, had seeped into the school in its early Weimar years through Johannes Itten and Georg Muche. At its core lay the belief that man's ultimate pursuit must be his own redemption through the perfecting of the physical world in order to attain spiritual and divine spheres. Breathing techniques were considered central and were performed through various physical exercises, chanting and praying. Such rituals were accompanied by bodily purges by way of fasting and a strict vegetarian diet, including large quantities of garlic.Followers would dress in monastic robes and would often shave their heads, as a means to enhance the soul. Yet growing dismay within the school towards the philosophy, especially from Gropius, who saw it as divisive and promoting the individual personality over collective work, led to Itten's departure in 1923 and the dwindling influence of Mazdaznan culture within the school.

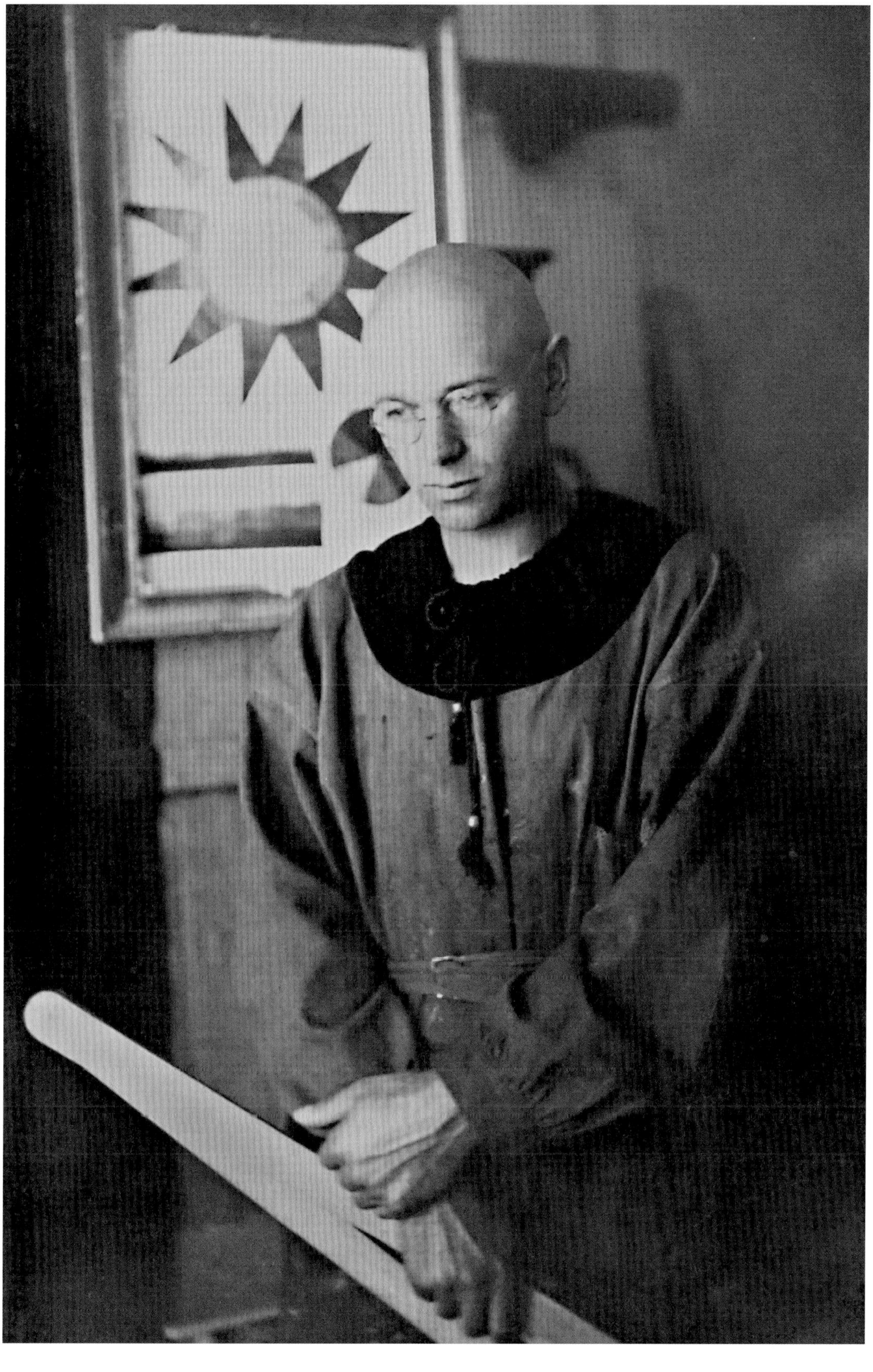

13
Paula Stockmar
Portrait of Johannes Itten, c. 1921
Bauhaus-Archiv Berlin

a return to the crafts

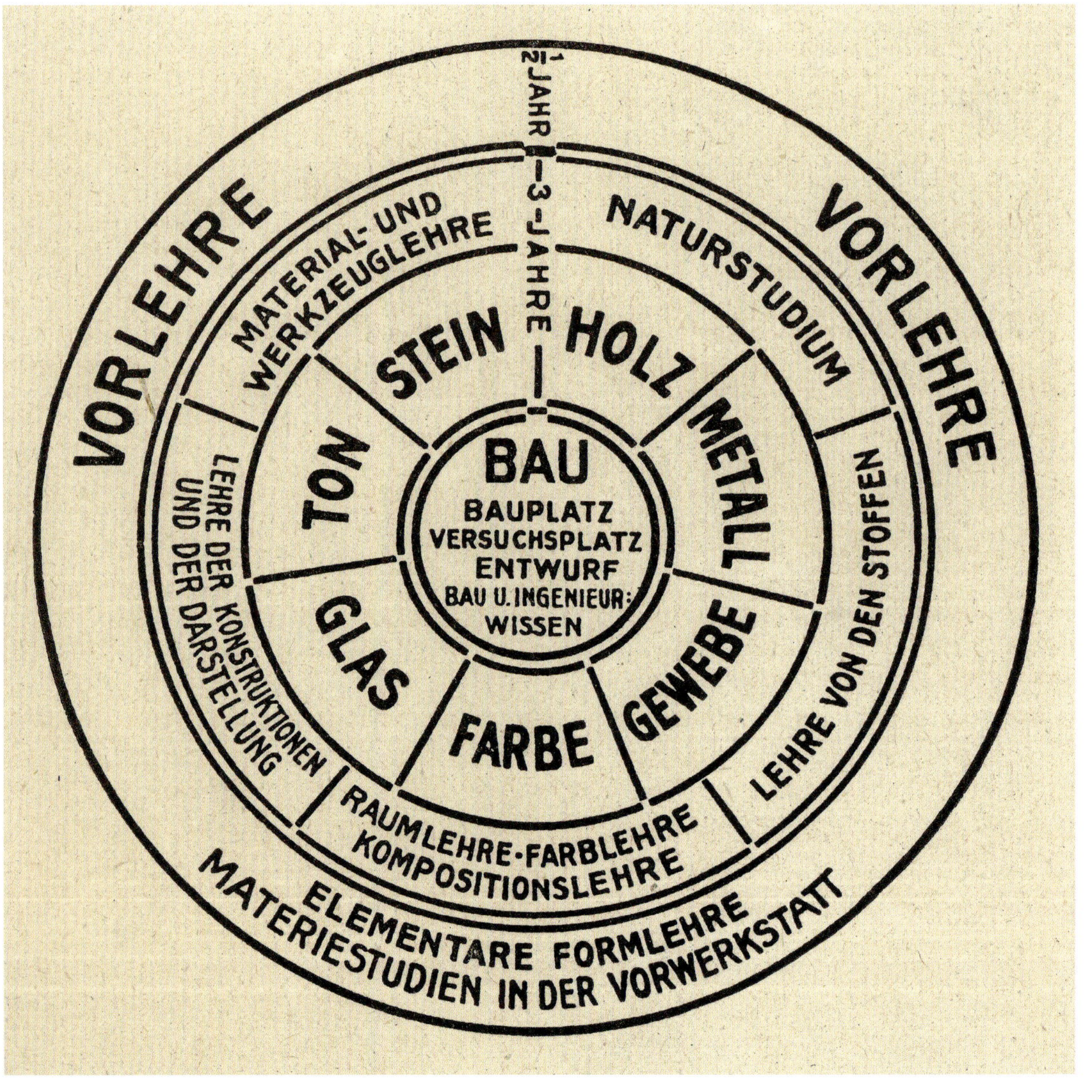

The Bauhaus was to be a school of invention rather than imitation. Initially, training centred on craft, drawing and painting instruction, but during the first few years of its existence the curriculum was reorganised. Represented by the iconic schematic diagram published by Gropius in the school's statutes of 1922 (fig. 14), integrated practical craft training and theoretical tuition would be offered, phased over a three to five-year period of study, which commenced with mandatory (from 1920) preliminary instruction under the guidance of Bauhaus master Johannes Itten. Itten's preliminary course concept was the backbone of Bauhaus education and evolved to become one of the school's most profound and widely dispersed legacies. Classes were divided into main areas: visual analysis, material study and colour theory. Itten's teaching was esoteric, emphasising the sensory nature of visual perception, and encouraged students to liberate their individual creative power before moving on to advanced practical workshop training.

Workshop tuition focused on developing skills in a range of materials: wood, stone, glass, textiles, paint, metal and clay. Each workshop was led by an artist, the 'master of form', whose role was to stimulate student creativity, and an expert craftsman who taught technical and manual skills. Practical training was complemented by theoretical courses exploring basic material and design principles such as form, colour, composition, space and construction, which built on the foundations of the preliminary course. Due to financial constraints, new workshop facilities were slow to set up, with the exception of printing, bookbinding and weaving, which had existed previously. The pottery workshop was located at an off-site studio in Dornburg, and run by Max Krehan, a master craftsman. He taught with Gerhard Marcks, who had experience working with ceramics factories prior to his appointment. Alongside Lyonel Feininger and Itten, Gropius built an impressive faculty drawn from international avant-garde circles. Paul Klee, Wassily Kandinsky, Oskar Schlemmer and Georg Muche all joined the Bauhaus within its first few years.

Gropius's experimental model of education aimed to address the tension between industrial production and artistic expression and proposed that all creative work should be rooted in building, explored collectively and on every scale. Although Gropius failed to initiate formal architecture training in the Weimar years, his vision to develop sites for experimental building was first realised with his client Adolf Sommerfeld, whose commission of a new house resulted in productive work for the students under Gropius's direction. Workshops were encouraged to develop prototypes and accept commissions that would, it was hoped, bring the school closer to industry and generate much-needed revenue. Student designs were sold to raise funds for the school as well as provide personal income for those experiencing extreme hardship in the aftermath of the war.

Gropius organised free meals, clothing and support for students who were destitute and unable to pay for their tuition or everyday needs. Despite such privations, communal gatherings in the form of evening lectures, parties and seasonal celebrations brought to life his aim to foster friendly relations between students and masters. Itten's motto 'Play becomes party – party becomes work – work becomes play' characterised the new community that flourished at the Bauhaus.

14
Walter Gropius
Schematic presentation of the Bauhaus curriculum, 1922
Bauhaus-Archiv Berlin

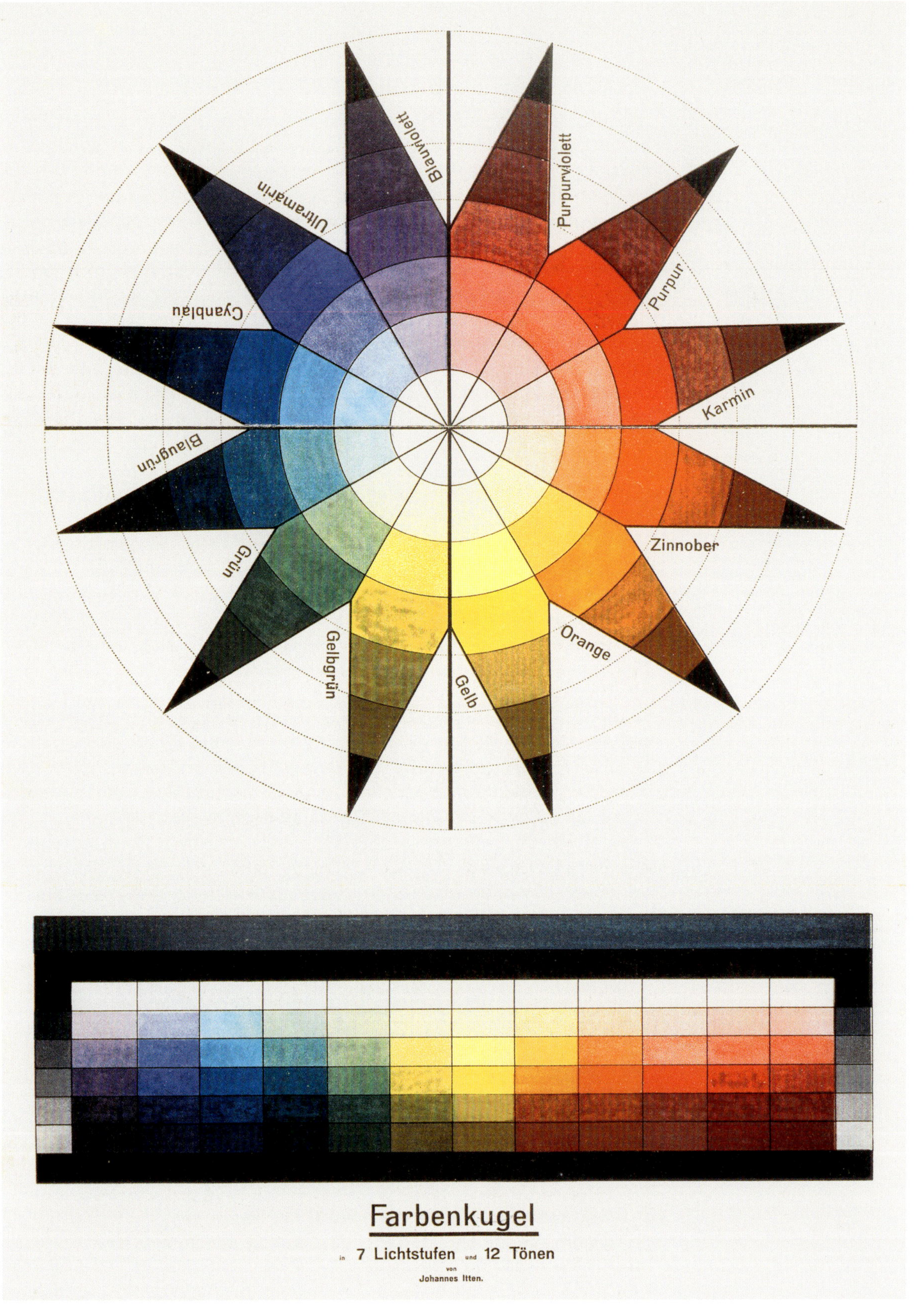

15
Johannes Itten
Colour sphere in seven light stages and twelve tones, from Bruno Adler, ed., *Utopia. Dokumente der Wirklichkeit* (*Utopia: Documents of Reality*), Weimar, 1921
Lithograph on card
47.3 × 32.2 cm
Bauhaus-Archiv Berlin

16
Nicolai Wassilieff
Spiral Tower (preliminary course exercise), c.1921
Bauhaus-Universität Weimar,
Archiv der Moderne
Photographer unknown

In preliminary course exercises devised by Johannes Itten, students worked with materials such as wood, metal, glass, paper and fabric, combining and arranging them to gain an understanding of their different qualities and how to create compositions with them. These studies resulted in two-dimensional collages and three-dimensional constructions, the majority of which have not survived except in photographs. Students often could not afford to buy materials, so they scavenged items from rubbish bins or local dumps to use in their course work. Itten felt that the employment of non-art items helped students to get beyond conventional thinking about art. Students who showed an affinity for a particular type of material would be admitted to the relevant workshop upon completion of the preliminary course.

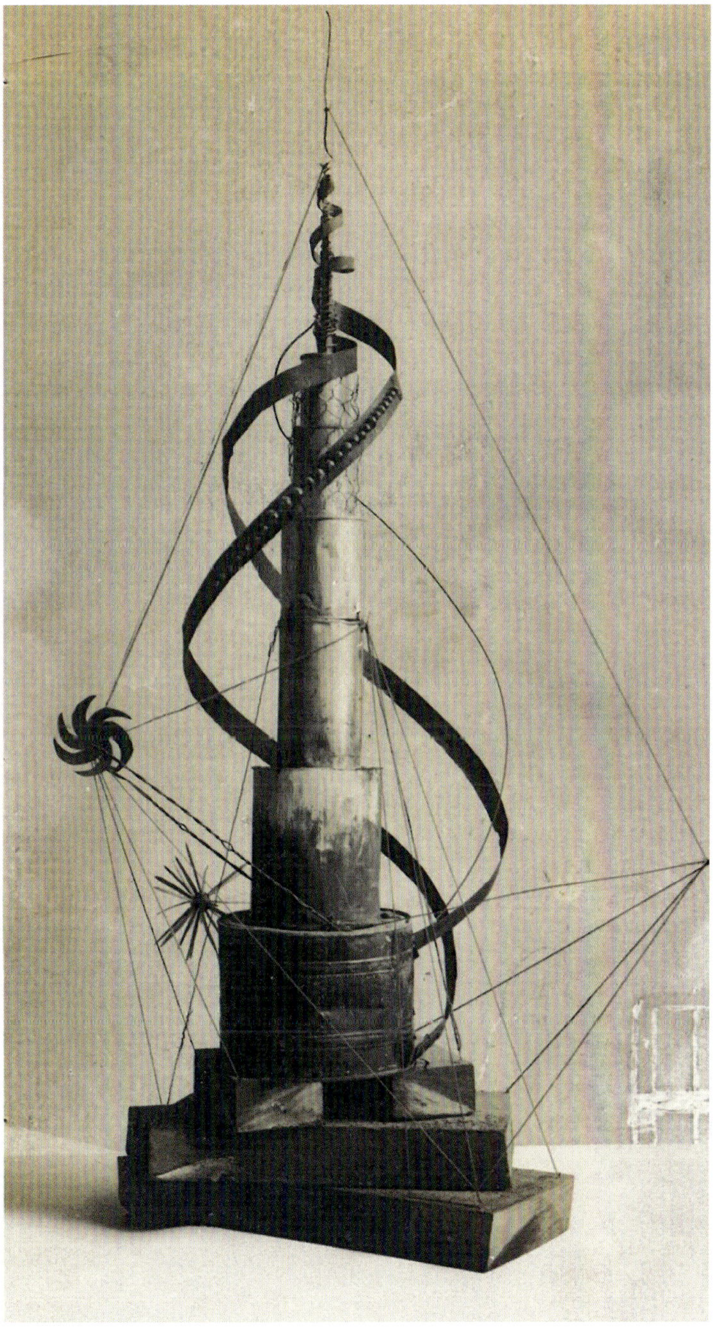

the bauhaus in weimar a school of creativity and invention

michael siebenbrodt

The world's first international fair, the Great Exhibition of 1851 in London, housed in John Paxton's Crystal Palace, is considered to be one of the most important historical points of reference for the Bauhaus concept, brought to fruition by Walter Gropius, in particular with the pedagogical support of Johannes Itten at the Staatliches Bauhaus in Weimar, beginning in 1919.[1] This Great Exhibition focused public attention on a globalised and increasingly industrialised world, with all its socio-economic and cultural problems. To counter the noticeable loss of quality that had occurred in everyday utilitarian products during the transition from handcrafted to machine methods of production, often with unskilled workers, a Europe-wide education offensive was launched and collections of exemplary models were established that would in turn one day become arts and crafts museums and schools for the arts. The first such institution was the South Kensington Museum of 1852, today's Victoria and Albert Museum, with its affiliated National Art Training School, followed by the arts and crafts museums in Vienna in 1863, Nuremberg in 1869, Hamburg and Leipzig in 1874. Among the protagonists of this movement were Gottfried Semper, as well as the founders of the Arts and Crafts movement in England, John Ruskin and William Morris.

Another line of pedagogical reform tradition goes back to the Enlightenment at the end of the eighteenth century. For instance, in 1776, at the initiative of the publisher and industrialist Friedrich Justin Bertuch and Johann Wolfgang von Goethe, the Großherzogliche freie Zeichenschule (The Grand-Ducal Free School of Drawing) was founded in Weimar. Here, children and young adults, both boys and girls, but particularly young apprentices, were schooled in the arts at no cost in order to promote craftsmanship and trade and to make them more competitive by developing the level of their creative quality.

This approach was also pursued by the reform movement of the Jugendstil (Art Nouveau) around 1900, which took up the discussion anew concerning the relationship between art and technology, integrating concepts of reform pedagogy in doing so. The Vereinigte Werkstätten für Kunst im Handwerk München (United Workshops for Art in the Craftsmen's Trade in Munich, 1897), the Deutsche Werkstätten Hellerau (German Workshops in Hellerau, 1899) and the Wiener Werkstätten (Vienna Workshops, 1903) brought dedicated entrepreneurs and artists together to further such a production process. The year 1902 witnessed the founding of the Debschitz School (training and experimental studios for the applied and decorative arts) in Munich, the training and experimental workshops of the school of arts and crafts in Stuttgart and the Reimann School in Berlin.[2] These ideas were also followed by Henry van de Velde, who had been called to Weimar by the Grand Duke in 1902 in order to advise the handcraft trade in the Grand Duchy in matters of design. Yet the same year, Van de Velde opened his private arts and crafts seminar (with a studio and counselling service for students), which was so successful that in 1907, the Grand-Ducal Saxon School of Arts and Crafts was to evolve from this and would be housed in a new school building. Just as in a commercial design studio, the ideas and products submitted by young craftsmen were further developed through teamwork and subsequently produced in factories. Van de Velde established a modern design doctrine that went beyond the academic copying of pattern books or models. Moreover, beginning in 1907, he set up workshops for bookbinding, pottery, metal and textiles, which the Bauhaus was able to take over in parts.[3]

Walter Gropius was actively engaged in the debates that took place within the Deutscher Werkbund, founded in 1907, where he had been a member since 1910. Particularly in the Arbeitsrat für Kunst and in the Novembergruppe, he was involved in discussions with other artists and intellectuals in Berlin in 1918–19 on the need for educational reforms after the November Revolution in the burgeoning Weimar Republic. These ranged from the introduction of the comprehensive school and the working school for all children, to the art school reform from which the Bauhaus programme was derived.

Gropius was familiar with all of these successful school and educational models. Thus he postulated in the Bauhaus programme not only the unity of all artistic disciplines, the *Große Bau* (Grand Design), but also demanded equal chances for all students regardless of gender, nationality, religion, ideology, previous education or social origin. And he charged his school with the task of promoting the talents of everyone who studied there. Besides professional training in the areas of the fine arts as well as applied arts and architecture, attention was also given to the broad spectrum of the performing arts: music, dance, theatre, festivals and performances, which was supported by the stage workshop that was open to all Bauhauslers.[4]

From the arts and crafts schools Gropius took over the tried-and-true workshop principle as the pedagogical basis for his new type of school of design. Under Gropius's new leitmotif of 'Art and Technology: A New Unity', the Bauhaus workshops were to be further developed into 'laboratories for industry', beginning in 1922.[5] The training workshops were supplemented with production workshops, not only to generate income for the school, the teaching staff and the students during economically difficult times, but also to ensure the practical orientation of the education and training.

Among the central pedagogical principles at the Bauhaus Weimar was the pluralistic approach, which was not oriented to a uniform Bauhaus style, but to the formation of different styles showing the hand of each individual student. Thus at the Bauhaus in 1922, it was possible to study the essentials of design, form and colour as 'subjective explorations' with such avant-garde artists as Johannes Itten, Paul Klee, Wassily Kandinsky and Oskar Schlemmer. In addition, this could be supplemented with a course given by the student Ludwig Hirschfeld-Mack. The dual principle followed in the workshops for studying with the Bauhaus artists as the masters of form on the one hand and the con-servative master craftsmen on the other, created poles of tension, between which each student had to navigate his or her way.[6] Such plurality is in keeping with the Bauhaus's internationality and its worldwide avant-garde network, with half of its teaching staff and masters coming from abroad, as did up to a third of its students.

Creative play and creativity training also comprised a part of Bauhaus pedagogical 'inventions', which integrated the educational reform experiences of Pestalozzi, Fröbel and Montessori into higher education for the first time.[7] After all, the Bauhaus was probably the first school to train and practice project-oriented cooperative work and teamwork beyond the boundaries of the workshops and the institution. Even today, this may be witnessed in virtually all of the Bauhaus buildings ever carried out, but also in the numerous design objects – ranging from the teapots by Theodor Bogler with their various wicker and metal handles, to the famous table lamp with glass foot – with Carl Jakob Jucker, Gyula Pap and Wilhelm Wagenfeld all sharing in its development.[8]

Next to Gropius as director, Swiss-born Johannes Itten was the most important instructor in the initial phase of the Bauhaus until 1921–22. He played a substantial role in setting up the workshops at the early Bauhaus and as a master of form he directed the stone sculpture, weaving, cabinetry, stained-glass and wall-painting workshops. Moreover, he developed and directed the famous Bauhaus preliminary course, the introductory and trial semester for prospective Bauhaus students.[9] Additionally, he was the only trained pedagogue at the Bauhaus, with a broad range of teaching experience. By 1912, when he completed his studies as a teacher on the secondary level, he had already been a primary-school teacher, directed a men's choir, studied art and music at the École des Beaux-Arts and at the Conservatory in Geneva, as well as put two years of maths and sciences behind him at the University in Bern.

Concerning his own work in the pedagogy of art, Itten's studies with Adolf Hölzel at the Stuttgart Art Academy, beginning in 1913, constituted a seminal experience. Hölzel's analyses of paintings, his colour theory and his theory of contrasts formed the basis for Itten's teaching at the Bauhaus.[10] As early as 1915, Itten instructed Hölzel's female students in painting before going on to teach at a private art school in Vienna at the end of 1916. A charismatic teacher, he became acquainted with Alma Mahler, who encouraged him to study esotericism, as well as Indian and Far Eastern religions. It was through her that Itten also got to know her second husband Gropius during the winter of 1918.

In February of 1919, Gropius invited Itten to work as a master at the future Bauhaus in Weimar, and Itten then moved there the following October to take up his new teaching position. Fifteen of his Viennese students accompanied him to Weimar. For the newly enrolled students, who came from all over the world and from the most diverse educational backgrounds, Gropius and Itten suggested a trial semester, from which the prerequisite preliminary course developed. Itten set himself three tasks that he wanted to accomplish with this: 'To determine the creative gifts of the students, to facilitate their occupational choices and to teach them the elementary means of design that would be needed in their future profession.'[11]

In retrospect, however, the preliminary course was far more than this, being geared towards the universal, holistic development of the personality, striving towards a 'new' man by means of mind and sensibility training, and containing intellectual stimulations and challenges in all areas. Without the pressure of the regular professional study course, with its regulated forty-eight-hour week, including thirty hours in the workshop, the students in the preliminary course were able to, and indeed were encouraged to, discover their own personalities, their strengths and weaknesses, their gifts and talents. At the same time, this constituted a seminal phase for getting to know one another, since the course was a veritable melting pot for young people ranging from sixteen-year-old secondary-school graduates to trained craftsmen, students already educated at the arts and crafts schools or art academies, up to those with doctorates. It even included forty-year-old Bauhaus candidates, who were searching for goals in life after the war and the revolution, and among all of these, up to fifty percent were women. The numerous foreign students were given the chance to improve their knowledge of German in this trial semester and to take an active part in the many discussions on the development of a new specialist design language. It was from working closely together every day during this trial semester that the close-knit Bauhaus community developed. The resulting life-long friendships and partnerships often helped to ensure survival in the most difficult political and economic times.

Itten taught the preliminary course introduction into Asian techniques of mental training. As a follower of the Mazdaznan doctrine,[12] he began each class with breathing and concentration exercises. The lessons in meditation served to focus one's inner self and make it easier to concentrate on new tasks. Immediately following this were movement concentration exercises, during which the students, mostly using both hands, executed studies of rhythm in charcoal or chalk on large-format paper. The object was not to create works of art, but to coordinate the head with the hand and to include the entire body in this process, similar to the way a drummer is trained. Only in the next step were these rhythm studies used to capture movements in their essential visual elements, such as playing a violin or the leap of a tiger, and to portray them in a spontaneous act of drawing from memory. It is no coincidence that the results are similar to Chinese or Japanese brush painting. Such mental training was supplemented with advice on healthy nourishment through forgoing meat, alcohol and drugs, how to care for the body and good hygiene, all according to the stipulations of the Mazdaznan doctrine.

Departing from the biological and medical knowledge of the day, according to which only a small percent of man's brain capacity and sense organs were made use of, Itten established his sensibility training in the preliminary course. It involved linking the training of sight and touch with his teaching of the basics of design. The black-and-white scales that have come down to us today document the task of portraying as many shades of grey as can possibly be differentiated by the human eye. The comparable touch plates also served the purpose of learning how to produce the finest differentiations in surfaces or arranging various materials in a row and then, with closed eyes, recognising them by touch. The sense of hearing was mostly trained outside of the preliminary course in the stage workshop and as part of the numerous musical activities of the instructors such as Lyonel Feininger, Klee or Schlemmer, and of the students themselves, culminating in the founding of the Bauhaus band by Andor Weininger.[13]

Itten introduced his complex epistemological concept of education in his publication *Analyses of the Old Masters*,[14] which corresponded to Gropius's postulate concerning *Wesensforschung* (ontological research). Using works of art from all epochs and civilisations (in the black-and-white reproductions and slide projections that were customary at the time),[15] the students were to analyse these works and learn to understand them. By means of mathematics, specifically with geometry and algebra, the relationships of forms and measurements were to be comprehended 'objectively'. Language afforded an opportunity for precise, neutral description as well as the subjective interpretation of the work. Finally, abstract drawing presented a third, essential level for accessing the work of art. These exercises were supplemented with Itten's theory of contrasts – both as an intellectual and a creative principle – in order to emphasise both difference and differentiation: cold-warm, light-dark, large-small, smooth-rough, loud-quiet, bitter-sweet, good-bad. In their studies of nature, the students had to visually capture and comprehend objects, materials and movements with such precision that they would subsequently be able to reproduce them from memory. Of course, such a method of analysis could also be used to examine all of the other creative forms and architectural phenomena and problems, and could even be applied to the students' own works as a critical feedback.

Ultimately, creative play and creativity training is reckoned to be one of the most important elements of Itten's Bauhaus preliminary course. In free play with materials beyond traditional contexts of form and function, the students were to liberate themselves from the customary educational constraints and academic conventions. Using household rubbish and refuse from Weimar craftsmen's businesses, as well as natural materials found in the forests or fields, the students created fanciful objects, by means of which they began developing their own individual design signatures.[16] This element of play also afforded the students the opportunity for an open-minded approach to working with the various materials, and finding one's favourite materials to work with in order to then choose one of the Bauhaus workshops to attend: metal, wood, stone, clay, glass, textiles, paint. The creative and playful element was to remain in the preliminary courses of László Moholy-Nagy and Josef Albers even after Itten had departed, but it was supplemented with more systematic research into the relationship of material, structure, technology, function and form.

This comprehensive approach to education is what makes Bauhaus pedagogy, and the preliminary course in particular, interesting in today's education debate. It is a concept for lifelong learning on a solid 'craftsman-type' basis that involves a high degree of teamwork and a view to social responsibility in keeping with Gropius's motto, namely, to develop architecture and products that ensure, with a minimum of material, energy and work hours, a maximum of beauty and purpose and which are to be affordable by the broad masses.[17]

By becoming members of the Circle of Friends of the Bauhaus, Albert Einstein and numerous other scientists and artists demonstrated that it was not only a small avant-garde school for designers, but also stood for a new type of modern university in a democratically organised industrial society and globalised world.

1 Michael Siebenbrodt, 'Die Werkstätten. Fundament der Bauhauspädagogik und der Designentwicklung am Bauhaus', in Ute Ackermann, Ulrike Bestgen (eds), *Das Bauhaus kommt aus Weimar*, 2009, p. 73f.

2 Kai Buchholz, Justus Theinert, *Designlehren. Wege deutscher Gestaltungsausbildung*, Arnoldsche, Stuttgart, 2007.

3 Karl-Heinz Hüter, *Henry van de Velde. Sein Werk bis zum Ende seiner Tätigkeit in Deutschland*, Akademie-Verlag, Berlin, 1967, p. 32f.

4 Michael Siebenbrodt (ed.), *Bauhaus Weimar. Entwürfe für die Zukunft*, Hatje-Cantz Verlag, Ostfildern-Ruit, 2000; Thomas Föhl, Michael Siebenbrodt (eds), *Bauhaus-Museum Weimar* (English Edition), Deutscher Kunstverlag, Munich and Berlin, 2006.

5 Walter Gropius, 'Grundsätze der Bauhausproduktion', in *Neue Arbeiten der Bauhaus-Werkstätten*, Verlag Albert Langen, Munich, 1925, pp. 5–8.

6 Rainer Wick, *Bauhaus-Pädagogik*, Dumont-Verlag, Cologne 1982, and the author's subsequent publications on this topic.

7 These three pedagogues and educational reformers addressed the development of childhood creativity, and discovered play as a pedagogic process of learning. In 1805 Fröbel worked for a time in one of Pestalozzi's educational institutions, before going on to found the first kindergarten in 1840.

8 See Siebenbrodt, *Bauhaus Weimar*, op. cit., pp. 24–25, 32–42 concerning the field of architecture, p. 132, 134–135, 147, 151, 153, 162–164 with respect to design.

9 Willy Rotzler (ed.), *Johannes Itten. Werke und Schriften*, Orell Füssli Verlag, Zurich, 1972.

10 Hans Georg Gmelin, *Der Hölzelkreis bis 1914*, exhibition catalogue, Kunsthalle Bielefeld, 1974; Marion Ackermann, Gergard Leister: *Kaleidoskop. Hoelzel in der Avantgarde*, Kehrer Verlag, Heidelberg, 2009; Hans-Dieter Mück: *Adolf Hoelzel 1853–1934. Wegbereiter der Abstraktion*, Utenbach Verlag/ARTeFACT/Artus, Apolda, 2009.

11 Johannes Itten, *Der Vorkurs* (1962), quoted in Siebenbrodt, *Bauhaus Weimar*, op. cit., p. 272.

12 The sect-like Mazdaznan religion was founded by Otto Hanisch (born in Tehran in 1844 and died in Los Angeles in 1936) in the US at the end of the nineteenth century. It was to spread into Europe from 1907 on. As a hybrid religion, it represents a Western reception of Asian philosophical notions and life practices.

13 Michael Siebenbrodt, 'Jazzkapelle und Gesamtkunstwerk. Musik am Bauhaus in Weimar', in: Hellmuth Th. Seemann, Thorsten Valk (eds) *Übertönte Geschichten. Musikkultur in Weimar*, Wallstein Verlag, Göttingen, 2011, pp. 121–42.

14 Johannes Itten, 'Analysen alter Meister', in Bruno Adler (ed.), *Utopia. Dokumente der Wirklichkeit*, I/II, Utopia-Verlag, Weimar, 1921.

15 Small collections of these glass negatives may be found today in the Archiv der Moderne at the Bauhaus University Weimar and at the Stiftung Bauhaus in Dessau.

16 Johannes Itten, 'Mein Vorkurs am Bauhaus. Gestaltungs- und Formenlehre', Otto Maier Verlag, Ravensburg, 1963; Johannes Itten, 'The Foundation Course at the Bauhaus', in Gyorgy Kepes (ed.), *Education of Vision*, George Braziller, New York, 1965, p. 104 f.

17 See Gropius, 'Grundsätze der Bauhausproduktion', op. cit.

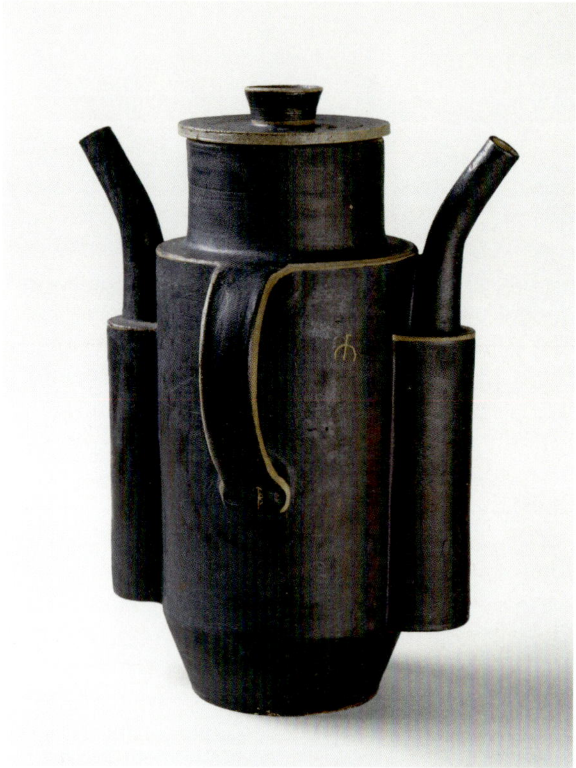

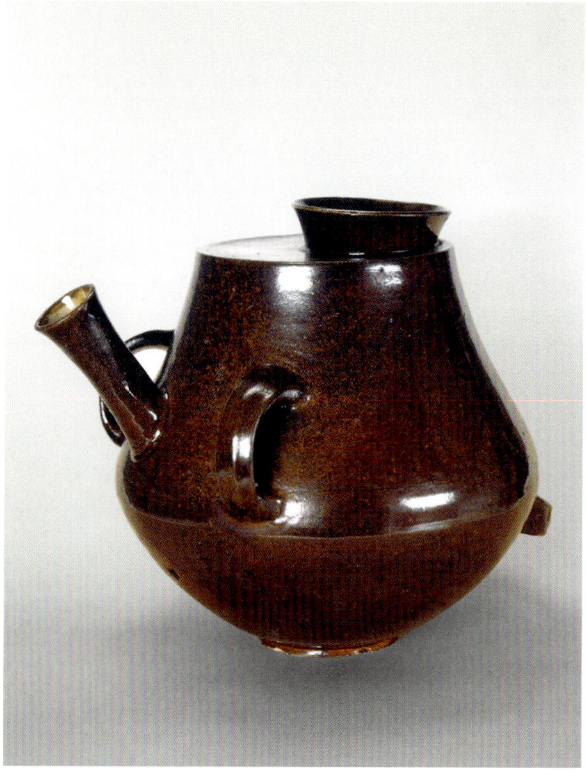

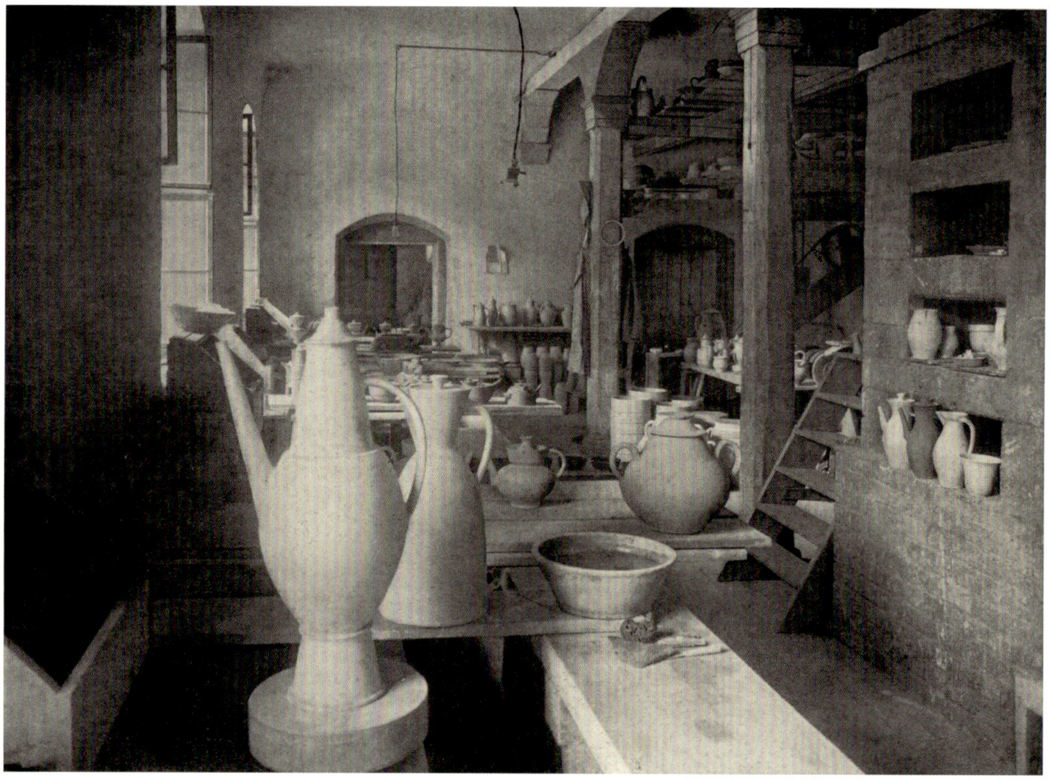

17
Theodor Bogler with slip decoration by Gerhard Marcks
Double pitcher, 1922
High-fired glazed earthenware, free thrown and assembled with painted slip decoration on exterior and glazed interior
Height: 31.8 cm
Klassik Stiftung Weimar, Bestand Museen

18
Otto Lindig
Bulbous pitcher with off-centre inlet opening, 1922
High-fired earthenware, free thrown and assembled, glazed exterior and interior
Height: 33 cm
Klassik Stiftung Weimar, Bestand Museen

19
Bauhaus pottery workshop, 1923
Bauhaus-Archiv Berlin
Photographer unknown

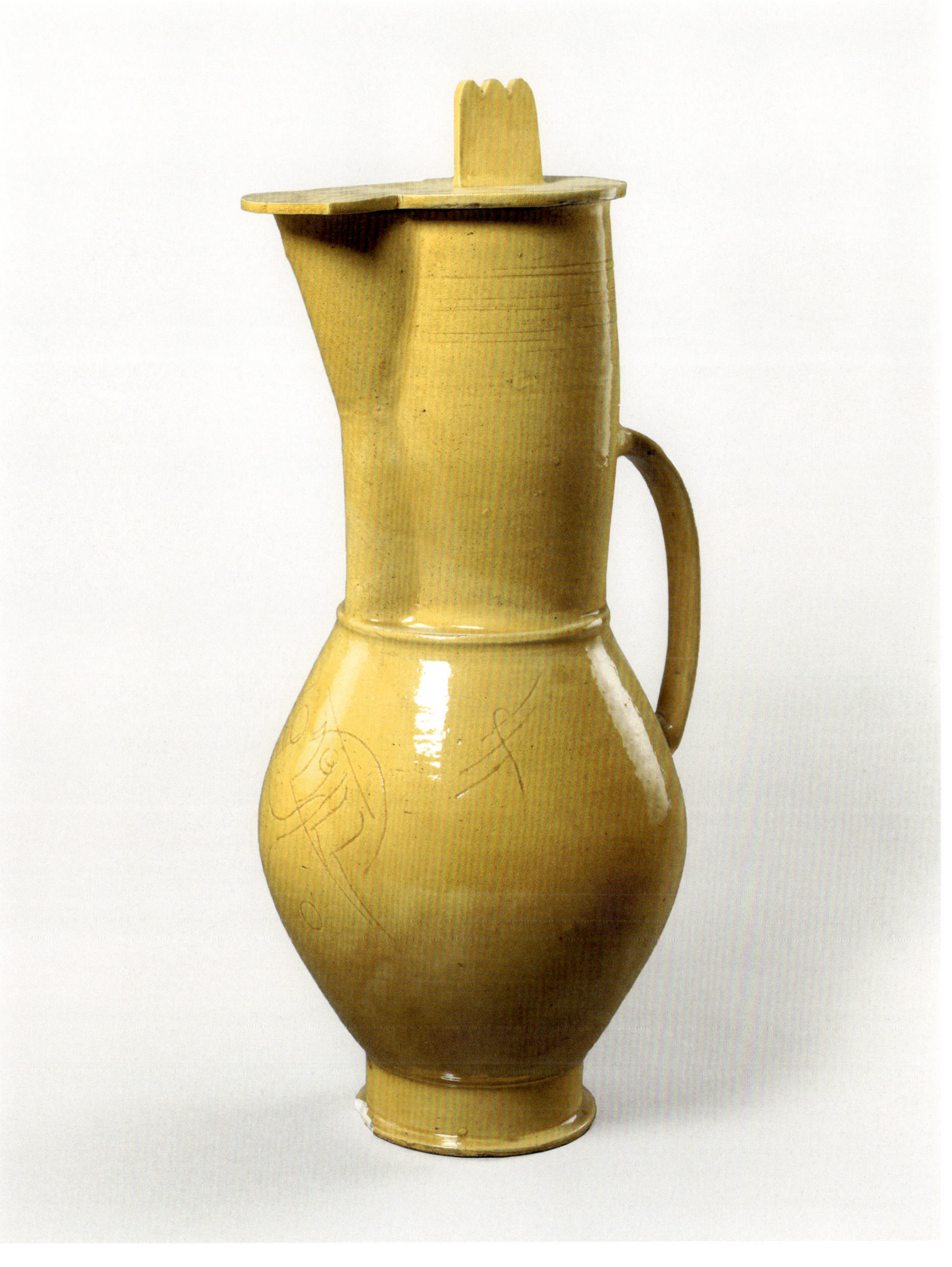

20
Otto Lindig
Tall jug with handle and incised decoration, 1922
High-fired earthenware, free thrown and assembled, with yellow transparent glaze
Height: 50 cm
Klassik Stiftung Weimar, Bestand Museen

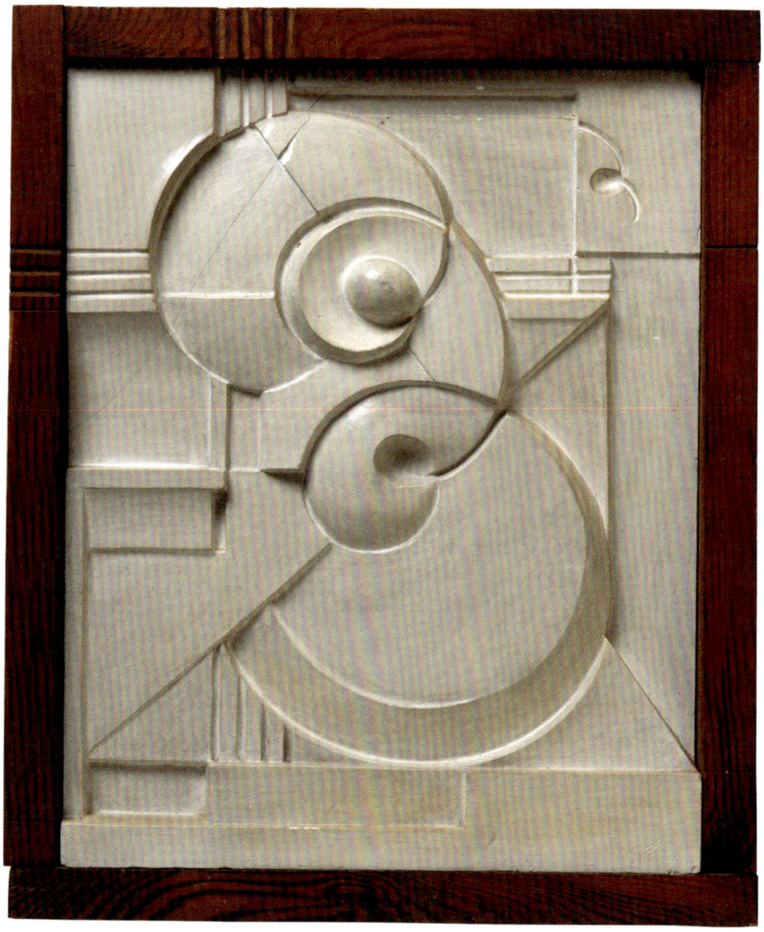

21
Theobald Emil Müller-Hummel
Relief with spiral motif, 1922
42.9 × 35 × 4.7 cm
Lacquered plaster, carved wooden frame
On long-term loan to Klassik Stiftung Weimar, Bestand Museen

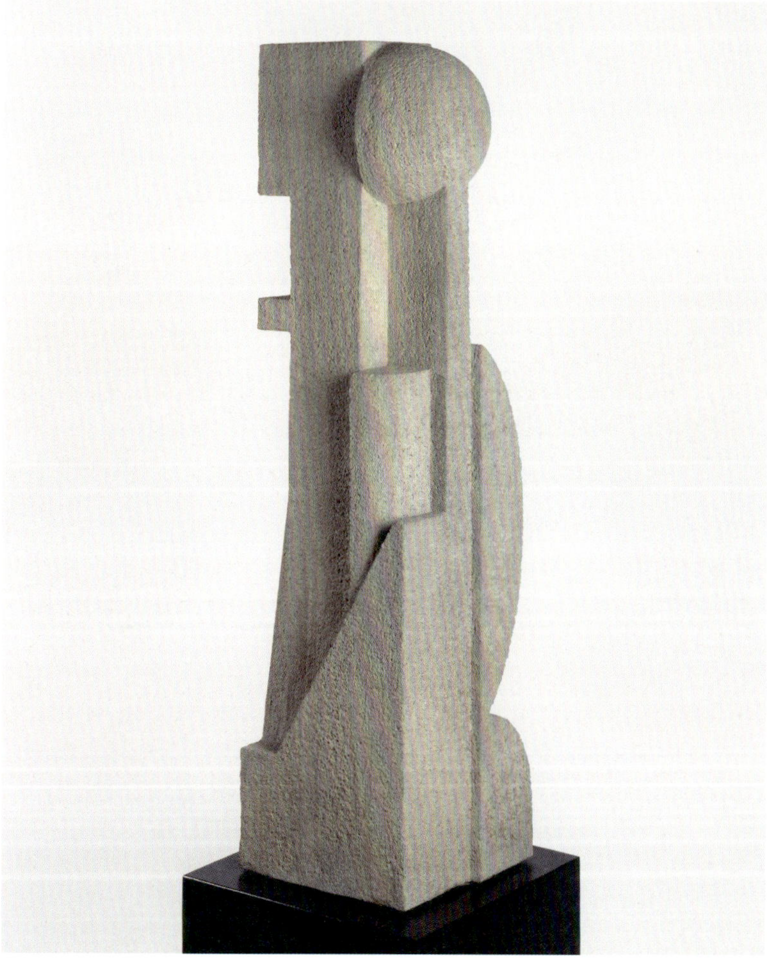

22
Otto Werner
Architectural sculpture, 1922
Chiseled Dorla shell limestone
Height: 128 cm
Bauhaus-Archiv Berlin

23
Oskar Schlemmer
Relief H, 1919
Plaster
67 × 28.2 × 2.8 cm
Private Collection
Courtesy Bühnen Archiv Oskar Schlemmer

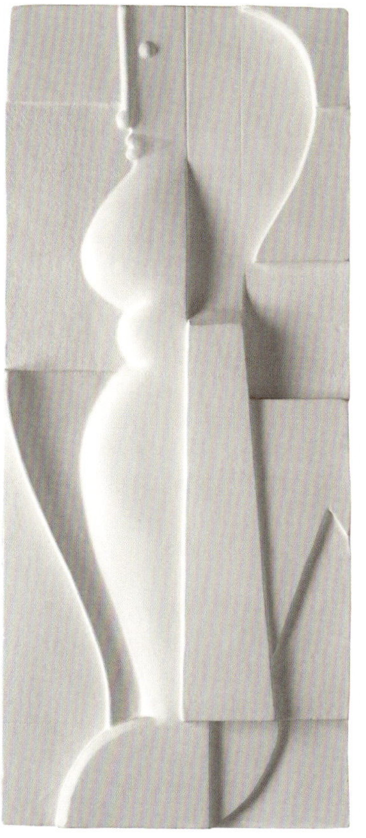

24
Stone sculpture workshop, 1923
With reliefs by Schlemmer and sculpture by Werner in mid-ground and sculpture by Schlemmer at far right
Bauhaus-Universität Weimar, Archiv der Moderne
Photographer unknown

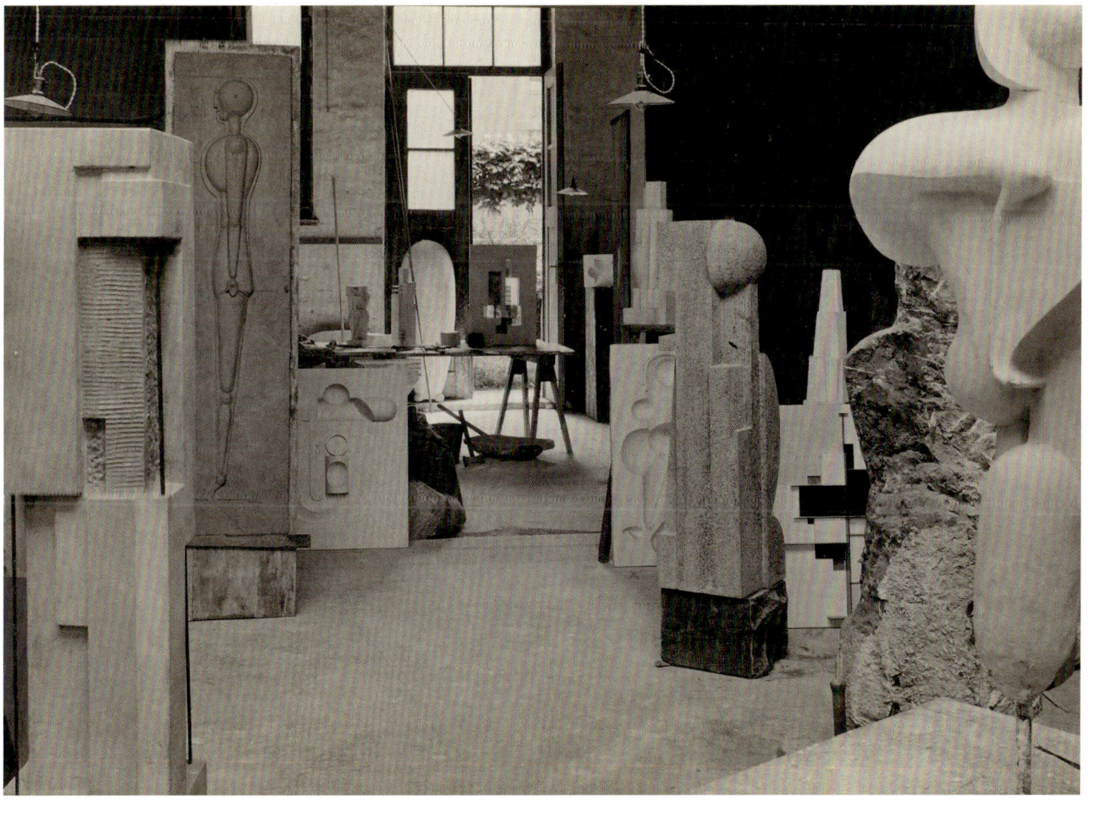

25
Sculpture workshop, 1923
Bauhaus-Archiv Berlin
Photographer unknown

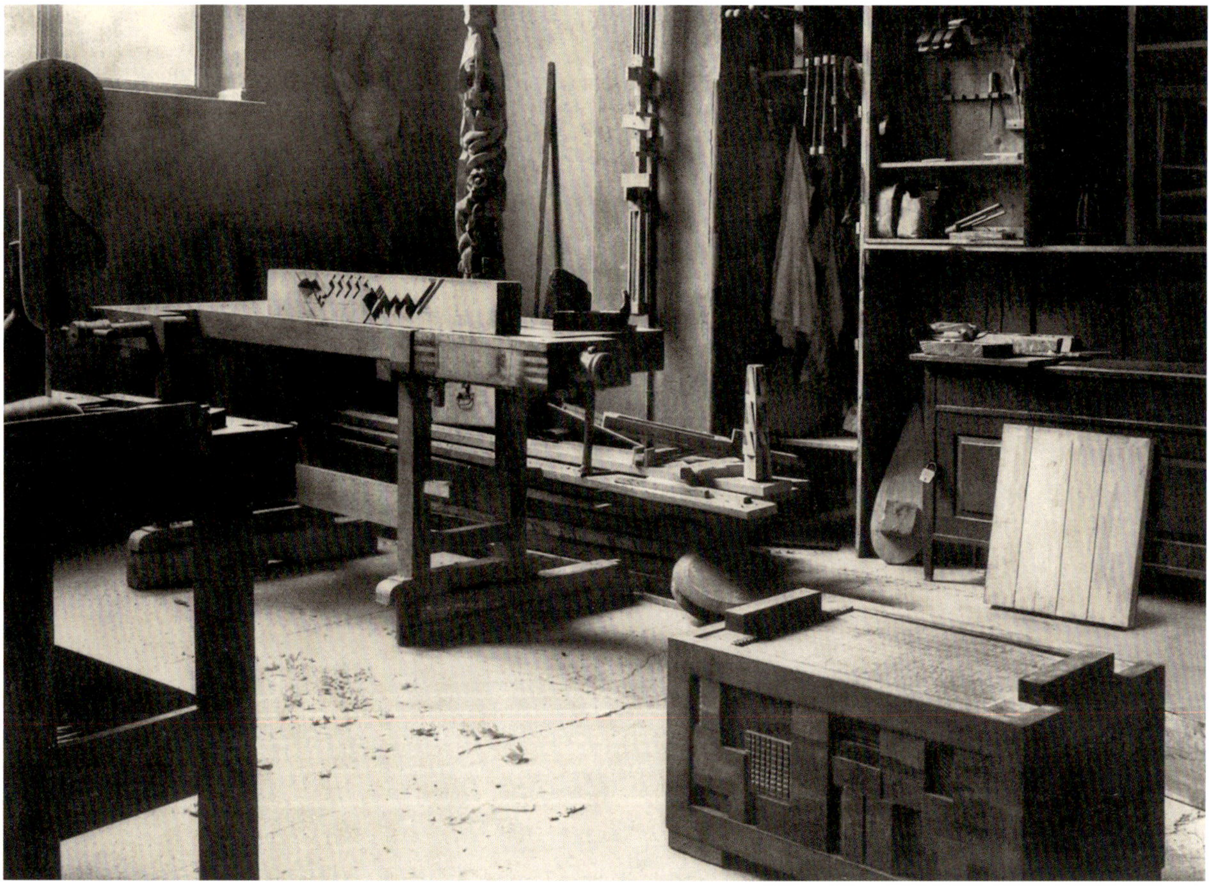

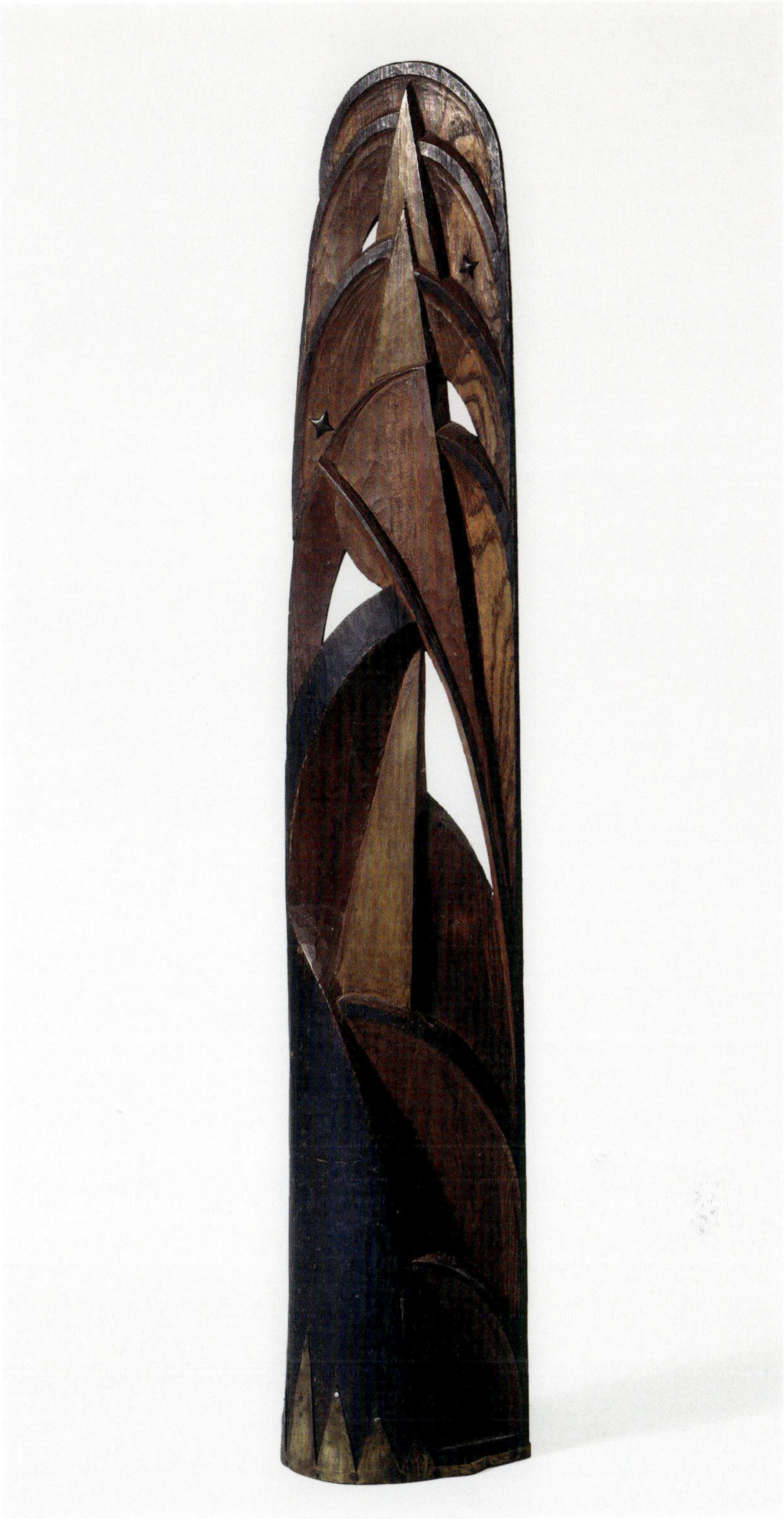

26
Theobald Emil Müller-Hummel
Pillar with cosmic vision, 1919–20
Carved and painted wood with
brass fittings
91.4 × 16.4 × 8.6 cm
On loan-term loan to Klassik Stiftung
Weimar, Bestand Museen

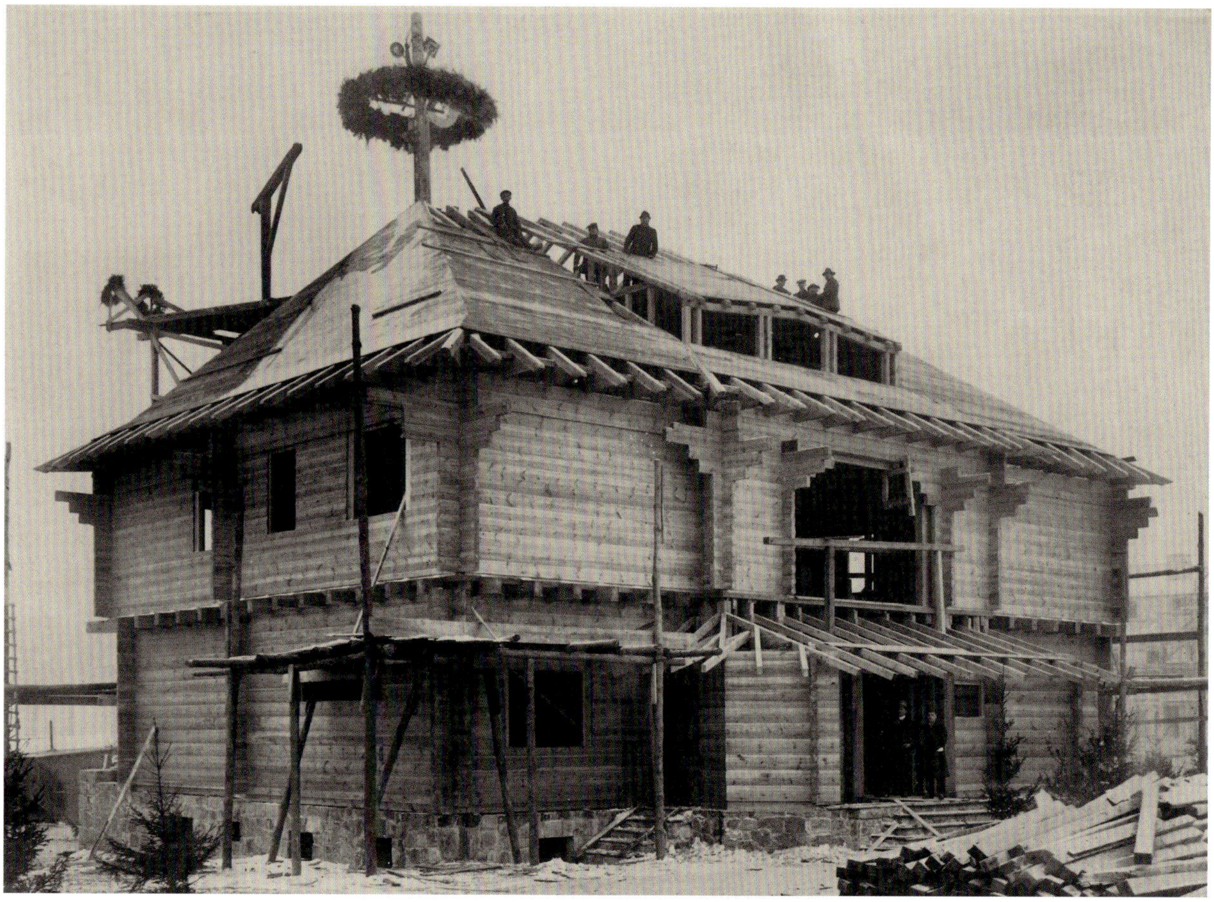

27
Sommerfeld House, Berlin-Steglitz, designed by Walter Gropius and Adolf Meyer
Construction site at the time of the topping-out ceremony, marking the completion of the structural framework, 18 December, 1920
Gelatin silver print
12.4 × 16.7 cm
Bauhaus-Archiv Berlin
Photographer unknown

'Architects, painters and sculptors must recognise anew and learn to grasp the composite character of a building both as an entity and in its separate parts', said Gropius, and with the Sommerfeld House, built in 1920–21 for Berlin timber merchant Adolf Sommerfeld, his goal was realised. The greatest communal expression of early Bauhaus ideals and the first project to enable ideas to be tested on a building site, its design drew on a range of stylistic sources, from German vernacular architecture to Frank Lloyd Wright's Prairie Houses. All the workshops, except pottery, were engaged in its realisation. Students closely involved in its interior design and decoration included Joost Schmidt, whose elaborate geometric carving covered the entrance hall, cladding, doors and decorative fascias; Josef Albers created a large staircase window, fusing a mixture of small latticed and large crystalline stained-glass panels; Marcel Breuer designed a table and chairs, and Dörte Helm an appliqué curtain.

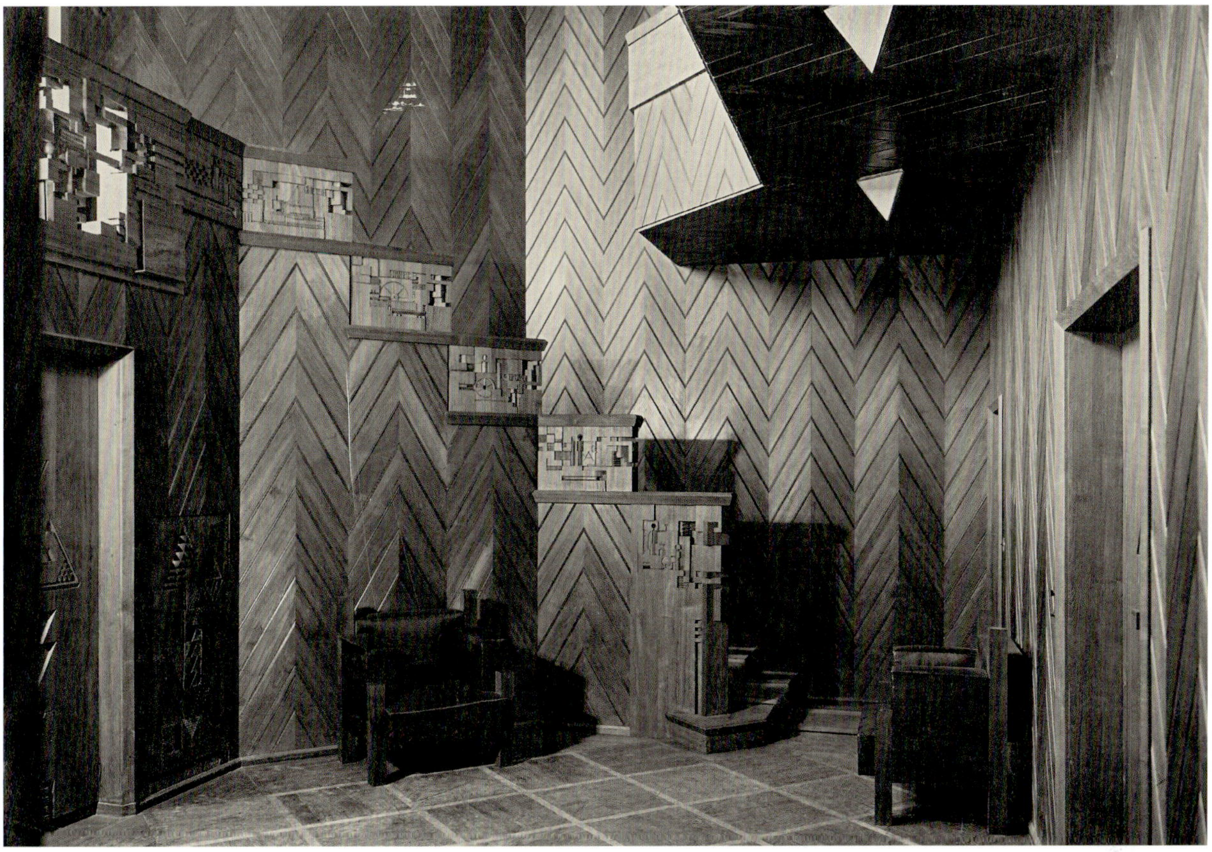

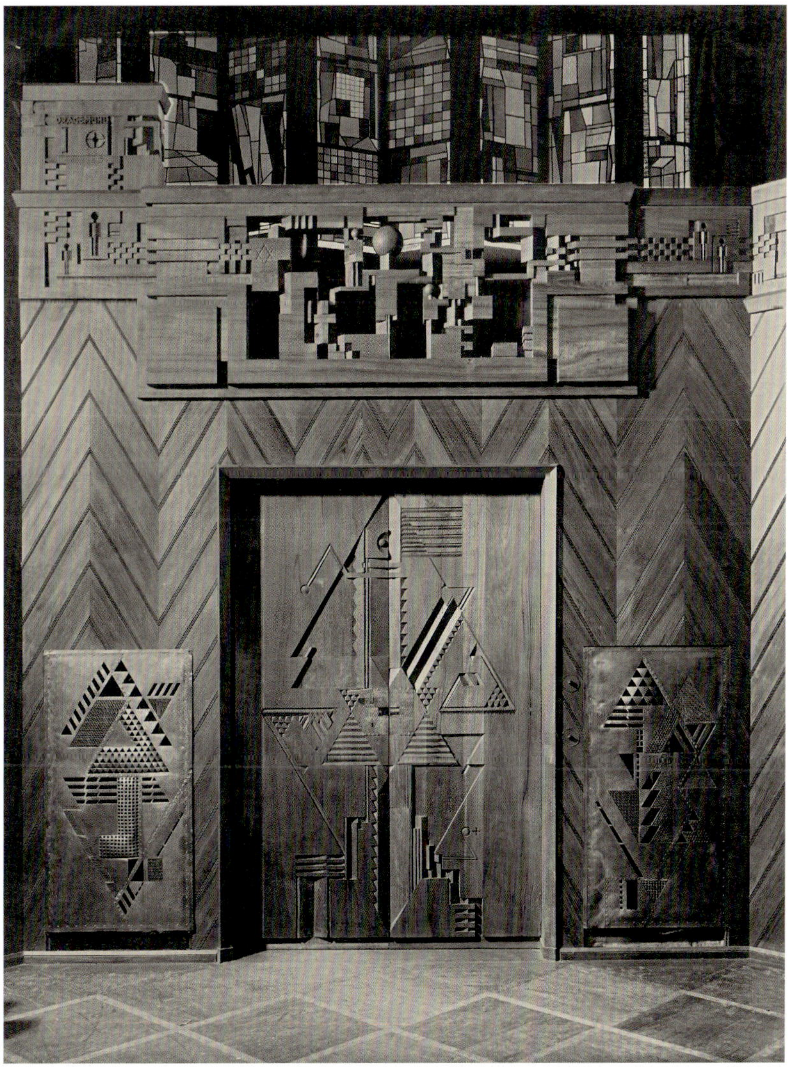

28
Sommerfeld House, Berlin-Steglitz, designed by Walter Gropius and Adolf Meyer
Vestibule with staircase designed by Joost Schmidt and furniture by Marcel Breuer, c.1923
Gelatin silver print
16.9 × 22.7 cm
Bauhaus-Archiv Berlin
Photographer unknown

29
Sommerfeld House, Berlin-Steglitz, designed by Walter Gropius and Adolf Meyer
Wooden door with relief designed by Joost Schmidt, glass window in background designed by Josef Albers, c.1923
Gelatin silver print
22.9 × 17 cm
Bauhaus-Archiv Berlin
Photographer unknown

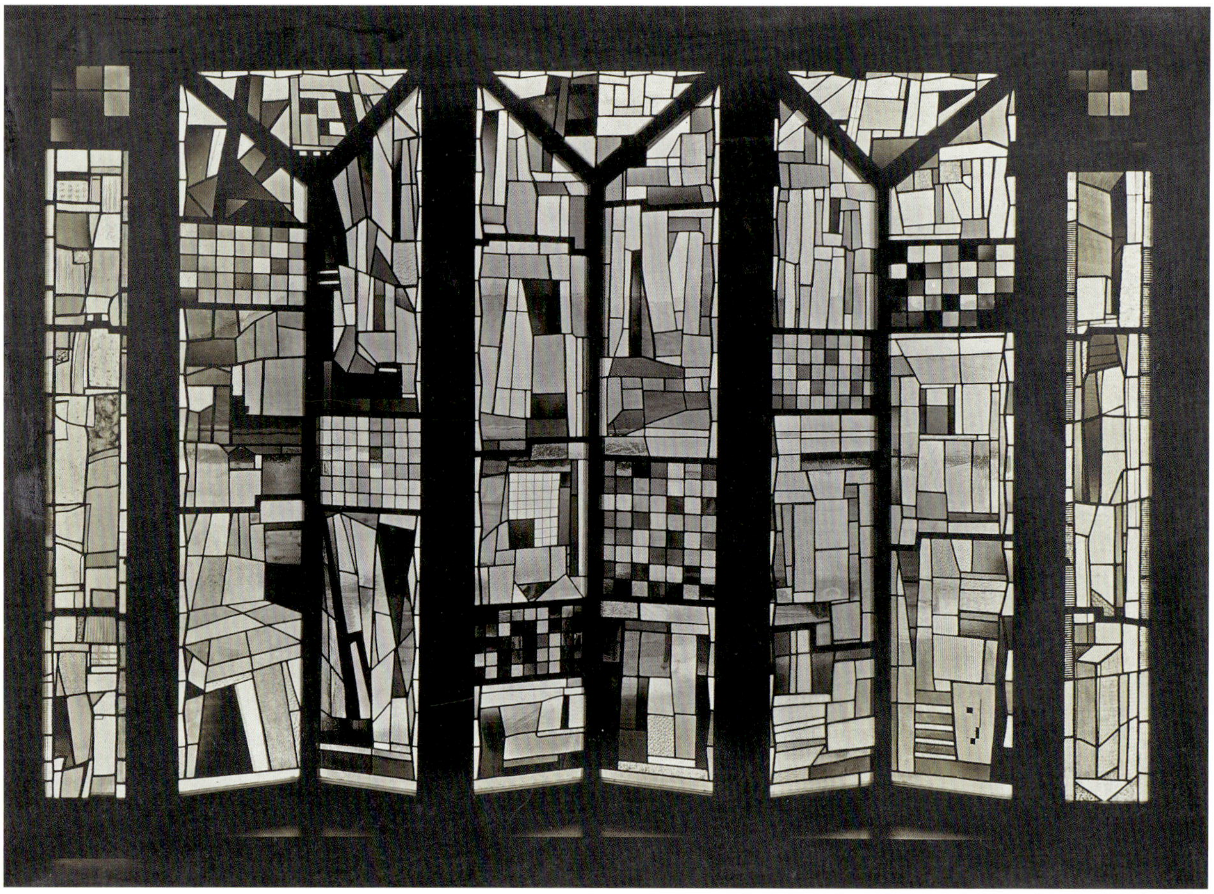

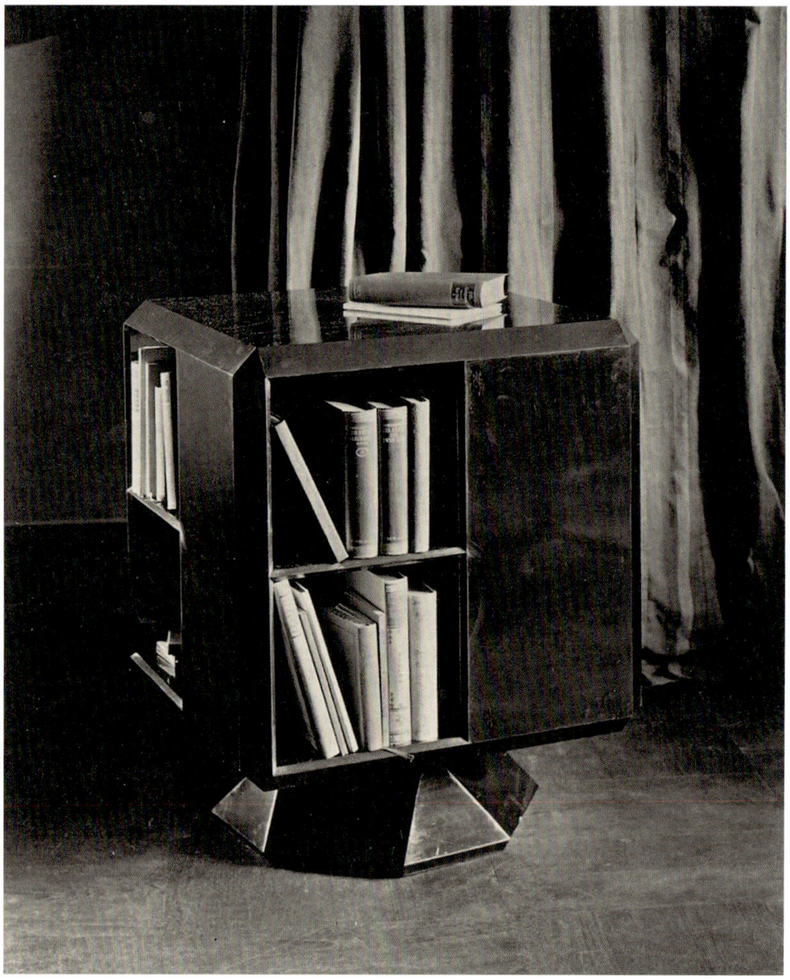

30
Sommerfeld House, Berlin-Steglitz, designed by Walter Gropius and Adolf Meyer
Staircase window designed by Josef Albers, c. 1923
Gelatin silver print
17 × 22.8 cm
Bauhaus-Archiv Berlin
Photographer unknown

31
Sommerfeld House, Berlin-Steglitz, designed by Walter Gropius and Adolf Meyer
Swivelling bookcase designed by Walter Gropius and Adolf Meyer, c. 1923
Sommerfeld Family, London
Photographer unknown

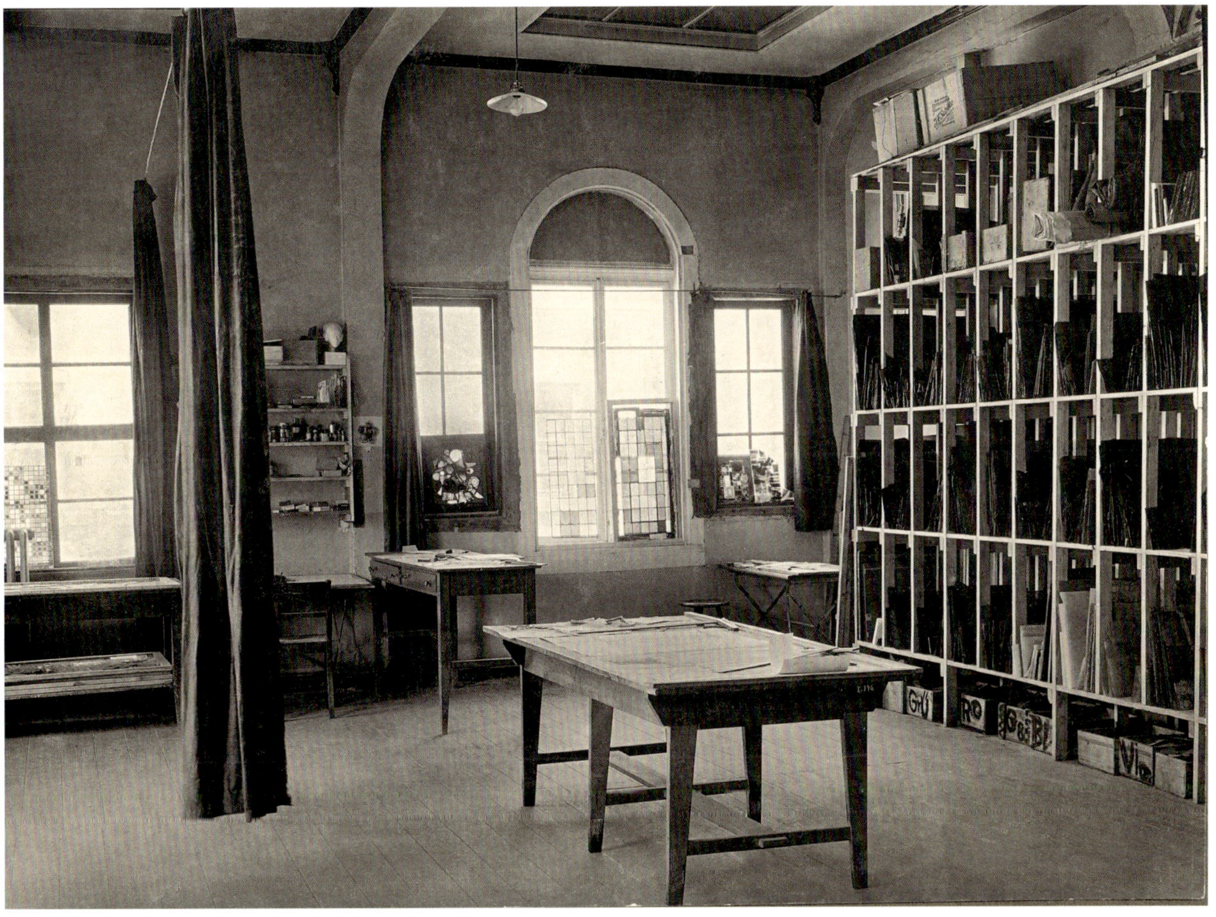

32
Stained-glass workshop, 1923
Bauhaus-Universität Weimar,
Archiv der Moderne
Photographer unknown

33
Artist unknown
Scene in Bethlehem, 1920
Tracing paper collage
49.2 × 42.7 cm
Klassik Stiftung Weimar,
Bestand Museen

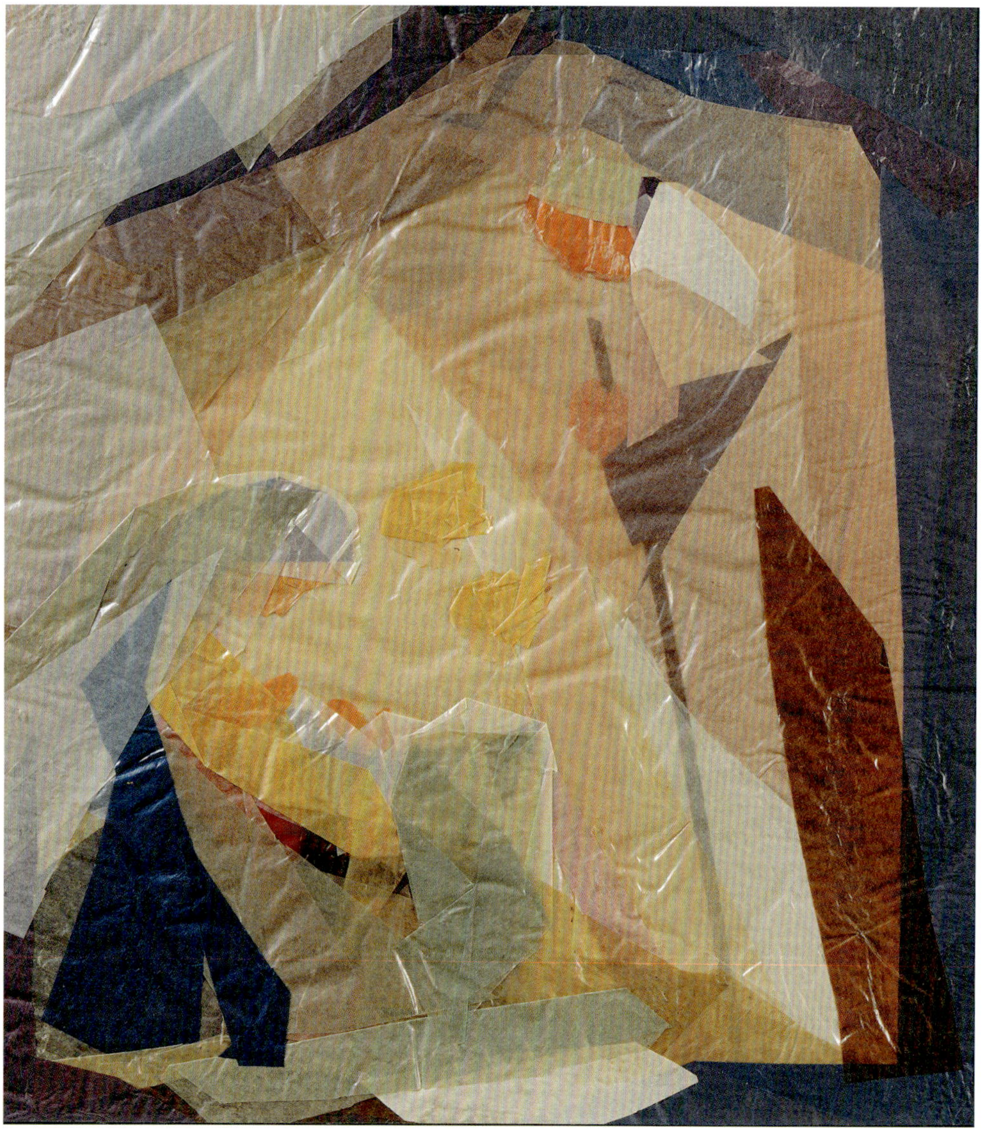

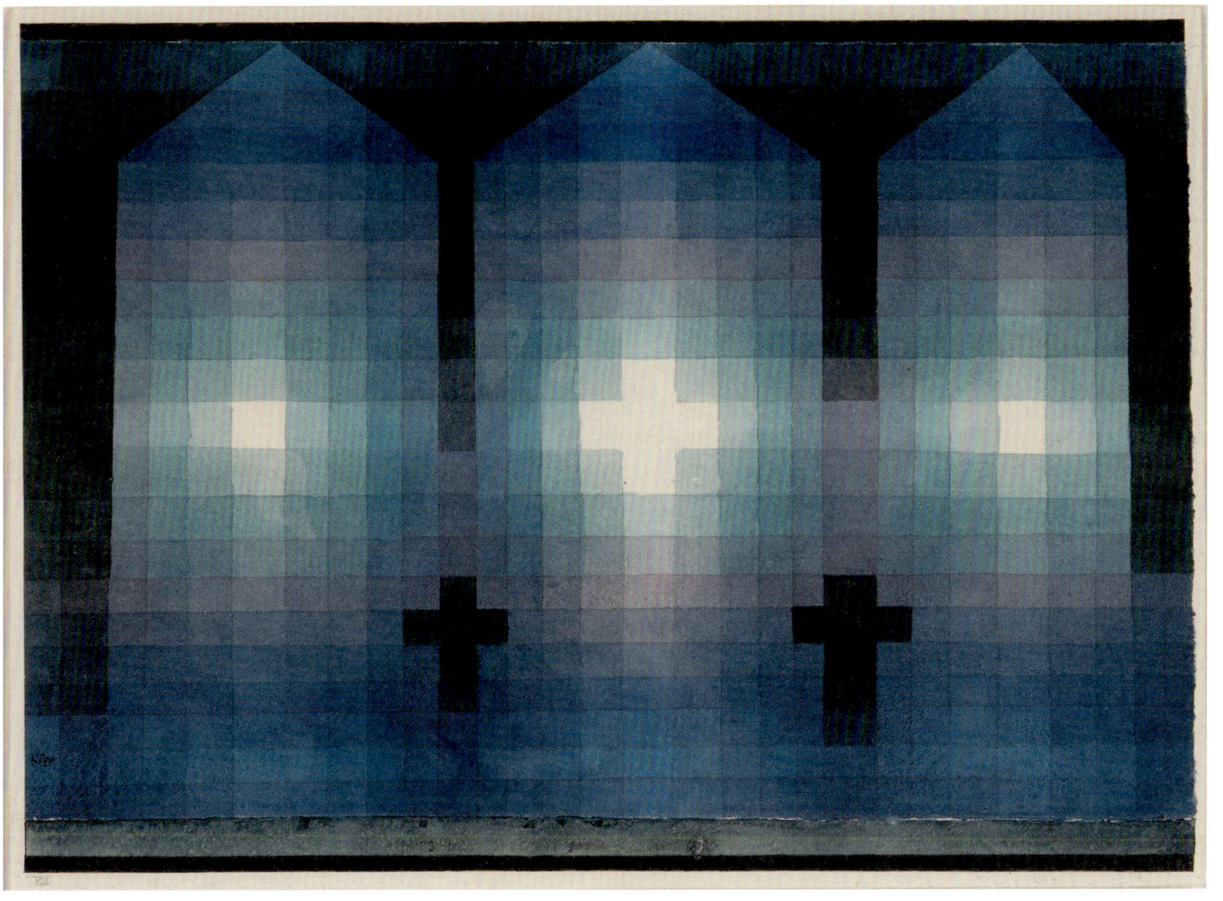

34
Paul Klee
Tomb in Three Parts, 1923
Watercolour and pencil on paper
33 × 45.1 cm
Philadelphia Museum of Art
The Louis E. Stern Collection 1963

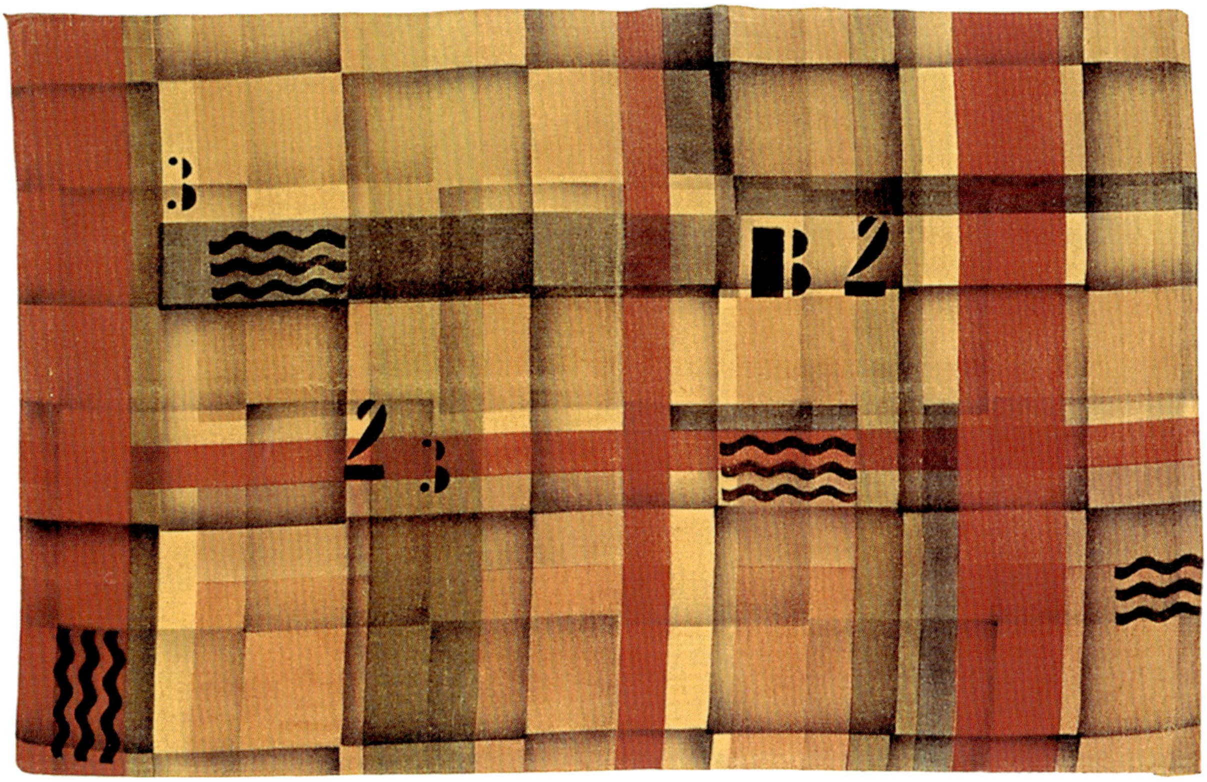

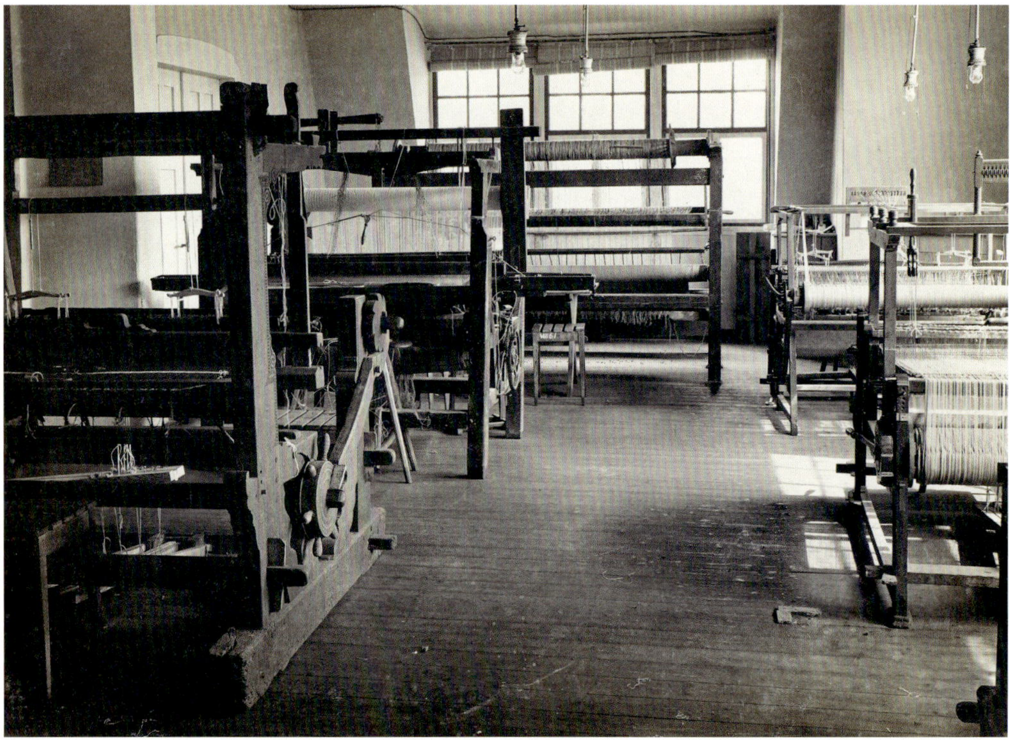

35
Felix Kube
Fabric, c.1921
Linen weave and cotton
60 × 38 cm
Bauhaus-Archiv Berlin

36
Weaving workshop, c.1923–24
Bauhaus-Universität Weimar,
Archiv der Moderne
Photographer unknown

gunta stölzl
diary entry, bauhaus, weimar

Just two days, and how rich they've been already. The first evening there was a wonderful party; one immediately sensed what sort of spirit flourishes here, a party to celebrate the opening of the dining hall. A large hall, white-clad tables, green walls, music; we were met with cheerful music. The people, who have come here to create in earnest, are all still strangers, but they want to get to know each other; is there a better way to do so than simply by happily passing the time together, dancing and playing? We were very exited about this beginning; of course, the whole Munich bloc sat together, faculty and students: a big, colourful hodgepodge. First, there was a marvellous free dinner. Then there was a shadow play of some delightful Morgenstern Lieder, a capital idea–and brilliantly silhouetted; then a shadow play showing the construction of the dining hall, also fabulously witty and imaginative, there was real artistry in it. Then there was dancing. It wasn't beautiful dancing, but wild and frolic-some, like dancing on a colourful meadow...

Oh, sometimes I wish I were among people, creating forms, shaping life, making people–and children–oh, how marvellous that must be, and I freeze up when I think about my kind of art. Will the world ever bloom for me like that; someday–oh, I'd like to give myself–but I know that I have to wait, look into myself, all of myself. My little garret is just right for that; you cannot see outside, it envelops you and doesn't permit you to gaze into the distance–but into the depths–I need to look deep inside in the upcoming months.

The party was a lively beginning; we were all carried away by it, and then came the serious works from Gropius. We are faced with a vacuum; it has to be filled, it has to be built, and every hand is needed. Don't shrink from chaos, but take from it things that seem to use to represent life, and give shape to them. Then he told us about the different opportunities the school already offers for artistic and professional development.

Itten–here great things are starting to become clear to me; mysteries, wider contexts appear visible; things I vaguely feel are entering my consciousness and now I can start to develop them.

His first words were about rhythm. First, one has to train one's hand, make the fingers flexible; we do finger exercises just as pianists do. We begin to feel what makes rhythm come into being, endless circular motions, starting with the tips of the fingers, the movement flows into the wrist, the elbows, the shoulders, up to the heart. One has to feel it in every stroke, every line; no more drawing without feeling, no more half-comprehended rhythm. Drawing is not replicating what we see, but instead letting flow through the entire body that which we feel through external stimulus (as well as through purely internal stimulus, of course). It then comes out again as something that is definitely one's own, some artistic creation or, more simply, pulsating life. When we draw a circle, the emotion of the circle has to vibrate throughout the entire body.

Diary entry, 18 October, 1919

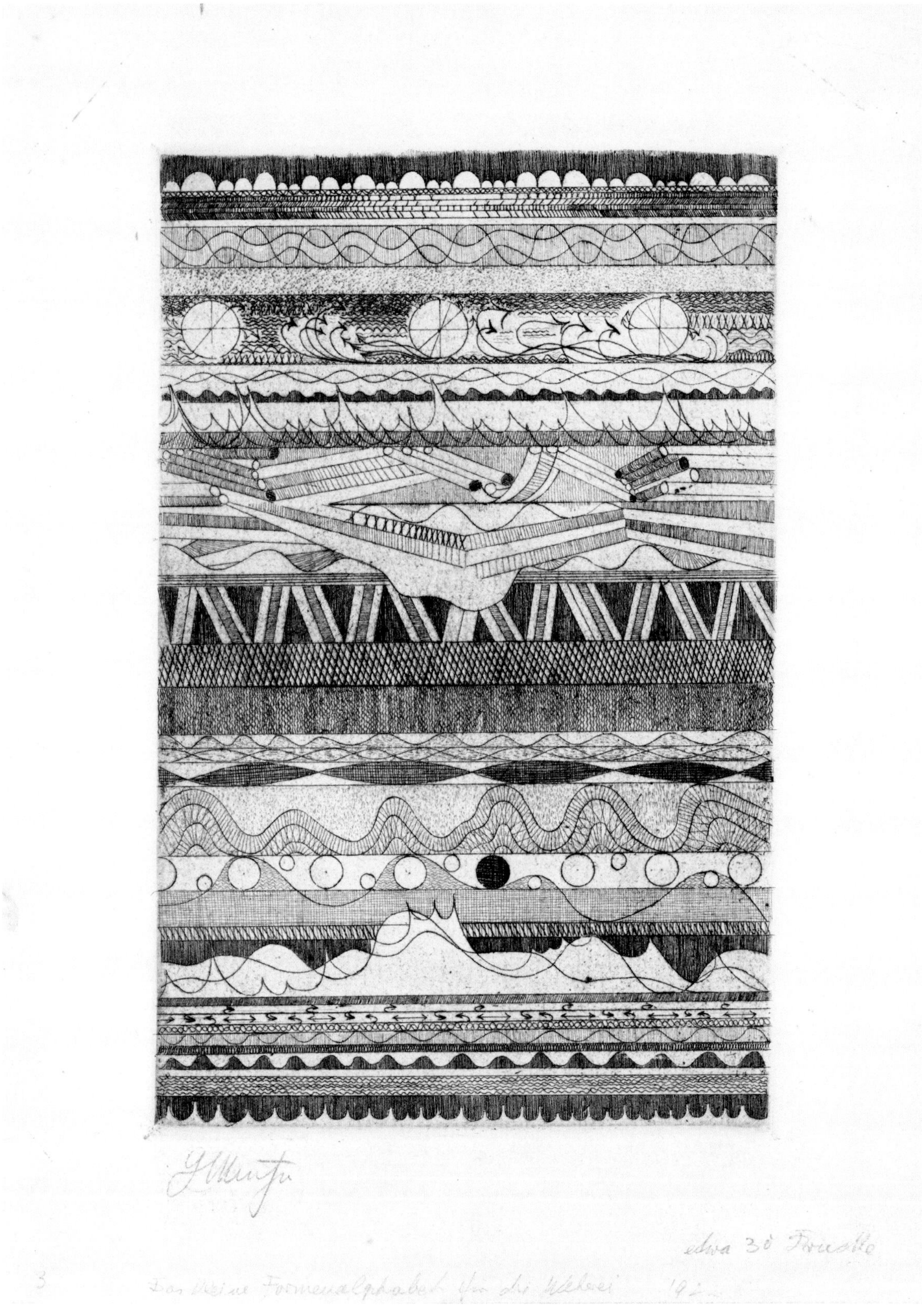

37
Georg Muche
The Small Form Alphabet for the Weaving Workshop, 1922
Etching
32.6 × 23.2 cm
Bauhaus-Archiv Berlin

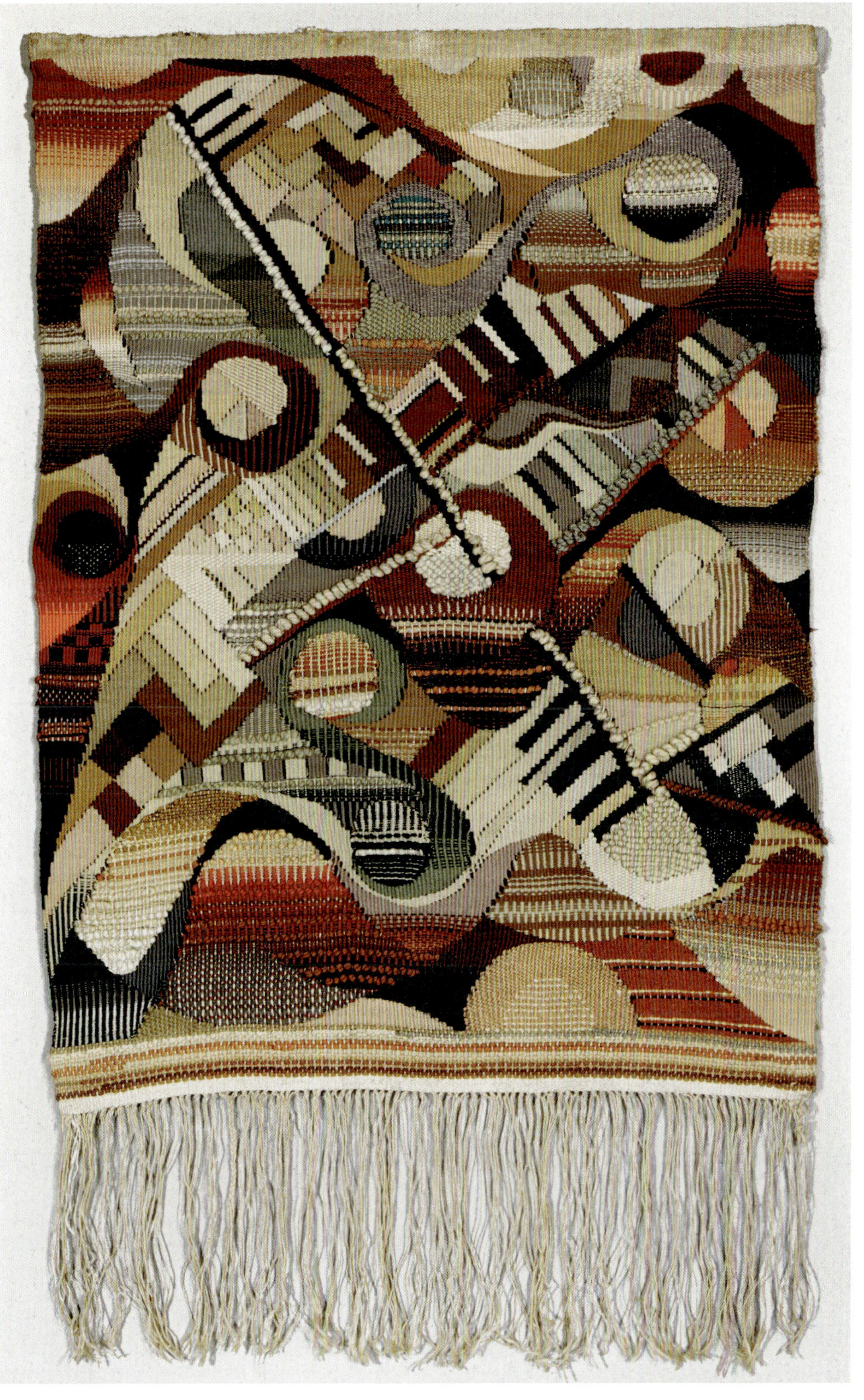

38
Hedwig Jungnick
Gobelin with abstract shapes, 1921–23
Linen, cotton, chenille, artificial silk,
wool and flattened silver wire
125 × 90 cm
Klassik Stiftung Weimar,
Bestand Museen

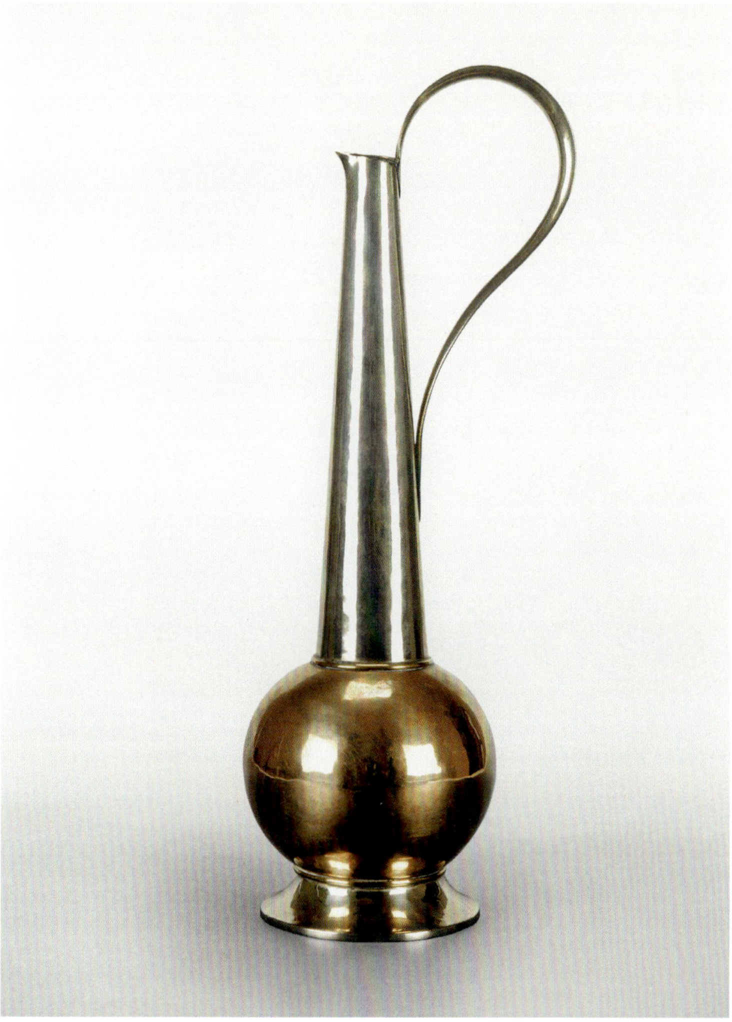

39
Gyula Pap
Liqueur pitcher, 1923
Copper, bronze and nickel silver
Height: 33.3 cm
Klassik Stiftung Weimar,
Bestand Museen

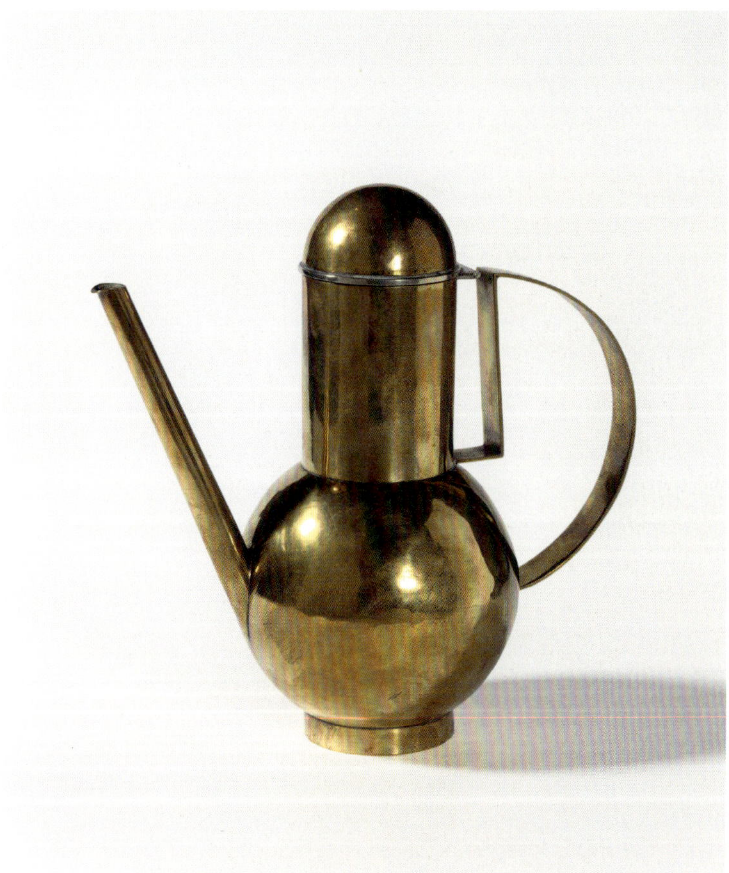

40
Wolfgang Rössger and Friedrich Marby
Spherical pitcher, 1924
Brass, tombac, nickel silver
with silver-plated interior
Height: 19 cm
Klassik Stiftung Weimar,
Bestand Museen

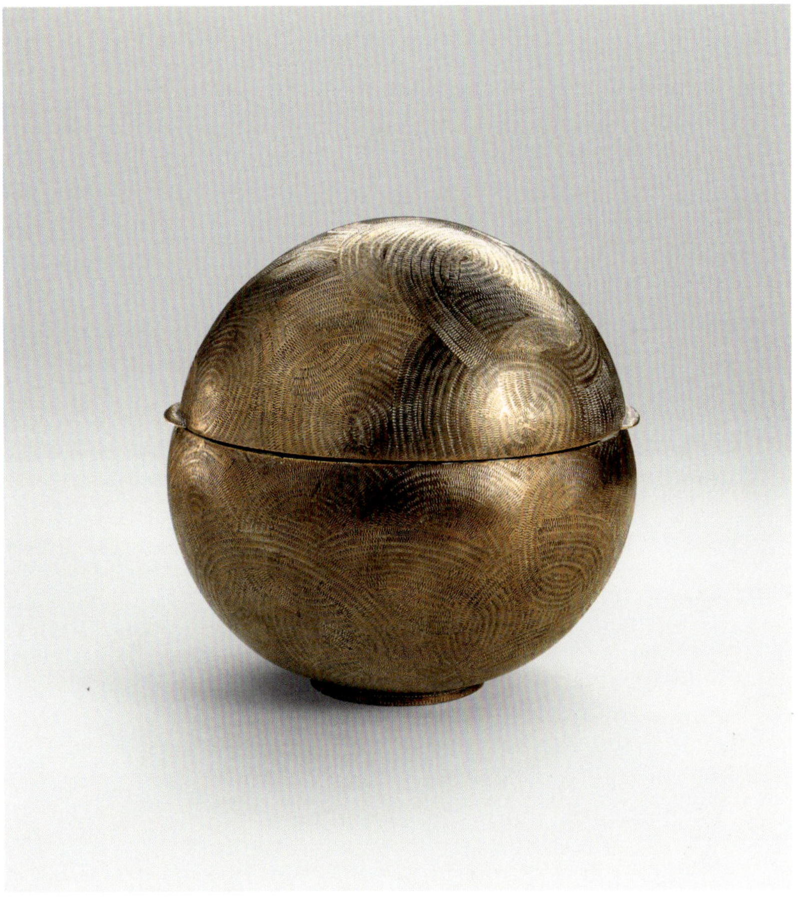

41
Naum Slutzky
Spherical tin, 1920
Copper with pewter interior
Height: 16 cm
Bauhaus-Archiv Berlin

42
Metal workshop, 1923
Bauhaus-Universität Weimar,
Archiv der Moderne
Photographer unknown

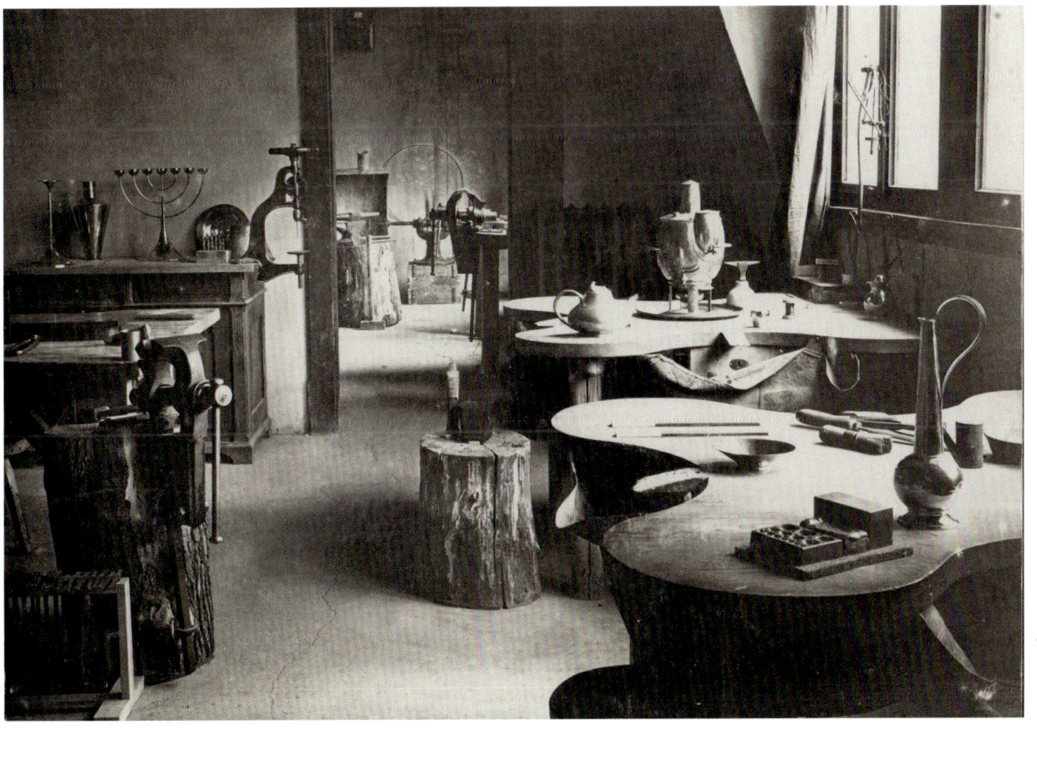

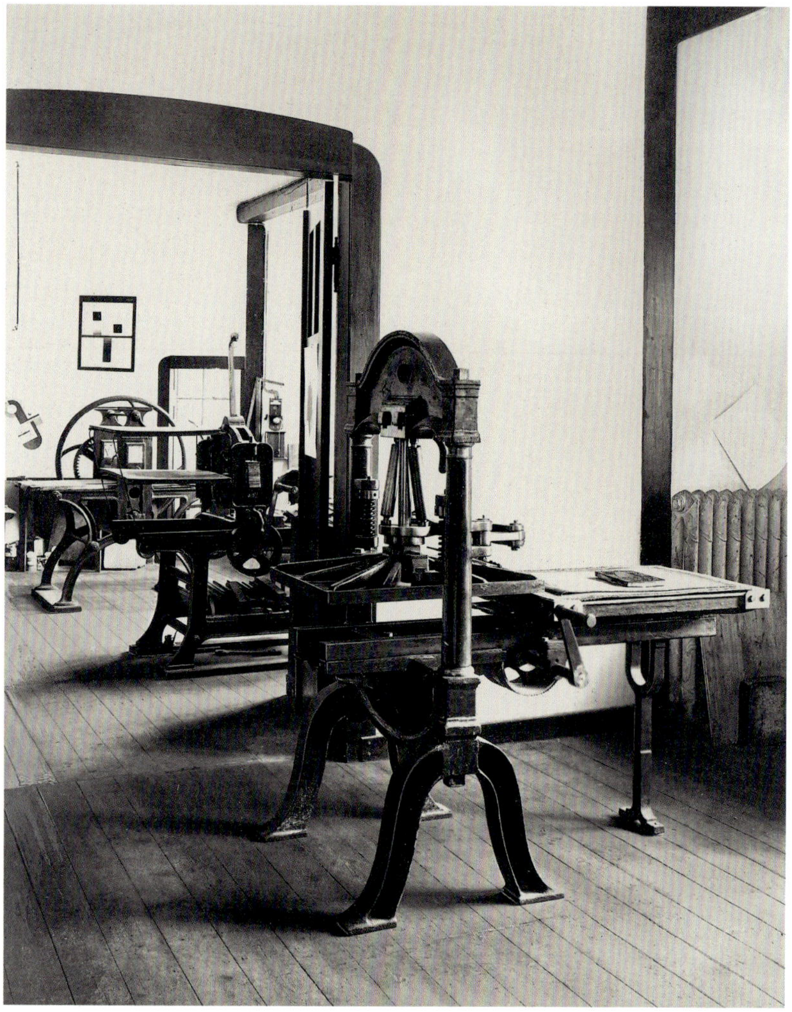

43
Printing workshop, 1923
Bauhaus-Universität Weimar,
Archiv der Moderne
Photographer unknown

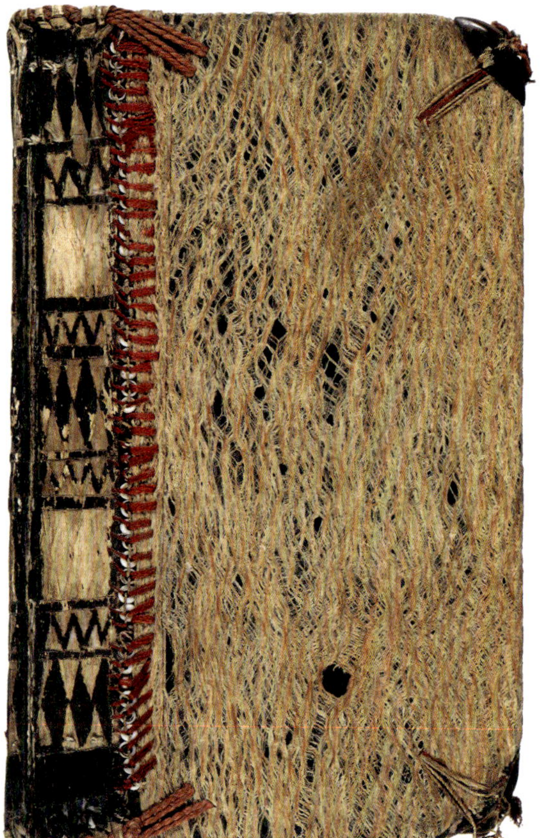

44
Anni Wottitz
Hand-binding of commercially printed book *Afrikanische Märchen* (*African Fairy Tales*), Carl Meinhof, ed., Jena 1921, 1922–23
Tree bark, plant materials, thread, mirror, shells and paper
21 × 13 × 3.3 cm
Bauhaus-Archiv Berlin

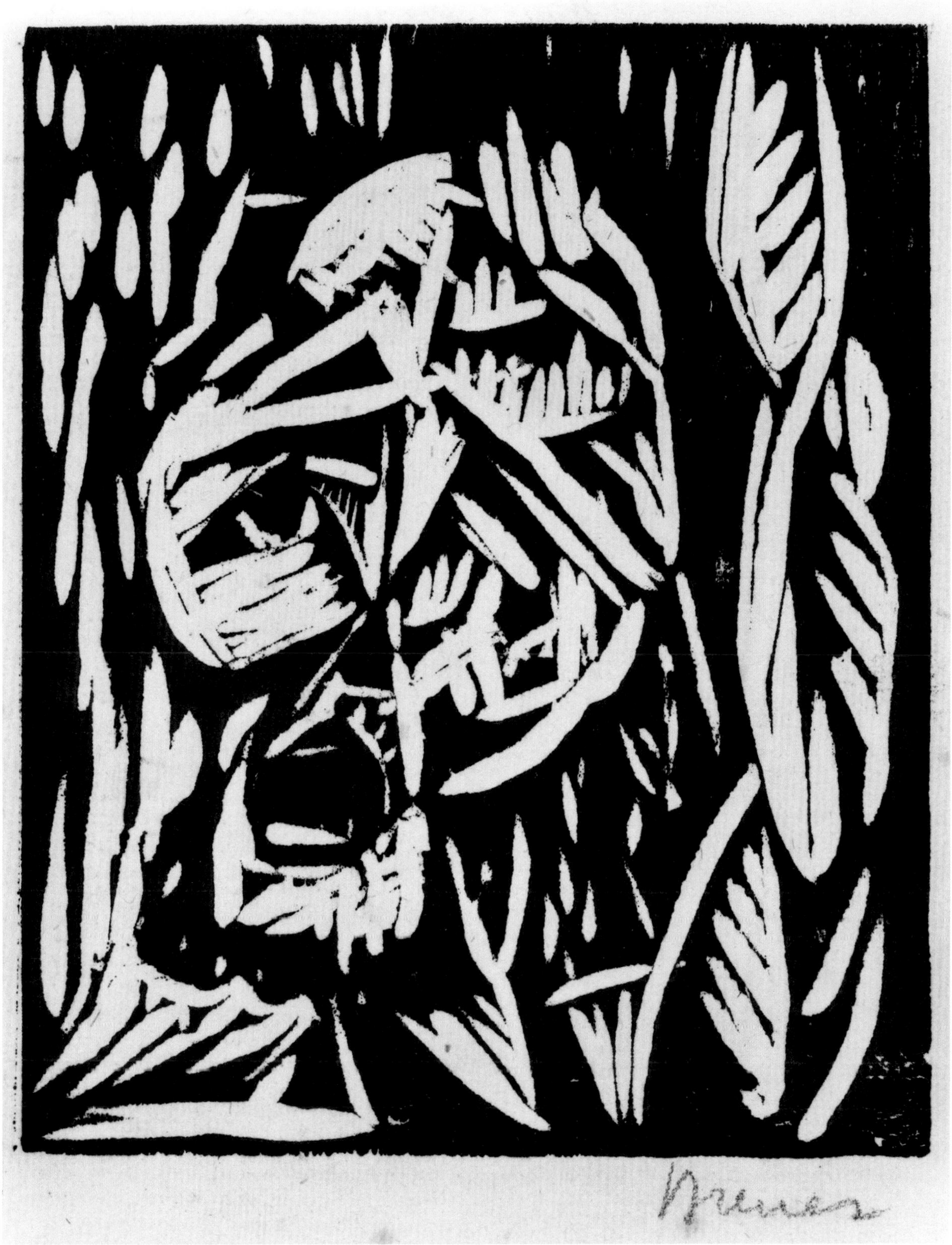

45
Marcel Breuer
Head, c.1920
Woodcut on paper
14.8 × 11.9 cm
Bauhaus-Archiv Berlin

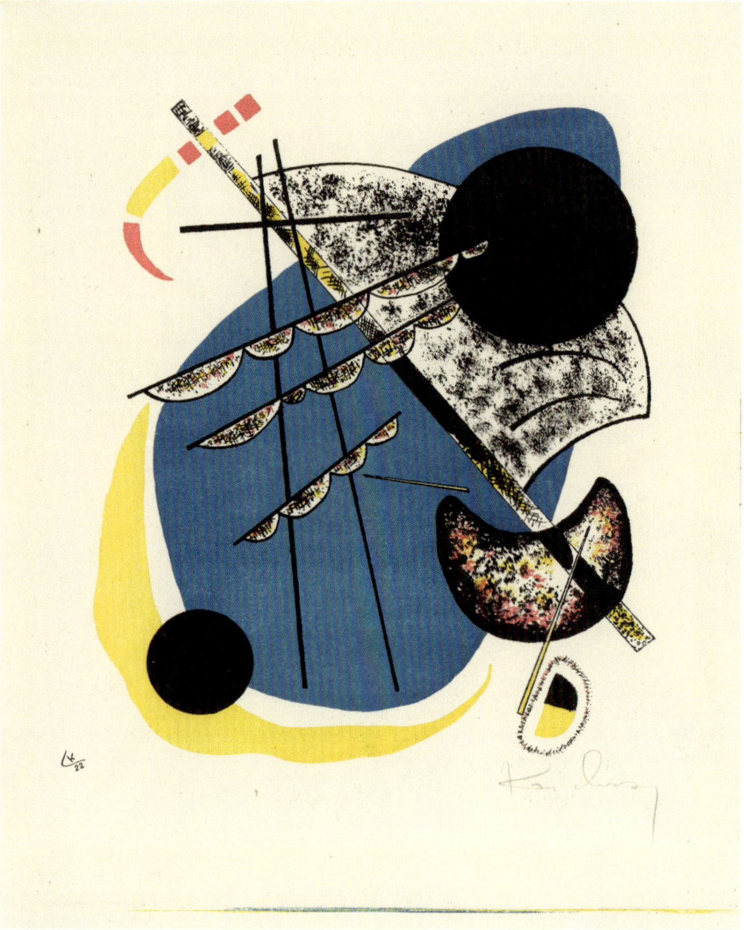

46
Wassily Kandinsky
Kleine Welten II (*Small Worlds II*), 1922
Lithograph from a portfolio
of twelve prints
35.8 × 28 cm
The Museum of Modern Art, New York
Purchase 1941

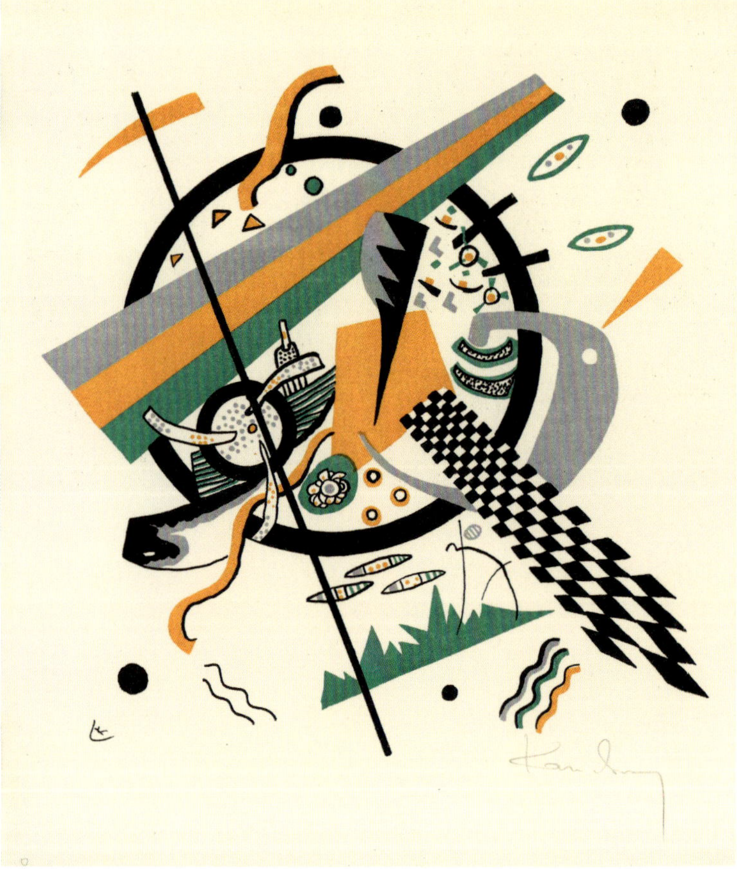

47
Wassily Kandinsky
Kleine Welten IV (*Small Worlds IV*), 1922
Lithograph (transferred from woodcut)
from a portfolio of twelve prints
33.6 × 28.9 cm
The Museum of Modern Art, New York
Gift of Abby Aldrich Rockefeller 1940

48
Wassily Kandinsky
Kleine Welten VI (*Small Worlds VI*), 1922
Woodcut from a portfolio of twelve prints
36.7 × 31.4 cm
The Museum of Modern Art, New York
Gift of Abby Aldrich Rockefeller 1940

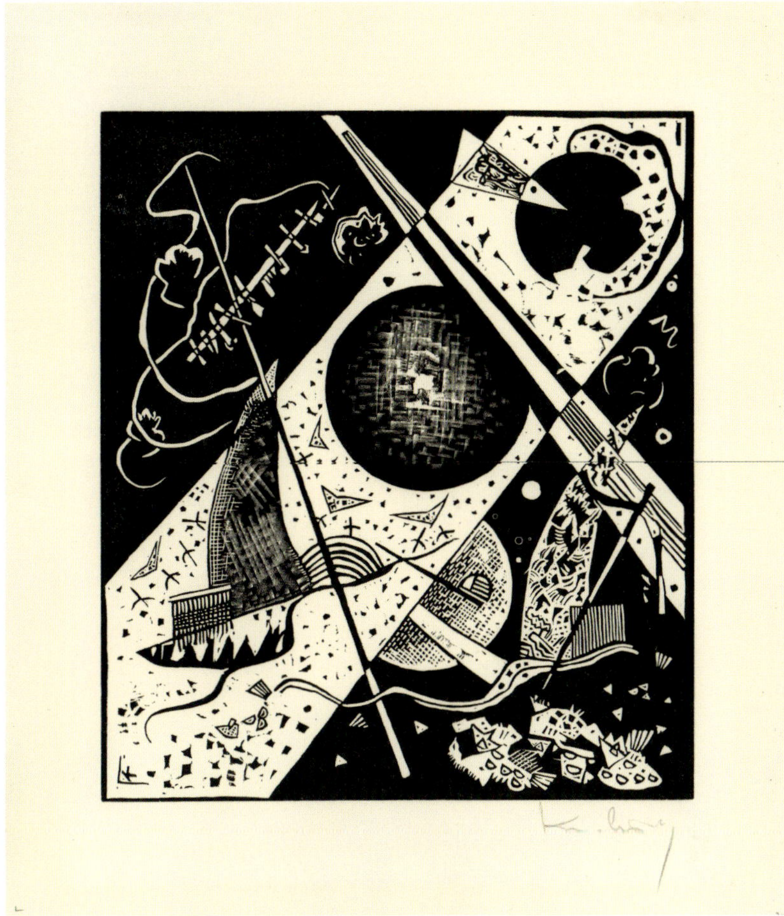

49
Wassily Kandinsky
Kleine Welten XI (*Small Worlds XI*), 1922
Dry point from a portfolio
of twelve prints
30.3 × 26.8 cm
The Museum of Modern Art, New York
Gift of Abby Aldrich Rockefeller 1940

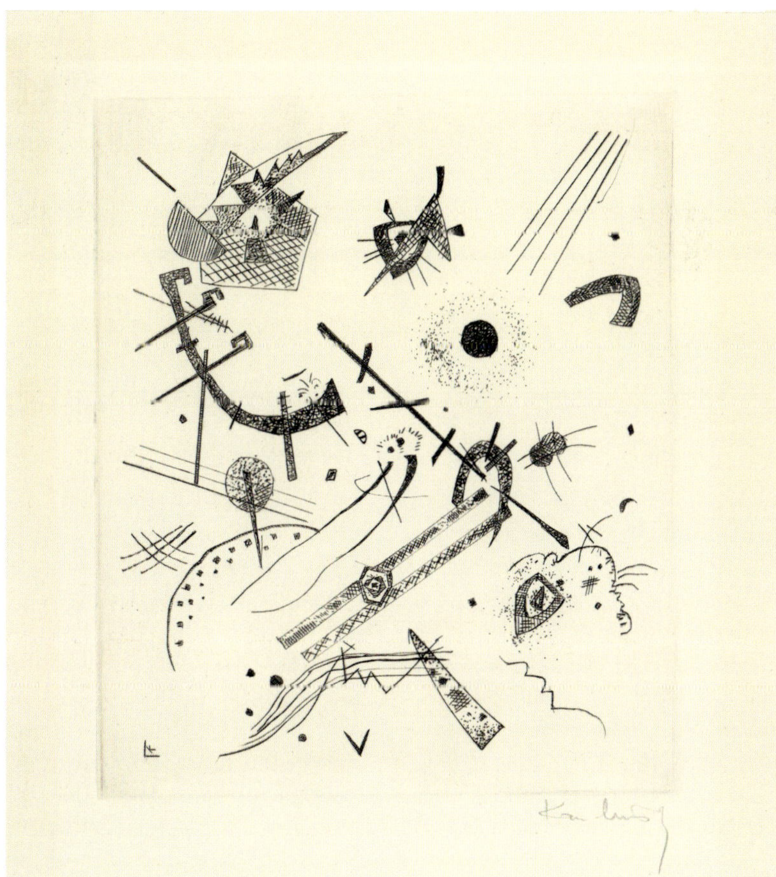

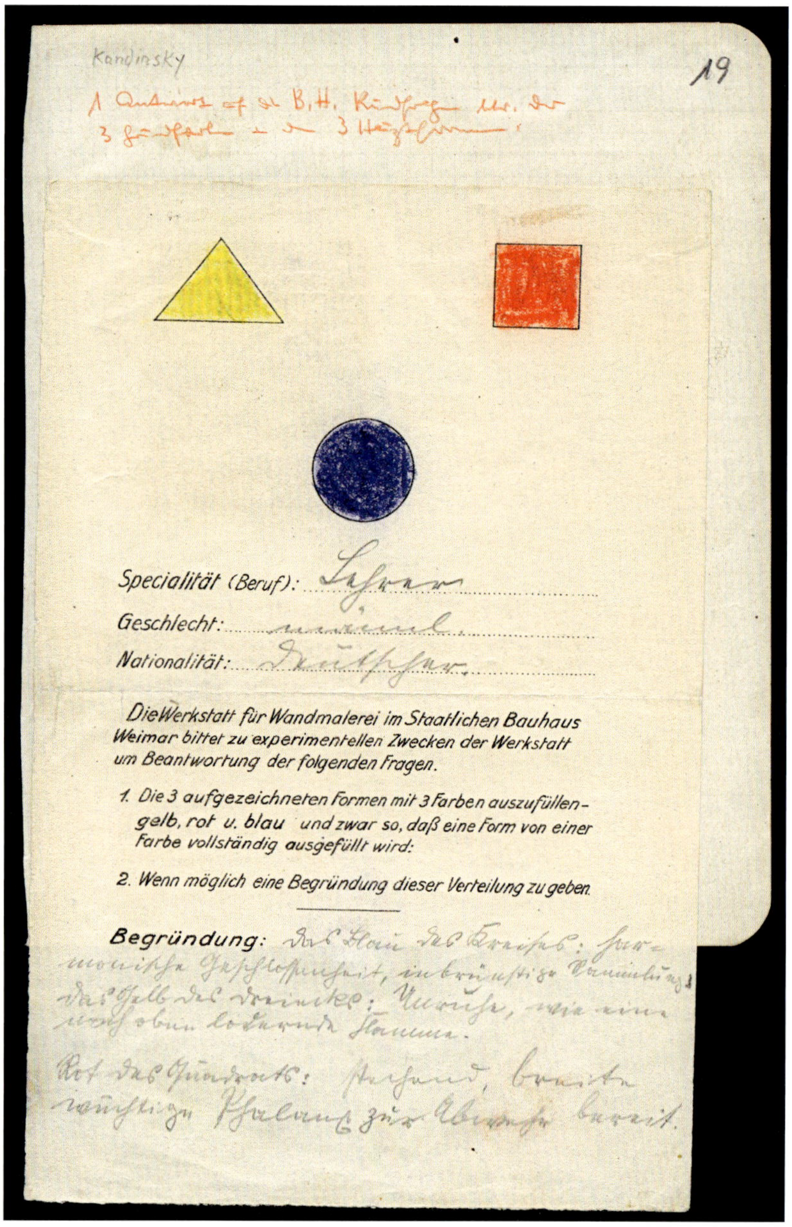
Kandinsky

19

Specialität (Beruf):

Geschlecht:

Nationalität:

Die Werkstatt für Wandmalerei im Staatlichen Bauhaus Weimar bittet zu experimentellen Zwecken der Werkstatt um Beantwortung der folgenden Fragen.

1. Die 3 aufgezeichneten Formen mit 3 Farben auszufüllen – gelb, rot u. blau und zwar so, daß eine Form von einer Farbe vollständig ausgefüllt wird:

2. Wenn möglich eine Begründung dieser Verteilung zu geben.

Begründung:

50
Artist unknown
Wassily Kandinsky's questionnaire issued by the wall-painting workshop on the relationship between primary colours and elementary forms, c. 1922–23
Lithograph on paper with pencil and coloured pencil
23.3 × 15.1 cm
Bauhaus-Archiv Berlin

As head of the wall-painting workshop, Kandinsky issued a questionnaire to students and other masters. He asked participants to match each of the basic geometric forms – triangle, square and circle – with one of the primary colours by filling it in with yellow, red or blue, and to provide a rationale for their choices. The artist who completed the questionnaire illustrated here corroborated Kandinsky's assumptions: a 'sharp' yellow for the triangle, an 'earthy' red for the square and a 'spiritual' blue for the circle. Kandinsky was concerned with the sensory perception of form and colour and the relationship between them. Since the publication of his book *Concerning the Spiritual in Art* (1911), Kandinsky had been interested in how colour could produce psychological effects and result in spiritual experiences.

wassily kandinsky
the fundamental elements of form

The work of the Bauhaus is devoted in general to the emerging unity of various areas that until recently were still considered strictly separate from each other.

These newly converging areas are: art in general, primarily so-called 'fine art' (architecture, painting, sculpture); science (mathematics, physics, chemistry, physiology, etc.); and industry, in the form of technical possibilities and economic factors.

- The work in the Bauhaus is synthesis.
- The synthetic method naturally embraces the analytical one. The interrelation of these two methods is inevitable.
- The instruction in the fundamental elements of form must also be built on this basis.
- The general problem of form must be divided into two parts:

1 Form in its narrower sense – plane and space.
2 Form in its broader sense – colour and the relation to form in its narrower sense.

In both cases the work has to begin with the simplest shapes and systematically progress to more complicated ones. Hence, in the first part of the investigation of form the plane is reduced to three fundamental elements – triangle, square, and circle – and space is reduced to the resulting fundamental space elements – pyramid, cube, and sphere. Since no plane and no space can exist without colour, that is, since form in the narrower sense must, in reality, immediately be investigated as form in the broader sense, the division of the problem of form into two parts can be made schematically. On the other hand, the organic relationship between the two parts must be recognised from the outset – the relationship of form to colour and vice versa.

The science of art, which is still in the process of developing, can give practically no explanations of this problem from art historical point of view, and thus, for the time being, the way indicated will have to be paved first.

Hence, every single investigation is confronted by two equally important tasks:

1 The analysis of the given phenomenon, which must be observed in isolation from the other phenomena as far as possible.
2 The interrelation between the phenomena that were first studied in isolation from each other – synthetic method.

The first, narrow and limited as much as possible; the second, broad and unlimited as much as possible.

From Staatliches Bauhaus Weimar 1919–1923, *Bauhaus Verlag, Weimar – Munich, 1923, p.26*

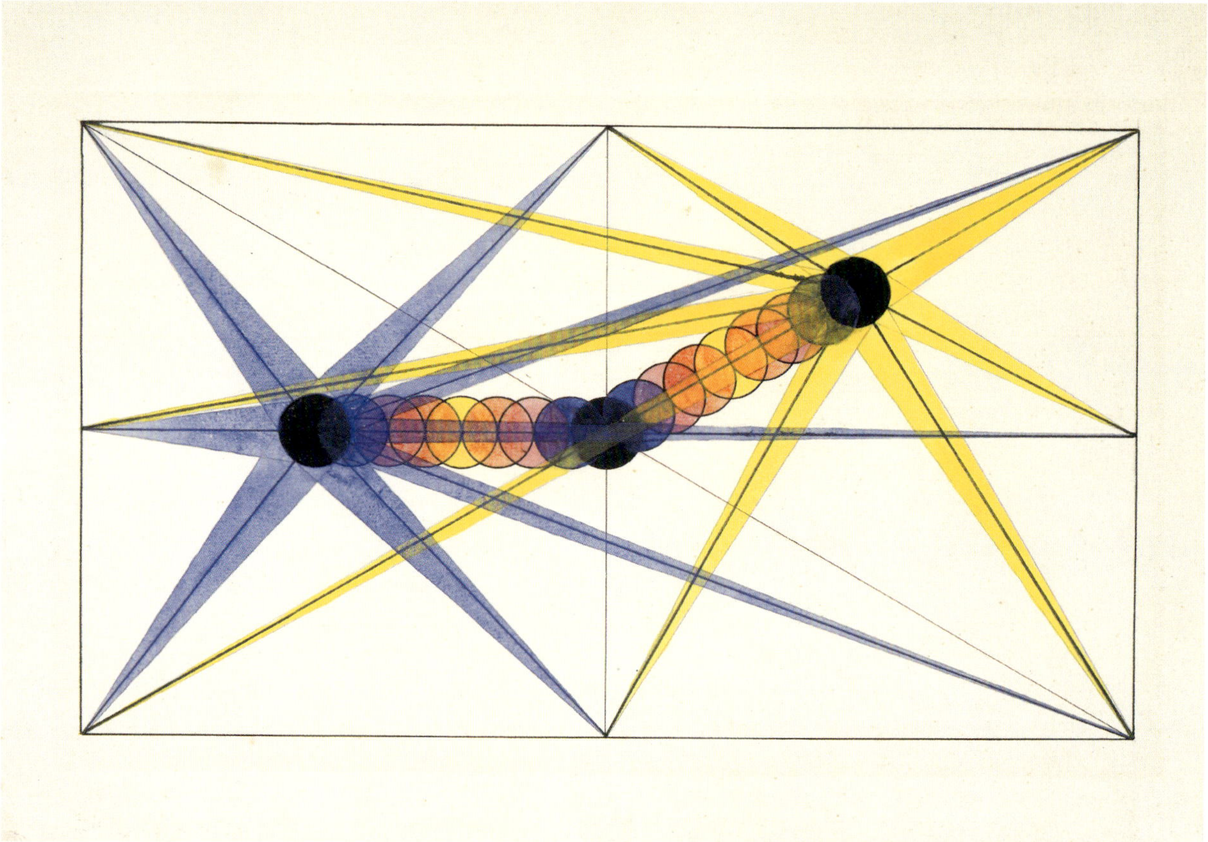

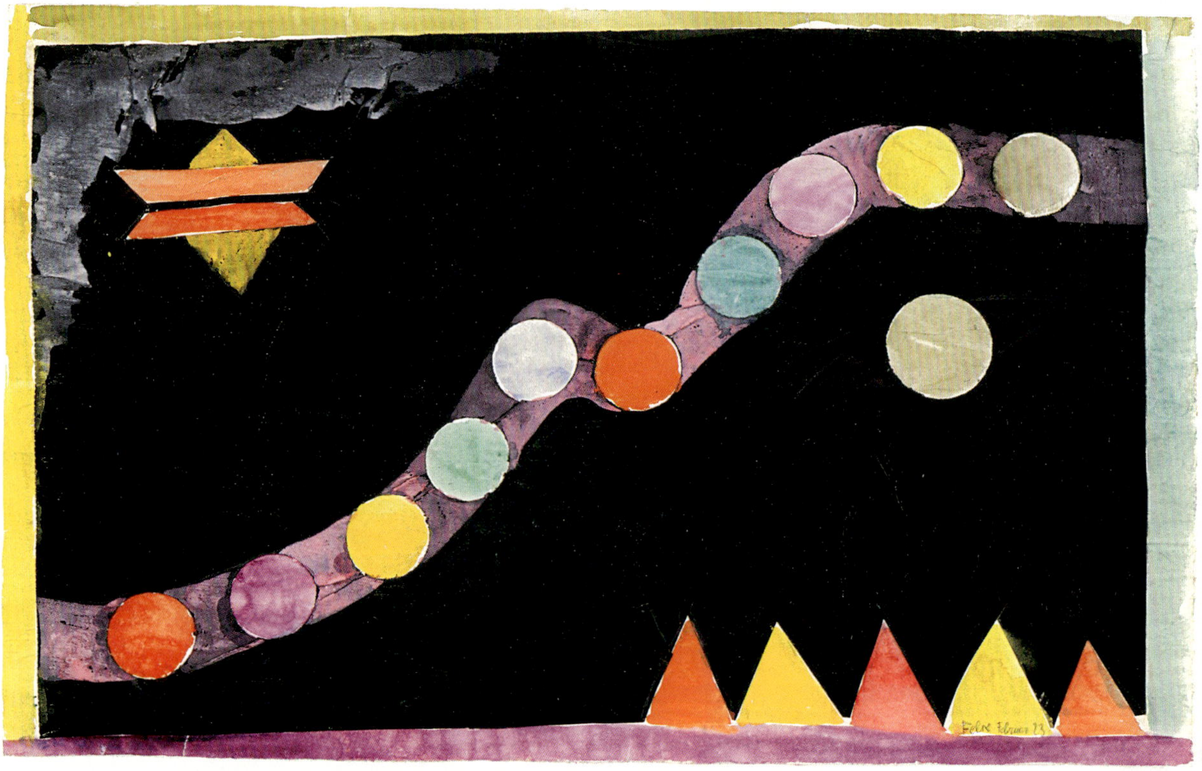

51
Lena Meyer-Bergner
Radiation/drifting centre from
Paul Klee's preliminary course, 1927
Watercolour and ink on paper
23.3 × 32.7 cm
Bauhaus-Archiv Berlin

52
Felix Klee
Untitled (*with stone, chain necklace, sun and tents*), 1923
Watercolour, gouache and collage on paper
32 × 50.3 cm
Bauhaus-Archiv Berlin

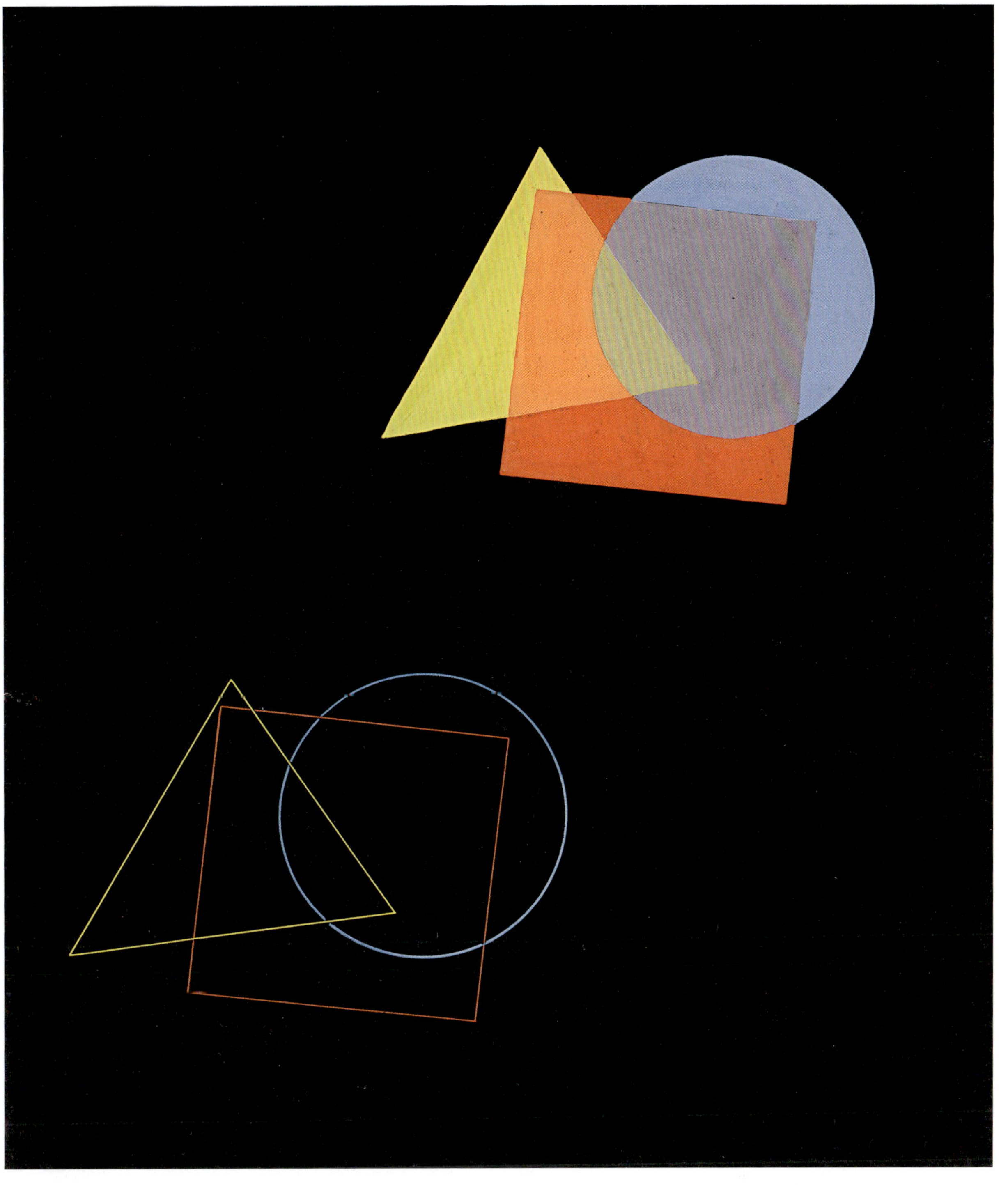

53
Eugen Batz
The spatial effect of colours and forms from Wassily Kandinsky's preliminary course, 1929–30
Tempera over pencil on black paper
39.2 × 32.9 cm
Bauhaus-Archiv Berlin

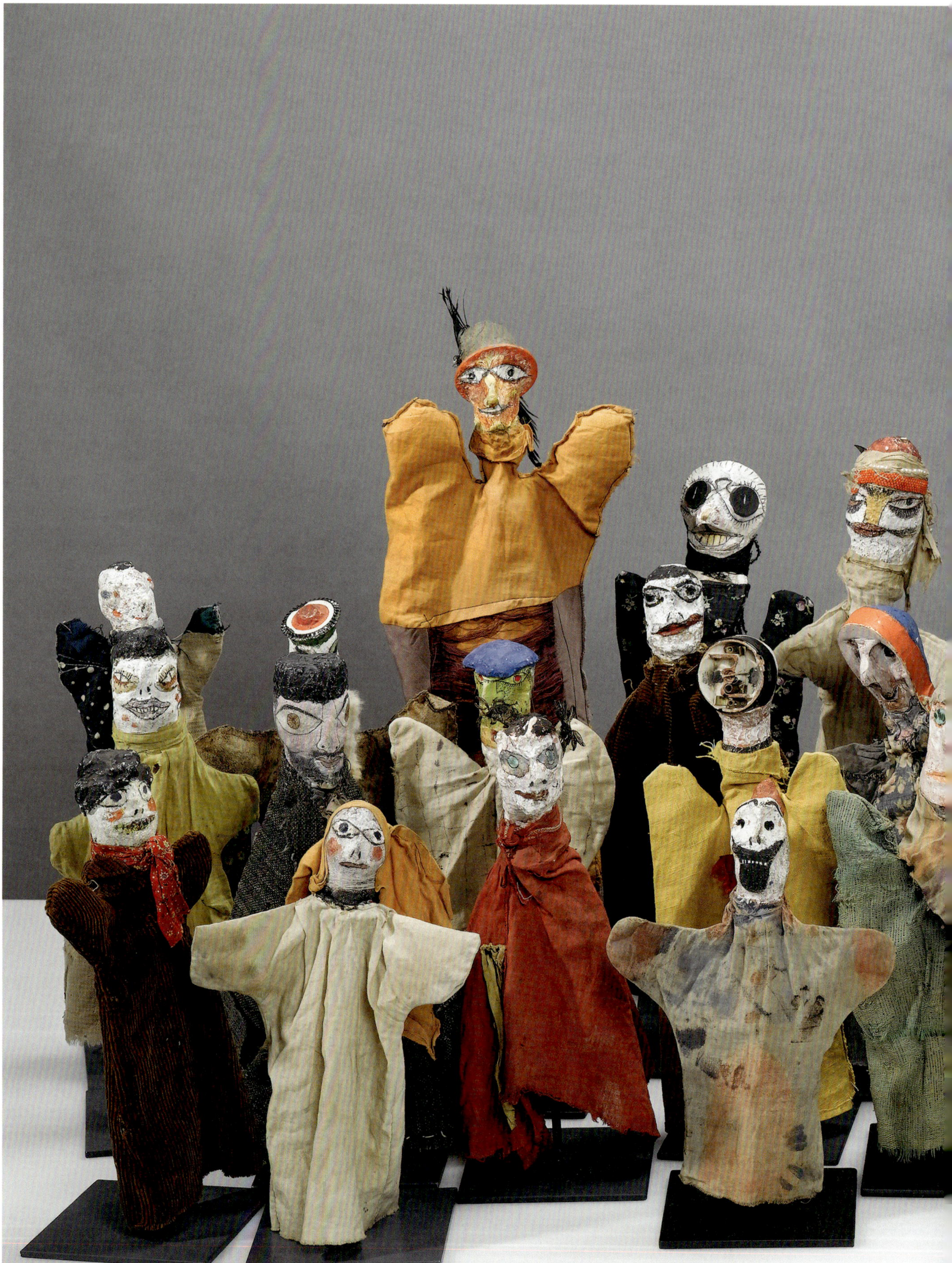

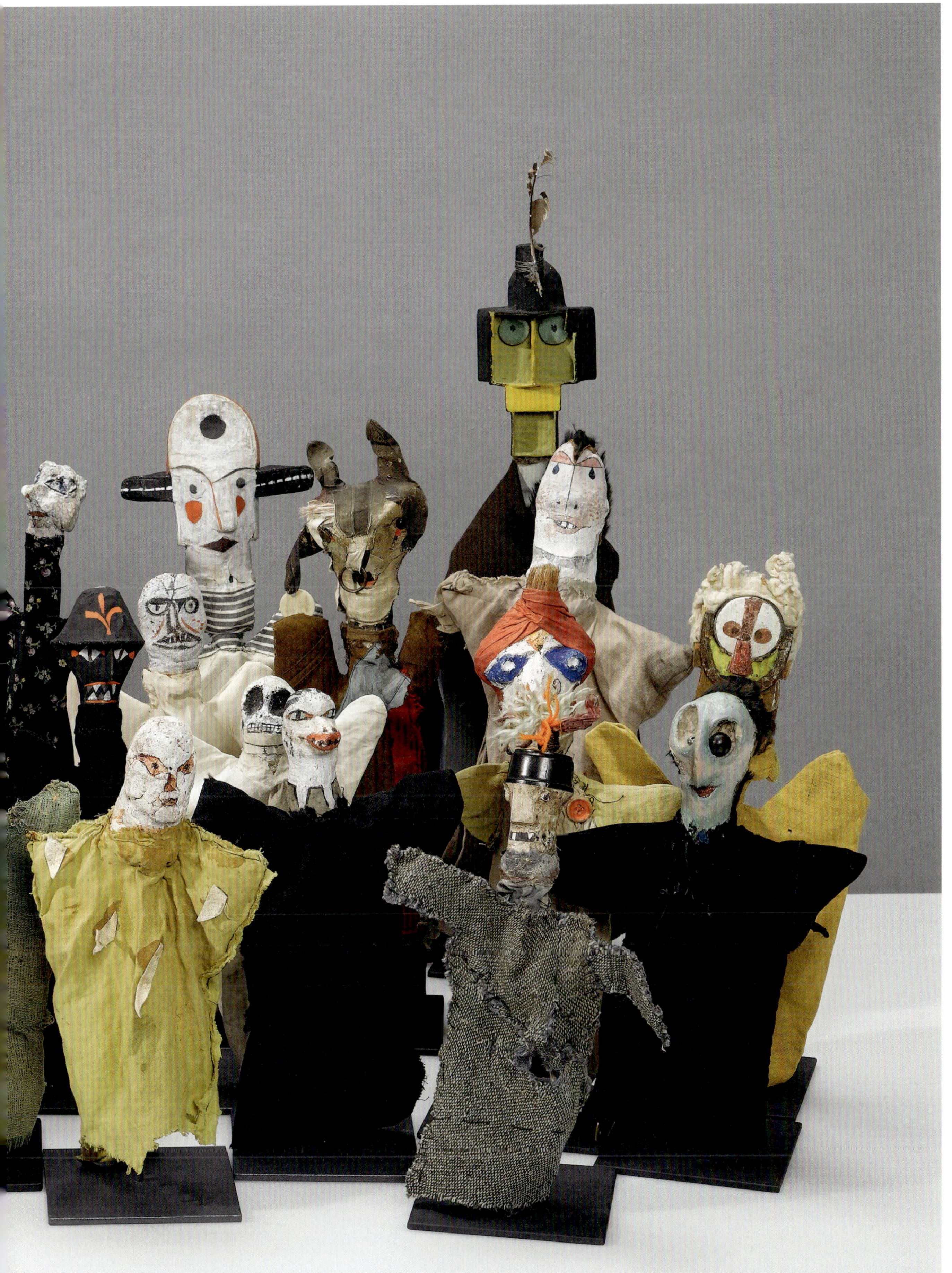

previous page
54
Paul Klee
Puppets made for Felix Klee, 1916–25
Plaster and papier-mâché heads, hand-sewn fabric and found objects
Height: 28 to 58 cm
Zentrum Paul Klee, Bern
Livia Klee Donation

55
Kurt Schmidt and Toni Hergt
The Little Hunchback, puppet in a series of eight for the play *Die Abenteuer des kleinen Buckligen* (*The Adventures of the Little Hunchback*) performed at the Bauhaus Weimar in 1923
Design: Kurt Schmidt,
Fabrication: Toni Hergt and
Stage direction: Oskar Schlemmer, 1923
Wood and iron wire
30 × 15.5 × 10 cm
Puppentheatersammlung
Staatliche Kunstsammlungen, Dresden

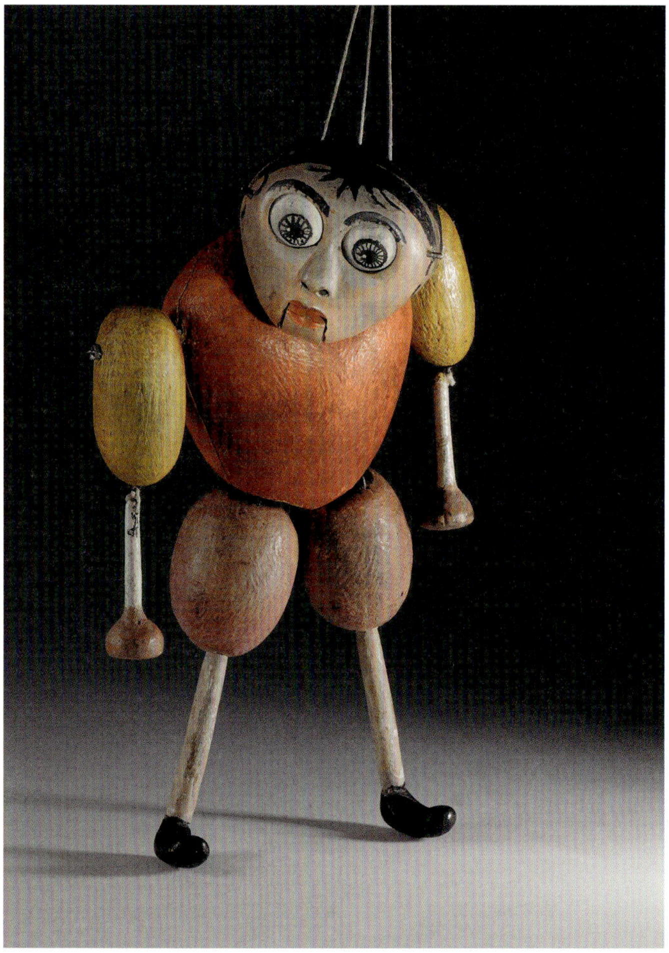

56
Alma Buscher
Dolls, 1923–24
Plaited straw, lacquered wood, knitted mixed fibres
Height: 54 cm and 55.5 cm
Die Neue Sammlung – The International Design Museum Munich

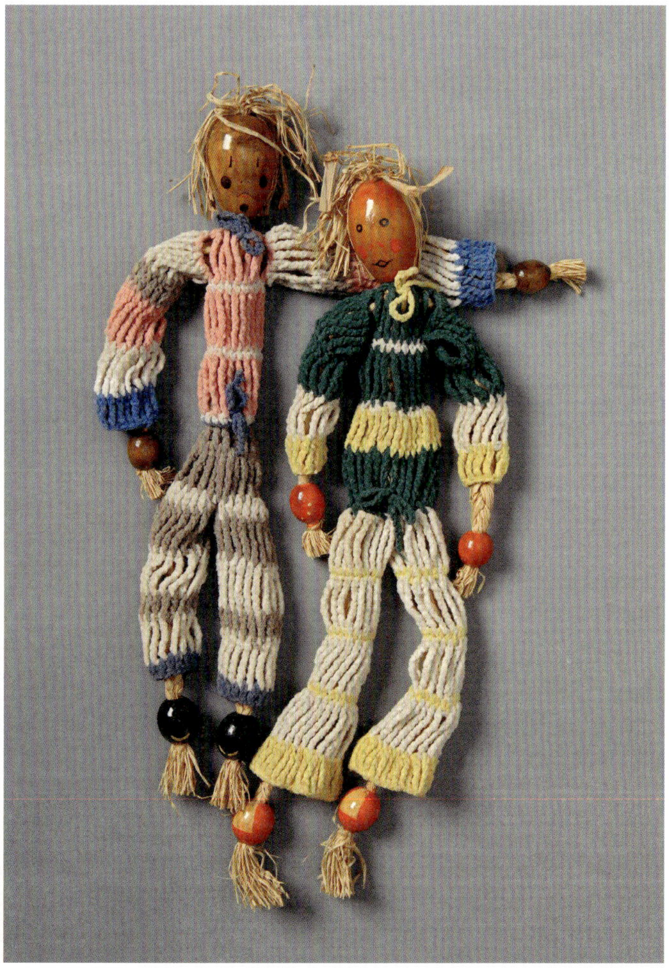

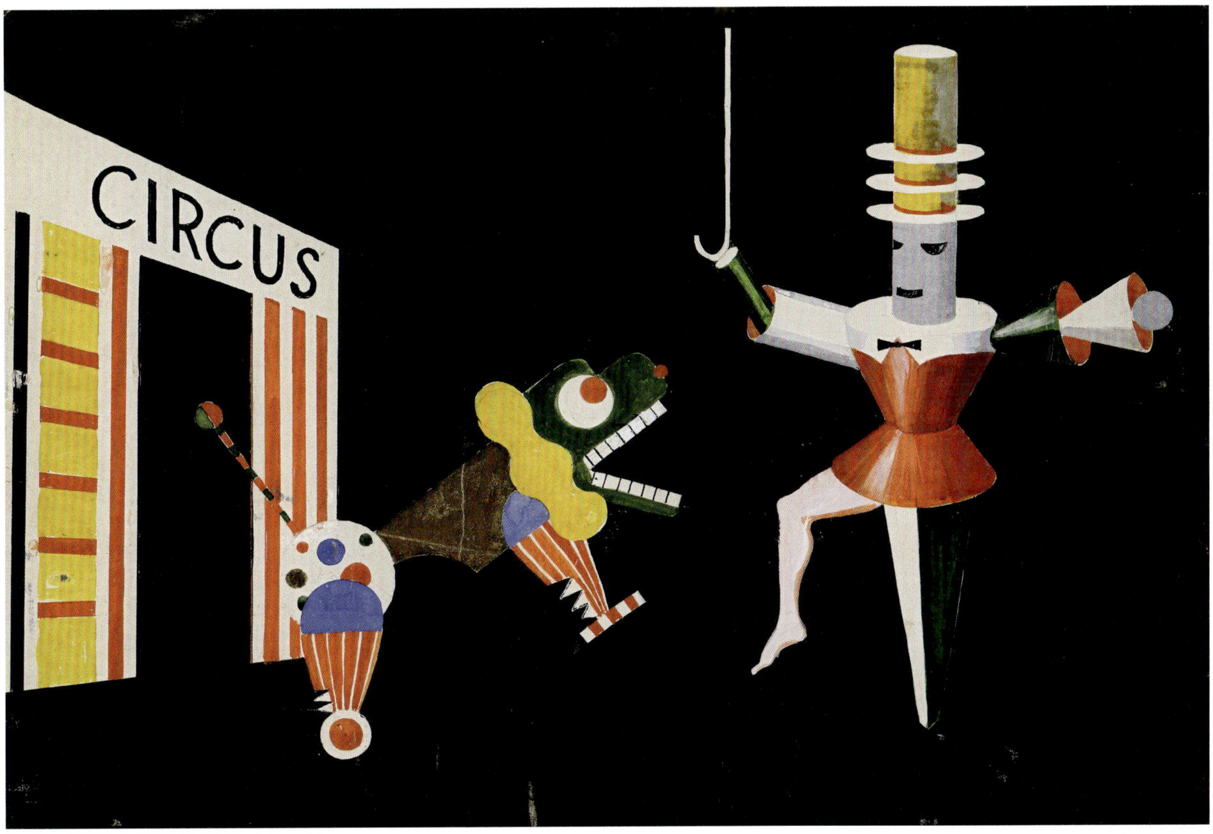

57
Xanti Schawinsky
Circus, c.1924
Tempera, ink and aluminium paint
on paper
34.5 × 50.5 cm
Bauhaus-Archiv Berlin

Play was considered an important underlying principle at the Bauhaus as a means of reconnecting the artist with the child. Paul Klee's series of fifty puppets (of which thirty still exist) created for his son Felix, is a good example of this notion. Made from an array of found materials, they are based on literary characters as well as people from Klee's own circle (the *Big-eared Clown*, for instance, is said to be based on Oskar Schlemmer). Their enigmatic names are emblematic of the artist's delight in child-like playfulness and provide a glimpse into the intimate relationship between the artist and his son. Other Bauhaus members such as Kurt Schmidt, a student in the stage workshop, saw in the art of puppetry opportunities to experiment more formally with artistic principles. His *Little Hunchback*, one of a series of puppets for Schlemmer's production of *Die Abenteur des kleinen Buckligen* (*The Adventures of the Little Hunchback*) from the *Tales of the 1001 Nights*, expressed basic notions of form and colour with its rounded body shape and bold colours.

salute to the square

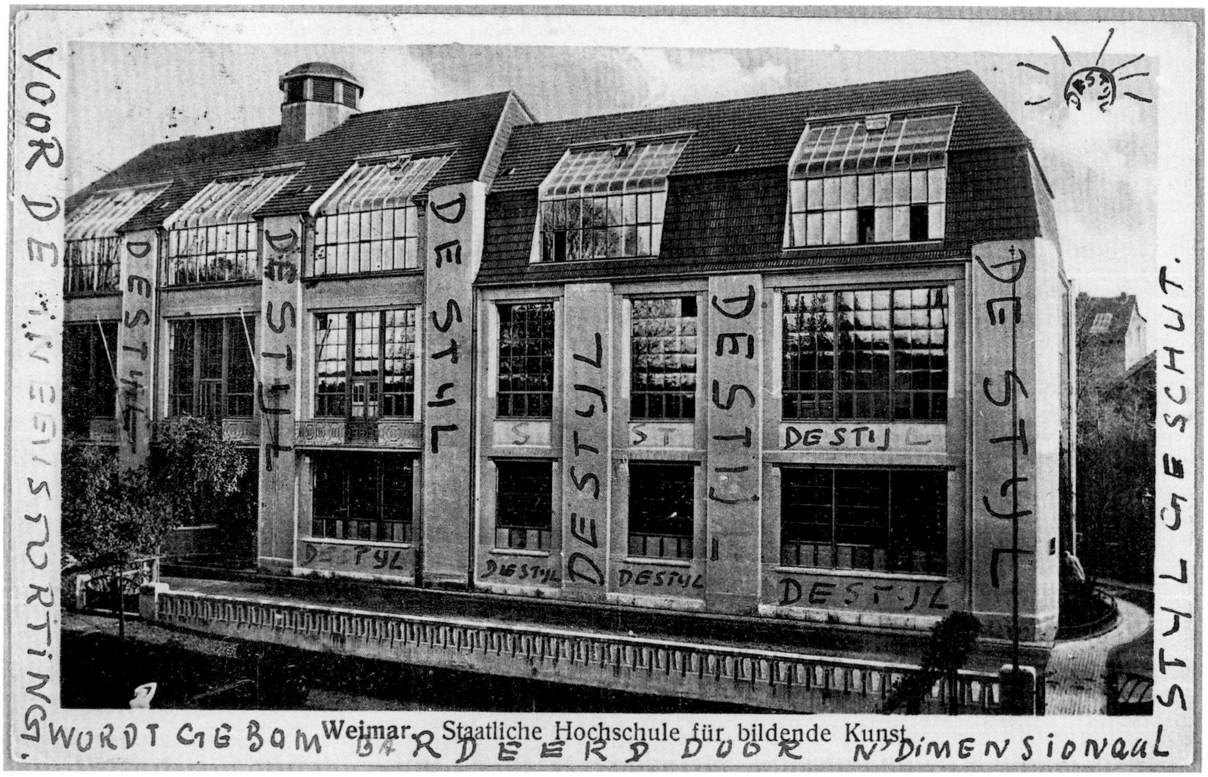

The year 1923 marked an important turning point for the Bauhaus. The school had shed its Expressionist image and emphasis on craft and now embraced a more rational, ordered aesthetic influenced by the abstract geometric forms of Constructivism and De Stijl and by mechanical production processes. This new direction was accompanied by changes in the school's faculty. In spring 1923, Gropius replaced Itten, who had been the source of much internal conflict, with László Moholy-Nagy, a Hungarian Constructivist painter living in Berlin. Gropius had been impressed by Moholy's first exhibition at Der Sturm gallery in 1922, featuring paintings, metal sculptures and reliefs.

The change in direction at the Bauhaus was set in motion in April 1921 when the Dutch artist Theo van Doesburg, founder of De Stijl, moved to Weimar with the aim of promoting his movement among the school's masters and students. Van Doesburg hoped to obtain a teaching position from Gropius, but when a job did not materialise, he launched his own private De Stijl course in Weimar and attracted a number of Bauhaus students, including Karl Peter Röhl, Werner Graeff, Farkas Molnár, Sándor Bortnyik, Peter Keler and Andor Weininger. In September 1922, Van Doesburg organised the International Congress of Constructivists and Dadaists in Weimar, bringing together leading figures from the two movements, including Hans Arp, Hannah Höch, El Lissitzky, Lucia and László Moholy, Hans Richter, Kurt Schwitters and Tristan Tzara, among others. Under Van Doesburg's influence, a group of Hungarian Bauhaus students – Marcel Breuer, Alfred Forbat, Molnár, Gyula Pap and Weininger – formed a group called KURI (an acronym for Construction, Utilitarian, Rational, International).

The influence of De Stijl and Constructivist tendencies came at a time when the Bauhaus was under pressure to earn revenue by producing goods that could be sold, and more importantly manufactured by German industrialists. The school's main funder, the local Thuringian state government, stipulated that the Bauhaus should hold a major exhibition to demonstrate its achievements. Masters and students spent months preparing for the 1923 Bauhaus exhibition, which was accompanied by a catalogue and presented in the school building and local museums. It featured the Haus am Horn, a model house designed by Georg Muche and furnished by the workshops, as well as a week of live performances, including Oskar Schlemmer's *Triadic Ballet*, an evening titled 'The Mechanical Cabaret', and concerts of avant-garde music. Gropius opened the exhibition on 15 August with a lecture 'Art and Technology: A New Unity', a slogan that signalled the school's new direction.

Although the 1923 Bauhaus exhibition was not a financial success, it drew thousands of visitors and received extensive press coverage, ensuring the circulation of Bauhaus products in the mass media and serving to cement the school's reputation if not its economic position.

58
Theo van Doesburg
Postcard to Antony Kok,
12th September, 1921
Ink on postcard
9 × 14 cm
Archive of Theo and Nelly van Doesburg (Donation Van Moorsel), RKD, The Hague

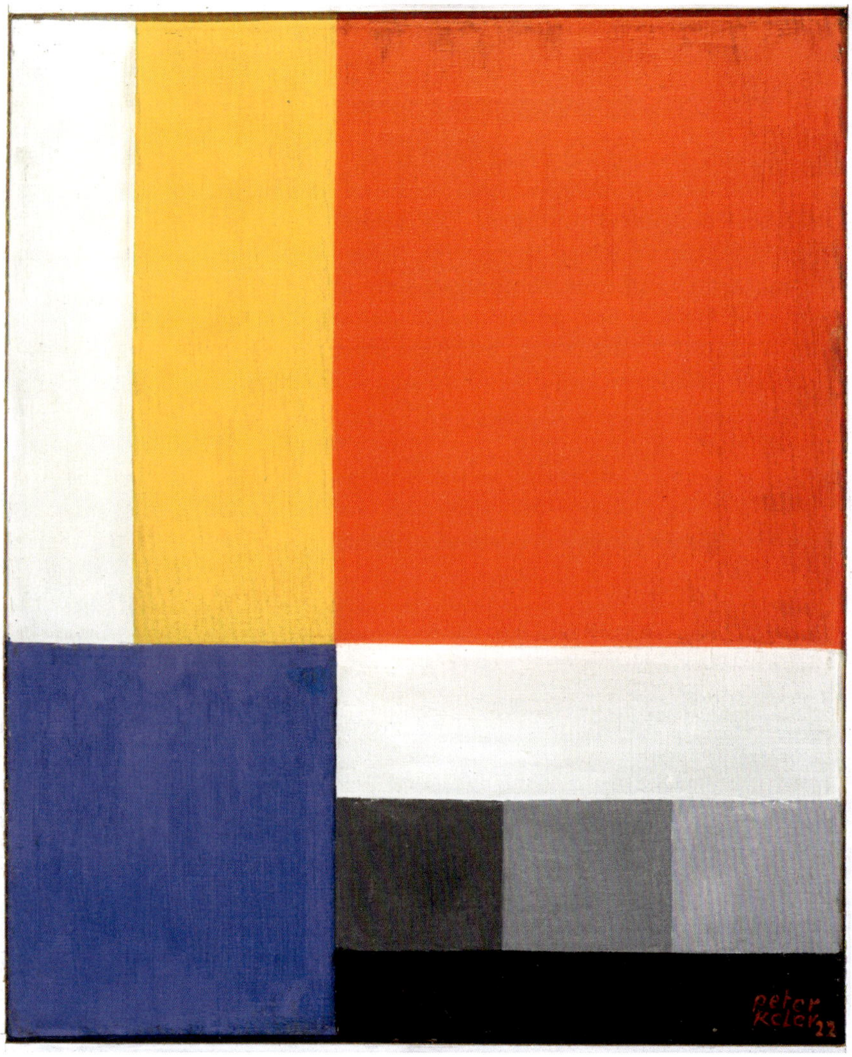

59
Peter Keler
De Stijl 1, 1922
Oil on canvas
54 × 43.5 cm
Klassik Stiftung Weimar,
Bestand Museen

60
Farkas Molnár
Design for a single-family house, 1922
Tempera over pencil on paper
24 × 33 cm
Bauhaus-Archiv Berlin

61
Alexander (Sándor) Bortnyik
Untitled (*Geometric Forms in Space*),
1923
Oil on canvas
46.4 × 60 cm
The Museum of Modern Art, New York
The Riklis Collection of McCrory
Corporation 1985

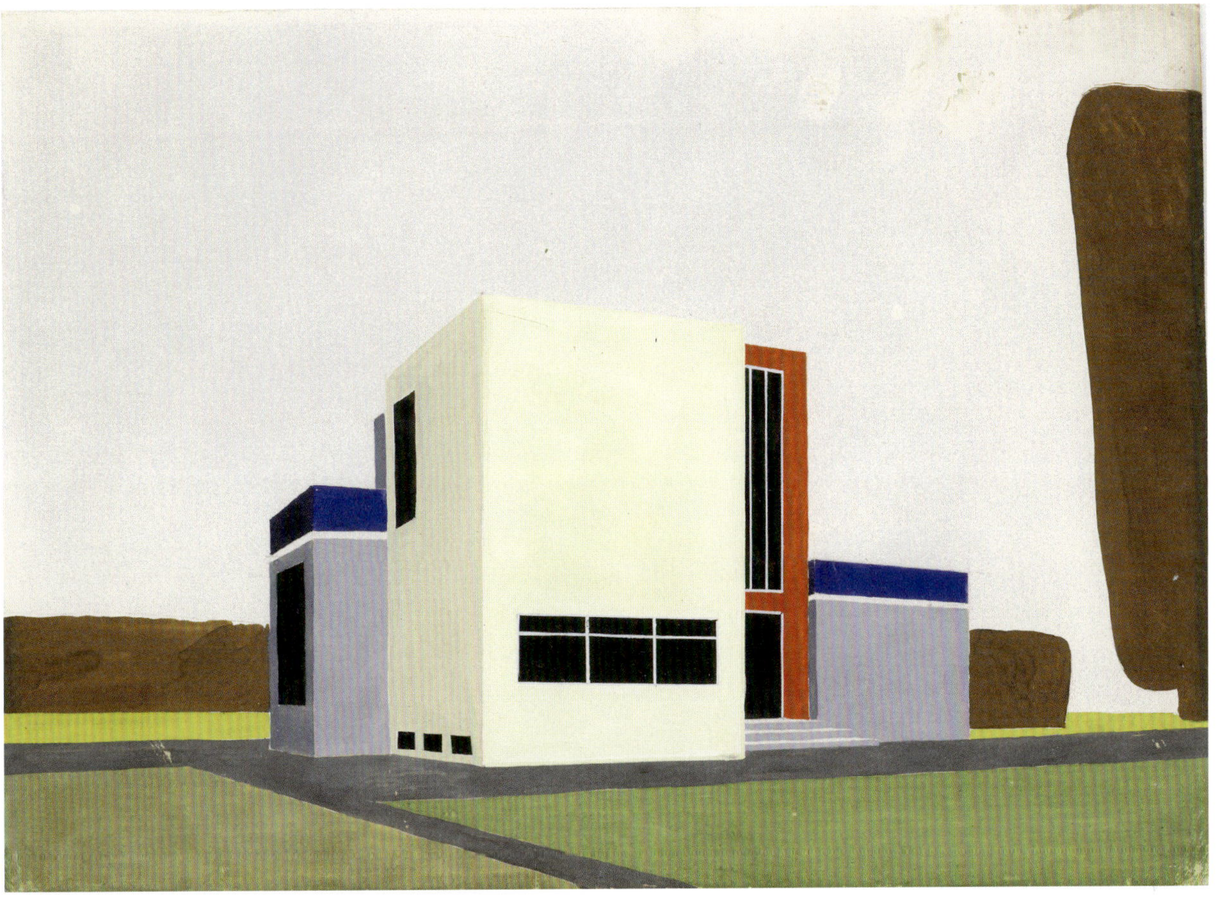

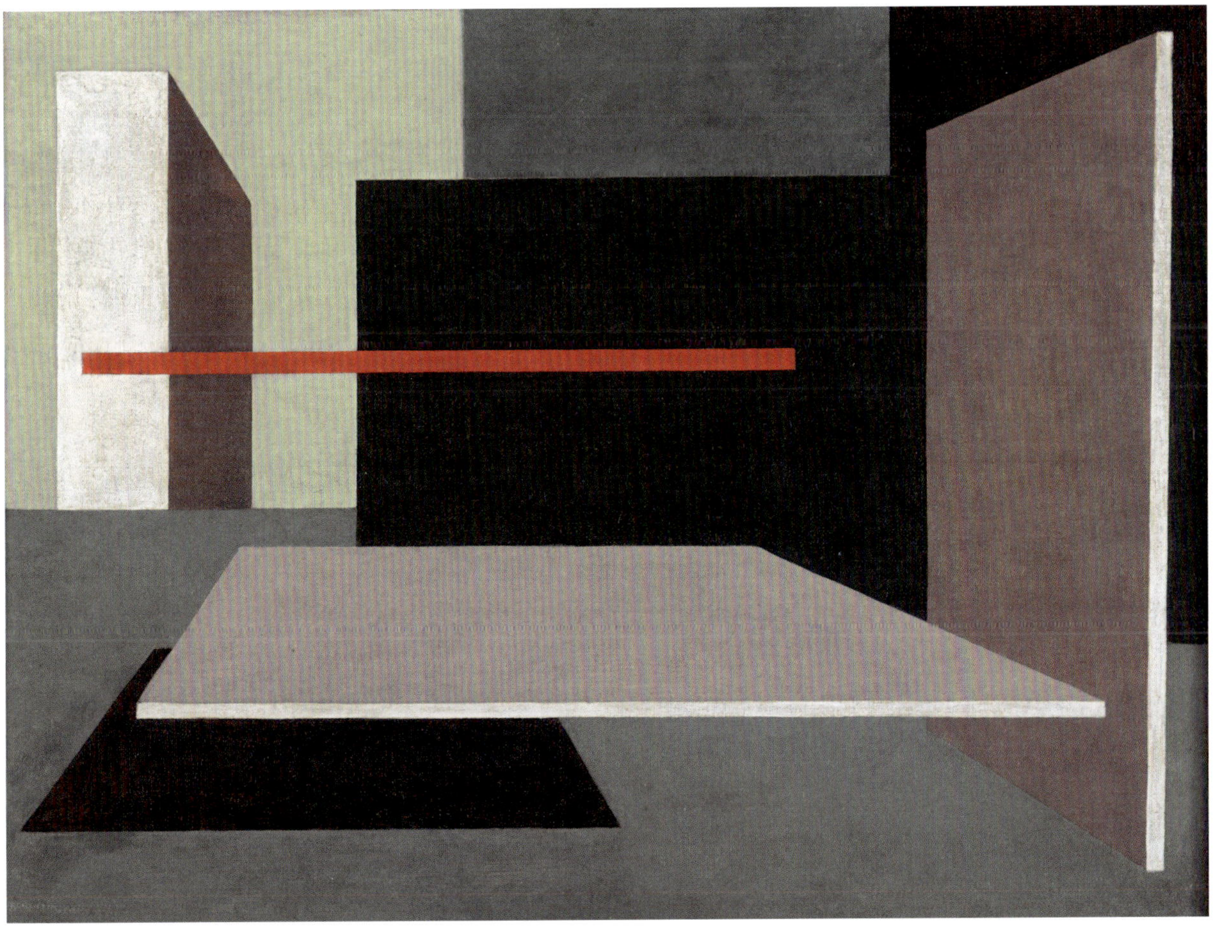

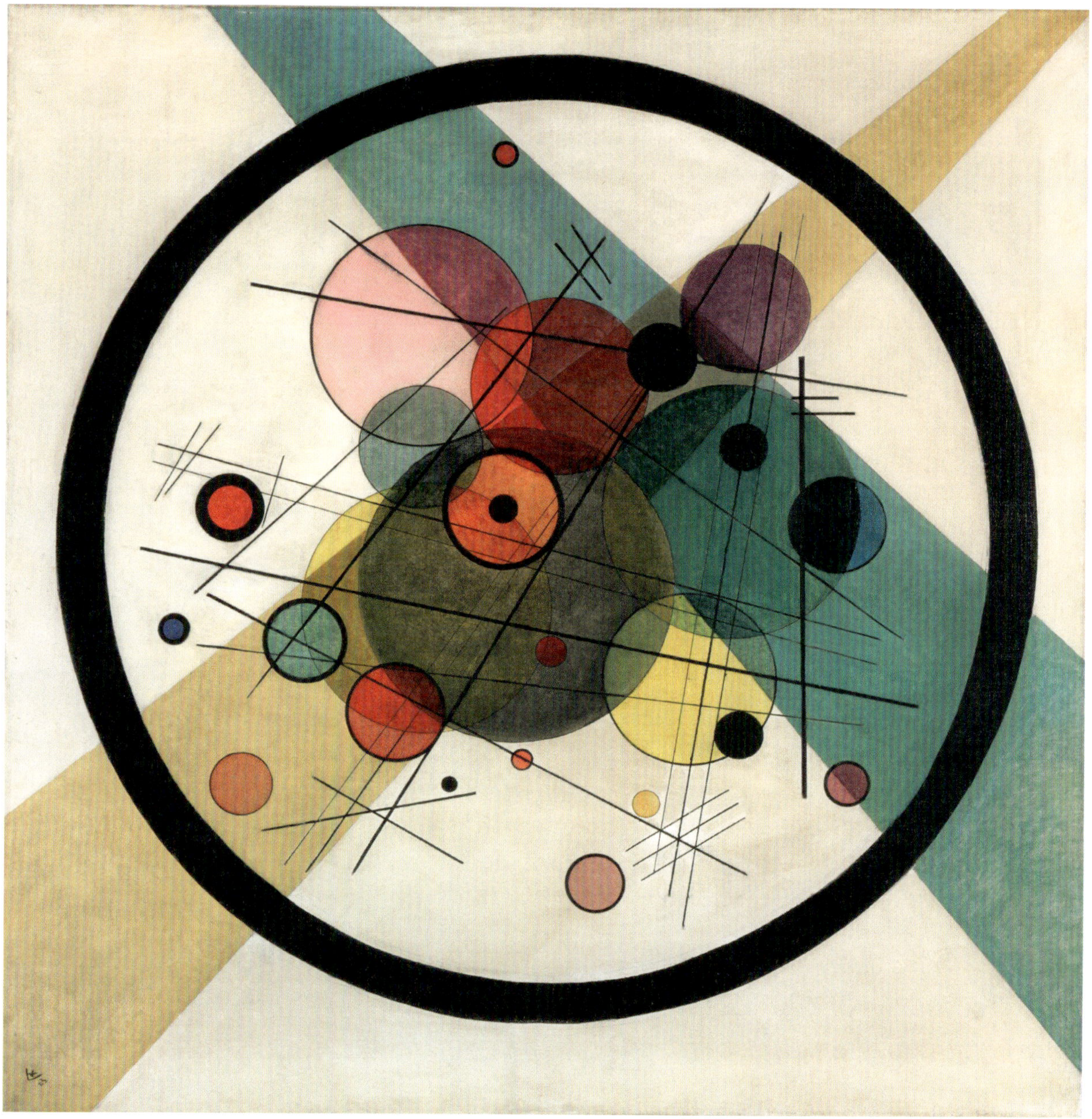

62
Wassily Kandinsky
Circles in a Circle, 1923
Oil on canvas
98.7 × 95.6 cm
Philadelphia Museum of Art
The Louise and Walter Arensberg Collection 1950

By the time Kandinsky joined the Bauhaus faculty in the summer of 1922 he was moving away from the amorphous forms and mottled colours of his Expressionist canvases and towards incorporating harder-edged geometric shapes, influenced in part by his contact with Russian Constructivists in Moscow, where he spent the war. In Weimar, he led the wall-painting workshop and taught classes on the theory of form. In its use of intersecting lines and overlapping geometric shapes, *Circles in a Circle* has affinities with work by the Constructivist painter Moholy-Nagy. Kandinsky, however, employed a wider range of colours to create a sense of movement and depth and believed that the circle had a 'link with the cosmic'. 'Of the three primary forms', he wrote, 'it points most clearly to the fourth dimension'.

63
László Moholy-Nagy
Composition Q IV, 1923
Oil on canvas
76 × 96 cm
Max Bill Georges Vantongerloo Stiftung,
Zumikon, Switzerland

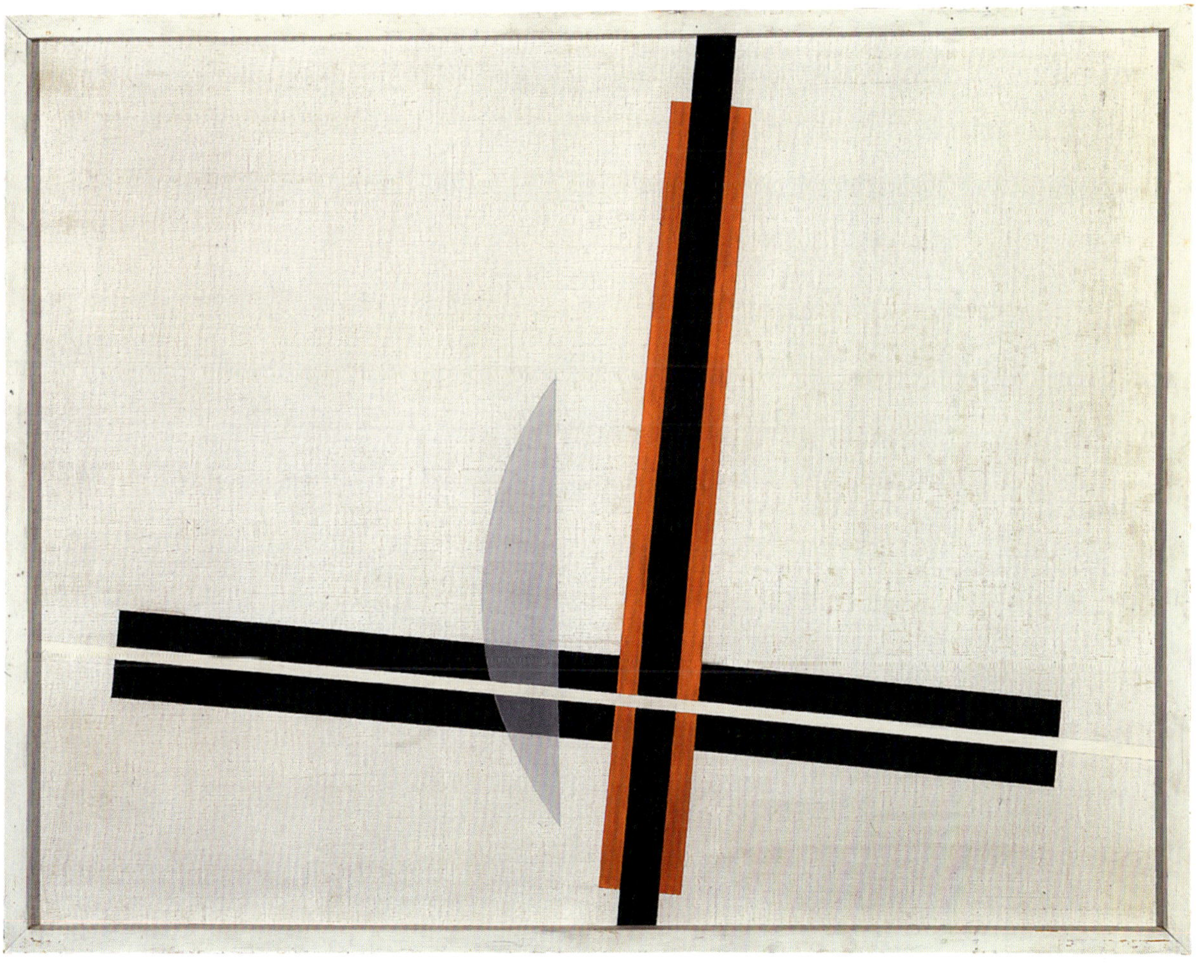

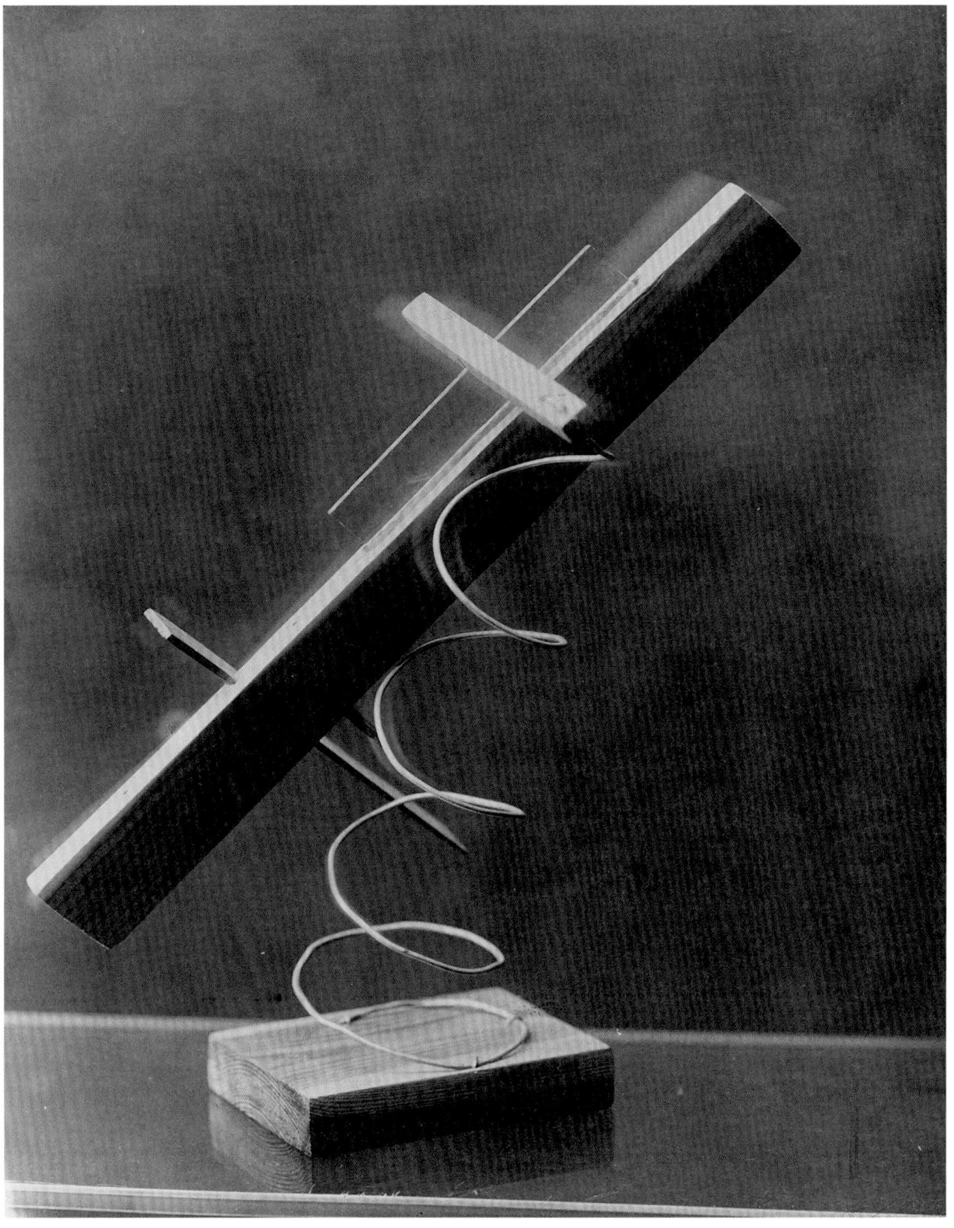

64
Lucia Moholy
Balance study by Corona Krause
from László Moholy-Nagy's preliminary
course, 1923 (printed 1993)
Gelatin silver print
24 × 18 cm
Bauhaus-Archiv Berlin

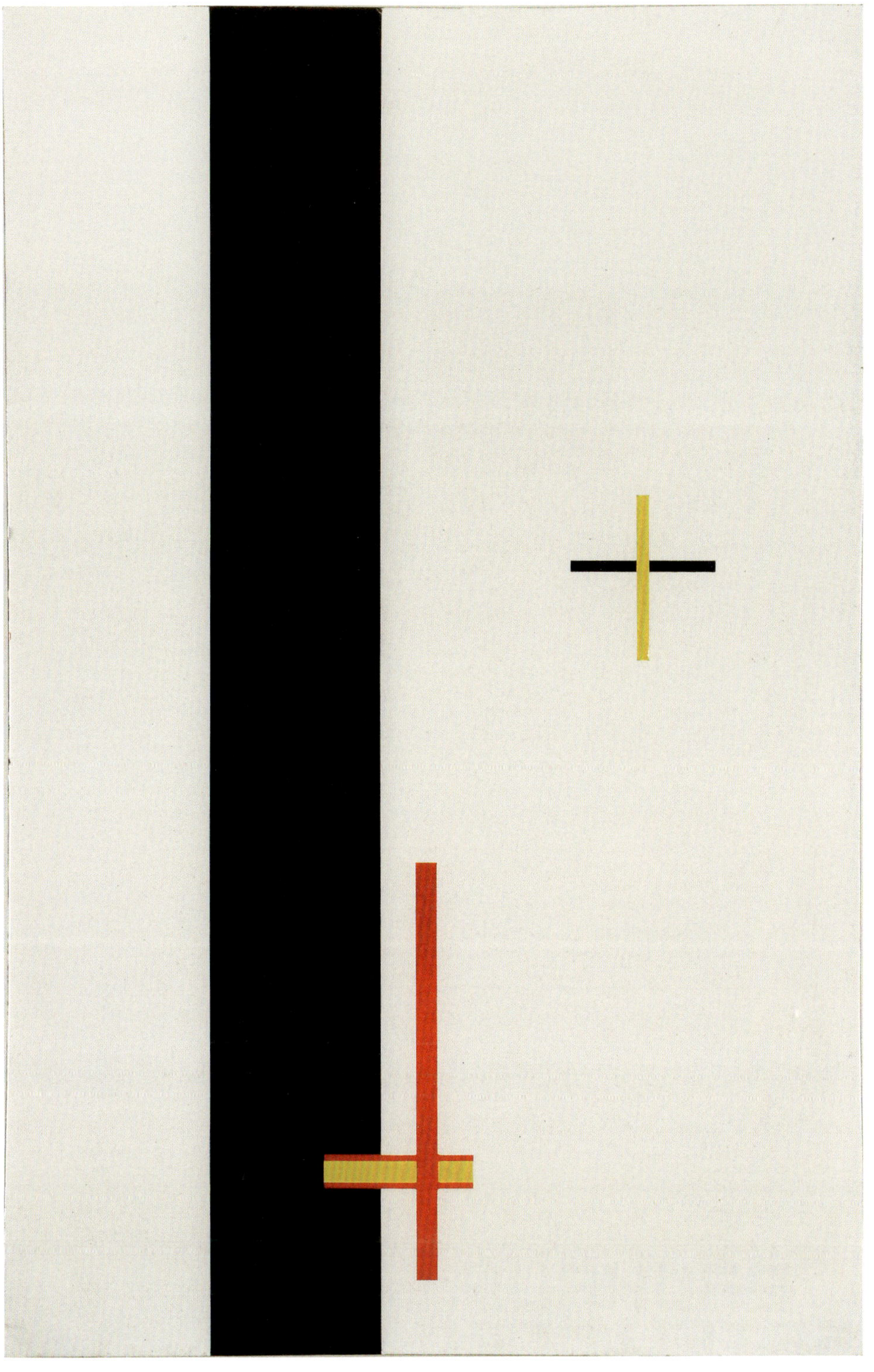

65
László Moholy-Nagy
Construction in Enamel 1 (EM1), 1923
Porcelain enamel on steel
94 × 60 cm
Collection Viktor and Marianne Langen

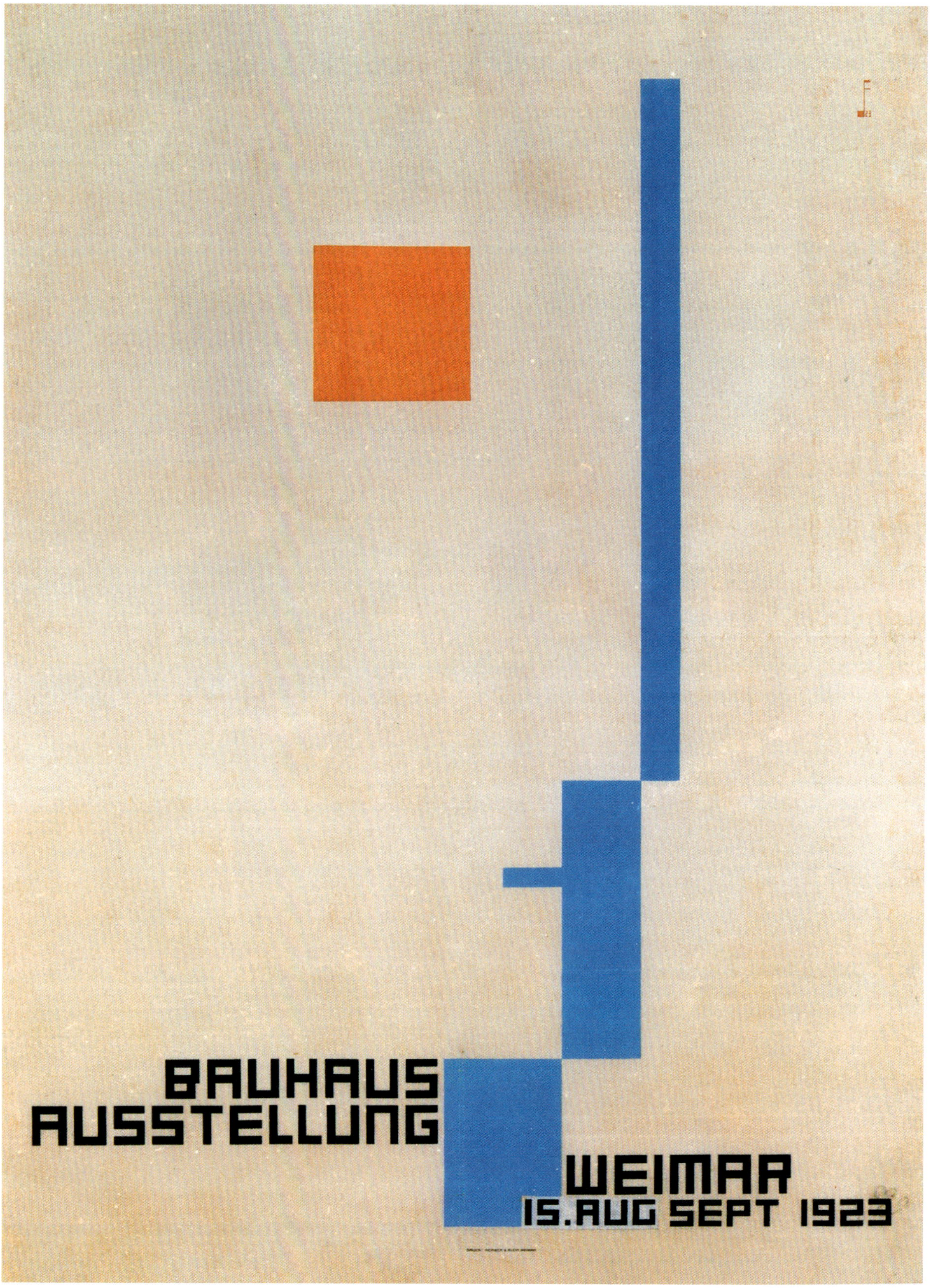

66
Fritz Schleifer
Poster for the 1923 Bauhaus exhibition, 1923
Lithograph on paper
100 × 73 cm
Herzogenrath, Berlin

67
Oskar Schlemmer
Bauhaus Signet, 1923
Lithograph on paper
25 × 30.2 cm
Bühnen Archiv Oskar Schlemmer/
The Oskar Schlemmer Theatre Estate
Collection C. Raman Schlemmer

gerhard marcks
on the planned bauhaus week

The Bauhaus week has begun! Posters in all the transcontinental trains!

The President is coming to the opening. The hotels are overcrowded with foreign visitors. One thousand homes had to be evacuated for the art critics. The Bauhaus Internationale is being played in every square. Everyone smokes Bauhaus brand. Big speculations are shaking the Stock Exchange.

And the reason for all this? In the museum there are a few cabinets full of little pots and little woven things. This is what Europe is all excited about. Poor Europe!

That, for what it is worth, is my opinion of the Bauhaus week 1923.

Faithfully,
G. Marcks

Letter addressed to the Council of Masters, 22 september, 1922

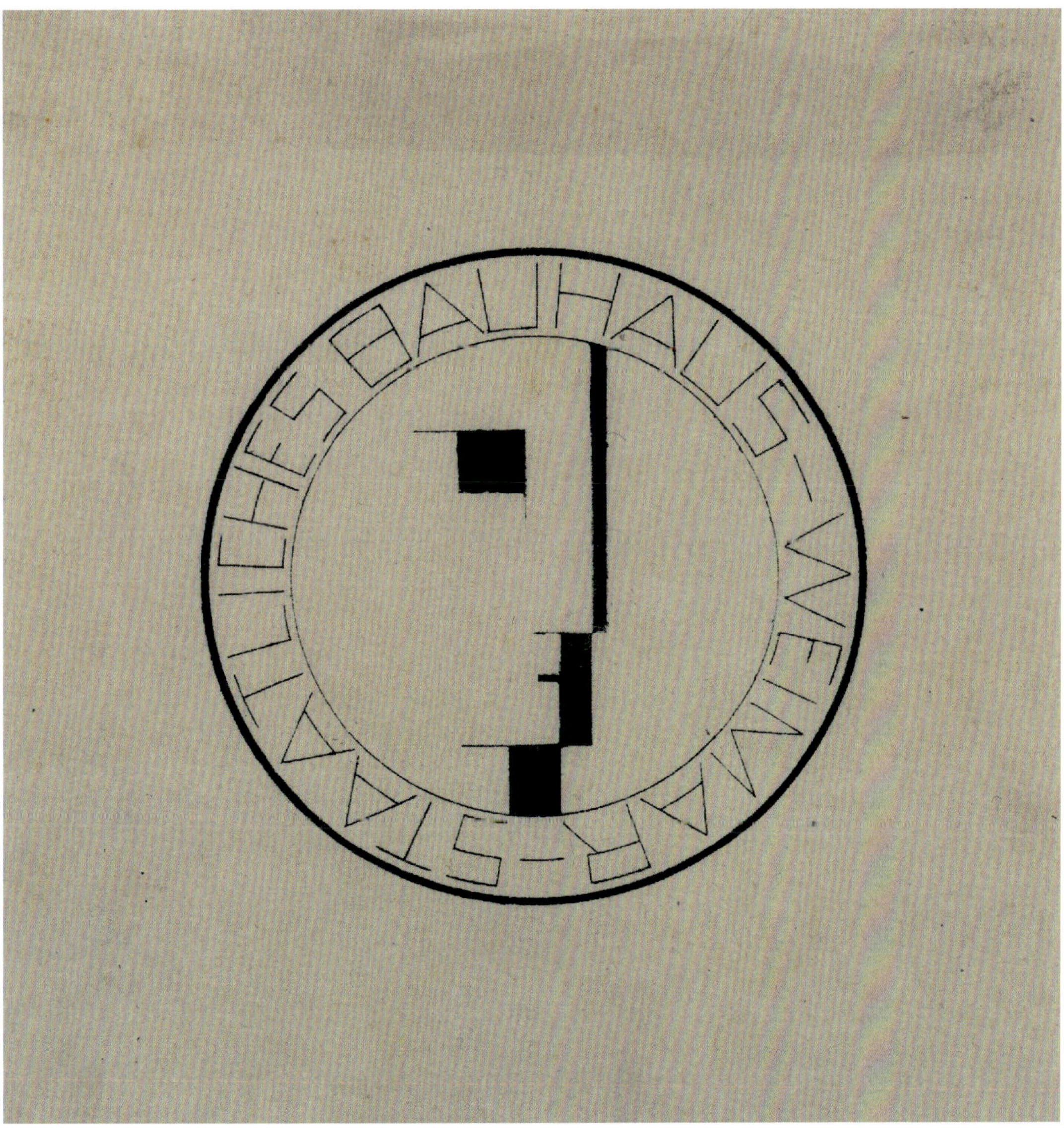

reinventing the bauhaus the 1923 bauhaus exhibition as a turning point in the direction of the school

éva forgács

Calling!

The first Bauhaus exhibition, planned for the summer of 1923, must, first of all, demonstrate the work and goals of the Bauhaus for the broader public, and appeal to these circles to demonstrate that we are intent not to withdraw in a resigned or arbitrary manner but to participate creatively and helpfully in the life of the community.

If we wish to survive, we need to concentrate all future work on this task. From today on, a state of emergency takes effect, linking the work of each individual and each workshop to the idea and realisation of the exhibition. The elected committee is empowered to execute this with the consideration of all particular wishes and interests.

—Muche, Schlemmer, Hartwig, Schwerdtfeger, Breuer, Gropius[1]

This document, signed by members of the faculty and the student body, dates from 13 October 1922, and marks the official beginning of the preparations for the 1923 Bauhaus exhibition.[2] It contradicts Walter Gropius's own account that 'In 1923 the Thuringian Legislative Assembly (Landtag) asked for a Bauhaus exhibition ... [which] was contrary to the intentions of the Director who would have preferred to postpone a public display until more mature results had been obtained.'[3] Although Gropius's words have been widely accepted in the Bauhaus literature, and it seems reasonable that the Thuringian government, supporter of the Bauhaus, would wish the school to be more popular with the local community, it appears that the Director initiated the project himself and had many reasons to do so.

External political pressure, Klaus-Jürgen Winkler reminds us, had repeatedly raised the issue of an exhibition since May 1922 at the latest, and had met with consistent resistance at the Bauhaus.[4] Gropius himself had entertained the idea from the earliest days of the school, that work in the Bauhaus had to be hidden from the public eye and introduced to it only when fully developed, as an extraordinary surprise.[5] However, Gropius's decision to organise a comprehensive exhibition was a response to the internal debates and conflicts of the school, rather than to political adversaries. The exhibition was intended to mark the shifting of emphasis at the Bauhaus from an introvert expressionist art and handcrafts-based programme to designing for the public by building working contacts with industry. It was also meant to prove the importance of architecture at the Bauhaus, to counterbalance the fact that the school lacked a department of architecture.

Throughout the year 1922, the Bauhaus was marred by the growing conflict between Gropius and Johannes Itten, who, having introduced his quasi-religion Mazdaznan to the school and having won over the majority of the students, had strong ambitions to rule.[6] It was also marred by the discontent and hostile activities of some of the teachers after being denied votes in the Masters' Council; the critique and even attacks of Theo van Doesburg, who attracted a number of dissatisfied Bauhaus students to his rival course during his stay in Weimar; and, last but not least, the adamant hostility of the conservative-nationalist Weimar establishment and public, incessantly expressed in many quarters. Gropius needed a school-wide effort to reinstate the inner cohesion of the Bauhaus.

Gropius's conflict with Itten reached a breaking point in February 1922, when the director addressed the faculty in a circular asking them to support him in 'the fusion, not in the separation'[7] of Itten's expressionist-individualist approach and his own intended contacts with industry. The hiring of Paul Klee and Oskar Schlemmer in 1921 was intended to counterbalance the overbearing influence of Itten and like-minded Expressionists Lothar Schreyer and Gertrud Grunow. By 1923 the latter three had left the Bauhaus, and Itten's replacement by the Constructivist László Moholy-Nagy, along with the hiring of Kandinsky and the new syndic Emil Lange, set the stage for a public show that would present the new spirit of the school. The exhibition was Gropius's monumental effort to hold the Bauhaus together at a point when it was at risk of disintegration. The fault line ran between the painters who wanted greater spirituality, and the technical workshops, where material experiments were underway.[8]

That Gropius launched the appeal for an exhibition in autumn 1922, whereas the Parliament addressed it only in spring 1923, establishes a clear chronology.[9] This is also confirmed, among many other documents, by Gunta Stölzl, who recalled '*Gropius's decision* that we should risk an exhibition in the summer of 1923',[10] as well as by Hans Maria Wingler, who also referred to the 1923 exhibition as resulting from a decision of the Masters' Council.[11] A strong reason for setting the date of the show for the summer of 1923 was the annual conference of the Deutscher Werkbund, scheduled in Weimar for the same time. The Werkbund was to bring to Weimar exactly those architects to whom Gropius was the most eager to prove that his years at the Bauhaus had not been wasted, and that he was able to resolve the Werkbund's dilemma of artistic autonomy versus social usefulness. The motto that Gropius worded for the event was: 'Art and Technology: A New Unity.'

The slogan was a masterpiece of modern political communication, with equal emphasis on individual words and the entire statement. 'Art' suggested respect for traditions and recommended a reinvented Bauhaus to the town and state officials, and was meant to reassure the artists in the Bauhaus. 'Technology' held the promise of modernisation and practicality, a spirit of change. And regardless of whether one preferred art or technology, 'unity' was the rhetoric of reconciliation. The slogan was a ringing authoritative statement, the real implications of which were, however, not lost on the artists' circle of the Bauhaus masters. 'Exactly what we didn't want',' said Lyonel Feininger to Gerhard Marcks when he glimpsed the slogan on a poster at the Weimar train station.[12]

Pragmatism and modernisation implied the lessening of the role that art was playing in the school. It was Schlemmer who voiced reproach for the fading out of what he understood as the original Bauhaus idea, speaking of the symbol of the 'socialist cathedral' degraded and replaced by a simple family house. 'It remains a question', he wrote, whether our work has to be defined by social and ethical ideas, or by the fact that the workshops exist and once they are there, they need to be kept working.'[13]

Claiming that art and technology can be married, and that the artists in the Bauhaus would embrace their craftsmen colleagues was a utopia, and perhaps it was its very impossibility that inspired Gropius to set this desired synthesis as a goal for the divided Bauhaus population. As long as there was a faraway ideal to be achieved, the controversies of the present could, at least nominally, be subordinated to that shining, superior concept. And at stake was the school's survival. The Bauhaus needed to be reinvented. Both art and craftsmanship had to give way to designs for industrial production, and the exhibition demonstrated that this was not impossible – even if art, in the sense in which Schlemmer, Feininger, Klee, and Kandinsky understood it, was marginalised. In spite of the slogan 'Art and Technology' were not married in the event. Even the show's centre-piece, Haus am Horn, a proposed family home of the future, hardly included a painting, while the painters' works were shown in a traditional exhibition in a museum.

The Bauhaus exhibition took place in several venues between 15 August and 30 September 1923. The vestibule and staircase of the main Bauhaus building were decorated by Schlemmer and students of the wall-painting workshop like Alfred Arndt and Josef Maltan. Joost Schmidt added reliefs. The wall-painting workshop was repainted by Herbert Bayer and Rudolf Paris, and the other workshops opened to visitors displaying their objects. Art was conspicuously relegated into the Weimar Landesmuseum, where an exhibition of paintings by the Bauhaus students and faculty included works by Joseph Albers, Bayer, Marcel Breuer, Paul Citroën, Feininger, Ludwig Hirschfeld-Mack, Itten, Kandinsky, Klee, Marcks, Moholy-Nagy, Georg Muche, Hinnerk Scheper, Schlemmer, Schreyer, Schmidt and others.[14] A series of print portfolios, the *Meistermappe 1923* was also published: twelve woodcuts by Feininger; Kandinsky's *Small Worlds* (fig. 46–49); twelve lithographs by Farkas Molnár and Henrik Stefán; and Marcks's woodcuts illustrating the Edda songs (fig. 5), while a number of postcards designed by both faculty and students went on sale. Posters by Schmidt, Fritz Schleifer (fig. 66), Albers, and others, were displayed all over town. They all included Schlemmer's Bauhaus Signet, a geometric face that associated architecture, rigorous simplicity and formal discipline (fig. 67). Schmidt's poster also referenced Russian Constructivism with red, black and grey on a white ground, and the diagonal position of the stylised human figure. Other designs using the primary colours were evocative of De Stijl's aesthetic. The fundamental document of the exhibition was the Bauhaus's publication *Staatliches Bauhaus in Weimar 1919–1923*, with a cover designed by Bayer, layout by Moholy – opening a new era in Bauhaus typography – and texts by Gropius, Klee, Kandinsky, Grunow, Moholy and Schlemmer.

The exhibition *International Architecture* featured designs, photos and models of works by De Stijl, Russian-Soviet experiments, a pre-fab housing concept by Walter Gropius and Adolf Meyer,[15] and placed special emphasis on the work of Le Corbusier, who organised and designed the display of his own exhibits himself.[16] Student works like Molnár's *Red Cube House* and other imaginative Constructivist designs were also shown.

The Bauhaus week inaugurating the exhibition opened on 15 August with Gropius's keynote speech 'Art and Technology: A New Unity'. Minister of the Interior Dr Edwin Redslob and Minister of Education Max Greil were present. During the following days, Kandinsky lectured 'On Synthetic Art', and J.J.P. Oud on 'New Building in Holland'.[17]

Schlemmer's *Triadic Ballet*, a stylised stage work in three parts with costumes that turned the dancers, or parts of their bodies into spherical, tubular and other geometric forms,[18] was performed in the Deutsches Nazionaltheater Weimar on Thursday 16 August at 8pm, with specially composed music by Paul Hindemith. At an evening called 'The Mechanical Cabaret,' the Bauhaus student Kurt Schmidt's *Mechanical Ballet* was staged, with music by Heinz Stuckenschmidt, who was a visiting faculty member at the Bauhaus at the time. In sync with the stage works that combined geometry and movement was the *Reflecting Colour-Light-Play* of Bauhaus student Kurt Schwerdtfeger. He developed it from his fellow student Ludwig Hirschfeld-Mack's earlier discussions with master Josef Hartwig.[19] Gropius, writing about the *Reflected Light Compositions* of Hirschfeld-Mack[20] saw this invention as analogous to the abstract films of Viking Eggeling, Hans Richter and Walter Ruttmann, since it brought abstract forms and colours into movement on a screen through the superimposition of transparent coloured panels in front of floodlights. 'Yellow, red, green, blue in glowing intensity, move about on the dark background of a transparent linen screen up, down, sideways in varying tempi. They appear now as angular forms: triangles, squares, polygons – and again in curved forms – circles, arcs and wave-like patterns. They join, and overlappings and colour-blendings result',[21] Hirschfeld-Mack wrote. He also composed music experimenting with synchronised colours and sounds.[22]

Musical events included the first performance of Hindemith's set of songs based on Rainer Maria Rilke's *Marienleben*, the debut of Ferruccio Busoni's *Six Short Pieces* for piano, a performance of Ernst Křenek's *Concerto Grosso*, and the second German performance of Igot Stravinsky's *The Soldier's Tale*, conducted by Hermann Scherchen in the presence of the composers.[23] The concerts added gravitas to the image of the Bauhaus, indicating that the school was deeply imbedded both in the tradition and the modernisation of German and European culture. Not only was Klee a professional musician and concert master, and Kandinsky the close friend and correspondent of Arnold Schönberg, but most of the Bauhaus faculty and many of the students had an impressive education in both classical and contemporary music.

The main event of the exhibition was the experimental Haus am Horn, named after the street where it was built. It was painter Georg Muche's design, voted for by the students instead of Gropius's own plans; technical help came from Gropius's office, which entrusted Adolf Meyer with the engineering and building of the house. Opposed to the existing building style in Germany, the square, white, flat-roofed house, 'overlooking the romantic setting of Johann Wolfgang von Goethe's garden house',[24] proposed supra-national modernity and a suburban lifestyle, one of privacy. It also represented Palladian Classicism with a nod to Weimar Classicism,[25] traditions that differed from Germany's preferred pitched roofs, adapted to frequent rain and snow. The simplicity of the building was an example of affordable constructions, necessitated by post-war economic conditions.

The living room, a cube within a cube, occupied the innermost space so that its ceiling had to be raised in order to accommodate windows. Every piece of furniture and equipment was designed and made in the Bauhaus. Each object, like the architecture, was simple, rational, and functional, although not yet streamlined, and was designed, as was the building, with the possibility of industrial production in mind.

Outstanding were Alma Buscher's multi-functional furniture for the children's room and her equally modular toy building blocks, Breuer's dressing table and interior design for the woman's bedroom, Gyula Pap's single-line floor lamp, and Theodor Bogler's simple functional pottery for the kitchen that left behind, on Gropius's urging, the 'single-piece aesthetic' of craftsmanship.[26] Signature objects that summed up the 1923 Bauhaus exhibition's spirit were the two versions of the table lamp (1923–24) by Wilhelm Wagenfeld and Carl Jucker (fig. 96), and Josef Hartwig's chess sets (1922–24: figs. 85–86), emblematic for their consistent rationalism pointing to a future of universally shared formal vocabulary and functional aesthetics.

The Haus am Horn functioned as a laboratory, testing the next phase of development at the Bauhaus. Schlemmer was correct in pointing out that it brought the ideal of the 'socialist cathedral' down to earth – although the word 'socialist' had to be erased from all press matter[27] – calling it a *Wohnmaschine* (living machine). It was a demonstration of what Gropius laid out in the *State Bauhaus*: 'We want to create a clear organic architecture, whose inner logic will be radiant and naked, unencumbered by lying façades and trickeries; we want an architecture adapted to our world of machines, radios, and fast motor cars, an architecture whose function is clearly recognisable in the relation of its forms.'[28]

It was Gropius's vision that saved the Bauhaus from falling into the abyss of inner controversies, and propelled it in a direction that, although moving away from the aesthetic high ground of the artists, promised to embed it into the fabric of society. The exhibition was a professional success and a political failure. It received many excellent reviews and, in spite of the cresting inflation, several hundred visitors daily, figures that multiplied during the Bauhaus week. But the local conservative-nationalist press, led by the journalist Mathilde von Freytag-Loringhoven and the Weimar architect Arthur Buschmann, remained ice-cold and hostile, deriding the exhibition as the work of outsiders, anti-German and, as far as the Haus am Horn was concerned, 'an attempt to return to the primitive art forms of inferior races',[29] foreshadowing the demise of the Bauhaus in Weimar in 1924, and, ultimately, in 1933.

With 'Art and Technology: A New Unity' Gropius meant to adapt the Bauhaus to the new realities. In retrospect, it was the first of his many later adjustments of the original Bauhaus idea to the fast-changing 'dominant spirit'[30] of the shifting historical times. For this unlikely 'new unity' he conceptualised the broad framework of 'the essential oneness of all things'[31] to reconcile elements that had previously been deemed antithetical. Saving the school, he won a short-term practical, rather than theoretical, victory, while emancipating technology in the Bauhaus led both to further successes and to deeper internal conflicts.

1 'Aufruf an alle Bauhäusler', 13 October 1922, Archivalien des Staatsarchivs Weimar, Bestand Staatliches Bauhaus, file 184. Printed in Karl-Heinz Hüter, *Das Bauhaus in Weimar*, Akademie Verlag, Berlin, 1976, pp. 235–36. All quotes, unless otherwise indicated, are the author's translation.

2 Earlier documents indicate preparations even before this. See Gerhard Marcks, letter dated 22 September 1922, in Hans M. Wingler, *Das Bauhaus 1919–1933, Weimar, Dessau, Berlin*. Gebr. Rasch, Berlin, 1962, p. 69, (reprinted in this catalogue, p. 77) and Lyonel Feininger, letter to his wife, dated 5 October 1922 ibid., p. 68.

3 Walter Gropius, Ise Gropius, Herbert Bayer (eds), *Bauhaus 1919–1928*, The Museum of Modern Art, New York, 1938, p. 80. Translator's name is not indicated.

4 For a detailed, account, see Klaus-Jürgen Winkler (ed.), *Bauhaus Alben*, Verlag der Bauhaus-Universität, Weimar, 2006–09, vol. 4, 'The Great Bauhaus Exhibition', pp. 19–25.

5 Walter Gropius, 'Rede bei der ersten Ausstellung von Schülerarbeiten des Bauhauses', June 1919, in Hüter, *Das Bauhaus Weimar*, op. cit., p. 211.

6 In 1919 Itten wrote in a letter: 'I can already claim the best minds at the school ... I am going to wipe the slate clean. For the past week I have been ruling the whole Bauhaus ... I have turned the whole institute into a flexible, malleable entity, and my task is now to create direction and order out of all this mobile malleability. This gives me joy.' Johannes Itten, letter to Mathias Hauer, 5 November 1919, in Willy Rotzler, *Johannes Itten*, Kunsthaus Zurich, Zurich, 1964, p. 68.

7 Walter Gropius, 'The Viability of the Bauhaus Idea', circular addressed to the Bauhaus masters, 3 February 1922, in Wingler, *Das Bauhaus 1919–1933*, op. cit., p. 51.

8 For the internal personal dynamics of the Bauhaus during the tumultuous time of the exhibition, see Éva Forgács, *The Bauhaus Idea and Bauhaus Politics*, Central European University Press, Budapest, London, New York, 1995, esp. chapters 7, 8 and 9.

9 'Landtag von Thüringen. Stenographischer Bericht', in Hüter, *Das Bauhaus in Weimar*, op. cit., p. 244. For successive parliamentary debates about the Bauhaus that urged for an exhibition but did not provide sufficient funding, see Winkler, *Bauhaus Alben*, vol. 4, op. cit., pp. 19–20; Barbara Miller-Lane, *Architecture and Politics in Germany 1918–1945*, Harvard University Press, Cambridge, Mass., 1968, 'The Controversy over the Bauhaus', pp. 69–86; Forgács, *The Bauhaus Idea and Bauhaus Politics*, op. cit., chapter 9,' If we intend to survive', pp. 98–103.

10 Gunta Stölzl, manuscript, in *Gunta Stölzl – Weberei am Bauhaus und aus eigenen Werkstatt*, Bauhaus-Archiv, Berlin, 1987, p. 105. Emphasis added.

11 Wingler, *Das Bauhaus 1919–1933*, op. cit., p. 6.

12 Gerhard Marcks, 'My Short Stay in Weimar', in Eckhard Neumann (ed.), *Bauhaus and Bauhaus People*, Van Nostrand Reinhold, New York, 1993, p. 30.

Oskar Schlemmer, letter to the
13 Masters' Council, 30 October 1922, in Wingler, *Das Bauhaus 1919–1933*, op. cit., p.72; Hüter, *Das Bauhaus in Weimar*, op. cit., p.236.

14 Walter Scheidig, *Bauhaus Weimar 1919–1924. Werkstattarbeiten*, Edition Leipzig, Leipzig, 1966, p.35; Reginald R. Isaacs, *Walter Gropius, Der Mensch und sein Werk*, Gebr. Mann Verlag, Berlin, 1983, p.35.

15 Scheidig, *Bauhaus Weimar 1919–1924*, op. cit., pp.34–35.

16 Isaacs, *Walter Gropius*, op. cit., p.299.

17 The Museum of Modern Art, *Bauhaus 1919–1928*, op. cit., p.80. Gropius' talk, according to his biographer Reginald R. Isaacs, attracted many of the architect's friends and colleagues, including Peter Behrens, Bruno and Max Taut, Hans Richter, Naum Gabo, Erich Mendelsohn, El Lissitzky and Hermann Muthesius. (Isaacs, *Walter Gropius*, op. cit., p.470, note 212.)

18 Klaus-Jürgen Winkler, *Bauhaus Alben*, vol.4, op. cit., p.23.

19 Wingler, op. cit., 340.

20 The Museum of Modern Art, *Bauhaus 1919–1928*, op. cit., p.65.

21 Hirschfeld-Mack in *Berliner Börsenkurier*, 24 August 1924, quoted by W. Gropius, in The Museum of Modern Art, *Bauhaus*, op. cit., p.65.

22 See his 'Dreiteilige Farbensonatine' (Ultramarin-grün) in Wingler, *Das Bauhaus 1919–1933*, op.cit., p. 98.

23 Scheidig, *Bauhaus in Weimar 1919–1924*, op. cit., p.299, also lists *Toccata and Chaconne* by Křenek.

24 Karin Wilhelm, 'Typing and Standardization for a Modern Atrium House. The Haus am Horn in Weimar', in Bauhaus-Archiv Berlin/Museum für Gestaltung, Stiftung Bauhaus Dessau, and Klassik Stiftung Weimar (eds), *Bauhaus: A Conceptual Model*, exhibition catalogue, Hatje Cantz, Ostfildern, 2009, p.150. Trans. Benjamin Carter, Benjamin Letzler, Ian Pepper, and John Southard.

25 Ibid., p.151.

26 Hubert Kittel, 'From Bauhaus Pottery to Laboratory for Industrial Product Development', in ibid., p.158.

27 See Karen Koehler, 'The Bauhaus Manifesto Postwar to Postwar', in Jeffrey Saletnik and Robin Schuldenfrei (eds), *Bauhaus Construct*, Routledge, London and New York, 2009, p.20. Koehler (p.21) quotes Schlemmer's later note defending his 1923 wording: 'didn't the majority of the German people want to build the Cathedral of Socialism in 1918? Weren't the revolution and the constitutional democracy launched in the name of the people's state? And what is a people's state other than socialism? Furthermore: does socialism necessarily imply the Social Democrats or the Communist Party? Isn't socialism a concept, an ethic, not limited to any specific party?' (quoted from Schlemmer, in Tut Schlemmer (ed.),*The Letters and Diaries of Oskar Schlemmer*, trans. Krishna Winston, Wesleyen University Press, Middletown, CT., p.200).

28 Walter Gropius, 'The Theory and Organization of the Bauhaus', in The Museum of Modern Art, *Bauhaus,* op. cit., p.27. Originally 'Idee und Aufbau des Staatlichen Bauhauses Weimar', in *Staatliches Bauhaus in Weimar, 1919–1923*, Bauhaus Verlag, Weimar and Munich, 1923.

29 For a detailed description of the local reception, see Barbara Miller-Lane, *Architecture and Politics in Germany, 1918–1945*, Harvard University Press, Cambridge, Mass., 1968, in particular 'The Controversy over the Bauhaus', pp.69–86. This quote, p.76.

30 Walter Gropius, 'The Theory and Organisation of the Bauhaus', in The Museum of Modern Art, *Bauhaus*, op. cit., p.20.

31 Ibid.

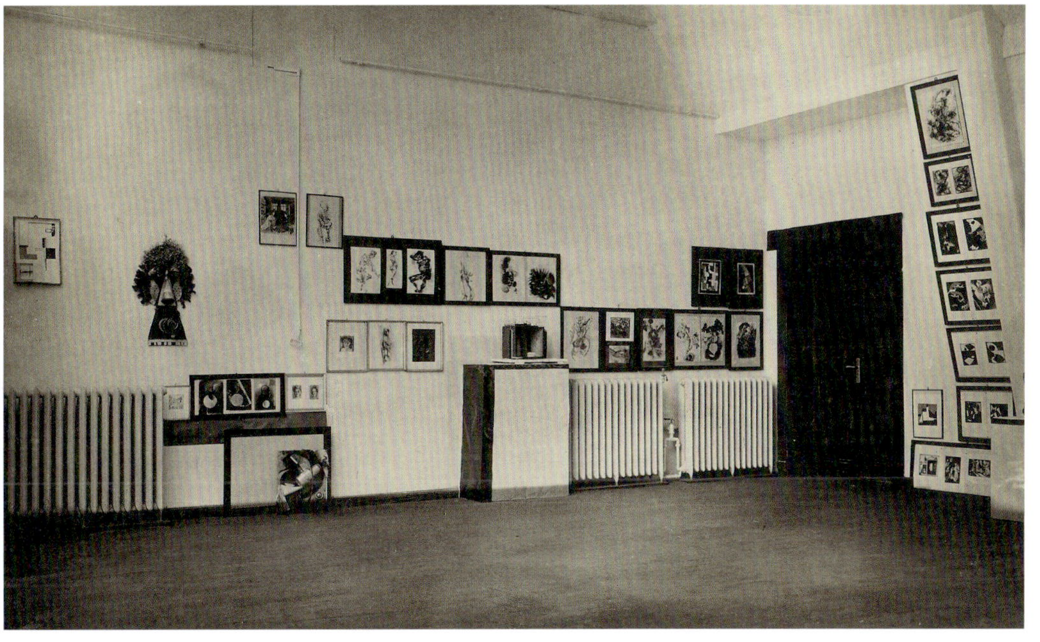

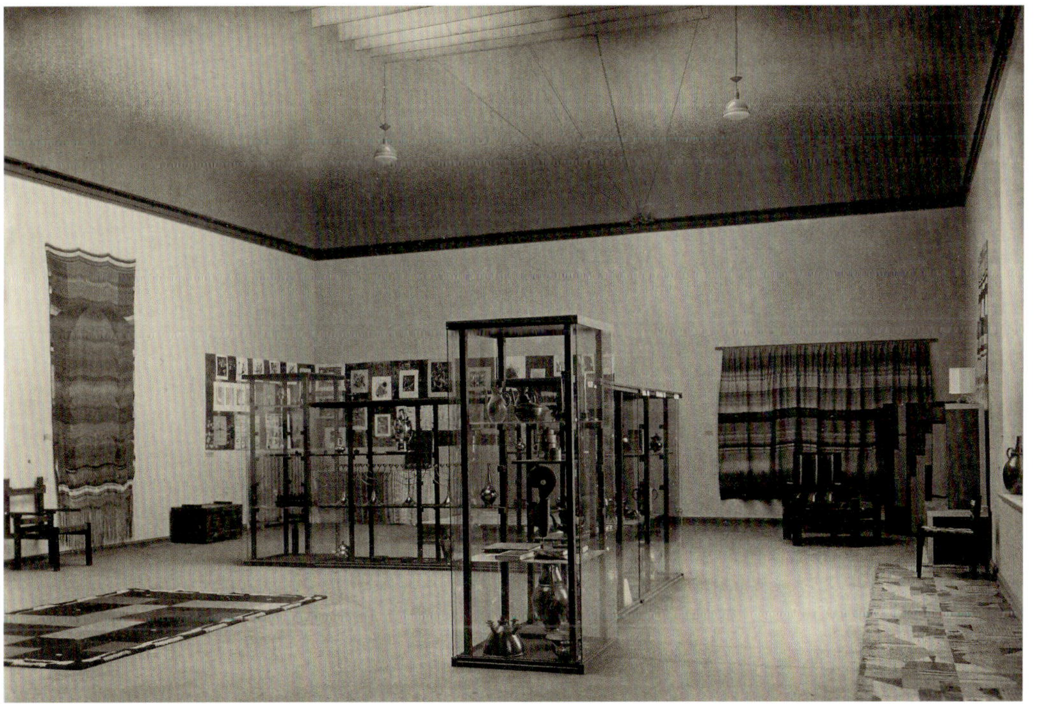

68
Exhibition of preliminary course work, displayed in the Weimar building at the 1923 Bauhaus exhibition, 1923
Bauhaus-Universität Weimar, Archiv der Moderne
Photographer unknown

69
Exhibition of workshop products in the studio room at the 1923 Bauhaus exhibition, 1923
Bauhaus-Universität Weimar, Archiv der Moderne
Photographer unknown

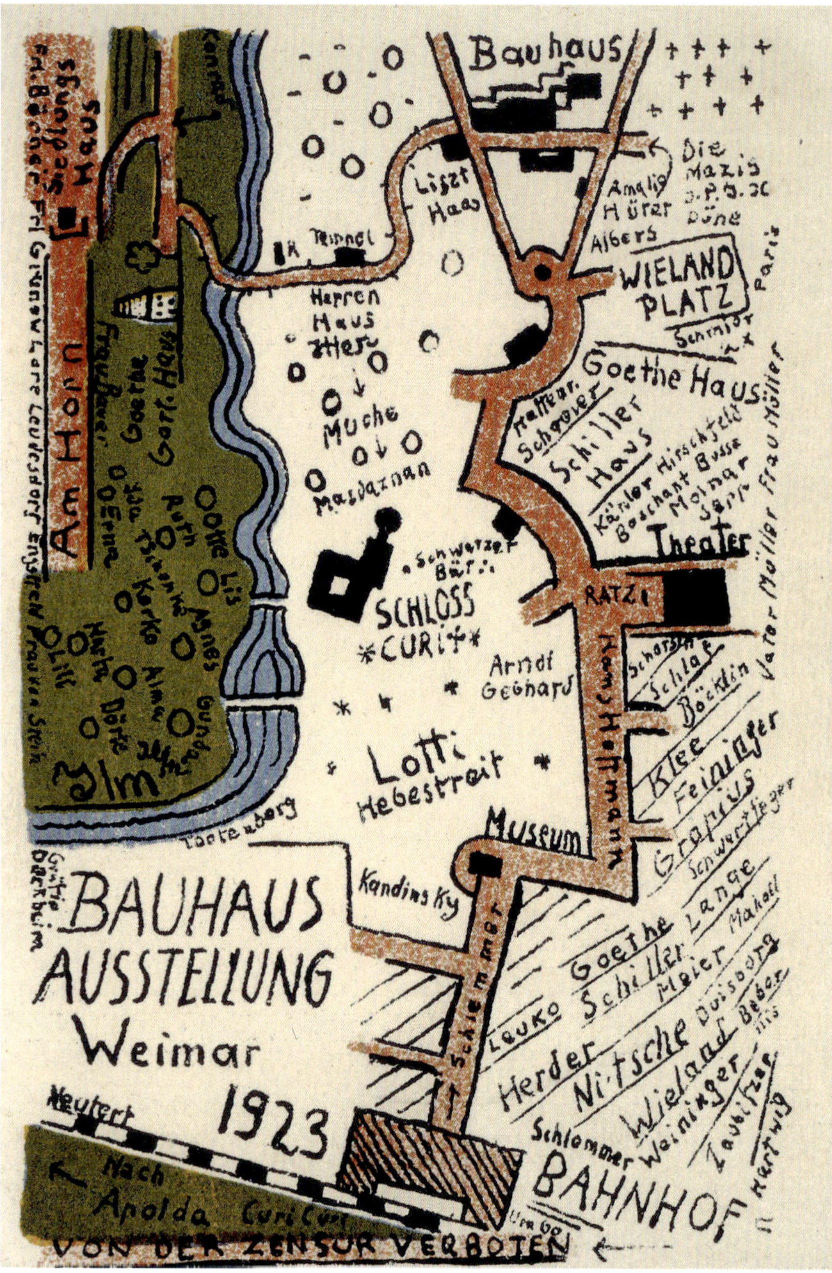

70
Kurt Schmidt
Postcard no. 19 for the Bauhaus exhibition in Weimar, summer 1923
Colour lithograph on card
14 × 9.4 cm
Bauhaus-Archiv Berlin

walter gropius
breviary for bauhaus members (draft)

Art and technology, a new unity! Technology does not need art, but art very much needs technology – example: architecture! They differ in nature; therefore their addition is not possible, but their common creative source must be explored and rediscovered by those who are endeavouring to establish the 'new idea of building'. The means: thorough preparatory training for these people in the crafts and technology. The crafts are thus merely an indispensable means to an end. Specialisation only after completion of preliminary training.

In order to design a thing so that it will function correctly, we [first] have to investigate its nature. The elements aiding the study of the nature of a thing are not only the laws of mechanics, statics, optics, and acoustics, but also the laws of proportion. These are a matter of the world of the intellect. In order to achieve precision here, we must consciously seek to make the personal factor more objective, but every work of art carries the signature of its creator. From the multiplicity of equally economical solutions – for there is not just one in each case – the creative individual selects the one that suits his personal feelings and taste….

Excerpt from manuscript, spring 1922

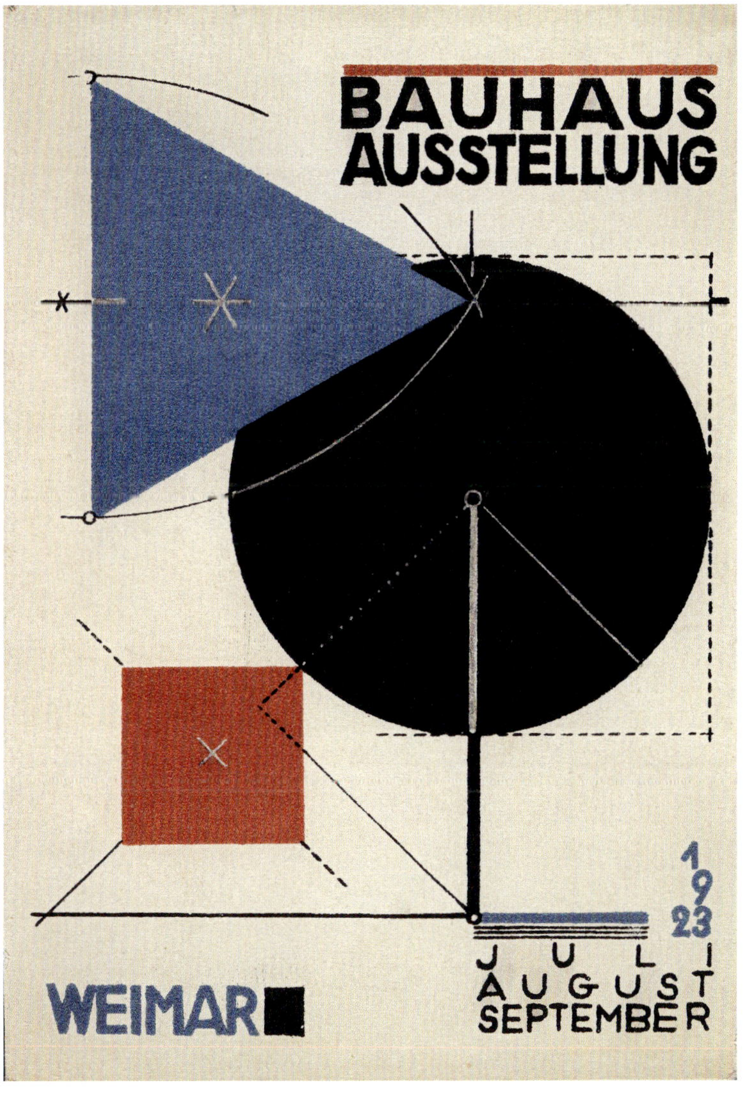

71
Herbert Bayer
Postcard no. 11 for the Bauhaus exhibition in Weimar, summer 1923
Colour lithograph on card
15.4 × 10.4 cm
Bauhaus-Archiv Berlin

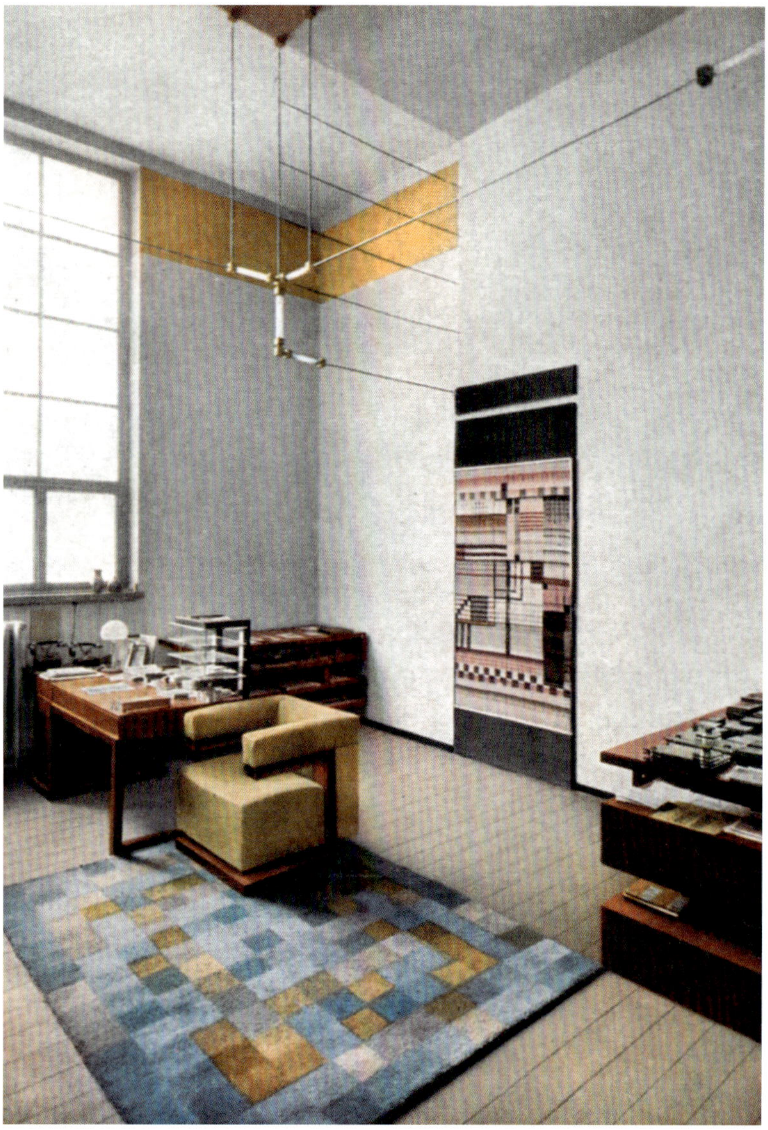

72
Lucia Moholy
Walter Gropius's director's office, 1924–25
Reprinted in *Neue Arbeiten der Bauhauswerkstätten*, 1927
Bauhaus-Archiv Berlin

73
Walter Gropius and Herbert Bayer
Isometric rendering of Walter Gropius's office at the Bauhaus Weimar, 1923
Lithograph on paper
24.6 × 24.2 cm
Stiftung Bauhaus Dessau

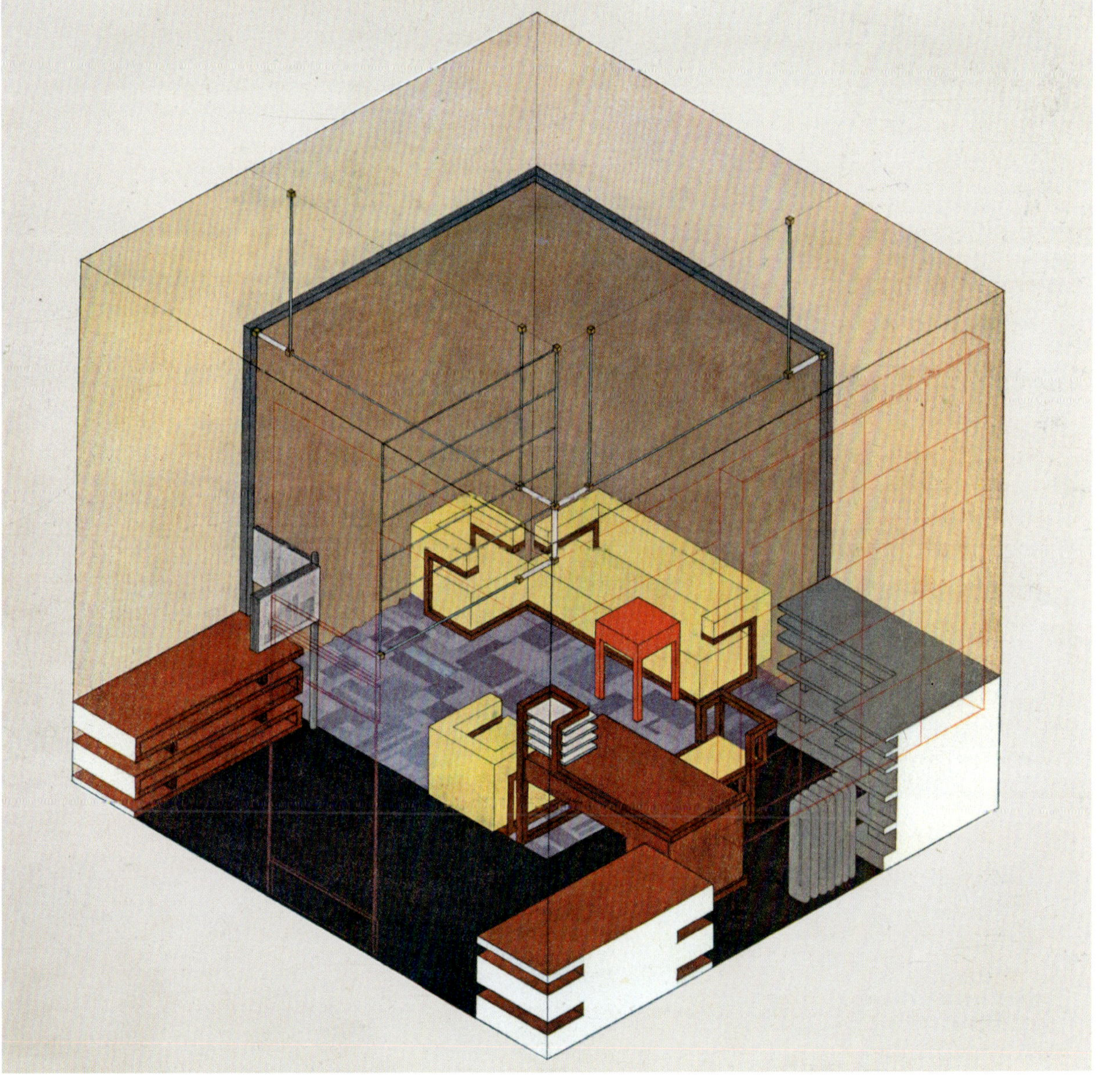

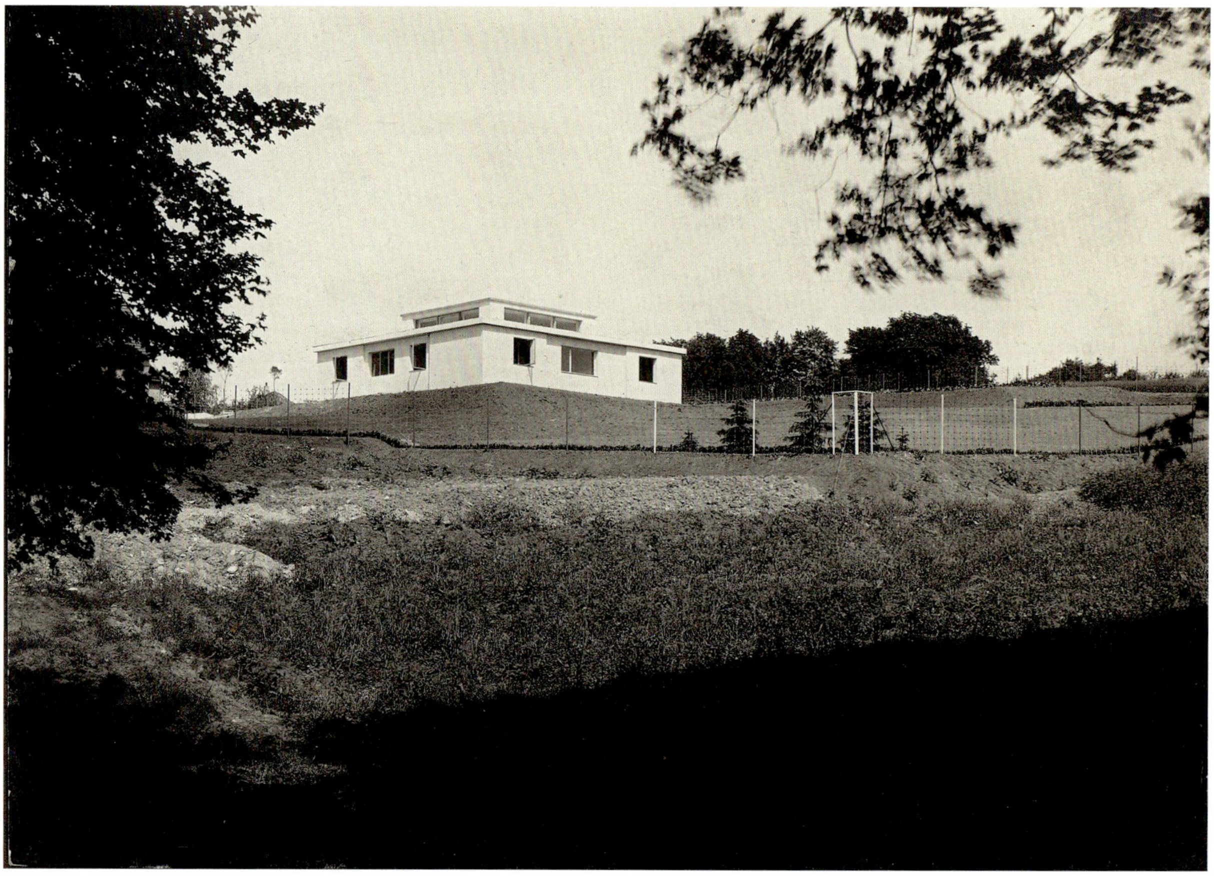

74
Haus am Horn, Weimar, 1923
Bauhaus-Universität Weimar,
Archiv der Moderne
Photographer unknown

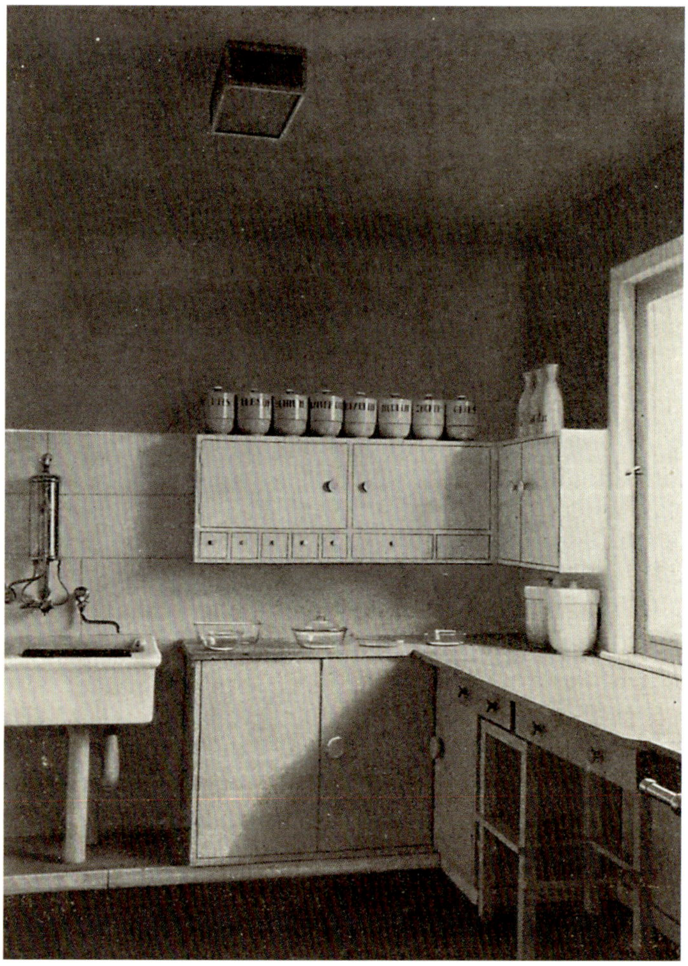

75
Kitchen in the Haus am Horn
designed by Benita Otte, 1923
Bauhaus-Universität Weimar,
Archiv der Moderne
Photographer unknown

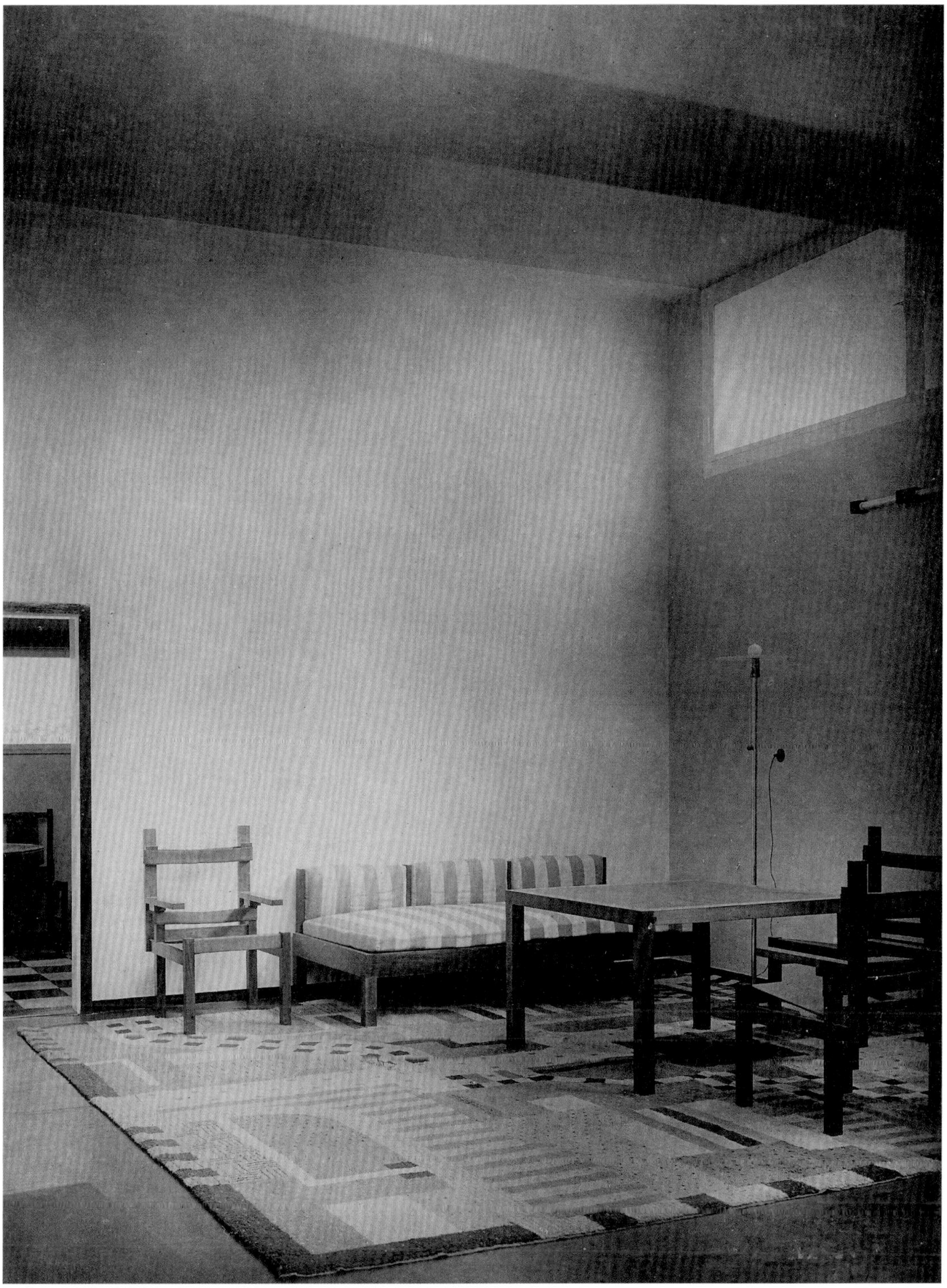

76
Interior of the living room in the Haus am Horn with furniture by Marcel Breuer, floor lamp by Gyula Pap, carpet by Martha Erps and wall lamps by László Moholy-Nagy, 1923
Bauhaus-Universität Weimar, Archiv der Moderne
Photographer unknown

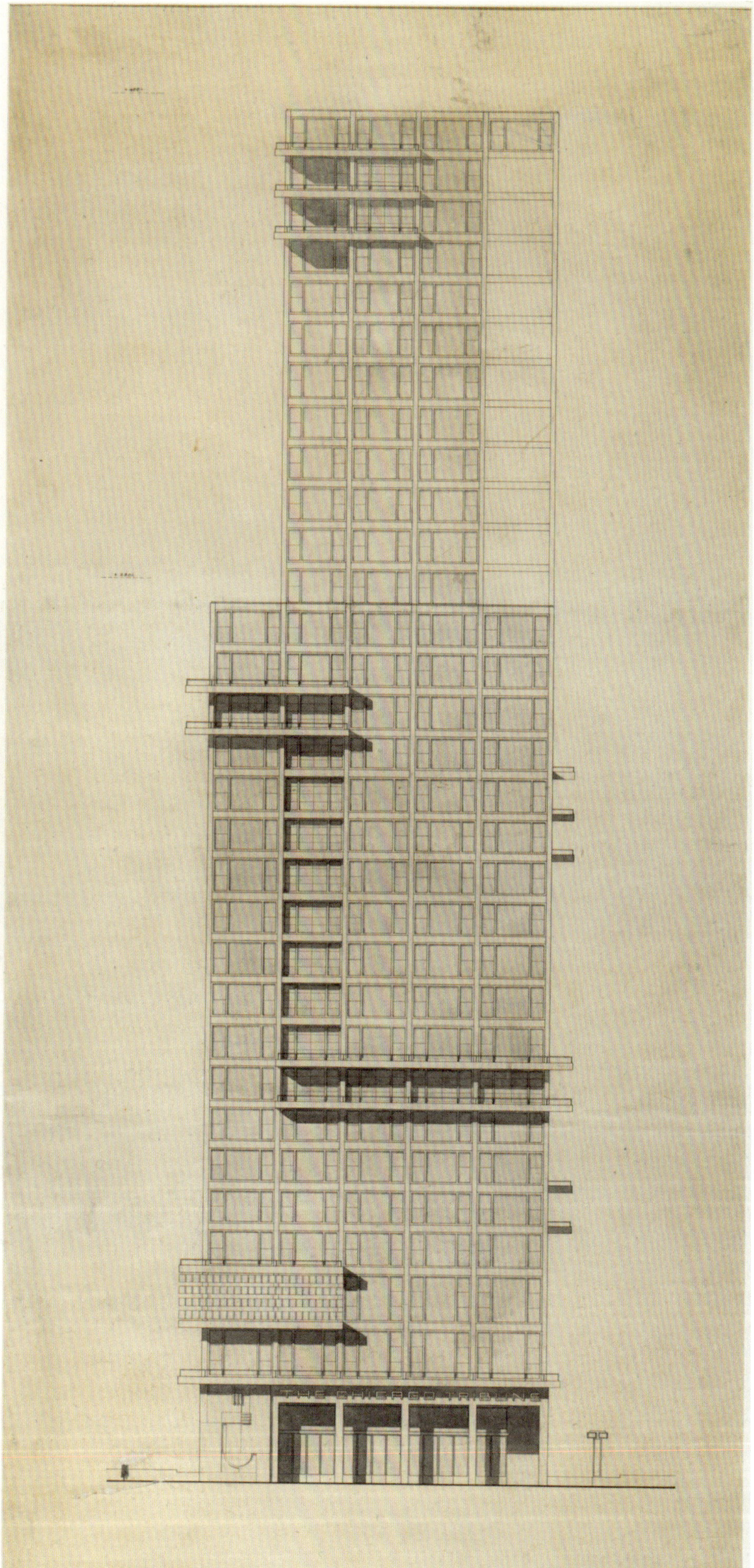
THE CHICAGO TRIBUNE
SIDE ELEVATION MICHIGAN AVE.

77
Walter Gropius and Adolf Meyer
Competition entry for the Chicago Tribune Tower, elevation, 1922
Ink and wash on paper, mounted on board
151.5 × 75.8 cm
Harvard Art Museums/Busch-Reisinger Museum. Gift of Walter Gropius

78
International Architecture exhibition, 1922, displayed in the Weimar building for the 1923 Bauhaus exhibition
Bauhaus-Universität Weimar, Archiv der Moderne
Photographer unknown

79
Models of prototype modular houses by Walter Gropius and Fred Forbát, 1922–23, displayed in the Weimar building for the 1923 Bauhaus exhibition
Bauhaus-Universität Weimar, Archiv der Moderne
Photographer unknown

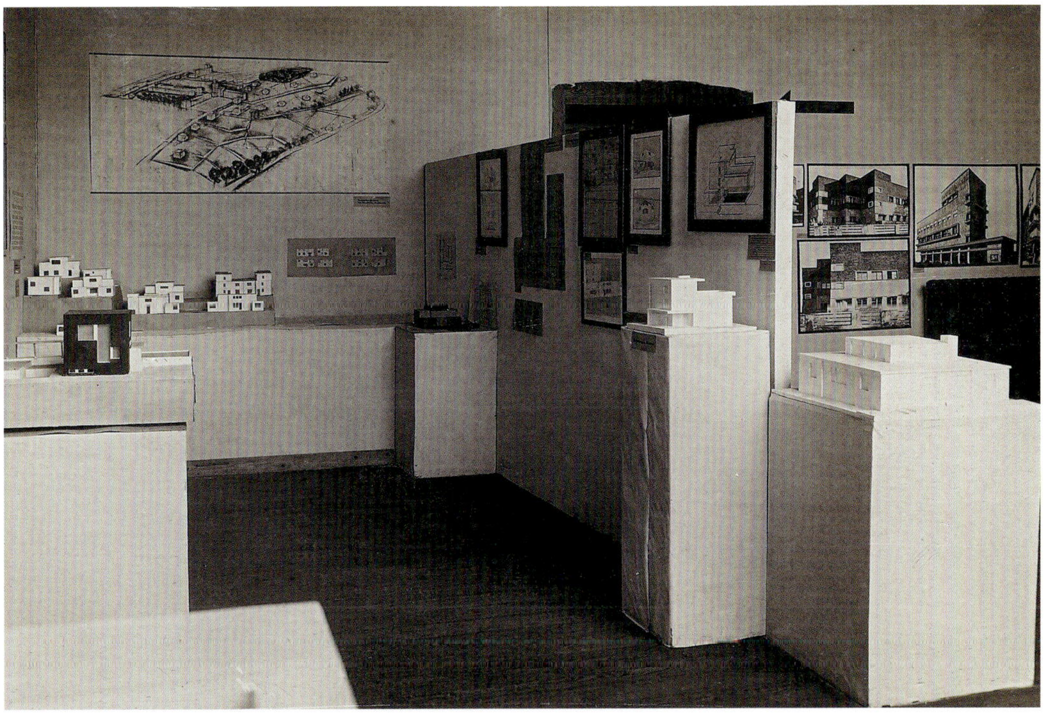

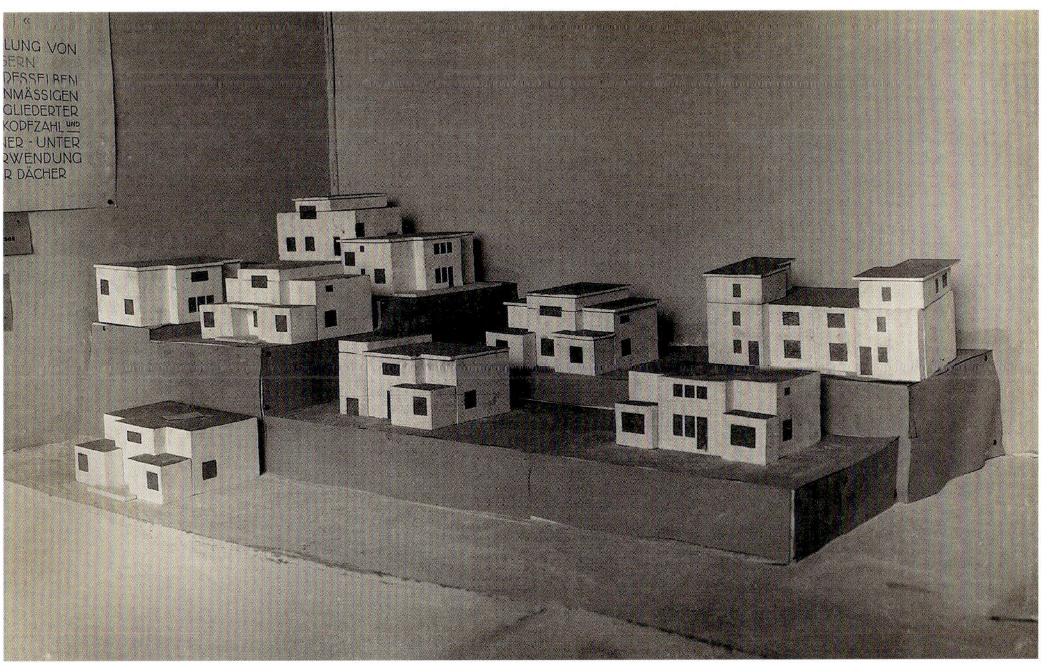

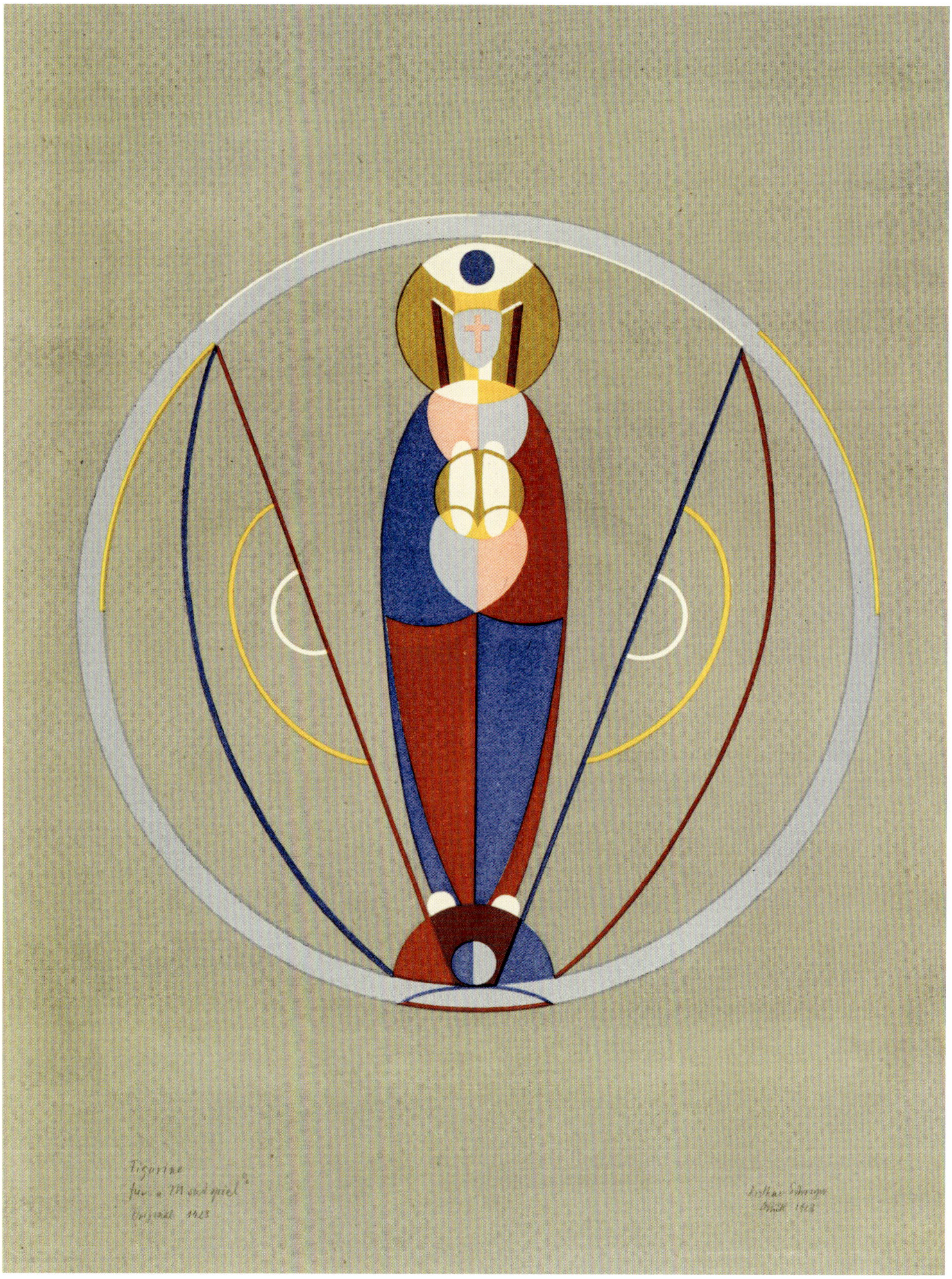
Figurine
Original 1923

80
Lothar Schreyer
Maria im Mond (*Mary in the Moon*),
costume design for *Mondspiel*
(*Moon Play*), 1923
Colour lithograph
39.8 × 29.8 cm
Bauhaus-Archiv Berlin

When Schreyer presented the dress rehearsal of his play *Mondspiel* (*Moon Play*) to the rest of the Bauhaus in February 1923, it sparked a furore. It was the first time he had shown his work since being appointed master of the stage workshop in 1921. The play's cultic and expressionist ideas, which had dominated the Bauhaus at its inception, by then had come to stand against the school's more modernist and commercially driven agenda. Composed of 346 lines of verses, *Mondspiel* featured two characters in full body masks: Maria, a tall rigid figure in a geometric costume symbolising all-consuming love; and, at her feet, the Moon or *Tänzer mit dem Tanzschild* (Dancer with the dance shield), a male orator. The dialogue lost its conventional dramatic meaning through alliteration and rhyme, emphasised by the actors' varying intonations. For Schreyer, the abstraction of all conventional elements of traditional theatre enabled a meditative engagement between the physical world and the cosmos. Following his aborted attempts to stage *Mondspiel*, Schreyer resigned from his leadership of the Bauhaus stage workshop and, in October 1923, he left the school.

81
Oskar Schlemmer
Das Triadische Ballett, Figurinen als Teil der Revue 'Wiedner Metropol', im Metropol-Theater, Berlin
(*The Triadic Ballet, Figurines in the Revue* 'Wiedner Metropol' at the Metropol Theatre, Berlin), 1926
Vintage print, altered by the artist
23/23.3 × 29.5/29.2 cm
Bühnen Archiv Oskar Schlemmer/
The Oskar Schlemmer Theatre Estate

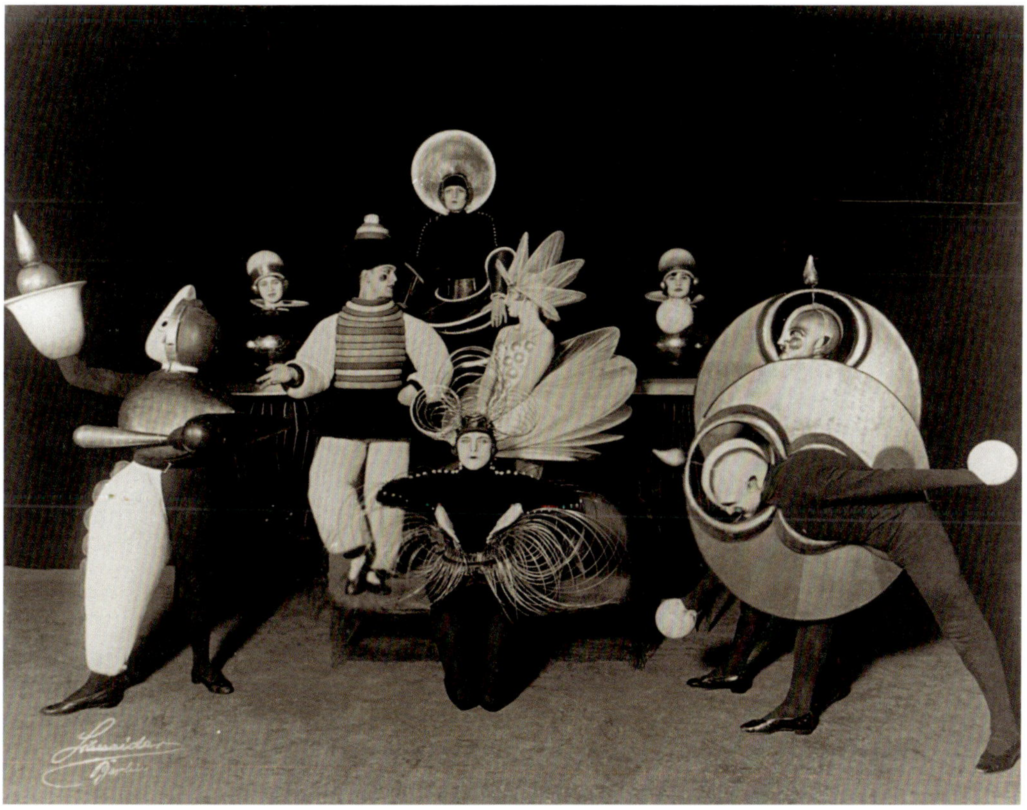

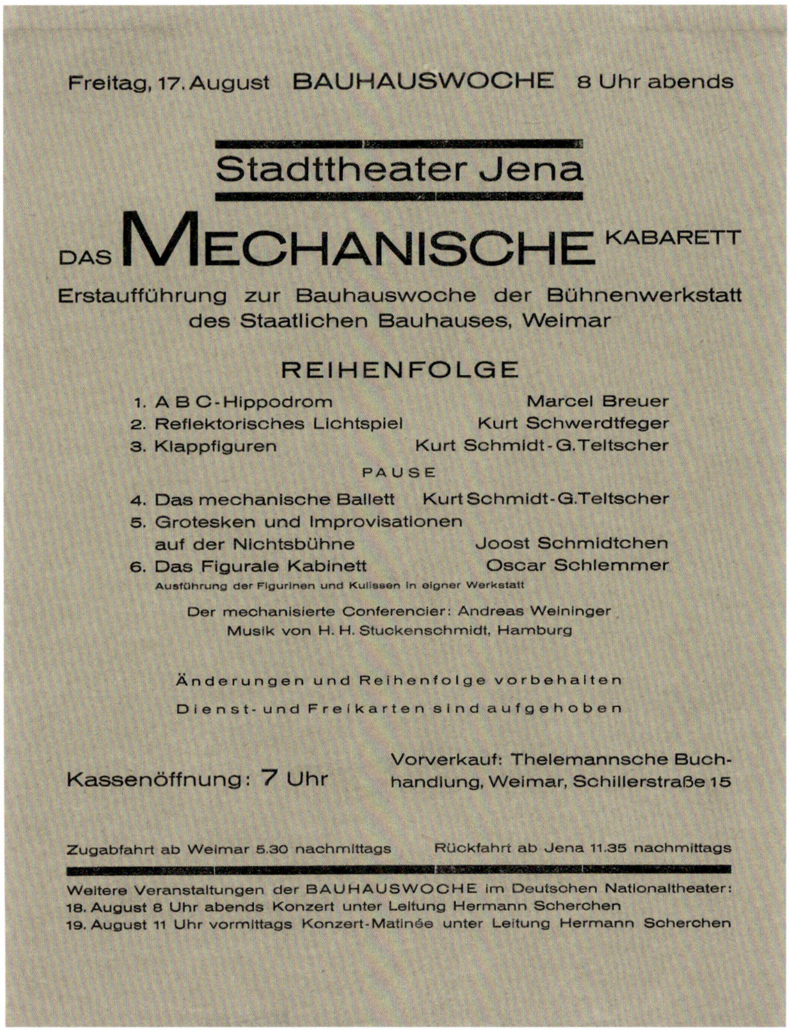
Freitag, 17. August BAUHAUSWOCHE 8 Uhr abends

Stadttheater Jena

DAS MECHANISCHE KABARETT

Erstaufführung zur Bauhauswoche der Bühnenwerkstatt des Staatlichen Bauhauses, Weimar

REIHENFOLGE

1. A B C-Hippodrom — Marcel Breuer
2. Reflektorisches Lichtspiel — Kurt Schwerdtfeger
3. Klappfiguren — Kurt Schmidt-G. Teltscher

PAUSE

4. Das mechanische Ballett — Kurt Schmidt-G. Teltscher
5. Grotesken und Improvisationen auf der Nichtsbühne — Joost Schmidtchen
6. Das Figurale Kabinett — Oscar Schlemmer

Ausführung der Figurinen und Kulissen in eigner Werkstatt

Der mechanisierte Conferencier: Andreas Weininger
Musik von H. H. Stuckenschmidt, Hamburg

Änderungen und Reihenfolge vorbehalten

Dienst- und Freikarten sind aufgehoben

Kassenöffnung: 7 Uhr

Vorverkauf: Thelemannsche Buchhandlung, Weimar, Schillerstraße 15

Zugabfahrt ab Weimar 5.30 nachmittags — Rückfahrt ab Jena 11.35 nachmittags

Weitere Veranstaltungen der BAUHAUSWOCHE im Deutschen Nationaltheater:
18. August 8 Uhr abends Konzert unter Leitung Hermann Scherchen
19. August 11 Uhr vormittags Konzert-Matinée unter Leitung Hermann Scherchen

82
Artist unknown
Programme for *The Mechanical Cabaret* at Stadttheater Jena, Bauhaus week, 17 August, 1923
Letterpress
24.5 × 18.5 cm
Bauhaus-Archiv Berlin

83
Kurt Schmidt
Design based on the performance of *The Mechanical Ballet* by Kurt Schmidt, Georg Teltscher and Friedrich Wilhelm Bogler, 1923
Paint on card
20.6 × 29.3 cm
Puppentheatersammlung, Staatliche Kunstsammlungen, Dresden

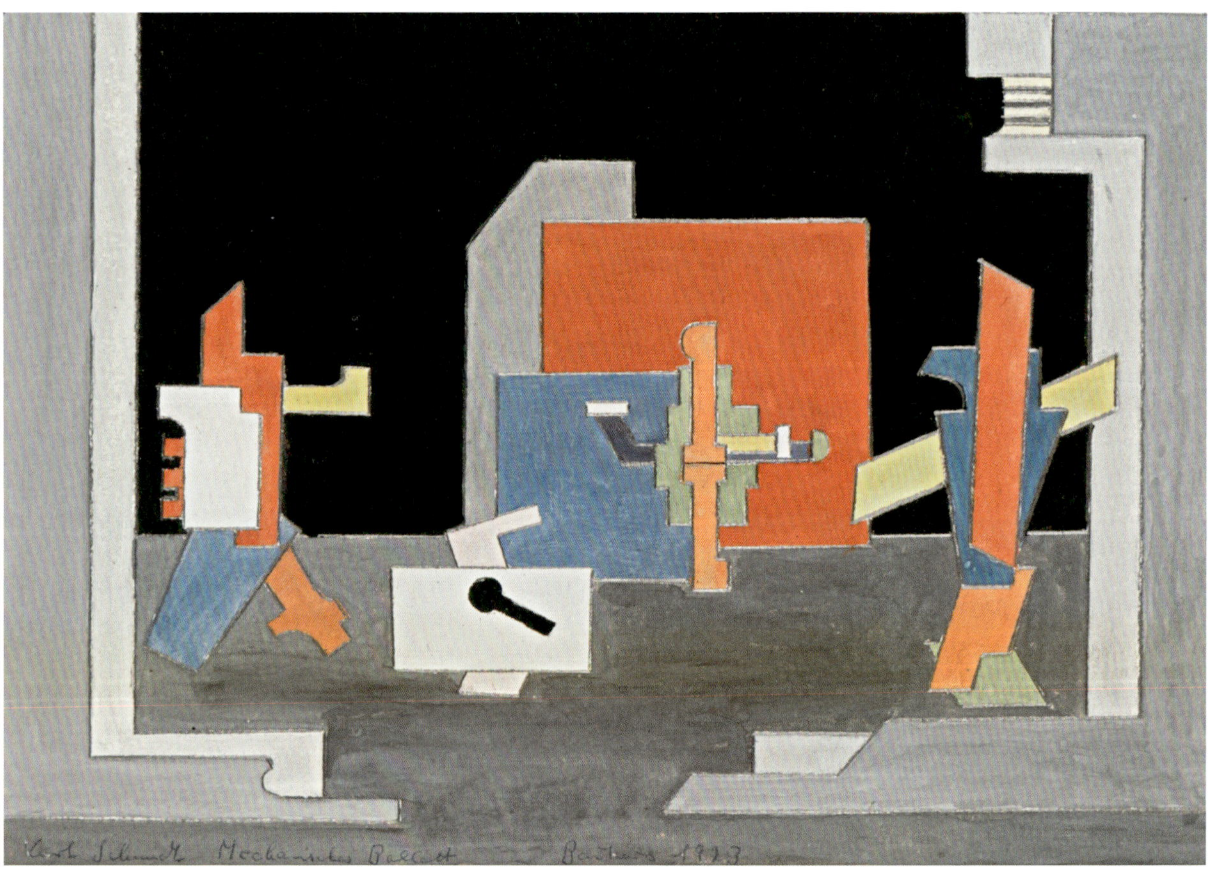

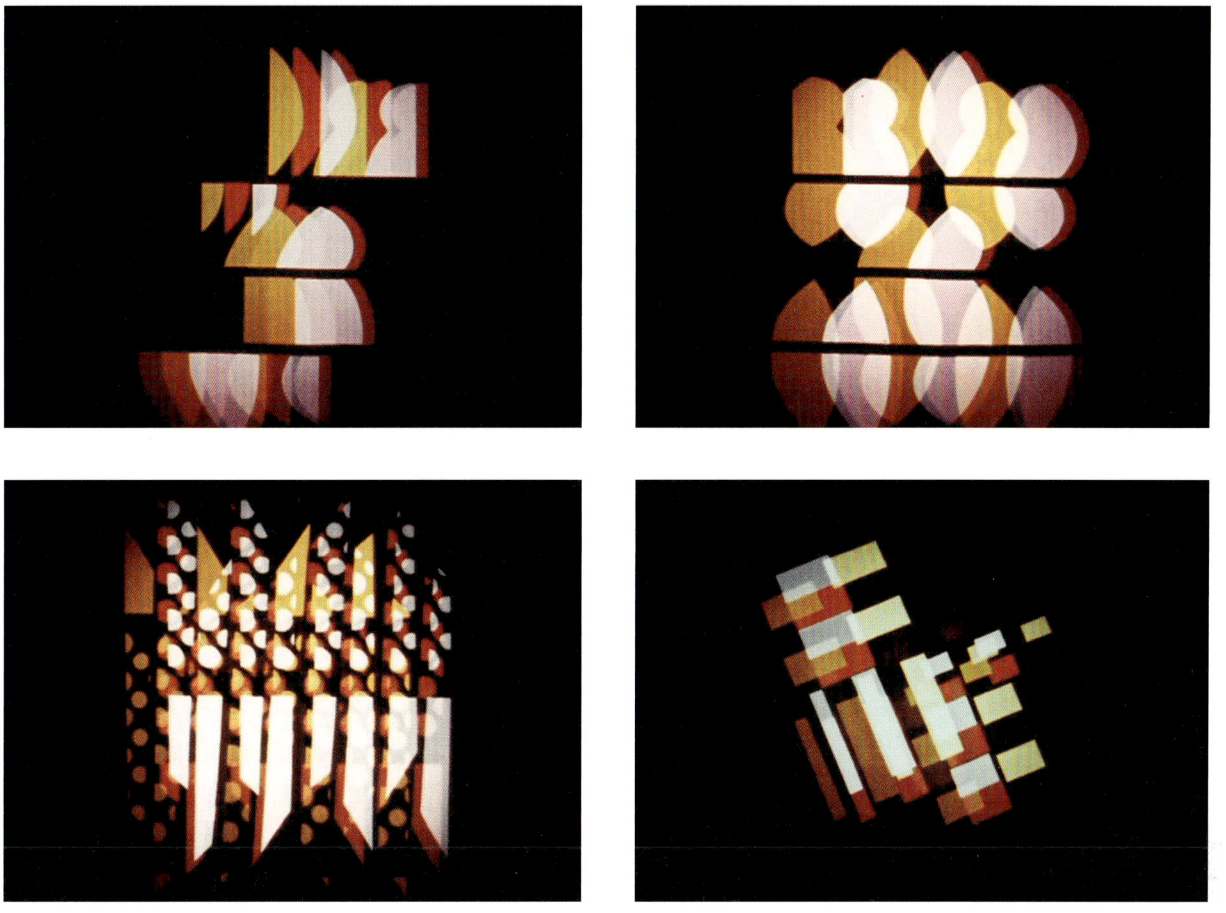

84
Kurt Schwerdtfeger
Stills from *Reflektorische Farblichtspiele* (*Reflecting Colour-Light-Play*), 1968
Film of 1966 restaging based on his 1922–23 Bauhaus performances

Colour, form and space were notions central to the Bauhaus's artistic principles. In 1922, Schwerdtfeger, a young student in the sculpture workshop, created a device known as the *Reflektorische Farblichtspiele* (*Reflecting Colour-Light-Play*). This mechanical system, which found its origins within the tradition of shadow theatre, consisted of a series of coloured lights that were operated through a keypad of switches in accordance with an accompanying musical score. The projection of coloured light would illuminate screens of various shapes and textures that were moved around by participants. Schwerdtfeger's idea for the *Reflecting Colour-Light-Play*, which originated at the Lantern Festival in 1921 and was first staged in 1922 at Kandinsky's home, would later be performed at the Jena Theater in 1923 as part of the Bauhaus week. When a dispute arose with his peer Ludwig Hirschfeld-Mack, who had undertaken similar experiments, Schwerdtfeger decided to leave the Bauhaus. The legacy of these experiments can be placed within the history of early twentieth-century avant-garde abstraction.

85
Josef Hartwig
Chess set (model XVI),
1922 (pieces and box),
1929 (board)
Pieces: Lime wood, partially stained, base with felt underlay
Box: Lime wood with metal
Board: Teak, mahogany and other types of wood
Each piece: 7.5 × 2 × 2 cm;
Box: 10 × 20.4 × 14.2 cm;
Board: 22 × 45.7 × 45.7 cm
Stiftung Bauhaus Dessau

Hartwig's chess set, first designed in 1922 and developed into two further versions, was one of the most successful products of the Bauhaus. The simple design of each piece was dictated by its status and function within the game. Volume and height signify rank, while form corresponds to the possible ways in which the pieces can move across the board. In the final version, model XVI, for example, the sphere atop the queen's cuboid body represents her mobility and contrasts with that of the rotated cube of the king, which can only move one square at a time. The latter two versions were intended for industrial production, and the apparent logic of Hartwig's design was given emphasis in the related advertising material. The *Katalog der Muster* (Catalogue of Designs) states that, in distinction to earlier figurative chess pieces that were difficult to move around without prior understanding of the game, the Bauhaus chess pieces, made up solely of cubes and spheres, were universally legible. The packaging by Joost Schmidt similarly sought to break with the past – a compact cardboard box housed the tightly arranged cuboid forms and further emphasised the quotidian nature of the Bauhaus set.

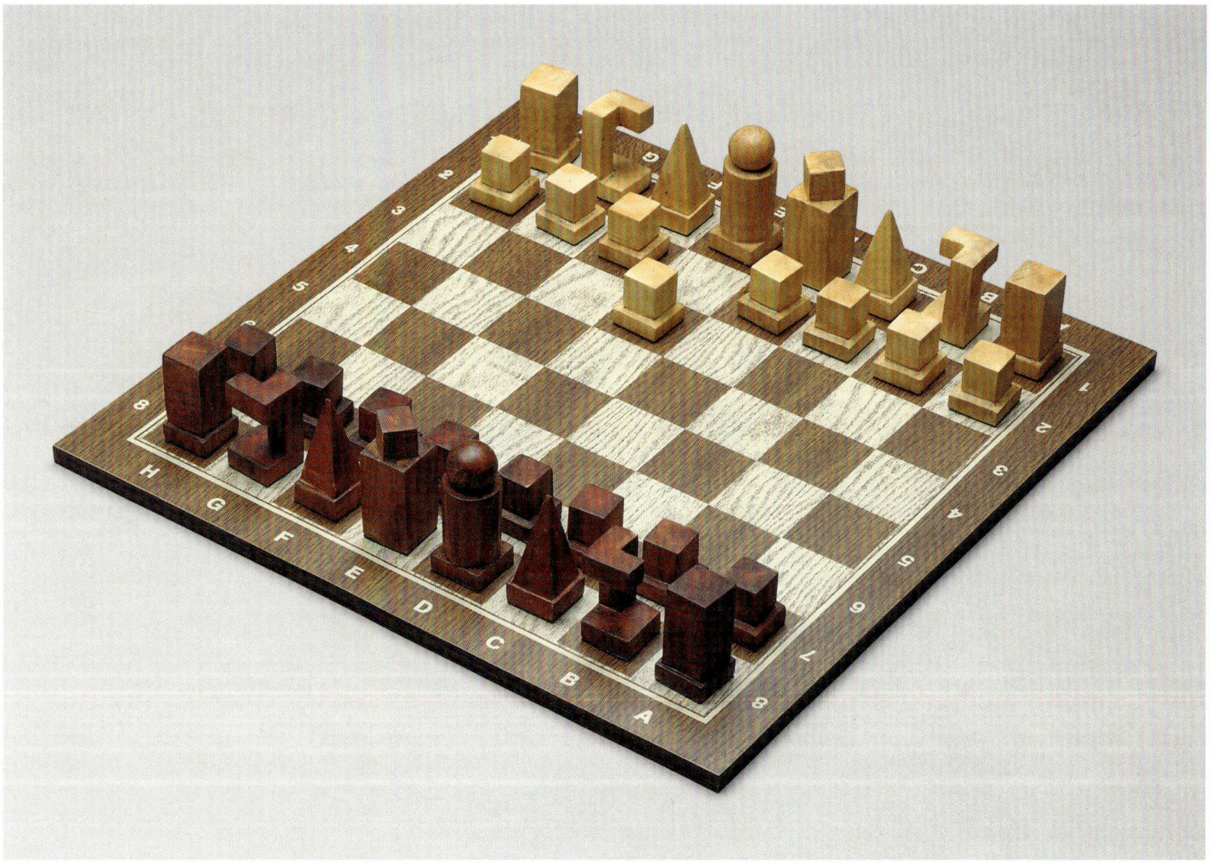

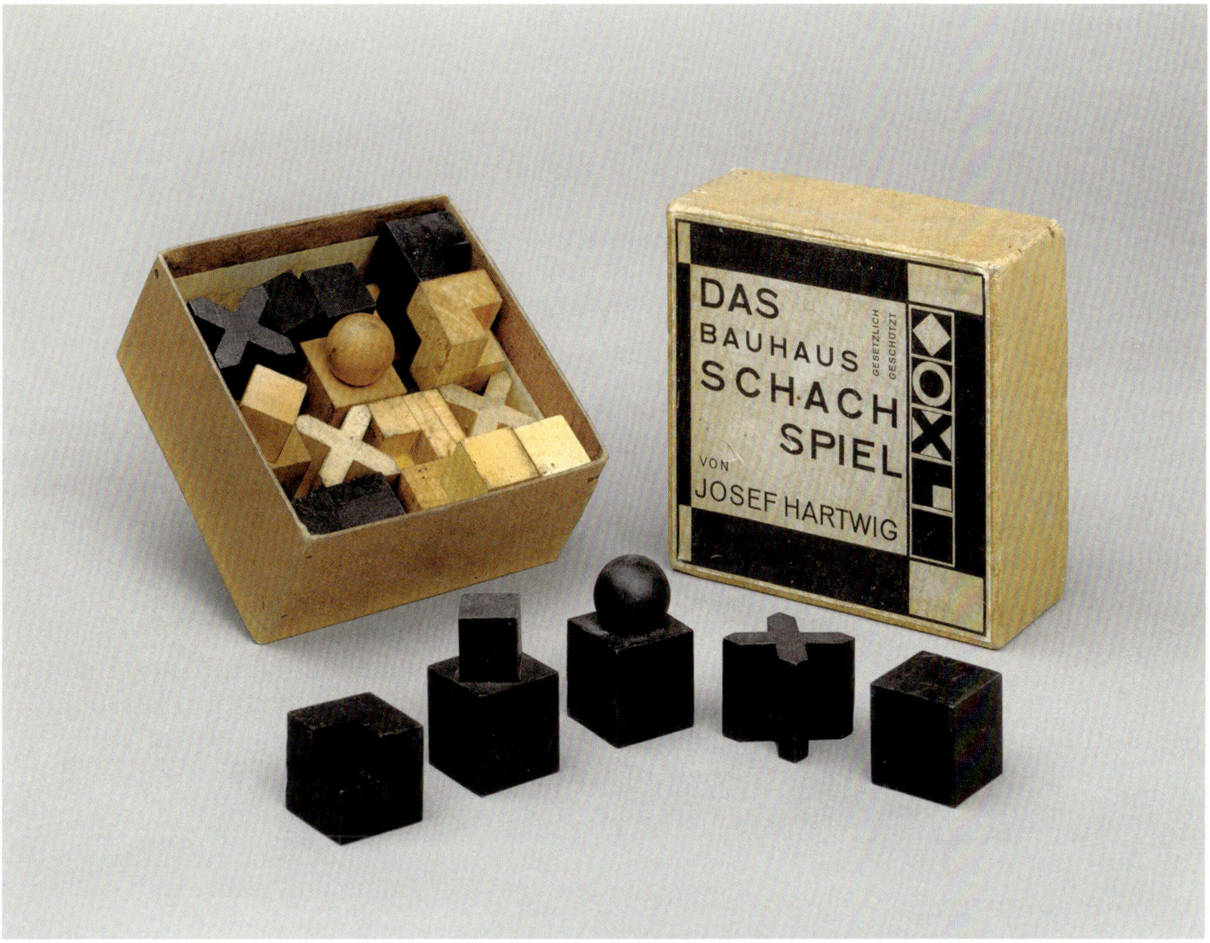

86
Josef Hartwig
Chess set (model XVI) with cardboard box designed by Joost Schmidt, 1923–24
32 pieces: pear wood, cardboard and paper
5.5 × 12.5 × 12.5 cm
Centre Pompidou, Paris
Musée National d'Art Moderne/
Centre de Création Industrielle
Gift Clarence Westbury Foundation 1999

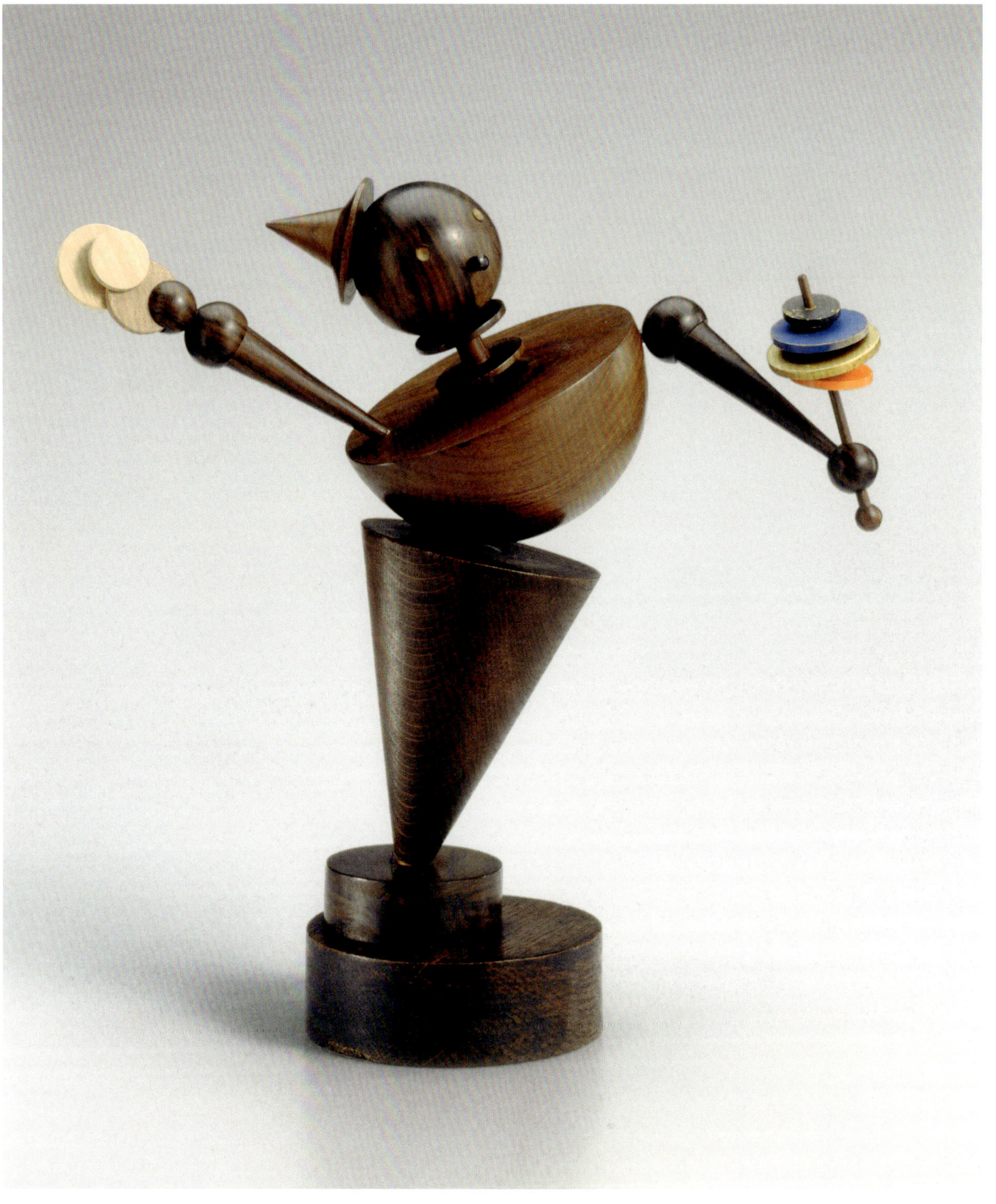

87
Eberhard Schrammen
Little mascot, 1924
Paint and varnish on wood
Height: 37 cm
Bauhaus-Archiv Berlin

88
Alma Buscher
Ship building toy, 1926
Paint and lacquer on wood
21 pieces, largest: 13.8 × 27 × 3 cm
Die Neue Sammlung – The
International Design Museum, Munich

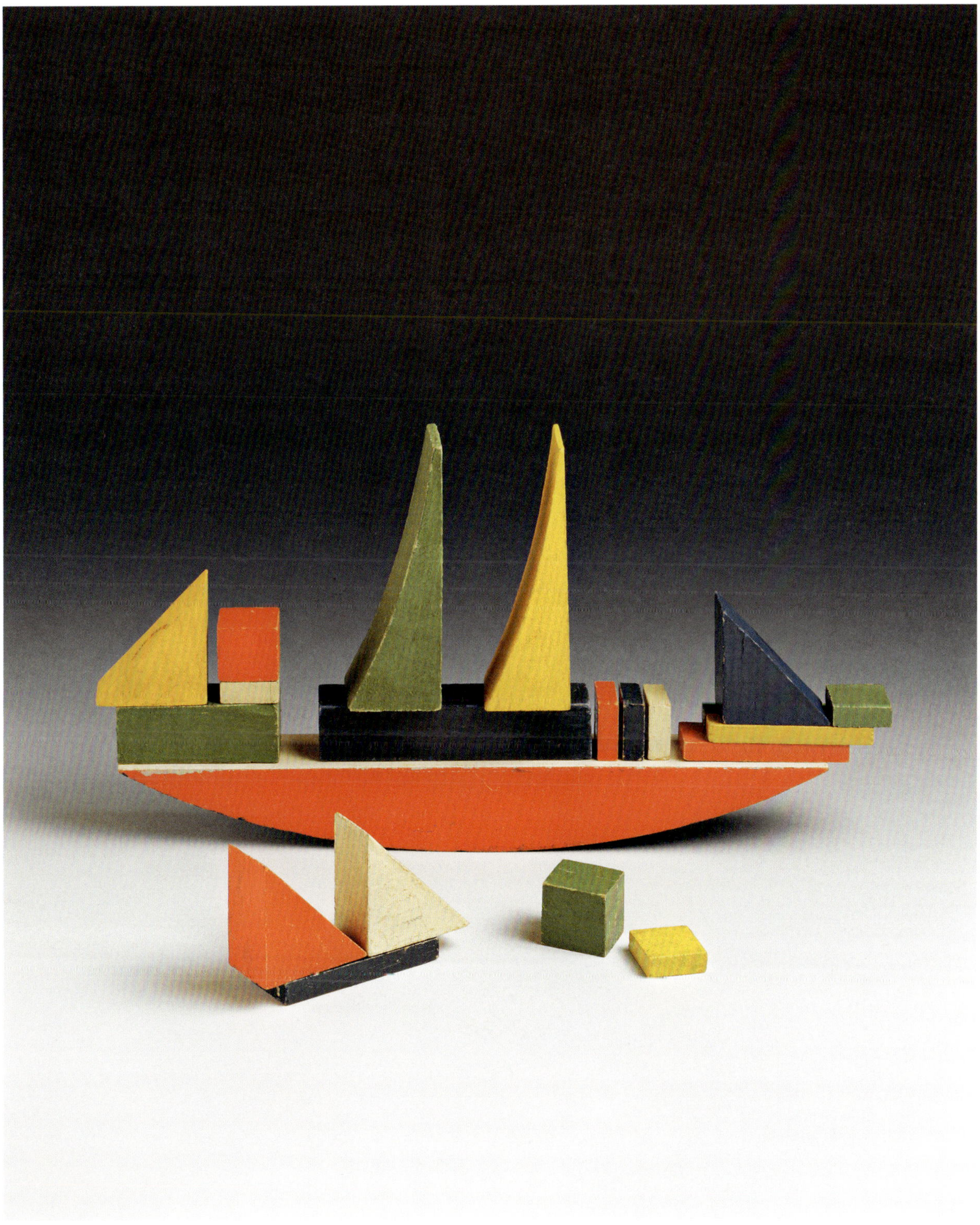

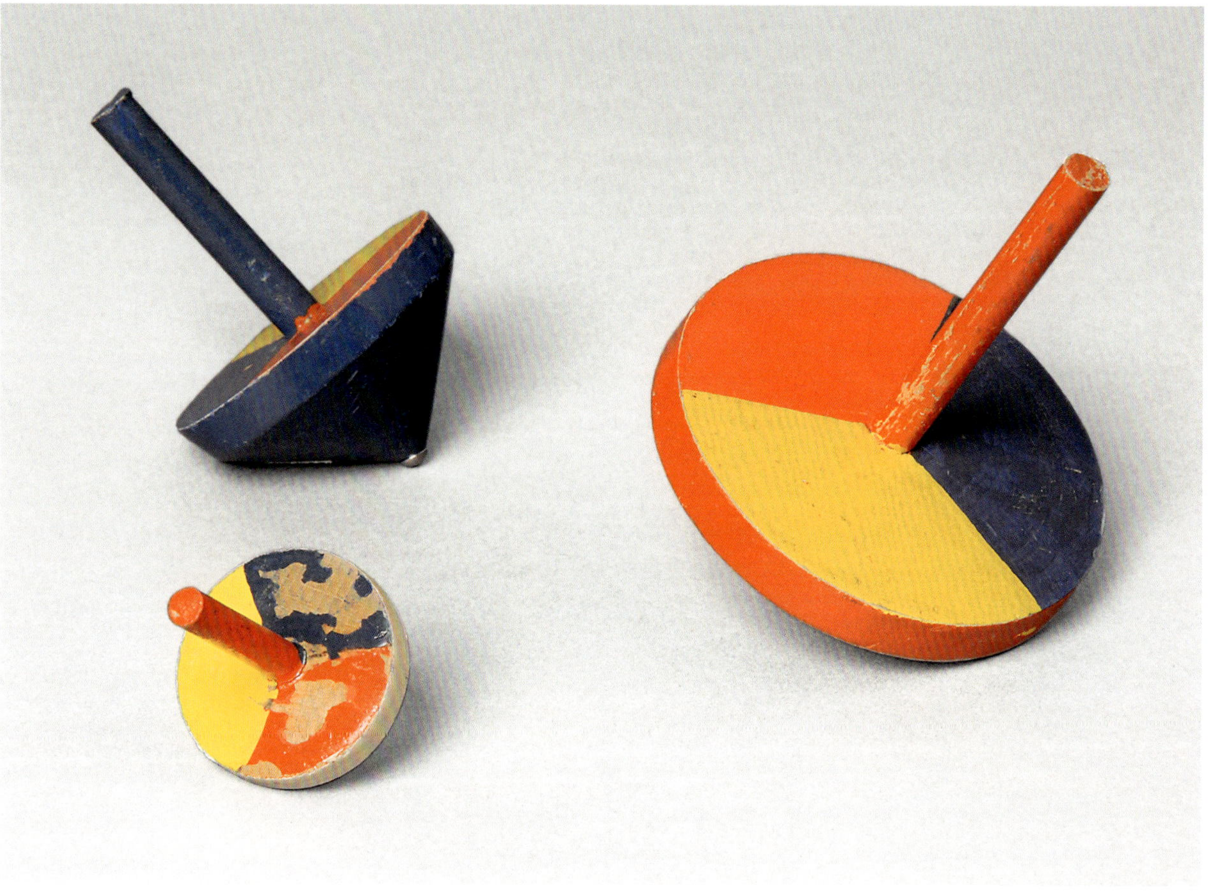

89
Ludwig Hirschfeld-Mack
Three spinning tops, 1924
Paint and lacquer on wood
10 × 7.6 cm; 9 × 6 cm; 6 × 4 cm
Die Neue Sammlung – The International
Design Museum, Munich

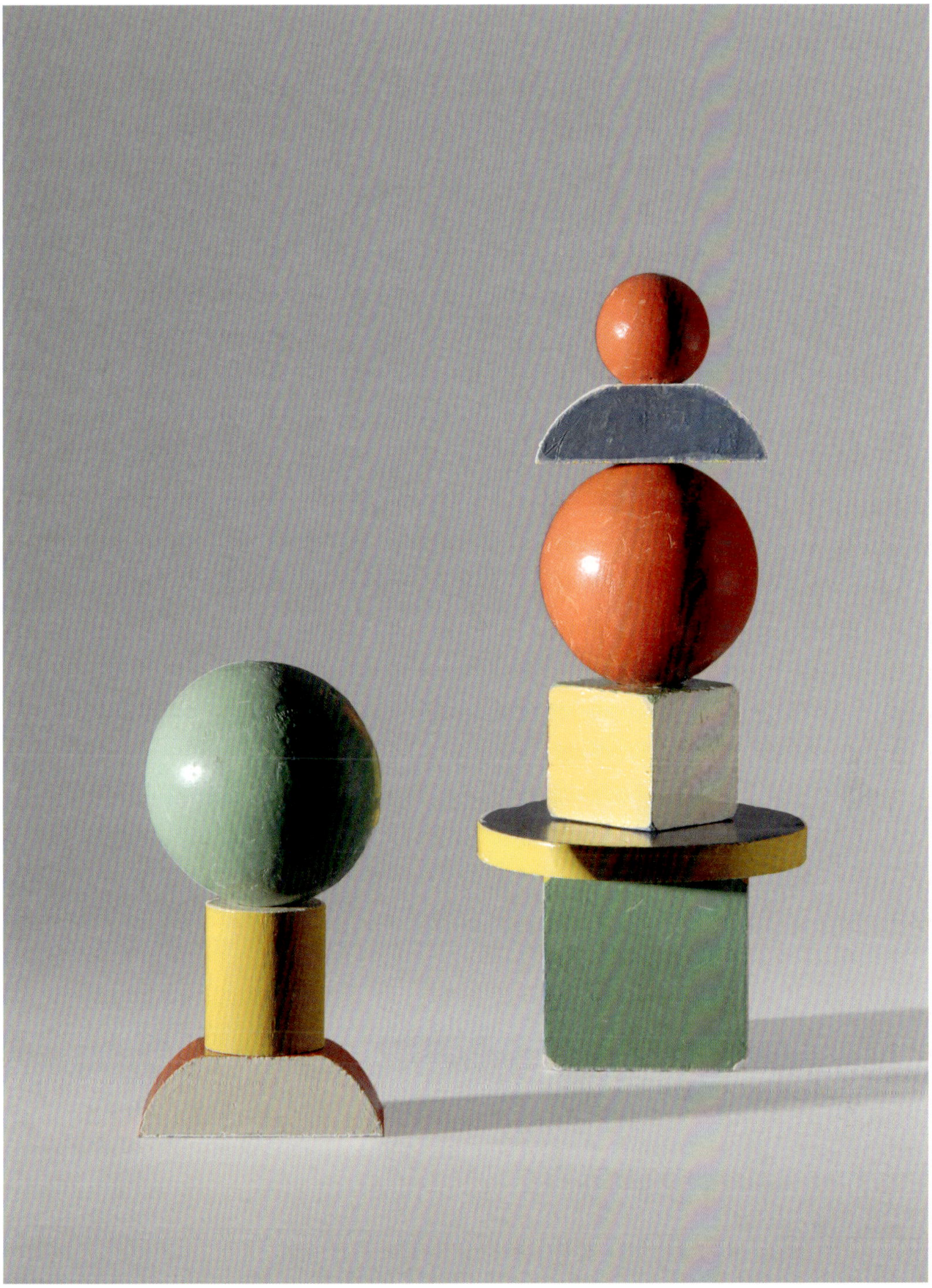

90
Alma Buscher
Wooden building blocks, 1923–24
Paint and lacquer on wood
9 pieces, largest piece: 13.8 × 27 × 3 cm
Die Neue Sammlung – The International
Design Museum, Munich

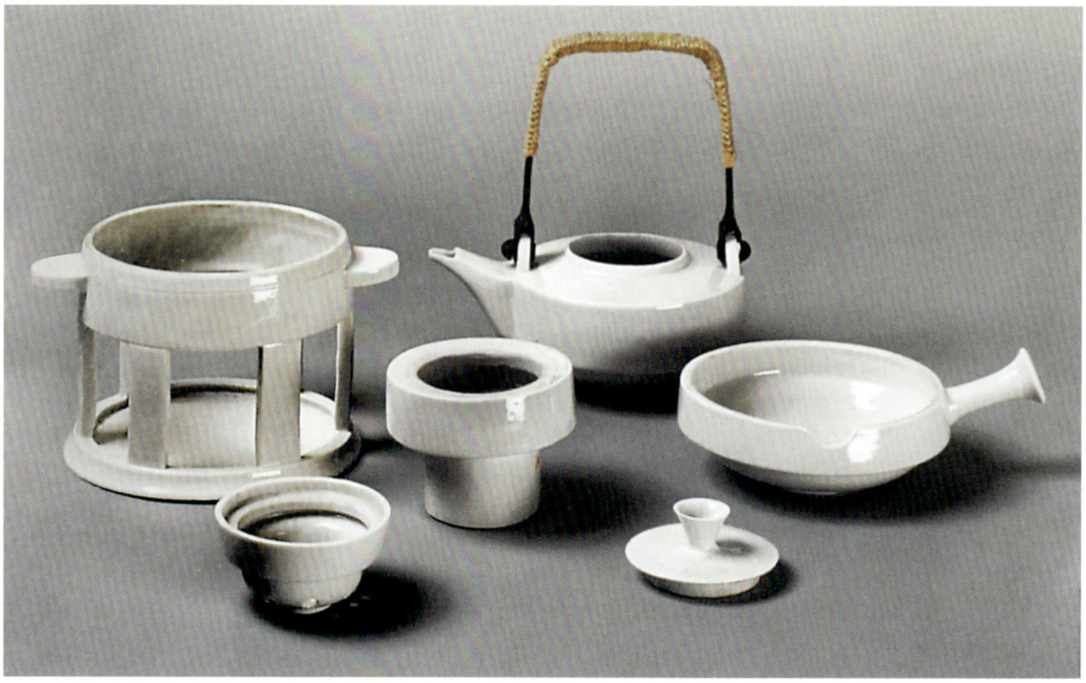

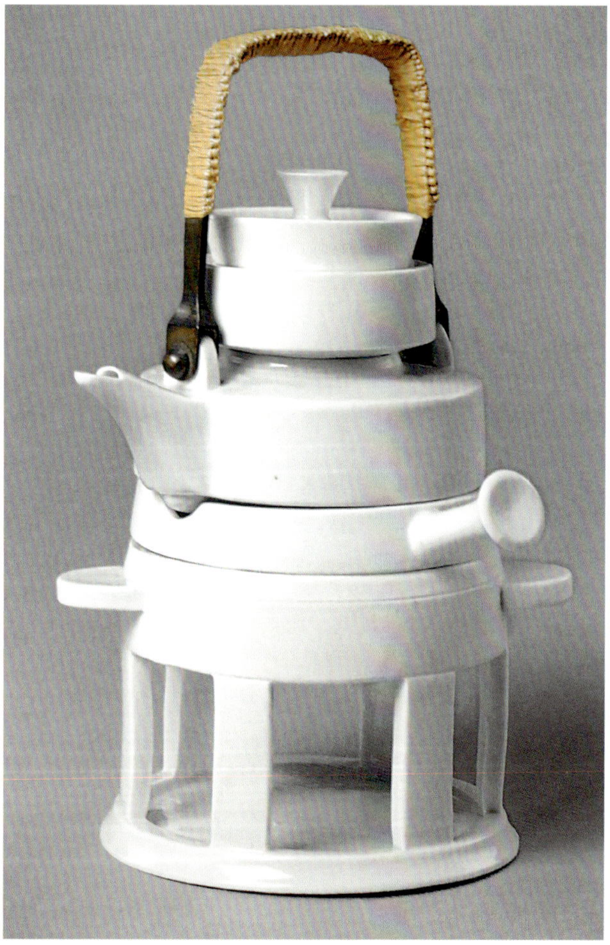

91
Theodor Bogler
Coffee machine displayed
in its component parts, 1923
Porcelain, cast and assembled
Height: 21.5 cm
Klassik Stiftung Weimar,
Bestand Museen

92
Theodor Bogler
Coffee machine, 1923
Warmer, bowl, pot, filter
fitting, strainer and lid
Porcelain, cast and assembled
Height: 21.5 cm
Klassik Stiftung Weimar,
Bestand Museen

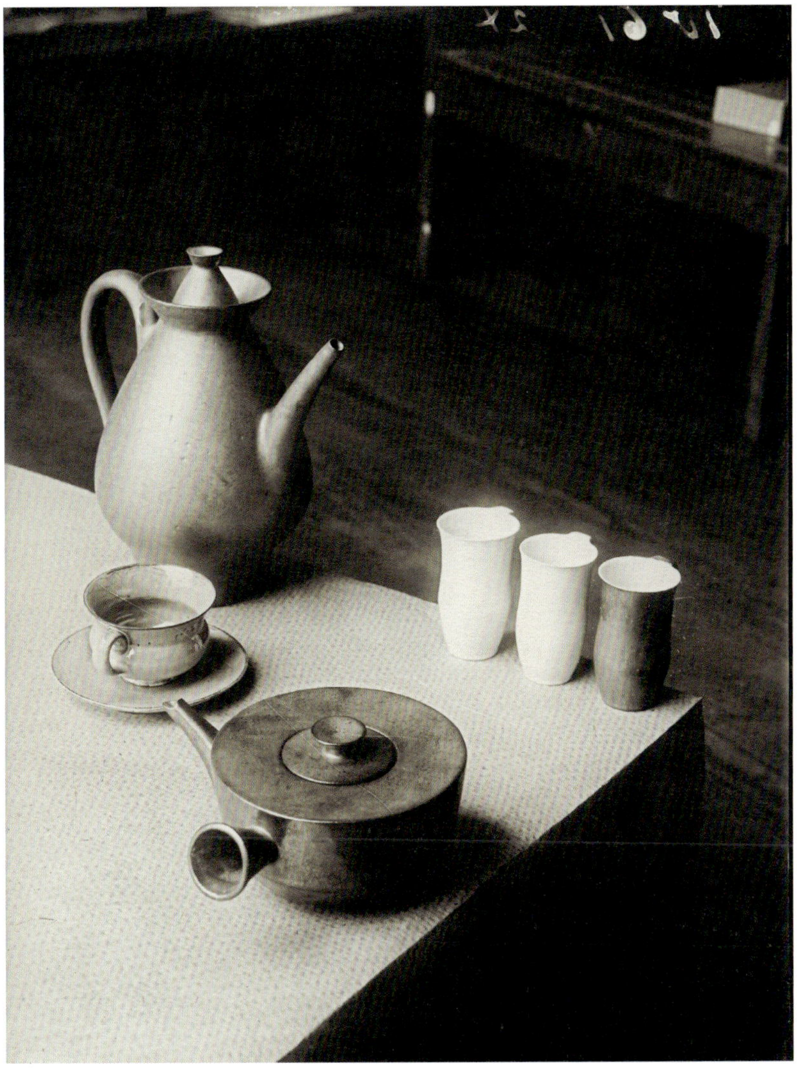

93
Lucia Moholy
Coffee pot and cup by Otto Lindig, combination teapot by Theodor Bogler and tumbler with handle by Marguerite Friedländer-Wildenhain, designed 1923, produced 1924, (photograph printed c. 1950s)
Gelatin silver print
18.4 × 13.3 cm
Bauhaus-Archiv Berlin

94
Theodor Bogler
Teapot (L1), 1923
Stoneware, cast and assembled, white glaze
Height: 12.7 cm
Klassik Stiftung Weimar, Bestand Museen

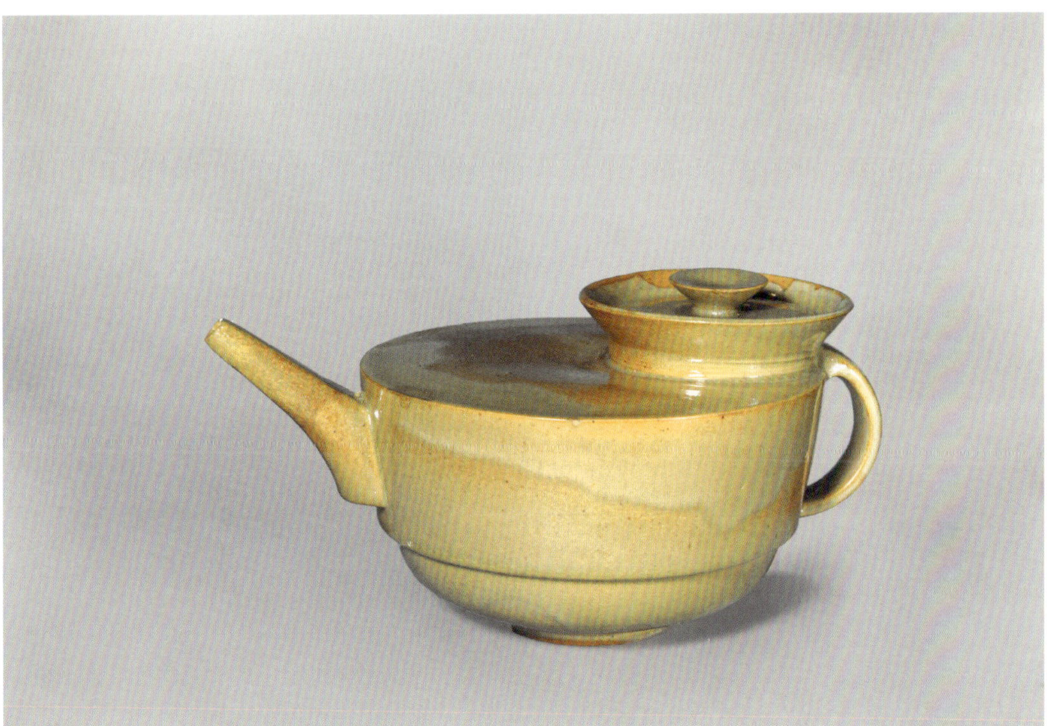

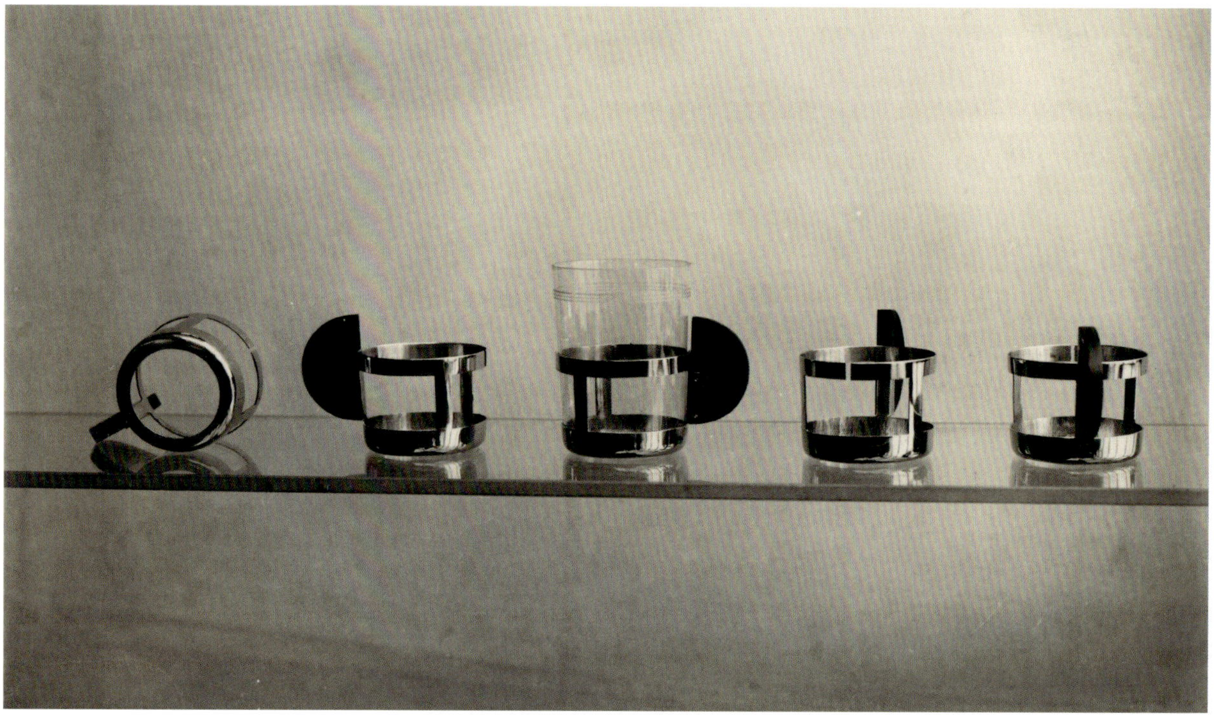

95
Lucia Moholy
Tea glass holder (MT 58)
by Max Krajewski, designed 1924,
1924 (photograph printed c.1950)
Gelatin silver print
13 × 18.1 cm
Bauhaus-Archiv Berlin

96
Lucia Moholy
Two desk lamps by Wilhelm Wagenfeld
and Carl Jakob Jucker, glass version
(MT 9/ME 1) metal version (MT8/ME 2)
designed 1923–24, 1924-25
(photograph printed 1993)
Gelatin silver print
23.7 × 18.1 cm
Bauhaus-Archiv Berlin

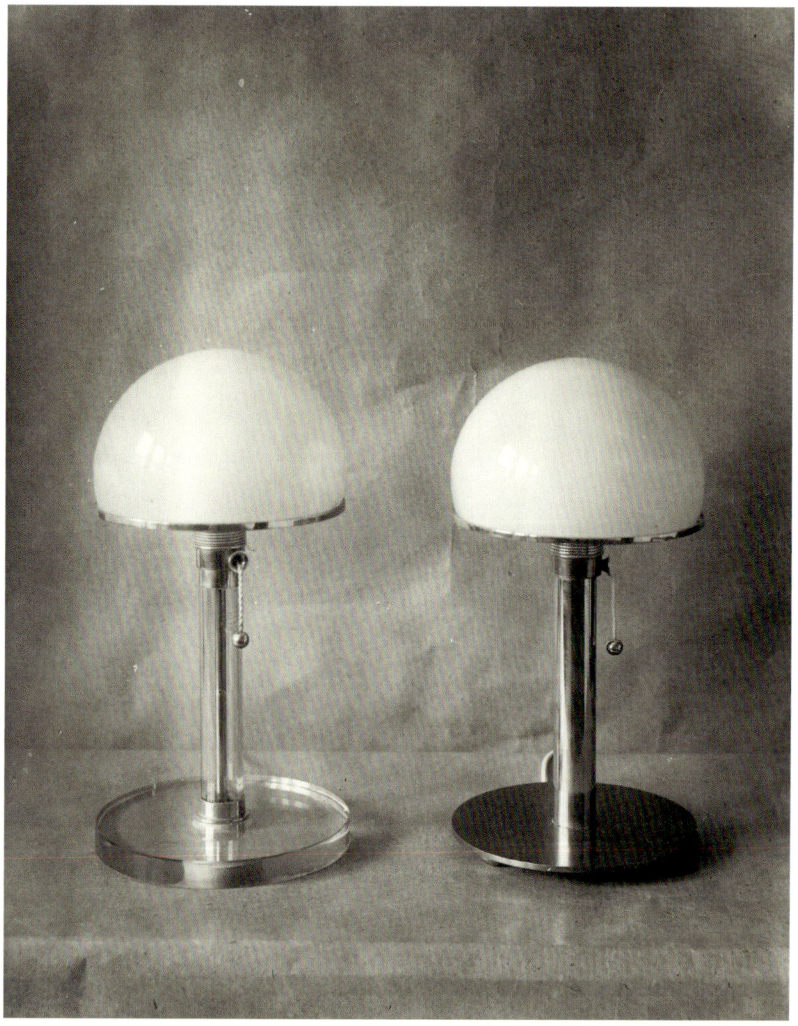

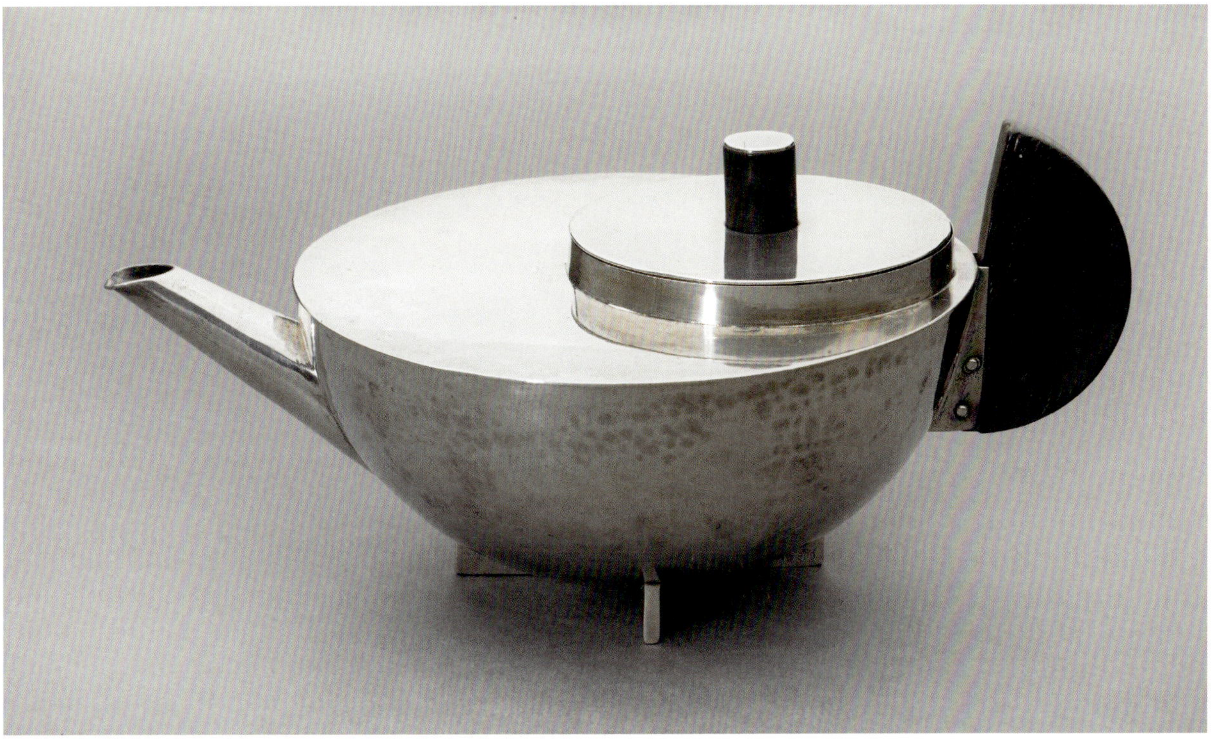

97
Marianne Brandt
Tea infuser, designed 1924, fabricated 1925–29
Silver and ebony
7.3 × 10.6 × 16.1 cm
The British Museum, London

98
Marianne Brandt
Tea infuser, c. 1924
Silver and ebony
13.5 × 10 × 10 cm
Private Collection

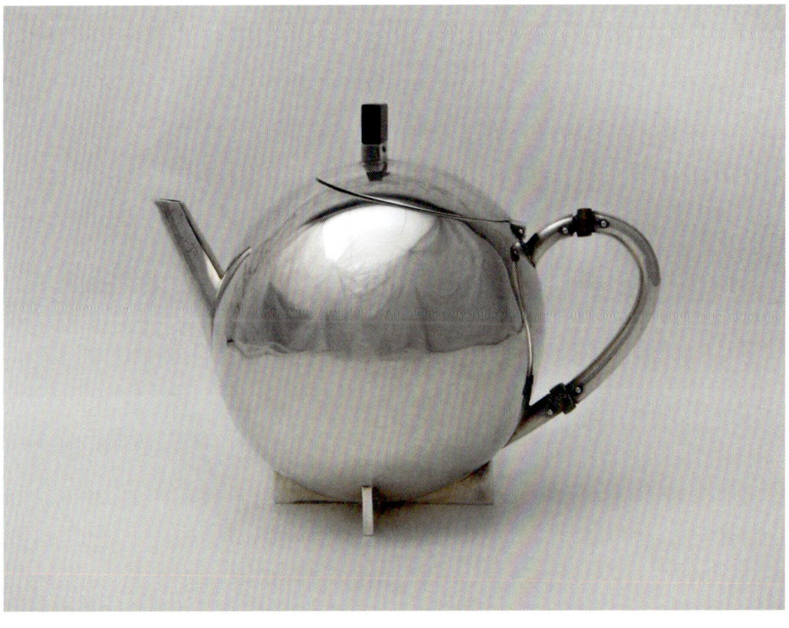

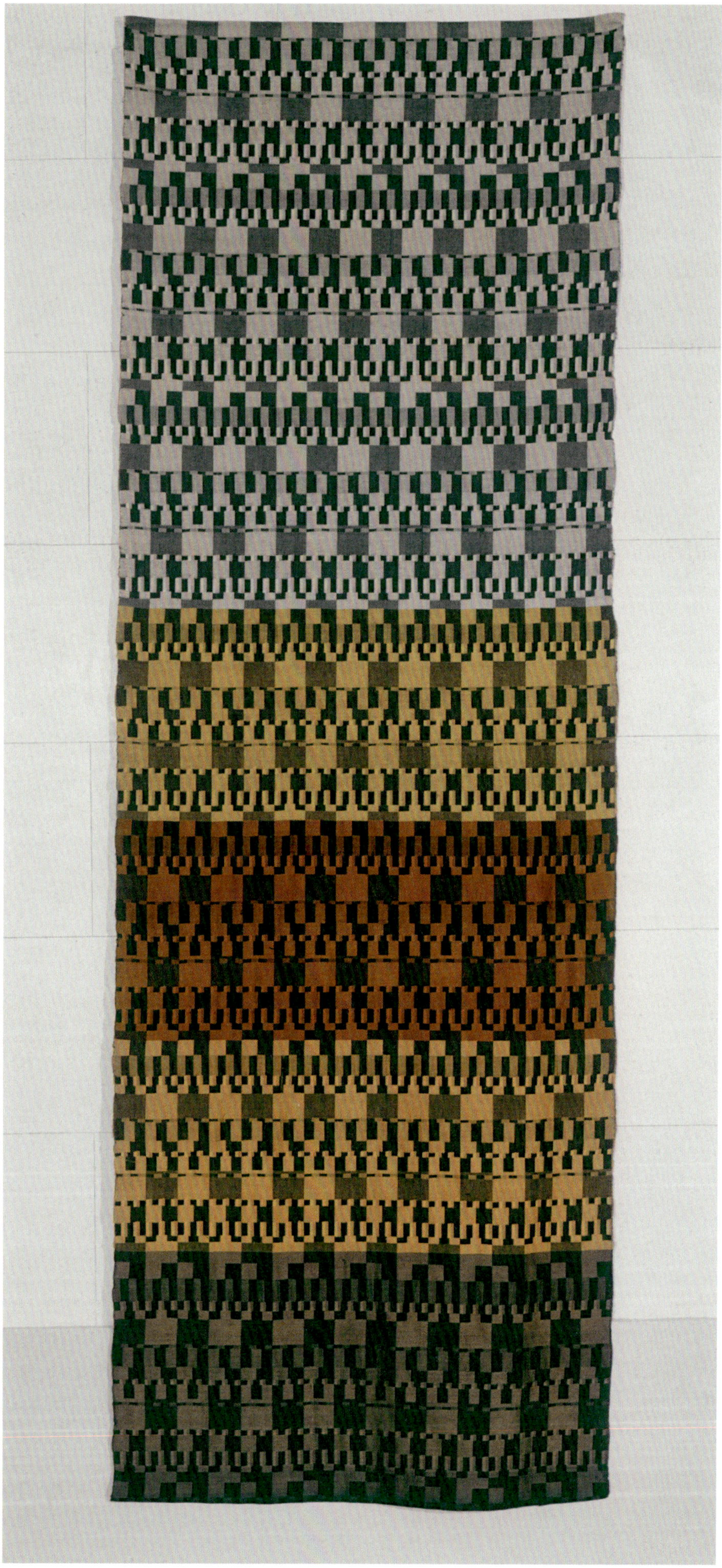

99
Agnes Roghé
Fabric to be sold by the metre, 1923–24
Jacquard material, twill weave
and cotton
280 × 95 cm
Klassik Stiftung Weimar,
Bestand Museen

100
Gunta Stölzl
Wall hanging with striped structure, 1923
(copy by Helene Börner 1925)
Linen weave, wool and synthetic silk
204 × 125 cm
Klassik Stiftung Weimar,
Bestand Museen

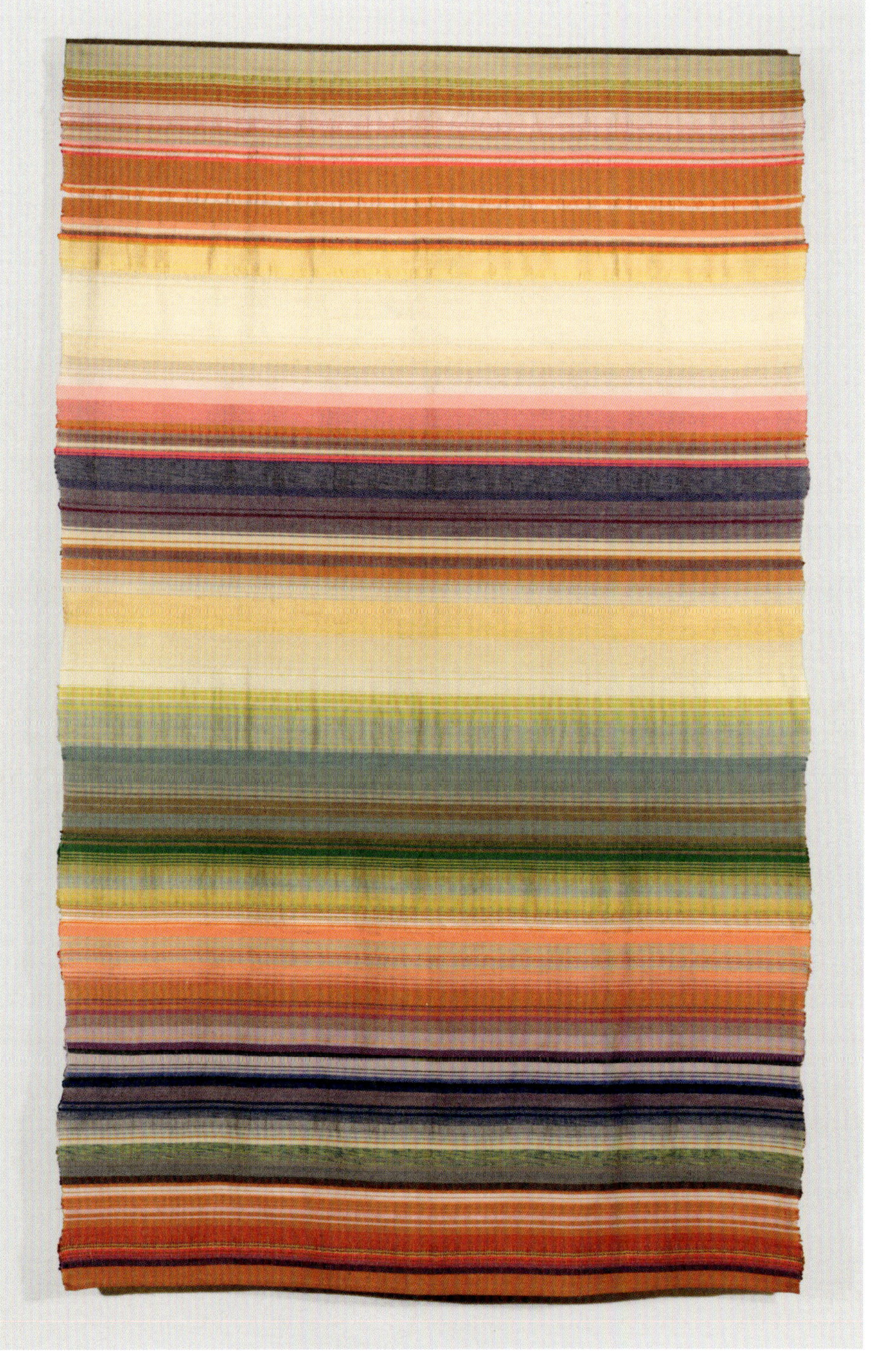

instruments of communication

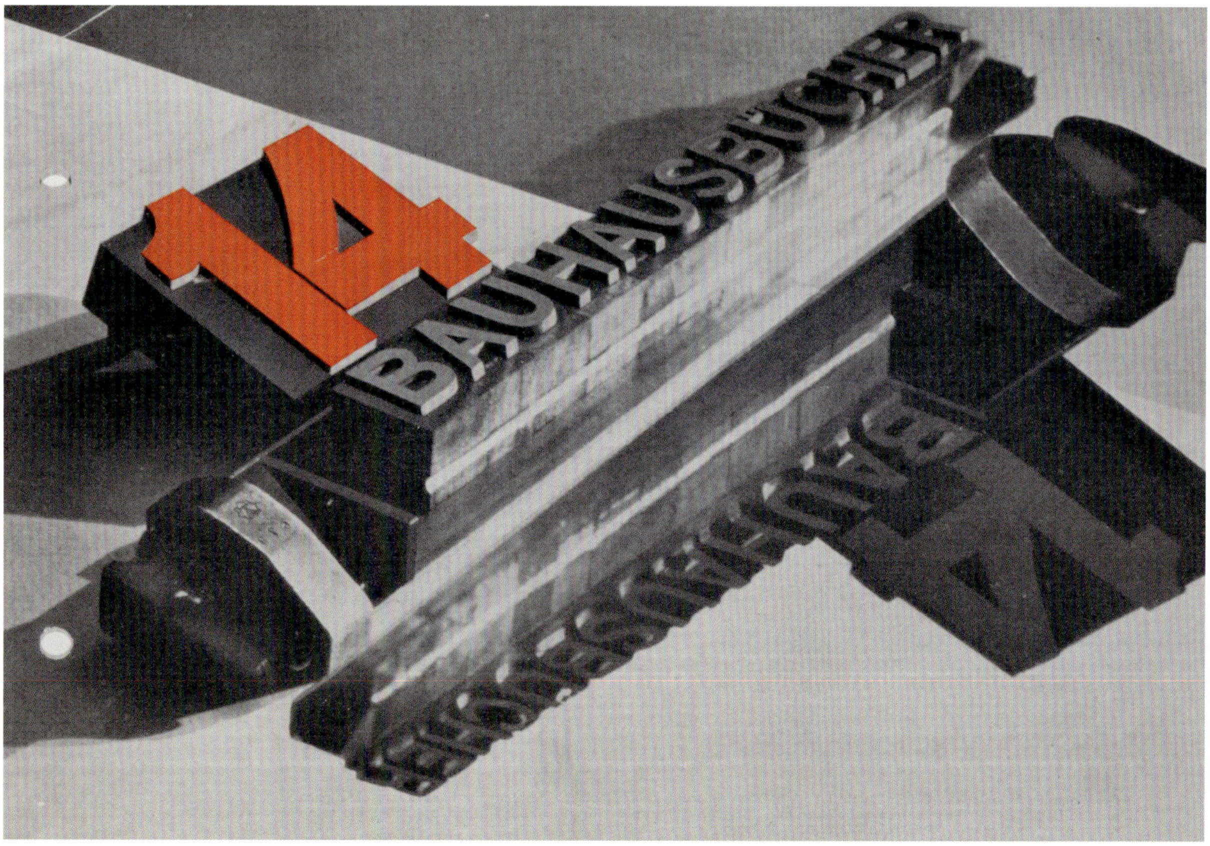

The Weimar Bauhaus printing workshop was inherited from the Grand-Ducal Saxon Academy of Fine Arts, and training focused on traditional techniques such as etching, woodcut and engraving. Graphic art prints by Bauhaus masters and students were produced to generate income for the school, as well as *Neue Europäische Graphik* (New European Graphics), a five-part series of print portfolios by leading avant-garde artists from across the continent. Students also designed and printed materials for school events and activities, from posters advertising the first Bauhaus lecture evenings to promotional literature for festivals.

László Moholy-Nagy joined the Bauhaus in the spring of 1923 and led the preliminary course and metal workshop. He was responsible for a radical change of direction in the Bauhaus identity, seen most evidently in the print material produced for the 1923 Bauhaus exhibition and in the formation of the Bauhaus Verlag (Bauahus Press). His aesthetic ideas chimed with Gropius's call for a unity of art and technology and swiftly replaced the eclectic style of early Bauhaus print, now taking its cue from the avant-garde experiments of De Stijl and Russian Constructivism. Moholy sought to create a new visual language appropriate to machine production and the communication needs of the modern world. His innovative design vocabulary emphasised precise and functional typography, clear layout, the use of simplified elementary forms such as bars and rules to organise information and give function to ornamentation, as well as strong contrast in form and colour.

From 1923, Moholy's radical formal language underpinned the school's identity. Bauhaus students Herbert Bayer and Joost Schmidt were the most prolific in their exploration of these new graphic design principles in their work for manufacturers or mass-market advertising. When the school moved to Dessau in 1925–26, they would go on to become 'junior masters', leading the reconceived typography, advertising and print workshop and introducing tuition in lettering to the suite of preliminary courses.

Designers of the period were preoccupied with developing economic type designs. Investigations into phoenetic alphabets and calls for the implementation of a singular, and therefore efficient, lower case alphabet had stemmed from the thinking of orthographic reformers of the previous century. Bayer introduced DIN industrial paper size standards to school print material, and in 1925 developed a 'universal' typeface, all lower case, constructed using a few simple geometric forms. He proposed dispensing with the German capitalisation of nouns, arguing that in speech, there is no difference between an upper or lower case letter.

Bauhaus educators also played a major role in the shaping of intellectual ideas of the period. The formation of the Bauhaus Verlag in 1923 helped disseminate their thinking and that of the avant-garde circle associated with the school more widely, especially through the production of a series of *Bauhausbücher* (Bauhaus Books). Edited by Gropius and largely designed by Moholy, the first volumes discussed issues of contemporary art, design and architecture and were intended to expand the Bauhaus's pedagogical range to audiences outside the school and associated circle. Volumes by Piet Mondrian, Theo van Doesburg and J.J.P. Oud formed part of the first series of fourteen books published between 1925 and 1930. Further volumes covering all aspects of intellectual life were planned, including titles by Ludwig Mies van der Rohe, Le Corbusier, Karel Tiege and Friedrich Kiesler.

101
László Moholy-Nagy
Prospectus cover for
14 Bauhausbücher
(*14 Bauhaus Books*), 1928
Letterpress
14.8 × 21 cm
Stiftung Bauhaus Dessau

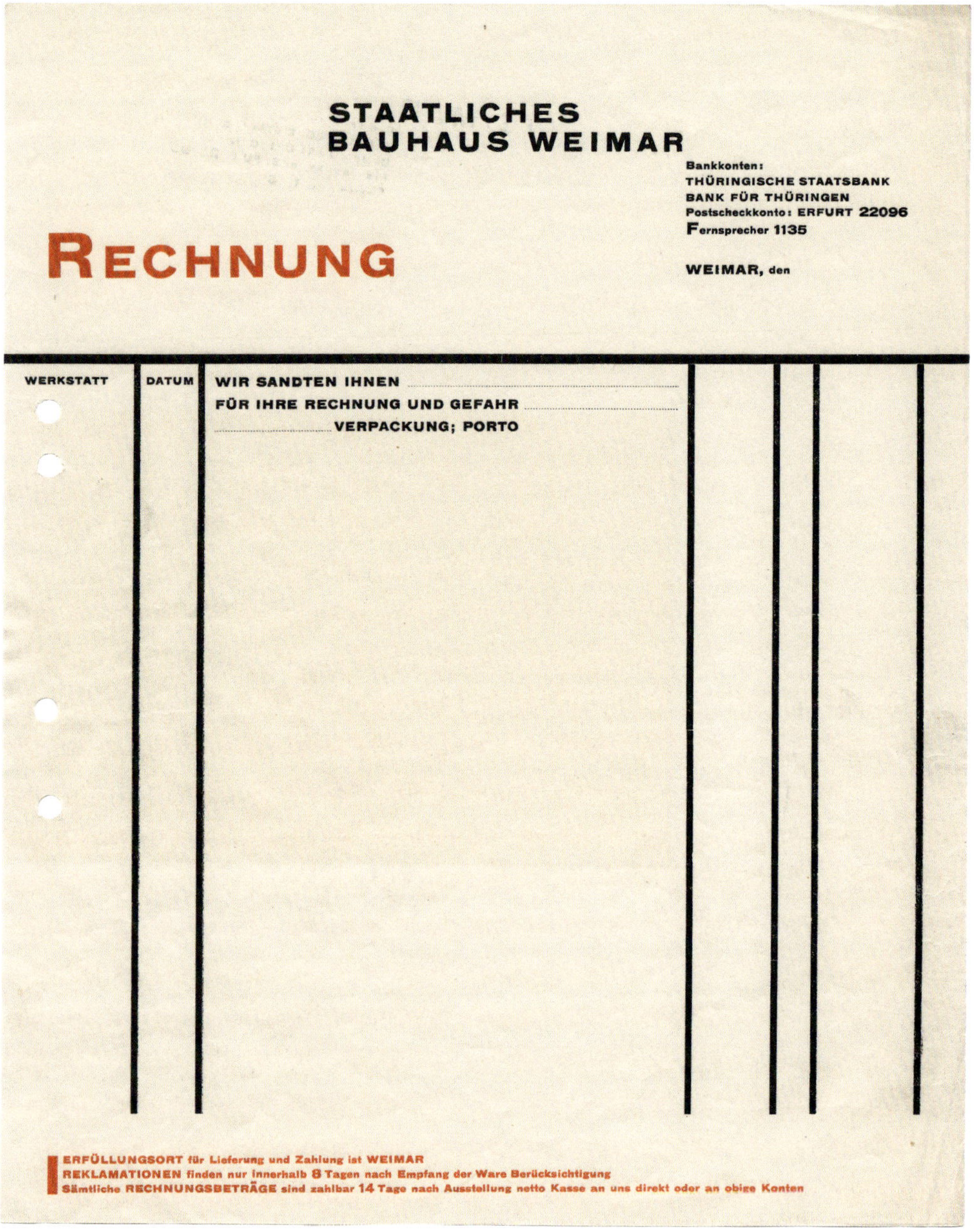
STAATLICHES
BAUHAUS WEIMAR

Bankkonten:
THÜRINGISCHE STAATSBANK
BANK FÜR THÜRINGEN
Postscheckkonto: ERFURT 22096
Fernsprecher 1135

RECHNUNG

WEIMAR, den

WERKSTATT | DATUM | WIR SANDTEN IHNEN ....
FÜR IHRE RECHNUNG UND GEFAHR ....
.... VERPACKUNG; PORTO

ERFÜLLUNGSORT für Lieferung und Zahlung ist WEIMAR
REKLAMATIONEN finden nur innerhalb 8 Tagen nach Empfang der Ware Berücksichtigung
Sämtliche RECHNUNGSBETRÄGE sind zahlbar 14 Tage nach Ausstellung netto Kasse an uns direkt oder an obige Konten

102
László Moholy-Nagy
Staatliches Bauhaus
Weimar invoice, 1923
Letterpress on paper
28.7 × 22.4 cm
Bauhaus-Archiv Berlin

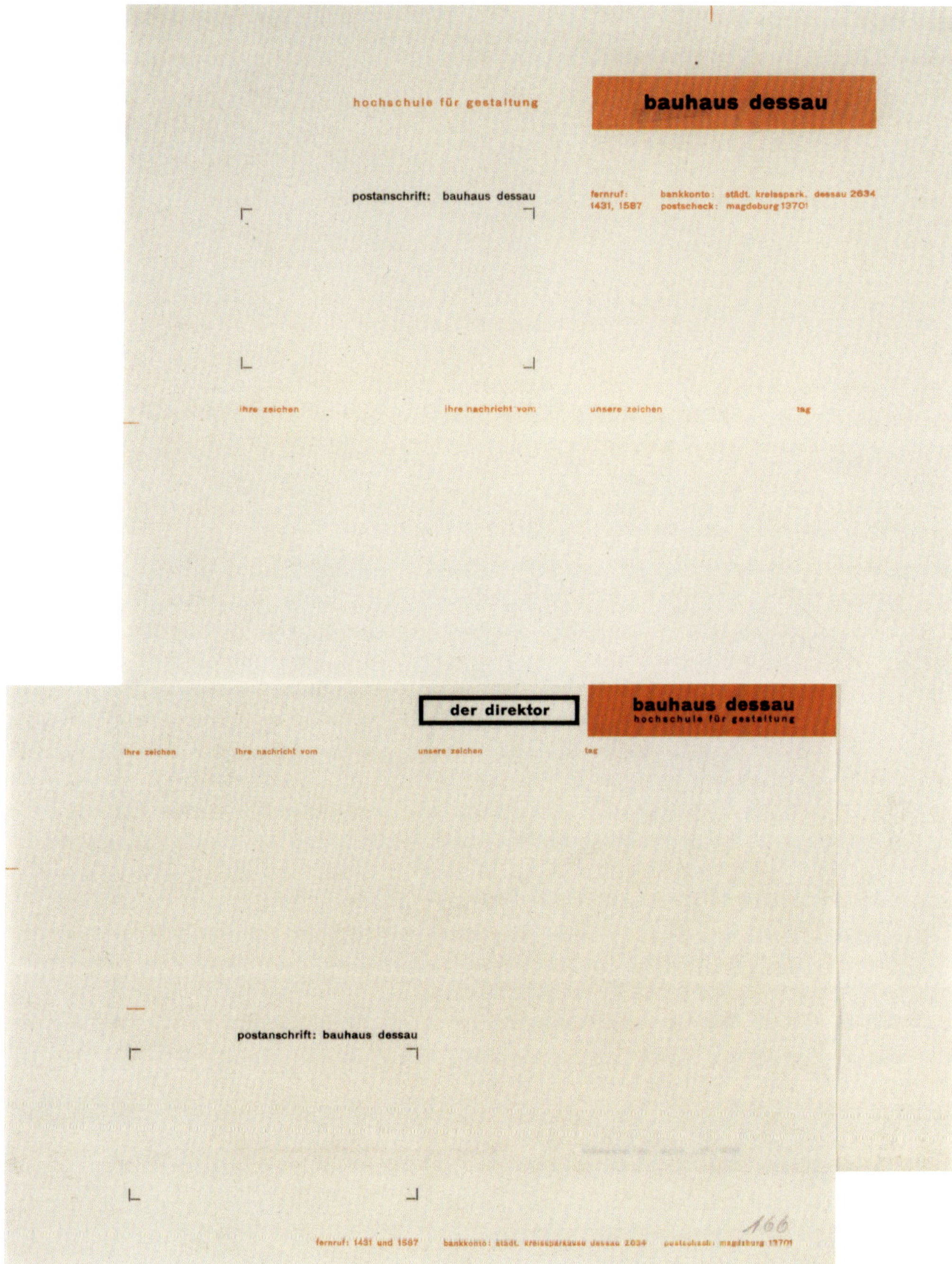

103
Herbert Bayer
Letterhead and envelope
from Bauhaus Dessau, 1927
Letterpress
29.4 × 21 cm
Bauhaus-Archiv Berlin

spread the word bauhaus instruments of communication

catherine ince

Throughout its history, the Bauhaus was dogged by financial difficulties and political pressure. To combat such threats, it forged a powerful identity that turned the Bauhaus name into a household word.[1] The Bauhaus's need to promote itself, sell its work and disseminate its ideas in the face of opposition and hardship demanded a strategic approach to design that could communicate its forward-thinking agenda. 'I would consider it a mistake if the Bauhaus were not to face the realities of the world and were to look upon itself as an isolated institution', said Walter Gropius.[2] While the Bauhaus's outward-looking perspective was driven by utopian aspirations addressing the challenges of modern living, this ambition reveals that fighting against such tendencies also played an important role in the construction of the Bauhaus brand.

Spreading the word involved cultivating a group of influential, cultured patrons, publishing the latest in avant-garde ideas, marketing and selling Bauhaus products, as well as organising exhibitions and events to promote the school and its progressive approach to art and modern education. The most significant testament to the development of a unified and influential Bauhaus identity is found in the 'products' conceived and designed by the school for its own needs. Workshops produced experimental furniture, textiles, lighting and other domestic items for the school's own requirements. A wealth of marketing materials, branded stationery, academic books, a Bauhaus magazine, posters and printed ephemera – whether promoting study at the school or inviting the public to join special festivities – all carried the Bauhaus message far and wide. The creation of the new Bauhaus campus in the city of Dessau demonstrated the school's avant-garde credentials and yielded the *Gesamkunstwerk* desired from the outset. The greatest opportunity for design was found, not in the collaborations sought with industry, but in the projects that the Bauhaus initiated in order to communicate its avant-garde message to the world.

The Bauhaus identity was transformed under the direction of new master László Moholy-Nagy, who joined the school in 1923. Moholy developed design principles in tune with Gropius's call at that time for greater synthesis between the arts and technology and the need to create a universal design language. In sharp contrast to the eclectic, expressionistic tendencies of the Bauhaus print workshop, Moholy embraced an experimental yet rational approach to design that took much from Russian Constructivism in its energetic use of form and bold colour. He privileged clarity of communication above all else: saying 'Typography is a tool of communication. It must be communication in its most intense form ... the new typography is a simultaneous experience of vision and communication.'[3]

Although Moholy's designs sometimes lacked the functionality to which he aspired, appearing instead aesthetically driven or purely symbolic and perhaps more to do with individual expression than the purity of communication,[4] Bauhaus print was to become characterised by a unified, design-led vocabulary. Bold elements such as the use of heavy bars and rules, sans-serif type and the 'dynamic' interplay of text, image and unprinted space dominated. Other elementary forms provided aestheticised yet functional ornamentation. Strong colour contrasts – principally using black and red – were foregrounded, certainly in relation to the aesthetics of avant-garde Constructivism, but also to the historic use of red as the second colour of printing in Germany since Gutenberg: 'In the context of social revolution', notes typographer Robin Kinross, 'it could take on new meanings'.[5]

In 1923 an exhibition was organised to demonstrate the Bauhaus's achievements since the school's inception in 1919. The print workshop produced posters, postcards and programmes advertising the exhibition, and Moholy, together with Gropius, designed and edited the catalogue, published by the recently established Bauhaus Verlag (Bauhaus Press). Reproductions of photographic images of Bauhaus work proliferated throughout; new theoretical texts by masters including Paul Klee, Wassily Kandinsky and Moholy himself (his essay was titled 'The New Typography') offered the reader a unique insight into the latest Bauhaus thinking. The cover – in bold, capital sans-serif letters – was designed by student Herbert Bayer, who, as well as designing exhibition print, completed new murals and directional signage for the Weimar building. Word and image – held together in a design composition reflecting the freshest ideas about visual communication – embodied the radical and wide-ranging intellectual approach that the Bauhaus sought to communicate. The exhibition and its specially conceived promotional materials were hugely influential. The young Swiss typographer Jan Tschichold, then aged twenty-three, visited the Weimar exhibition and was inspired by what he found. He went on to become one of the most important proponents of modernist typography and in 1928 published the seminal work, *Die neue Typographie* (*The New Typography*).[6] Designs for the 1923 exhibition document a decisive moment in the Bauhaus's history. It was a 'triumph of public relations'.[7]

Teaching at the Bauhaus was now to encompass 'a thorough practical, manual training in workshops actively engaged in production, coupled with sound theoretical instruction in the laws of design'.[8] Engaging with industry was to be a vital part of the creative education process. During the school's first few years, however, fruitful relationships with industry were slight. Workshop products were in fact handmade and largely unique objects. Some designs were batch produced in small quantities. In the absence of lucrative manufacturing partnerships, selling Bauhaus designs was viewed as an enterprise that would bolster the school's finances and help recoup monies borrowed to enable its founding. Additional income would also provide greater freedom from state financial – and therefore political – control. Initially, some workshop commissions came from masters and students on an individual basis – mostly for products needed to set up a new home. The school also required a number of new items, and orders were placed as necessary. One of the largest early orders for the pottery workshop was for the Bauhaus canteen, for example.[9] Others came in on an ad hoc basis from private clients, mostly middle-class professionals familiar with the school who could afford such expensive hand-crafted objects, or from companies with prior association, such as Gropius's former client Fagus.

As well as generating school income, Gropius expressed a desire to help alleviate the extreme poverty experienced by most of the students. Structured remuneration was put in place for students completing the serial production of products in the workshops.[10] In order to introduce business-like efficiency to school production, Gropius appointed Emil Lange, to control pay, pricing and licensing. Retail representatives were engaged to drive trade and in 1925 a limited trading company, Bauhaus GmbH, was set up to market and distribute Bauhaus products. Urged by retail representatives to think about publicity and promotion, the Bauhaus soon developed sales and advertising literature to promote its products to a wider market.[11]

The *Katalog der Muster* (Catalogue of Designs) was designed by Bayer using the principles of New Typography: an ordered and spacious composition of rational typography in combination with clearly reproduced photographs of selected objects (fig. 107–8). The brochure consisted of uniformly designed loose-leaf pages with functional ornamentation – such as circles, orange bars and thick black rules – employed to present standard information consistently. Each item was assigned a product code – contained within the circle – related to the object's relevant originating workshop: ME for the metal workshop, TI for the joinery workshop, and so on. The title page of the *Katalog der Muster* announced that products were distributed through Bauhaus GmbH.[12]

While aiming to appear business-like in print through the use of rigorous and systematic design principles and product coding (therefore implying operation on a large scale), some product descriptions emphasised the luxurious nature of the material or the fact that an object was made with attention to 'detailed handwork'.[13] Such paradoxes reveal the tension inherent in the Bauhaus's ideological ambitions and the practical means of production at their disposal. Bauhaus designs marketed as those best suited to mass reproduction were, in reality, exclusive, expensive hand-crafted objects for the wealthy consumer. One object included in the *Katalog der Muster* was Wilhelm Wagenfeld's now-iconic MT8 lamp, exhibited extensively by the Bauhaus in 1924 and attracting considerable international attention. While its critical success pointed to the consumer's desire for new forms of light fittings,[14] 'retailers and manufacturers laughed at our efforts' according to Wagenfeld. 'These designs which looked as though they could be made inexpensively by machine techniques were, in fact, extremely costly craft designs.'[15]

Like the metal, cabinetry or weaving workshop's, the need to generate income also impacted on the output of the print workshop. Much early print work was focused on the production and commercial sale of fine-art prints and limited-edition portfolios, which comprised collections by Bauhaus masters and leading artists from across Germany, Italy, Russia and France. Furthermore, the portfolios presented another opportunity to cement the image of the Bauhaus as a school of international renown, closely linked to the most progressive avant-garde artists of the day. Post-war financial disaster and hyperinflation meant, however, that anticipated revenue from print sales failed to materialise. Over time, a growing interest in advertising was increasingly viewed as the route to potential commercial success. Combined with the need to continue to raise the Bauhaus's public profile, graphic art gave way to advertising and the necessity for 'professional propaganda'.[16]

Although the formal study of advertising did not commence until the Bauhaus settled in Dessau, the intervening period saw the development of 'classic' Bauhaus graphic design, most visible in the marketing material for Bauhaus products as well as work for external clients and in the fruition of a range of publications from the Bauhaus Verlag. Design commissions for external clients were particularly taken up by students Bayer and Schmidt. Both would go on to become 'young masters' heading the soon to be established Bauhaus typography and advertising workshop, in 1925 and 1928 respectively. Schmidt completed a number of advertising designs for the Bauhaus-produced chess set by Josef Hartwig (figs. 85–86), as well as a competition-winning poster for the 1923 exhibition, which featured Oskar Schlemmer's Bauhaus Signet and hand-rendered type. For the company Yko, he designed marketing materials and printed packaging for their stationery goods (fig. 105). In 1923 Bayer conceived a series of *notgeld*, or emergency money, for the Thuringian state, during post-war hyperinflation. The *notgeld* exuded modernist design principles: restrained, functional, and without recourse to the nationalistic visual language or historic iconography that typified note design at the time.

Bayer went on in 1924 to develop corporate stationery for Puka Reklame (Puka Advertising) and promotional brochures for Gropius's former client, Fagus (fig. 106) in 1925 and later, for the company that fellow student Marcel Breuer set up to produce and distribute his now iconic tubular steel furniture. He also created a number of designs for three-dimensional advertising structures for speculative commercial clients, which evoke the mass-consumer spirit of the age. When the school moved to Dessau, he redesigned the Bauhaus's suite of administrative and promotional materials – from class timetables and student identity cards to prospectuses and branded stationery. Bayer, like Schmidt and Moholy, was influenced by De Stijl and Constructivist aesthetics, as well as the modes of mass-market advertising and communication that flourished in metropolitan cities in the machine age of the 1920s. Their work attests to the myriad influences on Bauhaus design in this period and the willingness to embrace the tools of mass communication to transmit the Bauhaus vision.

A series of academic books – the *Bauhausbücher* (Bauhaus Books) – was planned by Gropius and Moholy during the Weimar period of the school and they have come to represent the most influential examples of Bauhaus typographic design (fig. 110). They were intended as a collective set of volumes exploring theories of the time, as laid out in a *Bauhausbücher* prospectus from 1927:

> The publication of the Bauhaus Books is motivated by the recognition that all areas of design are interrelated. These books deal with problems of art, science and technology, and for the specialist working today they attempt to furnish information about the complex problems, working methods, and research results in various areas of design, thereby providing the individual with a criterion for his own studies and with the progress made in other areas. In order to tackle a task of this magnitude the editors have enlisted the cooperation of the most knowledgeable experts from various countries who are trying to integrate their specialised work with the totality of phenomena of the modern world.[17]

The Bauhaus Verlag had experienced financial difficulties and declared bankruptcy in 1924–25. Albert Langen Press was an established company based in Munich with professional distribution channels that stepped in to produce the series, allowing the school to continue its mission to reach a broad public.[18] Co-edited and largely designed by Moholy, the books were commercially printed in editions of 2–3,000 and in 1925 eight of the fourteen books eventually realised were produced. Bauhaus masters were responsible for five and other authors included Bauhaus associates such as Adolf Meyer and prestigious international figures, among them Piet Mondrian, Theo van Doesburg, J.J.P. Oud and Kazimir Malevich. It was Moholy who was principally concerned with gathering authors for new volumes, particularly those whose work represented a 'cross section' of the new age.[19] In a brochure for the Bauhaus Verlag, volumes 'in preparation' are detailed.[20] Had the publication of the *Bauhausbücher* not ceased in 1931, one would have enjoyed editions by Le Corbusier and Ludwig Mies van der Rohe on architecture, or Karel Teige on Czechoslovakian art. The *Bauhausbücher* typified Moholy's experimentation with design, typography and the photographic image. Volumes were consistent in format and material, but there was variation to interior layout and each cover was different from the next, designed to reflect the content of the books. Those by Van Doesburg (book 6) and Meyer (book 3) featured dust jacket artwork created by the guest authors themselves.

In stark contrast to the *Bauhausbücher*, designs for advertisements, invitations and posters to promote or facilitate Bauhaus extra-curricular activities yielded some of the most adventurous print experiments of the period. Exploring the graphic potential of type and image, Bayer and young students such as Xanti Schawinsky created exuberant ephemera that juxtaposed playful imagery with dynamic typography (fig. 153). Their designs screamed of a Bauhaus of delight and individuality, brimming with creative energy. Such enticing glimpses into the world of Bauhaus play were as important in shaping the Bauhaus identity as those materials conceived purposefully to communicate its progressive, utopian image worldwide.

Facilitating the new era of playful experimentation and interaction was the school's new purpose-built campus in Dessau. The school building and series of prototype live/work studios designed by Gropius were the ultimate expression of the school's ideals. They also achieved his goal of uniting the arts in one building. Former student and now young master Breuer and his students designed furniture and fittings; the metal workshop made the light fittings; Hinnerk Scheper, the recently installed head of the wall-painting workshop, developed the colour plan for the exterior and interior of the building, and the Bauhaus graphic identity was displayed prominently on the side of the building. Written in large floating letters running down the end of the studio block, and casting an offset shadow, the Bauhaus sign looked just like an experimental photograph taken by Moholy. Students exploring light and shadow and the strong vertical and asymmetric arrangements of New Vision photography used the building as a backdrop for their experiments. In 1926, the school also began to publish its own periodical, *Bauhaus* (fig. 112–13). The journal contained information about the school, its workshops, recent projects as well as articles by guest contributors and interviews with students. The first issue was designed by Moholy and featured extensive coverage and photography of the new school building, taken from new vantage points afforded by connections with the nearby Junkers aircraft factory.

Embraced by the Mayor of Dessau, Fritz Hesse, the Bauhaus was presented with an opportunity to position itself as a radical international powerhouse as never imagined before. New buildings, products, books, journals and promotional materials all served to cement the Bauhaus image in the minds of the intellectual avant-garde and general public alike.

1 Frederic J. Schwartz, 'Utopia For Sale', in Kathleen James-Chakraborty (ed.), *Bauhaus Culture: From Weimar to the Cold War*, University of Minnesota Press, Minneapolis, 2006, p. 125.
2 Walter Gropius, 'The Necessity of Commissioned Work for the Bauhaus', trans. Wolfgang Jabs and reprinted in Hans Wingler, *Bauhaus Weimar, Dessau, Berlin, Chicago*, The Massachusetts Institute of Technology, Cambridge, Mass., 1969, p. 51.
3 László Moholy-Nagy, 'The New Typography', originally published in *Staatliches Bauhaus Weimar, 1919–1923* and reproduced in Richard Kostelanetz, *Moholy-Nagy An Anthology*, Da Capo Press, New York, 1970, p. 75.
4 Norbert M. Schmitz, 'László Moholy-Nagy' in Jeannine Fiedler and Peter Feierabend (eds), *Bauhaus*, Könemann, Cologne, 2000, p. 294.
5 Robin Kinross, 'The Bauhaus again: in the constellation of typographic modernism', in *Unjustified texts perspectives on typography*, Hyphen Press, London, 2011, p. 250.
6 Ibid., p. 253
7 Frank Whitford, *Bauhaus*, Thames & Hudson, London, 1984, p. 138.
8 Walter Gropius, 'The Theory and Organisation of the Bauhaus', quoted in Herbert Bayer, Walter Gropius, Ise Gropius (eds), *Bauhaus 1919–1928*, Museum of Modern Art, New York, 1938, p. 23.
9 The extensive research outlined by Anna Rowland in 'Business Management at the Weimar Bauhaus' in *Journal of Design History* (vol. 1, no. 3/4, 1988) pp. 153–75 is relied on here to explain Weimar-period commercial ambitions and workshop production.
10 Ibid., p. 156.
11 Ibid., p. 161.
12 Author's translation.
13 Author's translation.
14 Christopher Wilk, *Modernism: Designing a New World 1914–1939*, V&A Publishing, London, 2006, p. 212.
15 Wilhelm Wagenfeld, quoted in Frederic J. Schwartz, 'Utopia For Sale', in James-Chakraborty (ed.), *Bauhaus Culture*, op. cit., p. 126.
16 Ute Brüning, 'The Weimar Art Print Workshop', in Fiedler and Feierabend (eds), *Bauhaus*, op. cit., p. 481.
17 Walter Gropius and László Moholy-Nagy, 'Prospectus "8 Bauhaus Books" by the Albert Langen Press, Munich (1927)', trans. Wolfgang Jabs and reprinted in Wingler, *Bauhaus*, op. cit., pp. 130–31.
18 Adrian Sudhalter, 'Walter Gropius and László Moholy-Nagy Bauhaus Book Series. 1927–1930', in Barry Bergdoll and Leah Dickerman (eds), *Bauhaus 1919–1933: Workshops for Modernity*, The Museum of Modern Art, New York, 2009, p. 198.
19 Magdalena Droste, *Bauhaus*, Bauhaus-Archiv Museum für Gestaltung, Berlin/Taschen, Hohenzollering, 2006, p. 138.
20 Gropius and Moholy-Nagy, 'Prospectus', op. cit., pp. 130–31.

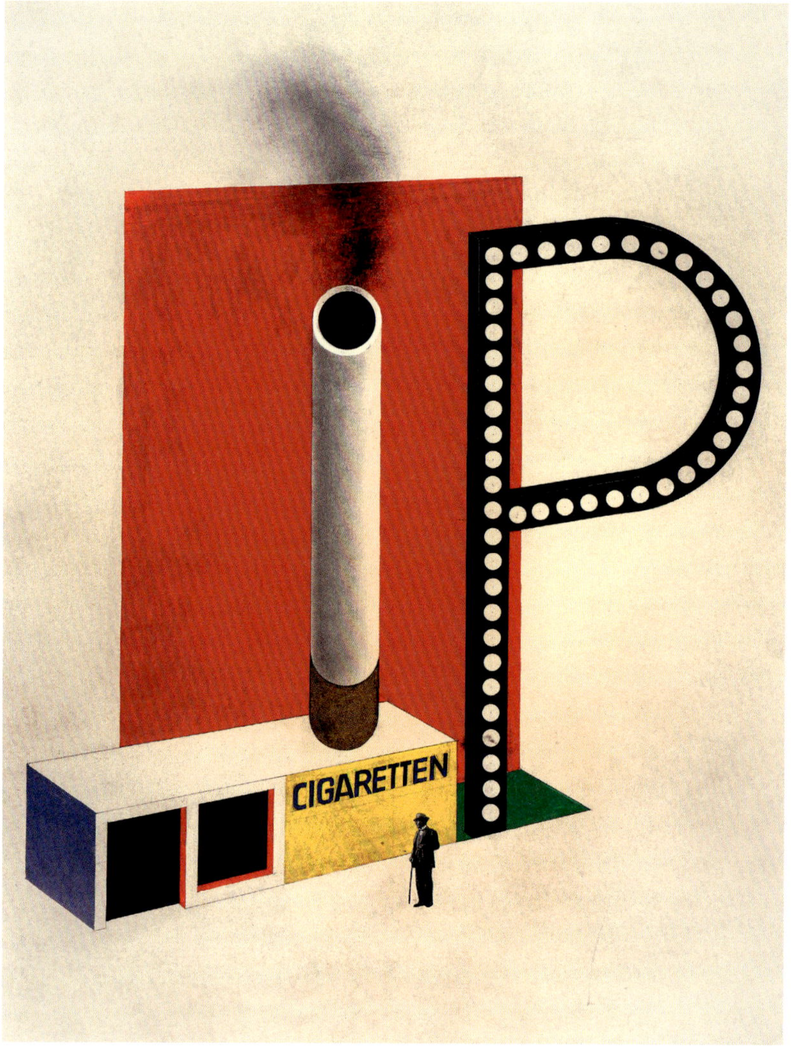

104
Herbert Bayer
Design for a Cigarette Pavilion, 1924
Ink, tempera, pencil and collage
on cardboard
50.5 × 38 cm
Bauhaus-Archiv Berlin

A giant cigarette puffs out smoke like an industrial chimney. Next to the low-rise pavilion an illuminated 'P', the size of a high-rise building, stands like a redundant letter from the 'Hollywoodland' sign. Bayer's design for a pavilion for the cigarette brand 'P' was made just one year after the iconic outdoor advertising campaign for the home of American movie-making was installed on the Hollywood Hills. The parallels between his 1924 designs for advertising stands, multi-media structures and kiosks and the outlandish manner of commercial advertising of the period are no coincidence. Bayer was testing the shifting colour planes of De Stijl and Constructivism in three-dimensions, while embracing the stylised and playful language of commercialised popular culture. *Design for a Cigarette Pavilion* encapsulates the Bauhaus ideals in one image: a rationalised formal language unified in a three-dimensional building and created in response to the rapidly changing needs and desires of everyday life.

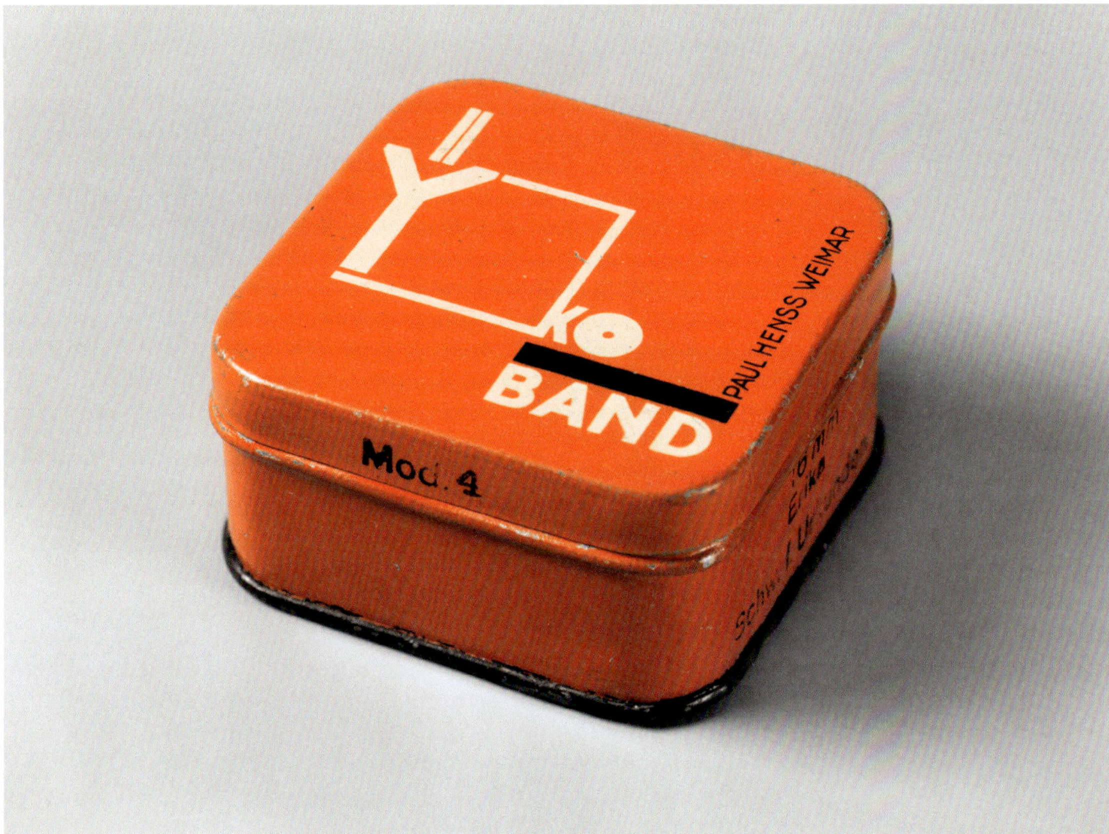

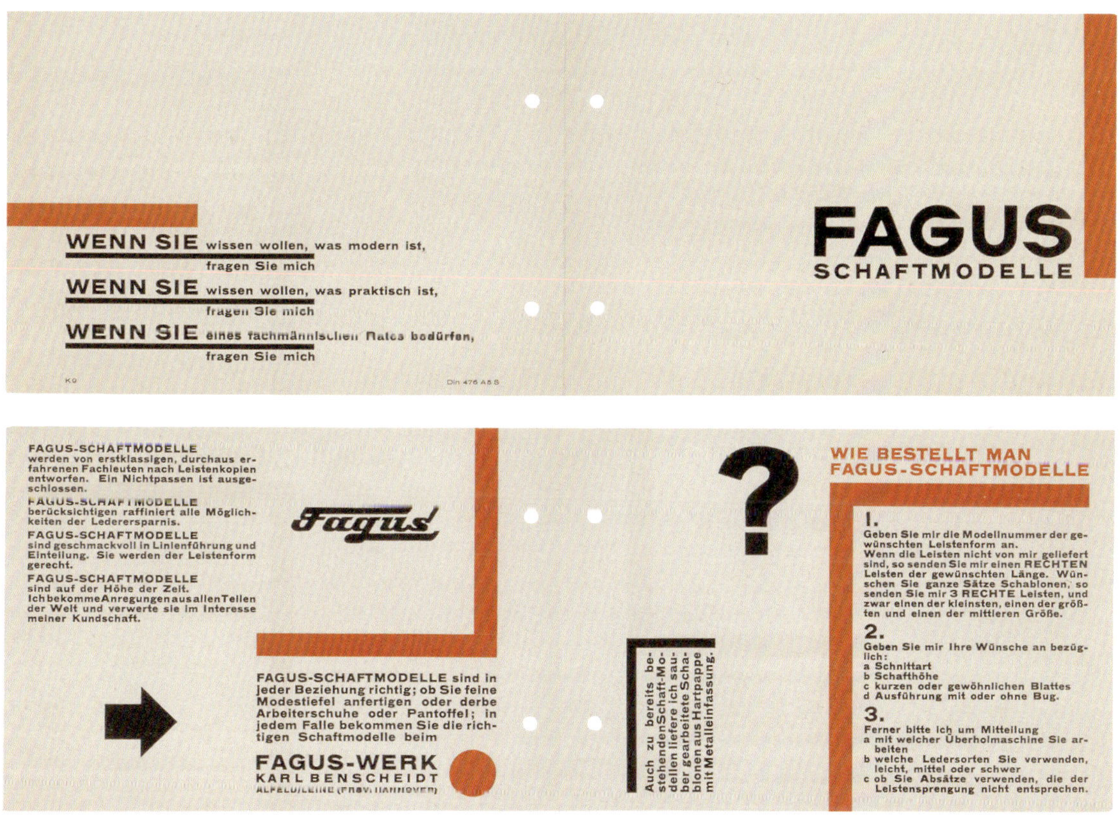

105
Joost Schmidt
Box for Yko-Band (Yko Tape), 1924
Tinplate box with lid
3.2 × 5.9 × 5.9 cm
Klassik Stiftung Weimar,
Bestand Museen

106
Herbert Bayer
Sales brochure for Fagus-Schaftmodelle
(Fagus Shaft Models), 1925–26
Letterpress on paper
21 × 14.8 cm
Stiftung Bauhaus Dessau

walter gropius and dr necker
staatliche bauhaus report on the economic outlook of the bauhaus

Until recently the Staatliche Bauhaus has been working essentially on experiments and on the production of prototypes. Every enterprise aiming at the manufacture of a new product must allocate a certain amount of time to its development. Most companies and workshops are merely concerned with the manufacture of some article or other which, after the completion of a series of experiments can be economically marketed provided the necessary funds are available. Of course modifications and improvements will still be made after that, but production continues without interruption.

The situation is different in an enterprise which is endeavouring to work out a new direction and new attitudes in a wider cultural area and which strives to apply them in practice. The concern is not with a single or even a number of articles, but rather the aim is to change the aspects of whole areas of production. It is obvious that this requires a longer period of experimentation and a greater amount of work. In the case of the Staatliche Bauhaus there is an additional difficulty. Unlike industry, it did not have the supply of capital necessary to do the work required of it. Instead, the Bauhaus had to produce, so to speak, everything from nothing. The costs for the experimental work were increased by the manufacture of many individual parts outside the Bauhaus, due to the fact that essential machines and tools, which are more vital in an experimental workshop than in any other workshop, were lacking. Furthermore, the Bauhaus had to buy its raw materials in small, uneconomical quantities. The larger part of the first earnings had to be spent on acquisitions in order to build up the proper machinery for production and thus was lost as working capital.

Under such conditions the profits of the Bauhaus workshops, if one were to hope for such at all during the period of experimental work, had to be low. The selling prices of the goods had to be greatly increased because of the poorly equipped workshops and the wasteful manner of purchasing in small quantities without any opportunity of taking advantage of favourable market conditions. The high prices made themselves felt in the decreasing number of sales.

In addition to these difficulties there was the complete dependence on the inflexible budget. Thus it was impossible to obtain new working capital in the form of loans at the time when it was needed most urgently. Due to the requests for new allocations or the arrangements for credits, much time was lost and good opportunities were missed.

Moreover, the open hostility against the Bauhaus for political reasons, because of artistic intolerance or because of lack of understanding, naturally also contributed a great deal to the weakening of the manufacturing set-up. No solid business enterprise can establish long-range ties with an undertaking whose existence is insecure.

In spite of all these problems, the Bauhaus has, for quite some time now, been on the road to economic recovery. The first prerequisite for this recovery was that a market be found for the products manufactured. The last industrial fairs were evidence of the increasing demand for Bauhaus products. Especially at the autumn fair in Leipzig ... a wide range of prototypes were bought which have already been reordered (a total of about 100 orders).

One series of Bauhaus goods has now been completed to the point where they represent final prototypes for which the experimental work is finished and industrial production can start ...

... Active sales are now hampered only by the lack of proper organisation of the production plant according to private-enterprise methods, lack of availability of adequate working capital, and the existence of an expensive loan. The sales machinery exists; that is, there are a number of salesmen already at hand as well as established connections to industry and retailers which guarantee secure and permanent sales and do not leave the Bauhaus dependent on occasional sales.

Weimar, 19 October, 1924
Supplement to a booklet published by the Thuringian State Treasury, September 1924

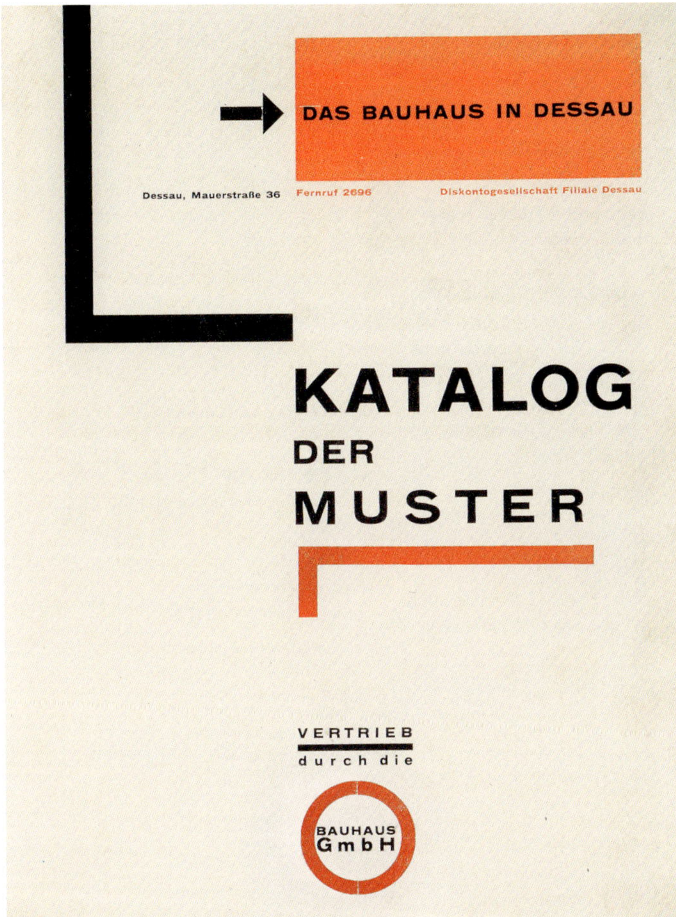

107
Herbert Bayer
Cover of *Katalog der Muster*
(Catalogue of Designs), 1925
Letterpress on paper
29.8 × 21 cm
Stiftung Bauhaus Dessau

108
Herbert Bayer
Page from *Katalog der Muster*
(Catalogue of Designs)
showing children's toy cupboard,
(TI 24) designed by
Alma Buscher in 1923, 1925
Letterpress on paper
21 × 29.7 cm
Bauhaus-Archiv Berlin

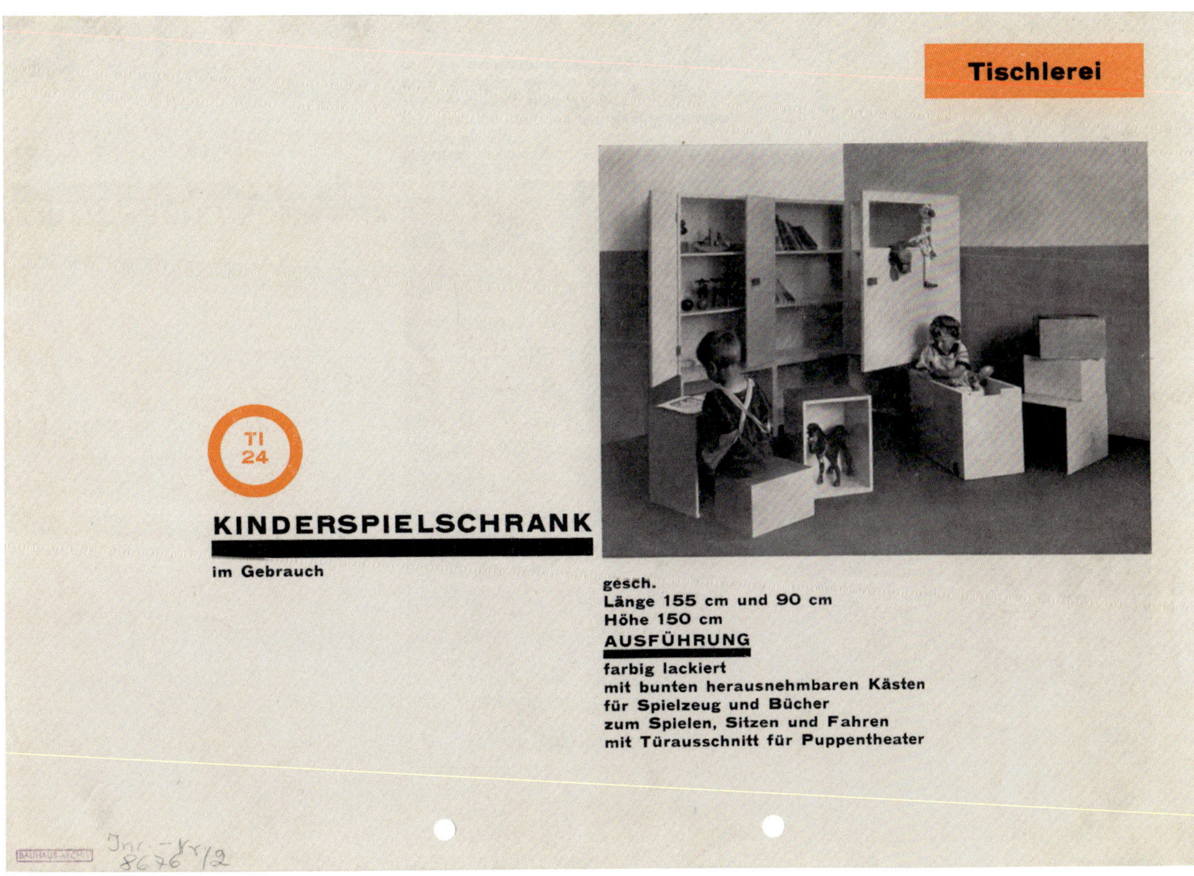

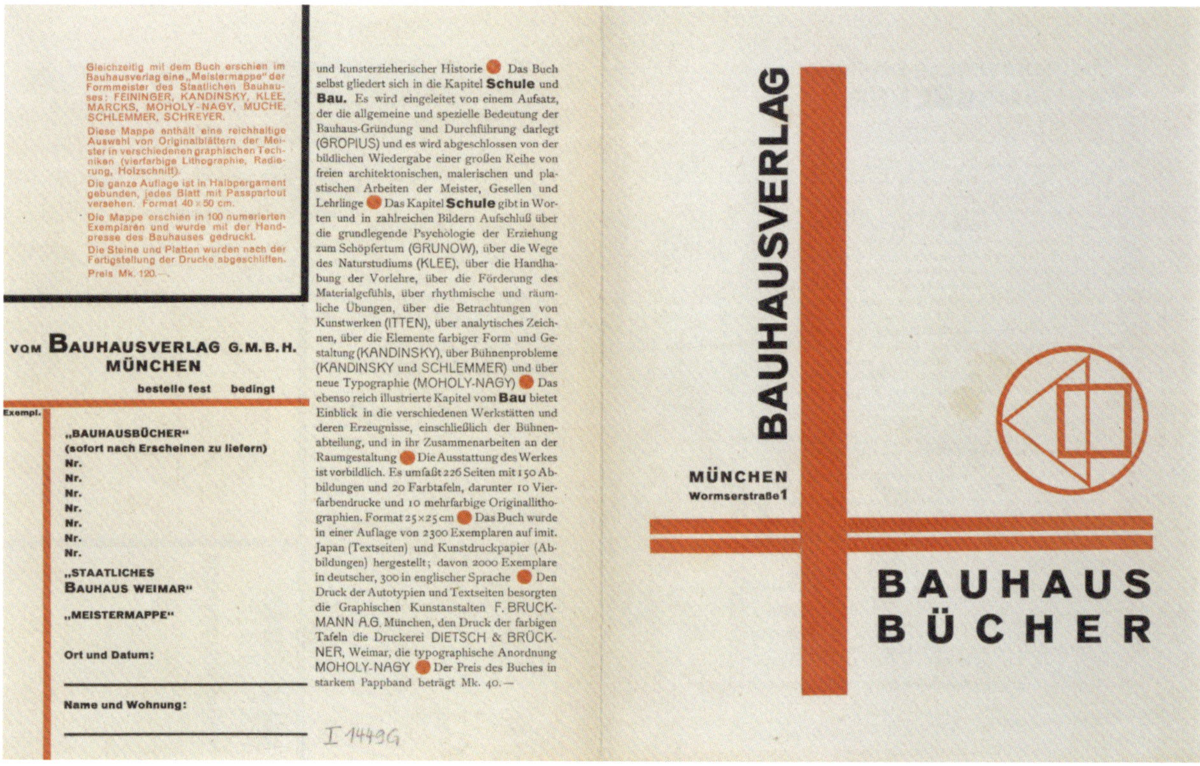

Gleichzeitig mit dem Buch erschien im Bauhausverlag eine „Meistermappe" der Formmeister des Staatlichen Bauhauses: FEININGER, KANDINSKY, KLEE, MARCKS, MOHOLY-NAGY, MUCHE, SCHLEMMER, SCHREYER.

Diese Mappe enthält eine reichhaltige Auswahl von Originalblättern der Meister in verschiedenen graphischen Techniken (vierfarbige Lithographie, Radierung, Holzschnitt).

Die ganze Auflage ist in Halbpergament gebunden, jedes Blatt mit Passpartout versehen. Format 40 × 50 cm.

Die Mappe erschien in 100 numerierten Exemplaren und wurde mit der Handpresse des Bauhauses gedruckt.

Die Steine und Platten wurden nach der Fertigstellung der Drucke abgeschliffen.

Preis Mk. 120.—.

VOM BAUHAUSVERLAG G.M.B.H. MÜNCHEN

bestelle fest bedingt

Exempl.

„BAUHAUSBÜCHER"
(sofort nach Erscheinen zu liefern)
Nr.
Nr.
Nr.
Nr.
Nr.
Nr.
Nr.

„STAATLICHES BAUHAUS WEIMAR"

„MEISTERMAPPE"

Ort und Datum:

Name und Wohnung:

und kunsterzieherischer Historie ● Das Buch selbst gliedert sich in die Kapitel **Schule** und **Bau.** Es wird eingeleitet von einem Aufsatz, der die allgemeine und spezielle Bedeutung der Bauhaus-Gründung und Durchführung darlegt (GROPIUS) und es wird abgeschlossen von der bildlichen Wiedergabe einer großen Reihe von freien architektonischen, malerischen und plastischen Arbeiten der Meister, Gesellen und Lehrlinge ● Das Kapitel **Schule** gibt in Worten und in zahlreichen Bildern Aufschluß über die grundlegende Psychologie der Erziehung zum Schöpfertum (GRUNOW), über die Wege des Naturstudiums (KLEE), über die Handhabung der Vorlehre, über die Förderung des Materialgefühls, über rhythmische und räumliche Übungen, über die Betrachtungen von Kunstwerken (ITTEN), über analytisches Zeichnen, über die Elemente farbiger Form und Gestaltung (KANDINSKY), über Bühnenprobleme (KANDINSKY und SCHLEMMER) und über neue Typographie (MOHOLY-NAGY) ● Das ebenso reich illustrierte Kapitel vom **Bau** bietet Einblick in die verschiedenen Werkstätten und deren Erzeugnisse, einschließlich der Bühnenabteilung, und in ihr Zusammenarbeiten an der Raumgestaltung ● Die Ausstattung des Werkes ist vorbildlich. Es umfaßt 226 Seiten mit 150 Abbildungen und 20 Farbtafeln, darunter 10 Vierfarbendrucke und 10 mehrfarbige Originallithographien. Format 25×25 cm ● Das Buch wurde in einer Auflage von 2300 Exemplaren auf imit. Japan (Textseiten) und Kunstdruckpapier (Abbildungen) hergestellt; davon 2000 Exemplare in deutscher, 300 in englischer Sprache ● Den Druck der Autotypien und Textseiten besorgten die Graphischen Kunstanstalten F. BRUCKMANN A.G. München, den Druck der farbigen Tafeln die Druckerei DIETSCH & BRÜCKNER, Weimar, die typographische Anordnung MOHOLY-NAGY ● Der Preis des Buches in starkem Pappband beträgt Mk. 40.—

I 1449G

BAUHAUSVERLAG

MÜNCHEN
Wormserstraße 1

BAUHAUS
BÜCHER

109
László Moholy-Nagy
Publishing prospectus for
Bauhausbücher (Bauhaus Books), 1925
Letterpress on paper
23.0 × 18 cm, folded
Stiftung Bauhaus Dessau

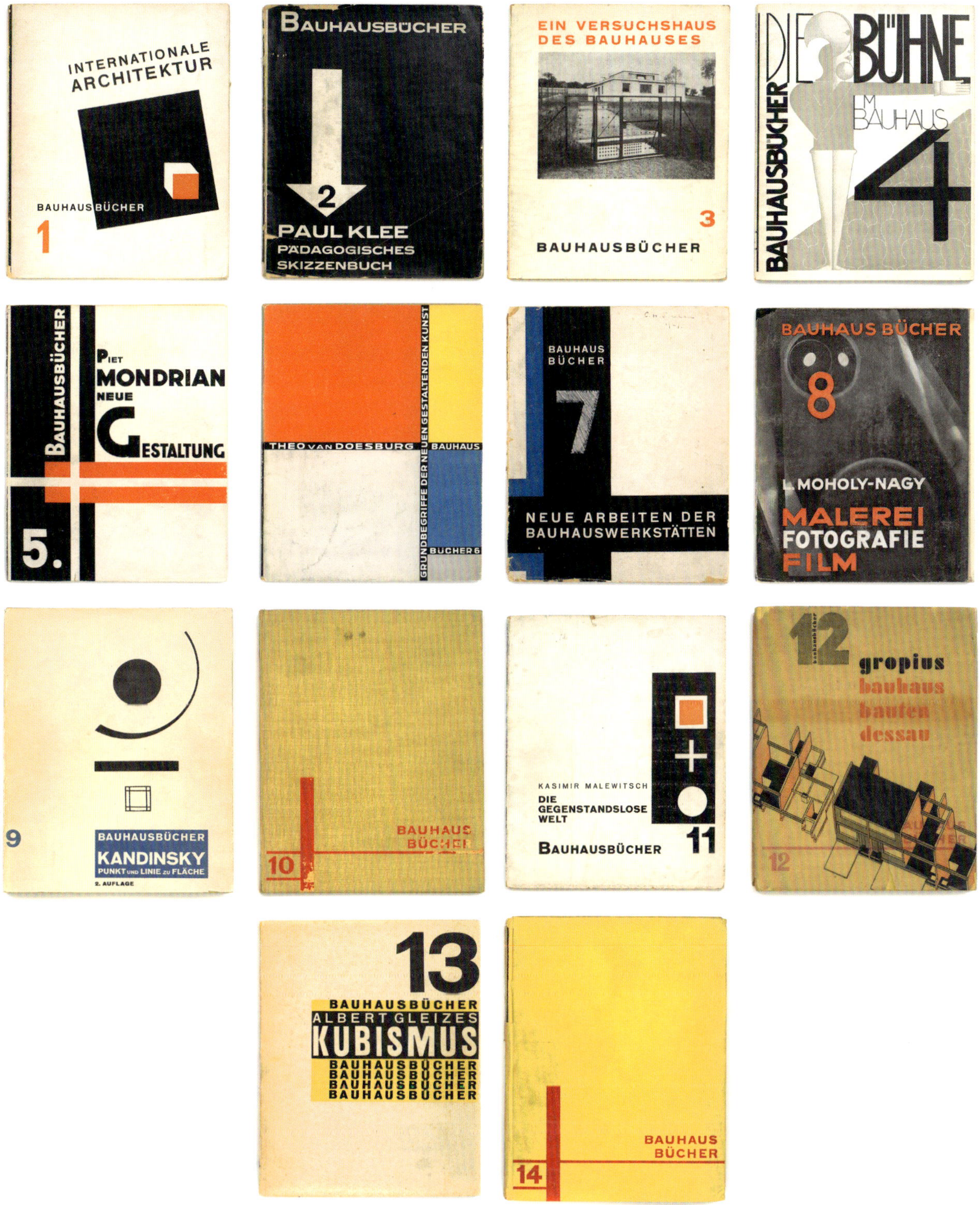

110
Various artists
Bauhausbücher (Bauhaus Books) *1–14*,
Munich: Albert Langen Verlag, 1925–30
Fourteen bound books, offset and lithography
23 × 17 cm, each

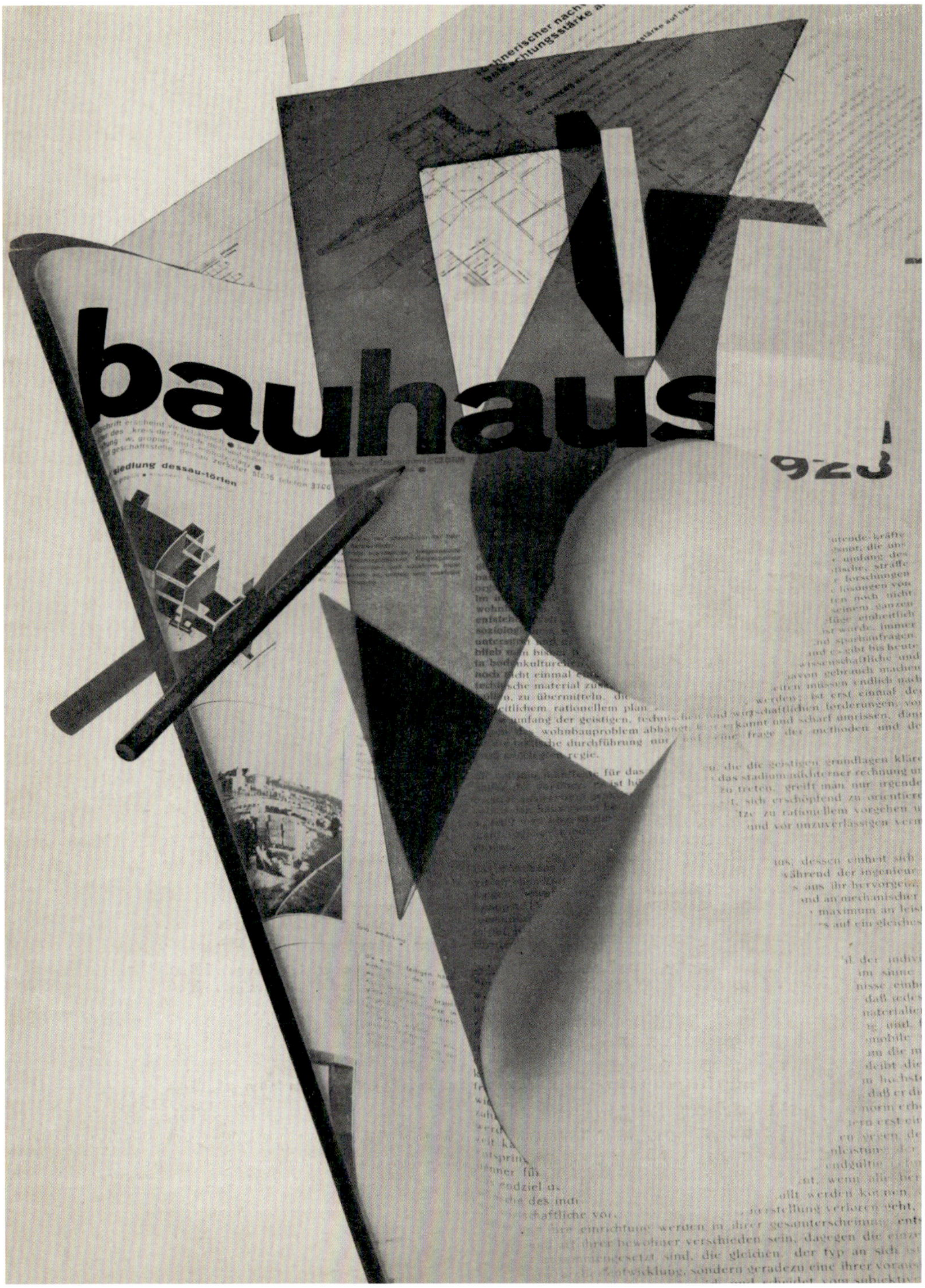

111
Herbert Bayer
bauhaus zeitschrift für gestaltung
(bauhaus magazine for design),
vol.2, no.1, 1928
Letterpress on paper
29.8 × 22 cm
Stiftung Bauhaus Dessau

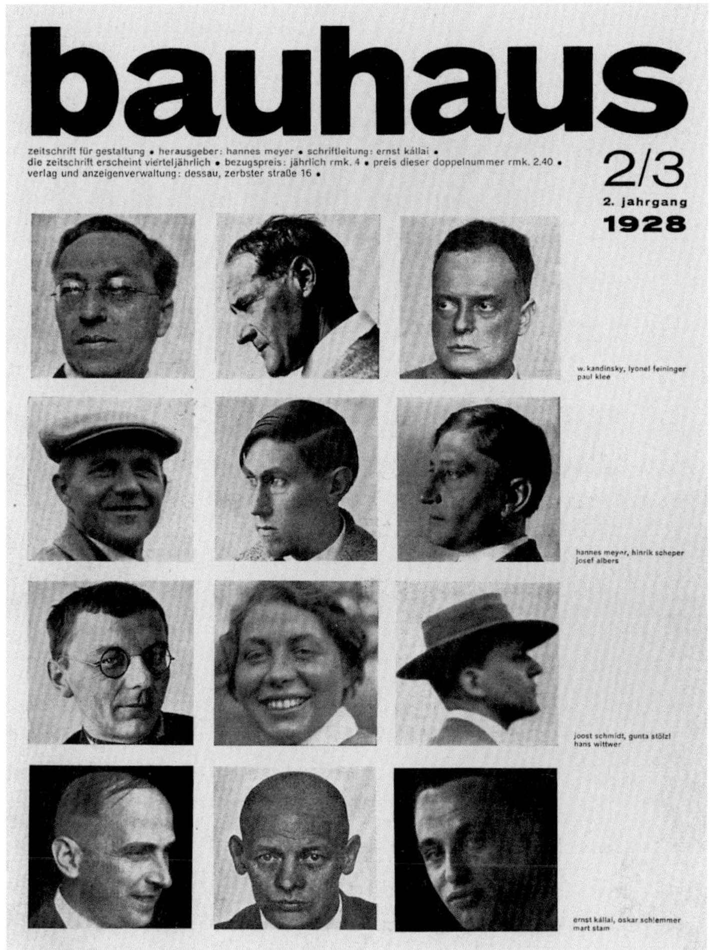

112
Hannes Meyer
bauhaus zeitschrift für gestaltung
(bauhaus magazine for design),
vol. 2, no. 2/3, 1928
Letterpress on paper
29.8 × 21 cm
Stiftung Bauhaus Dessau

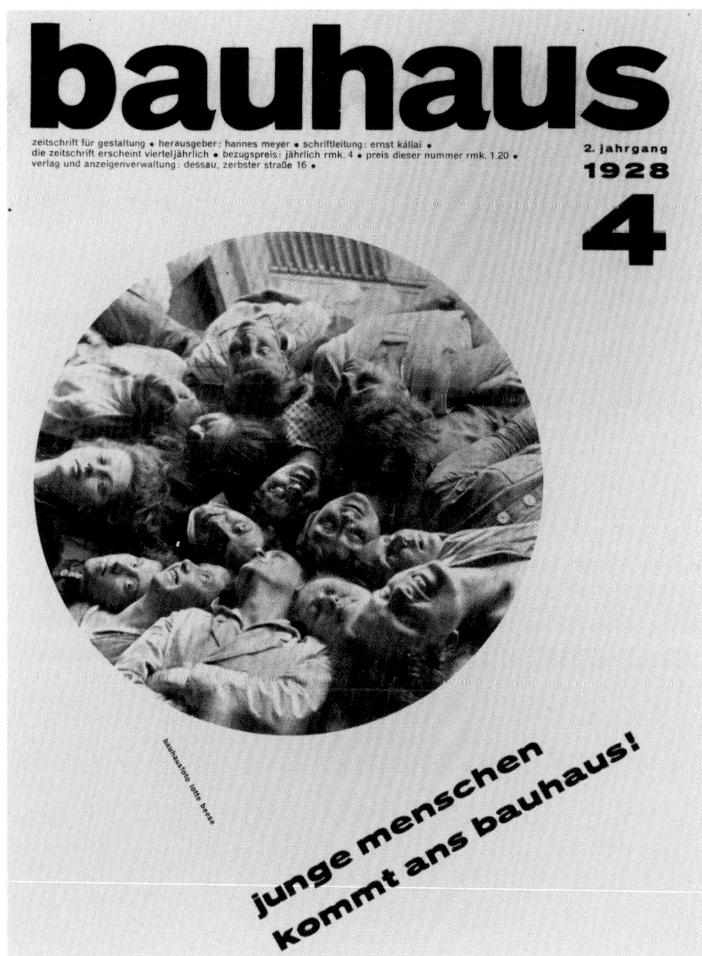

113
Hannes Meyer
bauhaus zeitschrift für gestaltung
(bauhaus magazine for design),
vol. 2, no. 4, 1928
Letterpress on paper
29.8 × 22 cm
Stiftung Bauhaus Dessau

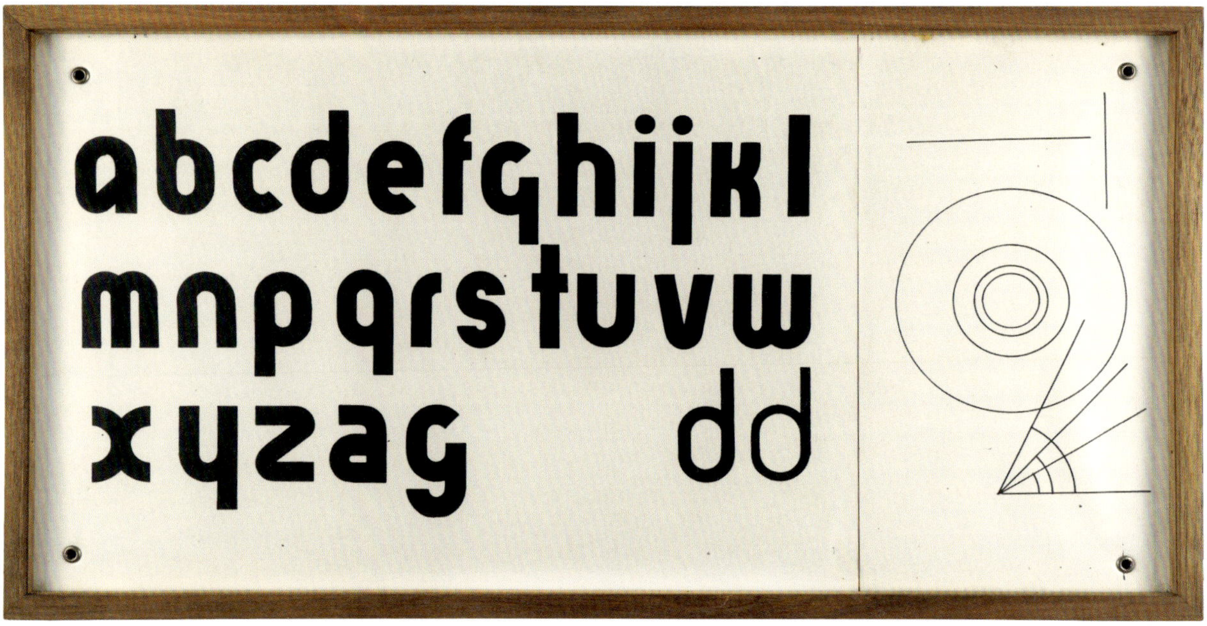

114
Herbert Bayer
Design for Universal lettering, 1925
Ink on paper
29.8 × 60 cm
Harvard Art Museums/Busch-Reisinger Museum. Gift of the artist

'We only use small characters because it saves time. Moreover, why have two alphabets when one will do? Why write capitals if we cannot speak capitals?' was the statement carried on Bauhaus letterhead paper. Following the move to Dessau, Bayer took primary responsibility for the design of the school's new identity and abolished the use of upper-case letters, a measure that was both economic and rooted in historic orthographic reform. His experimental Universal lettering set, and the modular alphabet later developed by Josef Albers, both aimed to change the norms of German printing by replacing heavy pages of gothic-style script with an internationally recognised, functional type design formed from simple interchangeable elements. Bayer refined his Universal alphabet over several years and the characters he published in 1927 feature more standardised geometric forms based on the circle. Despite his experiments, the Universal lettering was never produced as a metal font for letterpress printing.

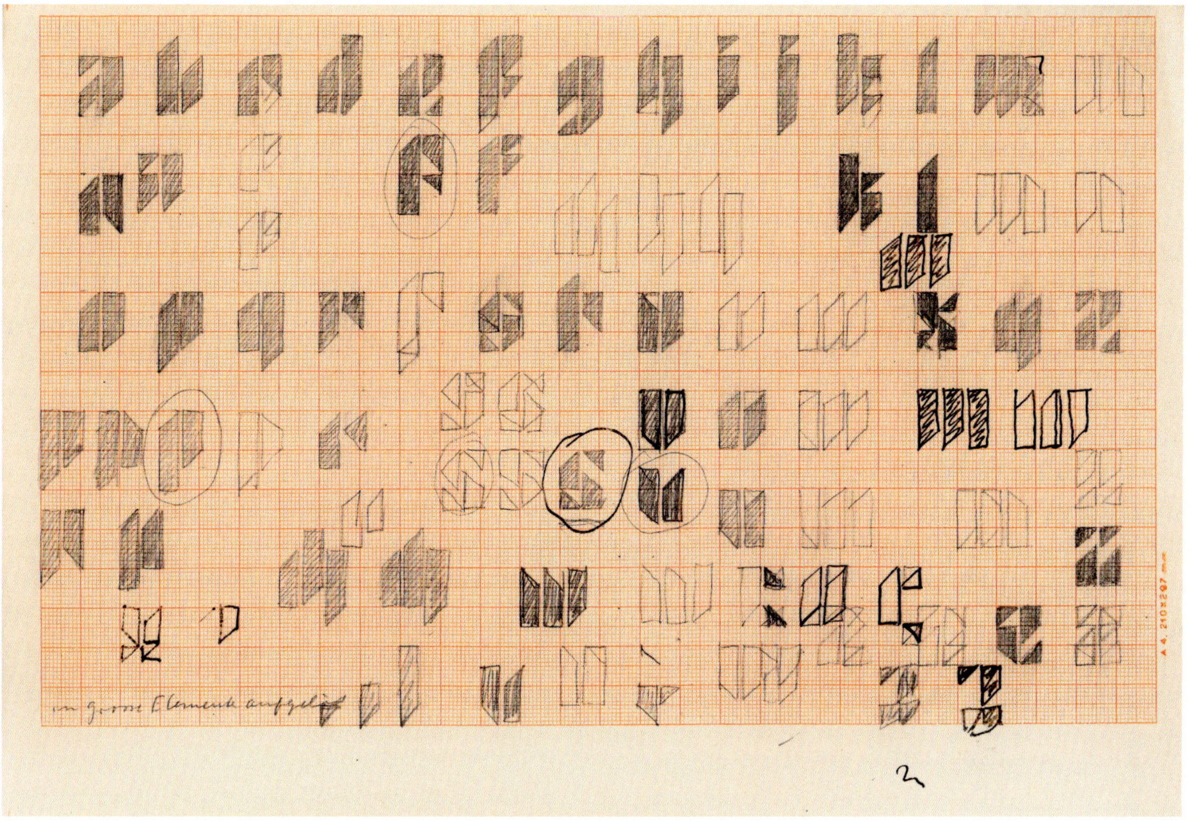

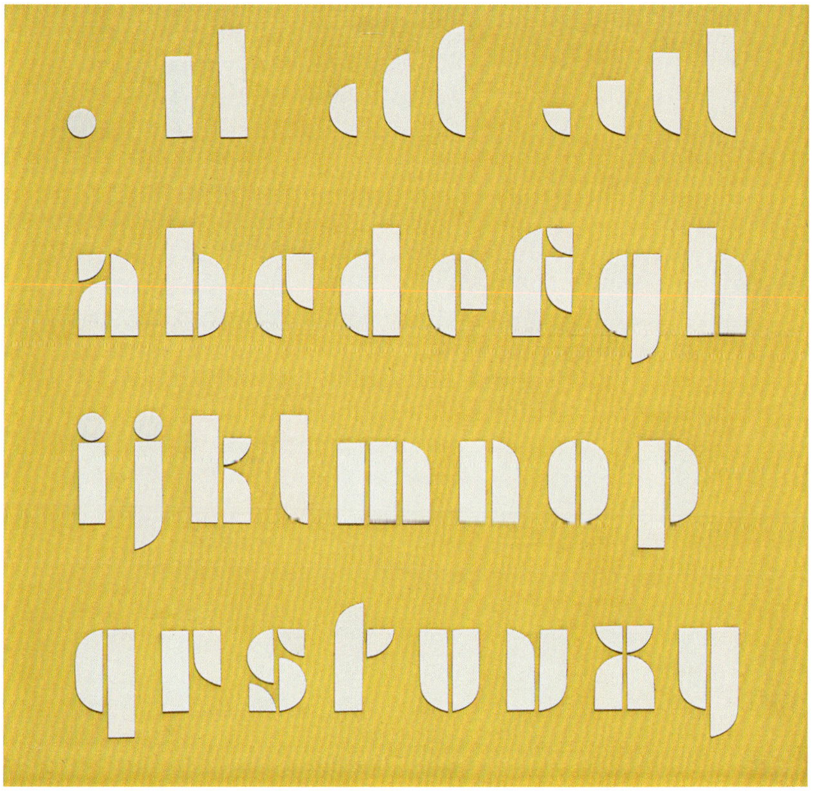

115
Josef Albers
Study for lettering, c. 1931
Pencil and black ink on graph paper
21 × 30 cm
The Josef and Anni Albers Foundation

116
Josef Albers
Combinatory letters, c. 1928
Glass lettering elements made by
Mettalglaz A.G., Offenburg/Baden
Milk glass, mounted on painted wood
61.3 × 60.6 cm
The Museum of Modern Art, New York
Gift of the Designer

circle of friends of the bauhaus
an invitation to join the 'circle of friends'

The Staatliche Bauhaus in Weimar, whose existence is still threatened after five years, is in need of participation and active help from all of its friends.

The Staatliche Bauhaus, originating from the union of an Academy of Art and a School of Arts and Crafts, has set itself the task of bringing art education – formerly isolated from the mainstream of everyday life – into close harmony with the practical demands of today. For that purpose, it has merged in its educational programme theoretical instruction with workshop training, which will be cultivated in light of today's technological and industrial methods of production. This was done with the thought in mind that today a whole series of isolated yet coexisting specialised occupations and creative endeavours are, in the final analysis, closely concerned with building. Hence, 'building' as a synthesis is the aim of the individual Bauhaus workshops (cabinetry, sculpture, wall-painting, glass, metal, pottery, weaving workshops, and architecture department).

This goal represents the justification for the existence, and the necessity for the present and future development, of the Bauhaus. After more than five years of activity, its actual accomplishments have proved that by the educational method and by the economical utilisation of the pedagogic results the theoretical aim as well as its practical realisation in the Bauhaus is correct. The significant response which its endeavours have found both inside and outside Germany demonstrates that a general intellectual movement is already emerging as a result of the Bauhaus experiments.

But since, for the time being, the Bauhaus still serves as a target for attacks that are jeopardising its peaceful work, we are calling for the formation of a circle of friends which will lend its unanimous moral and material support whenever the need for it arises. We therefore urge you and all those who are of the same heart and mind as we are to join the 'Circle of Friends of the Bauhaus' and to support its endeavours.

Anyone paying the minimum annual dues of 20 marks can become a member of the 'Circle of Friends of the Bauhaus.' For life membership a nonrecurring minimum amount of 100 marks is payable. Donations in excess of the minimum dues are rewarded with one original graphic print each, done by one of the Bauhaus masters: Feininger, Kandinsky, Klee, Marcks, Moholy-Nagy, Muche, Schlemmer. The selection is open to the donor. These graphics are especially made for this purpose by the Bauhaus and are not commercially available.

Dues and donations will be used for the furthering of Bauhaus production and for the extension of the Bauhaus movement. The administration of the funds is in the hands of Walter Gropius, the Director of the Staatliche Bauhaus, and two treasurers approved by the board (Bruno Wollbrück, book dealer in Weimar, and Countess Daisy zu Dohna, Weimar).

We are convinced that the Bauhaus will be better enabled to withstand the continually repeated attacks and complete without hindrance the work it has so promisingly started, the more firmly and unequivocally it unites its group of friends.

We would be grateful if you would advocate our cause among your acquaintances and if you would win further friends for it. For this purpose you will find a form for names attached which we ask you to return, after completion, to the Staatliche Bauhaus, Weimar.

Please send your contribution to the 'Bank of Thuringia.' Weimar, Hummelstrasse, for the account of the 'Circle of Friends of the Bauhaus.'

The Governing Board:

Prof. Peter Behrens, Berlin
Dr H.C.Gerhart Hauptmann, Agnetendorf
Dr H.P. Berlage, The Hague, Holland
Prof. Josef Hoffmann, Vienna
Prof. Adolf Busch, Berlin
Prof. Oskar Kokoschka, Vienna
Marc Chagall, Paris
Prof. Hans Poelzig, Potsdam
Prof. Dr Hans Driesch, Leipzig
Arnold Schönberg, Vienna
Prof. Dr Albert Einstein, Berlin
Adolf Sommerfeld, Berlin
Herbert Eulenberg, Kaiserwerth
Prof. Dr Strzygowski, Vienna
Prof. Edwin Fischer, Berlin
Franz Werfel, Vienna

Governing board of the 'Circle of Friends of the Bauhaus', 1924
Information leaflet

young people come to the bauhaus!

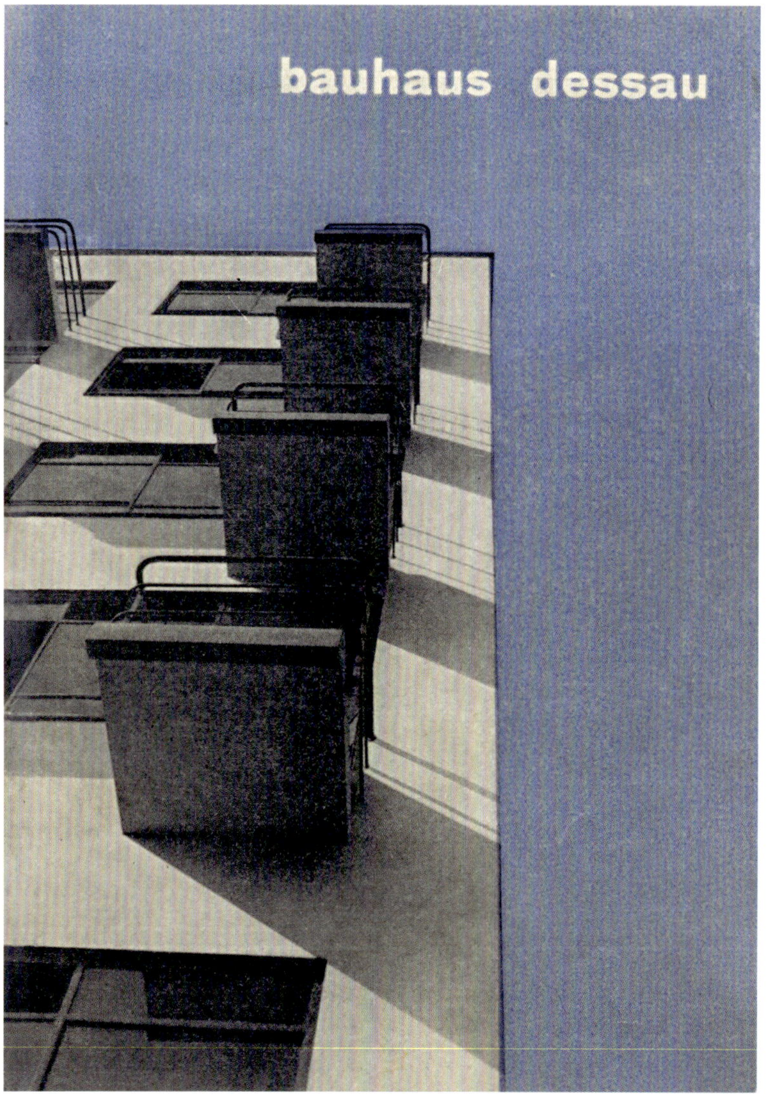

In 1924, after a swing to the right in the Thuringian state government, Bauhaus funding was cut dramatically and teaching posts were cancelled. The following year Gropius and his remaining staff resigned, and he began to look for alternative cities to accommodate the school. Dessau was a rapidly expanding socialist democratic city and home to several large manufacturers, including Junkers, makers of heating appliances and aircraft. Fritz Hesse, the city's liberal mayor, enticed Gropius and the school to the city and at the end of 1926 Bauhaus masters, students and hundreds of guests celebrated the opening of the new, purpose-built school building.

The Bauhaus Dessau building was designed by Gropius's private practice and crystallised modernist ideas on space, form and construction. A series of asymmetrically arranged cubic elements, the building is characterised by flat roofs, flexible plan and open internal spaces, reinforced concrete frame and a dramatic glass curtain-wall. Spaces in the new building were defined by their programmatic function. Open-plan workshop facilities and a library were located in the four-storey glass-walled studio block; the canteen and auditorium connected studios to the Prellerhaus, a block of twenty-eight student flats that provided sought-after accommodation on a rota basis. The Director's and administrative offices were linked, along a corridor, to a block of smaller teaching rooms built for the local Technical College. The new building was the ideal environment for a modern and progressive 'School of Design' – the designation applied from 1926 onwards – where students worked collectively and grappled with the social and economic issues of the age. Living, working and socialising became inseparable.

Gropius was also commissioned to design a trio of semi-detached houses for masters and a detached house for its director. These were situated along a tree-lined avenue a few streets from the school and their architectural language echoed that of the Bauhaus building. The interior decoration, light fixtures and signage of the Bauhaus Dessau and masters' houses were completed by the Bauhaus workshops. Tubular-steel furniture designed by Marcel Breuer – now junior master heading the furniture workshop – populated the school building and masters' houses from canteen and auditorium to studio and living room. New prospectuses, student identity cards and curriculum materials were designed, largely by Herbert Bayer, and in 1926 the first issue of the Bauhaus journal appeared. *Bauhaus* was edited by Gropius and Moholy, who also designed the first few issues, and included articles on school projects, topical issues, and, on occasion, interviews with Bauhaus students about their experience of studying at the school.

On moving to the new school building, training at the Bauhaus was re-oriented and workshops were rationalised. Students would now complete their one-year preliminary course before progressing to practical workshop instruction in metal, cabinetry, textiles, printing and wall-painting. Supplementary courses were offered covering a range of practical and theoretical tuition in, among other subjects, art and science, or technical draughtsmanship. Architecture training was finally offered, at first to students who in Gropius's words 'showed talent', and then more formally under the direction of new Bauhaus master Hannes Meyer, a Swiss architect hired by Gropius in 1927 to lead the newly established building department.

In Dessau the revitalised Bauhaus was 'a community to which each one of us gave what we had' said Paul Klee. The fervent joy and zest for life of this new community is seen in the animated, artful photography documenting the minutiae of daily life on campus.

117
Irene Bayer and Herbert Bayer
Prospectus for the Bauhaus Dessau, 1927
Letterpress on paper
20.9 × 14.6 cm
Stiftung Bauhaus Dessau

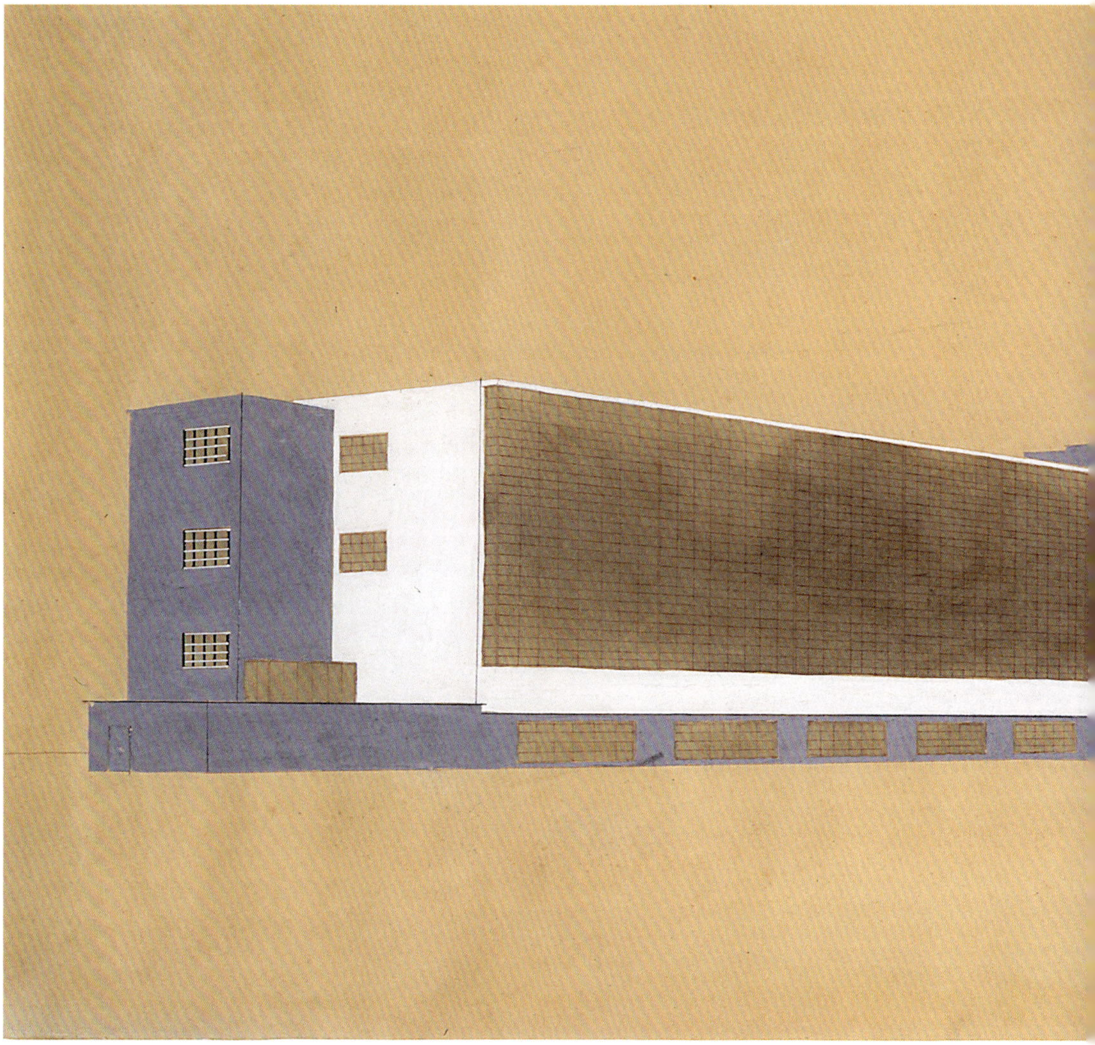

118
Hinnerk Scheper
Experiment with a coloured façade
of the Bauhaus building, view from
the south-east, 1926
Tempera over blueprint
33 × 78.5 cm
On long-term loan from the Scheper Family
to the Bauhaus-Archiv Berlin

When the Bauhaus moved to Dessau in 1925, the wall-painting workshop was headed by former student Scheper. Against the backdrop of a revived interest in using colour in architecture, the workshop moved from creating painterly murals and free, ornamental wall designs to an integrated design approach that brought architectural elements to the fore. Scheper's proposals for the colour treatment of the new Bauhaus building exterior were completed while it was under construction in 1926. The perspective shows the rear of the studio block and auditorium; the iconic Bauhaus sign was placed on the light grey four-storey block at the left of the drawing. Scheper's scheme combines large expanses of white and grey tones with flashes of red and yellow, accenting details such as window frames and balcony soffits. He also produced interior colour designs. Rooms were largely treated in neutral tones, with bright colour applied to ceilings and joists only. Architectural features in corridor spaces were highlighted in different colour combinations on each floor, in a scheme designed to aid orientation. The final colour treatment departed from his original proposals: the exterior colour was realised in a palette of black, grey and white.

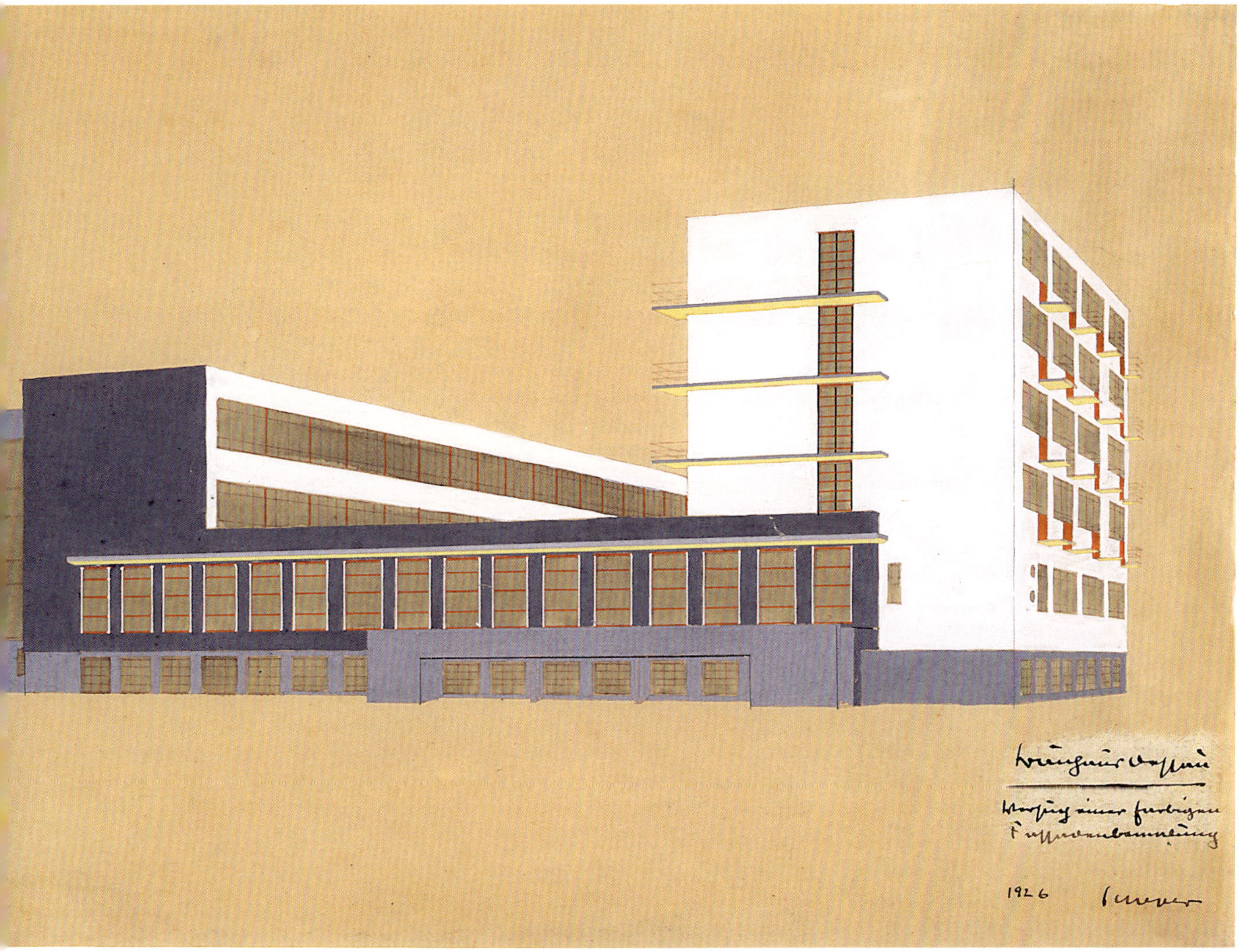
bauhaus dessau
versuch einer farbigen fassadenbemalung
1926
scheper

the bauhaus at home in dessau

philipp oswalt

For most people, the Bauhaus means not just tubular steel furniture and abstract paintings, but above all, the white, flat-roofed buildings in Dessau with which in 1926 the school clearly established itself for the first time as an integral part of modernist architecture. It is difficult, from our vantage point today, to imagine a better solution than its move to Dessau after the Weimar Bauhaus had been forced to close for political reasons in 1925. No other city was in a position to offer so much at once: here was a booming region with chemical and film factories, machine building and an aircraft industry offering promising possibilities for collaboration. The former princely residential city was doing its utmost to develop into a modern industrial location, not only in terms of economics, but also culturally. Vital protagonists such as the liberal mayor Fritz Hesse, the state head of historical monument preservation Ludwig Grote and the chairman of the Social Democratic group on the city council, all agreed that there was nothing more urgently needed in Dessau in 1925 than the Bauhaus. And thus they were prepared to finance it and to offer it a home that would be as comfortable as possible: a new school building, studios in which the masters could live and work, and not least, an additional lucrative building contract for director Walter Gropius's own architectural firm – a housing development project in Dessau-Törten.[1]

After the decision had been made that the Bauhaus in Dessau would not just continue as a communal Hochschule für Gestaltung (College of Design), but would also be in a position to make a fresh start there, Gropius further pushed for the restructuring of the Bauhaus that he had begun in Weimar in 1923 under the banner of 'Art and Technology: A New Unity'. Even though renowned artists such as Wassily Kandinsky, Paul Klee and Lyonel Feininger stayed on in Dessau as representatives of the avant-garde in order to attract students, it was ultimately a new generation that would determine the direction and everyday life at the school. In 1925, the first graduates were appointed as 'young masters'. The youngest of them all, Marcel Breuer, was only twenty-three years old at the time.

With its industrially and politically advanced environment, Dessau was a high-technology region, a German Silicon Valley of the 1920s. For the first Dessau years, the scope of this profound environmental change for the Bauhaus was fairly well hidden in its programmatic texts, since it was important to those in charge at the school to demonstrate a logical, stringent continuity. But the diary entries and letters of the Bauhauslers convey a different impression: Dessau was perceived as a mundane, impersonal and discouraging place. Swiss student Hans Fischli remembered 'grey streets with big cobblestones', 'two movie houses in dark, rear courtyards', 'an antiquated tram' and an industry filling the air with 'soot that made you cough' and an 'unpleasant, sweet smell'.[2] Soon though, the Bauhauslers discovered elements that made them more enthusiastic, including the nearby Elbe landscape and the gardens of Dessau and Wörlitz, to which the school devoted a one-page summary in one of its first Dessau brochures.[3] The change of atmosphere also promoted internal cohesion, even though the rooms made available in the new, overtly modernist Bauhaus building no longer had any of the *Gemütlichkeit* (cosy warmth) that had been present in Weimar, and the canteen, which had previously been run by the students themselves, ceased to be the 'living room' of all the Bauhauslers. While the Dessau Bauhauslers continued to exude an air of self-confidence derived from their self-perception as avant-garde bohemians, the form it took here had to be defined anew.

With the school building and the nearby masters' houses, where the 'old masters' lived and worked, the Bauhaus could tailor its designs to suit its own individual needs. For the first time, it was able to build on a grand scale, and in doing so, to demonstrate what it could achieve as an example of modern architecture that practically, vividly and impressively concentrated both Bauhaus work and Bauhaus life. A visitor coming from the railway station or from the city could see from far away the workshop wing with its 'Bauhaus' lettering and large glass-curtain façade. Next, the two-storey building bridging the street came into view, where the administration and Gropius's private architectural office were located. The highest part of the building, the Prellerhaus, with its twenty-eight studio apartments and many balconies for the students and young masters, stood as proof that the Bauhaus was not merely a school, but also a place for modern communal living. This took place not only in the apartments, but in the entire building, from the roof garden to the basement, where, besides a gymnasium, there were also communal baths and showers. Meals were taken together in the canteen on the ground floor or on the roof terrace. Each floor had a WC, a kitchenette, as well as a balcony facing south that everyone could use. The students and the young masters adapted to the spaces in a variety of different ways, as many documents serve to illustrate.

Despite the strong overarching architectural corporate identity, this was not an egalitarian community, however, but was structured and zoned according to a clear hierarchy, expressed in the different types of accommodation offered. Whereas the leading role of the old masters was confirmed in their villa-like studio homes, the young masters lived together with the students, directly adjacent to the workshops they now led. The atmosphere at the masters' houses, located about five-minute's walk away from the school building, was characterised by the more sophisticated lifestyle of the old masters, who had, even in those days, long since been established in the art market. The six semi-detached houses and the home of the director, located in a pine grove at the edge of a great eighteenth-century landscaped garden (now known as the Garden Kingdom of Dessau-Wörlitz) constituted an exclusive residential area for the prominent Bauhaus celebrities. But it was not only middle-class family life that took place here. Kandinsky, Klee, Feininger, László Moholy-Nagy, Oskar Schlemmer and Josef Albers were able to dedicate themselves to their art in their studios, where a number of outstanding works, paintings in particular, were created within a short period of time. Lucia and László Moholy set up a darkroom in their house so that they could pursue their photographic work and experiments. Next door was where the Feininger family lived, and the sons Theodore Lux (T. Lux) and Andreas, as well as the father Lyonel, were also beginning to execute photographic work. After the courses in independent painting had been set up, some of the masters' houses became places for teaching. They also served as excellent examples of the various artistic positions and lifestyles of their inhabitants, expressed in the furnishings and colour design of their interiors, so uniform from the outside. Whereas, for instance, Moholy and Albers chose their interior decoration to reflect Gropius's architecture, Kandinsky and Klee sought to counter it with their furniture and colour design.[4]

However, just as in the workshops the focus was now on the design and production of wares that could be manufactured in series, individual subjective experience was put aside in favour of 'objectivised' work. The goal was to get away from the 'wildly revolutionary Bauhaus creations'[5] and help contribute to the school's further development as effectively as possible. This was best accomplished with designs and perhaps even patents that could be marketed and sold by the Bauhaus GmbH, founded in 1925. According to the tenor of the new beginning in Dessau, unique and individual art – while not prohibited – was something best done in one's free time or in the 'independent painting classes' that had been instituted in 1927, taking place at the private studios of Klee and Kandinsky. The utopian and emotional enthusiasm for making the world a better place was ultimately turned towards practical and concrete design work in Dessau. Central to the school was not only the studio for free artistic design, or the lecture and seminar rooms for theory, but also the workshop, just as Gropius had formulated it in 1919: 'The school is to serve the workshop, it will be merged into it some day.'[6] The building was the three-dimensional version of the teaching diagram, in which the workshop, despite all of its borrowings from the aesthetics of industrial buildings, was not a place of Fordist serial production, but an experimental laboratory.

Gropius was aware of the pitfalls of the strong, practice-oriented approach. For this reason, he pressed for a continuation of the Bauhaus tradition of celebrations and festivities in Dessau. These took place on the building's 'festival level', whose focal point was the stage located between the assembly hall and canteen, the centre of the entire Bauhaus. It was enlivened above all by the stage workshop, whose most important task, in the final analysis, was less the development of dance at the Bauhaus and more to give shape to its festivities, together with the Bauhaus band.

To a greater extent than in Weimar, young people were now more heavily concentrated in the school building itself. They populated not only the workshops, the hallways, and the canteen, but in summertime the terrace or the balconies of the Prellerhaus. Because of the glass transparency of the building, nearly everything that happened inside could be seen from the outside – as if on a three-dimensional screen. And, aware that they were being watched, the Bauhauslers staged their appearances as a collective undertaking. The design of the interiors for modern man prepared and developed in Weimar could now be realised with the help of nearly all the workshops in such an intense and demonstrative fashion that the result must have evoked the impression of a unique building-wide exhibition. The occupants of these buildings on display, who – with the exception of the residents of the Dessau-Törten housing development, were the Bauhauslers themselves – played the role of the 'New Man' so longed for by the avant-garde as members of a better society living a new type of communal life.

A series of dry point etchings made by Farkas Molnár in 1923 anticipated the new relationship between man and architecture that was to be realised three years later with the Dessau buildings. Graceful young men and women move in antique nudity across the pages through wide spaces flooded with light. In *Georg and El Muche and the Haus am Horn*, the Bauhausler couple is shown before the 'model house' in Weimar. The immediate confrontation of new buildings and slender human figures symbolises the fresh start of architecture and the hopes connected with it, recalling the metaphoric images used by Gropius in his writings at the time, where he spoke of a 'clear, organic architecture' that is 'radiant and naked', 'unencumbered by lying façades and trickeries' and which by means of a 'new aesthetic of horizontals' brings the 'building masses' into an 'asymmetrical, but rhythmical balance'.[7]

For Schlemmer, the Bauhaus Dessau was an architecture that was in keeping with the model of the human figure that he developed in the pure artistic spaces of painting, sculpture and the stage. The building itself became a stage, a space for art, for living and working at the same time. Immediately after the Bauhaus building was completed, Schlemmer used it as a platform for various dances and plays, conceived as a composition of colour and form, centring on the visual, which in turn was to develop from the space of art to become a 'choreography of everyday life'.[8] The photographs that the Bauhaus students Erich Consemüller and T. Lux Feininger made of these stage experiments (under the direction of Schlemmer) not only document the work of the Bauhaus stage workshop, but also constitute staged photographic works of art, which make conscious reference to the proportion and shape of the architecture of the Bauhaus building. It is here that the real bodies of the Bauhauslers meet the visionary artistic concept of 'The Bauhausler' acted out on stage and elsewhere in the building. In doing so, they themselves become abstract figures, demonstrating through choreography and costume, as if in an artistic experiment, the role played by architecture. It is as though the prints of Molnár, thoroughly constructed in terms of perspective and dominated by modern architecture, were peopled by Schlemmer's artificial figures, which for their part have emerged from the fleeting sequences of their endless pictorial space to approach the actual human form.[9]

The exhibition character of the Bauhaus buildings in Dessau was underlined by a comprehensive accompanying programme designed to disseminate its ideas. This included the publication of a Bauhaus magazine and several Bauhaus books immediately before the new building opened on 4 December 1926, with nearly 1,000 guests in attendance. Subsequent to the opening, guided tours through the school were given, as well as through the Dessau-Törten housing development construction site. After visiting the Bauhaus building, figures from politics, art, science and economics were given a tour of the masters' houses. Demonstrations were also presented to the Housewives Association of the comfortable furnishings in the director's house. What the visitors were shown in the ensuing weeks and months was recorded in demonstration films, and in precisely calculated and staged sets of photographs sent to carefully selected press representatives and national and international artist colleagues. First came the local figures, ranging from the mayor Fritz Hesse and Ludwig Grote, to musicians and theatre people, engineers and industrialists such as Hugo Junkers. Other names read like an international *Who's Who* of 1920s modernism: the writers Ilja Ehrenburg and Tadeusz Peiper, the dancer Gret Palucca, the visual artists Kazimir Malevich, El Lissitzky, Naum Gabo, Amédée Ozenfant, George Grosz, Marcel Duchamp and Alfred Kubin, the art historians Adolf Behne, Walter Dexel, Will Grohmann, Sigfried Giedion, Rudolf Arnheim, Alois J. Schardt and Lu Märten, the art dealer Albert Flechtheim, the Guggenheims from New York, the architects Bruno and Max Taut, Rudolf Häring, Rudolf Bartning, Hendrik Petrus Berlage, Erich Mendelsohn, Arkadi Grigoryevich Mordvinov, the psychologist Hans Prinzhorn, the philosopher Otto Neurath, the filmmaker Dziga Vertov, the musicians Béla Bartók and Paul Hindemith, the conductor Leopold Stokowski, and the chemist and colour theorist Wilhelm Ostwald.[10]

Without such intensive public relations work, the enormous and immediately powerful effect of the Bauhaus Dessau would scarcely have been imaginable. Unmatched even today, the self-staging of the Bauhaus during the course of its first year outshines all of the subsequent perceptions of and changes to the school. In the public consciousness, the Bauhaus building has always been that white, transparent building populated by dynamic students as presented in 1926: an iconic anchor for Modernism, the epitome of a school building for modern design.

1 Ludwig Grote, 'Das Weimarer Bauhaus und seine Aufgabe in Dessau', in *Anhalter Anzeiger*, Dessau, 10 March 1925.

2 Hans Fischli, *Malerei Plastik Architektur*, Kunsthaus Zurich, 1968, p.19.

3 Bauhaus Dessau, brochure for teaching programme, 1927.

4 See Wolfgang Thöner, *Das Bauhaus wohnt. Leben und Arbeiten in der Dessauer Meisterhaussiedlung*, Seemann, Leipzig, 2002.

5 Gunta Stölzl, 'The Bauhaus Weaving Workshop' (1931), in Frank Whitford (ed.), *The Bauhaus: Masters and Students by Themselves*, Conran Octopus, London, 1992, p.86.

6 Walter Gropius, 'Antworten auf eine Umfrage des Arbeitsrates für Kunst', in *JA! Stimmen des Arbeitsrates für Kunst in Berlin*, Photographische Gesellschaft in Charlottenburg, Berlin, 1919, pp.30–33. Quoted in Hartmut Probst and Christian Schädlich, *Walter Gropius*, vol.3: *Ausgewählte Schriften*, Verlag für Bauwesen, Berlin, 1987, p.68.

7 Walter Gropius,'The Theory and Organization of the Bauhaus', in *Bauhaus 1919–1928*, The Museum of Modern Art, New York, 1986, pp. 27–28.

8 Concerning Farkas Molnár, see Eva Bajkay-Rosch, 'Die KURI-Gruppe', in Hubertus Gaßner (ed.), *Wechsel Wirkungen, Ungarische Avantgarde in der Weimarer Republik*, Jonas, Marburg, 1986, p.260.

9 Oskar Schlemmer, *Der Mensch. Unterricht am Bauhaus. Nachgelassene Aufzeichnungen*, Kupferberg, Berlin, 1969, p.20.

10 See Wolfgang Thöner, 'Choreographie des Alltags. Figuren der Moderne am Bauhaus und bei Neufert', in Walter Prigge (ed.), *Ernst Neufert. Normierte Baukultur im 20. Jahrhundert*, Campus, Frankfurt am Main u.a., 1999, pp.144–58.

119
Josef Albers
The Bauhaus buildings in Dessau with annotations by Josef Albers, c.1926
Pen on photographic reproduction
10.1 x 25.3 cm
The Josef and Anni Albers Foundation

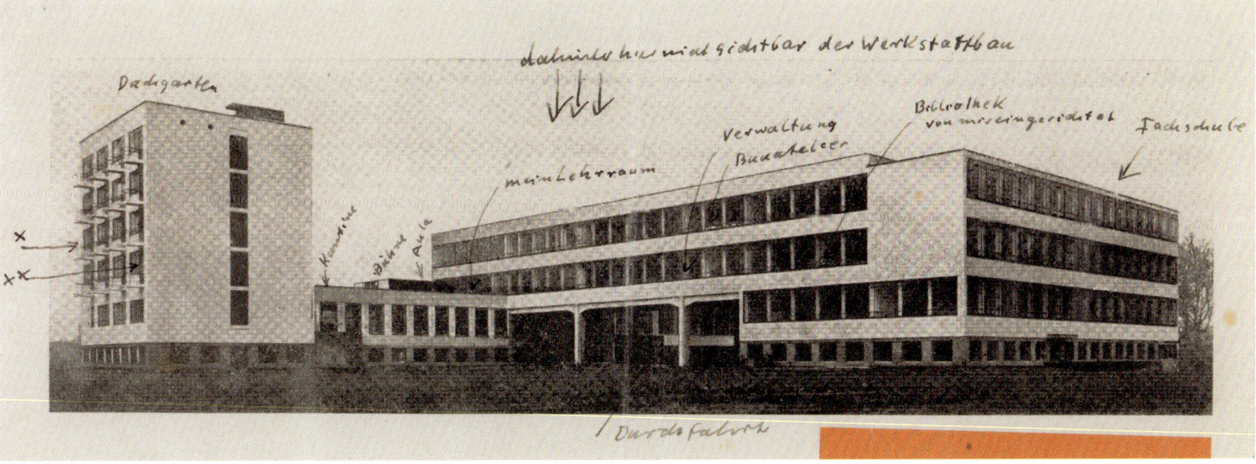

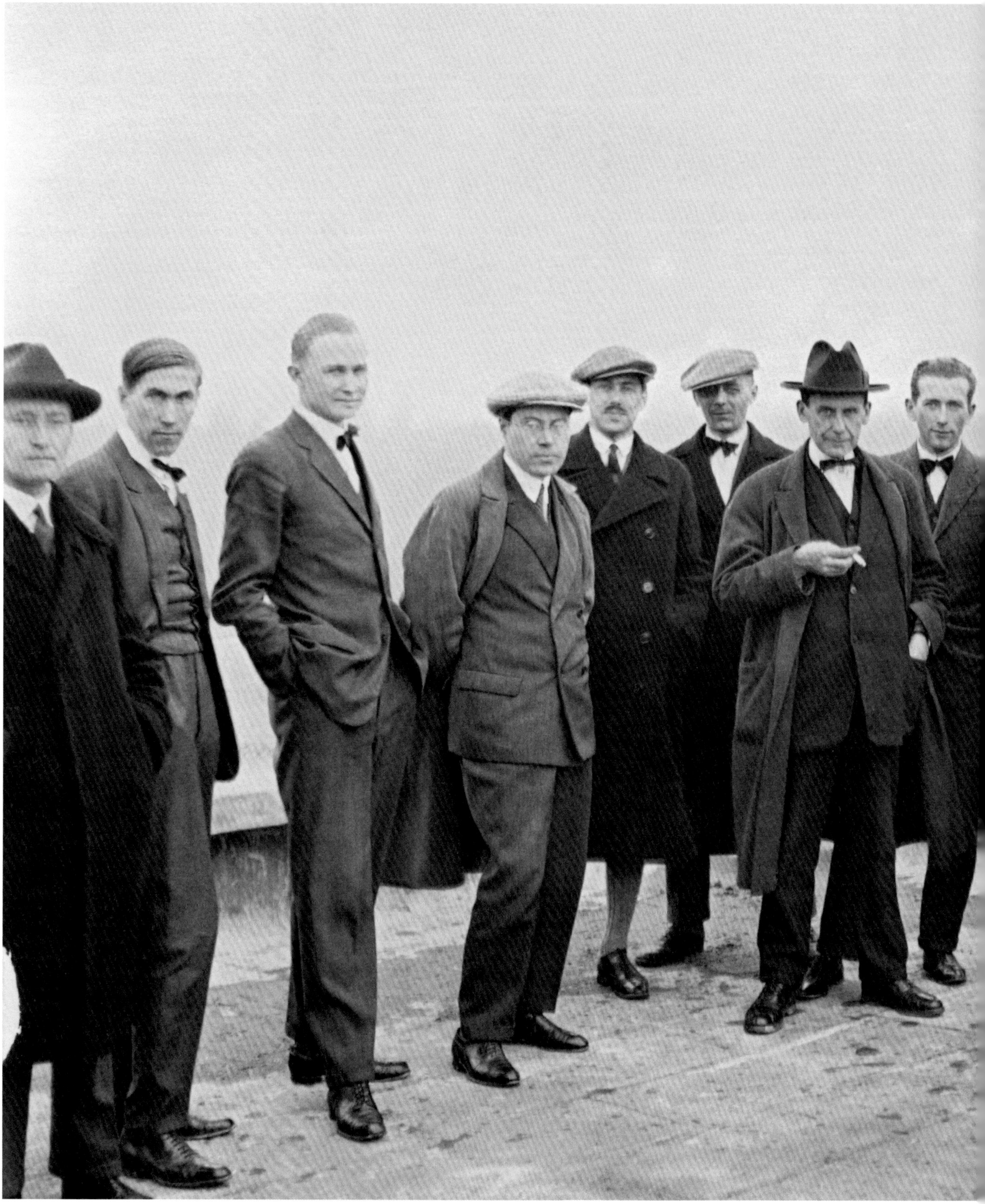

120
Masters on the roof of the Bauhaus building, 1926 (reprinted 1998)
From left: Josef Albers, Hinnerk Scheper, George Muche, László Moholy-Nagy, Herbert Bayer, Joost Schmidt, Walter Gropius, Marcel Breuer, Wassily Kandinsky, Paul Klee, Lyonel Feininger, Gunta Stölzl and Oskar Schlemmer
Gelatin silver print
18 × 24 cm
Bauhaus-Archiv Berlin
Photograher unknown

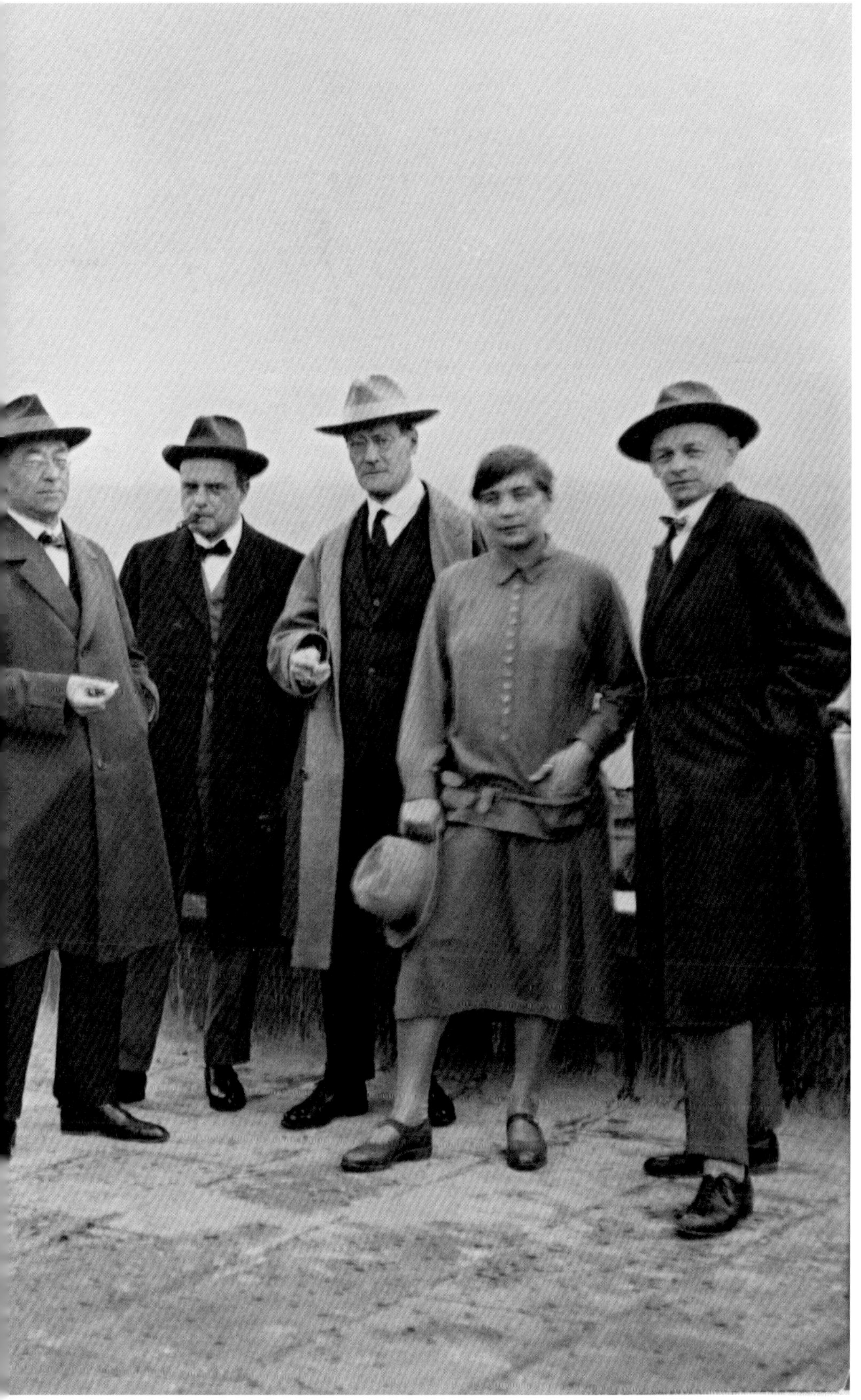

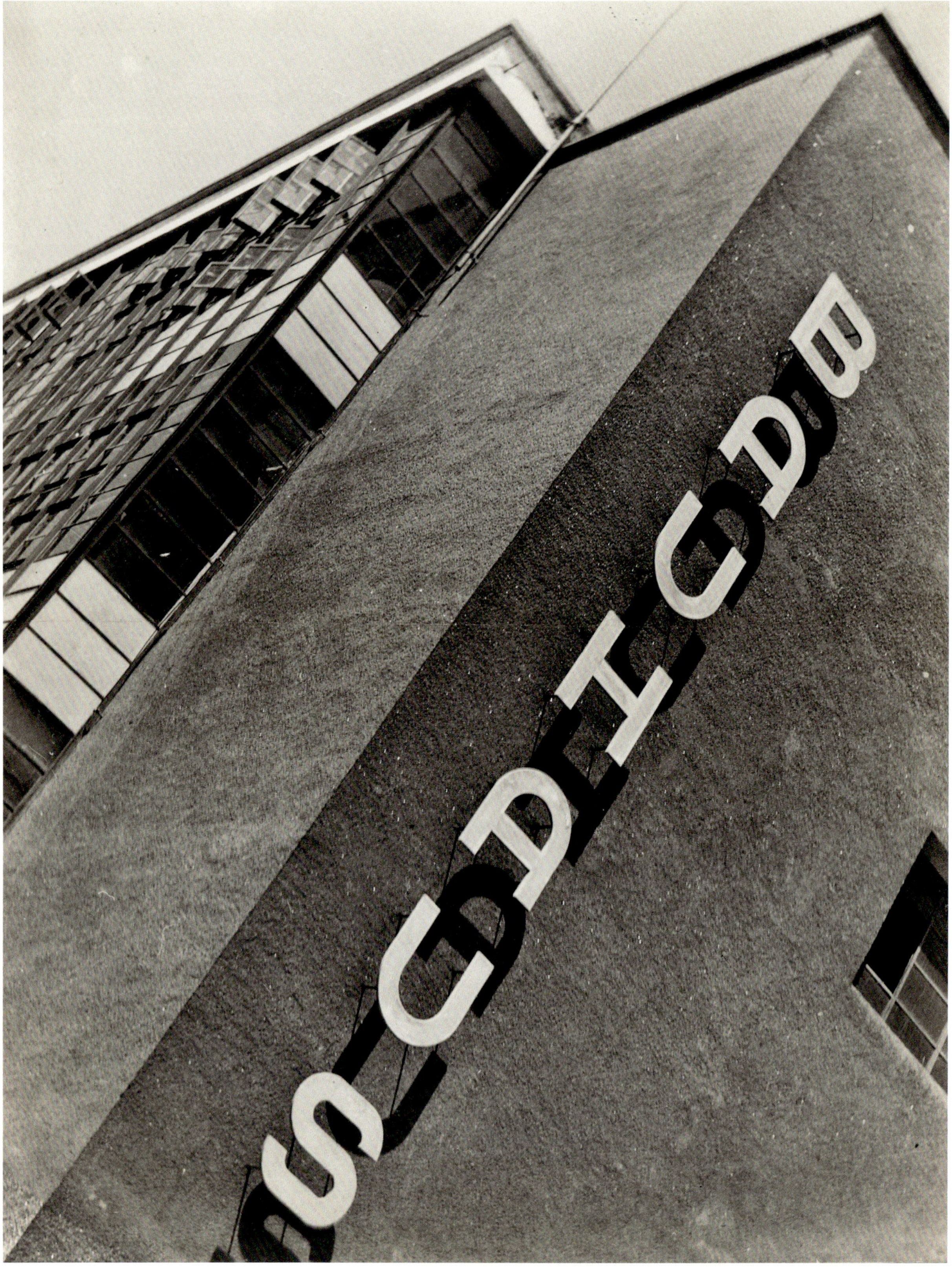

121
Iwao Yamawaki
Bauhaus building, 1930–32
Gelatin silver print
37.8 × 28 cm
Galerie Berinson, Berlin

122
Lyonel Feininger
Bauhaus building, Dessau,
balconies of the students' studios
from below, night view, 1929
Gelatin silver print
17.9 × 23.9 cm
Bauhaus-Archiv Berlin

123
Erich Consemüller
Auditorium with a view
to the vestibule, 1925–26
Bauhaus-Archiv Berlin

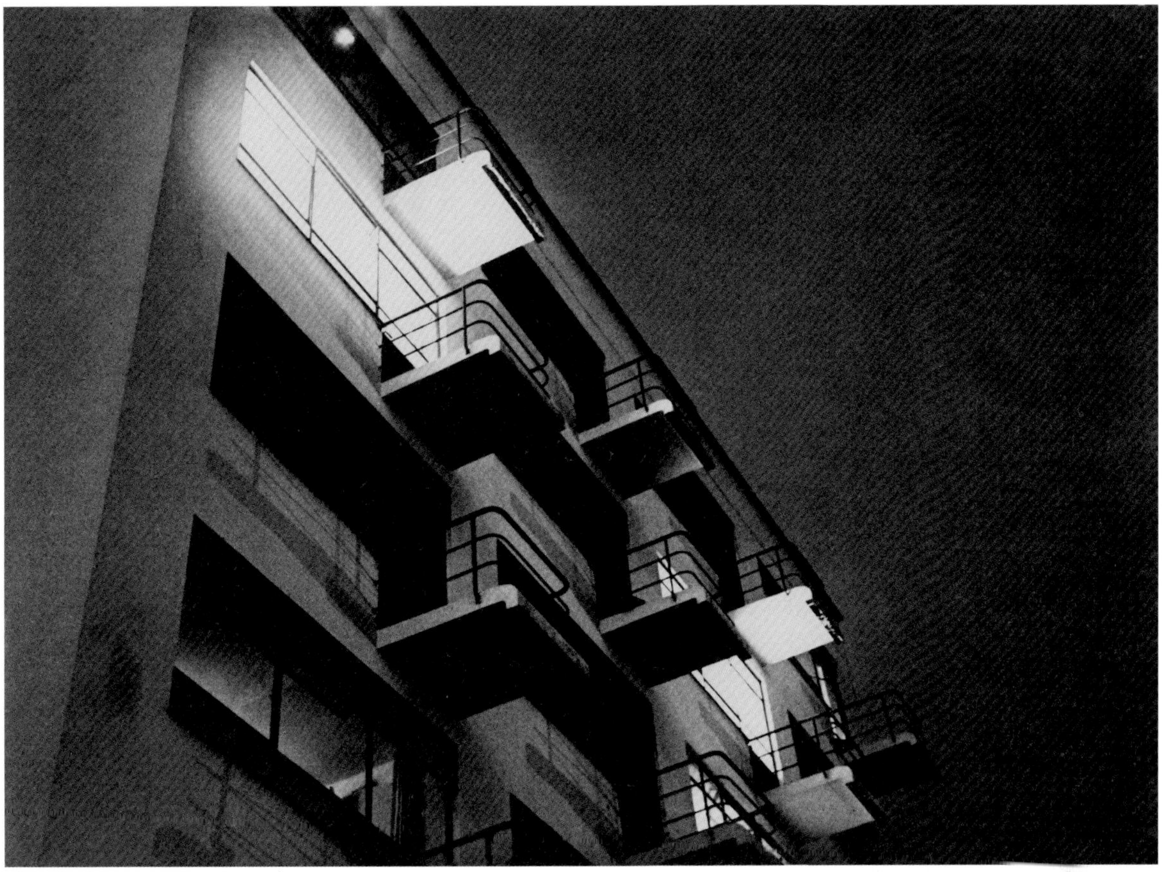

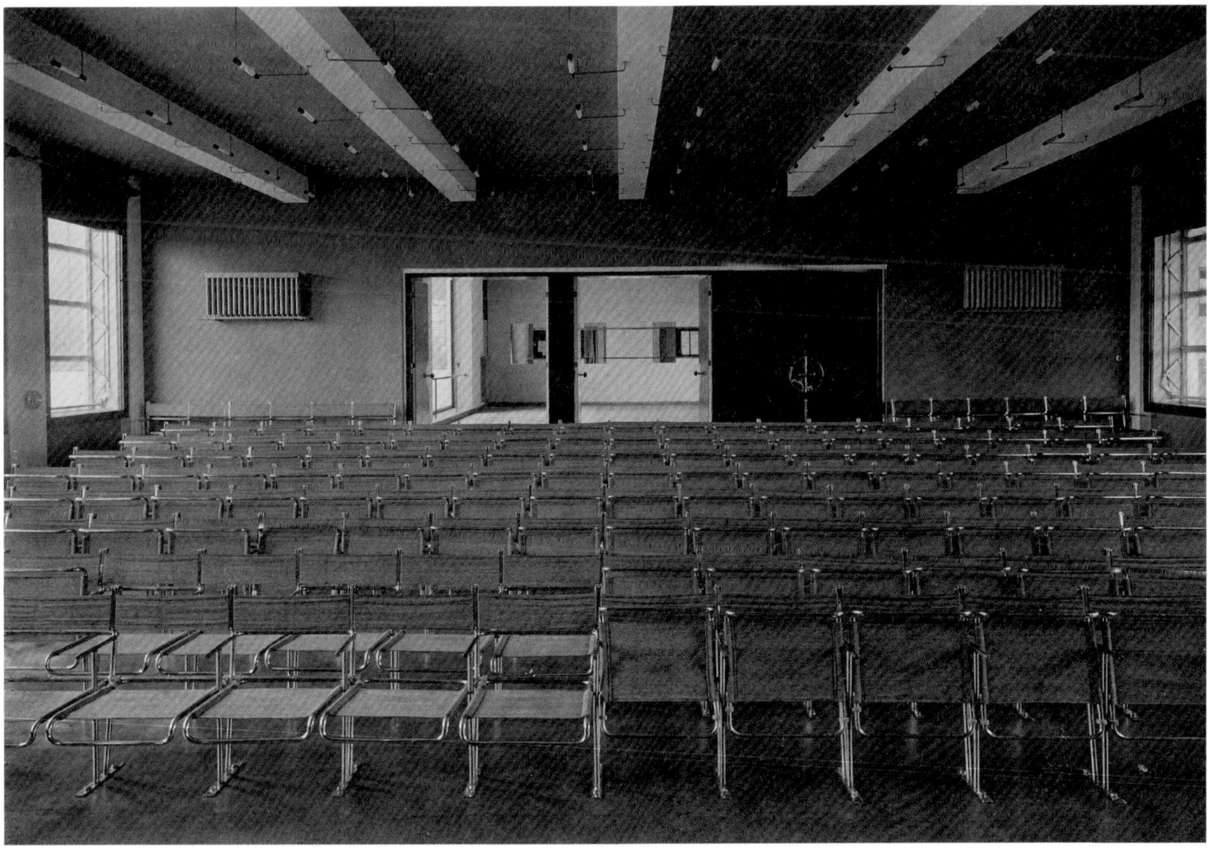

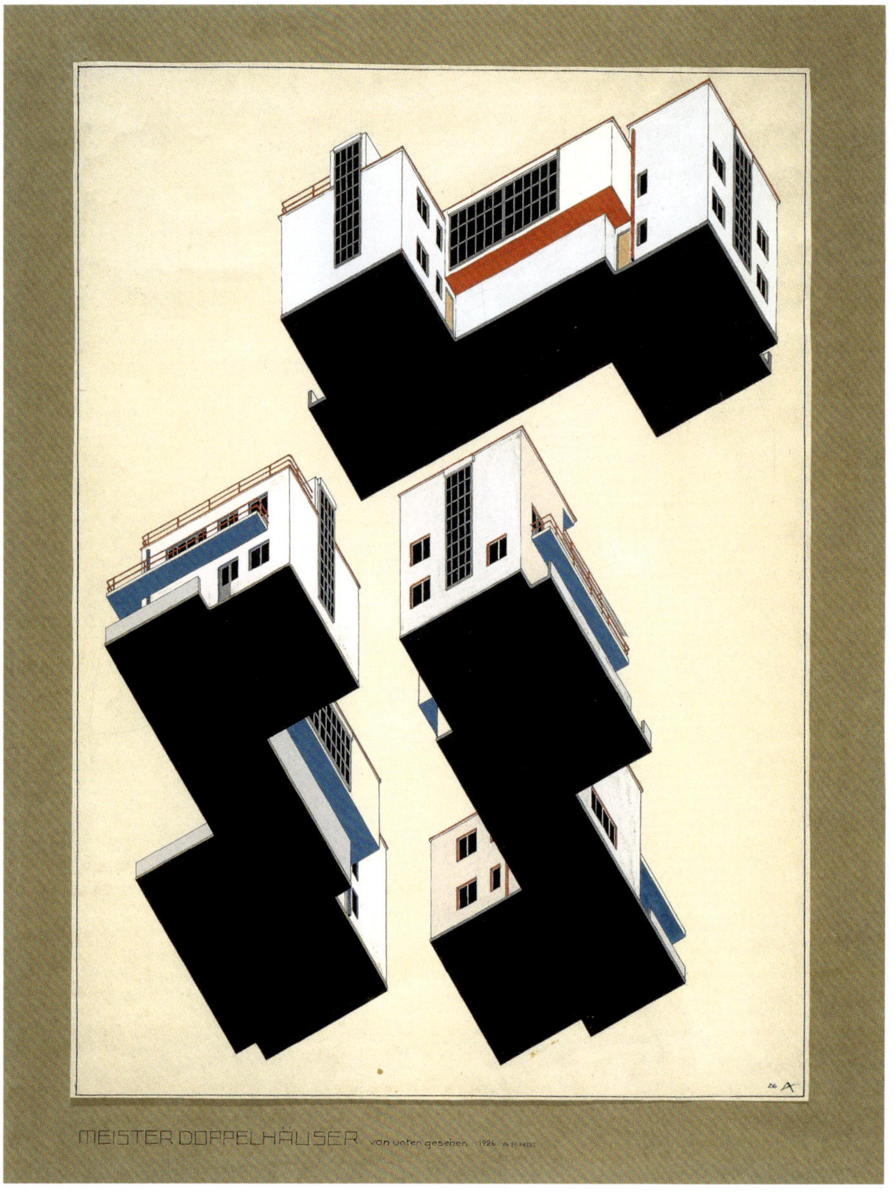

124
Alfred Arndt
Bauhaus masters' houses, Dessau,
colour scheme for the exteriors, 1926
Ink and tempera on drawing paper
75.7 × 55.8 cm
Bauhaus-Archiv Berlin

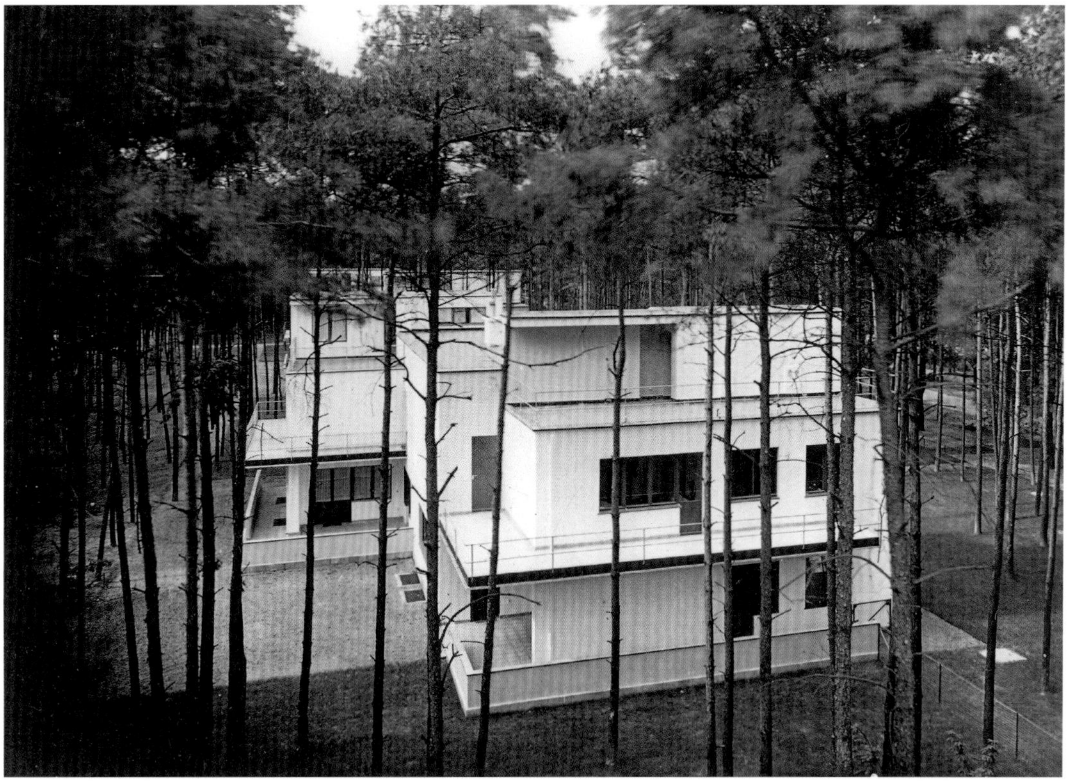

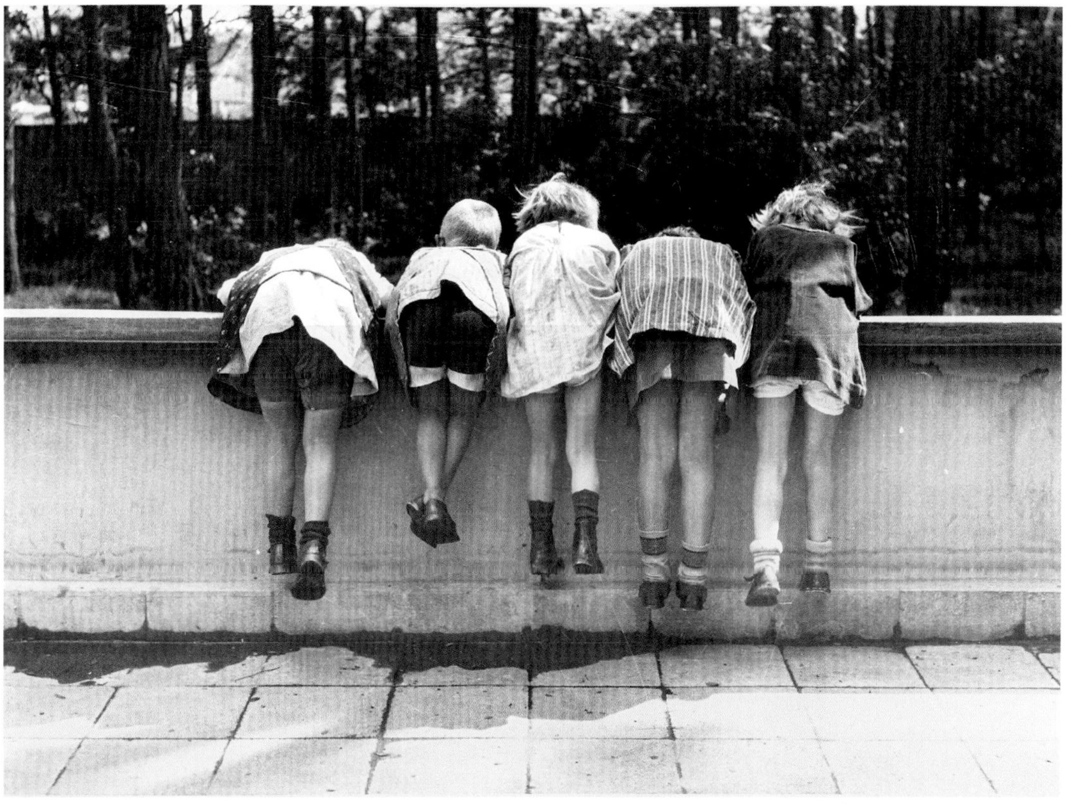

125
Lucia Moholy
Bauhaus masters' houses in Dessau, Moholy-Nagy and Feininger, viewed from above, 1926
Gelatin silver print
8 × 11.4 cm
Stiftung Bauhaus Dessau

126
Attributed to Ise Gropius
Children on the balustrade of a master's house, 1927
Bauhaus-Archiv Berlin

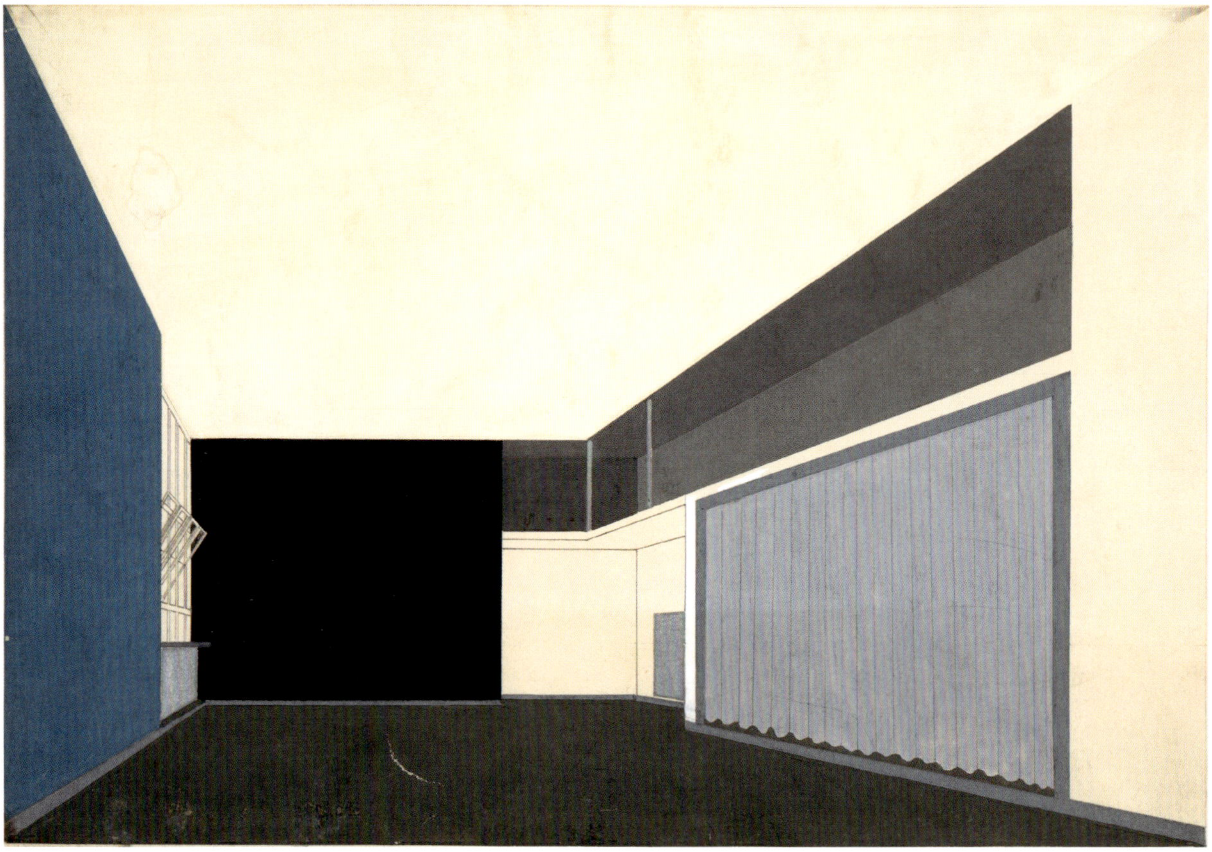

142

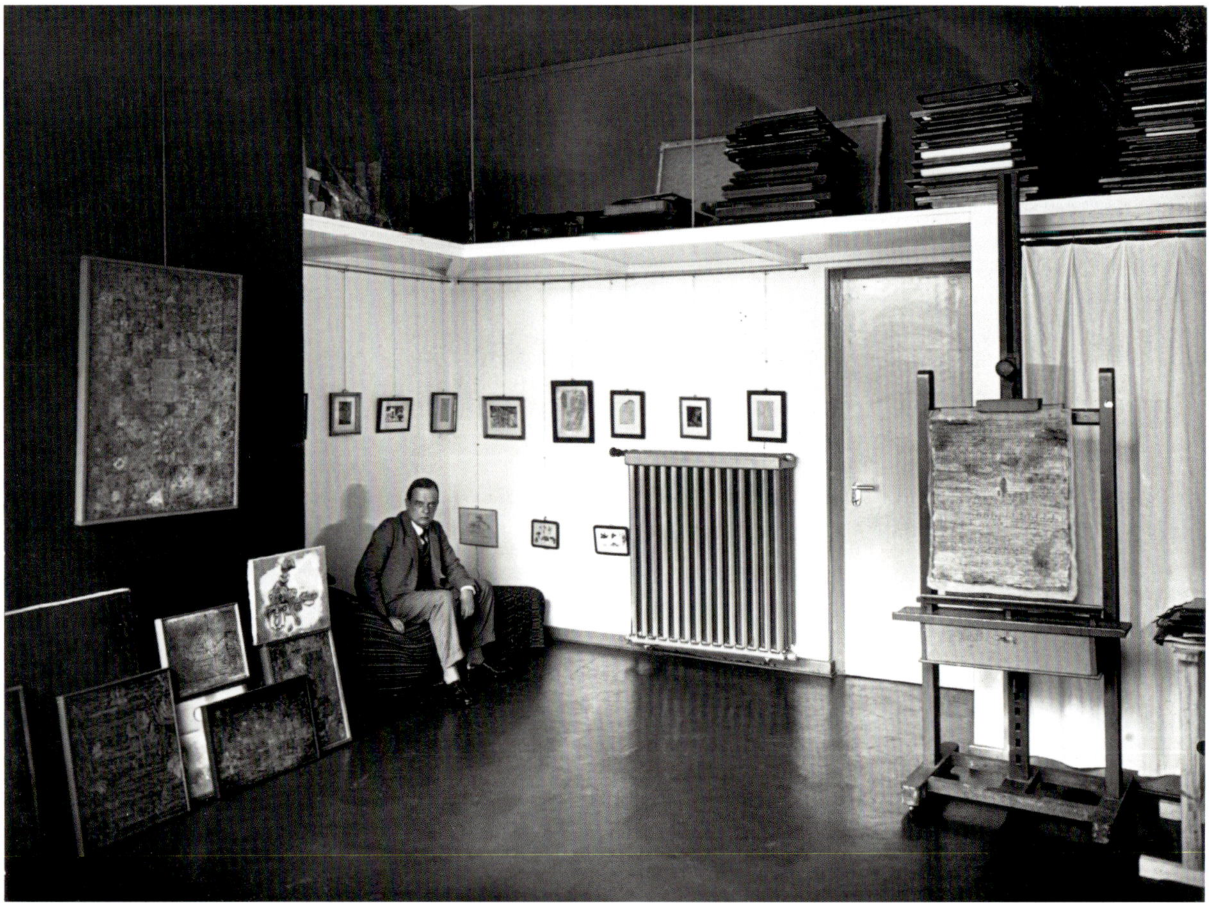

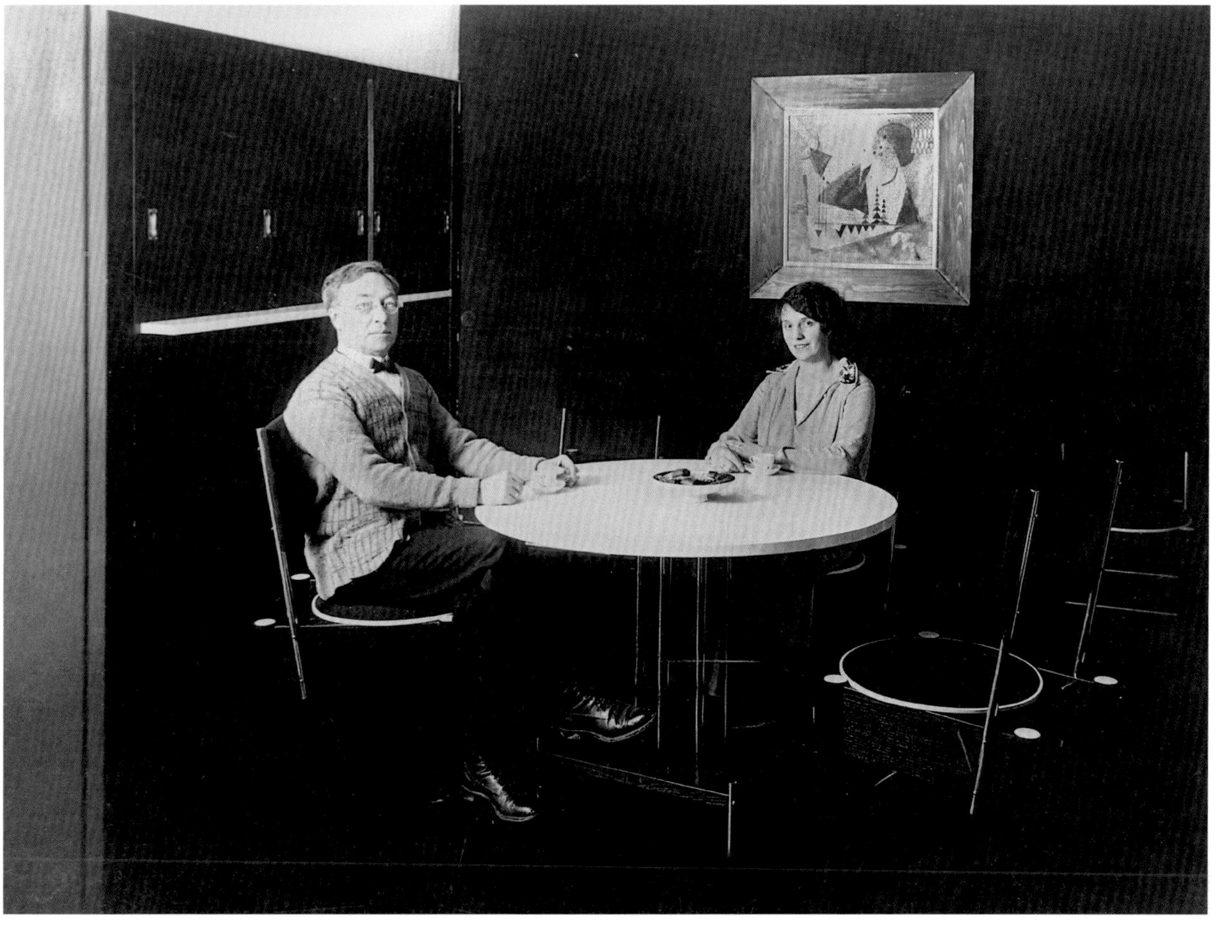

127
Fritz Kuhr
Bauhaus masters' houses, Dessau, colour scheme for Paul Klee's studio, perspective, 1926
Tempera, aluminium paint and pencil on paper
24 × 34 cm
Bauhaus-Archiv Berlin

128
Lucia Moholy
Paul Klee in his masters' house studio, 1927
Gelatin silver print
17.5 × 23 cm
Bauhaus-Archiv Berlin

129
Wassily and Nina Kandinsky in the dining room of their master's house, Dessau, 1927
Centre Pompidou – MnamCci – Bibliothèque Kandinsky
Photographer unknown

This photograph of Wassily and Nina Kandinsky in the dining room of their new master's house offers an insight into a modern mode of living that had come to epitomise the Bauhaus ideals: a simple, functional room. Kandinsky, however, added his own aesthetic touches with gold and black painted ceiling and walls, his painting *Three Sounds,* and wood and steel furniture based on the motif of the circle commissioned from Marcel Breuer. In accordance with Le Corbusier's ideas on modern architecture and living, function was the prime concern in Gropius's designs for the masters' houses. The simple white façades, the stark horizontal and vertical lines and the tubular-steel balcony railings were all chosen to create an efficient new lifestyle. Yet when the masters' houses were first opened to the public in 1926, many saw in them a more comfortable mode of living in comparison to the cold and sparse model of the Haus am Horn in Weimar. With their picturesque setting amidst tall pine trees, their large balconies and spacious reception rooms, the houses presented all the comfort and amenities of a middle-class dwelling equipped for both intimate family life and social gatherings.

author unknown
come to the bauhaus dessau, school for architecture and design

our bauhauslers
140 are of German origin
8 are from Anhalt
78 are from Prussia
26 are from Saxony
28 are from the rest of Germany
30 are foreigners, namely:
8 Swiss
4 Poles
3 Czechs
3 Russians
2 Americans
2 Latvians
2 Hungarians
1 German-Austrian
1 Dutchwoman
1 Turk
1 Persian
1 Palestinian
1 stateless person
119 are men
51 are women
14 are married
47 are between 17 and 20
90 are between 21 and 25
22 are between 25 and 30
11 are over 30 years old
1/3 need up to 50 marks per month
1/3 need between 50 to 100 marks per month
1/3 need between 100 and 200 marks per month
33 pay reduced school fees
25 are at home in the studio building
39 came to the bauhaus as apprentices
22 came to the bauhaus after their school-leaving examination
35 are in the preliminary course
7 are 'pure artists'
19 are active in the weaving workshop
54 are carpenters, painters, metalworkers
23 are keen on building
27 are in the advertising and print workshop
5 are in the bauhaus band
170 students

key information
The following are necessary for admission:
1 Curriculum vitae
2 photograph
3 medical certificate
4 criminal record check
5 evidence of financial support for the period of study
6 a selection of your work

fees
One-off admission fee
10 Reichsmark
Obligatory accident insurance fee
2 Reichsmark per semester

teaching fees per semester
First semester 100 Reichsmark
Second semester 60 Reichsmark
Third semester 50 Reichsmark
Fourth semester 40 Reichsmark
Fifth semester 30 Reichsmark
Sixth semester 20 Reichsmark
Seventh-ninth semester 10 Reichsmark
obligatory small flat-rate charge for bathrooms

in-house canteen
Full board with 4 meals daily 2 Reichsmark
breakfast 35 Pfennig
lunch 60 Pfennig
afternoon coffee 30–50 Pfennig
supper 60–75 Pfennig

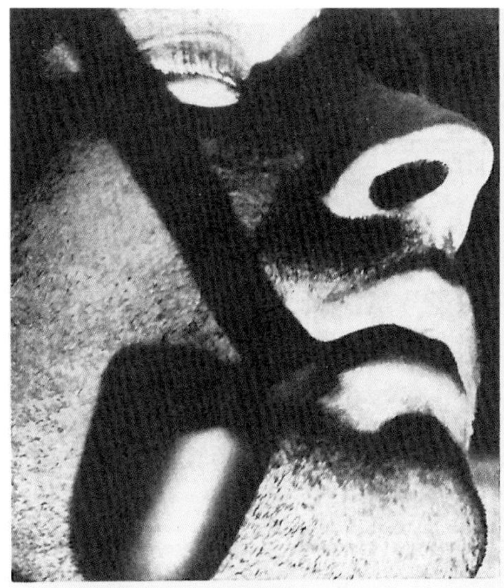

unsere bauhäusl

140 sind deutscher herkunft
8 sind aus anhalt
78 sind aus preußen
26 sind aus sachsen
28 sind aus dem übrigen deutschland
30 sind ausländer und zwar:
8 schweizer
4 polen
3 tschechen
3 russen
2 amerikaner
2 letten
2 ungarinnen
1 deutsch-österreicher
1 holländerin
1 türke
1 perserin
1 palästinenser
1 staatenloser
119 sind männlich
51 sind weiblich
14 sind verheiratet
47 sind im 17. bis 20. jahr
90 sind im 21. bis 25. jahr
22 sind im 25. bis 30. jahr
11 sind über 30 jahre alt
1/3 braucht monatlich bis 50 mark
1/3 braucht monatlich 50 bis 100 mark
1/3 braucht monatlich 100 bis 200 mark
33 sind vom schulgeld teilweise befreit
25 sind im atelierhaus heimisch
39 kamen als geselle ins bauhaus
22 kamen vom abitur ins bauhaus
35 sind im vorkurs
7 sind „reine künstler"
19 sind in der weberei tätig
54 sind tischler, maler, metallarbeiter
23 sind baubeflissene
27 sind in der reklame- und druckerei-werk
5 sind in der bauhauskapelle

170 studieren

merkblatt

zur aufnahme sind erforderlich
1. lebenslauf
2. fotografie
3. ärztliches gesundheitsattest
4. polizeiliches führungszeugnis
5. nachweis der unterhaltsmittel während der studienzeit
6. eine auswahl eigener arbeiten

gebühren
einmalige eintrittsgebühr rm 10.-
unfallversicherung obligatorisch pro semester rm 2.-

lehrgebühren pro semester
1. semester rm ~~80.-~~ 100,-
2. semester rm 60.-
3. semester rm 50.-
4. semester rm 40.-
5. semester rm 30.-
6. semester rm 20.-
7-9. semester rm 10.-

geringe pauschalgebühr für bäder obligatorisch

eigene kantine
volle pension bei 4 mahlzeiten täglich rm. 2.-
frühstück 35 pfg.
mittagessen 60 pfg.
nachmittags-kaffee 30—50 pfg.
abendessen 60—75 pfg.

merkblatt

wünschest du eine systematische schulung zur ku
suchst du die durchgangsstation zur neuen z
willst du lebensrichtig bauen lern
suchst du den ort energischer versuchsarb
brauchst du die gesellenprüfung als maler, tischler, schloss
willst du eine harmonische ausbildung dein eigen nenn
suchst du, ein fertiger handwerker, vertiefung deines könne
liebst du moderne kunst, abstrakt und sachli
suchst du deinen platz in der gesellsch
willst du weben, drucken oder fotografieren lern
suchst du umgang mit führenden geiste
bist du 17 oder 27 oder 37 jahre
träumst du von einer arbeitsgemeinsch
suchst du als studierende wahre gleichberechtigu
verlangst du nach einem ort produktiven studiun
quälen dich die probleme neuzeitlicher gestaltu
lockt dich die zusammenarbeit mit gleichgesinnt
willst du sparsam studiere

This is no cemetery. Here 28 bauhauslers are resting with their 28 Midgard lamps and their 28 gramophones in their 28 live-work studios in the so-called 'Prellerhaus'.

129
Hannes Meyer
Page from the brochure *bauhaus*, 1929
Letterpress on paper
14.8 × 21 cm
Stiftung Bauhaus Dessau

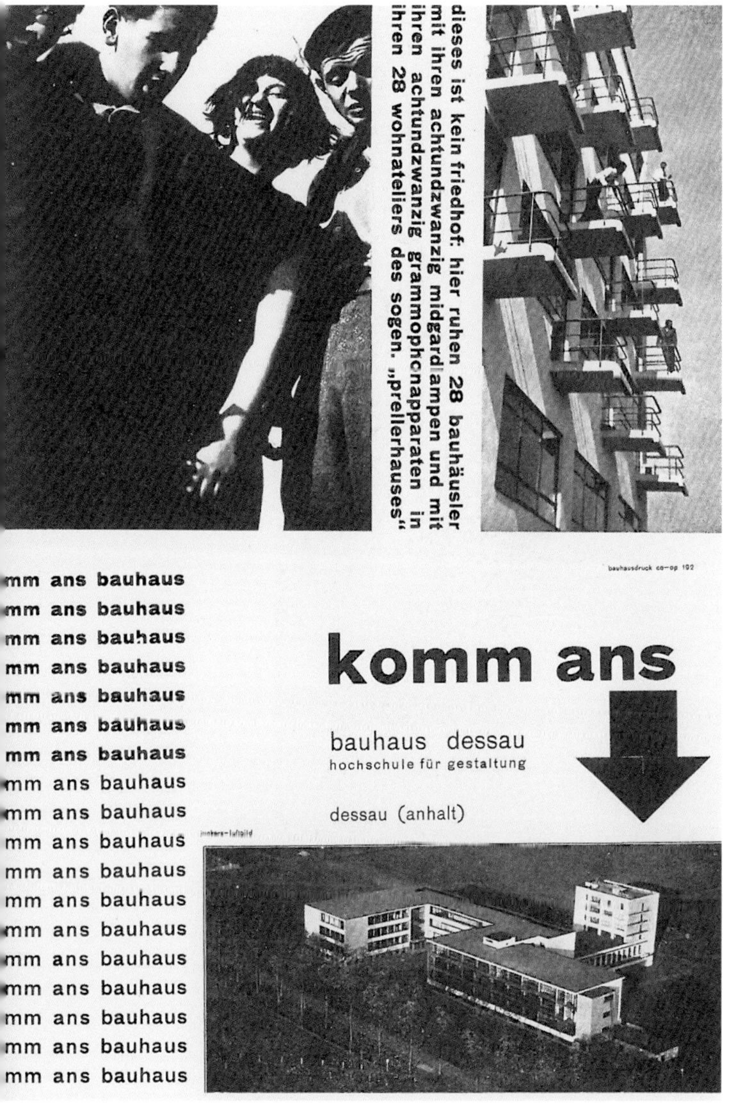

Would you like a systematic training in art?
Are you looking for a stepping stone to the new times?
Do you want to make buildings fit for living?
Are you looking for the place of determined experimentation?
Do you need to complete your qualifying examination as a journeyman painter, carpenter or metalworker?
Would you like to have a harmonious training?
Are you, as a qualified craftsman, seeking to deepen your skill?
Do you love modern art, abstract and functional?
Are you looking for your place in society?
Do you want to learn weaving, printing or photography?
Are you looking for contact with leading thinkers?
Are you 17 or 27 or 37 years of age?
Do you dream of a workers' co-operative?
Are you looking for true equality as a female student?
Do you require a place for productive study?
Do you struggle with the problems of modern design?
Are you attracted by working with like-minded people?
Do you want to study economically?

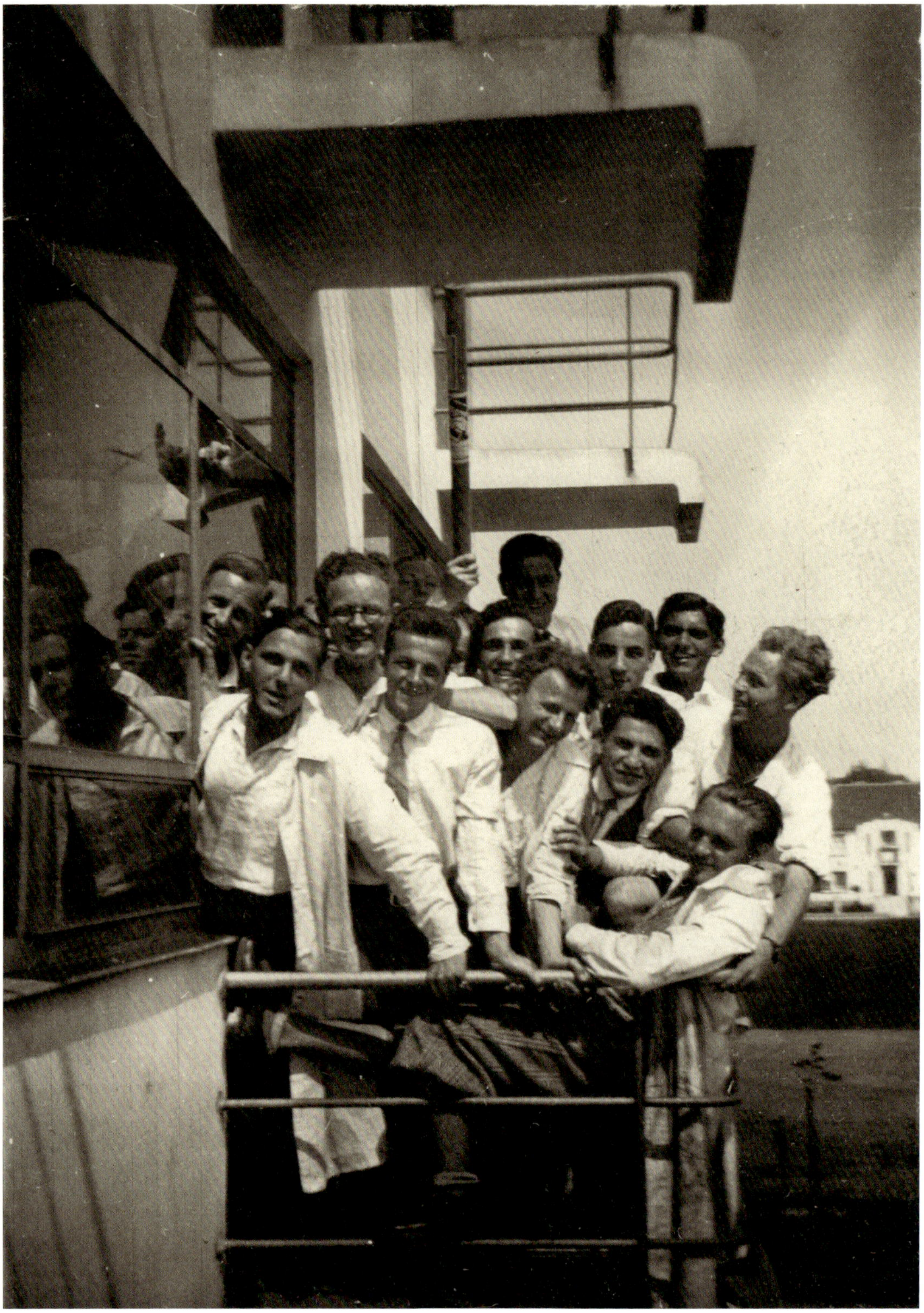

131
Fritz Schreiber
Students on a balcony at the Prellerhaus, Bauhaus Dessau, c. 1932
Gelatin silver print from photo album, mounted on card
Album page: 29.5 × 22 cm
Stiftung Bauhaus Dessau

132
T. Lux Feininger
The weavers on the bauhaus staircase, c.1927
Gelatin silver print
10.8 × 8.3 cm
Bauhaus-Archiv Berlin

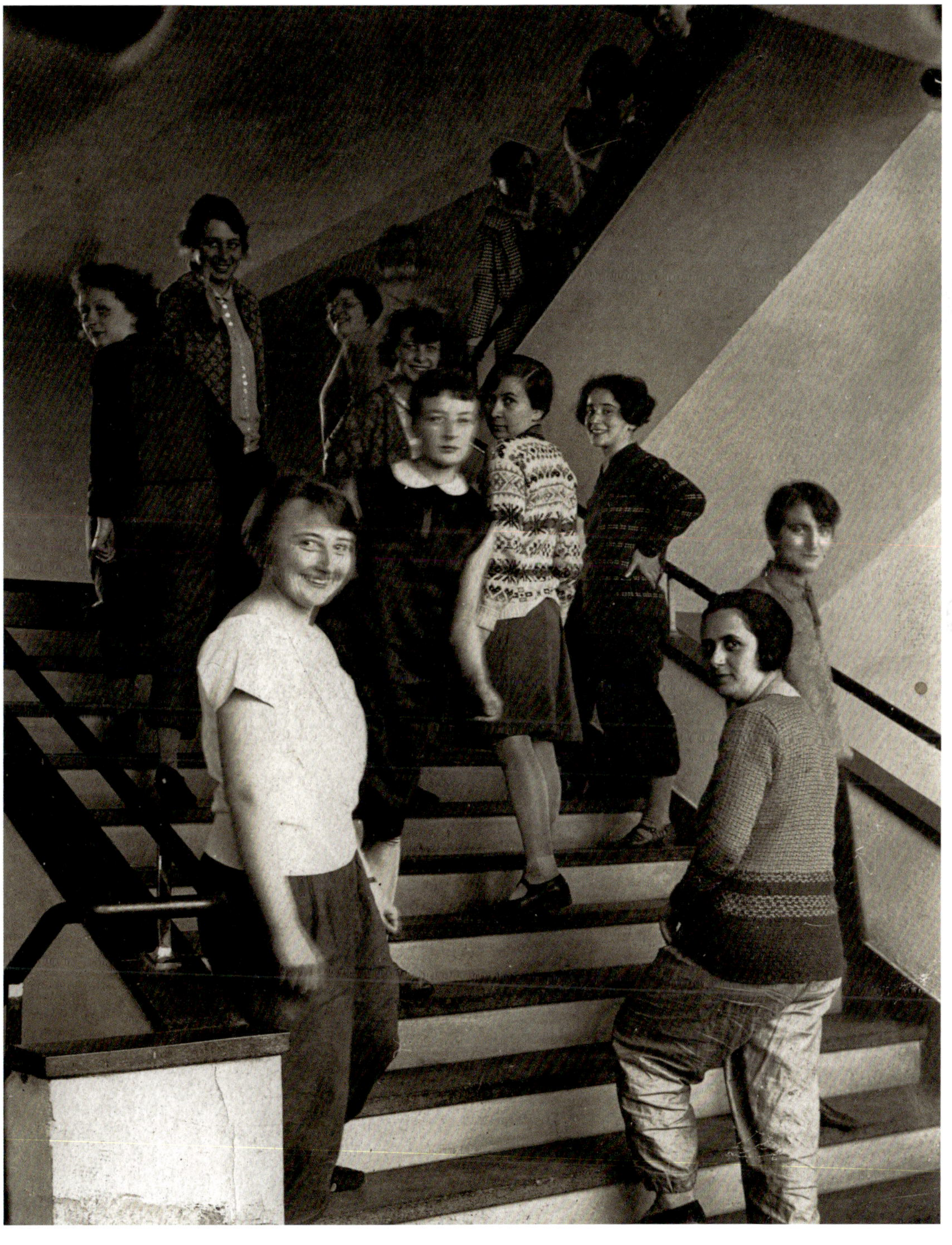

art as lifestyle theodore lux feininger's photographs of the bauhauslers

philip ursprung

In 1926, during a brief period of economic stability after several years of inflation and before the Great Crash of 1929, Theodore Lux Feininger enrolled at the Bauhaus. Only sixteen years old, he was one of the youngest students ever admitted to the school. It was certainly helpful that he was the son of the painter Lyonel Feininger, who was appointed to the Bauhaus faculty in 1919, and had therefore grown up 'with and at the Bauhaus',[1] which had just been forced to leave the conservative residential town of Weimar. The school was welcomed by the 'more urban' industrial city of Dessau, and the move 'increased the reputation of the Bauhaus considerably', as Lux Feininger later recalled in his autobiography.[2] The spectacular emblems of this new beginning were Walter Gropius's buildings for the school and the faculty. Lux Feininger, still a teenager, was proud to get his own room – he could even choose the colour it would be painted – in his parent's house, the semi-detached Meisterhaus (masters' house) no. 3, which the family shared with the Moholys. And he was equally impressed that a 'jazz band in smokings', coming to Dessau from Berlin, was performing at the opening ceremony of the new building in December 1926. The Bauhaus was definitively on the map.

After finishing the *Vorkurs*, the preliminary course, Lux Feininger enrolled in the experimental stage workshop of Oskar Schlemmer. He was attracted by the performances of this group, by the masks and costumes, the stage design, the movement of bodies through dark spaces. It was, as he put it, 'essentially a dancers' theatre and as such, sufficient unto itself', but 'it was also a "class," a locale of learning'.[3] Besides the stage workshop, it was again music, namely the jazz band, or *Bauhaus-Kapelle*, that fascinated the young student. He felt that 'the life at the Bauhaus was unthinkable without the musical background of its many parties – some improvised, others carefully and beautifully staged'.[4] Although he did not play an instrument yet, he was eager to join the band, and even bought himself a banjo. However, he had to wait until he had learned to play the clarinet before he was finally admitted. Only now, he felt, had he actually become 'a part of the life at the Bauhaus'.[5]

In retrospect it seems that Lux Feininger wanted to be both inside and outside the Bauhaus, to partake in its life and observe it from a distance. Perhaps this attitude was influenced by his father, who was half American, half German and who chose to stay at the Bauhaus in Dessau without actually teaching; he did not earn a salary but remained nominally a member of the faculty. Perhaps Lux Feininger's ambivalence was just due to his young age. He was undecided about his artistic future, but soon discovered photography as his 'niche'.[6] His older brother Andreas, originally trained as an architect and also interested in photography, helped him install a dark room in the basement of the house. Lux Feininger did not receive any instruction in the medium from the Bauhaus; the first photography course would not be taught until 1929, by Walter Peterhans.[7]

Lux Feininger first photographed the work of his fellow students and the performances in the stage workshop. Then he started to depict daily life at the Bauhaus – a subject in which, as he recalls, nobody else was interested. László Moholy-Nagy and his wife Lucia had set the tone with their dynamic interpretations of the modernist architecture. Herber Bayer and Josef Albers followed. And even Lyonel Feininger started to use the medium, inspired by his sons, to produce atmospheric representations of the building and its surroundings. It is obvious that these photographs had some influence on the student, but more interesting than the similarities are the differences. The photographs by the father, often taken by night, do not feature people and were obviously made with a tripod. And if Moholy depicted people at all, they were usually figures placed on the balcony to highlight the architectural quality of the buildings. The young Feininger, however, did exactly the opposite. In his images, made without tripod using a 9×12 glass-plate camera that he constantly carried with him,[8] the architecture is only a backdrop. For him, the modern architecture was not the spectacular object that seemed to make the photographer drop to his knees, and nor was it a source of exciting patterns and contrasts. It was instead a familiar environment that could be taken for granted.

For instance, when Feininger depicts two members of the jazz band – dancer Xanti Schawinsky and banjo-player Clemens Röseler – on the roof on a winter day, the entire building seems to rock. The camera is tilted and produces an oblique photograph in an expressionist style. But the intention of this framing is not to reflect on the inherent qualities of the new medium, but rather to create the illusion that the photographer and even the camera are driven by the music and have started to dance.

Unlike Moholy or others such as Marianne Brandt, who deal with the authority of photography as a new artistic medium, and put emphasis on the experimental character of their work, Lux Feininger has a more relaxed and playful relation to the camera. And unlike his father, who celebrates the authority of the institution, for instance by showing the brightly lit studio window contrasting with the dark night, the son captures the beauty and spontaneity of the students. When he takes snapshots during a football game, the buildings are depicted blurred, as if they were observing from afar what is happening around them. In his photographs, the Bauhaus turned from a space of education to a stage for lifestyle. Rather than an institution where art and crafts are taught, the Bauhaus appears as a place where life-style is designed. The photographs evoke the ideal of an autonomous, protected and free community. But they also prefigure the universal post-war lifestyle, with its emphasis on leisure and consumer culture.

This is certainly the reason why Feininger's early photographs are so appealing to today's public. Compared to those of Moholy, they found appreciation relatively late, towards the end of the twentieth century. They had featured in exhibitions since the 1980s, but only with the 2001 exhibition *Dancing on the Roof: Photography and the Bauhaus (1923–1929)* at the Metropolitan Museum in New York did they move centre-stage. For decades, these photographs had stood in the shadow of the ideology – and commodity value – of Bauhaus design, which was embodied by exclusive furniture, didactic principles and the problematic heritage of the International Style. Gordon Matta-Clark spoke for many artists of his generation when he criticised this legacy of the 'German design machine'.[9] And Tom Wolfe satirically described its fetishistic character in his book *From Bauhaus to Our House*, where he characterised Ludwig Mies van der Rohe's Barcelona chair as 'the holy object ... in a household where a fledgling architect and his young wife had sacrificed everything to bring the symbol of the godly mission into their home'.[10] In short, because the legacy of the Bauhaus was so ideologically loaded and the very concept of modernity was laid on the heroic 'master's' shoulders, there seemed to be no time for fun.

It is telling that the young Feininger refused simply to portray the famous masters, although the photo agency Dephot (Deutscher Photodienst) for which he worked would have liked to buy such material. When he took a picture of Schlemmer, for instance, he depicted him like a product of his own stage design, as if he himself were a mask, or a machine. However, today his photographs of cheerful vitality touch us in a different way from the controlled self-referentiality of the classical Bauhaus photography, precisely because they let us see a new aspect of this period. They provide a close-up view, so to speak. In the midst of an epic battle about the fate of modernist culture, while the directors of the Bauhaus, Walter Gropius, Hannes Meyer and Ludwig Mies van der Rohe struggled for the survival of the institution (and with each other), Feininger lets us observe groups of young students enjoying their daily life.

Nevertheless, it would be too simple to interpret these images as symptoms of the escapism that was typical of the Golden Twenties. Although the camera does not show the context of the Bauhaus – for instance, the Junkers aircraft plants that were at the basis of Dessau's prosperous economy, the many unemployed in the city, nor the signs of political confrontation – the perspective is far from naïve. Lux Feininger's images make clear that for artists of this generation – born in the early twentieth century and growing up quickly – study and work, leisure and self-promotion, fun and professional skills blend seamlessly together. They love to party with and without costumes. But even during a football game or a lunch break, they seem to be conscious how precious their activities are and the fleeting quality of their time at the Bauhaus. The camera is always present, as if even the most random detail of daily life were an artistic event that had to be preserved. The photographs show us that these young people have to perform, and have to be creative day and night, as if they could already foresee the pressure of immaterial labour and the 'creative industry' that arises half a century later. Life, so these photographs tell us, is precarious and becomes a matter of art, a resource ready to be marketed, consumed and designed.

A couple of months later, the credits that had been flowing into Germany from the US during the 1920s stopped when America itself was struck by the depression. The jazz bands would soon be silenced. Architecture students from the US still came to the Bauhaus, now mainly attracted by Mies, the new director. But Mies – in the 'law-and-order role of the administrator'[11] as Lux Feininger wrote – did not succeed in keeping the Bauhaus together. Many of the professors left, and the Bauhaus started to disintegrate. The political pressure within Germany grew, the National Socialist Party came to power, and through circumstance forced the Bauhaus to close, in 1933. By that time, Lux Feininger had already left for Paris to become a painter and would give up photography. The party was over.

1 T. Lux Feininger, 'The Bauhaus: Evolution of an idea', in Eckhard Neumann (ed.), *Bauhaus and Bauhaus People, Personal opinions and recollections of former Bauhaus members and their contemporaries*, trans. Eva Richter and Alba Lorman, Van Nostrand Reinhold, New York, 1993, p.183.

2 Theodore Lux Feininger, *Zwei Welten, Mein Künstlerleben zwischen Bauhaus und Amerika*, trans. Florian Bergmeier, Mitteldeutscher Verlag, Halle (Saale), 2006, p.73.

3 Feininger, 'The Bauhaus: Evolution of an idea', op. cit., p.193.

4 Feininger, *Zwei Welten*, p.90 op. cit. (author's translation).

5 Ibid.

6 Ibid, p.74.

7 See Katherine C. Ware, 'Photography at the Bauhaus', in Jeannine Fiedler and Peter Feierabend (eds), *Bauhaus*, Könemann, Cologne, 2000, pp.506–29.

8 See Jeannine Fiedler, 'T. Lux Feininger: 'I am a painter and not a photographer!', in Jeannine Fiedler (ed.), *Photography at the Bauhaus*, The MIT Press, Cambridge, MA, 1990, pp.45–48.

9 Gordon Matta-Clark, Note, Estate of Gordon Matta-Clark, on deposit at the Canadian Center for Architecture, Montreal. Quoted in Thomas Crow, 'Gordon Matta-Clark', in Corinne Diserens (ed.), *Gordon Matta-Clark*, Phaidon, London, 2003, p.102.

10 Tom Wolfe, *From Bauhaus to Our House*, Farrar, Straus, Giroux, New York, 1981, pp.60–61.

11 Ibid., p.110.

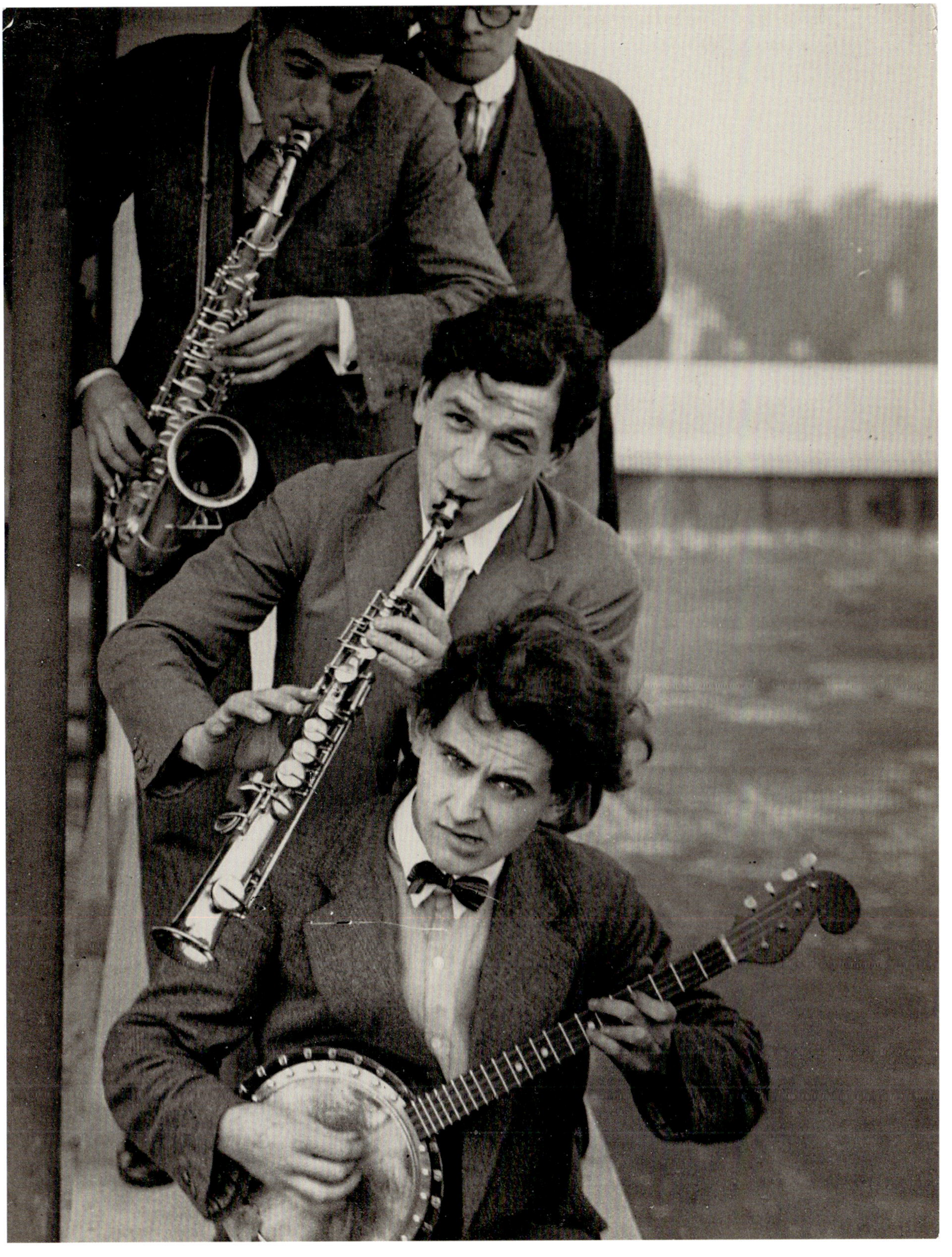

133
T. Lux Feininger
Members of the Bauhaus band (from top, Oskar Schlemmer, Werner Jackson, Xanti Schawinsky, Clemens Röseler), c.1928
Gelatin silver print
23.9 × 17.9 cm
Bauhaus-Archiv Berlin

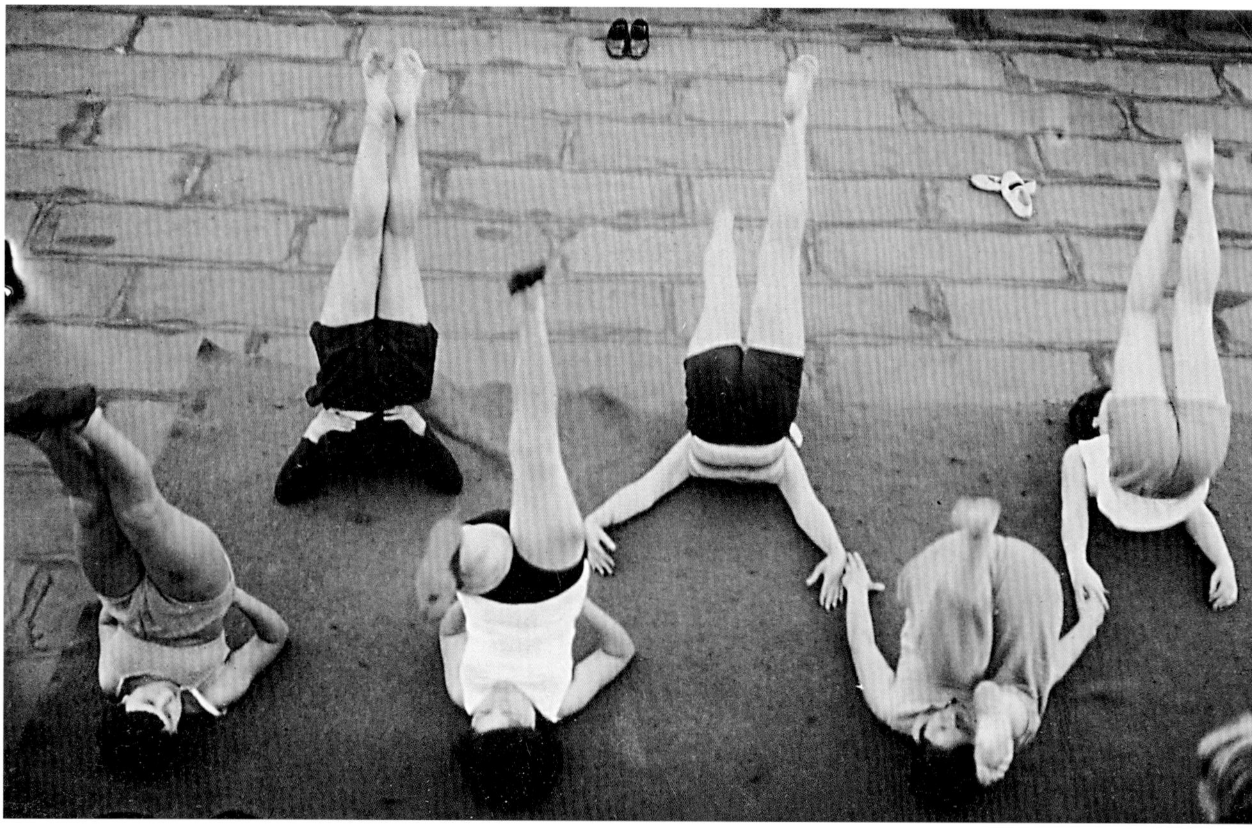

134
T. Lux Feininger
Women's gymnastics with Karla Grosch on the roof of the Prellerhaus, 1930
Gelatin silver print
8.8 × 12.1 cm
Bauhaus-Archiv Berlin

135
T. Lux Feininger
The jump over the Bauhaus/ Sport at the Bauhaus, c. 1927
Gelatin silver print
23.7 × 17.9 cm
Bauhaus-Archiv Berlin

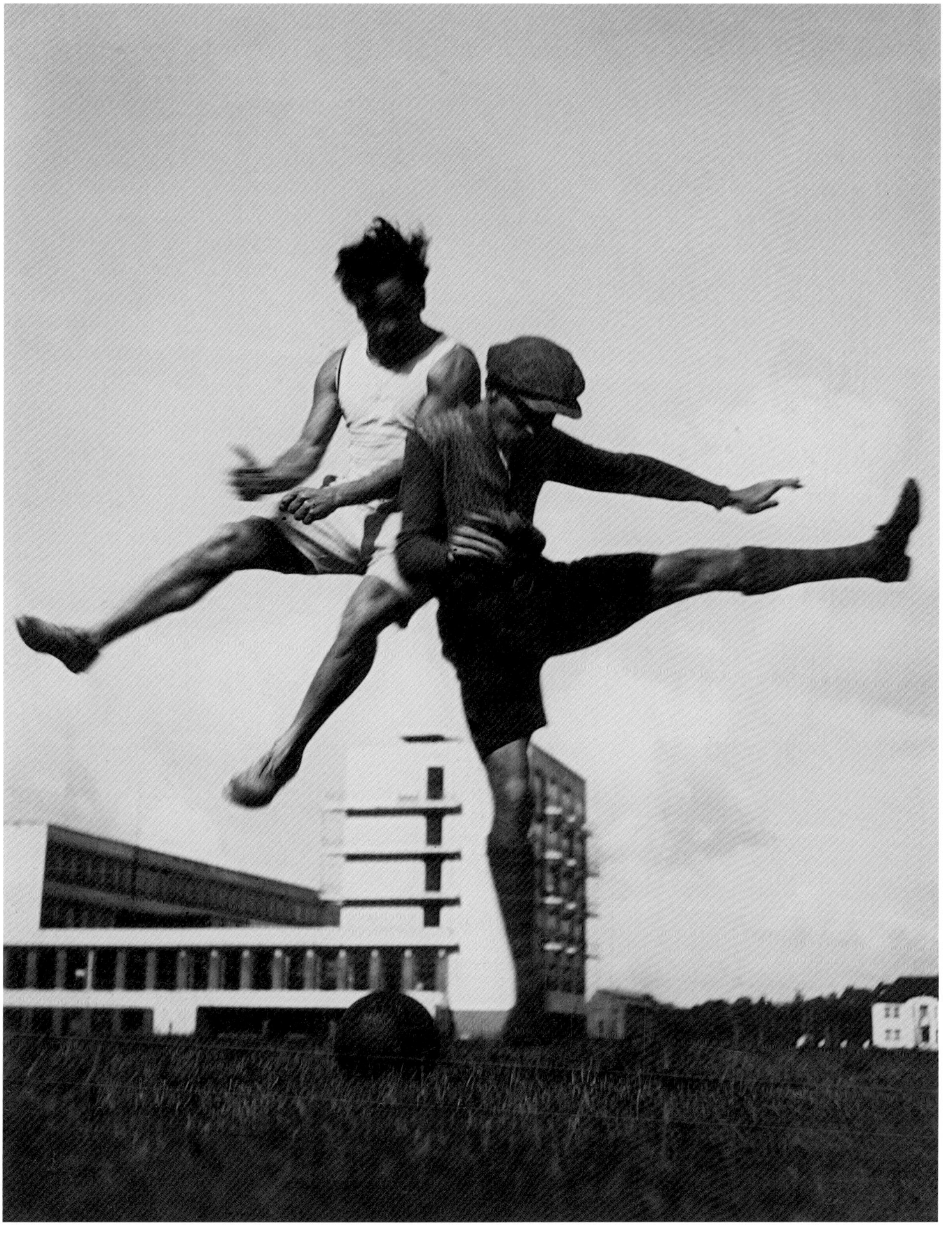

our play, our party, our work

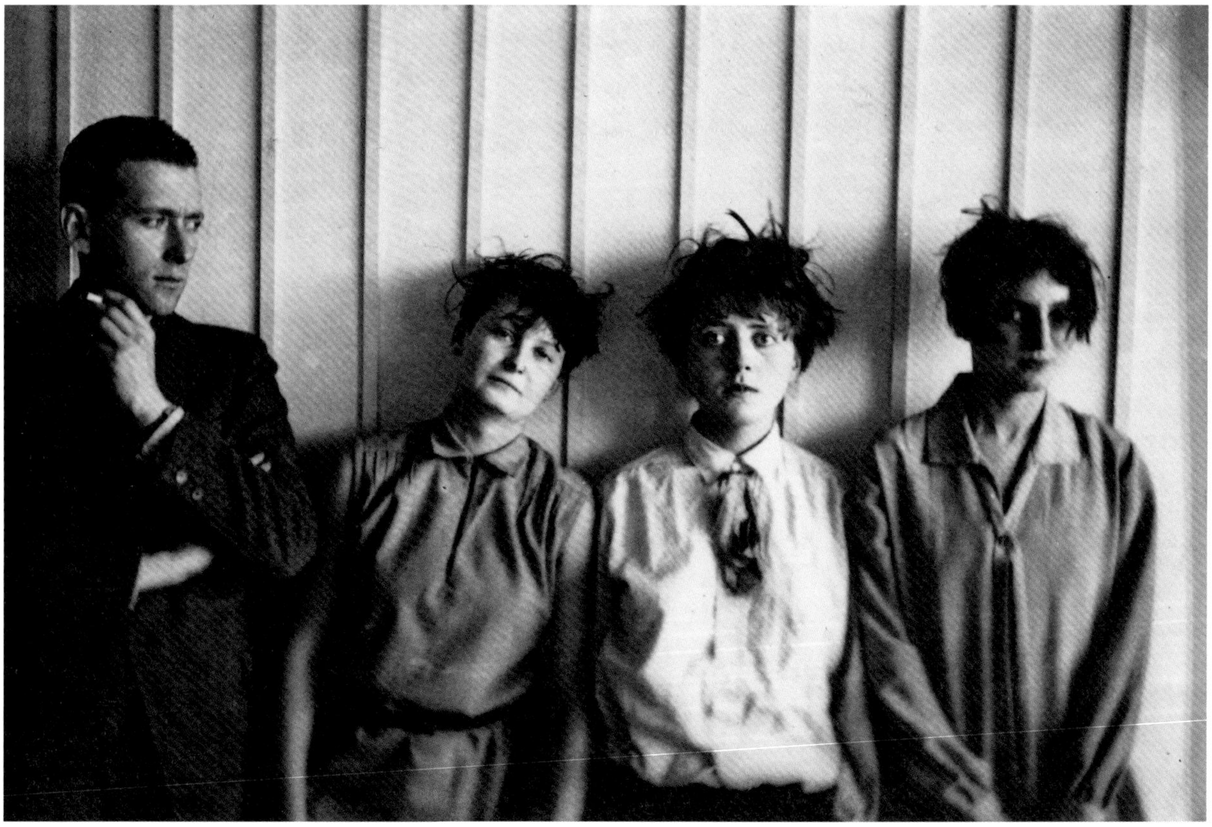

Once established, the Bauhaus was held together as much by the social gatherings and festivities that masters and students organised collaboratively as by Gropius's vision for a new art school. These celebrations served to promote contact between the school and the public, with attendance from locals and party-goers from further afield, making the school a lively cultural centre. Parties were also of central importance to Gropius's educational vision and from the outset he stressed the significance of extracurricular entertainment with the 'encouragement of friendly relations between masters and students outside of work'. Such festivities gave free rein to the masters and students to demonstrate their creativity and design invention, providing innumerable opportunities to conceive invitations, posters, costumes and decorations. An additional pedagogical aim of the festivities was the encouragement of play within teaching. Masters from Johannes Itten and Oskar Schlemmer to Paul Klee valued play as an essential ingredient of artistic creativity.

The Bauhaus parties moved from the imaginative improvisations and the rhythm of the seasons during Weimar, with the Lantern Festival in the spring and the Kite Festival in the autumn, to spectacular and monumental stage productions in Dessau. These large public parties were elaborately prepared around themes, such as the White Party (1926), in which everyone was instructed to appear in a costume 'dotted, chequered and striped', or The Beard Nose Heart Party arranged by the Bauhaus band. The highpoint of celebrations was in 1929 with the resplendent Metal Party. The school was given a glittering look and guests came attired in metallic objects from tin foil to frying pans and danced to the sound of bells. They entered the building by sliding down a large chute that deposited them in the first of several rooms decorated with silver spherical balls and reflecting walls faced with white metal. The lively creative activities entailed by these important social gatherings were recorded repeatedly in diaries, letters and photographs.

Varying from the formal photographs of Bauhaus masters taken by Josef Albers to more fleeting records of personal interactions between staff and students, photography became the prime medium with which to document life at the school.

The last Bauhaus parties were markedly different from those of previous years, largely due to financial pressures experienced by the school and the increasing need to use the parties as a source of income. The staging and creative endeavours remained constant, but gradually towards the latter part of the school's history, auctions and prizes were offered to raise funds.

136
Erich Consemüller
Marcel Breuer and his Harem, c.1927
(Marcel Breuer, Martha Erps, Katt Both and Ruth Hellos-Consemüller)
Gelatin silver print
11.2 × 8.2 cm
Herzogenrath, Berlin
On long-term loan to Klassik Stiftung Weimar, Bestand Museen

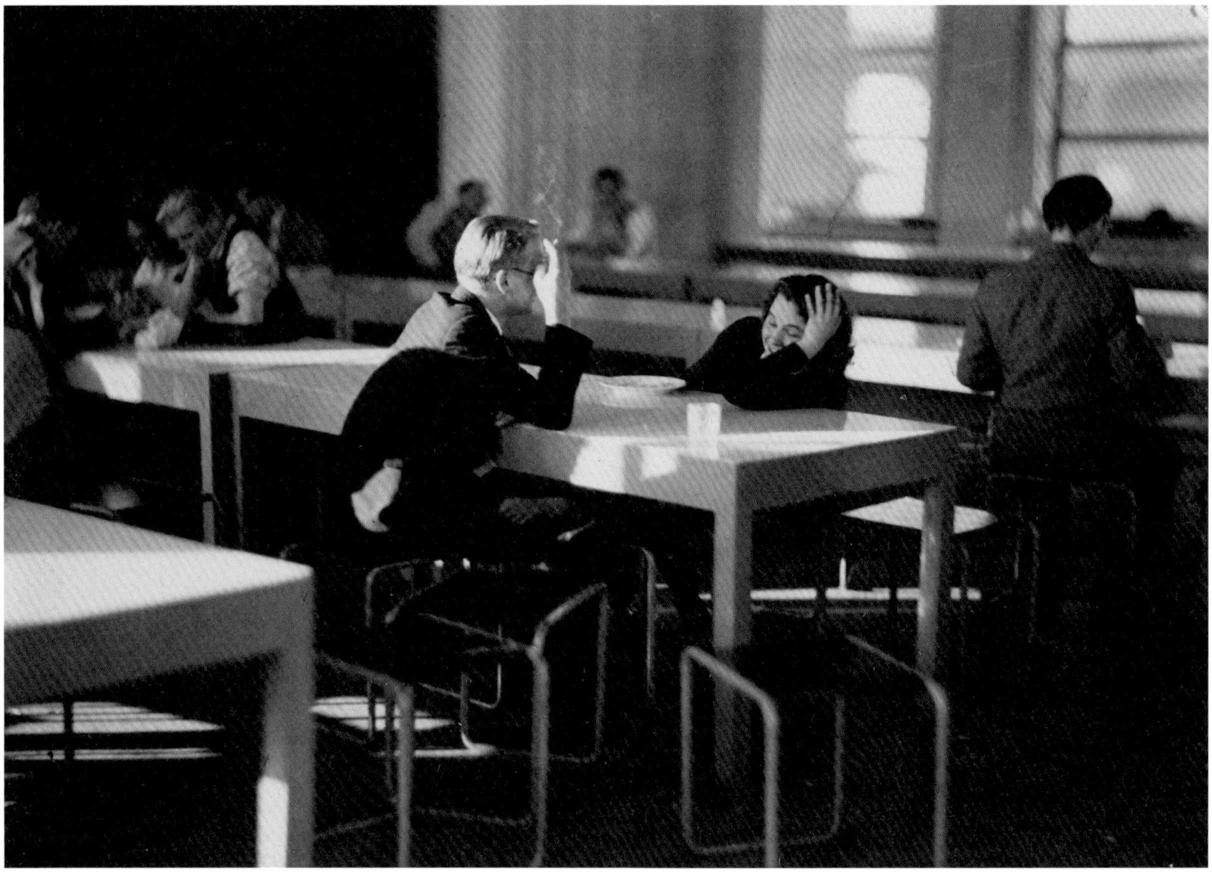

137
Iwao Yamawaki
Canteen after lunch, Bauhaus Dessau,
1930–32 (printed later)
Gelatin silver print
8 × 11.1 cm
Tate. Purchased 1996 with funds
provided by the Asia Pacific Acquisitions
Committee, 2010

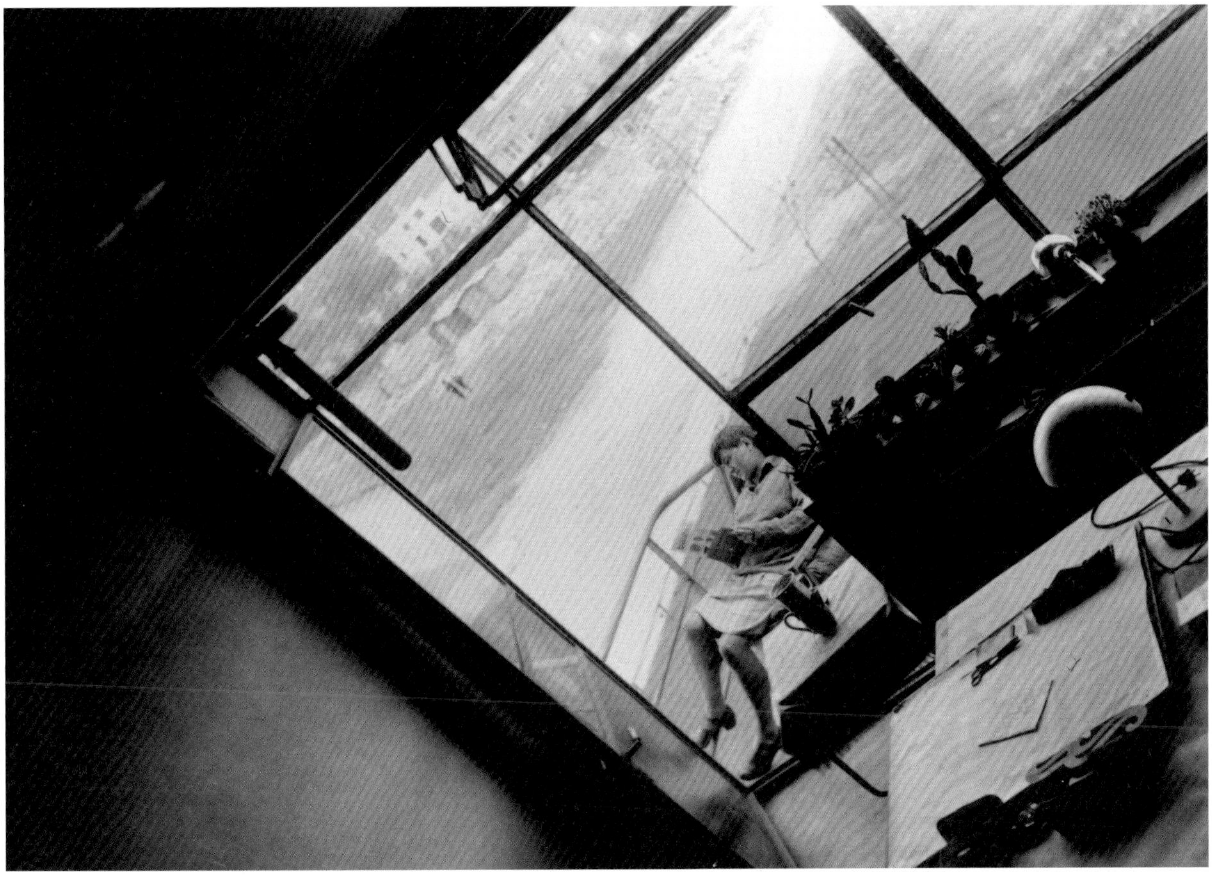

138
Werner Zimmermann
Marianne Brandt on the balcony of the Prellerhaus, Bauhaus, Dessau, 1928
Gelatin silver print
11.9 × 8.9 cm
Bauhaus-Archiv Berlin

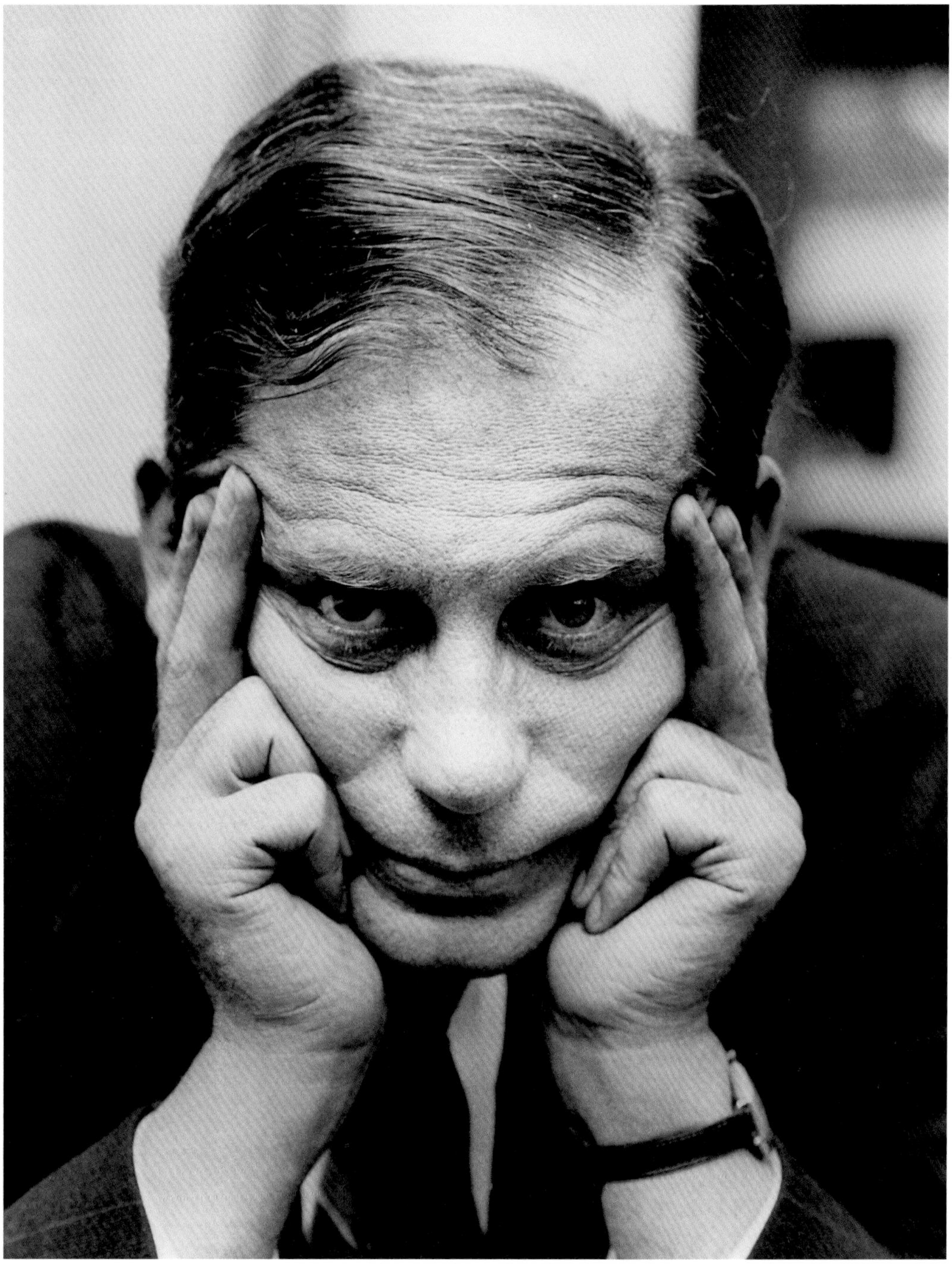

139
Lucia Moholy
Seated Portrait of Walter Gropius, 1927
(printed 1993)
Gelatin silver print
24 × 18 cm
Bauhaus-Archiv Berlin

140
Lucia Moholy
Self-Portrait, 1930
Gelatin silver print
23.9 × 17.9 cm
Bauhaus-Archiv Berlin

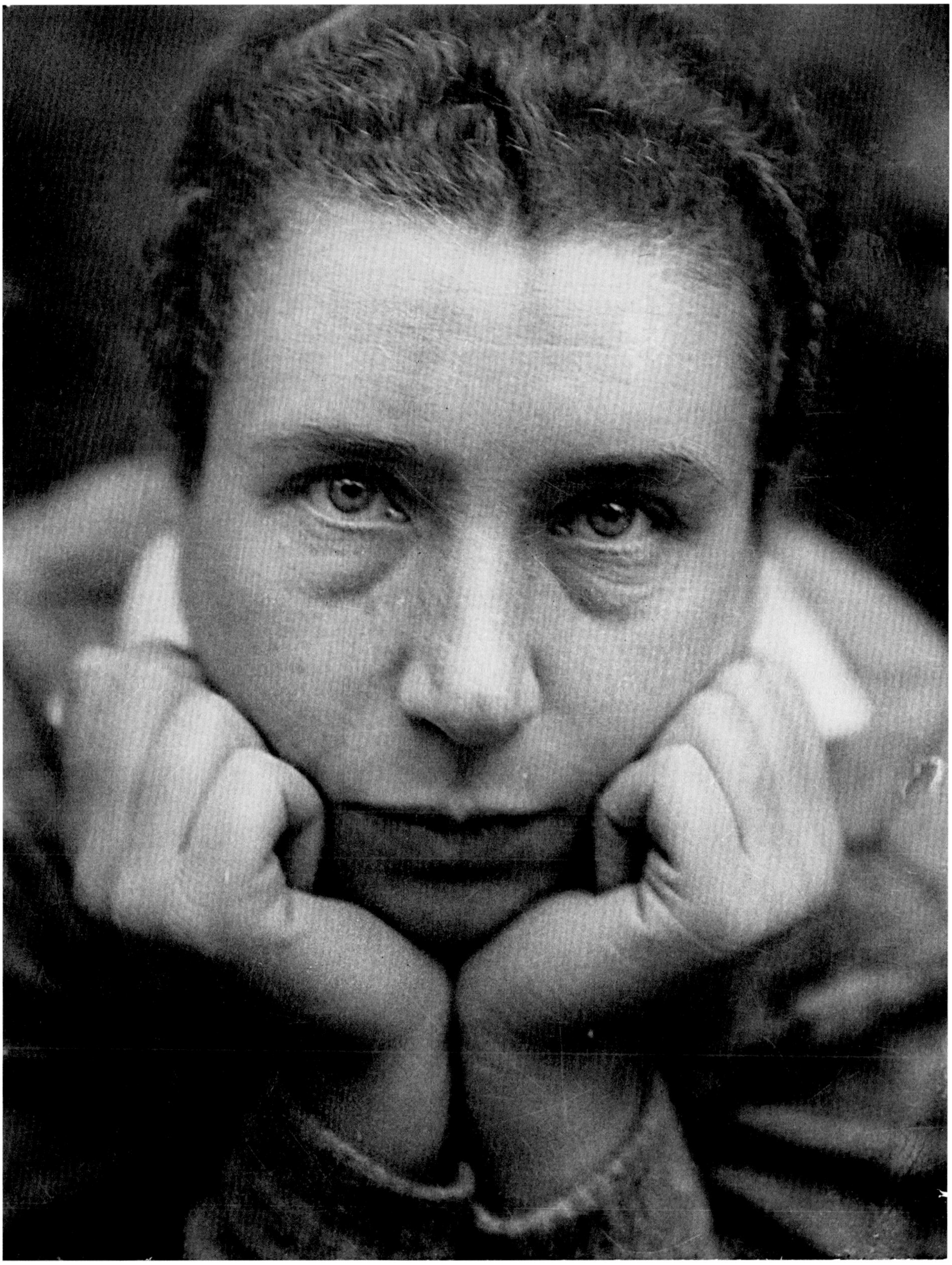

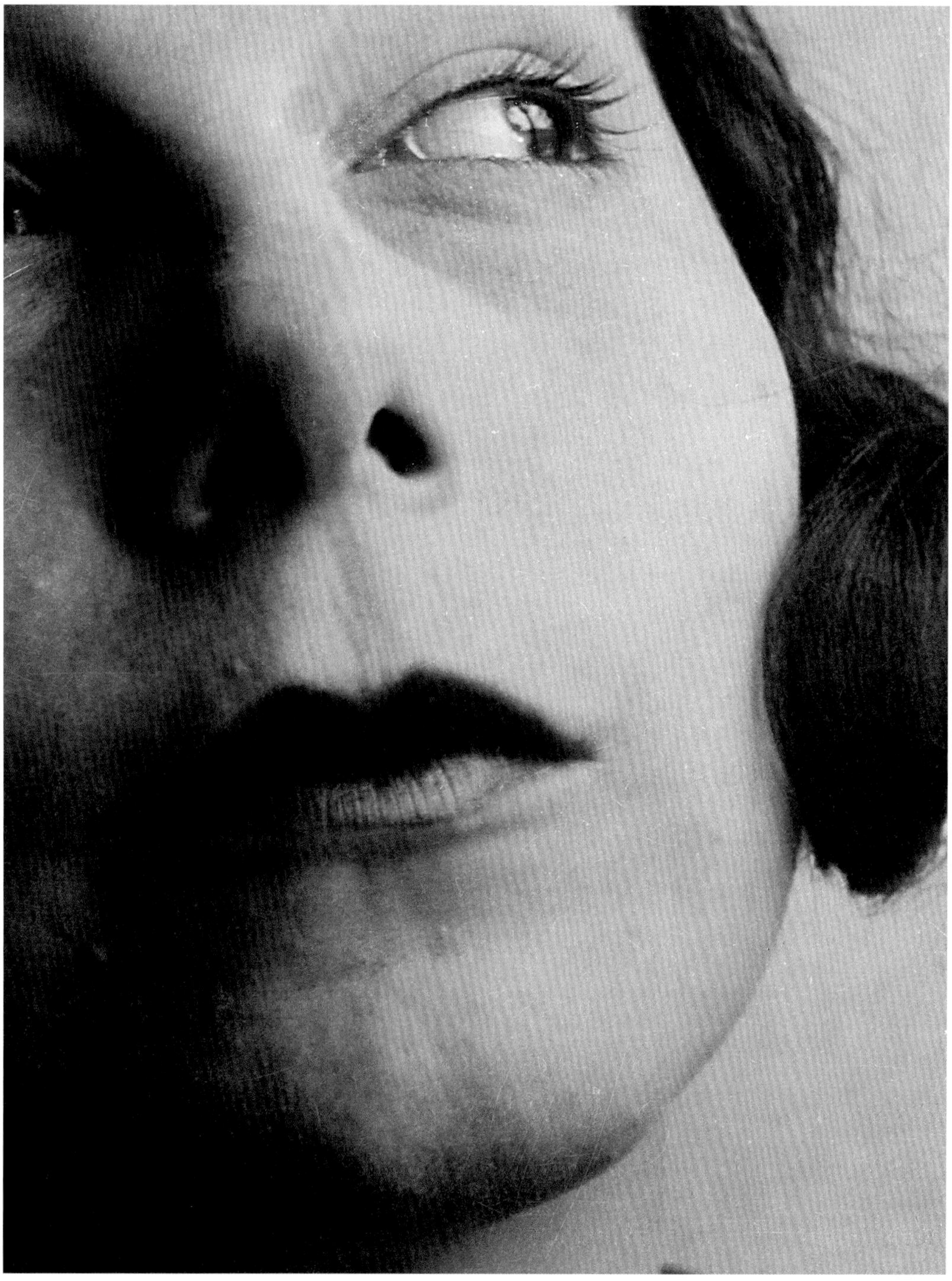

141
László Moholy-Nagy
Portrait of Ellen Frank, c.1929
Gelatin silver print
40 × 30 cm
Bauhaus-Archiv Berlin

142
Lucia Moholy
Portrait of Florence Henri, 1927
(printed 1970s)
Gelatin silver print
23.8 × 17.8 cm
Bauhaus-Archiv Berlin

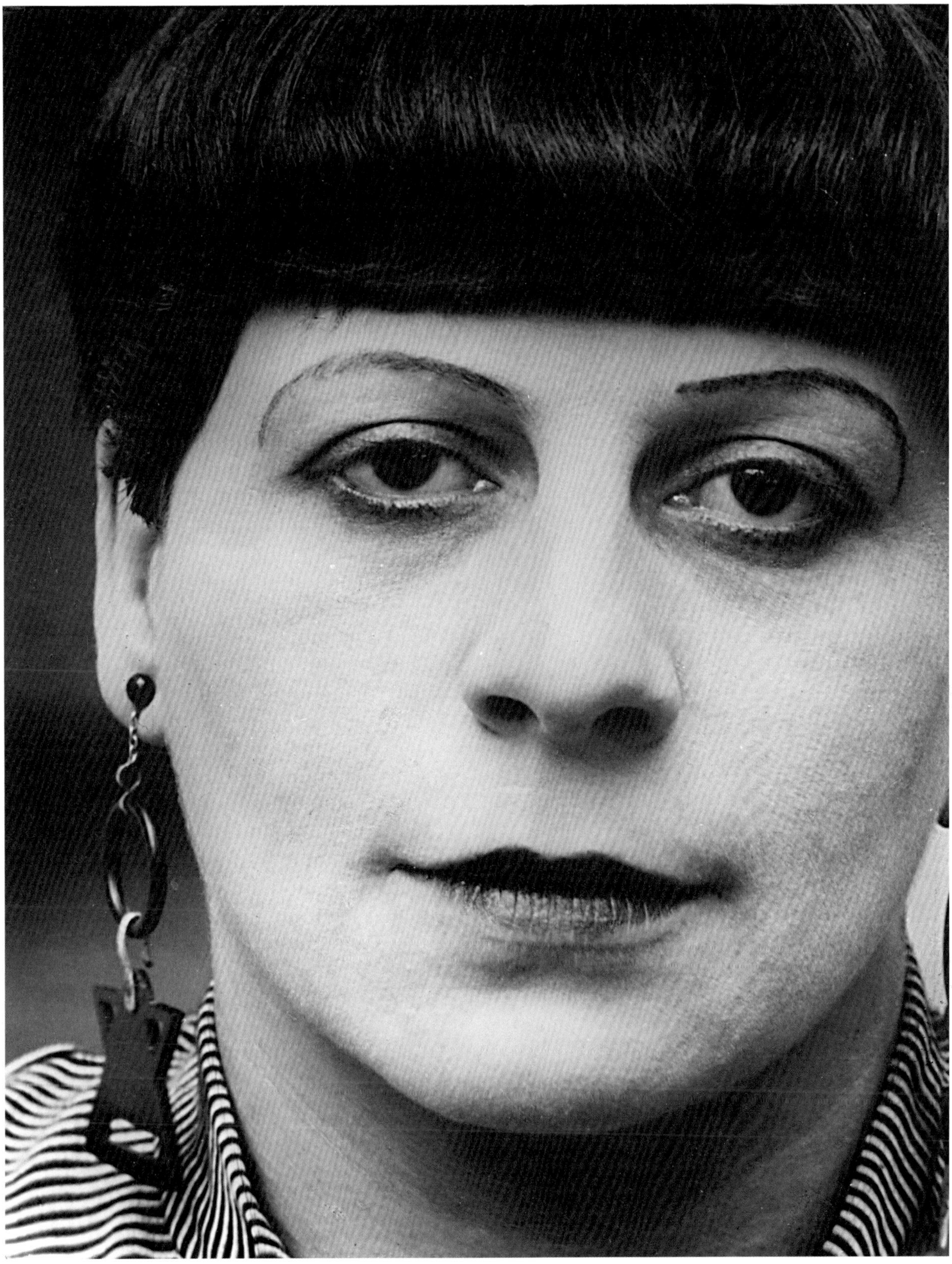

143
Josef Albers
Oskar Schlemmer, IV 1929; at Council of Master's, 1928;
Hans Wittwer, (Ernst) Kallai, Marianne Brandt,
preliminary course exhibition 1927–28;
Oskar and Tut, summer 1928, 1927–30
Gelatin silver prints, mounted on card
29.5 × 41.8 cm
The Josef and Anni Albers Foundation

Albers compiled a series of portraits of Bauhaus colleagues between 1929 and 1933. While the precise chronology of their creation and specific purpose is not known, the portraits, each comprised of informal photographs mounted on card of a uniform size, serve to capture the personalities of the individuals represented. The composition of each differs – the eleven images that Albers selected of Oskar Schlemmer cover a number of years of their friendship, while the twenty-two snapshots of Paul Klee, which were taken in close succession, are mounted side-by-side as though part of a filmstrip. The more intimate portrait of his wife Anni reclining in the sun is comprised of just two images taken from differing viewpoints. Five surprisingly intimate images of Gropius and Schifra Canaresi together in Ascona further show how Albers, through careful juxtaposition, creates portraits of considerable intensity and which as a group are indicative of the close and often intimate ties that existed between the individuals employed and associated with the Bauhaus. Albers first began to experiment with photography in early 1928 and the element of time and the potential of seriality – the creation of sequences of two or more images – are defining characteristics of his photography, as they were later to become of his painting and printmaking.

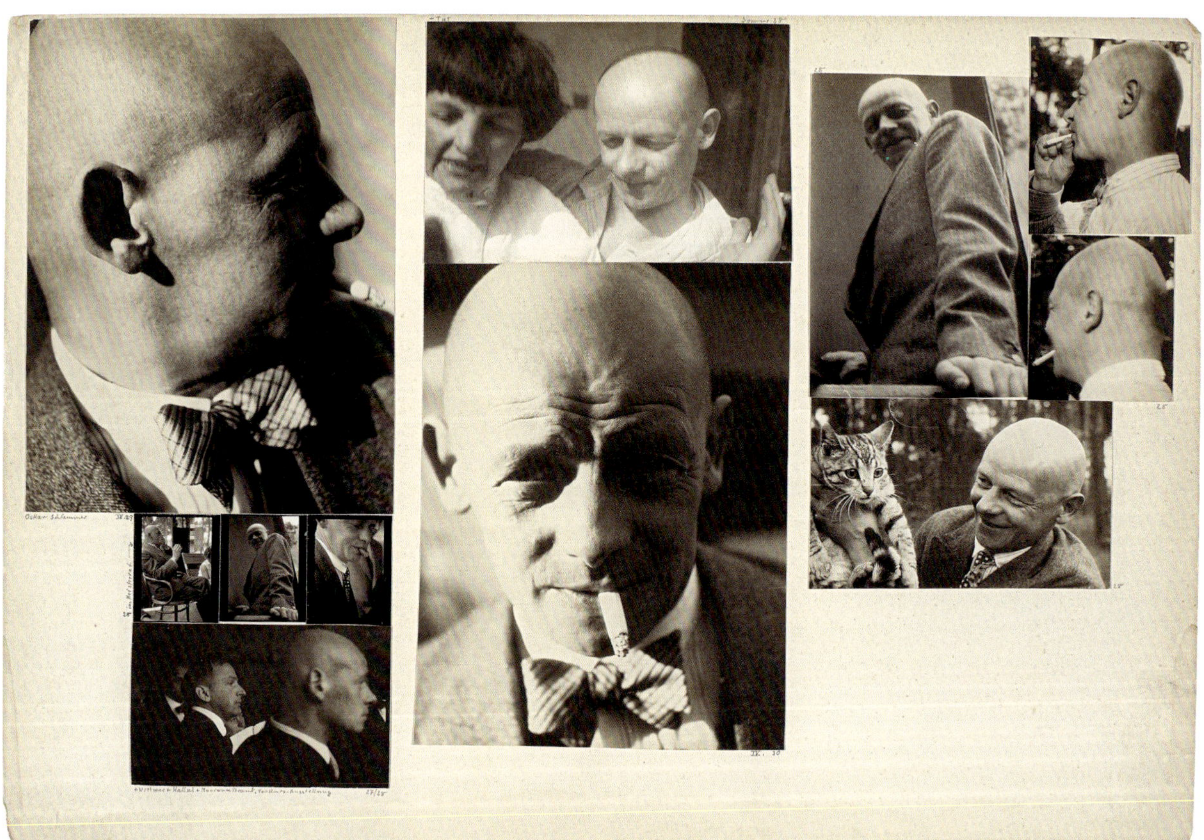

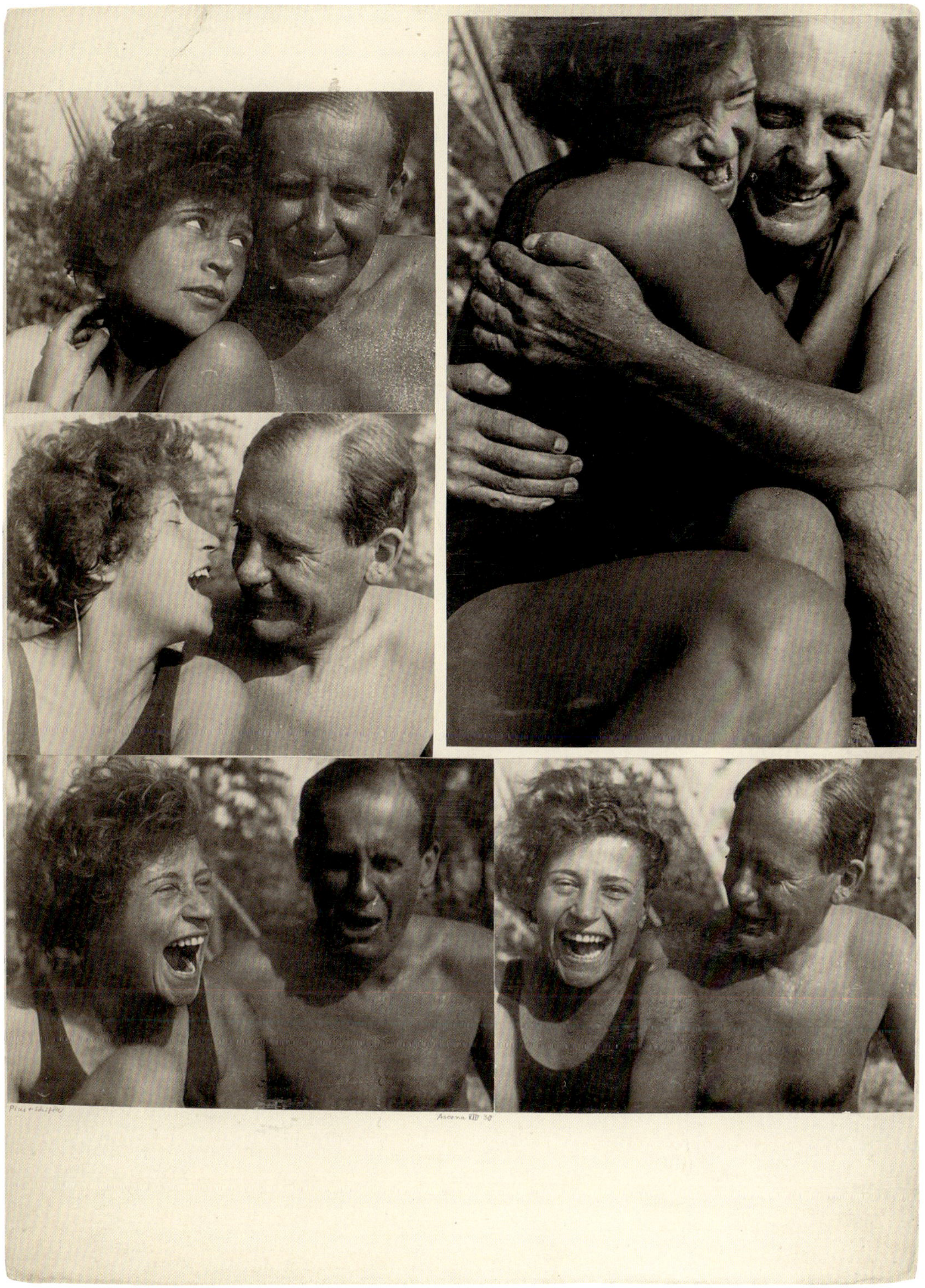

144
Josef Albers
Pius and Schifra, Ascona VIII 1930, 1930
Gelatin silver prints, mounted on card
41.8 × 29.5 cm
The Josef and Anni Albers Foundation

'square & flower: a new unity' bauhaus celebrations and bauhaus gifts

klaus weber

The Bauhaus was probably the only school ever to declare celebrating part of its curriculum. In his Bauhaus Programme of 1919, Walter Gropius expressly stated that amongst the goals of his new institute was 'the cultivation of friendly contacts between masters and students outside of work' and the 'establishment of a light-hearted ritual for these get-togethers'. From the very beginning, the objective had been to found not only a school, but also a community of people working and living together; not merely a pedagogical experiment but a social one as well. Thus events that would contribute to a sense of togetherness – such as 'theatre, lectures, poetry readings, music, and costume parties' – were encouraged. Students and teachers enthusiastically set about fulfilling this entertaining part of the Bauhaus Programme brief. 'Our Play, Our Party, Our Work' was the title given by Johannes Itten to his lecture of 1919. Felix Klee, who was the school's youngest student when he enrolled in the fall of 1921, fondly recalled the 'frenzy of pleasure' in Weimar: 'Every weekend at the Bauhaus there was a small party.'[1]

Bauhaus festivities are the stuff of legend. They began during the Weimar period with playful kite and lantern processions or with Dada-inspired performances, culminating in the magnificently staged Dessau carnival festivities such as the White Party or the Metal Party. There were external events like the *Neue Sachlichkeit* (*New Objectivity*) festival, which were organised together with friends at the arts and crafts school at Burg Giebichenstein in Halle. Also extra-territorial was the Beard Nose Heart Party organised by the Bauhaus band in Berlin in 1928. In 1925 the Last Dance had concluded the Weimar period, and the 1933 Carnival in Berlin would be the final Bauhaus festivity. With their elaborate decorations, spatial installations and fantastic costumes, accompanied by experimental theatre, music, dance and film, these events were always more than mere festivities. They constituted celebrations in the form of *Gesamtkunstwerke*, overall works of art. The repertoire of inspired silliness and whimsical inventions seems to have been inexhaustible.

Eyewitnesses of the day recounted the many sensations. Xanti Schawinsky, for example, reminisced about the spectacular stage appearances of Oskar Schlemmer at the Bauhaus festivities, as well as 'joost schmidt having a wrestling match with himself', nonsense proclamations such as 'square & flower: a new unity', which played upon Gropius's famous motto of 1923, Kurt Schwitters's guest appearance with his *Sonata in Primal Sounds*, and of course, Schawinsky's own 'jazz and step machine'.[2] The Hungarian Bauhausler Farkas Molnár emphasised as early as 1925 that the costumes at the Bauhaus festivities were 'always novel in design', adding that:

> There is nothing even remotely comparable that had ever been seen anywhere else ... Sometimes there were monsters towering storey-high, colourful, mechanical figures, where it is impossible to say where the head is. Darling girls in red cubes ... Kandinsky loved showing up as an antenna. Itten came as an amorphous monster, Feininger as two right-angled triangles, Moholy-Nagy as a segment pierced through by a cross, Gropius came as Le Corbusier, Muche as an unwashed apostle and Klee as the Song of the Blue Tree.[3]

A long slide beneath reflecting globes of glass, which allowed the guests at the Metal Party to glide along on rails, turned the Bauhaus building into a funfair attraction. The famous Bauhaus band, playing music that ranged from jazz to international folk, provided the turbulent sound-track to all of this, a 'fanatically rhythmical and penetrating din', according to its saxophonist Schawinsky: 'chairs, gunshots, hand bells, and giant tuning forks, sirens, and pianos prepared ... [with] any kind of tone-modifying materials supplemented the instrumental outfit'.[4]

There were always ample occasions for large and small celebrations: birthdays or weddings, the passing of examinations, greetings and farewells. The carnival in February was obligatory.

We also know of Christmas parties at the Bauhaus, at least in the early years. Felix Klee remembers that an improvised 'stepladder lent by the wall-painting workshop, with candles on cross-battens, served as a pseudo-Christmas tree'[5] and in 1920 Gropius read the Christmas story in front of a traditional backdrop, before distributing gifts to the people gathered there: 'A beautiful tree, lights and apples, a long white table, nicely laid and with big candles, a huge fir wreath, everything green. Beneath the tree everything in white, and upon this, countless gifts.'[6]

On mid-summer night in June 1921, for the first time there was a procession of fantastical paper lanterns illuminating the way through nocturnal Weimar, a 'swarm with the most diverse variations of geometric bodies and changing transparent colours'.[7] The kite festivals in September of the same year and the following one brought bizarre constructions to the Weimar streets, which were then flown in the sky above an open field: 'Two hundred flying objects in various colours and forms rise up in the air, held by a thin thread ... This is the joy of two hundred big and little children.'[8] The few photographs that remain, and the postcards printed for the kite and lantern festivals with images of wondrous lanterns and flying machines, at least give us a taste of these events.

But the absolute highlight in the festival calendar, and an annual occasion for a truly 'light-hearted ritual' was Gropius's birthday on 18 May. His wife Ise, describing one of these exuberant ceremonies in 1924, reports that:

> [Gropius] was showered with gifts from students and masters and celebrated with more spontaneity and enthusiasm than ever before ... Schlemmer conducted a huge choir in the most imaginative way, incredible caricatures of skyscrapers rose to the ceiling, each workshop brought its own gift and the masters presented him with a portfolio of paintings ... The band was in tremendous form and Walter was finally carried through the hall amidst deafening cheering.[9]

As Marianne Brandt adds of a similar event, sometimes 'the four bearers couldn't decide on the direction' [to take]'.[10] Of the many gifts from this triumphant birthday party, only that of the masters has been preserved: a portfolio containing six variations of a contemporary newspaper photograph by Lyonel Feininger, Wassily Kandinsky, Paul Klee, László Moholy-Nagy, Georg Muche and Schlemmer.[11] Schawinsky, always one of the main festival protagonists, tells of another birthday ritual for Gropius:

> ... on one of these stormy spring nights, we all showed up in front of his house, in a long retinue, each and every one of us outfitted with a huge angel-like halo and bearing a burning torch. summoned by the choir of angels, gropius came out to the terrace, puffing heavily on his cigar, and from out of the crowded semi-circle of torchbearers, andy's [Andor Weininger's] voice resounded: 'great chief, who guides us through the desert, we stand before you, you stand before us, we stand opposite each other. you are here, we are here as well. we are all here and there. the second hand of your clock of years has now advanced by another second, your wisdom has increased, o chief who leads this herd, you shepherd, you great daredevil! count on us, your grandchildren, your babies. We place our haloes upon the threshold of your forty-third year of life and suffering, ahoi! ahoi!' (amidst the wild cries of the torchbearers).[12]

No other Bauhausler was given so many gifts as often as the 'great chief', the first director. Whether this expressed esteem or venerations veiled in irony for 'Gropi' or 'Pius' is not altogether clear, however. Whatever the case, many of the presents given to him were too bulky or ephemeral to have survived – for example, the cannon for defending the Bauhaus, which he received in 1924, or the cactus made of cucumbers, its flowers fashioned from chocolate and cut radishes, that was presented to the cactus-fan Gropius as a gift in 1926. But photographs still exist to document the wild collection of objects placed on the gift table in his honour on 18 May 1926: among other things, a giant tin medal 'Pour le Mérite' for 'Pius I', a drawing of his horoscope, many paintings and collages (one of them four metres long), all kinds of workshop products, a paper ship as well as a little toy lorry, everything surrounded by rampant assemblages of wire, branches and scraps of material. Above it all we read: 'God bless handcraft.'

Some of the gifts shown on the photograph have been preserved by Gropius's estate. Fortunately, this also applies to a present handed over in the following year of 1927. Gropius even considered Herbert Bayer's spectacular collage for his forty-fourth birthday important enough to be displayed in the Bauhaus exhibition at The Museum of Modern Art, New York in 1938. This document is indeed unique, standing completely alone in the history of art. Known as *44 zärtlichkeiten in din* (44 displays of affection in German industrial standard format), it is an arrangement of numbered lip-prints of the Bauhaus teachers and students (fig.148). The forty-four colourful kisses for the director were sorted according to categories such as 'The Irresistibles', 'Norm sizes' or 'Beginners', the entire collage being foldable to a practical standard size. Among the oral expressions of fondness, either glued wildly inside, or arranged neatly in rows, a number of newspaper clippings were inserted, including one that read 'From Chaos to Design'.

When Gropius left the Bauhaus in March 1928, his farewell was also celebrated with a large party, though this time it would beyond a doubt have been tinged with melancholy. In a multimedia lecture staged for the occasion, Schlemmer presented a retrospective of the Gropius era. The parting gift was a monumental casket bearing the title 'The Bauhaus at 9. A Chronicle.' Once again, on twenty-one large-format panels, teachers and students unleashed their creative fireworks in Pius's honour, among them the charming self-portrait by Gunta Stölzl as a racing textile robot (fig.145) and Edmund Collein's famous photo-caricature of the overcrowded Prellerhaus (fig.149).

Of course, it was not only Gropius who was honoured in such ceremonies. Special birthday celebrations were organised for the other Bauhaus teachers. For instance, for Klee's fiftieth birthday in December 1929, his colleagues thought up a particularly spectacular way of handing over the present in Klee's house, thanks to the cooperation of the Dessau Junkers-Aircraft Factory. The artist himself reports, 'An aeroplane threw down gifts for me, breaking through the flat roof, the gifts landing in the middle of the studio.'[13] Precisely what these heavyweight packages contained is something we unfortunately do not learn.

Somewhat more modest were the gifts students gave to each other, or those that teachers gave to their students. In September 1930, for example, Stölzl designed individual 'honorary diplomas' for her weaving students, handing them out during a small costume party that is documented in photographs (fig.146). At least one of these diplomas has survived, bearing seven gold stars and with a colourful butterfly attached, for the recipient Margaret Leischner, who carefully kept it among her prized possessions over the years (fig.147).

Evidently there was not only a unique festival culture at the Bauhaus, but also a very special culture of gift-giving. Judging by the presents that have been preserved, they shared a character somewhere between art and amateur handcraft. Schawinsky defined such products in a decidedly objective way as having a 'collective or individually self-fabricated artistic or satirising tendency'.[14] The fact that there were real works of art among them is not surprising considering the creative potential at the Bauhaus itself. But even where the artistic value falls short of the entertainment level, it is precisely the improvised, episodic nature of such presents, with their spontaneous joy of creation, their humour, and their immediacy that provides authentic insight into life at the Bauhaus. A decisive role was played by the collage technique in all of this. It was through combining fragments of images and texts that one could unleash one's instinct to play, and where the most astonishing relationships of sense or nonsense could be developed. Added to this was the montage of diverse materials such as wood, fabrics, or metal foils, with which the students had become familiar from their texture studies with Johannes Itten or Moholy. What is striking is a revealing tendency towards elements that demonstratively contradict the purist aesthetics of the Bauhaus – this perhaps being a subliminal compensation for the prevailing dogma of sobriety and lack of adornment. Often we find lace papers, colourful decals, paper flowers, glitter and shiny foils, old-fashioned decorations such as little angels, sentimental landscapes and other elements from the realm of kitsch.

A surprisingly substantial number of the Bauhaus gifts have come down to us, the majority of which are in the collection of the Bauhaus-Archiv Berlin.[15] But at the time they were made, their creators will hardly have considered the possibility that their products would be kept, let alone become carefully preserved museum objects. After all, they had been made 'only for the moment, not for decades', as 'pure fun and nothing else'.[16]

1 Felix Klee, 'Meine Erinnerungen an das Bauhaus Weimar' in Eckhard Neumann (ed.), *Bauhaus und Bauhäusler*, DuMont, Cologne, 1985, p.82. Engl. trans., 'My Memories of the Weimar Bauhaus', in Eckhard Neumann (ed.), *Bauhaus and Bauhaus People*, Van Nostrand Reinhold, New York, 1985, p.42.

2 Xanti Schawinsky, 'bauhaus metamorphis', in ibid., pp.158–59.

3 Farkas Molnár, 'Das Leben im Bauhaus', in Periszkop, vol.1, 1925, no.4, quoted in *Wechselwirkungen, Ungarische Avantgarde in der Weimarer Republik*, Jonas-Verlag, Kassel, 1986, p.274.

4 Xanti Schawinsky, 'bauhaus metamorphosis', op. cit., p.157.

5 Felix Klee, 'My Memories of the Weimar Bauhaus'', op. cit., p.43.

6 Lis Abegg to Gunta Stölzl, 27 December 1920. Transcript in the Bauhaus-Archiv Berlin.

7 Farkas Molnár, 'Das Leben im Bauhaus', op. cit., p.273.

8 Ibid., p.272.

9 Ise Gropius to Manon Gropius, June 1924, Bauhaus-Archiv Berlin.

10 Marianne Brandt, 'Letter to the younger generation', in Neumann *Bauhaus and Bauhaus People*, op. cit., p.109.

11 Peter Hahn, 'A Cheerful Moment: The Gropius-Portfolio of May 18, 1924', in *Bauhaus: A Conceptual Model*, exhibition catalogue, Hatje, Cantz, Ostfildern, 2009, pp.171–76.

12 Xanti Schawinsky, unpublished autobiographical typescript, Bauhaus-Archiv Berlin, pp.126–27.

13 Quoted in Wulf Herzogenrath (ed.), *Paul Klee. Lehrer am Bauhaus*, exhibition catalogue, Kunsthalle Bremen, 2003, p.246. See also Nicholas Fox Weber, *The Bauhaus Group: Six Masters of Modernism,* Knopf, New York, pp. xiv–xvi and 196.

14 Schawinsky, unpublished autobiographical typescript, op. cit., p.126.

15 Klaus Weber (ed.), *Happy Birthday! Bauhaus-Geschenke*, exhibition catalogue, Bauhaus-Archiv Berlin, 2004.

16 Helene Schmidt-Nonne, 'Ein Geburtstagsgeschenk zum 18. Mai 1926 für Walter Gropius', in TM/communication 5, 1973, Bauhaus-Archiv Berlin.

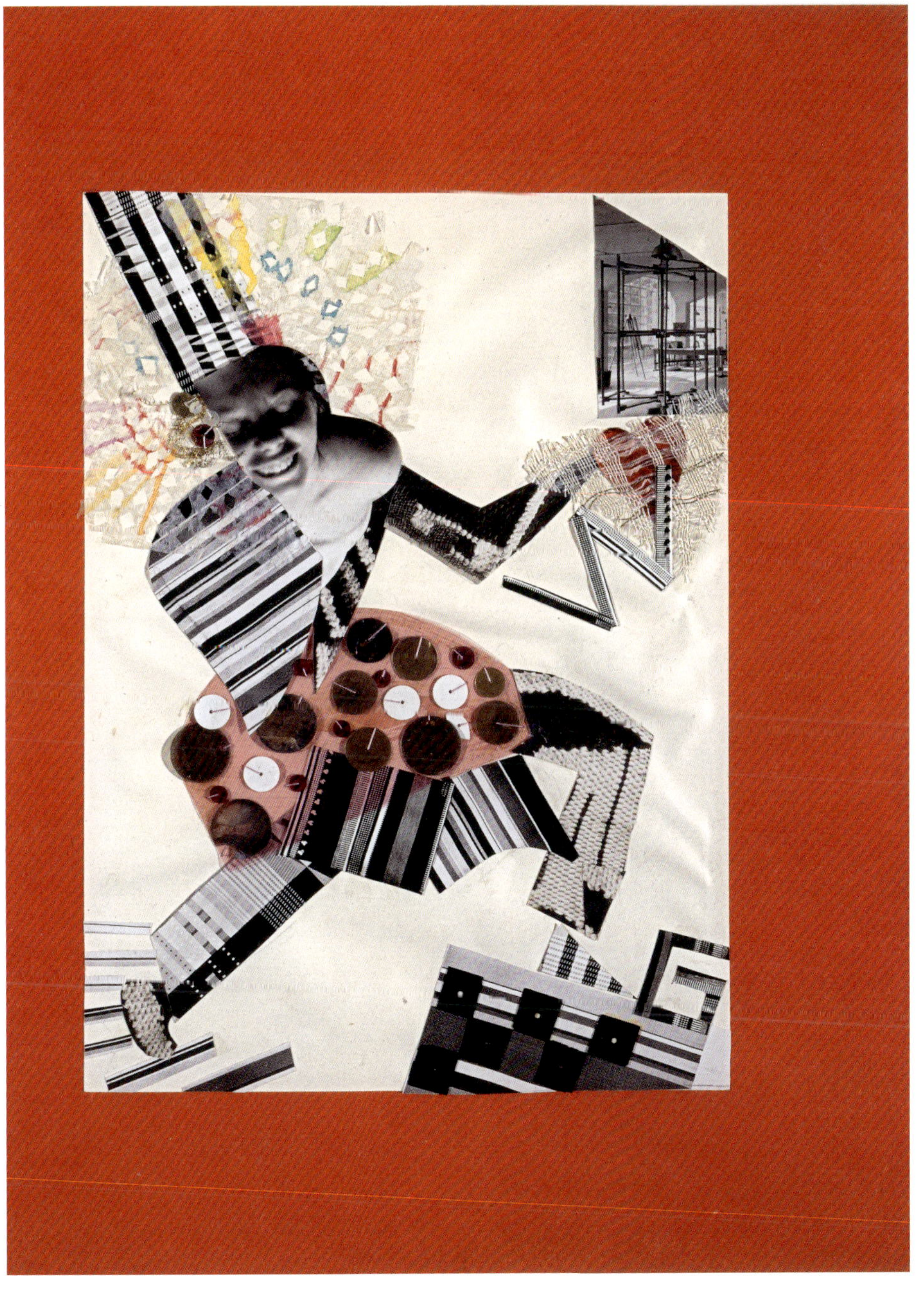

145
Gunta Stölzl
Self-portrait, 1928
Collage, mounted on card
29.5 × 21 cm
Bauhaus-Archiv Berlin

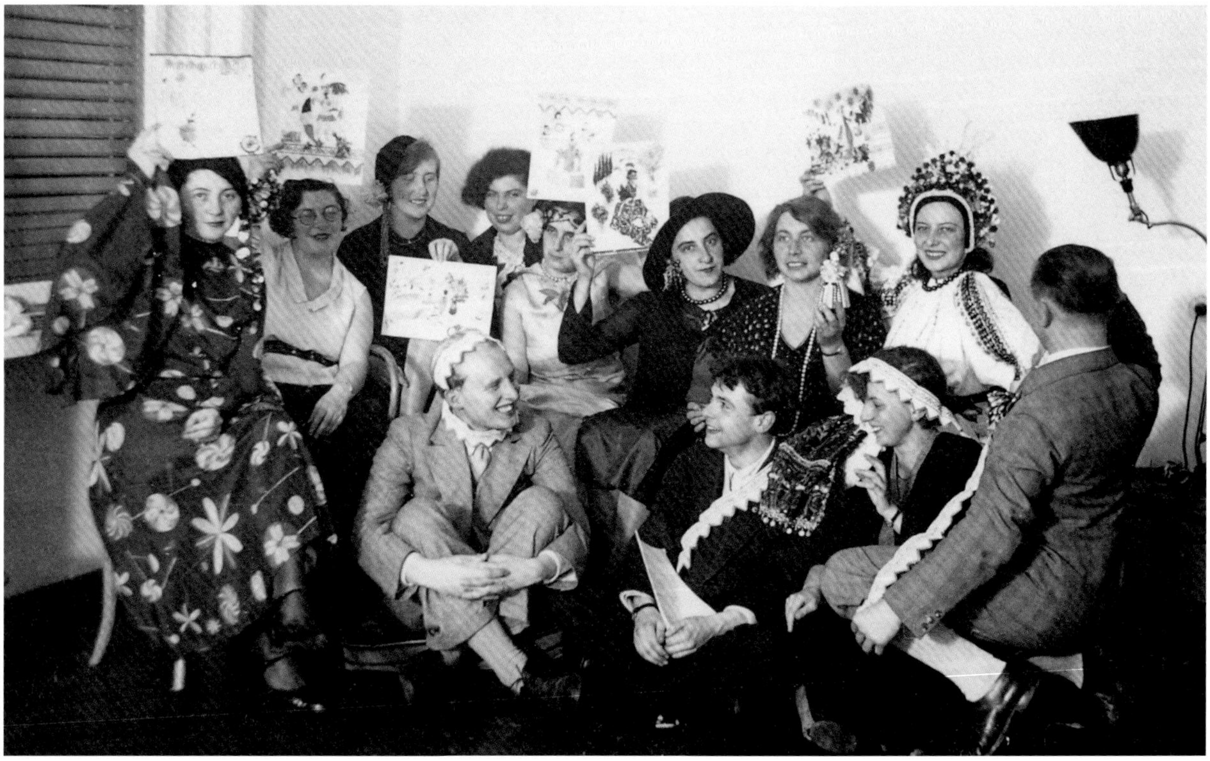

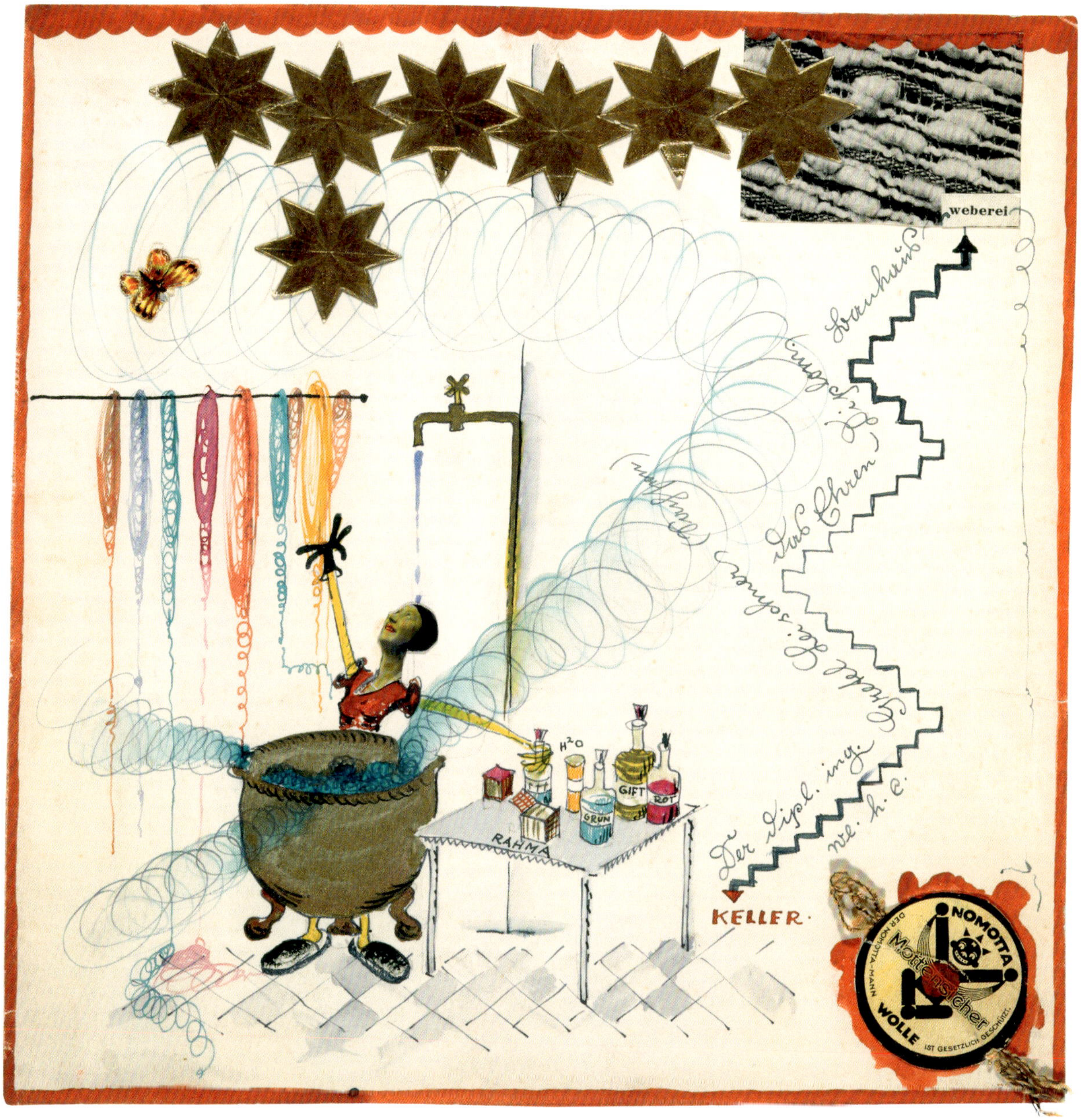

146
Gertrud Arndt
Celebration of the first diplomas in the weaving workshop, September 1930
Gelatin silver print, mounted on card
27.8 × 18.9 cm
Bauhaus-Archiv Berlin

147
Gunta Stölzl
Honorary diploma for Margaret Leischner, 1930
Collage, body colour and ink on paper
24.8 × 24 cm
Bauhaus-Archiv Berlin

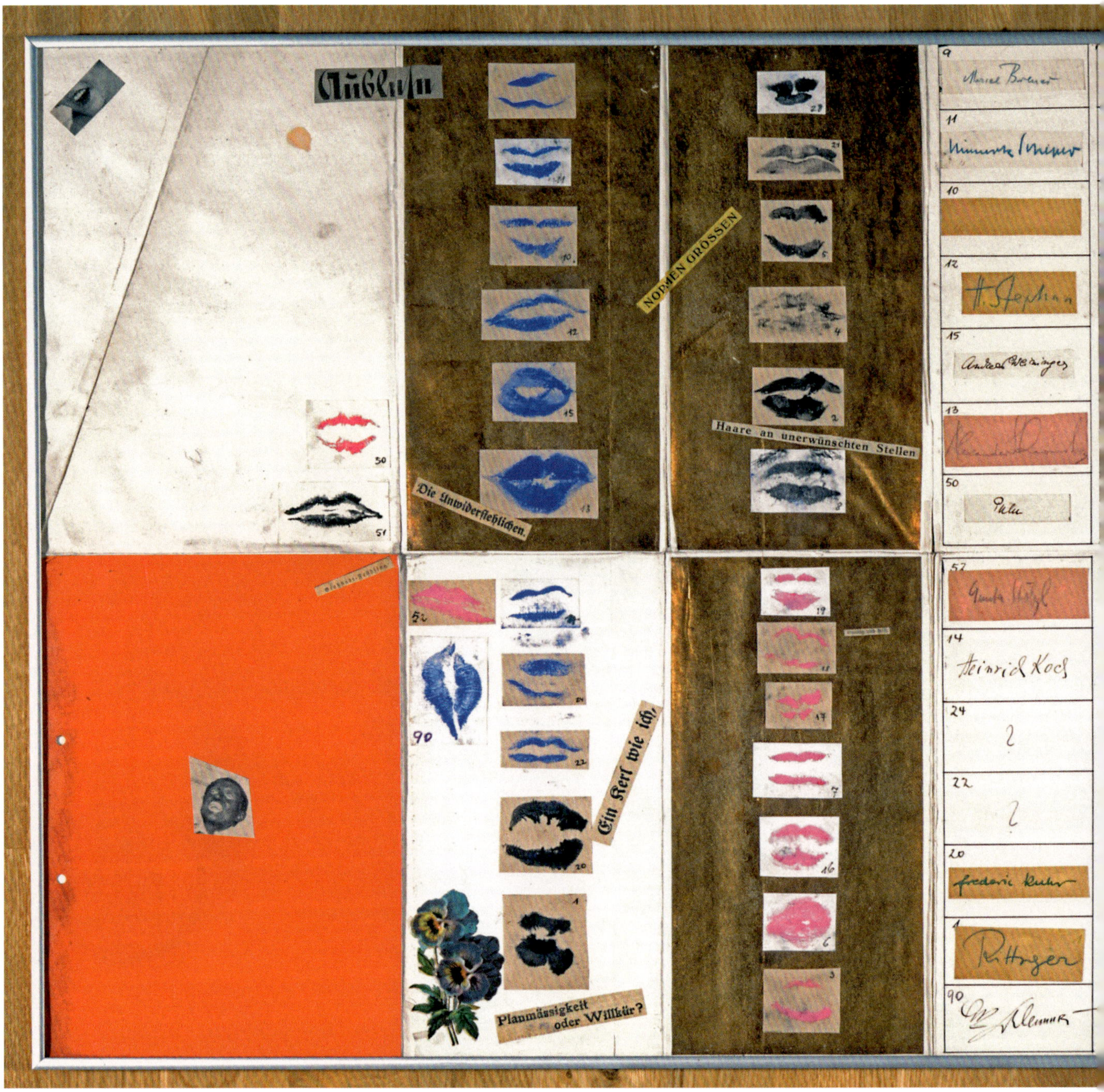

148
Herbert Bayer
Prospekt: der mund. 44 zärtlichkeiten in DIN (*Prospectus: the mouth. 44 caresses in DIN*), gift from teachers and students of the Bauhaus for Walter Gropius's 44th birthday, 18th May 1927
Collage on paper
59 × 125.5 cm
Bauhaus-Archiv Berlin

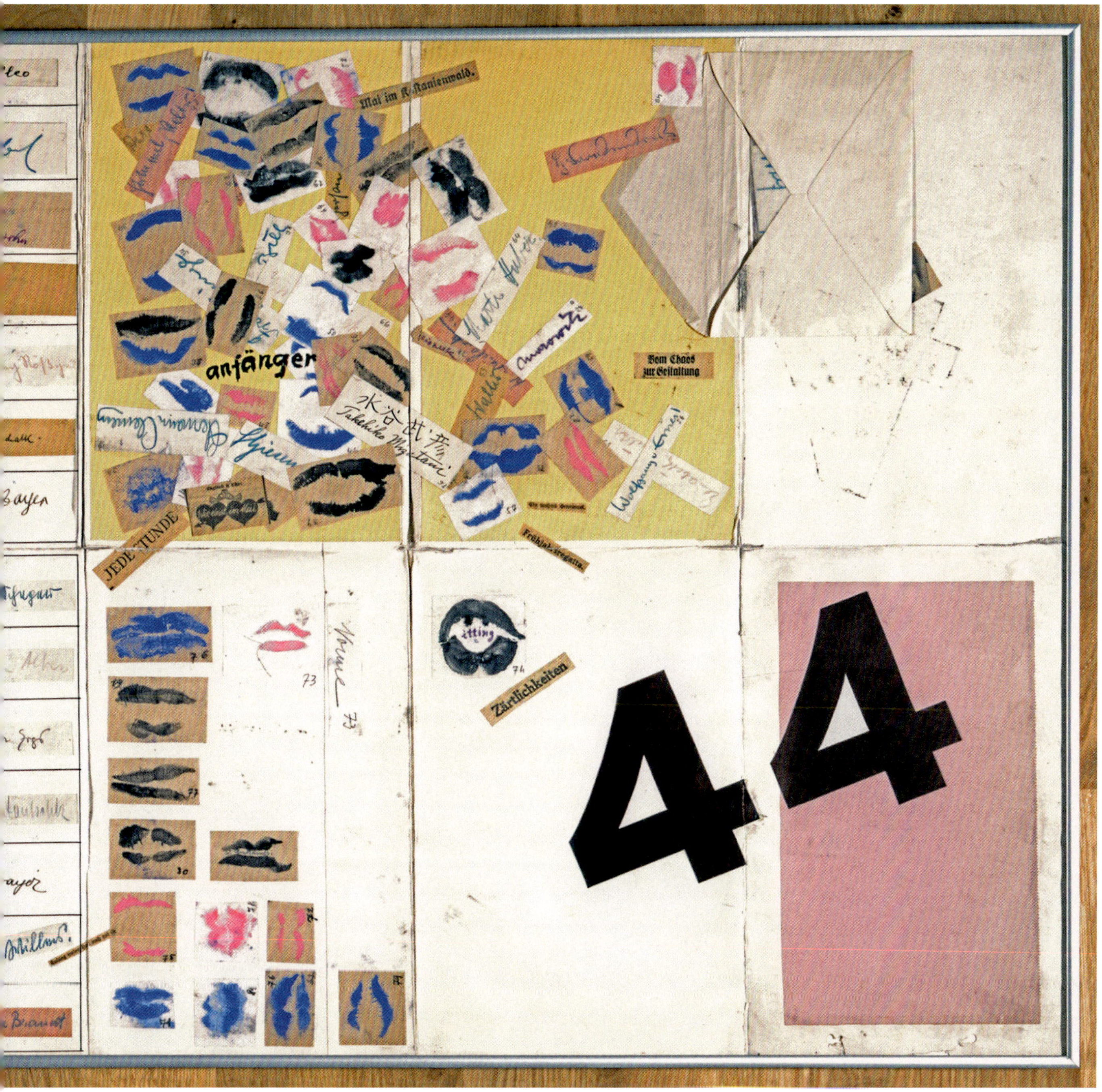

Mai im Kastanienwald.
anfänger
水谷武彦
Takehiko Mizutani
Vom Chaos zur Gestaltung
JEDE STUNDE
Frühlingsregatta
Zärtlichkeiten
44

149
Edmund Collein
Extension to the Prellerhaus,
from 9 *Jahre Bauhaus: Eine Chronik*
(9 *years Bauhaus: A Chronicle*), 1928
Photocollage with handwritten
stickers on paper
41.5 × 55 cm
Bauhaus-Archiv Berlin

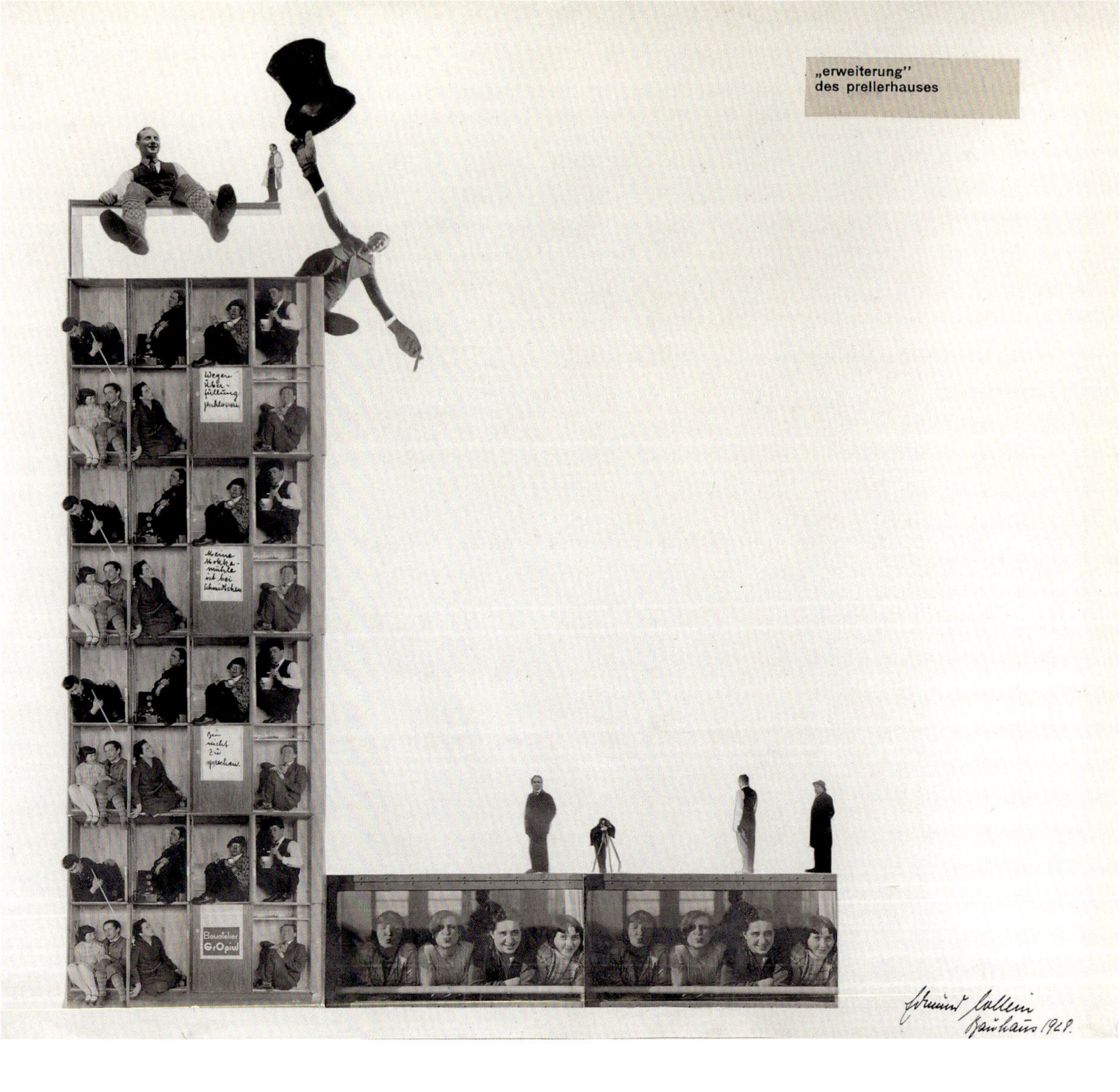

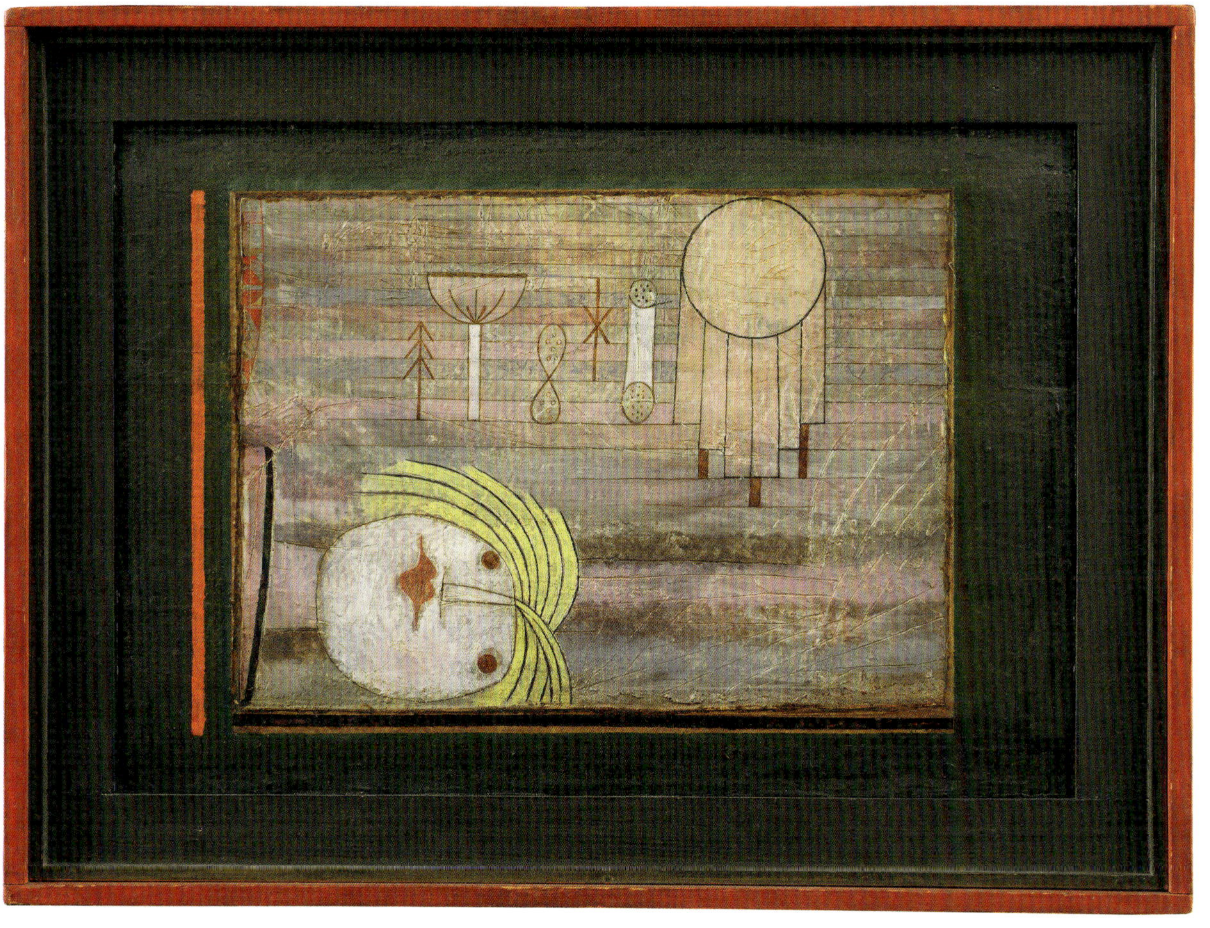

150
Paul Klee
Gifts for J, 1928
Oil, ink and gesso on canvas,
mounted on wood
40 × 55.9 cm
The Museum of Modern Art, New York
Gift of James Thrall Soby 1970

Klee's highly personal painting reflects the spirit of the school and the reverence of the students towards their master. In a manner fitting for a mystical, other-worldly man, students from the weaving workshop, including Anni Albers, hired a local Junkers aircraft and dropped gifts, wrapped in a package decorated like an angel, over the master's house on the occasion of his fiftieth birthday. Supposedly, the presents included a lamp made by Marianne Brandt, a print made by Lyonel Feininger and other objects from the cabinetry workshop.

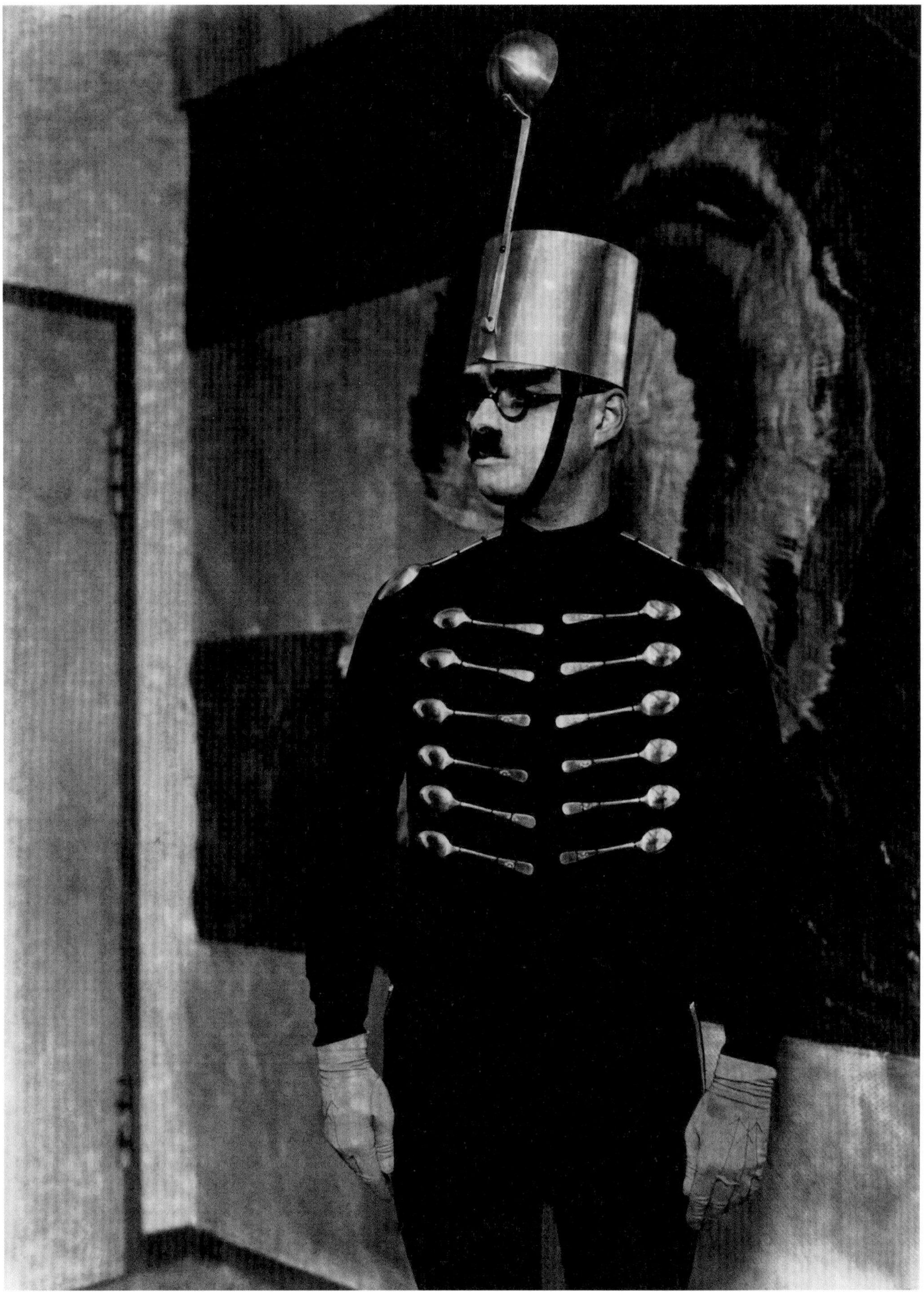

151
Nonsense Soldier, 1929
Bauhaus-Archiv Berlin
Photographer unknown

152
Attributed to Irene or Herbert Bayer
Neue Sachlichkeit Party, 1925
Gelatin silver print
13.9 × 8.8
Bauhaus-Archiv Berlin

Johannes Itten
our play, our party, our work

Play becomes celebration; celebration becomes work; work becomes play.
Our play should become work; our work, a celebration; and our celebration, play. I regard this as the supreme excellence of the human tasks.

Excerpt from a letter to Anna Höllering recounting his lecture to his students, Weimar, 15 December 1919

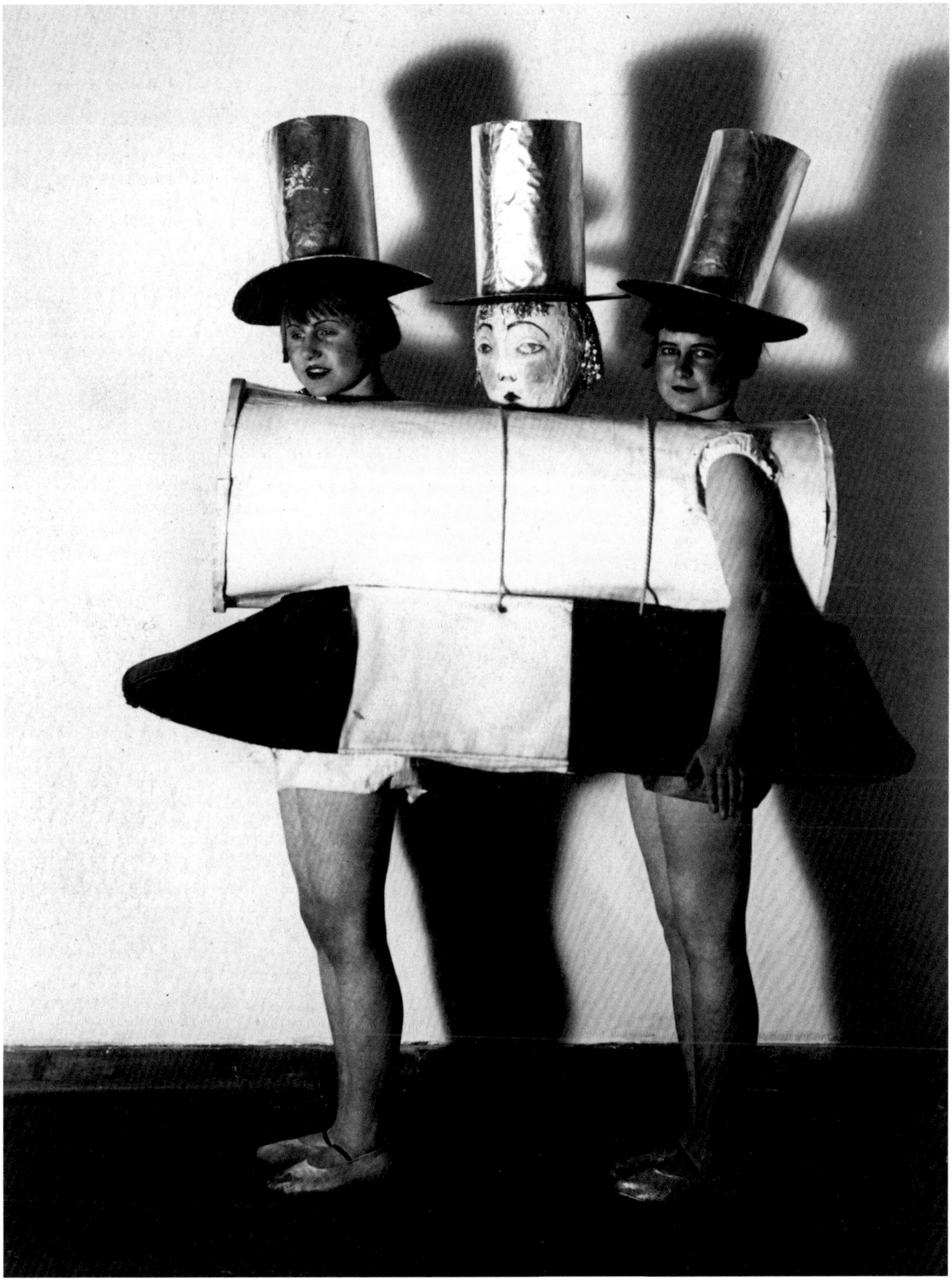

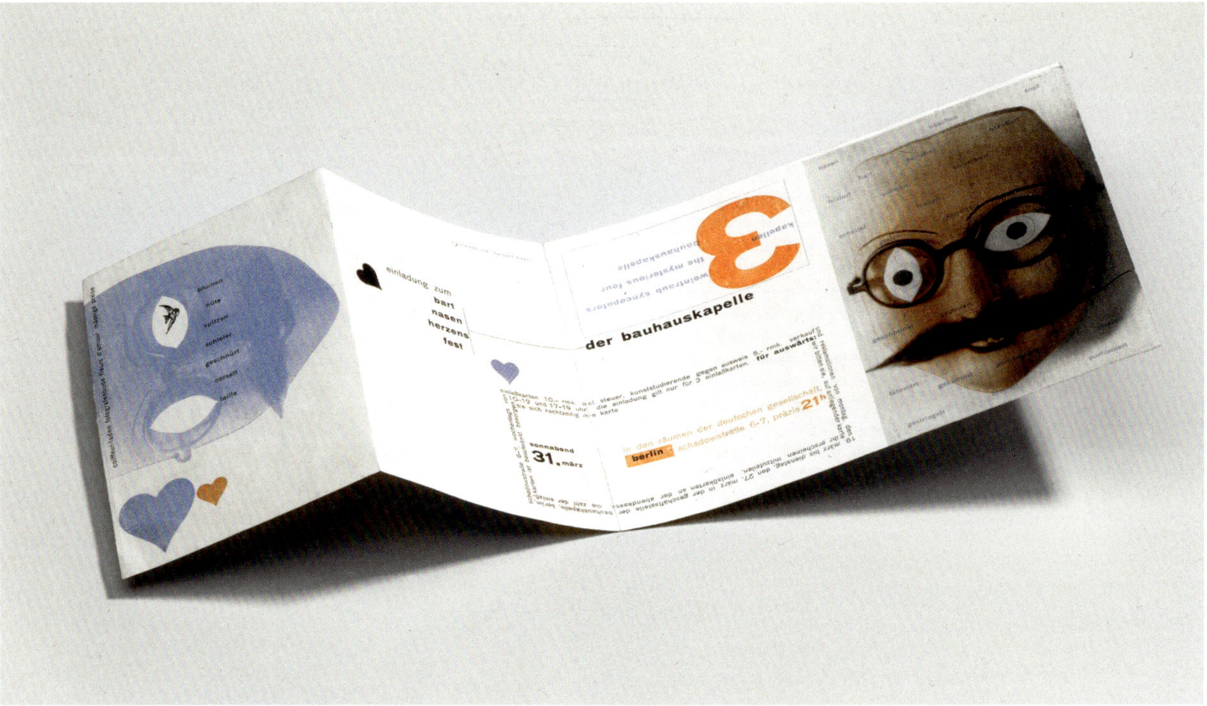

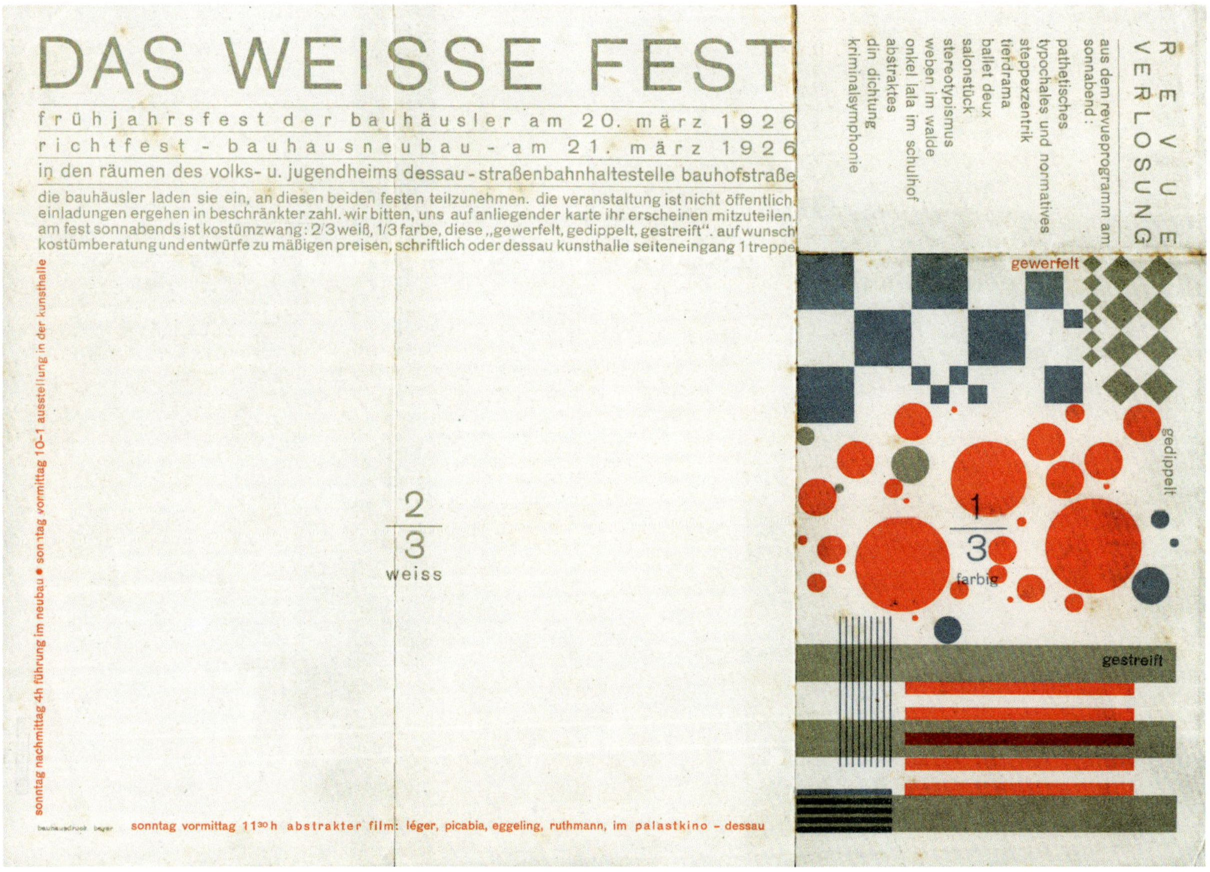

176

153
Herbert Bayer
Invitation to the Bauhaus band's Beard Nose Heart Party, 1928
Letterpress on paper
14.8 × 31.8 cm
Bauhaus-Archiv Berlin

154
Herbert Bayer
Invitation to the White Party, 1926
Letterpress on paper
20.9 × 28.8 cm
Bauhaus-Archiv Berlin

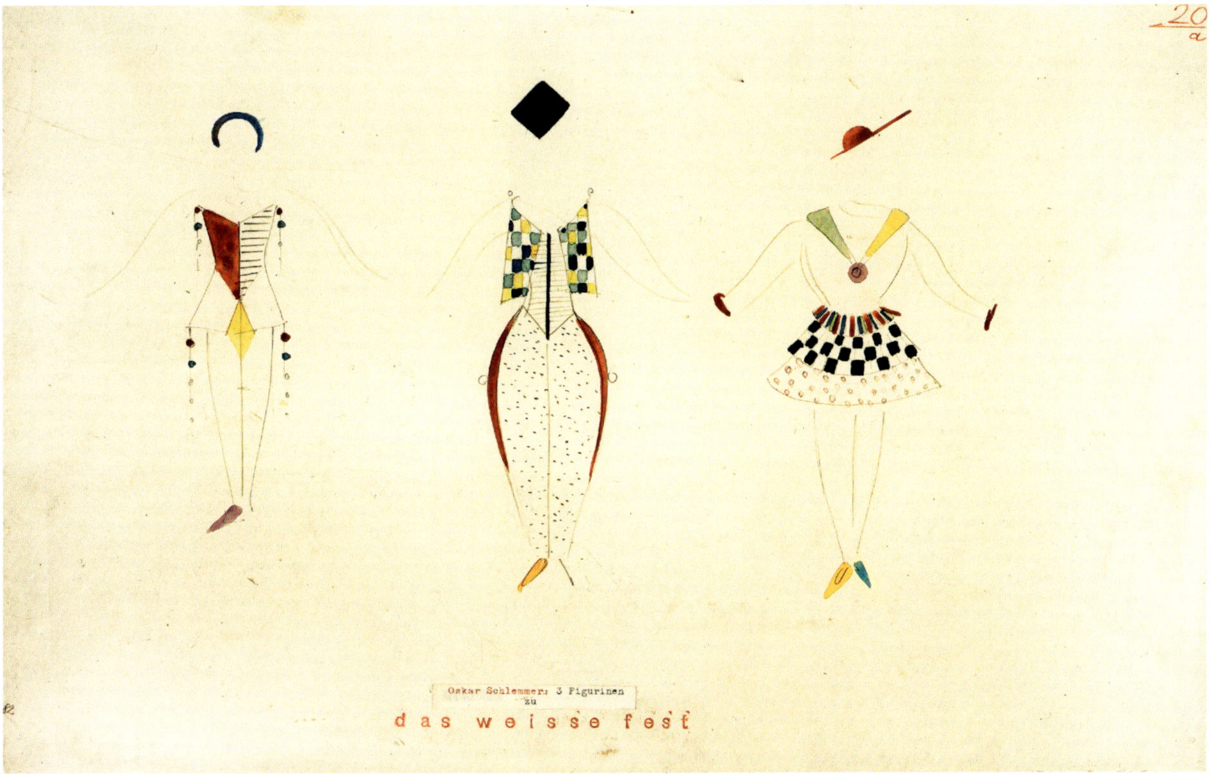

155
Oskar Schlemmer
Drei Figurinen zu das weisse Fest (*The White Festival, Three Figurines*), 1926
Watercolour and pencil
32.1 × 49.8 cm
Bühnen Archiv Oskar Schlemmer/
The Oskar Schlemmer Theatre Estate,
Collection UJS

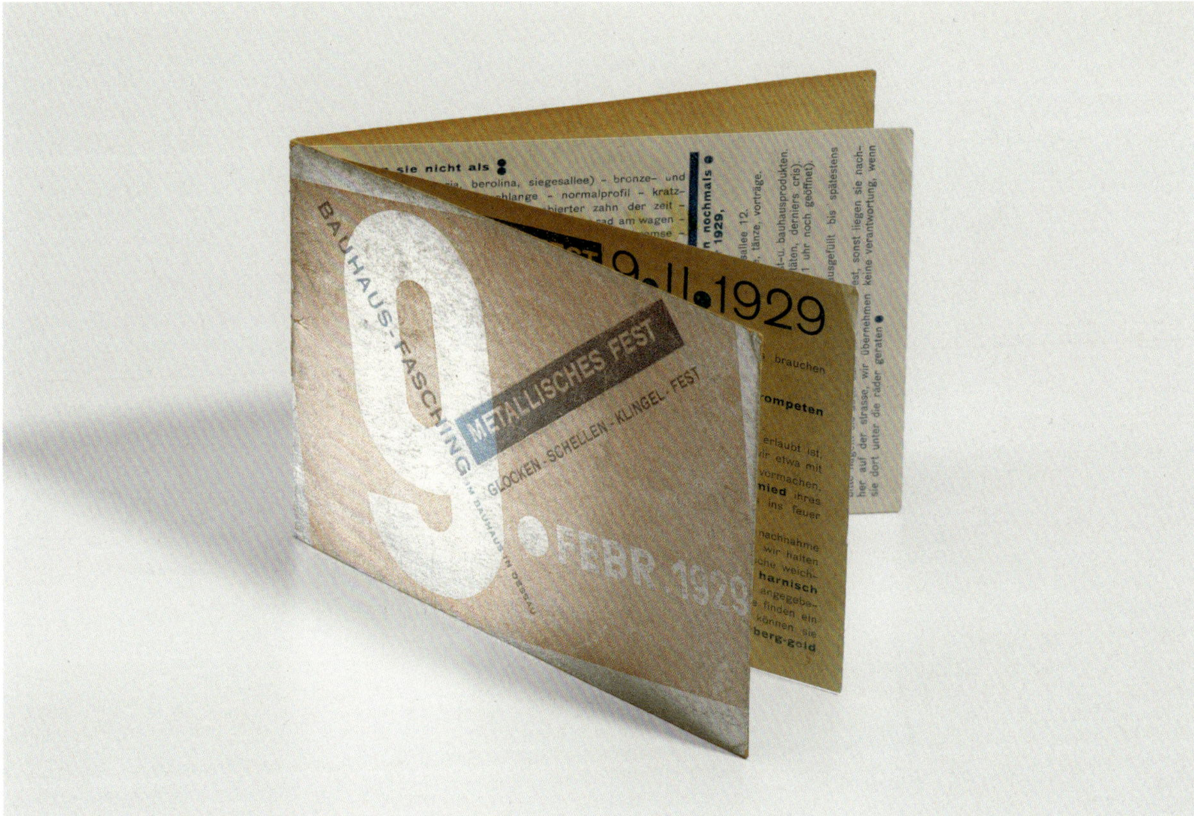

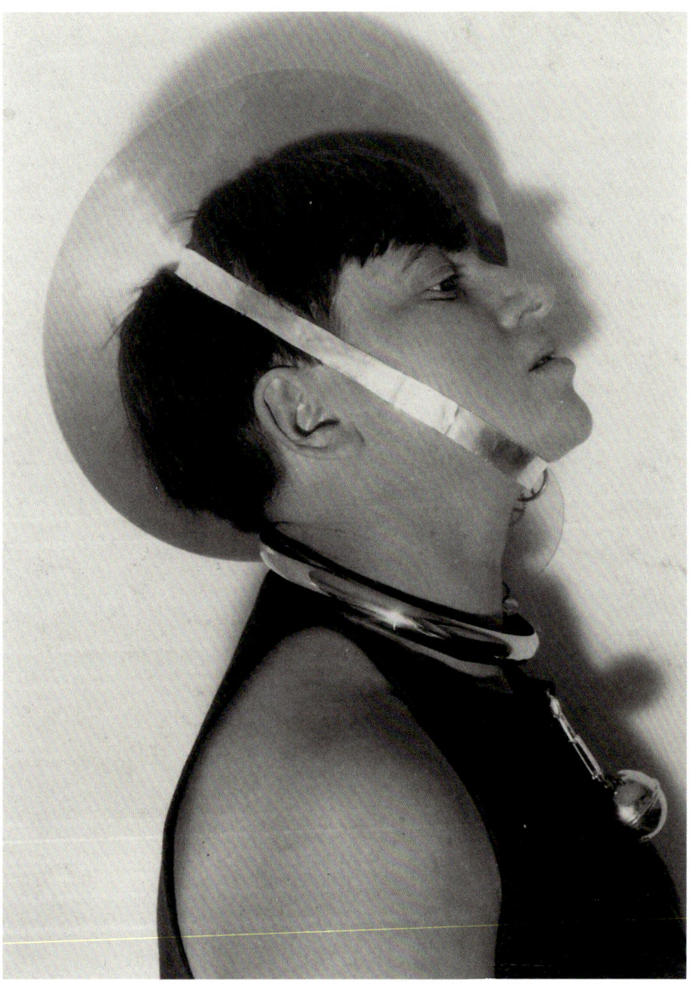

156
Johannes Niegemann
Invitation to the Metal Party, 1929
Letterpress on layered silver card
10.7 × 14.8 cm
Bauhaus-Archiv Berlin

157
Marianne Brandt
Self-portrait dressed for the Metal Party, 1929
Gelatin silver print
19.7 × 13.7 cm
Bauhaus-Archiv Berlin

158
Walter Funkat
Glass spheres (self-portrait in the Bauhaus vestibule, reflected in a sphere used to decorate the Metal Party), 1929 (printed 1986)
Gelatin silver print
23.7 × 17.7 cm
Bauhaus-Archiv Berlin

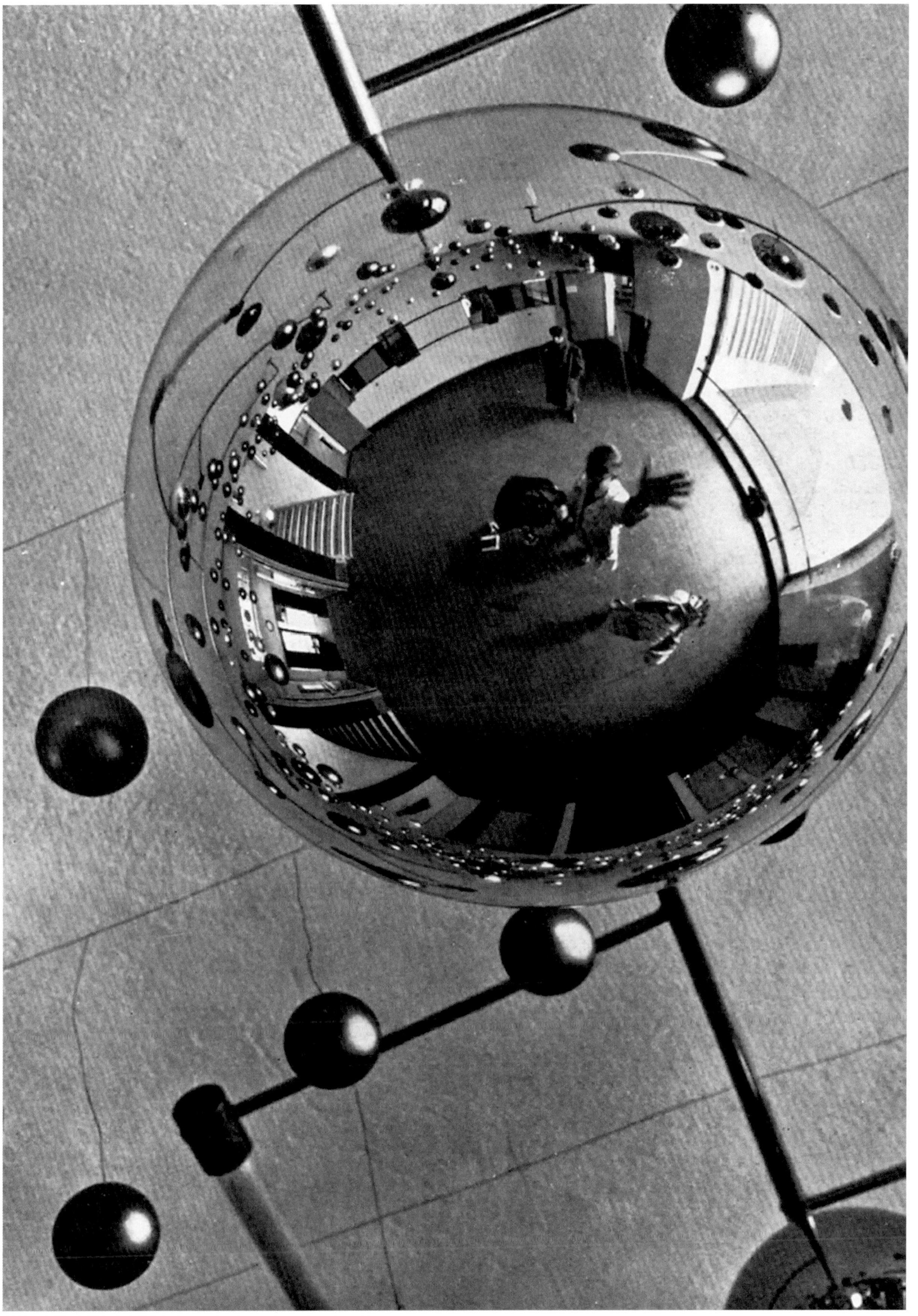

179

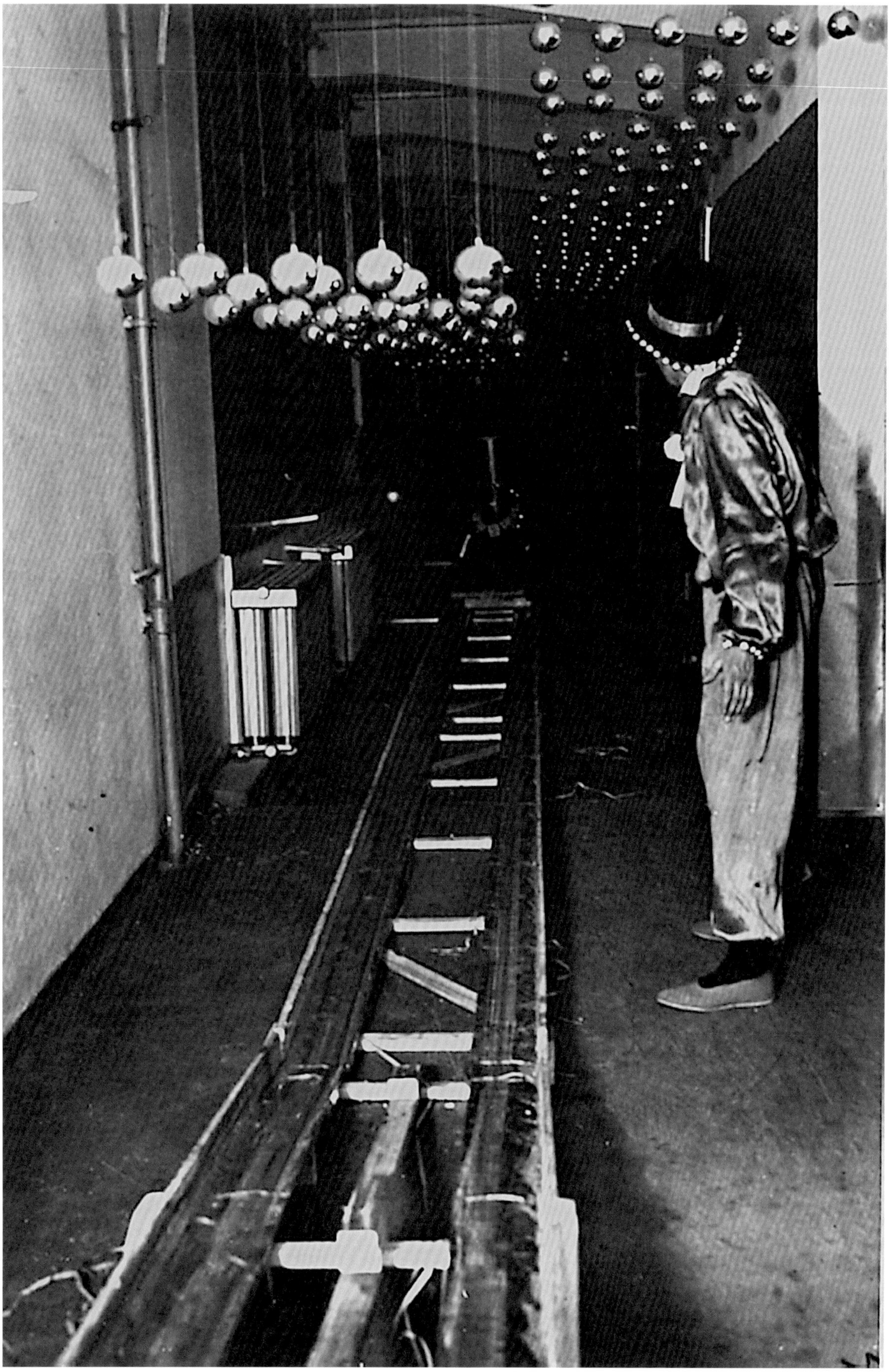

159
Robert Binnemann
Slide to the Metal Party at
the Bauhaus, Dessau, 1929
Designed by Xanti Schawinsky
Bauhaus-Archiv Berlin

author unknown
'something metallic': bauhaus celebration

With an elegant metal-coloured card, printed with the usual lower-case Bauhaus type, the Dessau Bauhaus and the circle of its friends issued invitations to a Metallic Festival. Metal is hard. But it is also sparkling and shiny. The festival last Saturday night proved to possess the latter qualities of metal ... The party sparkled and shone, and yet was of such friendly gaiety and merriment, without ever getting out of hand in any way, that all participants enjoyed it thoroughly. The entrance to the gaily decorated rooms was really ingenious. One entered the party via a chute that was built down from the connecting hallway between the two Bauhaus buildings. Here, even the most dignified personalities could be observed gliding down into the festive rooms, welcomed by the tinkling of bells and a big flourish played by a live four-piece village band which meant well but sounded terrible.... And then there was music in the air everywhere, and everything was aglitter wherever one turned. The rooms and studios of two floors, which normally are used for serious work, had been decorated with the greatest variety of forms placed together all over the walls, shinily metallic and fairy-like, the ceilings hung with bizarre paper configurations.... In addition music, bells, tinkling cymbals everywhere, in every room, in the stairways, wherever one went....

The government of Anhalt was represented by Prime Minister Deist and State Minister Dr Weber, and the city of Dessau by Mayor Hesse ... But the visitors did not come from Dessau alone. Many had come from Berlin, Leipzig, Halle, and other places. Most of them in metallic costumes. Rarely has Dessau seen such a great number of really original and magnificent costumes ... And wherever an evening suit did appear, it had at least some kind of metal decoration pinned on the lapels.

Thus the brilliance of sparkling lights and the music of happy dance tunes created a gay and colourful image: the chute, loved by young and old, the shooting gallery where the little man and his lady could test their marksmanship, the amusing laughing gallery, the champagne corners, and particularly the different rooms where the guests danced to the tune of some excellent bands – the Bauhaus's own band walking off with the prize. The performances in the lecture hall ... found an enthusiastic audience. A gay farrago of film pictures alternated with various stage presentations... An entertainer told amusing stories ... So everyone had great fun and enjoyed the party, and it was late when the first guests began to think about facing the piercing cold, which made the way home particularly unpleasant that night ...

From the newspaper Anhalter Anzeiger Dessau, *12 February, 1929*

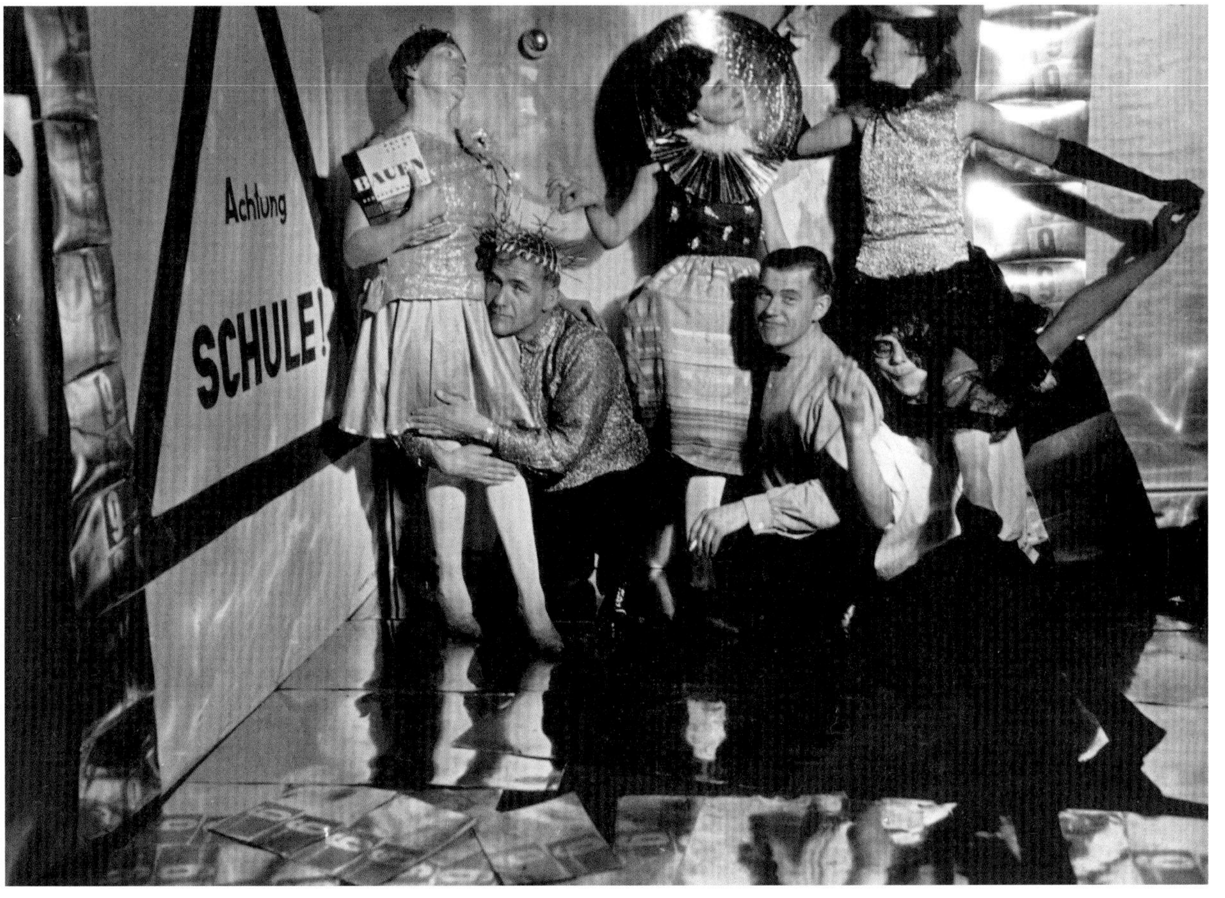

160
Attributed to Walter Funkat
Bauhausler at the Metal Party, 1929
Gelatin silver print
8.2 × 11.3 cm
Bauhaus-Archiv Berlin

161
Attributed to Marianne Brandt or Heinz Loew
Party meal at Bauhaus, Dessau, c.1927–28
Bauhaus-Archiv Berlin

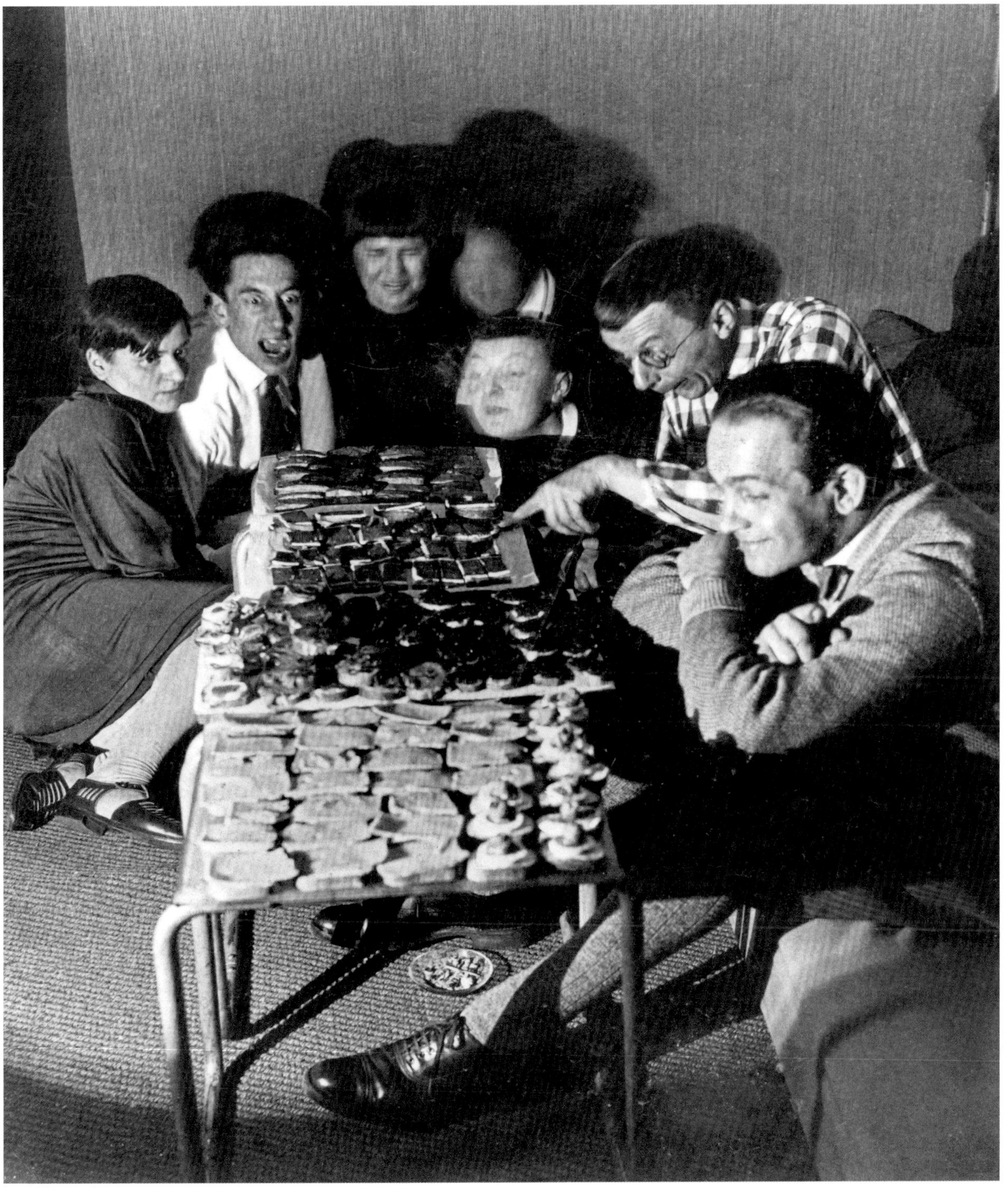

in the bauhaus kitchen

nicholas fox weber

When picturing the white surfaces and functional forms inside the Bauhaus, most people do not imagine the pervasive smell of garlic. But from 1919 to 1922, it was everywhere among the large group of students and faculty in Weimar: sweating out of their pores, on their clothes, in the air. Alma Mahler, wife of the school's founding director Walter Gropius, found it intolerable. When Anni Albers's uncles came from Berlin, they laughed about it. And it became a serious matter in school politics.

A faction of the students and faculty led by Johannes Itten adhered to the Mazdaznan doctrine – a way of life in accord with the teaching of Zoroaster, a Persian prophet born in 628 B.C., who viewed the universe as a cosmic struggle between *aša* (truth) and *druj* (lie). The goal of life was to sustain *aša* through good thoughts, words and proscribed activities. The adherents of Mazdaism at the Bauhaus not only followed their many rules rigorously, but condemned the violation of these rules by others. One of their requirements was vegetarianism.

Initially, Gropius extolled the health benefits of the regime. At this time, it was only his wife who recoiled from the redolent odour of garlic, cabbage, sprouts and other vegetables. Mahler, who had a sensitive gallbladder, refused to try 'the obligatory diet of uncooked mush smothered in garlic' for fear of a bilious attack,[1] and she was fond of pointing out to people that Itten himself often suffered from such attacks.

Many other people at the school objected to the rigorous rules of behaviour, which they felt encouraged a false sense of virtue. Paul Klee was troubled by Itten's role of holy figure, as leader of the Mazdaist sect. Klee was particularly critical of the sect's divisiveness, and the spell it cast over the entire school; Mazdaist rules, mainly those concerning food and diet, split the student body and faculty into two groups. In the spring and summer, the devotees of Zoroaster underwent major fasts that began with the taking of a powerful laxative. They would subsequently fast for as long as three weeks, consuming nothing but hot fruit juice. During these periods, they would repair to an orchard that the sect owned on a hill on the outskirts of Weimar, and there they would sing piously and tend the land surrounding their raspberry bushes and fruit trees. They also took ritual baths, piping hot, in the public bathhouse in Weimar and then rubbed themselves with ashes or charcoal. Their objective was to purify their outsides just as they had purified their insides through the fasting and laxatives. They even used a needle machine to puncture their skins before having their bodies rubbed with the same oil they had taken as a laxative. This was said to draw the impurities (what we would call 'toxins' today) out of the blood, causing the pinpoints in the skin to turn into pustules, which would be bandaged. The believers then exercised strenuously to induce a heavy sweat so that the ulcerations would heal, a process that often caused them to itch horribly for months.

In 1922, Itten managed to persuade the Bauhaus kitchen to follow Mazdaist rules for a while. He pushed to have all Bauhaus students adhere to the sect's practices, but Gropius opposed him. Everyone at the Bauhaus had to take a side, and Gropius finally prevailed, with the Council of Masters taking action so that Itten was required to confine himself mainly to teaching; he subsequently left the school. For the majority of Bauhauslers, the idea that a specific set of dos and don'ts, in the kitchen as in one's personal habits, could confer spiritual goodness was unacceptable. Food, like everything else, was considered an area of life that should be governed by principles of freedom, intelligence and a certain lightness of attitude that acknowledged the importance of pleasure. Food and the kitchen, furthermore, were central points of interest at the school, both because of their significance in and of themselves, and as a metaphor. Cooking was seen as similar to painting – the taking of raw ingredients and the application of correct technique, achieved through well-designed tools, to achieve palatable results.

Josef Albers, for example, the first student to become a master, said of his artistic method:

'I paint the way I spread butter on pumpernickel.' From there he would go on to extol the merits of good coarse dark German bread, contrasting its nutritional character and interesting texture to the empty airiness of white bread, which he likened to paper tissues. Food was like everything one designed: it should have character and enhance everyday existence. Later in life, Albers would call the selection of colours in his *Homages to the Square* 'recipes'. The idea went back to his Bauhaus years, where the notion of a meticulous formula or system behind creation, of planning and pre-meditation and the organisation of the elements, was seen as fundamental to making art and objects or taking buildings from the planning stage to the end result. The intention was to be deliberate and straightforward, to follow an organised approach, and to retain a lightness of touch and lack of self-importance about what one did.

Directness and candor were key on a purely visual level as well. Marcel Breuer designed impeccable kitchens, with the appearance of every appliance and cupboard honestly proclaiming what it was. In the metal workshop, tea glasses and other serving implements and utensils were streamlined. Clean aesthetics and functionalism were prized in every detail: modern materials like stainless steel and linoleum were celebrated. And while in most homes outside of the Bauhaus, living rooms were decorated with flowered wallpaper, damask curtains and chintz upholstery fabrics, at the Bauhaus the taste for smooth unadorned surfaces and forms that honoured purpose prevailed throughout the house.

The one faculty member who really knew how to cook was Klee, who was obsessed with the details of what he ate. When he was a teenager, the easiest way to get on with his cranky father was by drinking beer with him; Klee particularly prized 'wheat beer, which tastes utterly delicious, with a piece of lemon swimming in it'.[2] At such moments, one can feel Klee responding to the difference between wheat and hops, his seeing the yellow lemon as the essence of sunshine, his appreciating the sharpness of the citrus taste against the softness of the beer, his taking in the movement of the lemon. It matters that it was 'swimming' and not merely 'floating', that it was in motion rather than static. Food has much in common with painting: its need for contrasts, balances and counterbalances, the simple pleasures it presents.

Whenever Klee was apart from his wife Lily Stumpf, whom he married in 1906, he would write to tell her exactly what type of ham, for example, someone had served at lunch, delighting in such specifics when recounting a meeting with a friend as: 'good coffee. The skin on the milk was, thank God, so tough it stuck to the pot. But there were also macaroons – extra for me.'[3] Lily was a professional pianist; Klee a first-class violinist. As musicians, they knew the importance of nuance and measure, the way in which everything counts, and Klee treated the details of the kitchen as equally important. Like Albers, he was not interested in fancy food, but in the stuff of everyday life. He made a drawing for Lily of something he called 'caviar bread', which was so good that it had inspired him to take a holiday in a village near Bern because it was served at every meal in the modest pension there; he gave the bread its name not because it was topped with sturgeon eggs, but because, in its graininess, the humble bread had the quality of the greatest luxury.

Klee's taste in food was as eclectic as the subject matter of his painting, and he approached it with the same lust. Each detail has its own individual force, and a resplendent vitality, while at the same time existing in a rich relationship with all the other details. During World War I, when food was the essence of survival, he savoured 'a bowl of sauerkraut with blood sausage – the best dinner, very appreciated' and 'a lovely dinner consisting of tea, liverwurst, herring, chocolate, bread, apple-cake, apples, no hunger'.[4] This embrace of life, the longing for truthfulness over pretension, the whole-hearted zeal with which he experienced the everyday, was part of the spirit that he would bring to the Bauhaus a few years later, and that would be so essential to the school.

Near his air-force base in Cologne, early in December 1916, Klee 'had the good luck to find a little pub where I got veal ragout with potatoes, and bread with a thick layer of liverwurst on top. I was starving like a wolf.'[5] The more the experience of food satisfied his animal instincts, the better. His preferred dishes and ingredients were at times like the beasts and other images in his art: suckling pig, roast mutton, on numerous occasions a horrible-sounding 'sour liver', which he describes as 'very good, and useful on a winter night',[6] as well as cabbage, beets, lots of bread, and the inevitable potatoes, in various forms.

Early in 1917, Klee started putting his cooking ideas into letters to Lily. His approach had the creative flair that would infuse his teaching at the Bauhaus, and called for the understanding of materials and processes, and the willingness to be adventurous and take risks, which was seminal to the school's philosophy. Klee advised his wife on how to make what sounds like a coarse hash out of leftover roast meat and *steinpilzen* (porcini mushrooms): 'Cut some fat into small pieces when raw and put them through the sausage machine. Add some onions and potatoes. Fry on low heat, and use any other leftover in the sausage maker. Put the bones into the soup.'[7] As in Klee's art, it was essential to use everything and waste nothing, and to assemble a range of small parts authoritatively to make something whole and cohesive.

And the right food could have a direct impact on what he painted after eating it. Shortly after the armistice, when the making of art was easier than it had been for the previous four years, 'ein schön gebratenes Gockelchen' (a beautifully roasted chicken) that someone had sent to his house 'made for a nice, inspiring meal and provided me with the energy for a very colourful watercolour'.[8]

Klee first visited the Bauhaus in the autumn of 1920, the year after the school had opened in Weimar. By then, he was a well-respected painter, and Gropius was eager to have him come and teach at the new institution. Promised good studio space and a decent salary, Klee joined the faculty in Weimar in January of 1921. Once he was at the new school, he became increasingly preoccupied with what he ate. He wrote to his wife that the solution to living alone, before she and their young son Felix arrived in Weimar, was each day to make himself boiled eggs and eat them with poppyseed bread, ham and tea, and in the period before inflation became too rampant, to dine in a restaurant every evening. That strategy gave him the maximum time and energy to paint.

Then Felix arrived without Lily, and Klee employed a maid to help out. He adored her potato pancakes and instructed her on the best way to fry chops and exactly how to use a pullet to make soup. Especially when he invited Oskar Schlemmer for lunch, he wanted everything to be as good as possible, given that the ingredients could not be expensive.

Klee wrote to Lily that he needed the right foods to keep his moods in balance. He informed her that he was often famished, and that it was a struggle to keep his energy and spirits up. On one occasion, when he had been eating mainly wilted winter cabbage, he told her that at least there was enough leftover schnitzel to allow him to paint with force. He liked to throw together ingredients and cook them intuitively, making concoctions that had the right effect on him. He was proud of having prepared a true *sugo* – an Italian sauce based on tomatoes and ground meat – which was perfect with spaghetti. He prepared chicken in a heavy pot with onions and apples, and gave the canned peas that accompanied them some extra oomph by adding a homemade sauce composed essentially of butter and flour. The repasts were frugal and depended on the inventive recycling of ingredients: what had been the basis of a soup the previous evening was warmed up at lunchtime the following day, and then served cold at supper.

Above all, as in his art, Klee was obsessed with innards. He made risotto with a steamed calf's heart – drinking a glass of cooking wine as he stirred – and was pleased with tart kidneys and rice 'which behaved extremely well in a piquant wine sauce'. That description of their 'behaviour' was very much in keeping with his artistic approach, where inanimate objects were accorded personal traits. The leftover sauce from those well-behaved kidneys served Klee the next day in a minestrone with cabbage and onions. He delighted in reconstituting the same ingredients, in the way he reconfigured staircases and other recurring elements in his art. When he cooked offal, he responded with his painter's eye. Not only did the forms of hearts, kidneys, livers and lungs figure in his art, but he emulated the functions of these organs – the flow of blood and the intake of oxygen – in the processes he adopted on paper and canvas.

The most remarkable of Klee's culinary inventions was lung ragout, which he first made for a midday meal on a wintery Tuesday in January. Here he was more specific than usual about the timing, if as imprecise as always about the measurements:

> Tuesday ... a ragout of lungs spiced with blond spices. Recipe – start at ½ past 11 – boil a little water with some salt, add the whole lungs, 12 o'clock remove the lungs and slice finely on a board, 5 past 12 return the lungs to the pot. Ingredients added immediately: a chopped onion, some garlic, a strip of lemon peel, some horseradish, two carrots, butter and pepper. Ingredients at ¼ to 1: Flour dissolved in cold water, some vinegar, a lot of chopped parsley, a little nutmeg. Serve at 1 o'clock.[9]

Highly unusual, structured but playful, the two essentials of Klee's life – food and art – were of a piece, and it was important not to rule anything out as unacceptable.

When Gropius was designing the masters' houses in Dessau, Lily Klee asked for a stove fuelled by coal. Even though her husband was the principal cook, it was up to the mistress of the household to make the demand, and she knew that Klee liked to cook his stews and soups over coal. Tut Schlemmer, however, specified a gas stove. Georg Muche's wife, the Norwegian painter Erika Brandt, insisted on a new electric model. Nina Kandinsky, ever nostalgic for her native Russia, wanted only a *Kamin* – a wood-burning stove made of heavily ornamented black iron, which looked more suitable for a cosy dacha than a contemporary kitchen. For themselves, Ise and Walter Gropius opted for a streamlined stove in keeping with what was being made at the Bauhaus workshops.

The goal of the Bauhaus, of course, was to improve the experience of being human through the design of everything in one's surroundings. Each object one touches, the clothing one wears, the buildings one enters, and, above all, the vision and enchantment of great art, alter our existence, sometimes subtly, at other moments indelibly. The intelligence, grace, and artistry of design in one's kitchen, the cooking implements, the serving objects: all could invite feelings of balance and grace, of nourishment to the soul, a sense of harmony and psychological well-being in every aspect of daily existence. On the other hand, if executed carelessly, with impracticality or what might be seen as moral corruption, a sense of imbalance and discomfort would result. Since a well-nourished person who had enjoyed his or her last meal was likely to achieve better art and design, the Mazdaznan adherents stuck to their vegetable juices and garlic, while Klee continued to eat innards. The choice was personal, but the objective was the same in both cases: to improve human life. To that end, the Bauhaus saw the acts of making, eating, and serving food not just as essential, but as sacred.

1 Alma Mahler Werfel, *And the Bridge is Love*, Harcourt, Brace, and Company, New York, 1958, p.143.

2 Paul Klee, *Briefean die Familie*, vol.2, 1907–40, trans. Oliver Pretzel, Dumont, Cologne, 1979, p.813, May 9, 1916.

3 Ibid., p.768, July 20, 1911.

4 Ibid., p.831, November 9, 1916.

5 Ibid., p.838, December 2, 1916.

6 Ibid., p.839, December 5, 1916.

7 Ibid., p.861, April 1, 1917.

8 Ibid., p. 935, August 29, 1918.

9 Ibid., p.1259, January 9, 1935.

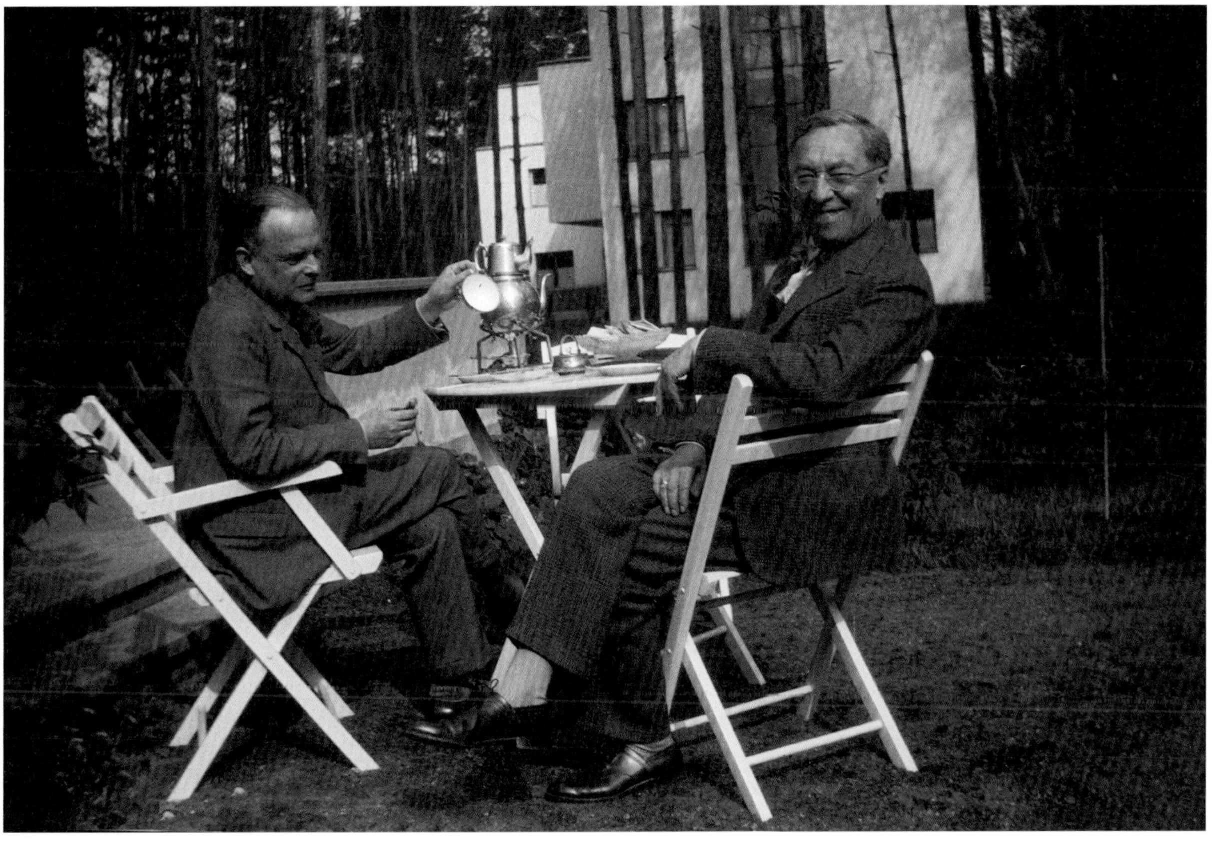

162
Paul Klee and Wassily Kandinsky at their masters' house, Dessau, c.1926
Centre Pompidou - MnamCci - Bibliothèque Kandinsky
Photographer unknown

163
Attributed to Irene or Herbert Bayer
View of the canteen terrace, Bauhaus Dessau, c. 1927 (printed later)
Gelatin silver print
25.3 × 20.4 cm
Bauhaus-Archiv Berlin

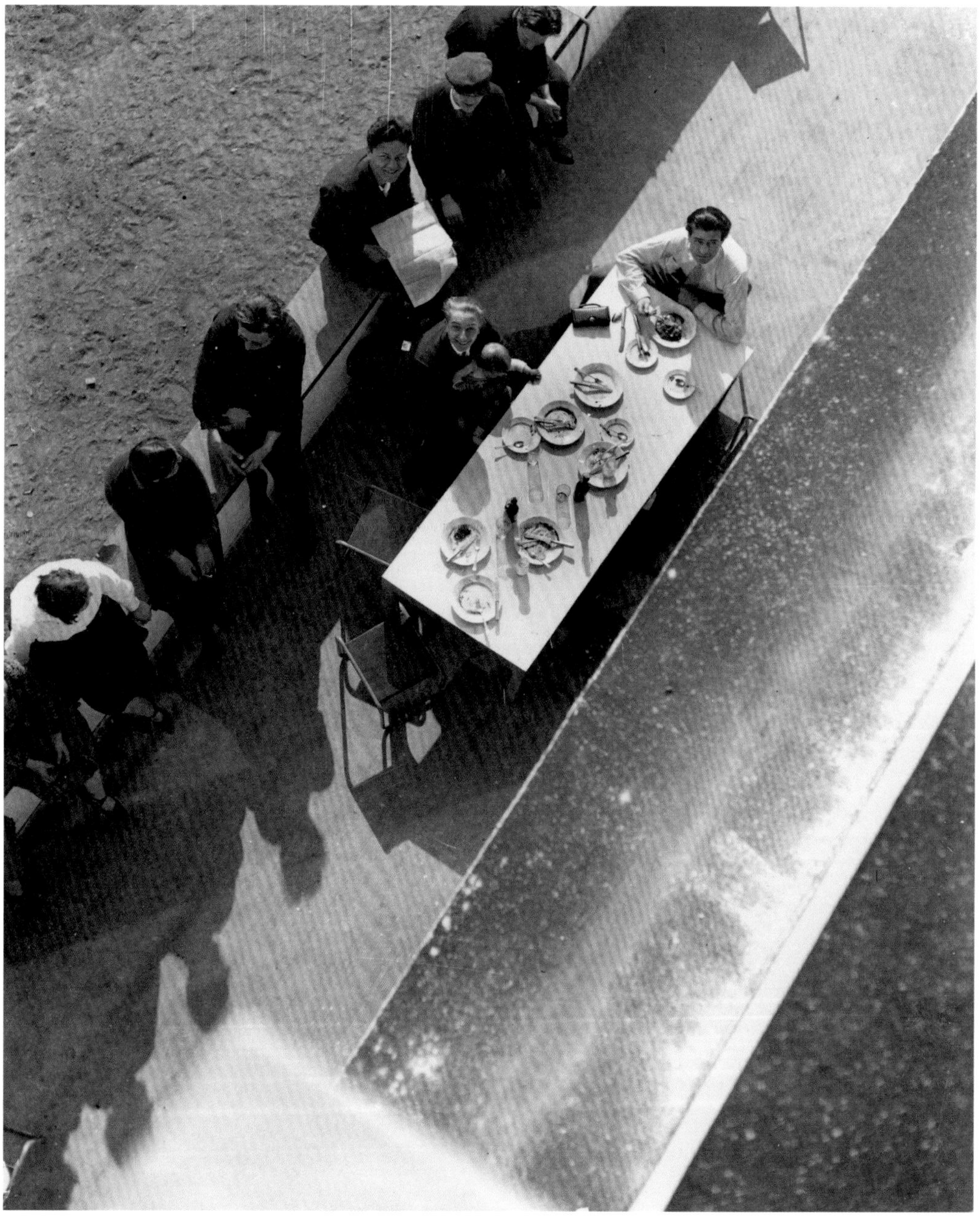

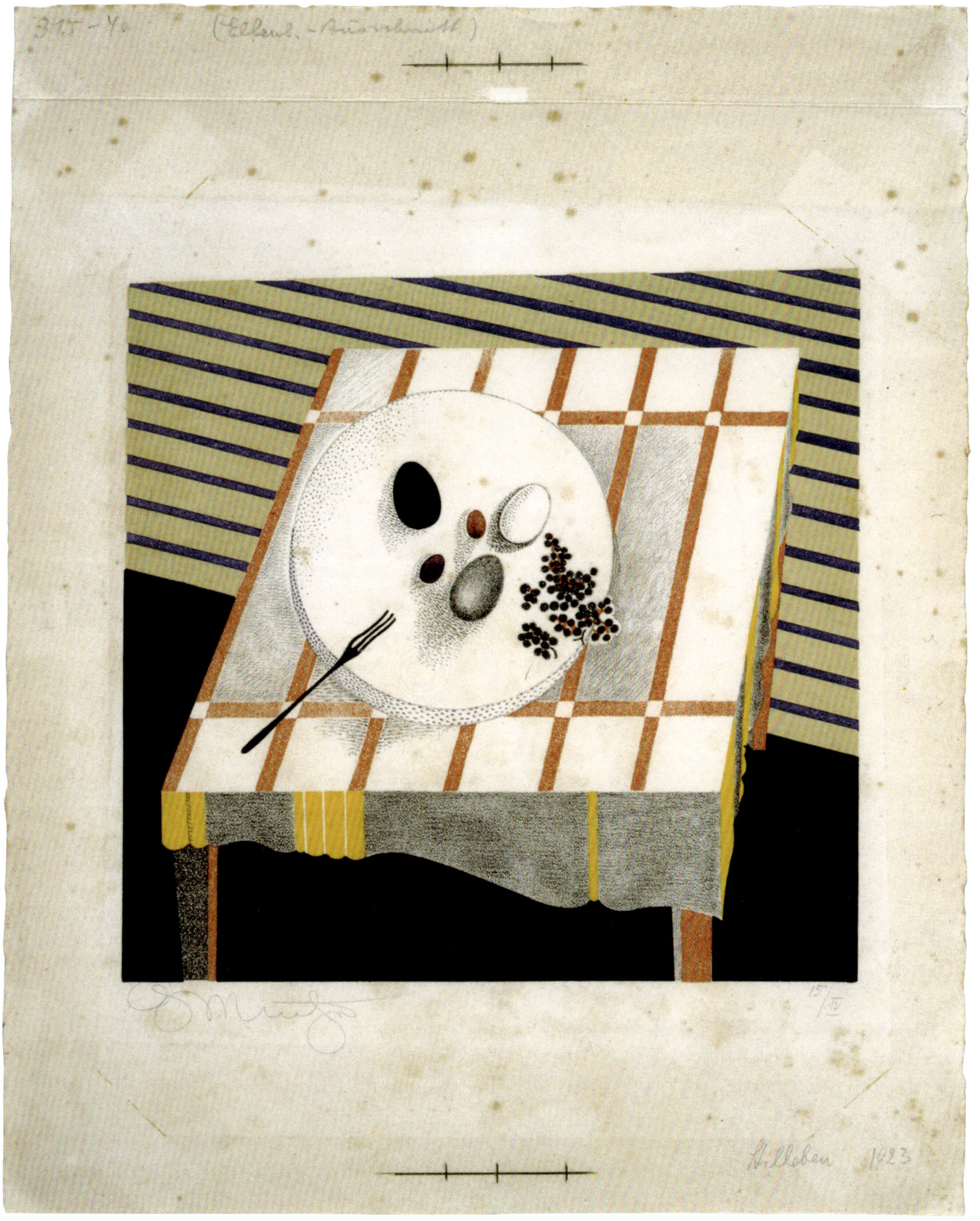

164
Georg Muche
Still-life, 1923
Colour lithograph on vellum
33.6 × 23.2 cm
Bauhaus-Archiv Berlin

stage, space, architecture

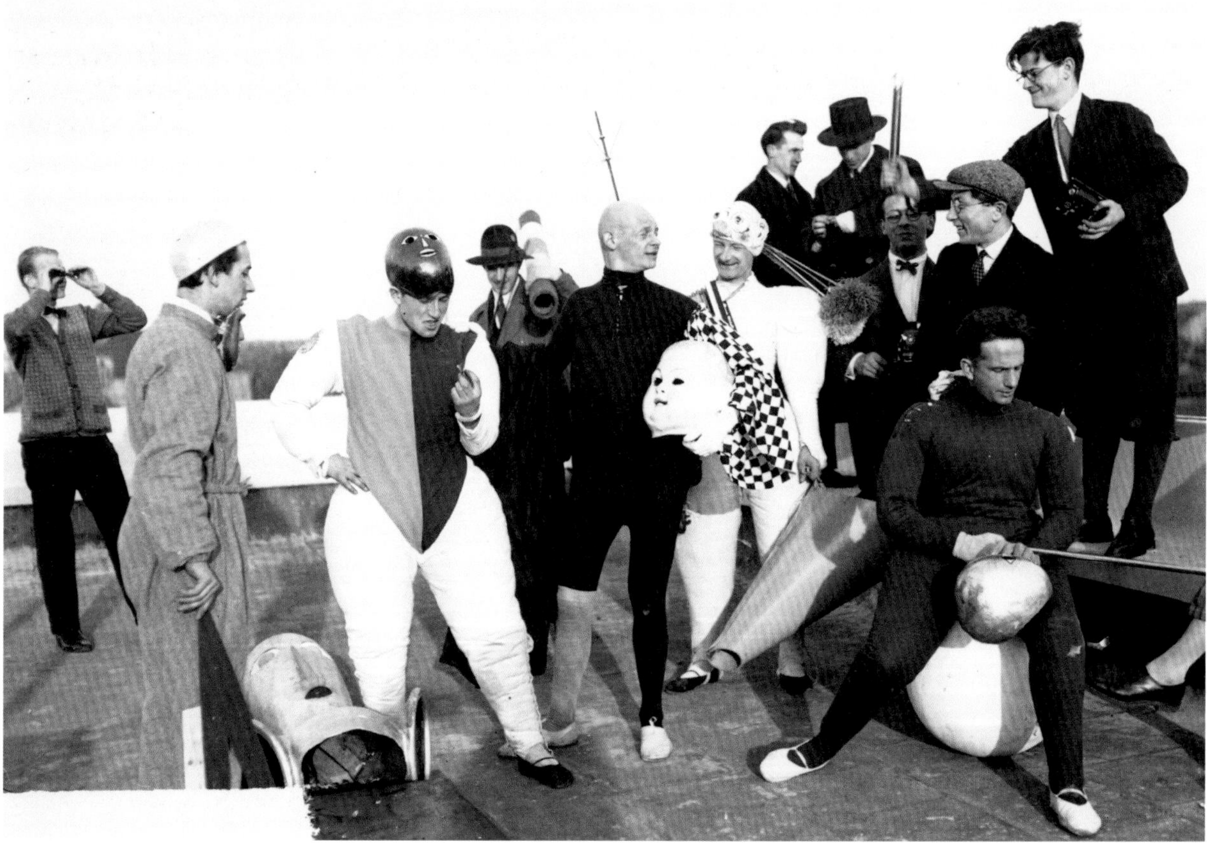

The school's ambition to unite all of the arts into a *Gesamtkunstwerk* or 'total work of art' found its outlet in the Bauhaus stage workshop, established in 1921. Functioning as an experimental laboratory, it combined architecture, painting, sculpture, music, dance and poetry to create, as Kandinsky noted, 'a monumental abstract art'. Although theatre was not included in the 1919 manifesto, by 1922 stage work was a key element of Bauhaus activities. Theatre also became the essential binding agent for social life at the school.

Lothar Schreyer was charged with setting up a stage workshop in 1921 and the Expressionist theatre performances under his supervision gradually came into conflict with the school's aim of achieving a synthesis of art and technology in 'pure' forms. The move towards a spatially orientated theatre, with a new abstract form for the stage, came under the direction of Oskar Schlemmer from 1923 to 1929. Schlemmer defined such theatre as an art of space and movement, equating human performers with other theatrical elements such as light, form and motion, and transforming dancers and actors into moving architecture, as seen in the series of performances and demonstrations at the Bauhaus week with *The Triadic Ballet* (1923) and in his later gestural and spatial dances.

Costumes were often conceived in sculptural terms, utilising exaggerated headdresses, masks, padded torsos or outfits made up of concentric hoops, all of which constricted the movement of the dancer but also served to heighten the visibility of the pose and to metamorphose the human figure into a sculptural form in space. In Kurt Schmidt's *Mechanical Ballet* (1923) abstract figures with brightly coloured cut-outs of geometric forms attached to their black leotards moved across the stage to modern music, creating an illusion of dancing automatons. These geometric, constructivist-inspired figures were an embodiment of the modern industrial world, invoking machines and technology.

In contrast to Schlemmer's creation of voluminous space, the reflected light experiments produced by Kurt Schwerdtferger between 1922 and 1925 sought to flatten space, to emulate painting with light. The series of coloured light projections, beamed through templates of cut-out geometric forms, produced kinetic, abstract designs of light in motion, which were sometimes accompanied by music.

With the publication of the first theatre journal *Bauhausbühne* (*Bauhaus stage*) in 1922, Gropius outlined his aims for theatre as 'a new scenic space ... based on the spirit of construction' that 'should unite movement, organic and mechanical bodies, form, light, colour, verbal and musical sounds'. The inclusion of a dedicated stage space within the school's new Dessau building reiterates the importance of the stage to Bauhaus creative experimentation during this period. Gropius's interconnected design and the centrality of its position – between canteen and auditorium – brought the stage into the heart of communal, everyday life. Other Bauhaus figures such as Kandinsky and Andor Weininger designed sets for theatre productions or explored the potential for new interpretations of theatrical space with conceptual stage designs for such leading figures as the director and producer Erwin Piscator.

Performances occurred in a variety of venues not only on the experimental stage of the Dessau building but also on its balconies and roofs, where students and masters cavorted before the camera both in and out of costume, as seen in the photographs by Eric Consemüller and T. Lux Feininger. The building as stage represents the holistic approach of the Bauhaus and its aim to unite under one roof architecture, formal design and visual art.

165
Attributed to Irene or Herbert Bayer
Members of the stage workshop on the roof of the Bauhaus Dessau. From left to right, Erich Consemüller (with light meter), Roman Clemens, Clemens Röseler, Heinz Loew (with hat), Oskar Schlemmer (wearing black), Andor Weininger, two unknown persons, Andreas Feininger (with camera), unknown, Werner Siedhoff (seated), T. Lux Feininger (with camera), 1928 (printed 1985)
Gelatin silver print
18 × 24 cm
Bauhaus-Archiv Berlin

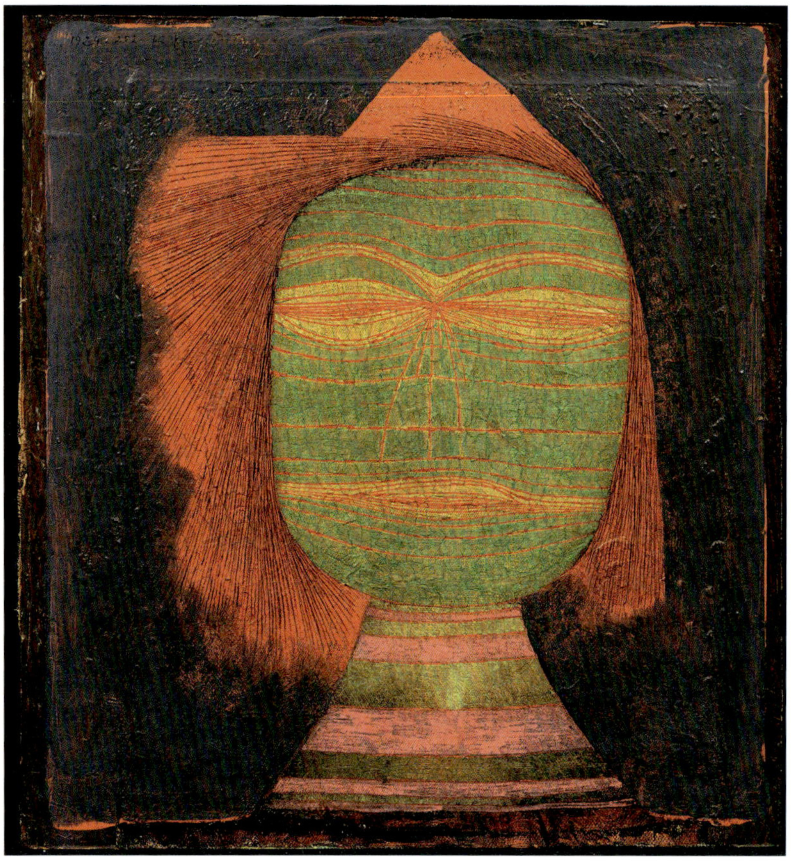

166
Paul Klee
Actor's Mask, 1924
Oil on canvas mounted on board
36.7 × 33.8 cm
The Museum of Modern Art, New York
The Sidney and Harriet Janis
Collection 1969

167
Oskar Schlemmer
Oskar Schlemmer als Musikalischer Clown mit Cello (Oskar Schlemmer as Musical Clown with Cello), 1926
Vintage print, inscribed and mounted by the artist
12.1 × 15.4 cm
Bühnen Archiv Oskar Schlemmer/
The Oskar Schlemmer Theatre Estate

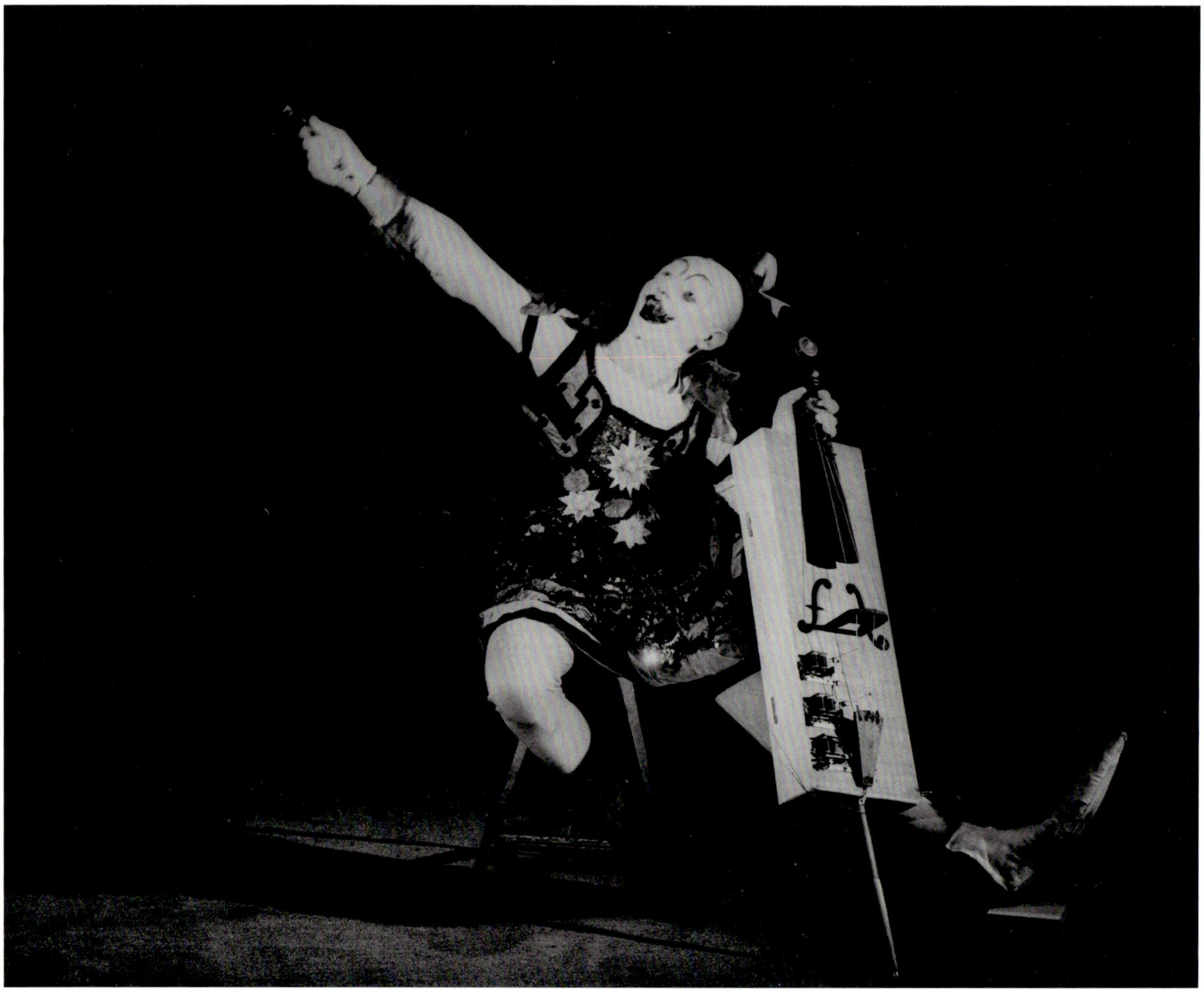

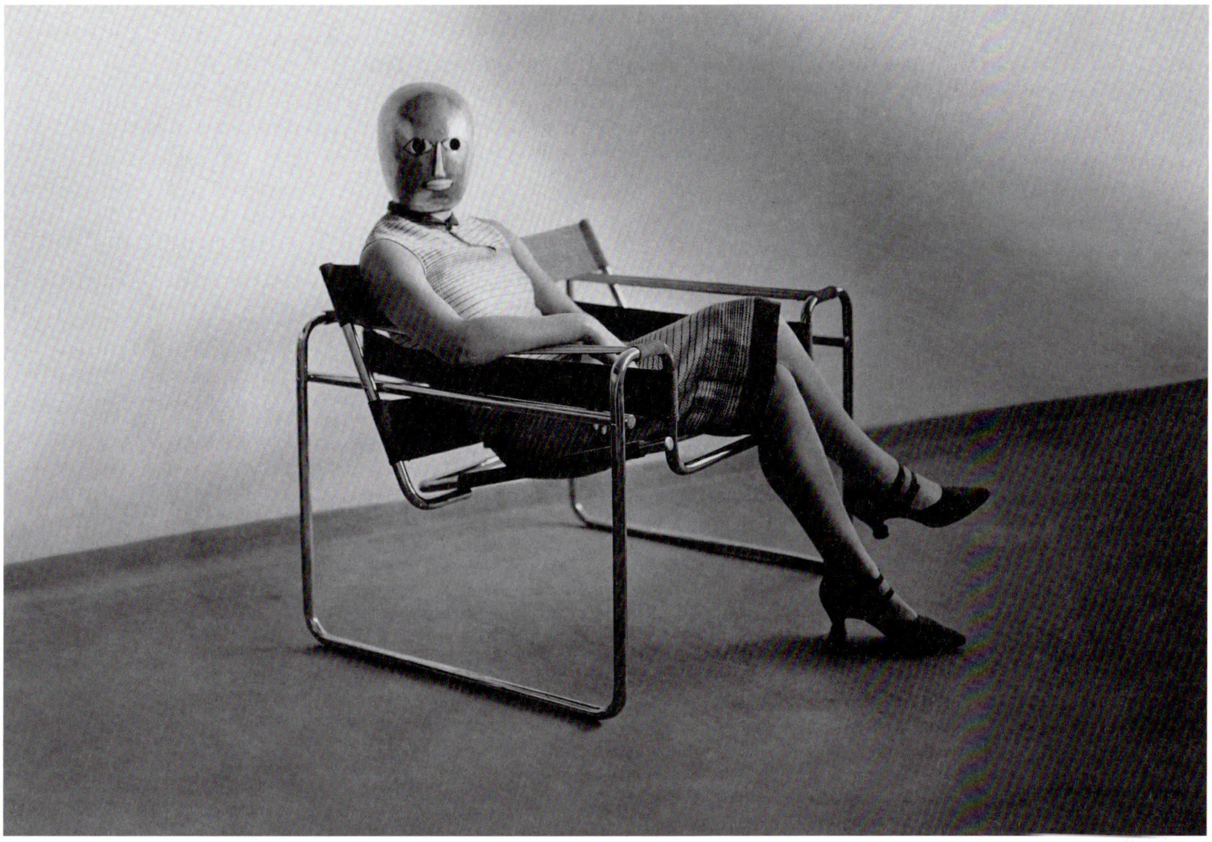

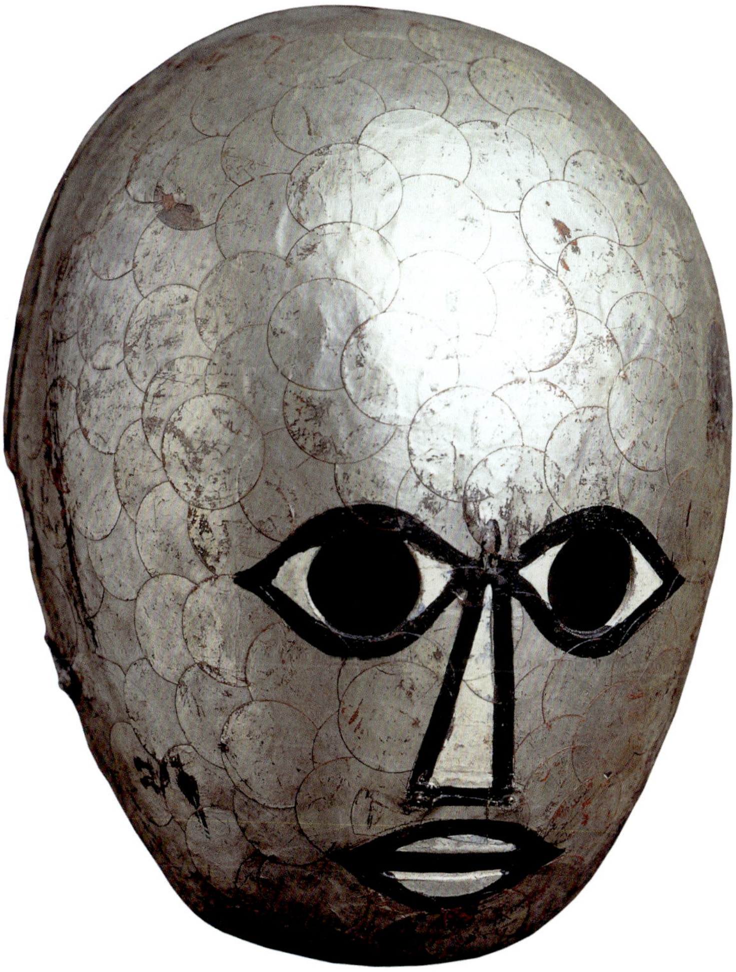

168
Erich Consemüller
Lis Beyer or Ise Gropius sitting on the B3 club chair by Marcel Breuer and wearing a mask by Oskar Schlemmer and dress fabric by Lis Beyer, c.1927
Gelatin silver print
12.9 × 17.9 cm
Herzogenrath, Berlin
On long-term loan to Klassik Stiftung Weimar, Bestand Museen

169
Oskar Schlemmer
Bauhaustanze, Maske (*Bauhaus Dances, Head Mask in Silver*), 1924–26
Papier mâché, silver, gouache
28 × 20 × 23 cm
Bühnen Archiv Oskar Schlemmer/
The Oskar Schlemmer Theatre Estate, Collection UJS

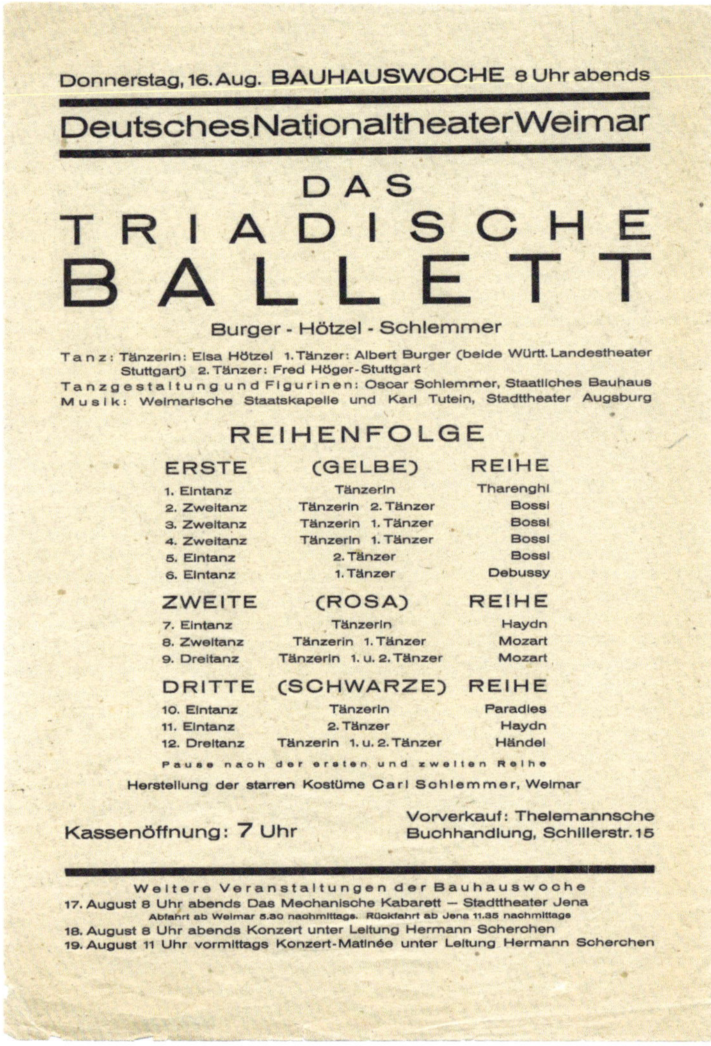

Donnerstag, 16. Aug. BAUHAUSWOCHE 8 Uhr abends

Deutsches Nationaltheater Weimar

DAS
TRIADISCHE
BALLETT

Burger - Hötzel - Schlemmer

Tanz: Tänzerin: Elsa Hötzel 1. Tänzer: Albert Burger (beide Württ. Landestheater Stuttgart) 2. Tänzer: Fred Höger-Stuttgart
Tanzgestaltung und Figurinen: Oscar Schlemmer, Staatliches Bauhaus
Musik: Weimarische Staatskapelle und Karl Tutein, Stadttheater Augsburg

REIHENFOLGE

ERSTE	(GELBE)	REIHE
1. Eintanz	Tänzerin	Tharenghi
2. Zweitanz	Tänzerin 2. Tänzer	Bossi
3. Zweitanz	Tänzerin 1. Tänzer	Bossi
4. Zweitanz	Tänzerin 1. Tänzer	Bossi
5. Eintanz	2. Tänzer	Bossi
6. Eintanz	1. Tänzer	Debussy
ZWEITE	**(ROSA)**	**REIHE**
7. Eintanz	Tänzerin	Haydn
8. Zweitanz	Tänzerin 1. Tänzer	Mozart
9. Dreitanz	Tänzerin 1. u. 2. Tänzer	Mozart
DRITTE	**(SCHWARZE)**	**REIHE**
10. Eintanz	Tänzerin	Paradies
11. Eintanz	2. Tänzer	Haydn
12. Dreitanz	Tänzerin 1. u. 2. Tänzer	Händel

Pause nach der ersten und zweiten Reihe

Herstellung der starren Kostüme Carl Schlemmer, Weimar

Kassenöffnung: 7 Uhr

Vorverkauf: Thelemannsche Buchhandlung, Schillerstr. 15

Weitere Veranstaltungen der Bauhauswoche
17. August 8 Uhr abends Das Mechanische Kabarett — Stadttheater Jena
Abfahrt ab Weimar 5.30 nachmittags. Rückfahrt ab Jena 11.35 nachmittags
18. August 8 Uhr abends Konzert unter Leitung Hermann Scherchen
19. August 11 Uhr vormittags Konzert-Matinée unter Leitung Hermann Scherchen

170
Artist unknown
Programme for Oskar Schlemmer's *Triadic Ballet,* Bauhaus week, 16 August, 1923
Bauhaus-Archiv Berlin

171
Oskar Schlemmer
Das Triadische Ballett, Tänzer türkisch I (*The Triadic Ballet, Turc I*), 1922 (1995)
Wool and silk fabric with mixed media
195 × 61 × 66 cm
Bühnen Archiv Oskar Schlemmer/
The Oskar Schlemmer Theatre Estate
Collection C. Raman Schlemmer

172
Oskar Schlemmer
Das Triadische Ballett, Drahtkostüm (*The Triadic Ballet, Wire Figure*), 1922 (1967)
Steel wire
214 × 140 × 118 cm, diameter 125 cm
Bühnen Archiv Oskar Schlemmer/
The Oskar Schlemmer Theatre Estate
Collection C. Raman Schlemmer

173
Oskar Schlemmer
Das Triadische Ballett, Tänzer türkisch II (*The Triadic Ballet, Turc II*), 1922 (1985)
Wool and silk fabric with mixed media
198 × 94 × 98 cm
Bühnen Archiv Oskar Schlemmer/
The Oskar Schlemmer Theatre Estate
Collection C. Raman Schlemmer

Figurines mounted on armature in steel wire, designed by U. Jaïna Schlemmer, based on the drawing 'The Symbols in Man, Dematerialization', 1924 by Oskar Schlemmer

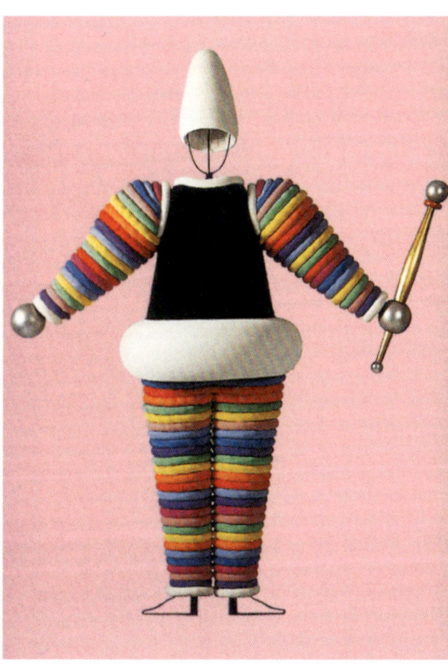

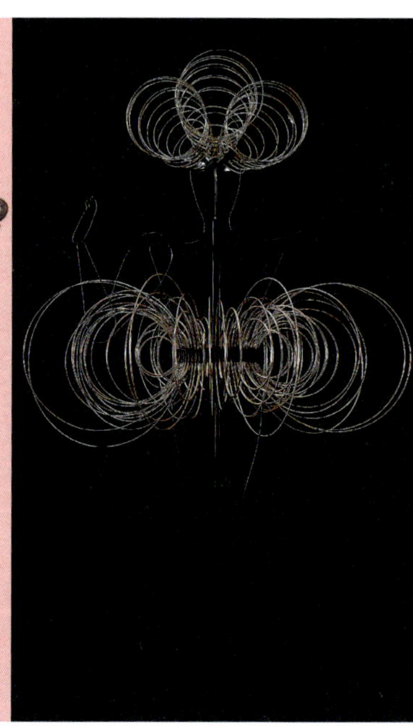

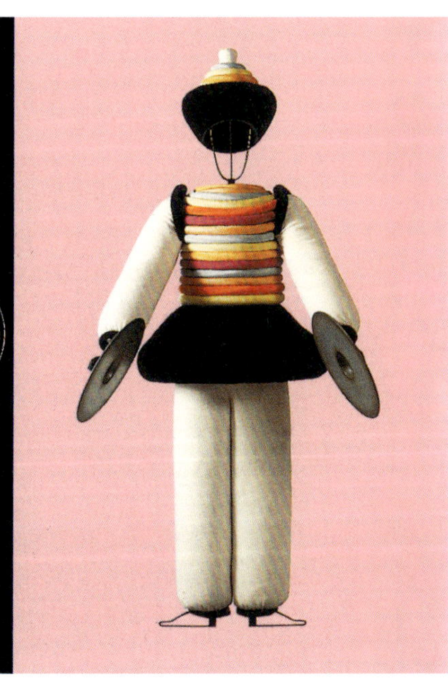

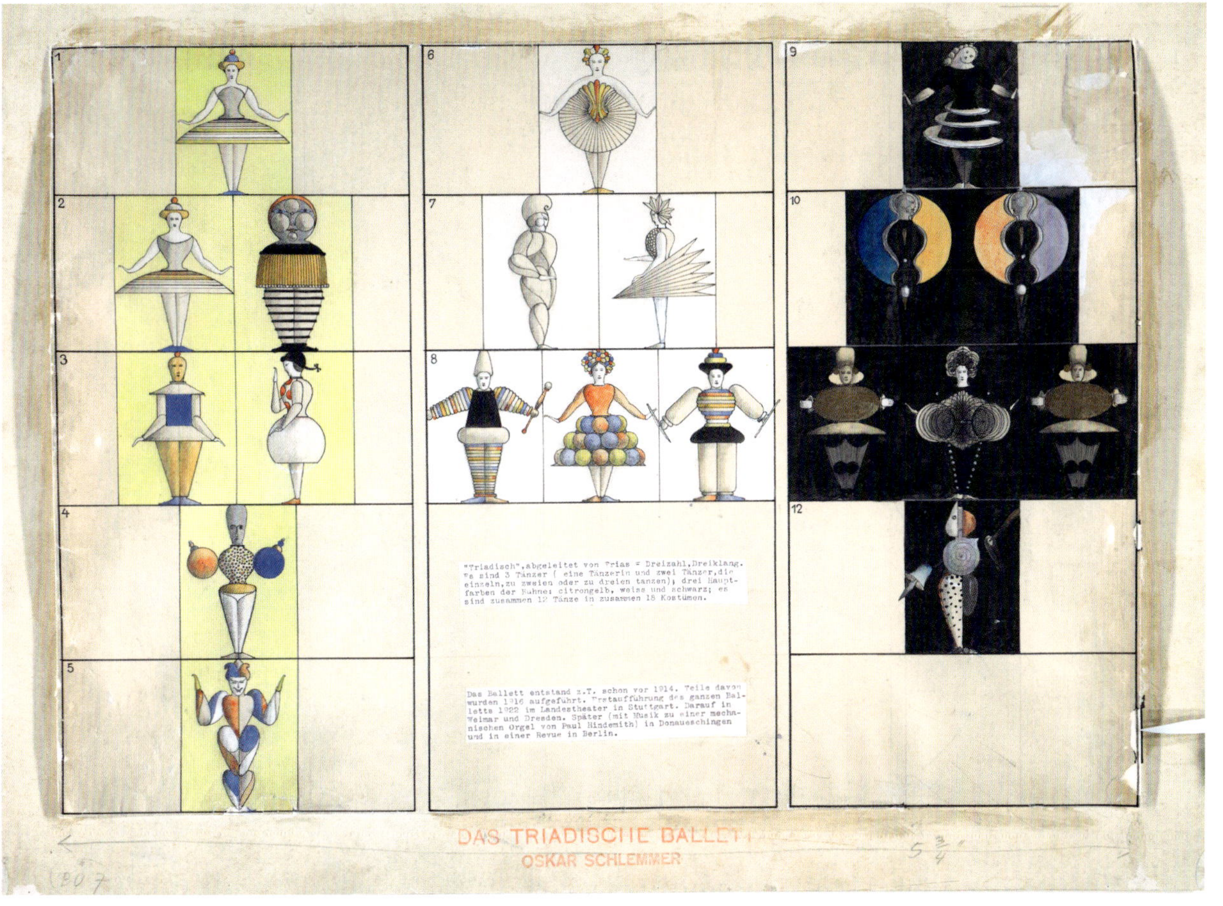

174 (illustration only)
Oskar Schlemmer
Das Triadische Ballett, Figurenplan
(*The Triadic Ballet, Plan of Figures*), 1924
Ink, gouache, metallic powder
and pencil with collage
38.6 × 53.7 cm
Harvard Art Museums/
Busch-Reisinger Museum

On exhibition
Oskar Schlemmer
Das Triadische Ballett, Figurenplan, 1924
Lithograph
16.8 × 23.2 cm
Bühnen Archive Oskar Schlemmer/
The Oskar Schlemmer Theatre Estate
Collection C. Raman Schlemmer

In 1912 Oskar Schlemmer first wrote about his concept for a complete dance performance entitled Dance Vision, parts of which were performed as *Das Triadische Ballett* (*The Triadic Ballet*) during World War I in 1916. Created and completed before Schlemmer joined the Bauhaus in Weimar in 1921, the world premiere of *The Triadic Ballet* was in Stuttgart in 1922, accompanied by music from three centuries. This symphonic dance is divided into three sections; otherwise there is no underlying action to the piece. The first section, on a lemon-yellow stage set, is serene-burlesque. The theme of the second, on a pink stage set, is festive-carried, while the theme of the third, on a black stage set, is mystical-fantastic. Three performers, two female and one male dancer, alternatively dance twelve dances.

In *The Triadic Ballet* it is the costume not the dancer that determines movement, conditioning the dancer to new expressions. As much as the static, sculptural costumes and masks inhibit the dancer's range of motion – in a synthesis of body and costume – they introduce, encourage and intensify specific new movements. The costumes become ambulant architectures. *The Triadic Ballet* and, in particular the figurine *The Abstract* are a *leitmotif* in the *Gesamtkunstwerk* of Schlemmer.

C. Raman Schlemmer

oskar schlemmer
the stage and the bauhaus

The endeavours of the Bauhaus to integrate art and artistic ideals with craftsmanship and technology by way of investigating the elements of design, and the attempts to direct all activities together toward architecture, naturally exert an influence on the work of the stage. For the stage is after all architectonic: it is ordered and planned, and it provides a setting for form and colour in their liveliest and most versatile form.

The stage was there on the very day the Bauhaus opened, because enjoyment in designing was there on that first day. This enjoyment was first expressed in the celebrations (the lantern party and the kite-flying party), in the invention of masks, the making of costumes and the decoration of rooms. And it was expressed in *dancing, dancing, dancing*! The music evolved from the Bauhaus dance, which developed from the clown dance into the 'Step'; from the concertina to the jazz band. From this 'dance for everyone' evolved the 'dance for the individual' and its reflected form on the stage: the chromatic-normal, the mechanised *ballet*. From inspiration, whim, and a mind to do something primitive, evolved *parodies* on existing theatre, opera, drama, circus, and variety shows. Such travesty has positive results: the understanding of the origin of the theatrical play, its conditions and laws. We are breaking conventions where they seem to be already shaky, and we are experimenting with creating new forms.

Where can we create such new forms?

In our particular field, with our particular means, by providing the eyes with what is due them: everything in the realm of the visual, the *show*. The elements of that realm are form, colour, light, space and movement.

The inherent laws of these elements, both the mathematically precise as well as the intangibly metaphysical, will aid our understanding of related and complementary elements, such as language, word, tone, and sound.

Our work is to serve research experiments, for which there is neither time nor inclination in the bustle of today's business scene. For the time being we intend to protect this work from the curiosity and the activity of the public. Whatever achievement, in our opinion, will have acquired significant value and will have taken definite shape, shall then no longer be kept from public view.

From the journal Offset, Buch und Werbekunst, *Leipzig, 1926, no.7*

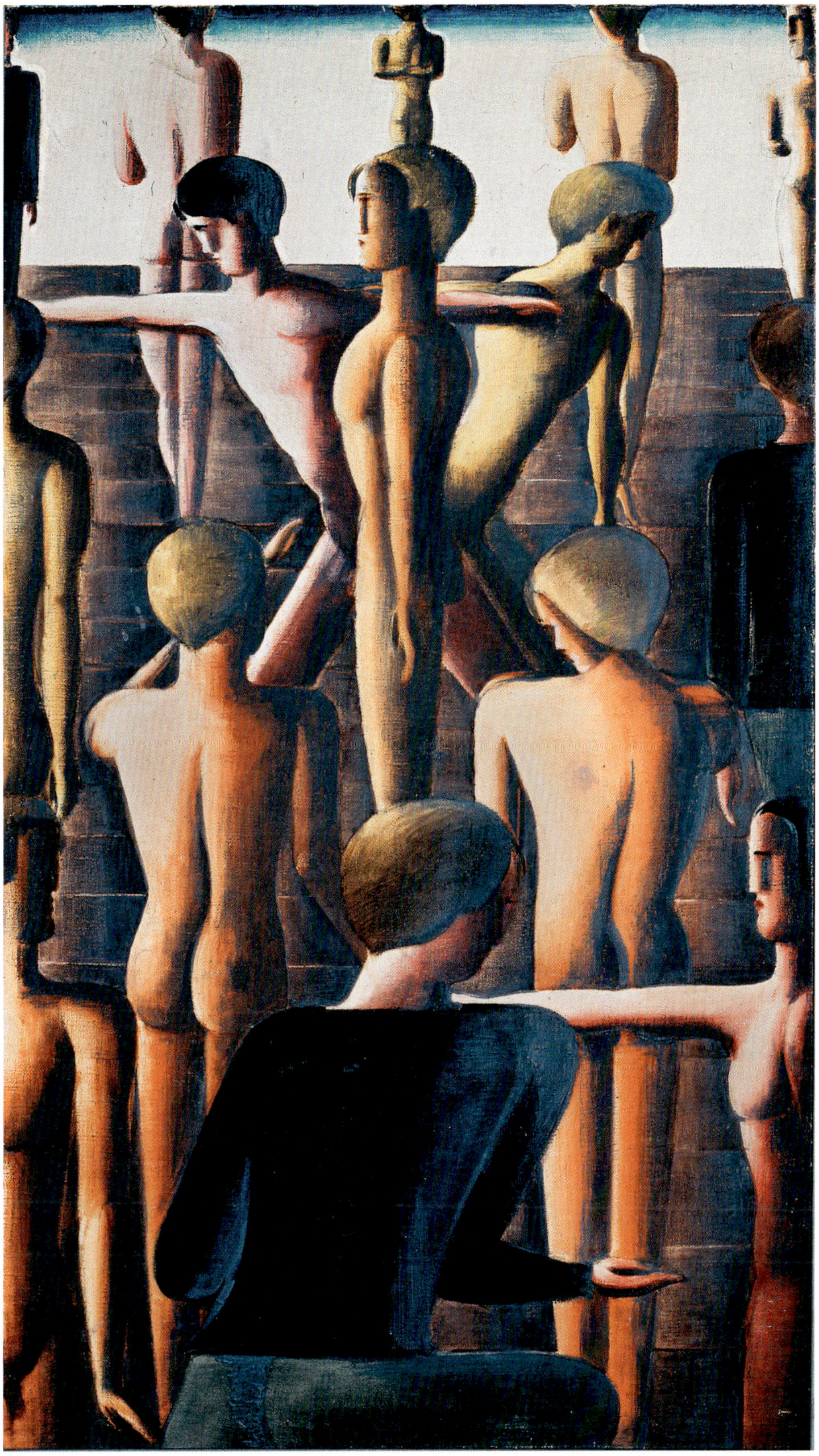

175
Oskar Schlemmer
Fünfzehnergruppe
(*Group of Fifteen Figures*), 1929
Oil on canvas
178 × 100 cm
Lehmbruck Museum Duisburg

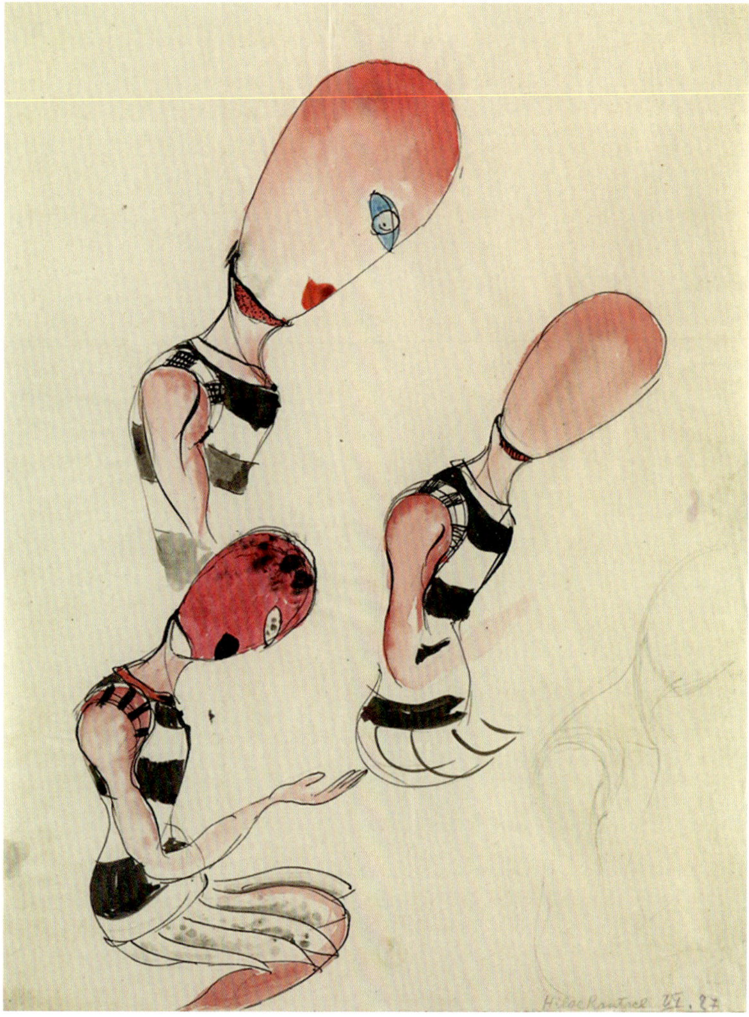

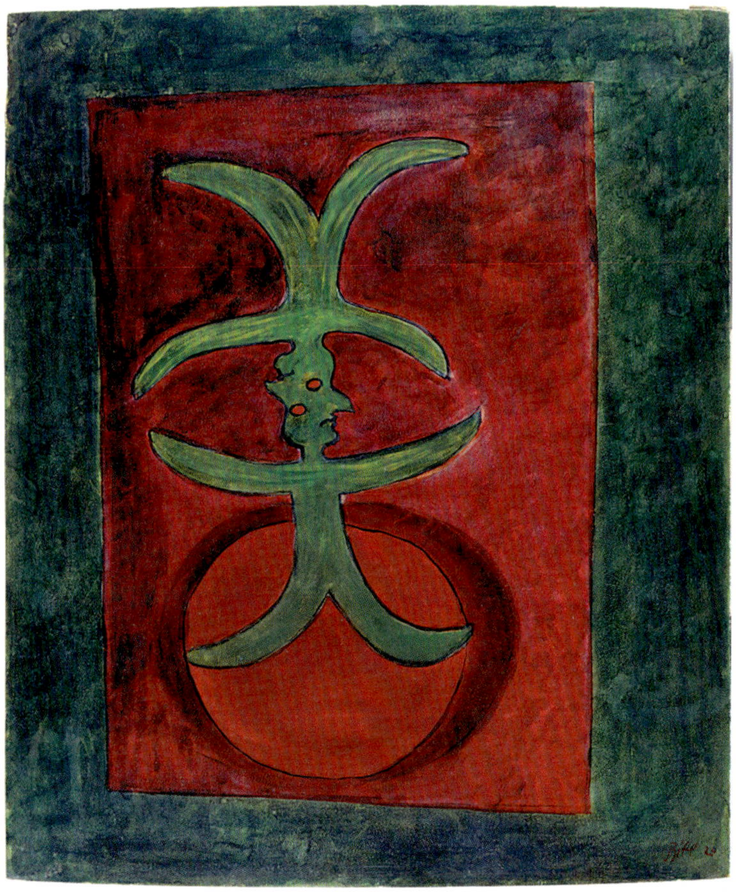

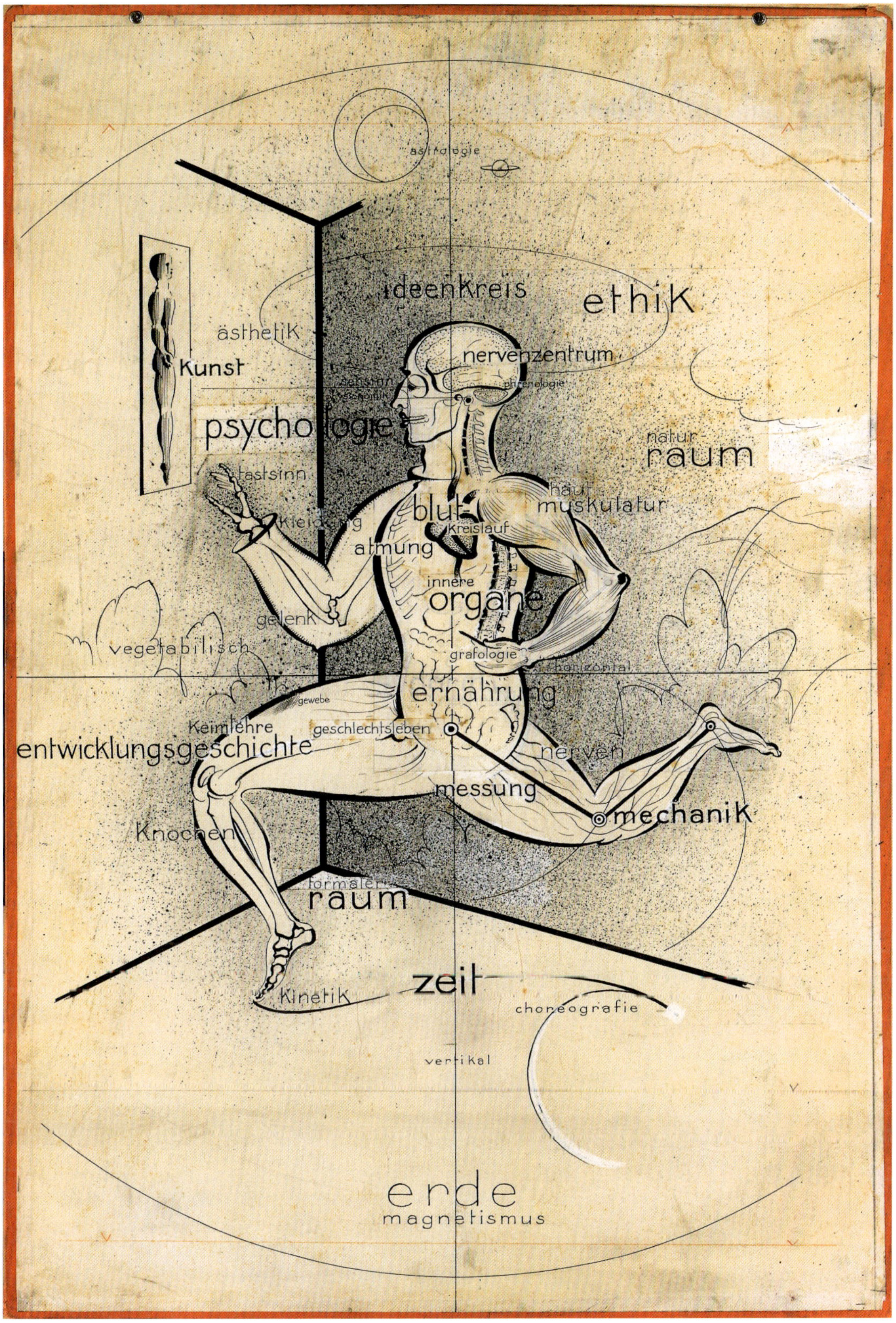

176
Hilde Rantzsch
Untitled, 1927
Watercolour and ink on paper
28.5 × 20.5 cm
Max Bill Georges Vantongerloo Stiftung, Zumikon, Switzerland

177
Max Bill
Siamese Twins – Acrobats, 1929
Oil on card
66.5 × 57 cm
Max Bill Georges Vantongerloo Stiftung, Zumikon, Switzerland

178
Oskar Schlemmer
Der Mensch im Ideenkreis
(*Man in the Sphere of Ideas*), 1928
Teaching Board, Stage Course 'Der Mensch/Man', Bauhaus Dessau
Pen, ink, gouache, fabric and colour pencil on paper, mounted on board
74.5 × 48.9 cm
Bühnen Archiv Oskar Schlemmer/
The Oskar Schlemmer Theatre Estate
Collection UJS

bauhaus lighthouse
der bau als bühne
das bühne als bau

melissa trimingham

Like a theatre stage, the Bauhaus building at Dessau articulated its spaces through the use of light. Glass walls hung like vast curtains, reflective from the outside, transparent from the inside, flooding the workshops with light; the staircases were wide glazed stages running between the floors; the high floating balconies of the Prellerhaus brought the outside in, and the inside out, provoking the most hair-raising photographs ever taken in Dessau. Huge windows dominated the white bedrooms. Subtle colouring around door frames and infinitesimal variations in moulded beams and columns were designed to pick up every ray of light, each nuance of shadow. This architecture defined by light was a social shaper in the Bauhaus community: Walter Gropius, who designed the building, made use of the windows to spy on the unfolding 'scene' below from his office up on the bridge connecting the two main blocks, and directly overlooking the Prellerhaus.

László Moholy-Nagy described photography as *Lichtgestaltung* (*lightplay*), the forming of light into new configurations, as an art that would supersede old-fashioned painting with pigments.[1] He designed and built his *Lichtrequisit für Elektrischen Bühne* (*Light Prop for the Electric Stage*) between 1922 and 1931 to create experiences of new gestalts of light and space in kinetic motion. In Weimar, in a similar fashion to Kurt Schwerdtfeger, Ludwig Hirschfeld-Mack excitedly projected cut-out shapes onto a two-layer screen with acetylene lamps to create his *Reflektorische Lichtspiele* (*Reflected Light Compositions*). And at Dessau, within the 'window' of his picture-frame stage, Oskar Schlemmer pulverised the elements of the stage, of which light was a fundamental gestalt.

Not only Schlemmer but the Bauhaus as a whole, and especially at Dessau, dissected the components of art. In a sense they dismantled the *Gesamtkunstwerk* (total work of art) into the simplest of forms in order to rebuild it with fresh understanding. 'One of the signs of our time is abstraction, which ... works to separate parts from the existing whole, leading them to absurdity, or raising them to their highest possibility', wrote Schlemmer.[2] Since light realises material form, one question the Bauhaus asked anew was how do we – indeed, how can we – experience light? Intimately connected to their obsessive analysis of the colour wheel (light, of course, realises colour too[3]), Bauhaus ideas about light drew on the latest modernist theories of perception. Although we can find parallels with then current ideas in gestalt psychology, Bauhaus interest in perception has to be seen against a background of competing idealist and materialist theories that were explored under the influence of Expressionist and Constructivist experimentation.[4] All these extremes, however, relied upon a quasi-scientific view of how reality was constituted, usually via gestalts or forms that combined and recombined to produce complex structures. The Bauhaus project was to understand the simplest gestalts and to build creative form from them.

The ultimate complex form was architecture, the supreme ethical project of the time, the tool to shape a decent society – a visible cause and effect of a new culture. If the building in Dessau was a stage, then the stage – situated between the social heart of the Bauhaus, the canteen, and its public face, the auditorium – was the building: an ever-changing space of cardboard and wood, a flexible laboratory to expound the elements of space, movement and light. The ultimate aim of the building was ethical: both aesthetic and socialist. Linking light to ethics may sound farfetched, but not at the Bauhaus. Light was the purest of space articulators in an institution ultimately devoted to the ethical shaping of space, i.e. architecture.

Light as an active force on a stage connects with a tendency to *present* and not to *represent*. As the German director Achim Freyer remarked of his *Bildertheater* (visual theatre), it is not a 'play with appearances, it represents nothing, it is what it is'.[5] The Bauhaus stage did not concern itself with narrative, characters and story, but with the exploration and articulation of space, and the stage at Dessau became the testing ground for the greater architectural project of the Bauhaus.

Schlemmer experimented with radiant light on stage as well as ambient light. For him, working on his personal, ethical and aesthetic project, which was nothing less than the revival of the German theatre (contingent in his terms with any revival of society and community), radiant light had an impact that took the viewer beyond mundane reality, just as the radiant beauty of the Old Masters was a virtual experience of heavenly grace. On one memorable night he filled the Bauhaus with radiant light at the Metal Party. He describes going outside and observing the building from a distance, lit up in the frost of a January night, gleaming, magical, an academy at last of 'United Form' achieved through illumination.[6] Schlemmer was not the only artist at the Bauhaus to bring these neo-Romantic ideals of ethics and aesthetics into the laboratory of light: other like-minded artists with an intense interest in light and colour on stage included Wassily Kandinsky and Moholy-Nagy.

Constructivist thinking, with which Moholy is normally associated, will not get us far in understanding his stage work, or indeed in grasping his total vision of art and theatre. He was closer to the thinking of some of his more Expressionist colleagues, including Kandinsky, than is generally thought, though his political zeal and uncompromising vision alienated him from many of them, especially Schlemmer. Moholy seemed able to retain the visionary but strip it of metaphysics. He wanted to push our senses, using light, beyond their accustomed limits. He continually refers to the untapped 'biological' capacity of man: 'the man of a given period is most perfect when the functional mechanism of which he is composed – the cells as much as the complex organs – is being used to the limits of its biological capacity'.[7] He had an extraordinary expectation of what the human consciousness could achieve; he can sound almost Bergsonian in his visionary and inspired optimism but is very far from Henri Bergson in his practical means of realisation: 'Art brings this about.'[8] He was also actively politically committed to this vision in a way that Bergsonian vitalism and expressionist metaphysics never even approached.

Moholy designed theatre sets before and after his Bauhaus years, but his interest at the Bauhaus was influenced by his developing ideas on space, motion and light. Schlemmer dominated the Dessau stage programme with his work on the human figure, but the potential of the stage space to open up new experiences for an audience was not lost on Moholy. As in his photography, in theatre he wanted not to reproduce but to produce: light was an active force in the theatre to realise new articulations of space, and not repeat (a concern for Schlemmer, too) the tired stage scenarios of silver moonlight or light-dappled forest.

Moholy's conception of the apperceptive and the associative is key to understanding the Bauhaus artists' use of stage light, however unsophisticated the equipment they had at their disposal. Associative effects of light, and indeed sound[9] connect to 'representational composition': 'dependent upon climate, race, temperament, education, rooted in association and experience'.[10] This leads to the representation, or more or less naturalistic 'reproduction', of life in both painting, photography and the stage – the silver moonlight on stage for example. 'Apperceptive' effect of light on the other hand is 'colour composition: the pure inter-relationships of colours and light values, similar to what we know in music as composition in acoustical relationships; this is the composition of universal systems, independent of race, temperament, education, rooted in biological laws.'[11] This leads to 'production' in painting, photography and the stage – that is, the creation of new *Gestalten* that open viewers' minds beyond the limits of their accustomed perception; this in turn promoted understanding of these universal systems as the mind opened up to more and more new gestalt patterns. Years later, James Gibson described how the light rays fill the space around us, bouncing off surfaces, a dense network of convergence and divergence, and how the convergence points enter the eye as an 'optical array'.[12] Put simply, it is as if Moholy wanted more, different and unaccustomed convergent points to enter our eyes – and, importantly, to be recognised by us. However, familiarity blunts perception. As Moholy said of his younger self: 'My eyes were not yet trained to see.'[13]

The *Lichtrequisit* (usually translated as *Light Prop*) was an apparatus developed during the 1920s. *'Requisit'* has a distinct theatrical overtone: *Requisiten* are stage props, a word used, for example, by Schlemmer to describe the hoops and boxes with which he worked. A 1.5-metre high version was manufactured by the electric company AEG to Moholy's specification and displayed in the Bauhaus section of the Deutscher Werkbund Exhibition of 1930 in Paris. Always rather shaky, even noisy, in operation, it was a machine basically consisting of revolving slatted discs and shapes apparently designed to reflect ever-changing patterns of shadow and light on the walls of its containing space (either box, room or stage).[14] Sibyl Moholy-Nagy gives a lively description of her first encounter with it in a room in Berlin near Alexanderplatz in the early 1930s, after Moholy had used the apparatus to make his abstract film *Ein Lichtspiel: schwarz weiss grau* (*Light Play: black white grey*): 'a construction – half sculpture and half a machine

– a combination of chromium, glass, wire and rods, in which I recognised the forms of the light display film (fig. 181). As it turned slowly, invisible lights flared on and off, producing gigantic shadows on the wall and ceiling.'[15] She gasped, to Moholy's delight, that it was almost as beautiful as the film itself.[16] In Paris he exhibited it in a box with a round viewing hole; small slowly flashing lights shone on it as it revolved, producing unexpected forms and shadows.

Moholy's contributions to the 1925 book *Die Bühne im Bauhaus* (*The Stage of the Bauhaus*), which he edited, fill out and develop his visionary plans for a stage production, the *Mechanischen Exzentrik* or (*Mechanised Eccentric*). What Moholy meant by 'eccentric' is a Dadaesque, non-logical, non-literary performance, but one not dominated by the human figure (as it was in Dada, and on Schlemmer's stage too). His long pull-out colour theatre score *Pariturskizze zu einer Mechanischen Exzentrik. Synthese von Form, Bewegung, Ton, Licht* (*Farbe*) *und Geruch* (*Sketch of a Score for a Mechanised Eccentric. Synthesis of Form, Movement, Sound, Light* [*Colour*] *and Smell*) promised an 'eccentric', illogical, immersive, and even humorous theatre experience. In his essay 'Theatre, Circus, Variety',[17] Moholy adds in other elements, including performers and set. He calls for 'pure and luminous chromatic tones' and film projections. The flares and sudden blinding effects of light, the startling black outs – all these, he says, are thought of 'in a sense totally different from anything in the current traditional theatre'.[18] Moholy had developed a vision that was peculiarly his own: one both biologically based and deeply ethical. He wanted not a *Gesamtkunstwerk* but a *Gesamtwerk*. Watching the *Mechanised Eccentric* would contribute to the necessary expansion of human perception that modern life demanded, a stretching of human abilities and capacities – a purposeful activity rather than a purely aesthetic experience.

Kandinsky's stage remained more rooted in expressionist metaphysics and he was perhaps closer to Schlemmer than to Moholy. His ideas draw on gestalt thinking that derived ultimately from Johann Wolfgang von Goethe, and the search for a unified work of art. He criticises Richard Wagner's stage as welding the artistic means (music, set, gesture, etc.) together externally and failing to touch the inner, necessarily abstract level (or 'necessity' as he calls it) where such diverse means (in simple gestalts) are able to resonate with each other.[19] As a result, in 1913, a few years before the Bauhaus opened, Kandinsky wrote the stage composition *Gelber Klang* (*Yellow Sound*), with its synthesis of coloured lights, abstract plastic forms and sounds, intended to stimulate the inner 'vibrations' of the viewer. Kandinsky remained hopeful that his early play would reach the stage of the Bauhaus, but Schlemmer did not take up the hint, since he himself had moved beyond what he felt was essentially the symbolism of Kandinsky's early script.

In fact, Kandinsky also moved on, absorbing more constructivist formal ideas, but he did not let go of his idea of setting his painterly abstract forms in motion. For the 1923 exhibition catalogue he wrote 'Abstract Synthesis on the Stage'[20] where he called for the melding of inner power, construction and composition.[21] This stage synthesis was supposedly rather more scientifically worked out than in *Yellow Sound* and paralleled the development in his painting into geometric, constructivist forms. In 1928 at the Friedrich Theatre Dessau, he produced an animated abstract stage set with moving colour blocks of triangles, spheres, lines (both wavy and straight), trapezoids and so on for Modest Mussorgsky's music, *Pictures at an Exhibition*. It was a 'painting evolving in time'.[22] As head of the wall-painting workshop between 1922 and 1925[23] he had maintained a desire for and interest in the 'temporal and spatial extension'[24] of his painterly ideas, and he continued to be interested in stage work. This, he said, was 'the period of the great analysis, which speaks out loud of the great synthesis'.[25]

Schlemmer tackled the analysis head on. He never played with stage light without a human being to illuminate, both literally and figuratively speaking. Light was crucial to his theatre:

> Let us rather open our eyes and expose our minds to the pure power of colour and light. If we can do this, we shall be surprised at how well the laws of colour and its mutations can be demonstrated by the use of coloured light in the physical and chemical laboratory of the theatre stage. With nothing more than simple stage lighting, we can begin to appreciate the many possibilities for the imaginative use of colour play.[26]

Moholy's later vision for a film studio/laboratory sounds similar:

> The studio for the manipulation of light will not, of course, be imitative like film studios of today. It will not be its ambition to transform plywood into forests or Jupiter lamps into sunshine. Work in that studio will proceed from the basic elements of the medium employed and the development of its inherent potentialities.[27]

In Dessau, working on his new tiny proscenium platform, with primitive equipment, Schlemmer insisted on putting the body centre stage. As in architecture, ambient light can act as a sculptural medium, transforming the shape, volume or texture of the object it illuminates, playing with the 'surface and border' information. This 'play' for Schlemmer could be the total content of a scene, modifying the amount of ambient rays, their direction and often their colour, working with transparent screens and the human body. Radiant light released this control. Schlemmer's piece *Metalatanz* (*Metal Dance*) was the stage equivalent to the Metal Party mentioned earlier: a feast of radiant light to blur the boundaries of space and its surfaces. In his stage design for Igor Stravinsky's *Les Noces* 1927–28, we also see his desire to experiment with more sophisticated technology using painted light screens.[29]

What Schlemmer ironically discovered was that the scientifically controlled experimentation with the 'ABCs' of borders and boundaries of the optical array that he began in *Raumtanz* (*Space Dance*) (three masked figures in padded plain suits smoothing out the human body to a uniform gestalt, articulating the space in carefully measured paces, centrally lit against uncontoured matt black) and in *Formtanz* (*Form Dance*) (where the same figures carry abstract geometrical forms of a stick, a hoop and a long bar) quickly spiralled into unexpectedly dynamic and mysterious territory, so that it is hard to correlate *Reifentanz* (*Hoop Dance*), for example, with the architectural project of the Bauhaus. *Hoop Dance* plays with ambient light but when set in motion is more Bridget Riley than Bauhaus. Here, dynamic form, structure with motion, the built-up *Gestaltung*, seems to have progressed beyond the Bauhaus project of analysing, controlling and understanding. Moholy never gave up the hope of nailing down the myriad of possibilities that space offered – sight, hearing, locomotion, equilibrium: 'I am convinced that sooner or later we shall have a genuine space system, a dictionary for space relationships, as we have today our colour system or as we have our sound system for musical composition.'[30] Schlemmer was always more doubtful.

Moholy talks of the 'psycho-physical effectiveness' of film[31] and the 'purely biological appeal'[32] that underlies the medium. A force or energy does seem to be communicated by certain images that are felt before they are 'thought' and which may not yield easily to subsequent logical analysis. They appear to touch a nerve and reveal a truth that is not easily articulated in words. Dancers revealed by a low-level light in absolute surrounding darkness, as an opening to a performance, when we know nothing of its context (which may be what audiences saw when the curtains opened on *Form Dance*) is an example of one such powerful image. And another I believe was the motile space of *Hoop Dance*. The problem is that today we believe that this perception is not biologically given but shaped by our embodied experience of the world. This immediate embodied perception is continually taking place in our lived perception of the world and continually unnoticed. As Maurice Merleau-Ponty wrote, 'It is the unreflected which is understood and conquered by reflection. Left to itself, perception forgets itself and is ignorant of its own accomplishments.'[33] The Bauhaus experimented with this layer of perception that normally 'forgets itself'. Understand the basic elements, they thought, and the resulting creative combinations, like musical notes in a symphony, will be infinite but analysable. Its project, however, was never realised.

Whilst we inevitably see Schlemmer and his colleagues as embedded in their era: modernist, experimental, quasi-scientific, analytical and often misguided, we can also choose to see them as verging on the extraordinary. Their experiments into flux, uncertainty and release – touching on discoveries about consciousness itself – were as embodied, intentional and dynamic as light.

1 László Moholy-Nagy, 'Light: A New Medium of Expression' [1939], *Architectural Forum*, LXX, Time Inc., reprinted in Richard Kostelanetz, *Moholy-Nagy*, Allen Lane, The Penguin Press, London, 1970, pp.151–55.

2 Oskar Schlemmer, 'Theater (Bühne)' [1927] in Walter Gropius and A. Wensinger (eds) [1925/1961] *The Theater of the Bauhaus*, trans. Arthur Wensinger, John Hopkins University Press, Baltimore and London, 1996, pp.81–101, originally published as 'aus einem vortrag von oskar schlemmer mit demonstrationen auf der bühne vor dem kreis der freunde des bauhauses am 16 märz 1927', in Walter Gropius and László Moholy-Nagy, *bauhaus* 3, pp.1–4. I have translated here directly from the original Bauhaus book since Wensinger's translation (which I have used elsewhere) in the Gropius and Wensinger 1961 edition is not clear.

3 See Norbert Schmitz, 'László Moholy-Nagy', in Jeannine Fiedler and Peter Feierabend (eds), *Bauhaus*, Könemann, Cologne, 2000, pp.292–301, who describes how pigment became for Moholy-Nagy a 'place for storing light', p.299.

4 See Rose-Carol Washton Long, 'From Metaphysics to Material Culture Painting and Photography at the Bauhaus', in Kathleen James-Chakraborty (ed.), *Bauhaus Culture from Weimar to the Cold War*, University of Minnesota Press, Minneapolis and London, 2006, pp.43–62, for an exploration of Kandinsky and Moholy-Nagy's mix of expressionist and constructivist influences; and Michael White, 'Mechano-Facture: Dada/Constructivism and the Bauhaus', in Achim Borchardt-Hume (ed.), *Albers and Moholy-Nagy: From Bauhaus to the New World*, exhibition catalogue, Tate Publishing, London, 2006, pp.79–84, on the mutual interplay of Dada and Constructivism.

5 Thomas Schober, *Das Theater der Maler*, M & P, Stuttgart, 1994, p.137.

6 Oskar Schlemmer, [A. Langen-G. Müller, Munich, 1958], in Tut Schlemmer (ed.), *Oskar Schlemmer Briefe und Tagebücher*, Verlag Gerd Hatje, Stuttgart, 1977, p.110. My translation.
7 László Moholy-Nagy, *Painting Photography Film* [1925], trans. Janet Seligman, Lund Humphries, London, 1969, p.30, originally published as *Malerei, Fotografie, Film*, Bauhausbücher 8, Albert Langen Verlag, Munich, 1927.
8 Ibid.
9 See Melissa Trimingham, *The Theatre of the Bauhaus: the Modern and Postmodern Stage of Oskar Schlemmer*, Routledge, London, 2011, p.143.
10 Moholy-Nagy, *Painting Photography Film*, op. cit., p.8.
11 Ibid.
12 James Gibson, *The Senses Considered as Perceptual Systems*, Houghton and Mifflin and Co., Boston, 1966, pp.193–94.
13 Krisztina Passuth, 'László Moholy-Nagy activist painter 1917–1921', in *lászló moholy-nagy*, exhibition catalogue, ACGB (Arts Council of Great Britain), London, 1980, p.7.
14 In the film *Eine Lichtspiel, schwarz-weiß-grau* [1930], to which Sybil Moholy-Nagy here refers, it is noticeable how prominent the apparatus is. In this way, it was a kinetic sculpture too, a large version of which would be watched by a theatre audience as much as the shadow and light effects it produced.
15 Sibyl Moholy-Nagy, 'The Light-Display Machine' [1950], in *Experiment in Totality*, MIT Press, Cambridge, Mass., 1969, pp.64 and 66–67, reprinted in Kostelanetz, *Moholy-Nagy*, op. cit., pp.147–48.
16 But not quite as good. This pleased him and justified his making the film.
17 László Moholy-Nagy, 'Theater, Circus, Variety' [1925], in ibid, pp.49–70, orginally published as 'Theater, Zirkus, Varieté', in Walter Gropius and László Maholy-Nagy, *Die Bühne im Bauhaus*, Albert Langen Verlag, Bauhausbücher 4, Munich, 1925, pp.45–56.
18 Ibid.
19 Wassily Kandinsky, 'On the Spiritual in Art' [1912], in Kenneth C. Lindsay and Peter Vergo (eds), *Kandinsky, Complete Writings in Art*, vol. 1, trans. Kenneth C. Lindsay and Peter Vergo, Faber and Faber, London, 1982, pp.257–65.
20 Wassily Kandinsky 'Abstract Synthesis on the Stage' [1923], in ibid., p.505.
21 Ibid., p.507.
22 Günther Berghaus, *Theatre, Performance and the Historical Avant-Garde*, Palgrave Macmillan, London, 2005, p.225.
23 Christine Mehring, 'Wassily Kandinsky Designs for Wall Paintings 1922', in Barry Bergdoll and Leah Dickerman (eds), *Bauhaus 1919–1933 Workshops for Modernity*, exhibition catalogue, The Museum of Modern Art, New York, 2009, pp.122–27.
24 Wassily Kandinsky, 'Abstract Synthesis on the Stage' [1923], 'On the Spiritual in Art', op. cit., p.504.
25 Ibid, p.506.
26 Schlemmer, 'Theater (Bühne)', op. cit., p.96.
27 László Moholy-Nagy, 'Problems of Modern Film' [1928–30], *Cahiers d'Art*, VII/6–77, Paris [1932], reprinted in Kostelanetz, *Moholy-Nagy*, op. cit., pp.133–34.
28 Gibson, *The Senses Considered as Perceptual Systems*, op. cit., 1966.
29 See *oskar schlemmer tanz theater bühne*, exhibition catalogue, Kunstsammlung Nordrhein-Westfalen, Düsseldorf, Kunsthalle Wien and Sprengel Museum Hannover, Gerd Hatje, Stuttgart, 1994, pp.246–53.
30 László Maholy-Nagy, 'The New Bauhaus and Space Relationships' [1937], in *American Art and Architecture*, CLI, reprinted in Kostelanetz, *Moholy-Nagy*, op. cit., p.109.
31 László Moholy-Nagy, 'Supplementary Remarks on the Sound and Colour Film', in *Telehor*, Brno, reprinted in ibid., p.141.
32 Moholy-Nagy, 'Problems of Modern Film', op. cit., p.133.
33 Maurice Merleau-Ponty, 'The Primacy of Perception and Its Philosophical Consequences', in John O'Neil (ed.), *Phenomenology, Language and Sociology*, Heinemann, London, 1974, p.19.

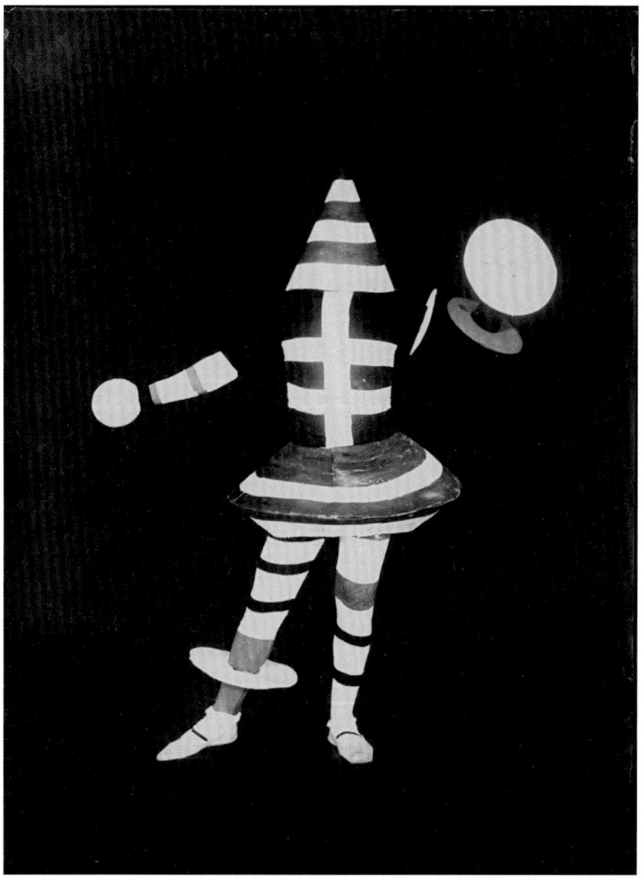

179
Lucia Moholy
Performers from Bauhaus stage production *Der Mann am Schaltbrett* (*Man at the Control Panel*) by Kurt Schmidt, 1924 (printed c.1950)
Gelatin silver print
Harvard Art Museums/Busch-Reisinger Museum. Gift of Walter Gropius

opposite page
180
Oskar Schlemmer
Bauhaustänze, Metalltanz (*Bauhaus Dances, Metal Dance*), 1929
Vintage print, altered and mounted by the artist
17.4 × 13 cm
Photographer Robert Binnemann
Bühnen Archiv Oskar Schlemmer/ The Oskar Schlemmer Theatre Estate

181
László Moholy-Nagy
Stills from *Ein Lichtspiel: schwarz weiss grau* (*Light Play: black white grey*), 1930
35 mm, black and white, sound, 6 minutes
Hattula Moholy-Nagy

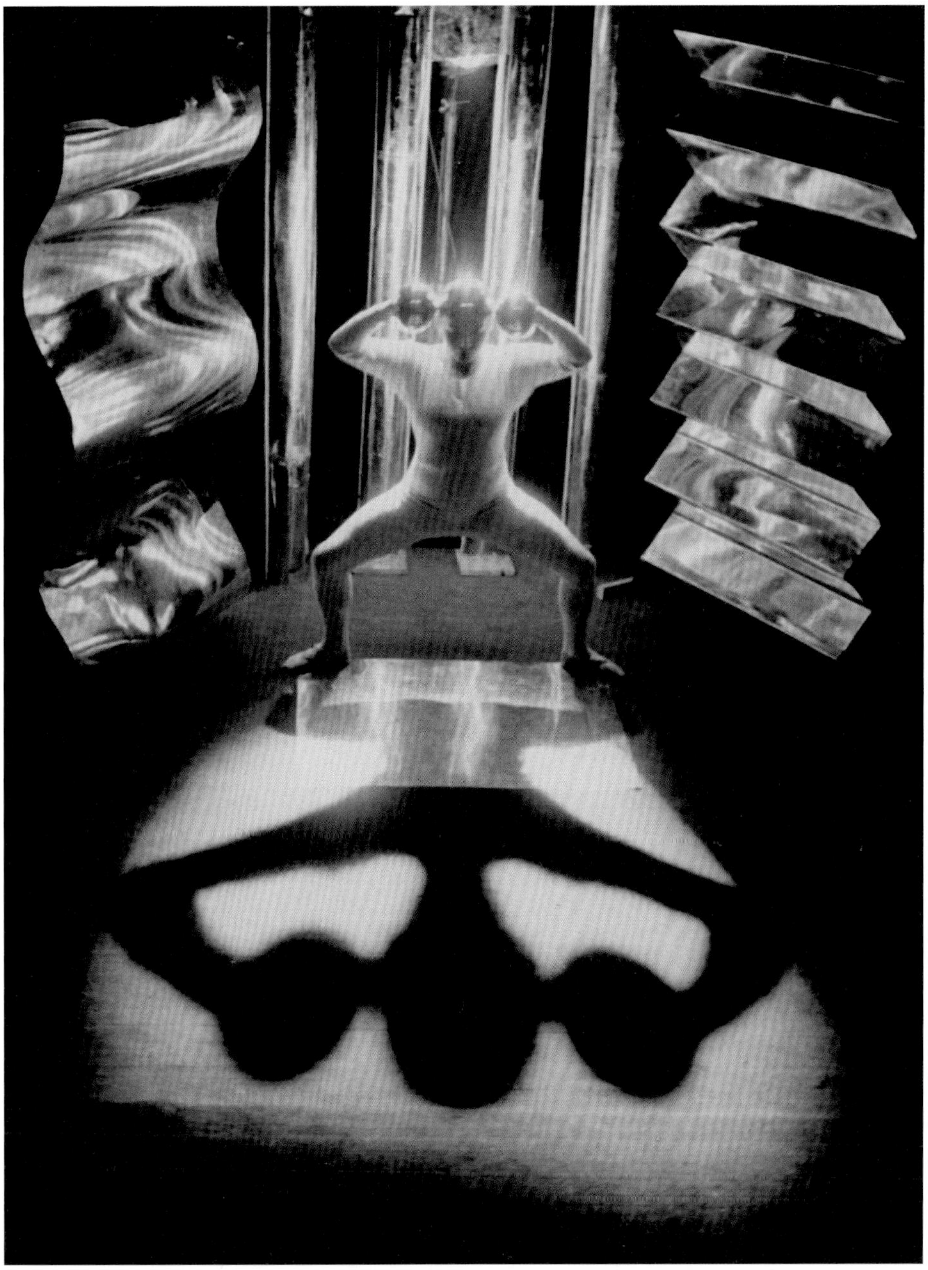

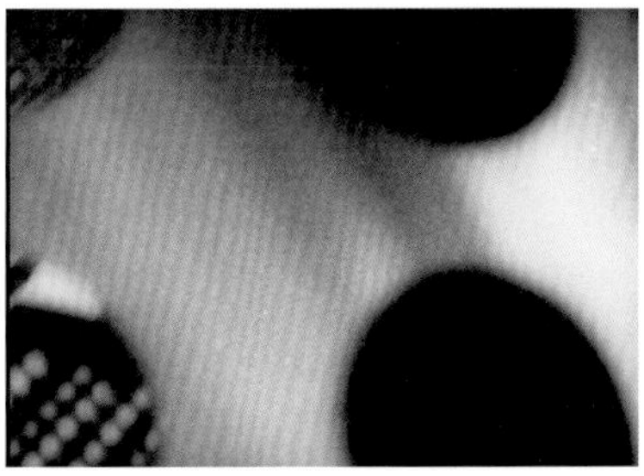

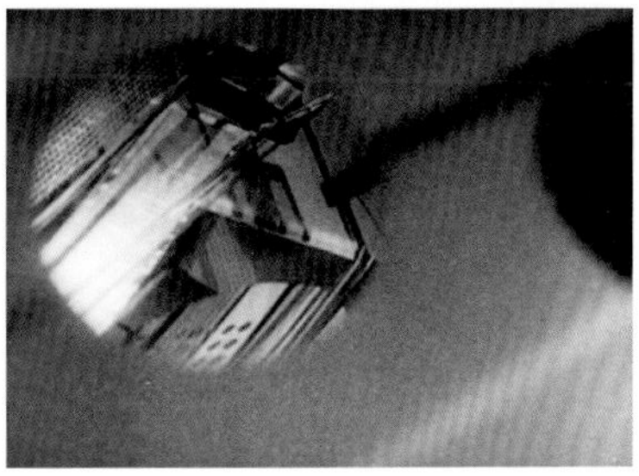

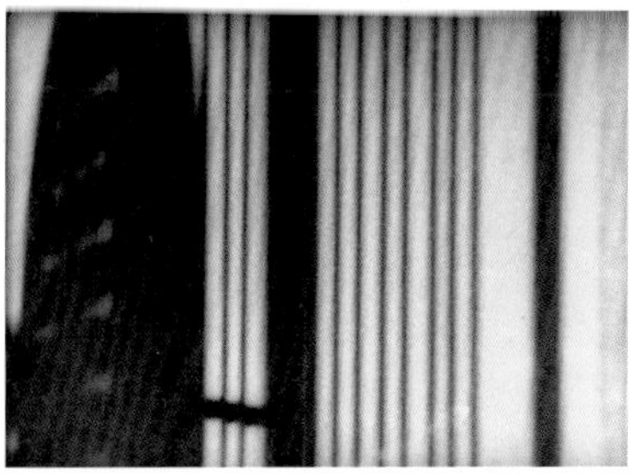

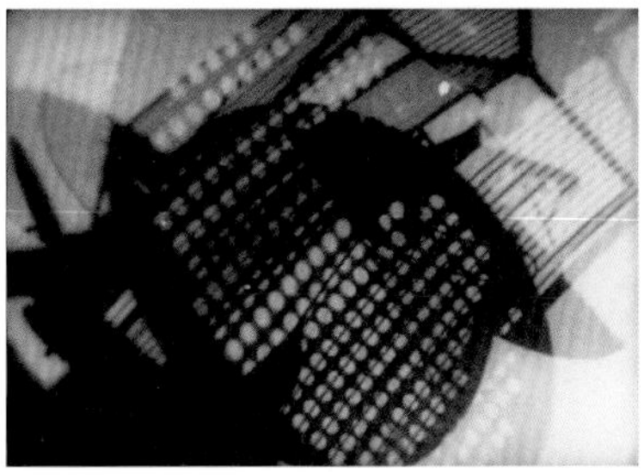

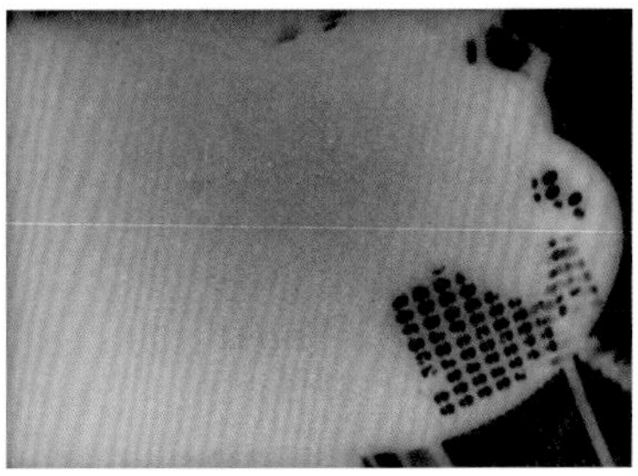

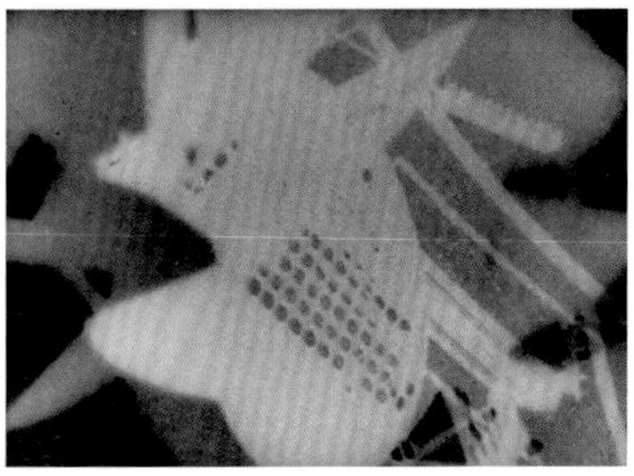

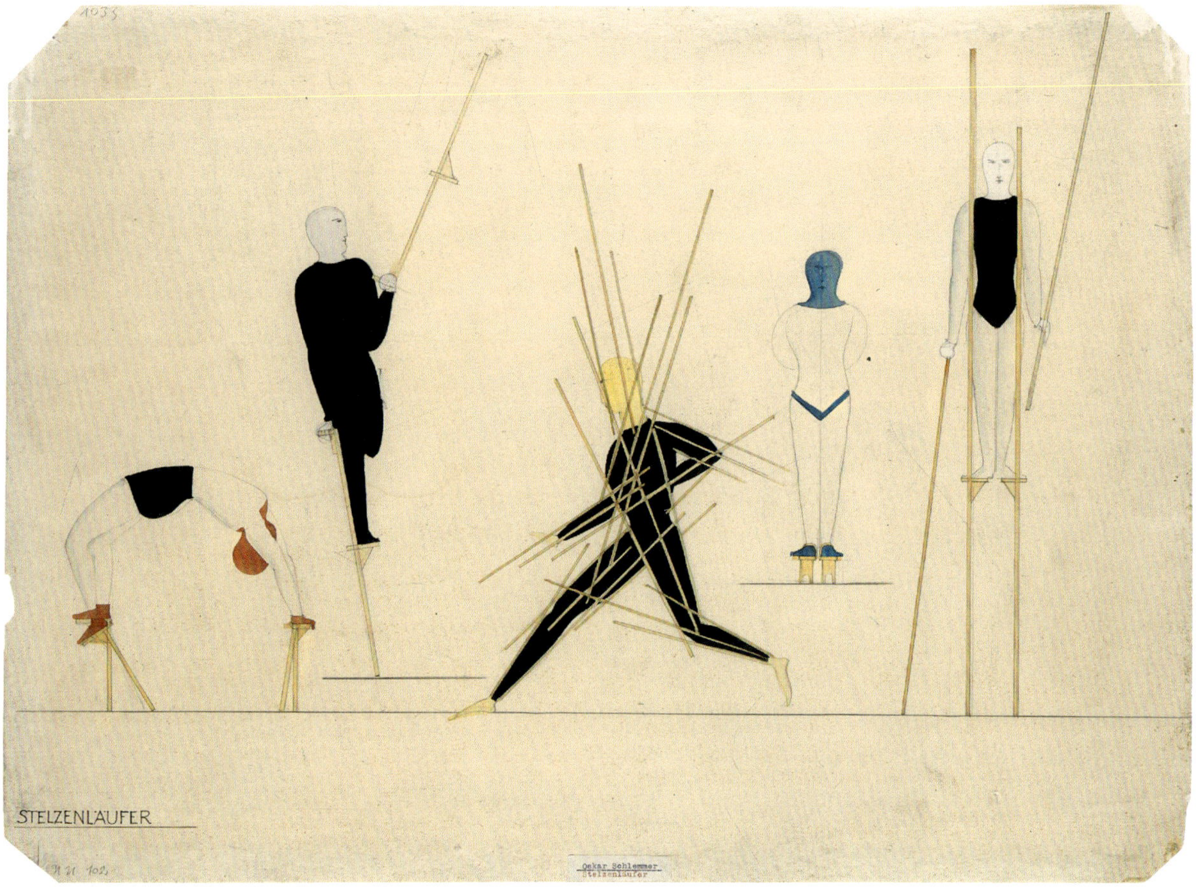

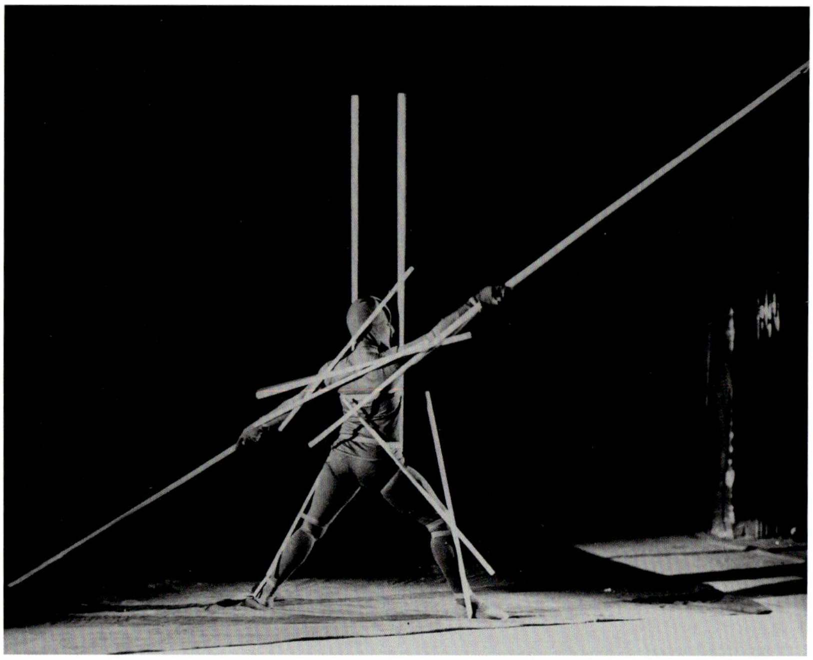

182
Oskar Schlemmer
Stelzenläufer (*Stilt Runner*), 1927
Watercolour and pencil
45.3 × 60.7 cm
Bühnen Archiv Oskar Schlemmer/
The Oskar Schlemmer Theatre Estate
Collection UJS

183
Oskar Schlemmer
Bauhaustänze, Stäbetanz (*Bauhaus Dances, Dance with Poles*), 1928
Vintage print, altered and mounted
by the artist
17.5 × 11.3 cm
Photographer T. Lux Feininger
Dancer: Manda von Kreibig
Bühnen Archiv Oskar Schlemmer/
The Oskar Schlemmer Theatre Estate
Collection UJS

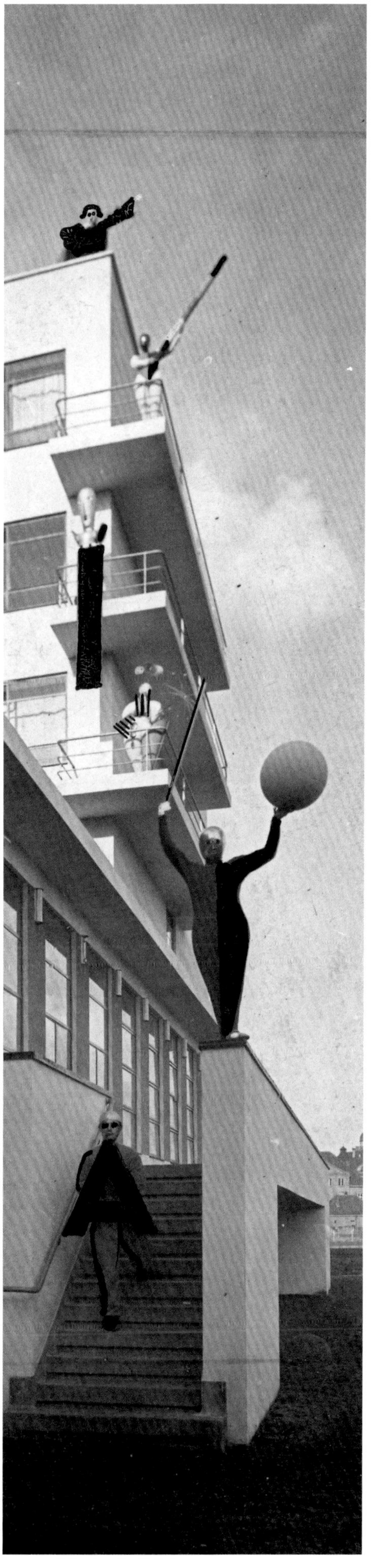

184
Oskar Schlemmer
Oskar Schlemmer's, *The Building as Stage,* 1928
Gelatin silver print
17 × 4,1 cm
Photograph attributed to T. Lux Feininger or Erich Consemüller
Bauhaus-Archiv Berlin

When Oskar Schlemmer was appointed as head of the Bauhaus stage workshop in 1923, he elaborated his own theory based on his *Typenfiguren* as well as on his experience with *The Triadic Ballet* and as a dancer. Schlemmer conceived the art of the stage as an art of space. Elements, such as space, light, colour, metal and glass, and forms, such as cubes, poles, hoops or just a glove, emphasised the dancers' movements. For some dances, a black stage with a diagram on the floor determined the space and underlined the directions of movement. Accompanied by music composed by Schlemmer, the dancers, Schlemmer himself and his students, wore masks in gold, silver or bronze and their costumes and props were in the primary colours of blue, red and yellow, complemented by black, grey and white.

For the new Bauhaus building in Dessau, Gropius designed a theatre space based on the specifications of Schlemmer, The stage could be open on both sides: to the auditorium in front and the canteen at the rear. As part of a *Gesamtkunstwerk*, Schlemmer envisioned the transformation of the total architectural structure into a total stage space: the *Building as Stage*. Schlemmer came closest to this concept in performances he staged on the roof terrace and in directing and orchestrating the experimental Bauhaus festivals, such as the White Party in 1926 and the Metal Party in 1929.

C. Raman Schlemmer

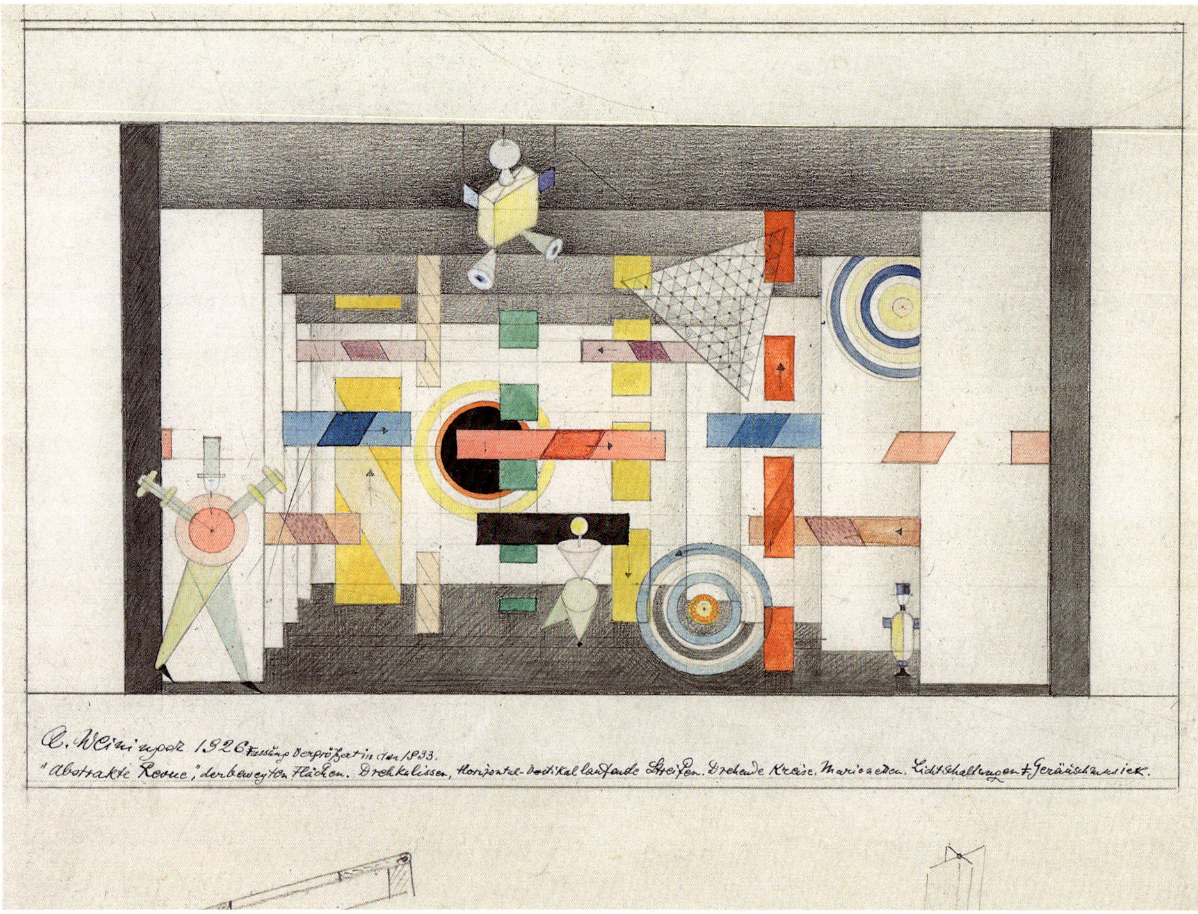

185
Andor Weininger
Scenography for mechanical stage-revue diagram with marionette figure: phase I – III, 1926
Pencil and watercolour on card
20.2 × 30 cm
Theaterwissenschaftliche Sammlung, Universität zu Köln

186
Wassily Kandinsky
II. Gnomus (*Gnome*). Second of sixteen movements for Modest Mussorgsky's *Pictures at an Exhibition* for performance at the Friedrichtheater, Dessau, April 11, 1929, c. 1930
Ink, tempera and watercolour on paper
20.5 × 35.8 cm
Theaterwissenschaftliche Sammlung, Universität zu Köln

187
Wassily Kandinsky
XV. Hütte der Baba-Jaga (*The Hut of Baba Yaga*). Fifteenth of sixteen movements for Modest Mussorgsky's *Pictures at an Exhibition* for performance at the Friedrichtheater, Dessau, April 11, 1929, c. 1930
Ink, tempera and watercolour on paper
39 × 56.5 cm
Theaterwissenschaftliche Sammlung, Universität zu Köln

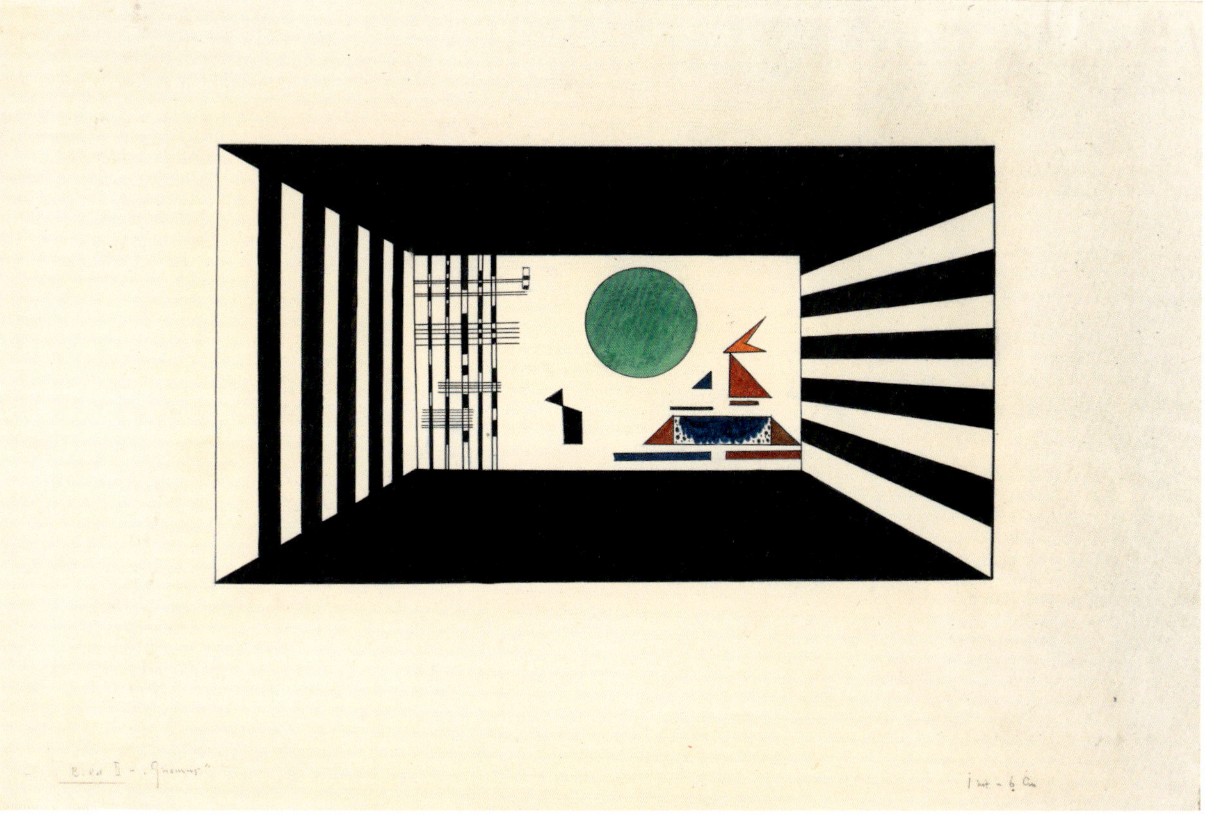

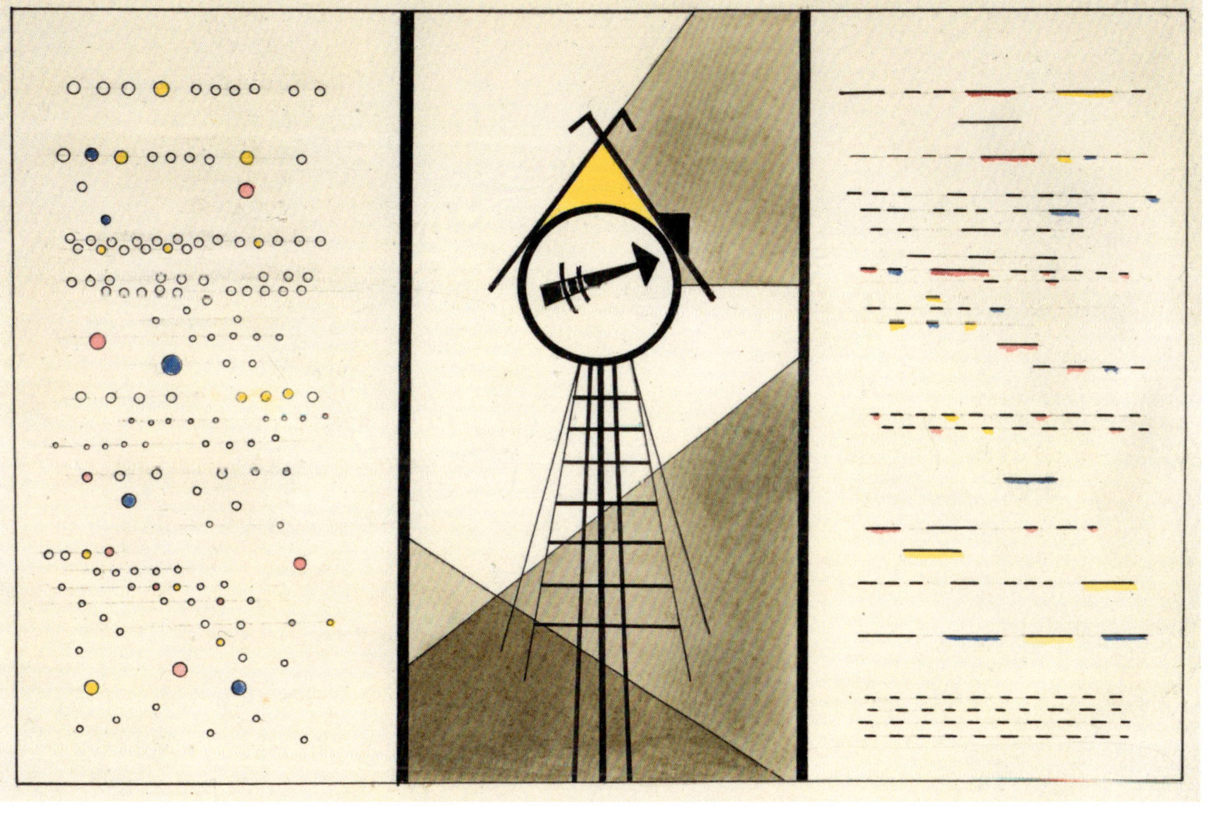

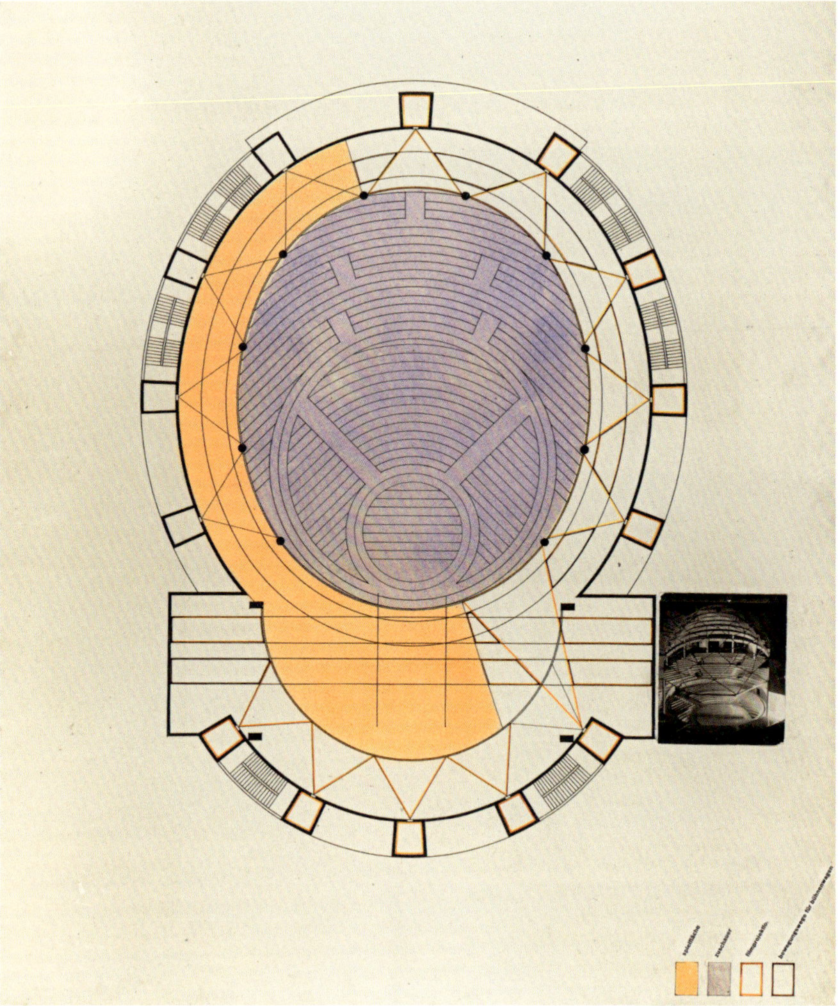

188
Walter Gropius, drawing by Stefan Sebök
Total Theatre, Berlin, 1926–27
Designed for Erwin Piscator
Photocollage, ink over blueprint
Theaterwissenschaftliche Sammlung,
Universität zu Köln

Gropius was commissioned by the radical left-wing theatre director Erwin Piscator to design a fully mechanised theatre. Piscator had already established a reputation for staging theatre where the action took place in the round and projected film and images were integral to the set. For Piscator, the *Total Theatre* was to go a step further to unite architecture and performance: 'What I had in mind was a theatre machine … an apparatus that would incorporate the latest lighting, the latest sliding and revolving scenery, both vertical and horizontal, numerous projection boxes, loudspeakers everywhere.' Gropius's design, developed with architect Stefan Sebök, other members of his office and Bauhaus colleagues, drew heavily on experience gained through the staging of experimental theatre at the Bauhaus. Oval in plan and with a parabolic roof shaped so as to optimise acoustic conditions, the theatre included walkways for processions or choirs, both within and behind the area occupied by the audience. Most notably, it featured a revolving platform that allowed the main circular stage to be moved from the proscenium to the centre of the auditorium and two further stages that could be shifted during a performance. After the financial crash in 1929, funding for the *Total Theatre* fell through and Gropius and Piscator are believed to have fallen out after the architect sought a patent for the mechanised stage claiming the design as entirely his own.

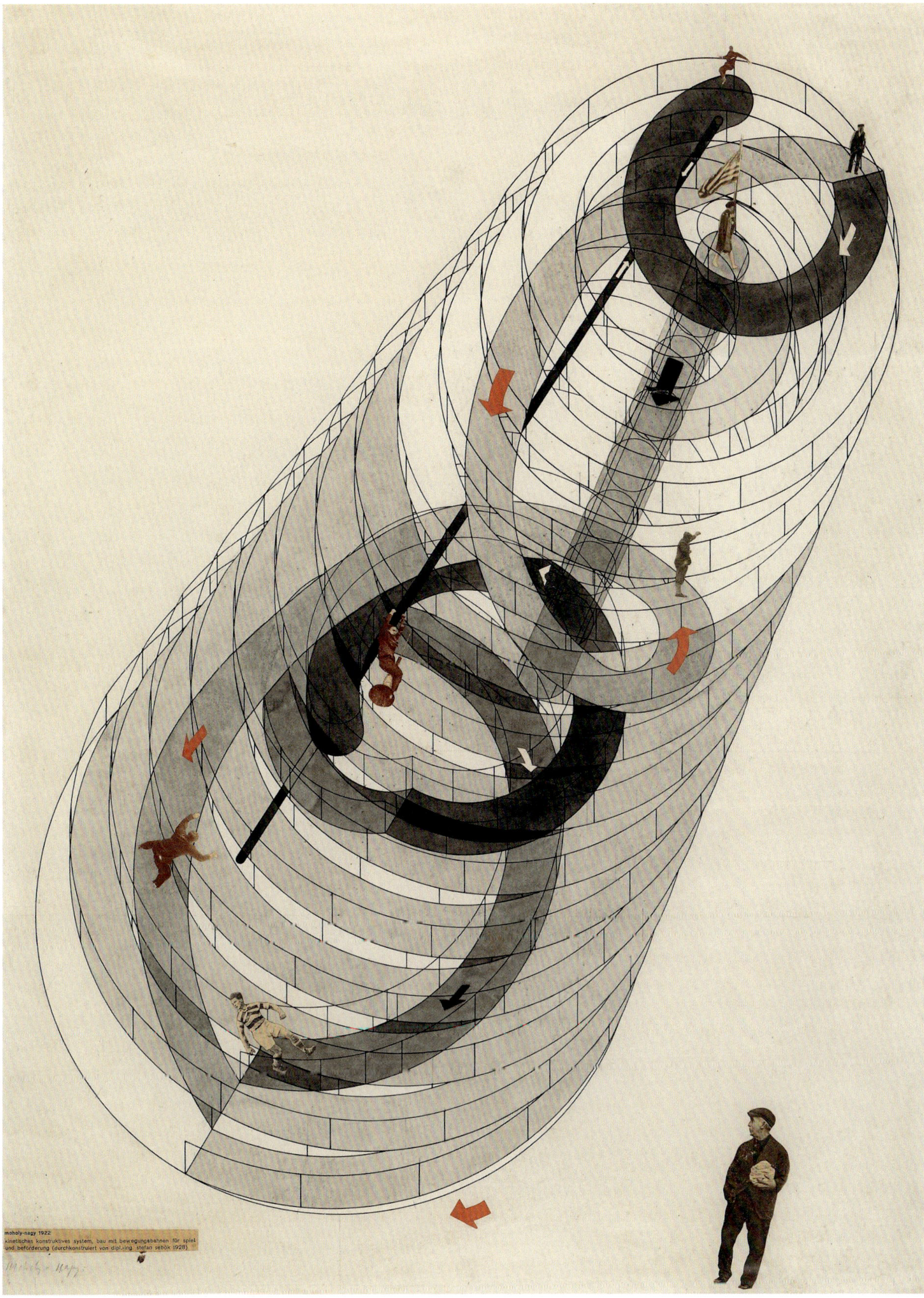

189
László Moholy-Nagy
Kinetic constructive system (structure for moving parts for play and movement), 1922–28
Photomontage, ink and watercolour on card
76 × 54.5 cm
Theaterwissenschaftliche Sammlung, Universität zu Köln

designing the modern world

212

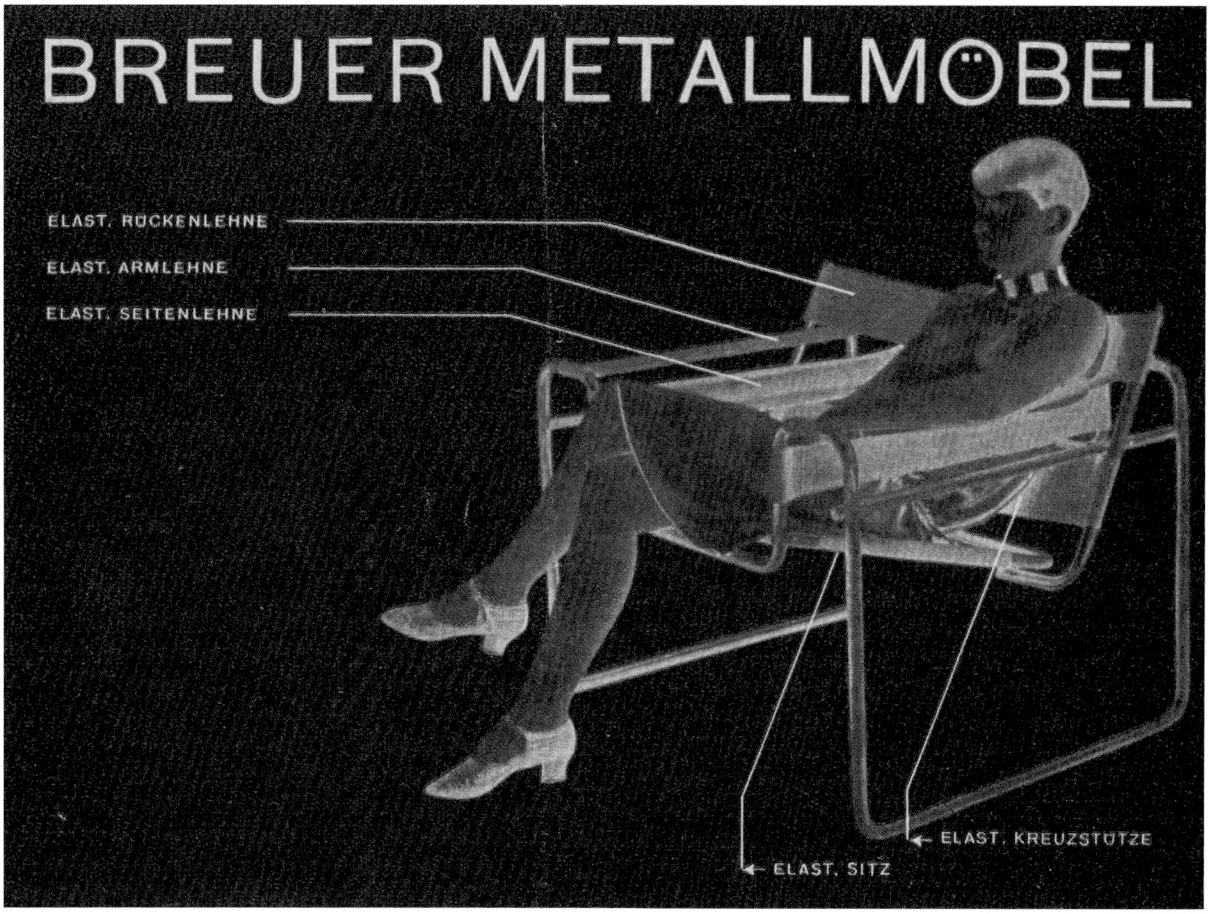

In 1926 the Bauhaus was awarded university status and given the designation 'Institute of Design'. Masters became 'professors' and the terms previously applied to students – 'apprentices' or 'journeymen' – were dropped. The following year the curriculum was reorganised and architecture, advertising, theatre, and free painting and sculpture became the cornerstones of Bauhaus teaching. Led by the newly appointed Hannes Meyer, the architecture programme encompassed building and interior decoration, within which the metal, cabinetry, weaving and wall-painting workshops were grouped. Theatre, under the direction of Oskar Schlemmer, finally occupied a prominent position in Bauhaus teaching. Advertising included typography, printing, and, from 1929, a dedicated photography course. Free art and pictorial design classes were taught by Paul Klee and Wassily Kandinsky in an attempt to revitalise the subordinated role of painting at the school. Teaching of the preliminary course continued under the direction of László Moholy-Nagy and Josef Albers.

Walter Gropius and Meyer were united in their belief that architecture should only be taught in conjunction with building and undertook large-scale projects, including the Gropius-designed Törten housing estate in Dessau, and the School of the German Trade Union Federation (known as ADGB) by Meyer and Hans Wittwer in Bernau.

In 1928 Gropius resigned as director of the Bauhaus, citing his desire to focus on his own architectural work. He was followed by Moholy, Bayer and Breuer, who left the same year to pursue private practice in Berlin. Meyer took over as director and although he maintained the key principles of Bauhaus pedagogy, emphasis shifted to a scientific and theoretical methodology instead of one based on the intellectual unity of the arts. His mission was to provide 'necessities not luxuries'. In his inaugural speech to students and faculty, Meyer, echoing Gropius, underlined the need for workshops to 'develop design ability' because 'we, as human beings, are living for no other reason than to solve the problems posed by life'. New workshop facilities equipped with sophisticated tools and machinery enabled students to experiment with production processes used in industry. The potential of new technologies and the problems of manufacturing were most enthusiastically explored in the metal, cabinetry and weaving workshops. Meyer continued Gropius's efforts to direct the workshops towards commercial productivity and new contracts were secured with lighting manufacturers and, eventually, wallpaper producers. Gunta Stölzl became the head of the weaving workshop in 1927 and introduced a systematic approach to workshop training. Students were exposed to all areas of the textile production process – from design and construction to dyeing methods and material purchasing. Marianne Brandt returned to the Bauhaus, after a brief sojourn in Paris, as a *Mitarbeiter* (associate) of the metal workshop.

Cabinetry workshop products characterised by lightness, consistency of design and technical innovation aimed to enhance and unify the interior architecture for which they were created. The chair was the furniture form used most readily to explore questions of design and economic manufacture within the context of everyday life.

Although seemingly disconnected, basic courses in colour and form theory continued to exert influence on workshop investigations. Emphasis was given to the production of prototypes for manufacture through, crucially, creative experimentation with not only materials and technology but also the formal, aesthetic and constructive principles that were the fundamentals of Bauhaus education.

190
Herbert Bayer
Brochure of *Breuer Metallmöbel* (Breuer metal furniture)
Loose-leaf sales catalogue for furniture offered by the Standard Möbel company, showing Breuer's B3 club chair of 1925, c.1927
Half-tone and letterpress on paper
14.8 × 21 cm
Bauhaus-Archiv Berlin

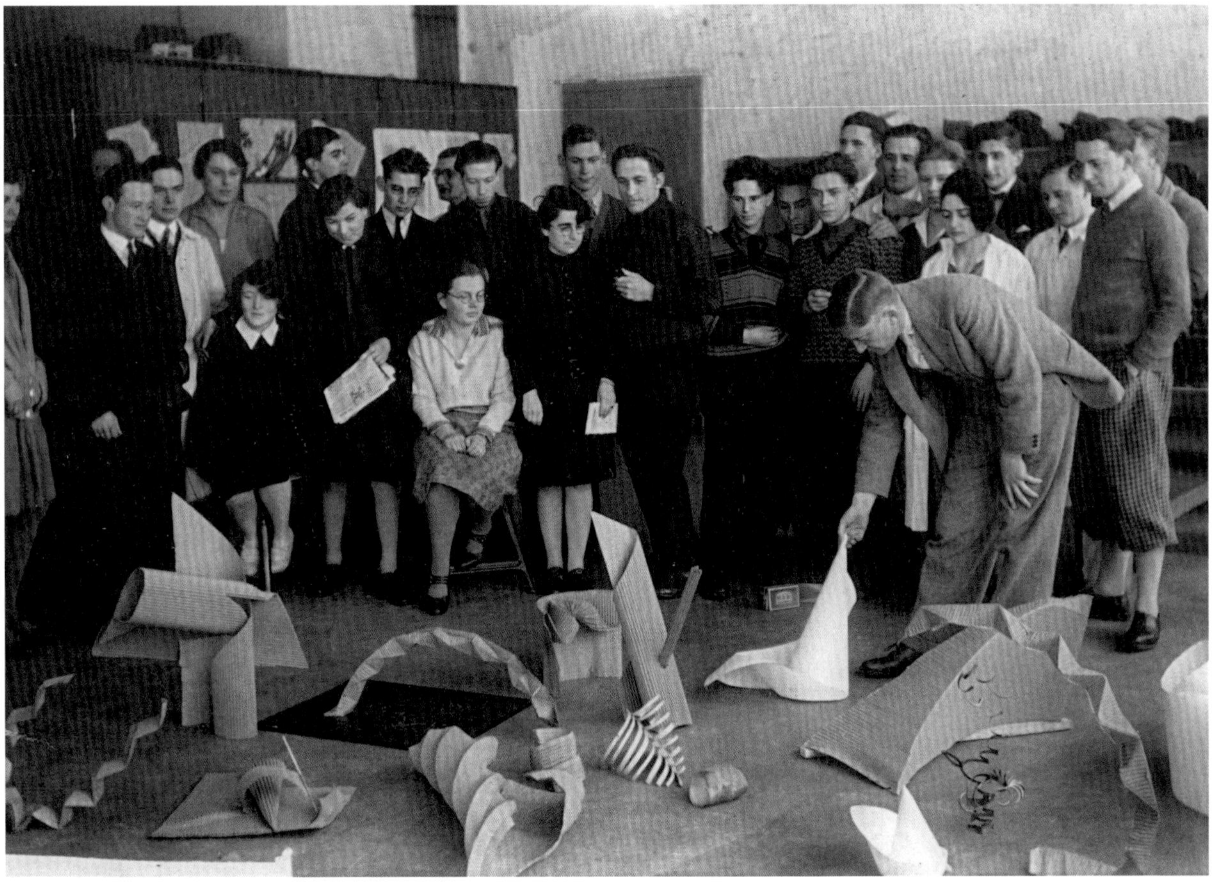

191
Umbo (Otto Umbehr)
Josef Albers and students in a group critique at the Bauhaus Dessau, 1928–29
Gelatin silver print
12.6 × 17.1 cm
The Josef and Anni Albers Foundation

192
Takehiko Mizutani
Material study from Josef Albers's preliminary course, 1927
Sheet brass
73.5 × 50 cm
Bauhaus-Archiv Berlin

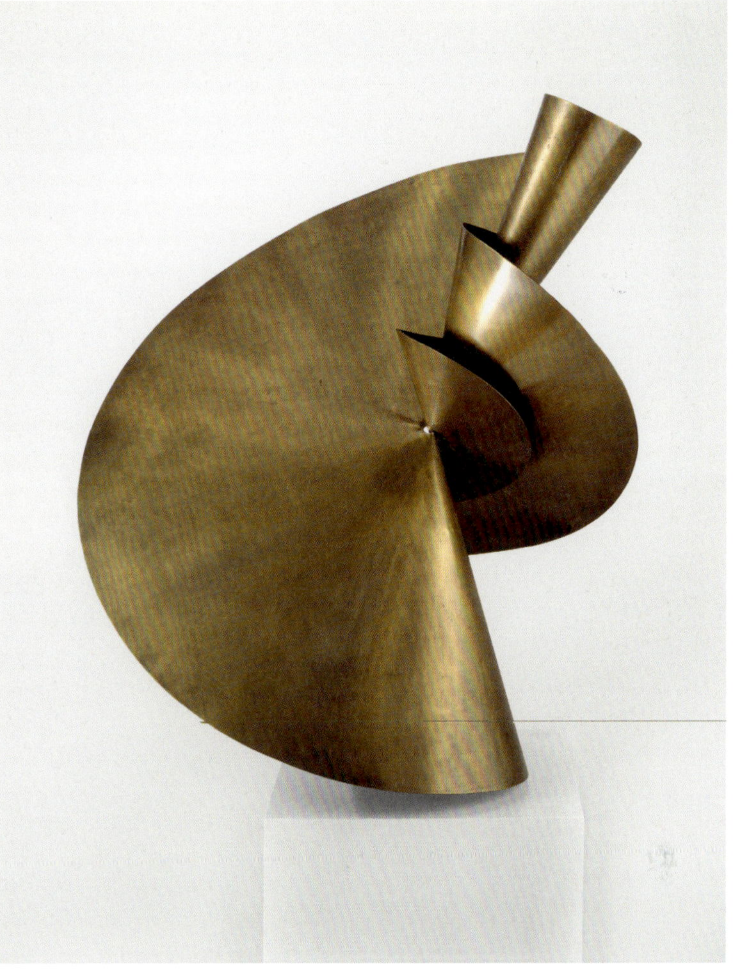

193
Artist unknown
Exercise from Josef Albers's preliminary course, n.d.
Industrially painted wire screen
30.5 × 12.7 cm
The Josef and Anni Albers Foundation

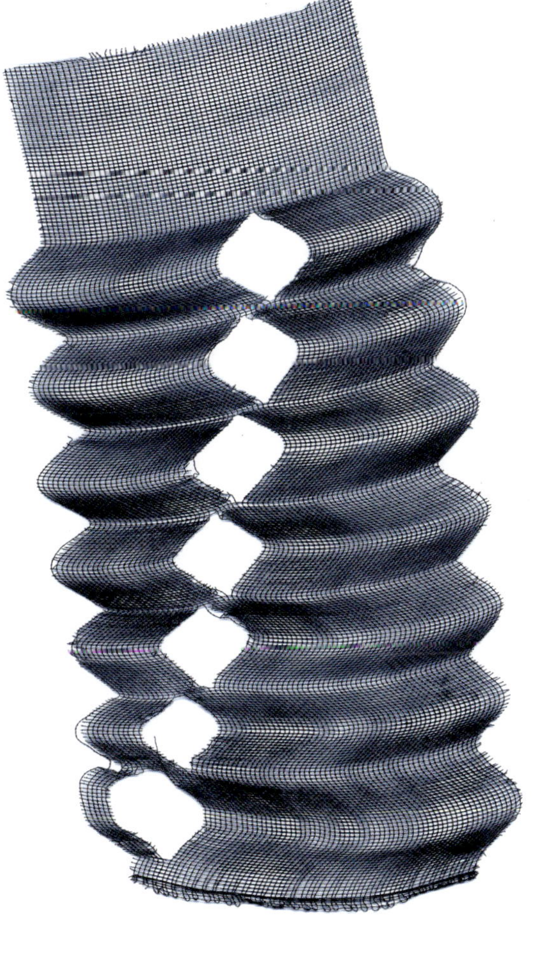

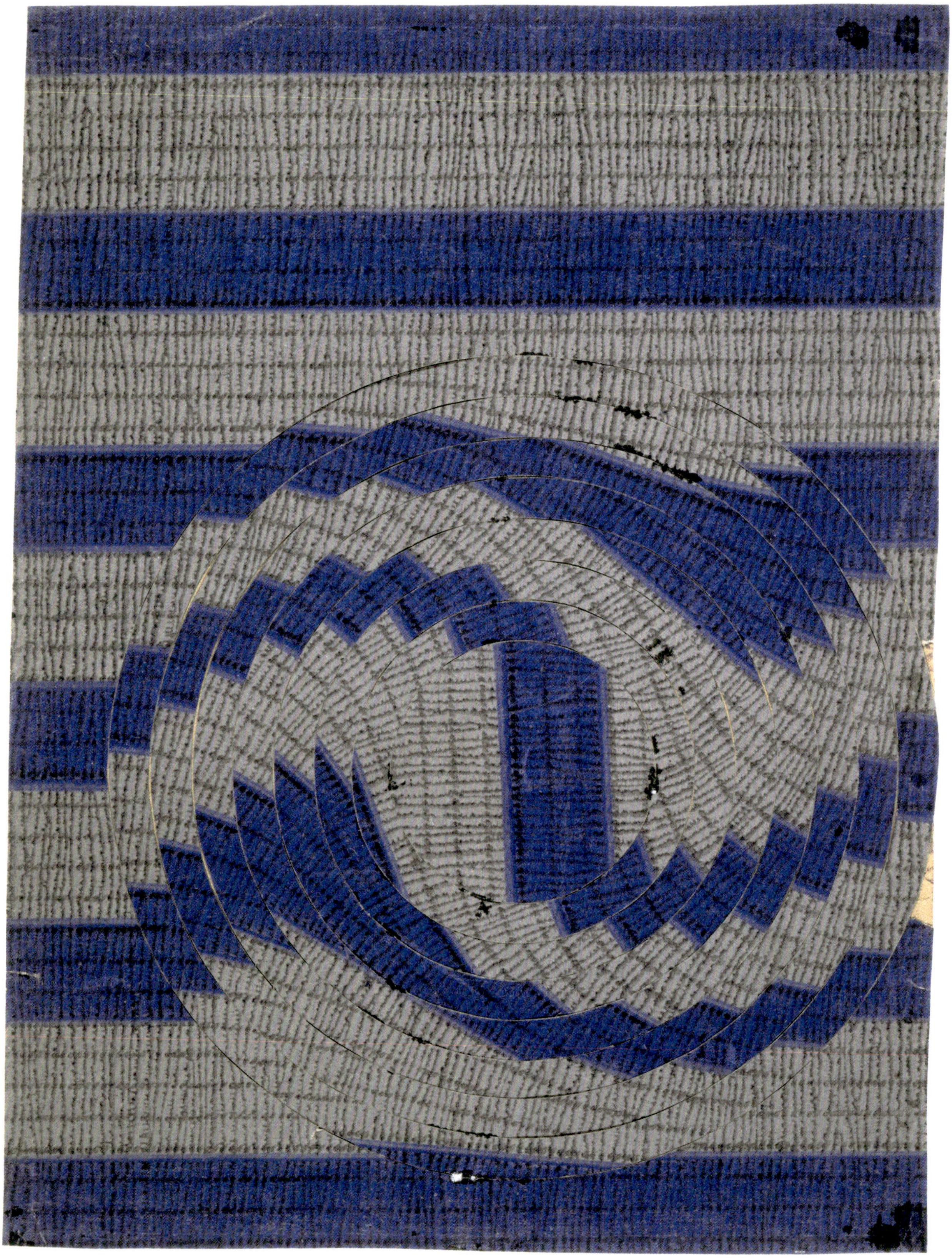

194
Monica Bella Ullman-Broner
Exercise from Josef Albers's preliminary course, 1929–30
Collage of patterned wallpaper on cardboard
31 × 22.9 cm
Bauhaus-Archiv Berlin

195
Artist unknown
Reordering study from Josef Albers's preliminary course, n.d.
Collage on newsprint
21 x 29.3 cm
The Josef and Anni Albers Foundation

196
Hajo Rose
Design for a fabric print pattern made from typewriter type, 1932
Type on paper
29.5 × 20.9 cm
Bauhaus-Archiv Berlin

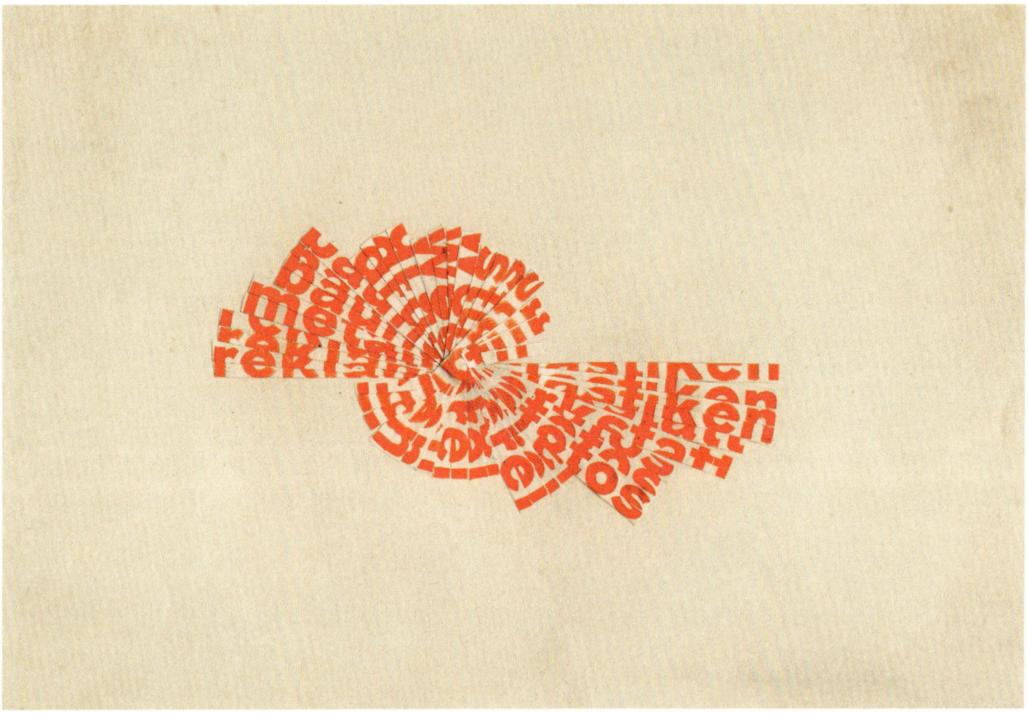

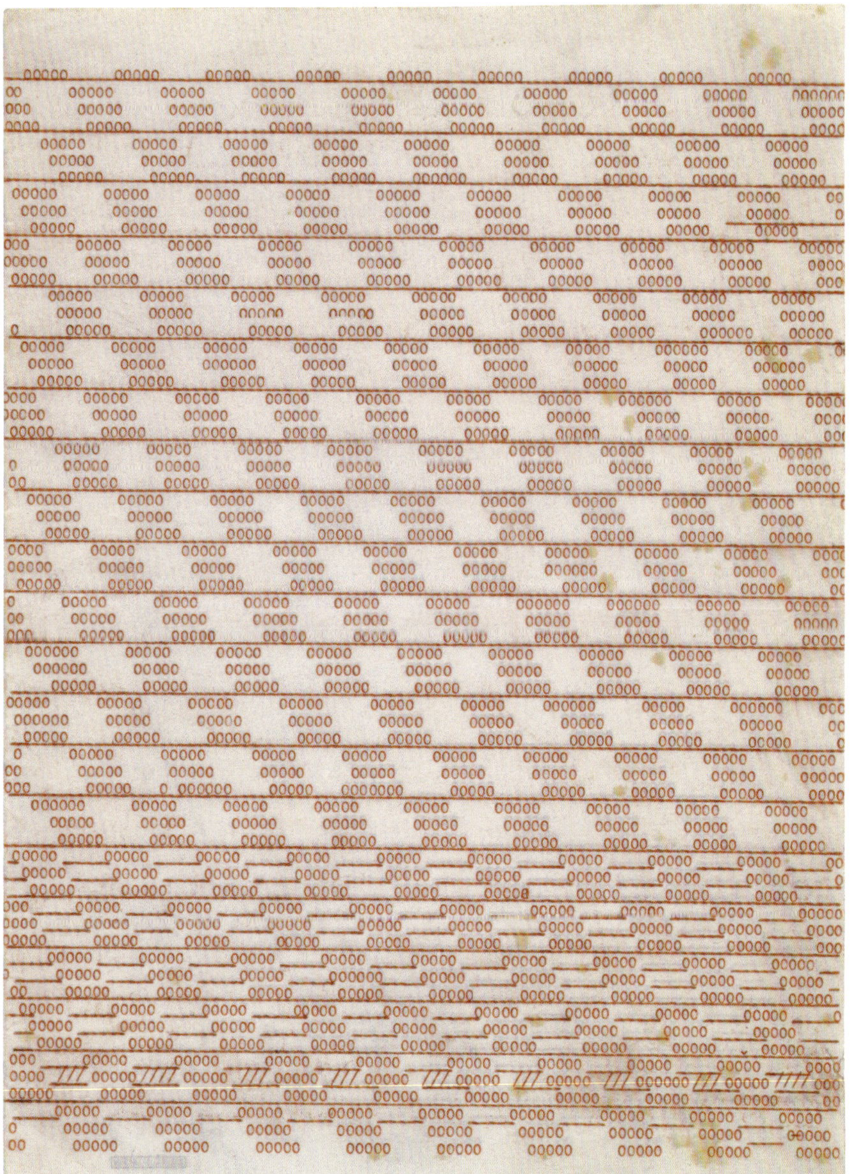

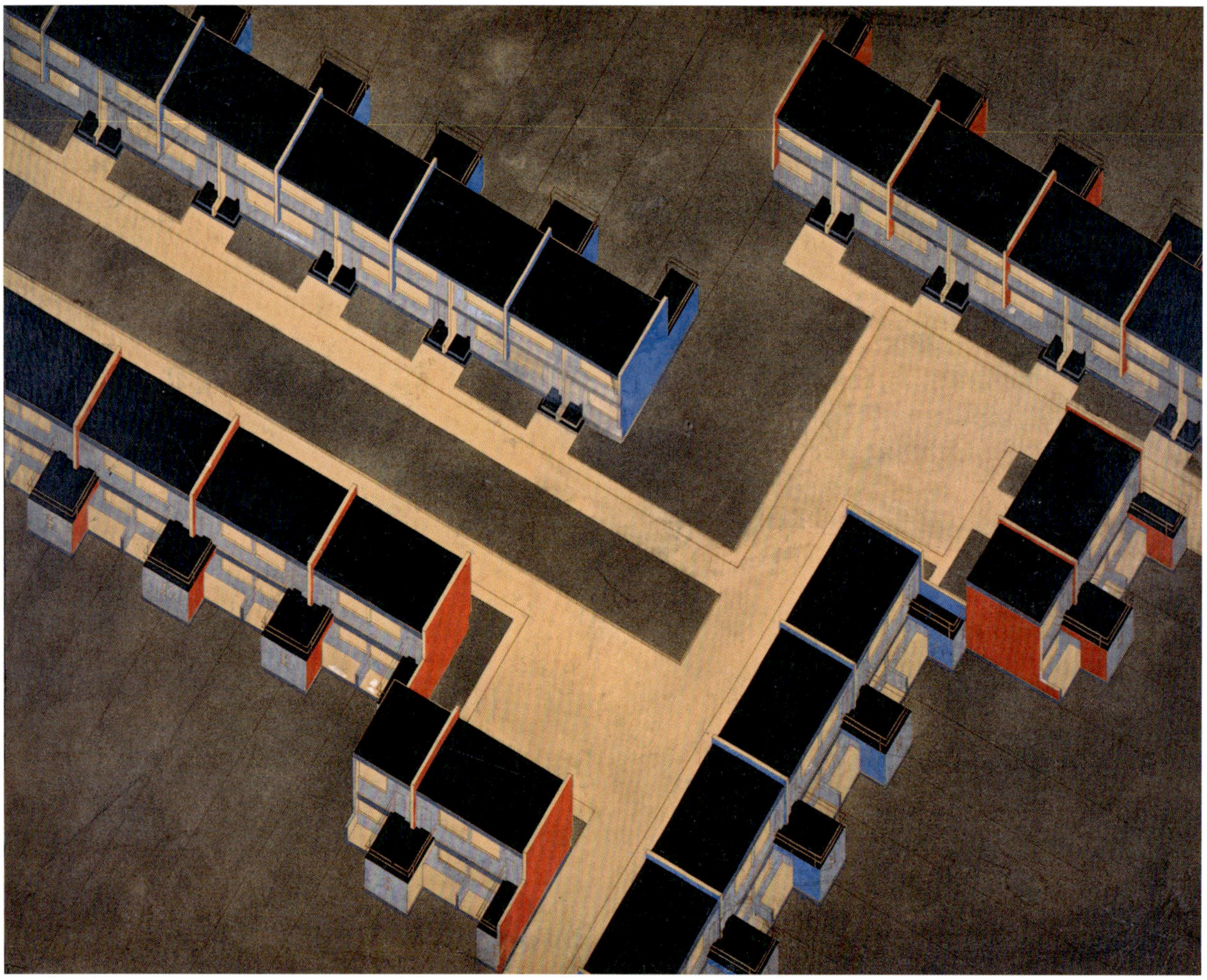

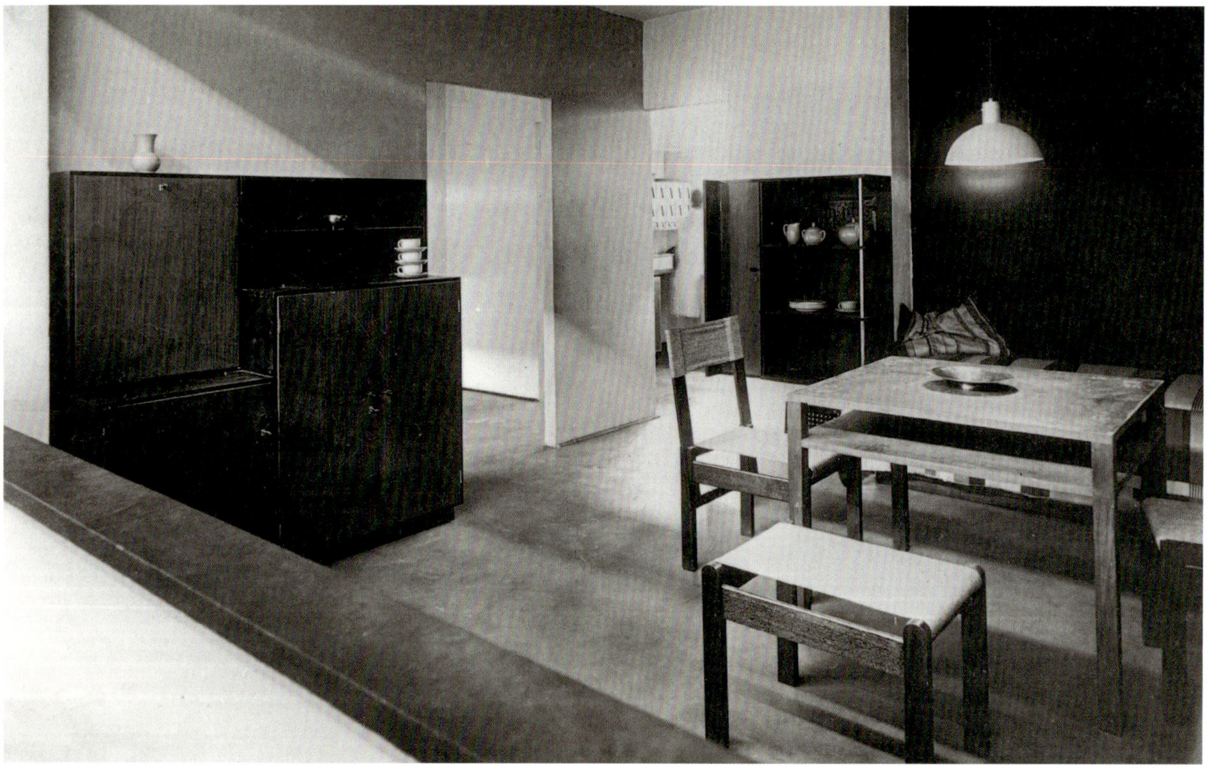

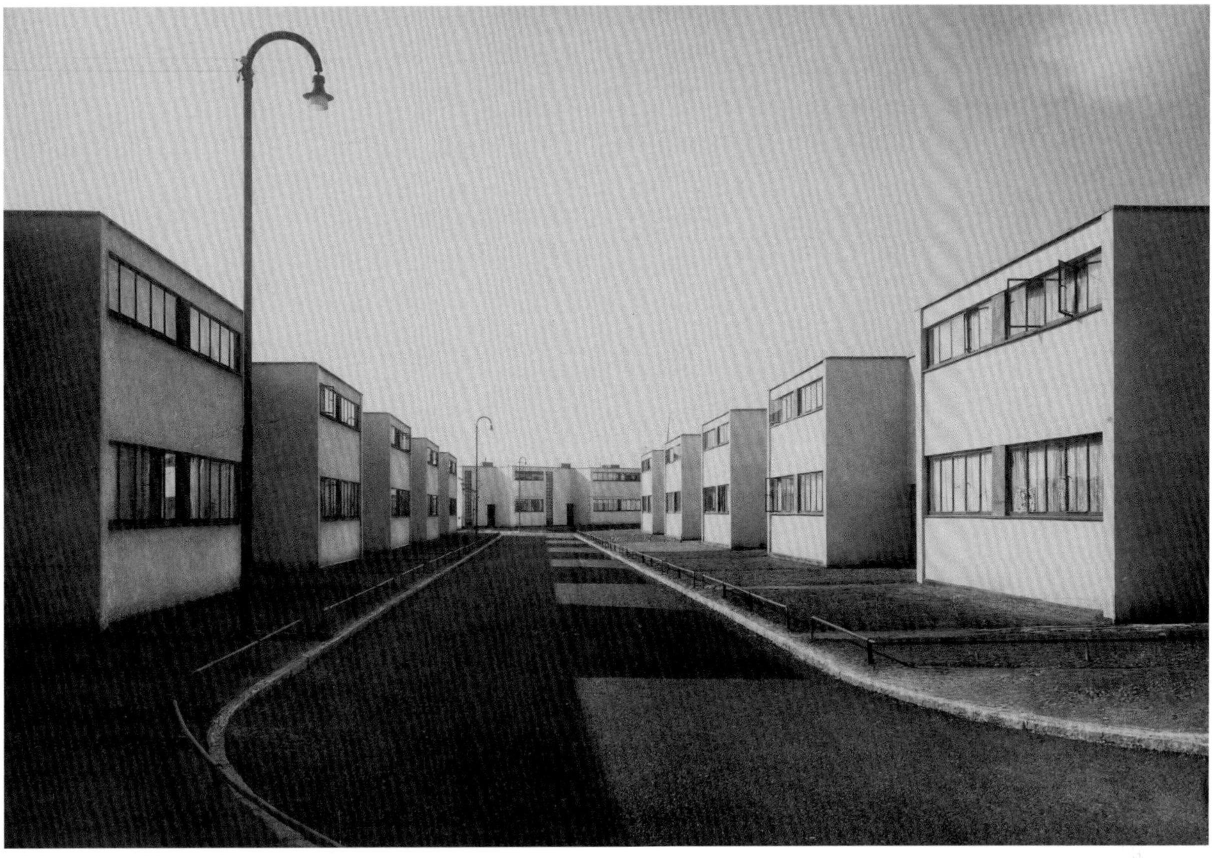

197
Walter Gropius
Törten housing estate, Dessau, 1926–28
Isometric construction scheme
Ink, paint and gouache on board
88.8 × 107.3 cm
Harvard Art Museums/Busch-Reisinger Museum. Gift of Walter Gropius

198
Törten housing estate, Dessau, 1926–28
Model interior for living room with standardised workshop-assembled furniture
Photographer Erich Consemüller
Bauhaus-Archiv Berlin

199
Törten housing estate, Dessau, 1926–28
Street of houses built in the second phase, with design improvements
Photographer Musche
Bauhaus-Archiv Berlin

Soon after his arrival in Dessau, Gropius was commissioned to build a new estate of affordable homes for the local working population. The estate was completed over a two-year period and comprised 314 single family houses on a semi-rural plot, grouped in units in a radial plan inspired by the English garden city. The project allowed Gropius to test the latest building materials and construction techniques, often adapted from industrial elements and methods. House types evolved as each phase was completed and residents quickly changed elements with which they were unhappy. Today, no house exists in its original form. In 1930 Hannes Meyer and the Bauhaus department of architecture designed balcony-access apartments as part of the planned extension of the estate, which were partially completed. Gropius's associate Carl Fieger built his own house on the estate, which aimed to test 'simplified housekeeping through good organisation' and featured furniture made in the Bauhaus workshops.

new masters and workshops in dessau

torsten blume

It all began in Weimar in 1919, with the idea of the *Großer Bau* (the grand building), which was eventually realised with the construction in 1925 of the new Bauhaus in Dessau. A community of artists and designers from various fields and genres collaborated to create their own environment for working, learning and living 'under the wings' of a new architecture that constituted far more than building design.[1] Walter Gropius's guiding principle and perspective for the Bauhaus took a universal artistic approach to exterior and interior design that opened up new methods in the building and furnishing of houses as well as introducing a reconciliation of technical and sensuous aspects. Ultimately, it produced a space that was perceived as a *Gesamtkunstwerk* – designed *in toto* and down to the last detail for a newly structured modern life.

In this respect, it is not surprising that for a long time the school was considered a place for a general sort of architectonics in which 'building' was understood as a universal creative activity for designing 'life processes'. It was not until 1927, when Hannes Meyer was appointed, that an actual department of architecture was established. But the goal of achieving architecture in concrete terms had always been present, not least due to the projects underway in Gropius's private architecture office. For instance, students and staff at the Bauhaus workshops had been involved with the furnishings of Sommerfeld House in 1920–21. With the erection of the new Bauhaus building and the other structures in Dessau, this practice was to attain its zenith and conclusion simultaneously, since the workshops were subsequently restructured and redefined. More decisively than before, they became 'productive workshops', their management for the most part being turned over to former students who had proven themselves in earlier furnishing projects, or distinguished themselves with their dedication to purely practice-oriented design.

The dual path of artistic and handcraft education that each student was required to complete before the apprenticeship certification exam conducted by the Chamber of Crafts and the *Meisterrat* (Council of Masters), remained in effect in Dessau. Although technical staff continued to work in nearly all the workshops, they no longer held leadership positions as they had in Weimar. The new masters, called 'young masters' (internally they were sometimes ironically referred to as 'little masters') now bore the sole responsibility for the overall programme of their respective workshops. Thus in Dessau this new generation of young teachers (the youngest, Marcel Breuer, was only twenty-three years old in 1925) began to exert their influence on the Bauhaus. Not only did they increase productivity at the school, but they also attracted significant appreciation from outside, proof that Gropius's ambition for the Bauhauslers to make their own independent contributions was paying off. Herbert Bayer, Hinnerk Scheper, Gunta Stölzl (whose position was not formally confirmed until 1927) and Breuer were now in charge of the workshops for printing, wall-painting, weaving and cabinetry respectively. Along with the metal workshop, which was run by László Moholy-Nagy, these workshops constituted the backbone of the 'productive workshops'. Thirty-year-old Moholy-Nagy was a technology enthusiast, artist and experimenter, who became one of the most important proponents of the new orientation of the Bauhaus. When Josef Albers was promoted to master in 1925, it was less a new beginning for him than an official recognition of his role as an instructor of the preliminary course, which he had been teaching with Moholy since 1923. The preliminary course now came to be known as the 'basic education course', having been extended to cover two semesters. For Joost Schmidt, his appointment as director of the sculpture workshop served to reward his role as a dedicated Bauhausler, who had proven himself an inspiring and versatile designer.

The atmosphere in the new Bauhaus was more business-like and further away from art, largely free of the romanticising and pompous undertones of the Weimar Republic. Work, training and life were more clearly organised within the one building. The debates on vegetarianism, personal fulfilment, Eastern culture and life reform, as well as on Americanism, progress and technology had become less heated. This was because in Dessau there was greater ambition, and pressure, to make products from the school's experiments that were marketable and ready for mass production. The Bauhaus GmbH company was founded in 1925 as a catalyst for this. It sold the products from the workshops, taking over the advertising and marketing. Of the company's revenue, part went towards the overall school budget and the rest to the Bauhaus masters and students for their labour and design. It was those workshops that could be expected to deliver design work suitable for building projects and the demands of industrial mass production that were continued in Dessau, while the workshops for pottery, glass-painting and bookbinding were not reopened.

Herbert Bayer, who had a lead role on the advertising team for the 1923 Bauhaus exhibition in Weimar, assumed leadership of the print workshop from Lyonel Feininger. Instead of artists' prints, he now focused on layouts, typography and advertising design. He pressed for the introduction of the lower-case lettering designed by Emil Porstmann, and the use of DIN (German industrial standard) norms for all printed matter. In keeping with the increased emphasis on public relations at the Bauhaus in Dessau, he concentrated his teaching on issues pertaining to advertising design, dealing also with psychological and economic aspects. By 1928, he had expanded the workshop into an 'advertising department' that handled not only the promotion and exhibition designs for the Bauhaus, but also took on outside contracts. After Bayer left the Bauhaus in 1928, Schmidt stepped in to head the workshop.

Breuer took over the cabinetry workshop that had previously been led by Gropius. The work he had submitted for the completion of his apprenticeship was furniture for the 'lady's bedroom' at the Haus am Horn in Weimar. In Dessau he continued to develop furniture types for mass production that he had started in Weimar. With the help of engineers from the Junkers aircraft factory in Dessau, he began to use bent-steel tubing as a basic material for making chairs. The cabinetry workshop also took on interior design for private homes, for example, that of the avant-garde theatre director Erwin Piscator. Breuer also attempted to market his tubular steel chairs independently, but without success.

The workshop for wallpainting, which Wassily Kandinsky had previously headed, was now led by Hinnerk Scheper. Prior to his Bauhaus studies in Weimar, Scheper had completed his training as a wall painter, studied at the Düsseldorf Art Academy and at the arts and crafts school in Bremen, and received his master-craftsman's diploma from the Chamber of Crafts in Weimar. In 1922, while still a student, he had taken charge of the chromatic design for the Weimar State Museum. This design, based on nuances of pastel colours and consciously taking its lead from the building's architecture, was ultimately the reason why Scheper and his wall-painting workshop received the commission to carry out the chromatic design for the Bauhaus building. Under Scheper's direction, all types of decorative painting were dropped in favour of designs that emphasised surface. The focus was on the examination and application of various types of paint, grounds and techniques, as well as brush-and-roller techniques.

Gunta Stölzl did not receive word until 15 June 1926 that she had become the head of the weaving workshop and it was only on 1 April 1927 that this was confirmed by contract. However, she had been informally recognised as the leading person in the workshop at the Bauhaus in Weimar, as her dedication to technical innovation had raised the level of education and training in this area. Nevertheless, official recognition by Gropius and the Council of Masters only came about after persistent interventions on the part of the female weaving students. The previous head, Georg Muche, had no technical knowledge of weaving or textile design, hardly developed any formal ideas for designing textiles, and had fulfilled virtually none of the functions of his position. In Weimar, Stölzl had been instrumental in the procurement of new weaving looms and other equipment (for example, for the dyeworks). Moreover, it was she who recognised early on that the weaving workshop lacked the knowledge needed to enter into production, and remedied this by attending, on her own initiative, courses on weaving and dyeing techniques at the Höhere Fachschule für Textil-Industrie zu Krefeld (Higher Technical School for the Textile Industry in Krefeld) in 1922 and 1924 in order to pass on this knowledge to her co-students. She orchestrated and oversaw the move of the weaving workshop from Weimar to Dessau. Essentially, it was down to her that the 'women's class', which had begun in 1921 with a rather general understanding of textile handcrafts, was able to develop into a professional weaving workshop in Dessau, and ultimately to concentrate on the design of functional, reproducible textiles for interiors: practical furnishing materials, curtains and wall and floor coverings. When the weaving workshop took up its work in Dessau, it was able to offer for sale to furniture producers and retailers 900 designs that had already been developed in Weimar. In Dessau, Stölzl restructured the weaving workshop to become a place for experimentation and production with a focus on cost effectiveness and the testing of new materials such as viscatape, cellophane, cellulose wire, bast fibre or paper yarn. Despite all of this, the weaving workshop did not turn into a little factory, but remained a place of work, experimentation and learning. Stölzl pursued a course different from that of Muche, who, regardless of his failure to appreciate what the women weavers had collectively amassed in learning on their own, was far from willing to give up leadership (for a long time enjoying the continuing support of Gropius). Unlike Muche, Stölzl was of the opinion that, for all the orientation towards mass production, the training was to be based on manual weaving, as she believed that one needed to work directly with the technology, to know how a loom functions, in order to get away from the perception of the woven fabric as a picture and recognise its inner, structural, technical logic – the laws intrinsic to the weave. To accomplish this, the handloom afforded far more opportunities for research and variation than the power loom, which would ultimately execute the designs.

As a Bauhaus student, Schmidt had been selected by Gropius to design the interior wood panelling for the Sommerfeld House in 1922. Schmidt also designed the vestibule of the school building for the Bauhaus exhibition in 1923. He succeeded Schlemmer as head of the sculpture workshop in 1925. Due to the lack of space, tools and financial resources, the sculpture workshop had a precarious status at first. It did not have a clearly defined mission for practice-oriented work, which reflected a general uncertainty regarding the up-to-date application of art in the public arena. Schmidt and his students were therefore initially active in outfitting the Bauhaus stage. His hopes of advancing his ideas for a 'mechanical theatre', however, were to be thwarted by Schlemmer, who had other notions. Only in 1928 did the sculpture workshop manage to reach a formal and material par with the other workshops. That same year, Schmidt became the head of the advertising workshop, parts of which he tried to merge with the sculpture workshop. He was a Bauhausler with many talents and inclinations, often acting beyond the scope of the workshop, and developing a complex course agenda. Despite the need to be economically pragmatic, he wanted the Bauhaus to remain a place of playful experimentation and invention. Beginning in 1925, while helping out at the print workshop, Schmidt taught a course in typography. Alongside this, he also developed a creative design theory of his own, which was implemented in the sculpture workshop, above all after 1928 as part of the 'elementary studies of spatial and sculptural relationships'.[2] He emphasised that his concern was not for making art, but for some form of basic, design-oriented research on sculptural issues. The goal was an 'awakening, developing, and intensifying of our capacity for imagining space, the conscious experience of spatial sensory perceptions' and 'the realisation of spatial notions'.[3] In the midst of the practice-oriented Bauhaus, Schmidt often had a hard time in conducting these aesthetic experiments, especially since he did not enjoy the standing of Klee or Kandinsky. And yet he was admired by many students as an inspirational and understanding partner in discussion.[4] He was able to secure his position by designing extensive amounts of print material, and after 1929, by taking on numerous Bauhaus exhibition designs.

In Josef Albers's *Werkgrundlehre* (basic teaching of crafts), students acquired knowledge of the 'handling of various materials and tools', in preparation for the course taught by Moholy on *Formgrundlehre* (basic teaching of forms), the essential content of which was the 'analysing of form elements ... a guide to abstraction' and 'constructive exercises in design'. With these two parts, the preliminary course, now called the 'basic education course', was prolonged, taking up the entire first year.[5] The article published in *Bauhaus* magazine in 1928 that dealt with his *werklicher Formunterricht* (teaching of forms and crafts) begins with the assertion:

> We find ourselves in an economically oriented period. In earlier times, it was more important to commit oneself to an ideology or a way of looking at the world. Today, it is impossible to exist ... without taking the economy into consideration. The economic form is of concern to us ... for the reason that the earlier overemphasis on emotional or historical forms has inevitably been followed by a need for rational form giving ... The economic form results from function and material. Prior to the cognition of the function, of course, there must be the study of the material. Thus, our form studies begin with the study of the material.[6]

Nonetheless, Albers later emphasised the importance of 'inventive building and discovery-oriented attention', for this experience is 'training for every kind of design' and calls for 'undisturbed, uninfluenced, that is to say, unbiased, experimenting, which means (initially) doing handcraft with the material in a purposeless, playful fashion. This is achieved by ... experimental work.' Suitable for this were 'materials or building elements, whose use, or application does not exist or whose treatment is unknown'. The economic orientation that characterised the Dessau workshops in general, also became a parameter in Albers's creative training:

As far as possible, each material is to be used without loss, without waste. Preliminary experiments are made using the smallest samples, and if the material is valuable, by using cheaper material replacements. Thriftiness leads to an emphasis on the lightness ... Nothing must remain left over in any form; otherwise the calculation has not been correct, because chance has played a role here, it is not accounted for and therefore, irresponsible, and in addition, banal, because it comes from habit.[7]

Subsequent to this, 'texture exercises' gave rise to 'more formal areas of work and possibilities for free creativity'. In these exercises exploring the 'inner energies of the materials', experiments and compositions were carried out 'more in the form of painting than building'.[8] Similarly to Schmidt, Albers consciously made his argument from a non-artistic standpoint, tying in with Moholy-Nagy's teaching concept, which aimed at a general schooling of sensory perception and creativity. All the same, Albers could scarcely deny his origins in artistic work. The decisive divergence, however, from Johannes Itten's preliminary course and the design practices of the early Bauhaus in general, is Albers's increased emphasis on the rational and social control of the sensory experiments with material and form, since 'subjective observation', the cultivation of one's 'own thought forms' and the promotion of the 'primal creative power of the individual'[9] can lead to narcissistic self-cultivation. The necessity for ridding oneself of habits, and overcoming too much specialisation by training the mostly atrophied sensory capacity of recognition was certainly not intended to lead to the isolation of the individual artist, but was to be developed and rationalised within a community of like-minded practitioners. Nevertheless, the expanded preliminary course in Dessau constituted an important counterbalance to the otherwise strongly practical orientation of the workshops. And thus it preserved the explicitly artistic and experimental fundaments, without which the Bauhaus would scarcely have been different from any other school of craft or design.

In this context, what was at least as important as the preliminary course was that the role of the early masters of form, and thus of the artists at the Bauhaus, was not overstated, though their significance was never fundamentally questioned. They continued to teach their elementary form courses up to the fourth semester, and after 1928 they offered 'classes in free painting'. Gropius had appointed these artists as leading masters because, in the geometrical base of their abstract painting, he believed that he had found a bridge connecting the functional design logic of technicians and engineers with the compositional logic of visual artists. This presumed correspondence between visual and technological function was repeatedly criticised and put into perspective over the course of subsequent Bauhaus history. As a structuring model, however, it was never entirely replaced, leading to a lack of real cooperation with industry. This is the reason why technical production know-how never reached the same level as the well-established artistic design teaching at the school. A true equality between artistic and technical education – for which the young masters stood as representatives and models – was ultimately to remain an ideal at the Bauhaus. However, this also prevented the tendency towards specialisation in the workshops from ultimately gaining the upper hand, and thus there was still room 'for fundamental ideas that give importance to human content and keep it alive', a crucial attribute at the school since 'as soon as the production of an object becomes purely a speciality and the working process is geared to trade, the educational process loses all vitality'.[10]

1 Walter Gropius, 'Programm des Staatlichen Bauhauses in Weimar', Pamphlet, Staatliches Bauhaus, Weimar, 1919. English translation printed in this publication on pp. 15–17.
2 See Rainer Wick, *Bauhaus Pädagogik*, DuMont, Cologne, 1988, p. 312.
3 Ibid.
4 See Heinz Loew, 'Joost Schmidt: Lehrer am Bauhaus', in Joost Schmidt, *Lehre und Arbeit am Bauhaus 1919–32*, Edition Marzona, Düsseldorf, 1984, p. 9.
5 See Rainer Wick, *Bauhaus Pädagogik*, DuMont, Cologne, 1988, p. 69.
6 Josef Albers, 'Werklicher Formunterricht', in *Bauhaus*, 2 1928, no. 2/3, pp. 3–6.
7 Ibid.
8 Ibid.
9 See Walter Gropius, 'Idee und Aufbau des Staatlichen Bauhaus Weimar', in Walter Gropius, *Staatliches Bauhaus Weimar*, BauhausVerlag, Weimar/München, 1923, p. 11ff.
10 László Moholy-Nagy, letter of resignation, 17 January 1928, in Frank Whitford, *Das Bauhaus. Selbstzeugnisse von Meistern und Studenten*, Deutsche Verlagsanstalt Stuttgart, Stuttgart, 1993, p. 254.

marcel breuer
metal furniture and modern spatiality

Metal furniture is part of a modern space. It is styleless, for it should express no intentional form beyond its function and the design its function requires. The new space should not represent a self-portrait of the architect nor from the outset the composure of the soul of its individual user.

Since the external world affects us today with the most intense and various impressions, we change the form of our lives in more rapid succession than in earlier times. It is only logical that our surroundings must undergo corresponding changes. We are approaching furnishings, spaces, and buildings which, to the greatest possible extent, are alterable, mobile, and accessible to various combinations. Furniture, even the walls of the space, are no longer massive, monumental, apparently permanently rooted, or in fact permanently installed. They are much more injected with air, drawn, so to speak, in space; it hinders neither movement nor the view through space. The space is no longer a composition, no rounded-off whole, since after all its dimensions and elements are subject to essential changes. One comes to the conclusion that any correct, usable object fits in the space in which it is needed, similar to how a living being fits in nature: a person or a flower. The reproductions show metal furniture of the same characteristic form, determined by the type of design, in the most various spaces: in the theatre, auditorium, atelier, dining room, and living room.

I have specifically chosen metal for these pieces of furniture to achieve the characteristics of modern spatial elements just described. The heavy, pretentious upholstery of a comfortable armchair has been replaced by tightly stretched fabric surfaces and a few easily dimensioned, springy, cylindrical brackets. The steel used, and particularly the aluminum, manifest conspicuously little weight given the large static demands made (the tensile stress of the fabric). The slit form increases mobility. All of the various types are constructed of the same standardised, elementary parts that can be disassembled and interchanged at any time.

These pieces of metal furniture should be nothing more than necessary instruments of contemporary life.

First published as 'metallmöbel und moderne räumlichkeit,' in das neue frankfurt, *no. I, 1928, II.*

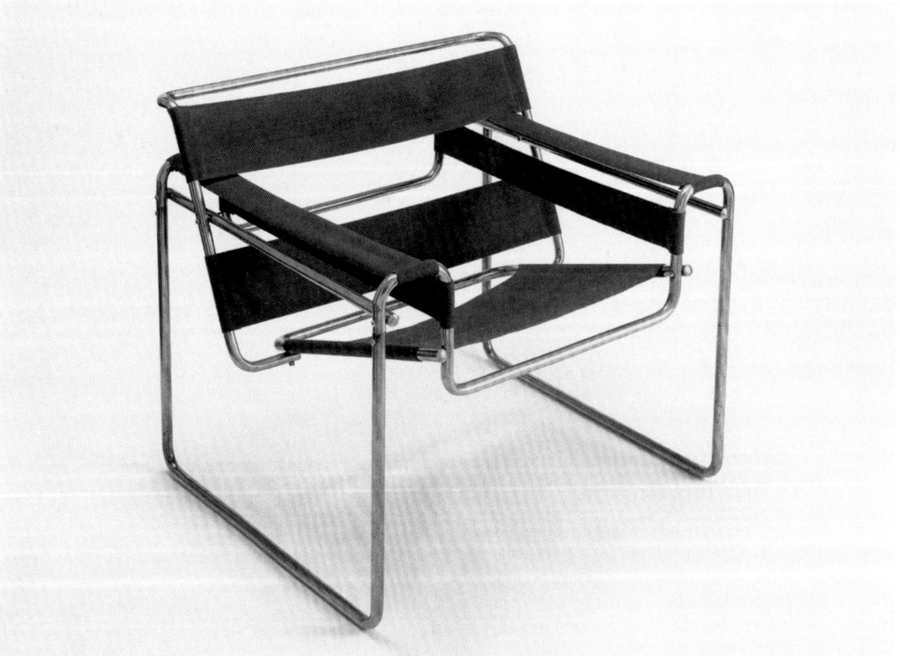

opposite page
200
Marcel Breuer
Club chair, 1925–26
Tubular steel, originally nickel plated (later chrome) and eisengarn (metalized yarn)
70.5 × 81 × 69.5 cm
Victoria and Albert Museum
Supported by the friends of the V&A

201
Marcel Breuer
Chair, 1926
Tubular steel and fabric
85.9 × 48.5 × 60.9 cm
Bauhaus-Archiv Berlin

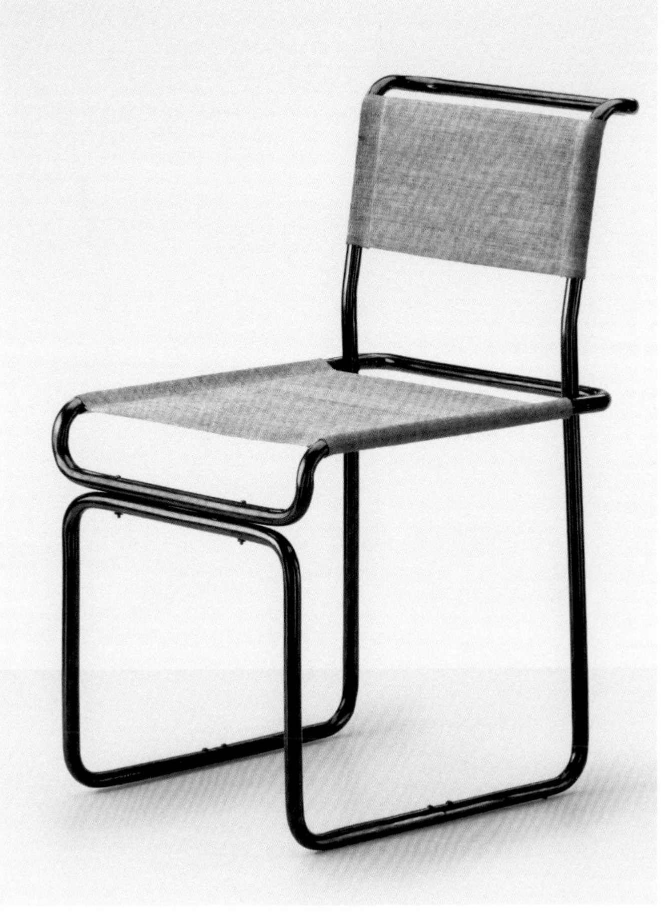

Inspired by the strength of his bicycle frame, Breuer was the first to pioneer the use of tubular-steel furniture. His earliest example was the club chair designed in 1925 and the new building in Dessau provided an opportunity to turn ideas of industrial production into reality. This model, Breuer's first tubular-steel chair without arms, was used throughout the school and particularly in the office areas and the masters' houses. Yet despite such extensive employment, it was never put into commercial production. Screws joining the seat to the back and leg unit protruded visually and tended to scratch the sitter's legs. Although not fully resolved, this design confirmed Breuer's interest in working on chairs and other furniture that used the sled or runner as a basic construction principle. Used for the club chair and nearly all his later designs, the continuous lengths of tubular steel achieved maximum strength from a minimum of material and a level of visual transparency that chimed with the modernist desire for interior spaces that were open and free-flowing. Breuer refined this design and in 1927 the model B5 was put into small batch production and sold by Breuer and Kalman Lengyel's Standard-Möbel.

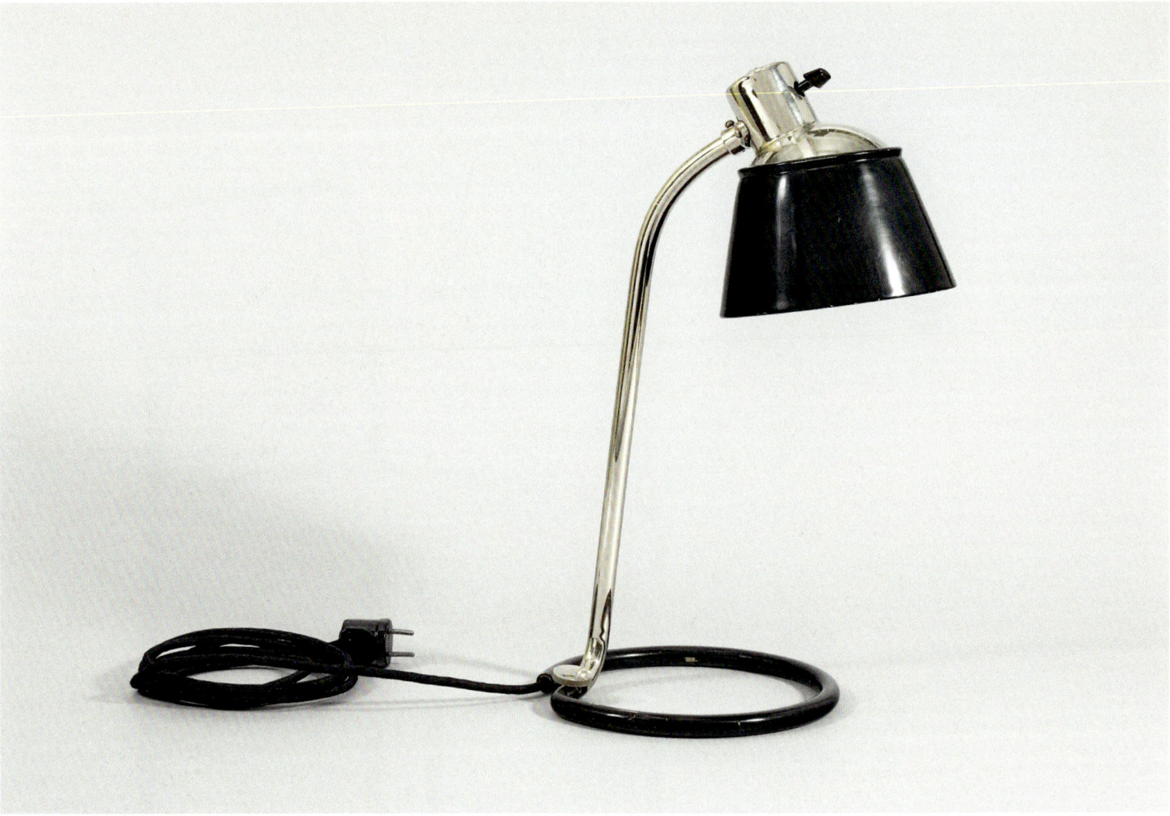

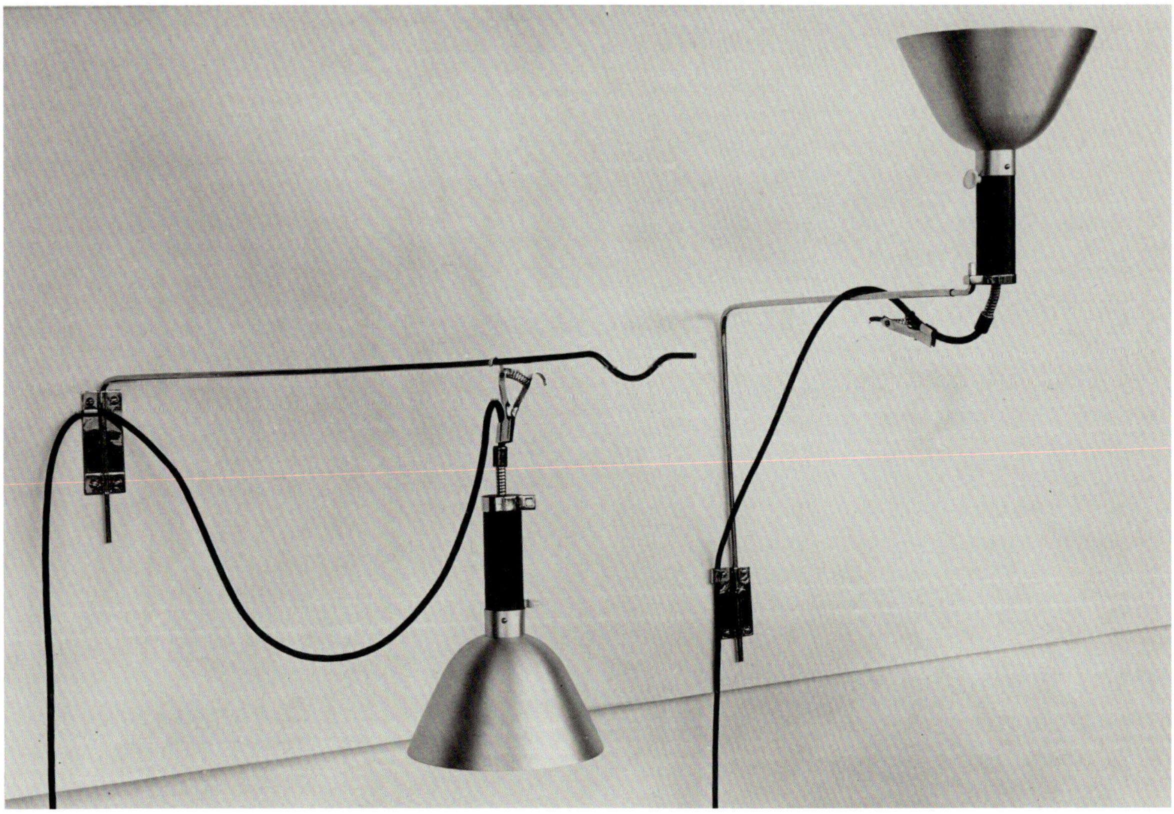

202
Heinrich-Siegfried Bormann
Kandem tube table lamp, No. 934, manufactured by Körting & Mathiesen, 1932
Nickel-plated-aluminium shade, tubular nickel-plated-brass arm and base, all external parts black lacquer
47 × 23 × 21 cm
Bauhaus-Archiv Berlin

203
Erich Consemüller
Wall lights by Marianne Brandt, ME 152, c. 1927
Gelatin silver print
10.1 × 16.5 cm
Herzogenrath, Berlin
On long-term loan to Klassik Stiftung, Bestand Museen

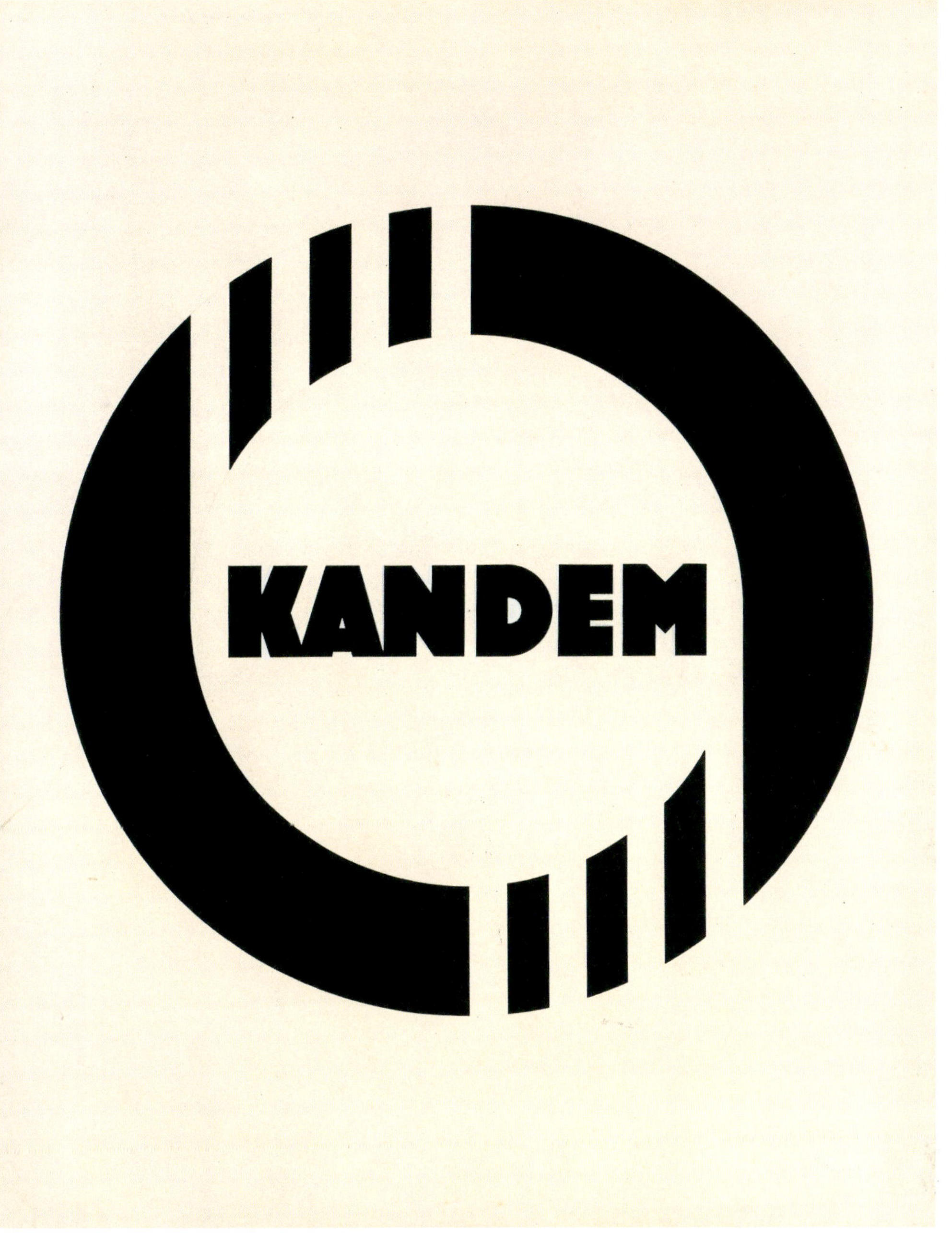

204
Herbert Schürmann
Design for a Kandem sign, 1932
Ink on paper
75 × 50 cm
Bauhaus-Archiv Berlin

The Bauhaus secured contracts with two lighting manufacturers, Schwintzer & Gräff and Körthing & Mathiesen, in 1927. Fifty-three designs ranging from desk to wall-mounted and ceiling lights were produced by Schwintzer & Gräff, yet the relationship with the company came to an end before 1930. For Körthing & Mathiesen, Hannes Meyer encouraged the development of a much more limited range of lights, which were manufactured under the Kandem name. Marianne Brandt and Hin Bredendieck designed a series of standardised lamps. The simple designs manufactured by Kandem were immediately commercially successful and the Leipzig-based company continued to produce Bauhaus designs into the 1950s.

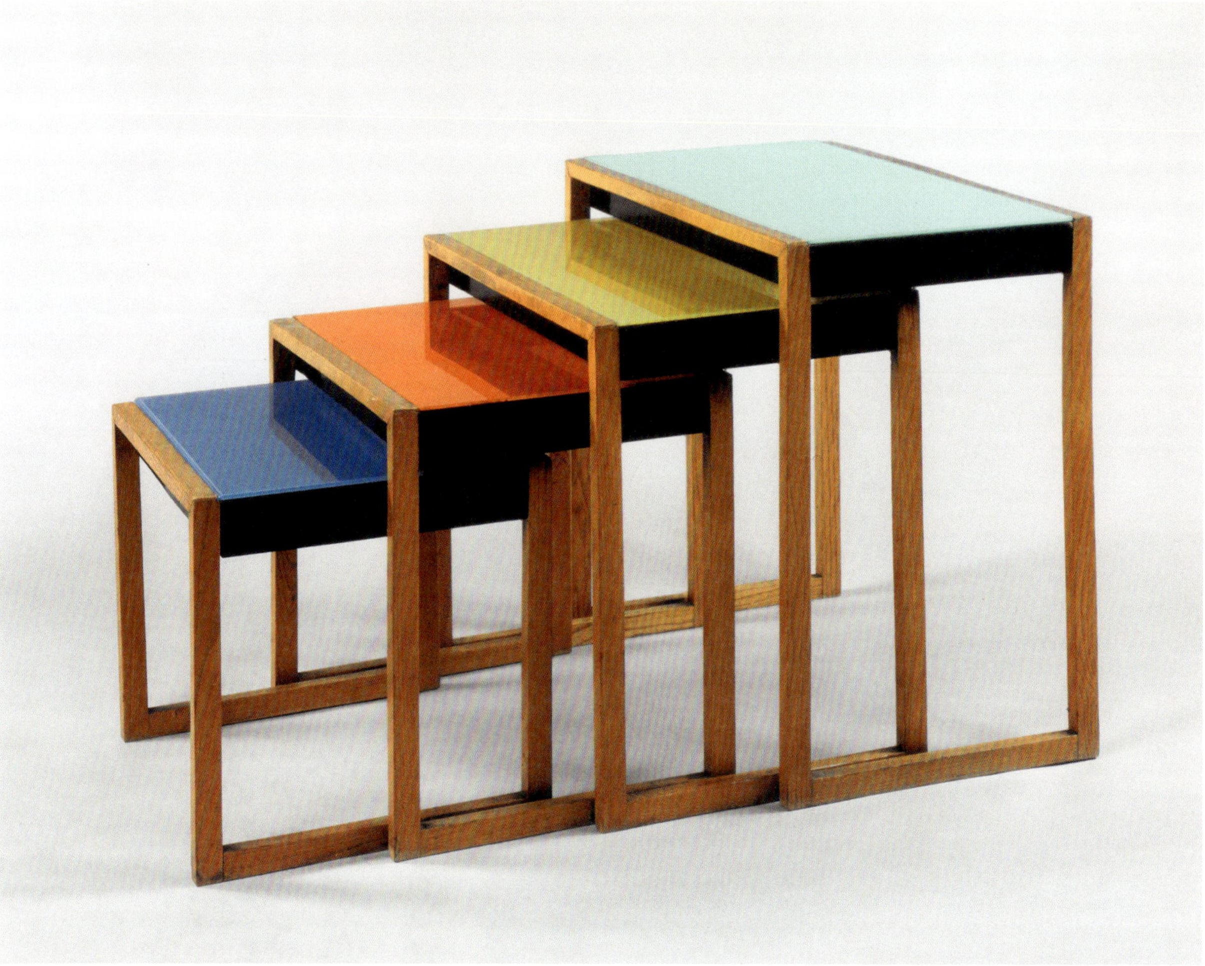

205
Josef Albers
Set of stacking tables, c.1927
Ash veneer, black lacquer, wood
and painted glass
Largest: 62.6 × 60.1 × 40.3 cm
Smallest: 39.2 × 41.9 × 40 cm
The Josef and Anni Albers Foundation

206
Josef Albers
Armchair from the Oeser House,
designed 1926, produced 1928
Solid mahogany and mahogany veneer,
beech wood, maple, with flat cushions
75 × 61.6 × 67.6 cm
Bauhaus-Archiv Berlin

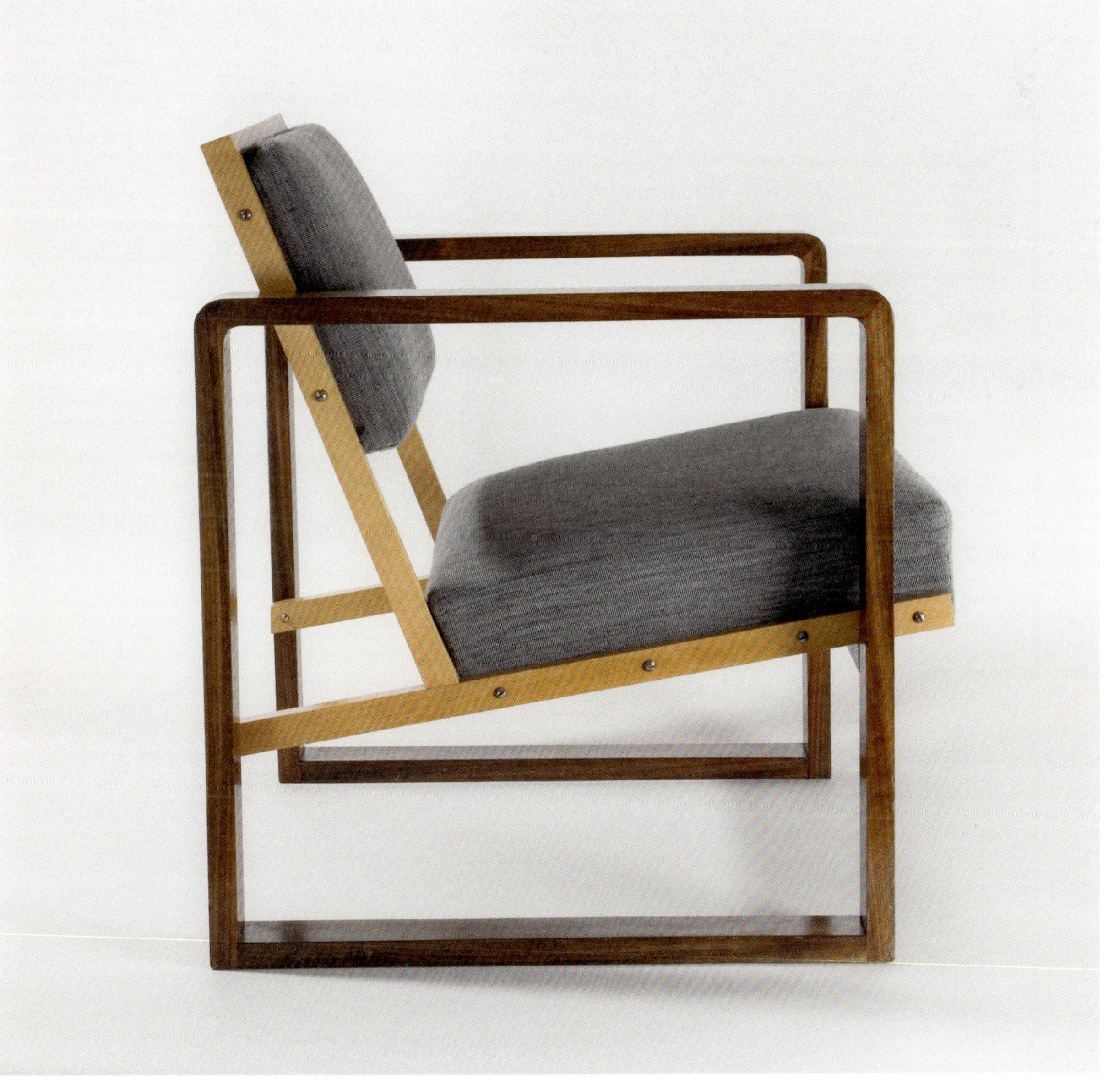

ernst kállai
ten years of bauhaus

It was ten years ago that Walter Gropius reorganised the Weimar School of Arts and Crafts and named the new school 'Bauhaus'. The success of his creation is well known. What, during the early years at Weimar, used to be the vehemently disputed activity of a few outsiders has now become a big business boom. Houses and even whole housing settlements are being built everywhere; all with smooth white walls, horizontal rows of windows, spacious terraces, and flat roofs. The public accepts them, if not always with great enthusiasm, at least without opposition, as the products of an already familiar 'Bauhaus style'. But in reality the initiative for this kind of architecture originated by no means at the Bauhaus alone. The Bauhaus is just one part of an international movement that developed quite a while ago, particularly in Holland. But the Bauhaus became the first school of this movement. It has been highly effective in disseminating its ideas and has been extraordinarily successful as a place for experimentation. The reputation of the institute has quickly spread and reached even the remotest corners of the country. Today everybody knows about it. Houses with lots of glass and shining metal: Bauhaus style. The same is true of home hygiene without home atmosphere: Bauhaus style. Tubular-steel armchair frames: Bauhaus style. Lamp with nickel-coated body and a disk of opaque glass as lamp shade: Bauhaus style. Wallpaper patterned in cubes: Bauhaus style. No painting on the wall: Bauhaus style. Incomprehensible painting on the wall: Bauhaus style. Printing with sans-serif letters and bold rules: Bauhaus style.

everything written in small letters: bauhaus style.

EVERYTHING EXPRESSED IN BIG CAPITALS: BAUHAUS STYLE.

Bauhaus style: one word for everything. Wertheim sets up a new department for modern-style furniture and appliances, an arts-and-crafts salon with functionally trimmed high-fashion trash. The special attraction is the name 'Bauhaus'. A fashion magazine in Vienna recommends that ladies' underwear no longer be decorated with little flowers, but with more contemporary Bauhaus-style geometrical designs. Such embarrassing and amusing misuses in the fashion hustle of our wonderful modern age cannot be prevented. His Majesty the snob would like something new. Very well. There are enough architects making the Bauhaus style into a new decorative attraction. The exhibition of cold splendor is back again. It has just been rejuvenated, has exchanged the historical robe for a sort of pseudo-technological raciness. But it is just as bad as before... The new Berlin despises the swollen marble and stucco showiness of the 'Wilhelmian' public buildings and churches, but it revels in the hokuspokus of megalomaniac motion-picture palaces, department stores, automobile 'salons' and gourmets' paradises with their shrieking advertisements. This new architecture, the slender nakedness of its structure shining far and wide and bathed in an orgy of lights at night, is by no means, so we are told, ostentatious; it is rather 'constructive and functional'. Hence, once more: Bauhaus style. But let us take heart. For small home owners, workers, civil servants, and employees the Bauhaus style also has its social application. They are serially packaged into minimum standard housing. Everything is very functional and economical. Furniture and household articles are within reach and, according to Westheim: the suicidal gas main is in their mouth....

Let us keep the slogan 'Bauhaus style', since it has already become a household word, even where it is no more than a cover for a corruption of originally more sincere intentions. With all due respect to the difference between these intentions and the commercialisation of the Berlin Broadway. It cannot be denied, however, that the work of the Bauhaus itself is in no way free of aesthetic overcultivation and of dangerous formalism. It is true that discarding all ornamentation and banning each and every curved plane and line in the design of houses, furniture, and appliances has led to the creation of very interesting, new, and simple forms. But whatever was obvious about these new functional forms has by no means always made as much sense. Rather, the products which were to be expedient and functional, technical and constructive, and economically necessary were for the most part conceived out of a taste-orientated arbitrariness decked out in new clothes, and out of a *bel-esprit* propensity for elementary geometric configurations and for the formal characteristics of technical contrivances. Art and technology, the new unity – this is what it was theoretically called and accordingly practiced – interested in technology, but art-directed. This is a critical 'but.' Priority was given to the art-directedness. There was the new formalistic willfulness, the desire to create a style at all costs, and technology had to yield to this conviction. This is the way those Bauhaus products originated: houses, furniture, and lamps which wrested attention primarily by their obtrusively impressive form and which, as a logical result of this characteristic, were accepted or rejected by the public and the press as being products of a new style, namely the Bauhaus style. But they were not accepted or rejected for being the products of a new technical development in the building or furniture industries. Of course the Bauhaus, in numerous programmatical and propagandistic publications, affirmed time and time again that the formal characteristics of its products were no more than the inevitable results of a 'strictly relevant' fulfillment of function, rather than an intention to create a style. Yet, a few years of practice were already enough even for the eyes of the younger Bauhaus generation to recognise that these products were outdated handcraft. This may be less florid than customary handcraft. But it is instead inhibited, prejudiced by a doctrinaire mock asceticism, stiff, without charm, and yet pretentious to the point of arrogance. Fellow-travelers who are smarter businessmen and are more unscrupulous have not hesitated to make frankly shoddy handcraft out of this somewhat clumsy trouble-child of the new functional design. Where is the dividing line between genuine and false Bauhaus style? The Bauhaus started things rolling with its aesthetic ambition; it must now accept the fact that others are going to add all the rest right up to the bitter end. Why is it that a similar fate does not threaten a swivel chair or the 'Zeiss' lamp? The reason is that these products are not born of the unity of art and technology but are genuine constructions evolved from industrial technology: they are creations of engineering. It would be revealing to ask one of the 'Zeiss' engineers for his opinion on the technical and illumination properties of the Bauhaus lamps.

Gropius established, among others, the following guide lines for the Bauhaus programme: 'The Bauhaus wants to assist in the development of present-day housing, from the simplest household appliances to the finished dwelling .... The Bauhaus workshops are essentially laboratories in which prototypes of products suitable for mass production and typical of our time are carefully developed and constantly improved ... The prototypes that have been completed in the Bauhaus workshops are reproduced by outside firms with whom the workshops are closely related .... The Bauhaus brings creatively talented people with ample practical experience into the actual course of production, people who have mastered both technical and formal problems, and who are to take over the preparation of models for production in industry and the crafts ...'

Excerpted from 'ten years of bauhaus', published in the journal die weltbühne, *berlin, no. 21, january 1930*

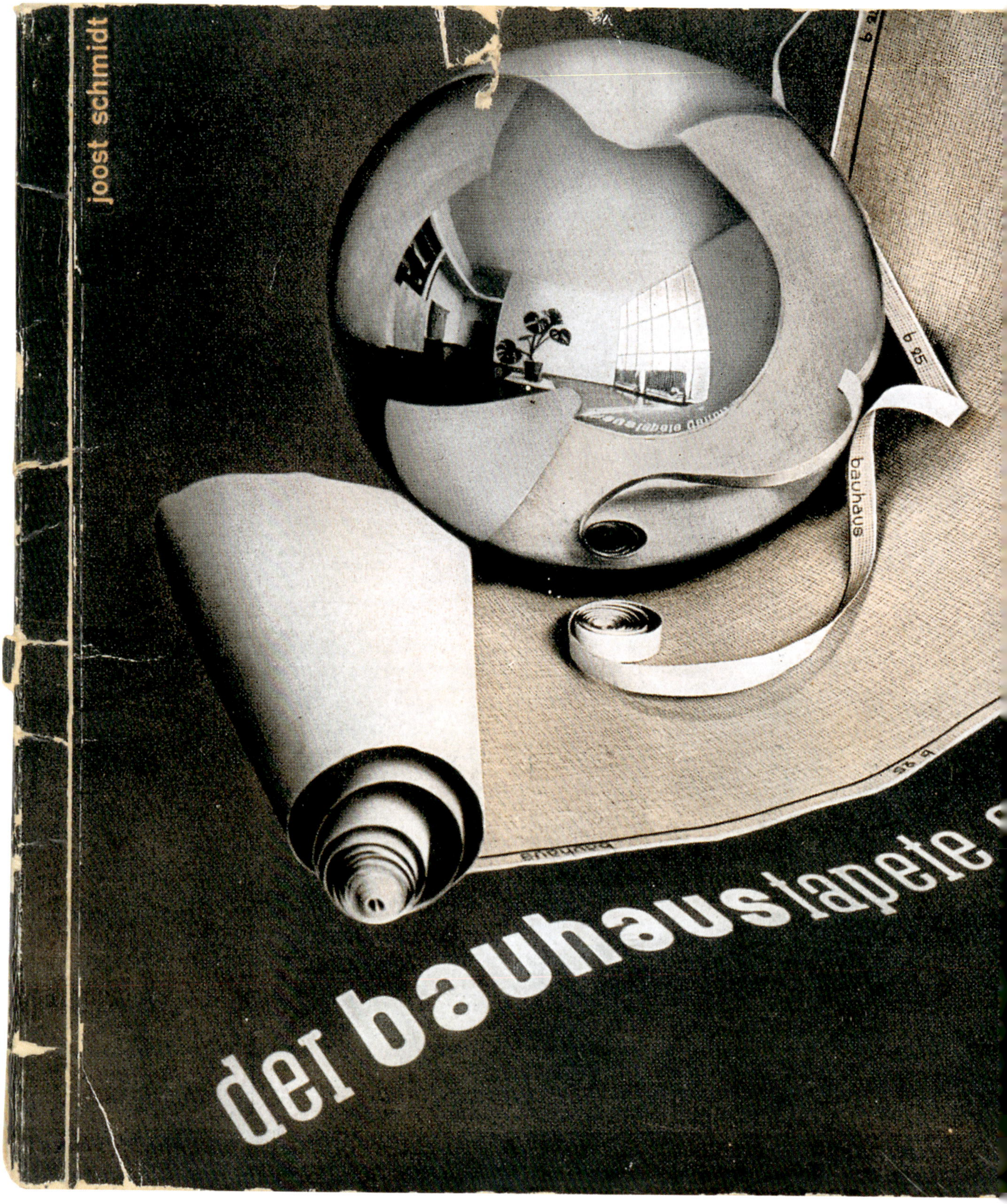
joost schmidt
der bauhaustapete
bauhaus

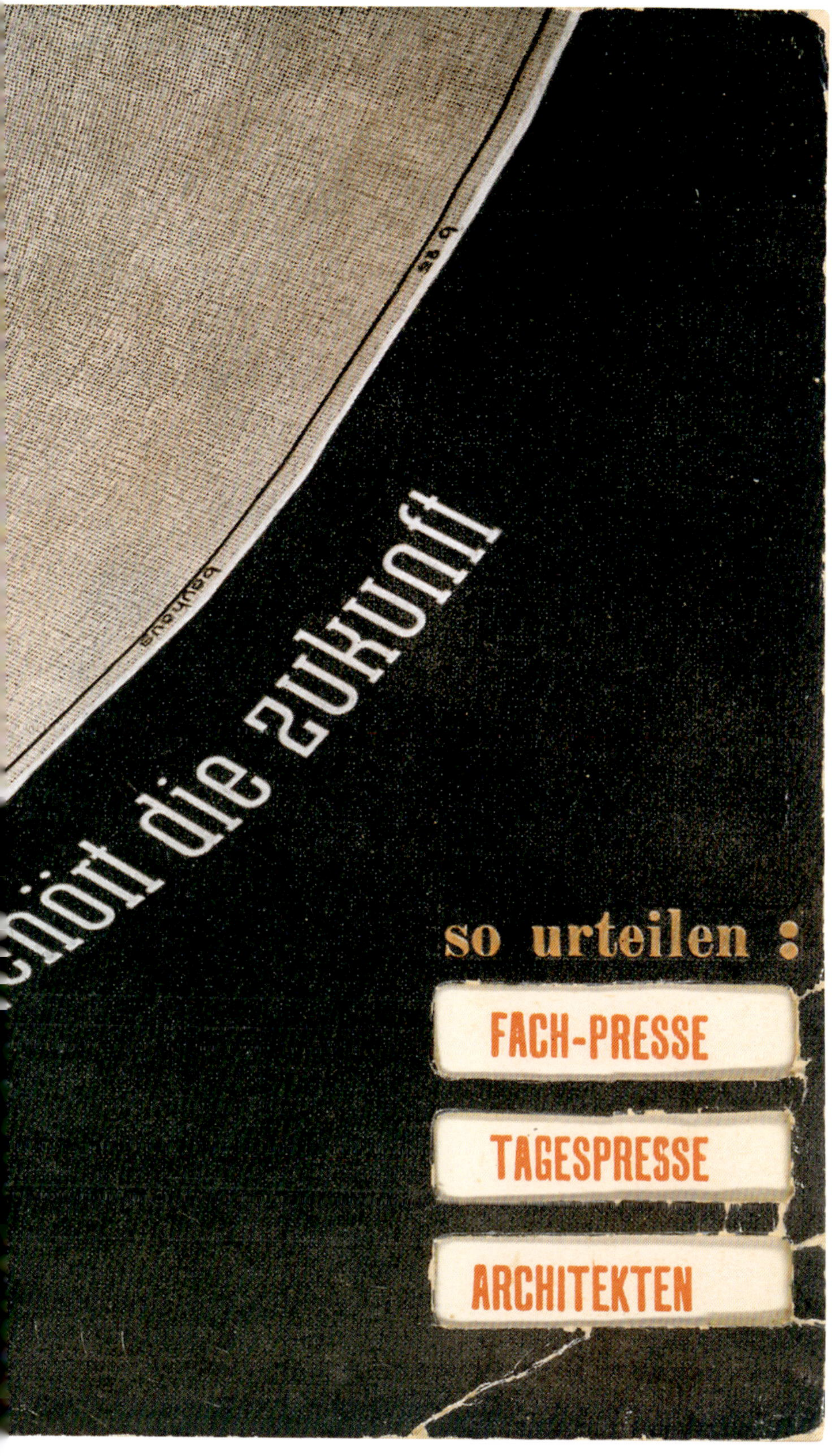

207
Joost Schmidt
Cover of the pamphlet *Der Bauhaus Tapete gehört die Zukunft* (*The future belongs to Bauhaus wallpaper*), 1931
Letterpress on paper
14.8 × 21 cm
Bauhaus-Archiv Berlin

208
Gertrud Arndt
Wall hanging, 1927
Double weave, cotton and rayon in seven colours
153 × 122 cm
Bauhaus-Archiv Berlin

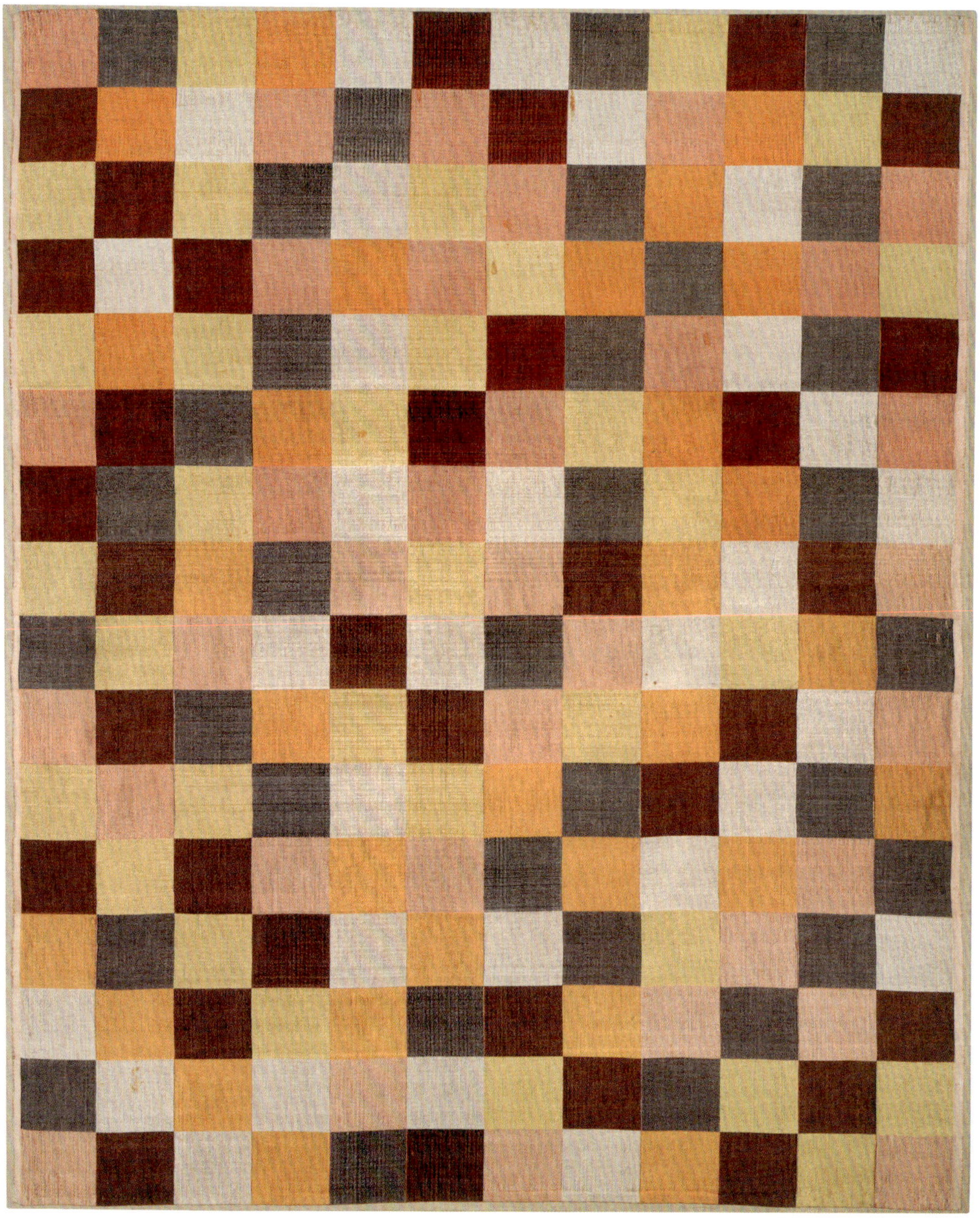

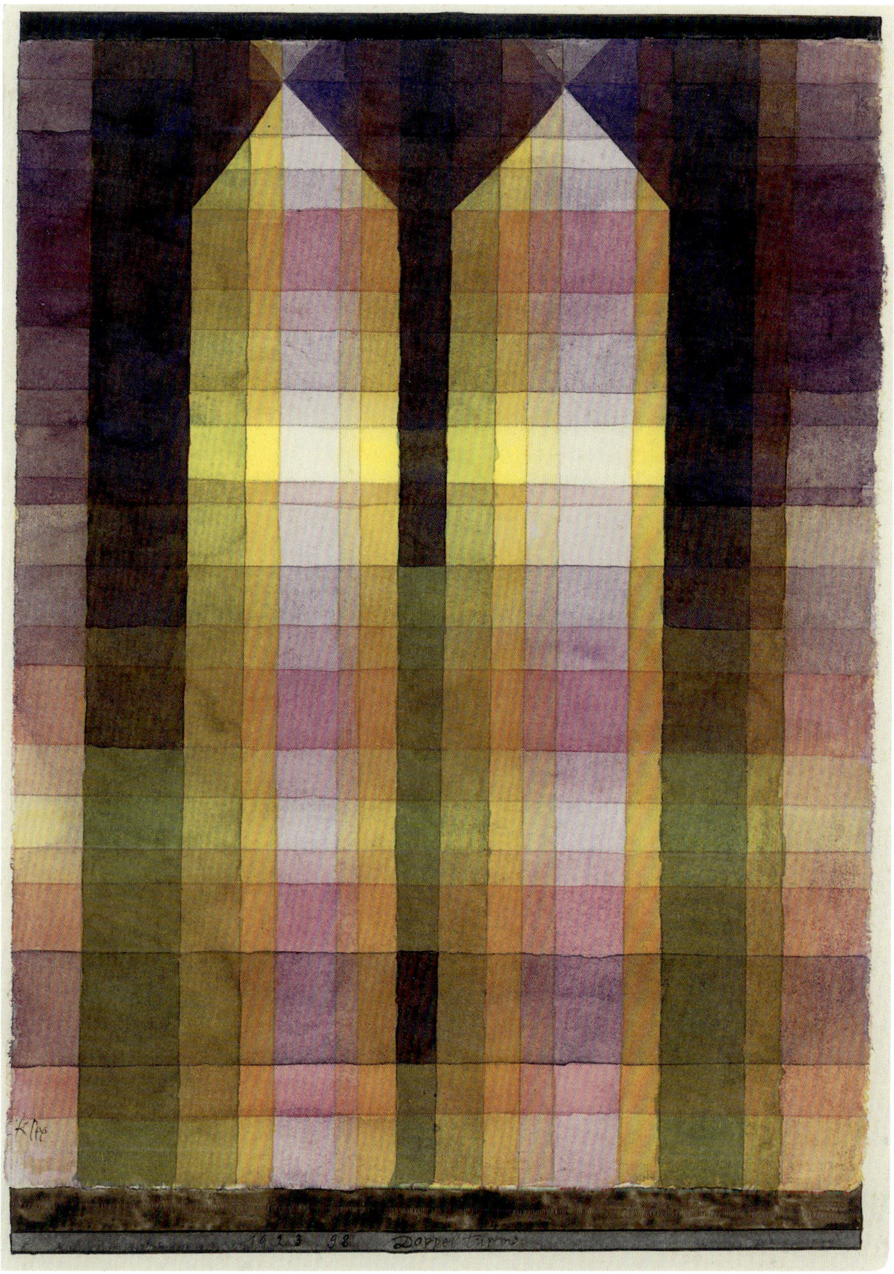

209
Paul Klee
Doppelturm (*Double Tower*), 1923
Watercolour and pencil on paper
30.9 × 23 cm
Private Collection. On long-term loan to the
Franz Marc Museum, Kochel am See, Germany

Painted during his time at the Bauhaus in Dessau, *Doppelturm* exemplifies Klee's fascination with abstraction and colour theory. His influence on the work produced by students and masters alike across the school, particularly within the weaving and stained-glass workshops, was considerable. The colourful, loose geometric forms bear a close relationship to the composition and colour of several weavings from this period. Klee's class on form for weaving students explored planar design, colour theory and materials, but it was his own work that made the strongest impression on the weavers. In particular, Anni Albers was very vocal in expressing her appreciation of his work and its impact on her own designs: 'What I learned from him, I learned from looking at his pictures ... I find that he probably had more influence on my work and my thinking by just looking at what he did with a line or a dot or a brush stroke.'

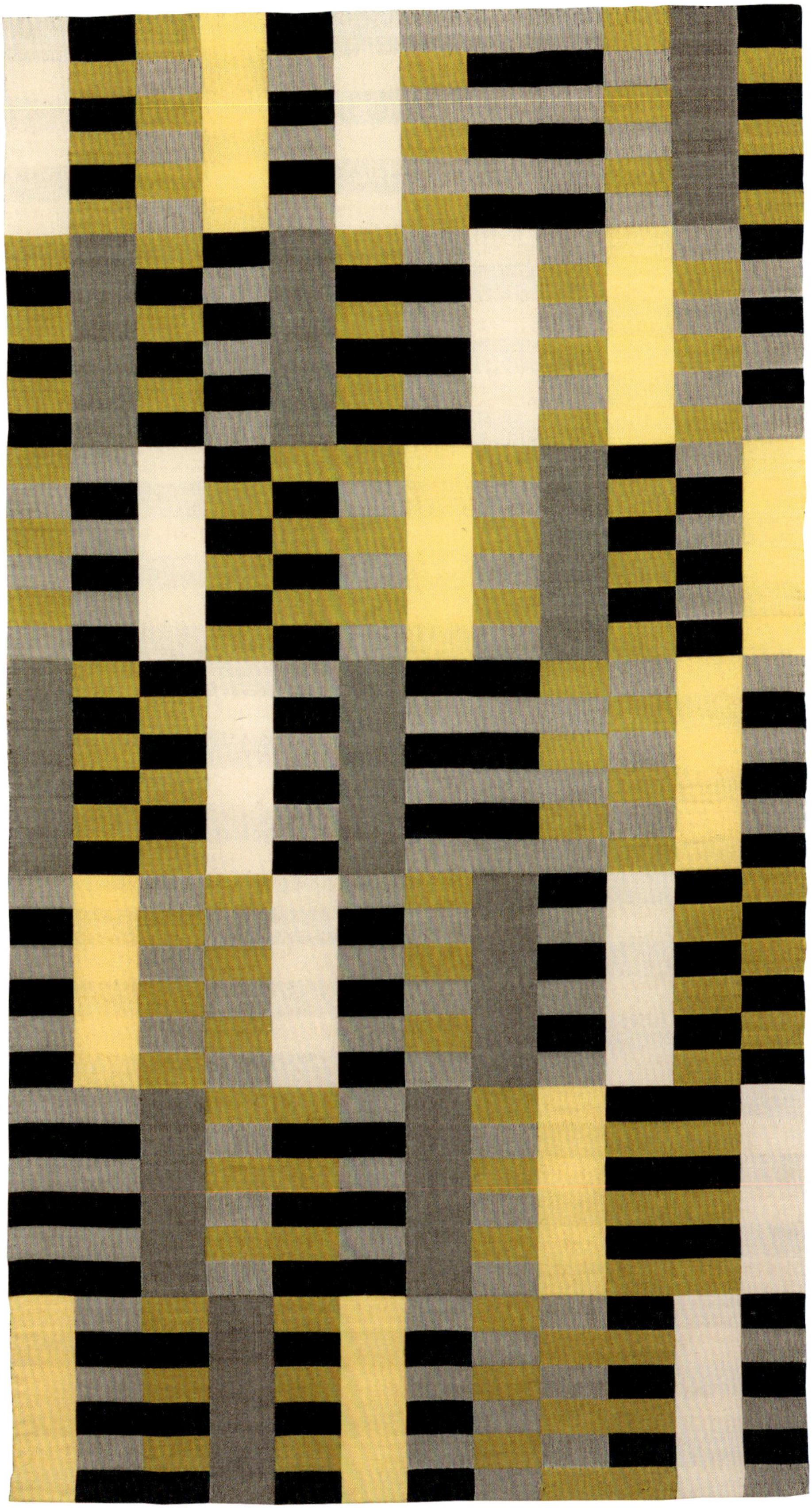

210
Anni Albers
Wall hanging WE 493/445, 1926
(remade 1964)
Triple-weave in black, white and
yellow cotton and synthetic silk
223 × 117 cm
Bauhaus-Archiv Berlin

211
Josef Albers
Factory A, 1925–26
Sandblasted flashed glass with black paint
35.5 × 45.7 cm
The Josef and Anni Albers Foundation

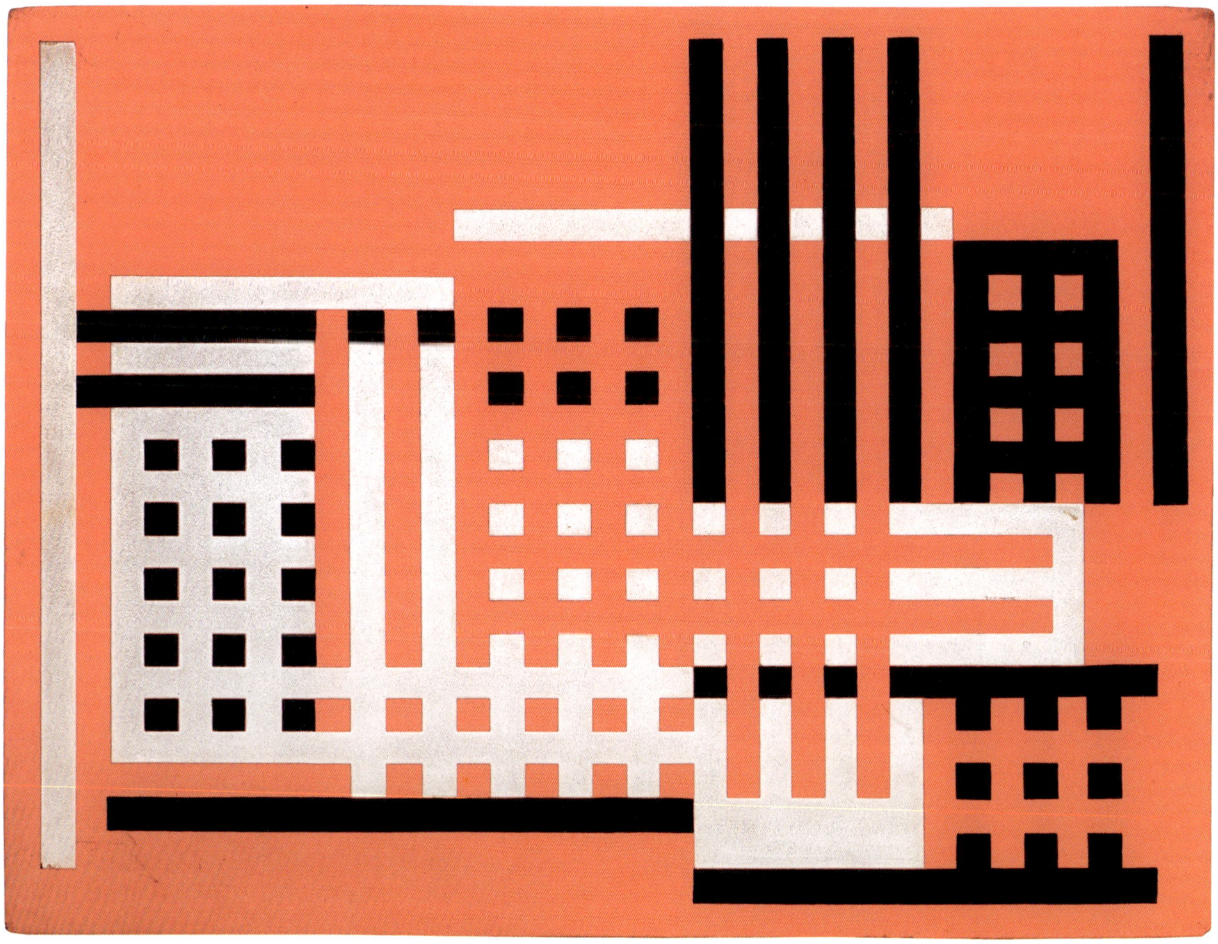

female careers at the bauhaus

anja baumhoff

Although it was one of the most advanced art schools of the Weimar Republic[1], the Bauhaus has always projected a male-dominated image. Despite this reputation, one third of its students were female. 1919 was after all, not only the founding year of the Bauhaus, but also the birth of the Weimar Republic, whose new constitution granted women the right to choose freely where to study. In this context, the question arises, what use were women able to make of this new opportunity? The weaver Gunta Stölzl and product designers Marianne Brandt and Alma Buscher each represent the various ways in which women could succeed at the Bauhaus: by networking, through patronage, or on their own account, but they also exemplify the pitfalls.

In his first speech as Bauhaus director in April 1919, Walter Gropius addressed a student body made up almost equally of men and women. He emphasised female equality and urged women to be as hard-working as male handcraftsmen, even though, he said, women had hardly achieved much artistic merit in the past. In the notes for his welcoming speech, Gropius explained that the tradition of female amateurism would not be accepted in the Bauhaus: 'No distinction between the beautiful and the strong sex. Absolutely *equal* rights, but also absolutely *equal* duties. No consideration for ladies; *at work all craftsmen.* I shall strongly oppose the limited occupation with pretty little salon pictures to pass the time.'[2] But while he did not want special treatment for 'ladies', contemporary German society did not welcome female craftsmen.[3] Gropius's philosophy therefore put his female students in an uneasy position. They found a way out of this dilemma through what was seen as a female occupation. Of all workshops, the weaving class best fitted contemporary gender stereotypes and it soon turned into a 'women's class'. Bauhaus master Oskar Schlemmer reflected these gender stereotypes with the teasing rhyme: 'Where there is wool/You'll find a weaving wench/If only to pass the idle hours at her bench.'[4] Most women either gathered in that class or were sent there after the preliminary course; the ones who resisted the pull were few and far between. But there were also those who wanted to work in a single-sex class, like Stölzl, who forged an exceptional career at the Bauhaus, becoming the one and only female junior master of the school.

After studying painting, glass painting, and ceramics for several years in Munich, Stölzl came to the Bauhaus in 1919. She passed the preliminary course and moved into the weaving workshop, which remained her territory from then on. 'Our first experiments were "painted fabrics"', she remembered, 'finely segmented with many colour shades, a lush palette.'[5] In 1926, in her first publication, she wrote: 'Does woven fabric present a challenge for mankind's creative desire? Yes!'[6] At the Bauhaus it posed a particular challenge, since it did not fit easily with the white, flat-roofed architecture or to the modern cantilever chairs that other students were producing.

Stölzl reached the position of master by building up an extensive network. As her daughter, Monika Stadler, wrote:

> At the height of her career, Gunta Stölzl resolutely crossed out the word *student* on her Bauhaus identification card and, in her own handwriting, replaced it with the word *master*. She had attained this position [as head of the weaving workshop] through her own efforts, backed by the votes of the members of her workshop – not by being called to the post – and despite the procrastination and hesitation of the Bauhaus masters, who, as recent research has shown, would never have considered accepting a woman into their faculty. Consequently, she did not describe herself with the German word *Meisterin*, a female master, but with the [masculine term] *Meister*, or master.[7]

Stölzl was outspoken and popular and participated in most of the Bauhaus activities, from the many festivities, parties and dances to the soup kitchen in Weimar. She retained life-long friendships with many Bauhauslers, among them Benita Otte, Gertrud Arndt, and Oskar Schlemmer. The reason why most of the weaving students supported her wish to head the workshop was because they were women, who saw that for one third of the students, there was literally no chance of promotion, while the male students could at least hope to gain one of the rare positions as junior master, as did Marcel Breuer, Ludwig Hirschfeld-Mack and Herbert Bayer. While the Bauhaus masters tended to ignore this problem, the students staged a coup, forcing the current weaving master, the painter Georg Muche, to leave. In 1927 Stölzl officially took his place. A few years later she too left the Bauhaus, after she had found a swastika painted on her door. She moved to Switzerland in 1931, where she set up the Handweberei Flora (Flora Handweaving Studio) in Zurich, remarried and raised her two daughters.[8]

Brandt was one of the most outstanding talents of all Bauhaus students and her designs are still impressive today. She had studied fine art before she joined the Bauhaus and later remembered:

> In 1924, when on the advice of Moholy-Nagy I transferred from the preliminary course to the metal workshop, they had just begun to produce objects capable of being mass-produced though still fully handcrafted ... At first I was not accepted with pleasure – there was no place for a woman in a metal workshop, they felt. They admitted this to me later on and meanwhile expressed their displeasure by giving me all sorts of dull, dreary work. How many little hemispheres did I most patiently hammer but of brittle new silver, thinking that was the way it had to be and all beginnings are hard? Later things settled down, and we got along well together.[9]

Brandt's now internationally famous designs for metal ashtrays, tea and coffee services as well as tableware, the famous Kandem lamps and other household objects were originally manufactured under a Bauhaus licence. Her use of metals and glass was revolutionary and her designs helped the Bauhaus to gain a leading role in the area of product design.[10] After Gropius and the Hungarian Constructivist painter László Moholy-Nagy left the Bauhaus, she even headed the metal workshop for a year, negotiating some of the most important Bauhaus contracts for collaborations with industry. But in 1929 she resigned from the post, with the newly established Bauhaus diploma in hand.[11] Her reasons for leaving were multiple as Magdalene Droste states:

> It was difficult for Brandt to develop a professional female habitus as a designer even in the relatively liberal environment of the Bauhaus ... [because] the metal workshop was a male territory: a [prestigious] battleground among men. Although Brandt surprised her male colleagues by mastering all technical aspects of the workshop and producing the largest number of objects, she lost the fight for real power and symbolic recognition at the Bauhaus. Developing a professional female habitus was even more challenging in the world beyond the school, where there were almost no arenas for a female metalworker to assert authorship. For Brandt, her time at the Bauhaus was the highpoint of an ultimately nonexistent career.[12]

After the Bauhaus, Brandt worked for three years as a designer for the metal factory Ruppelwerke in Gotha, Thuringia, before she withdrew to her home town Chemnitz, where she lived through the Nazi period without attracting much attention. In 1949 she was appointed to the faculty of the College of Fine Arts in Dresden, as instructor in wood, metal and ceramics, but two years later she moved to the Institute for Applied Art in Berlin, where she taught for three more years before returning to Chemnitz to retire in 1954.[13] Today, Brandt's achievements are fully recognised, but at the time she owed her career to the patronage of Moholy. Without him, she could not have lived up to her full potential. And although he, as well as Gropius, tried to support her after the Bauhaus, they could do little for her from abroad.

Unlike Brandt, the designer Alma Buscher had no one in particular to support her, and nor was she dependent on anybody – we shall see if this was a strength or a weakness. Before enrolling at the Bauhaus, she studied at an arts and crafts school in Berlin for several years.[14] Like Stölzl and Brandt, however, she had to start with the preliminary course. She was channelled into the weaving class, but soon switched to the cabinetry workshop.[15] There she was so successful that she was allowed to design the children's room for the Haus am Horn, a family home of the future, built as part of the school's major exhibition of 1923. Supported by the apprentice Erich Brendel from the cabinetry workshop, she designed the complete nursery and play room while simultaneously collaborating with Ludwig Hirschfeld-Mack on his lighting and colour experiments, which were part of the stage workshop under the leadership of Schlemmer. Intended for a corner, her toy cupboard made up of modular and flexible blocks featured tall white shelving, a door with an aperture allowing it to become a puppet theatre, and coloured boxes usable both for and as toys, i.e. for storage and as oversized building blocks. The whole ensemble was multifunctional and could be adapted to different uses once a child had grown up. In addition, she created a chest of drawers that could be turned into a writing table.

It was for this exhibition that Buscher also produced her most successful design object – a ship-building toy or *Bauspiel* (fig. 88), made up of building blocks of different shapes and sizes in the primary colours, along with white and green – which is still being sold today.[16] Buscher echoes the association of art and play insisting that her toys merely supported children's tendency for free play. Her design philosophy must be seen in the context of its time. By the early twentieth century, the theories of educational reform put forward by Friedrich Fröbel and Johann Heinrich Pestalozzi were entering broad segments of German society and also influenced the Bauhaus's preliminary course. 'The educational use value of the *Bauspiel* is most explicit in that it introduced children to the modern modular construction, and did so with efficiency appropriate to the functionalist tendencies of the Bauhaus.'[17]

It is striking how well Buscher's designs reflect the Bauhaus idea of a unity between art and function by combining the representational mode of three-dimensional modern furniture with the abstract visual designs of the two-dimensional modernist style. But despite this, her achievements were long overlooked. One reason for this might be that her oeuvre was small, another that her clientele was so too: as a woman who designed children's toys, she seems to have been underestimated by the Bauhaus as well as by later historians. With her toys Buscher developed an emphatic sign of what a Bauhaus pedagogy might look like if combined with pure planes in primary colours. Under the banner of simplification for the sake of educational reform, she had created some-thing that could have become a best-selling item, but Gropius was afraid that a toy might come to represent the Bauhaus. To his mind, architecture was more appropriate to carry the Bauhaus banner. And though her designs were exceptionally successful, the Bauhaus's support for her dwindled away. In 1927 the Council of Masters told her that her work was 'peripheral' and thus did not warrant support.[18] Clearly, performance alone did not suffice to merit success – students had to fit in socially as well. Buscher had married and given birth to a baby girl. It is likely that the school did not expect her to continue working. Disappointed by this reaction, she left the Bauhaus and supported her husband's career as an actor. While raising two offspring she continued to design paper cut-outs for children, which were published by the Pestalozzi-Fröbel company and are still made today. In 1944 she died during a bombing raid near Frankfurt.

All three women were exceptionally successful at the Bauhaus, but only Stölzl managed to establish a career after she left. Drawing on her contacts, she made a new start abroad with the help of two former Bauhaus students, Gertrud Preiswerk and Heinrich Otto Hürlimann. Brandt, Buscher and Stölzl all designed objects that are still in production today – an achievement few designers accomplish – but this was not enough to grant them success, whether inside or outside the Bauhaus. Comparing their strategies, it seems that networking topped both patronage and skill in a Bauhaus woman's career.

1 Wulf Herzogenrath and Stefan Kraus (eds), *Bauhaus Utopien. Arbeiten auf Papier*, Hatje Cantz, Ostfildern-Ruit, 1999, p. 11.

2 Papers of Walter Gropius no. 7/10, Bauhaus-Archiv Berlin. Quoted in Anja Baumhoff, *The Gendered World of the Bauhaus. The Politics of Power at the Weimar Republic's Premier Art Institute, 1919–1932*, Peter Lang, Frankfurt and New York, 2001, p. 53.

3 Gropius explained in a letter to Annie Weil of 22 February 1921: 'In our experience it is not advisable for women to work in the heavy industrial workshops, such as carpentry etc. However, it is our policy to discourage women from studying architecture.' See Anja Baumhoff, 'What's in the Shadow of a Bauhaus Block? Gender Issues in Classical Modernity', in Christiane Schönfeld (ed.), *Practicing Modernity. Female Creativity in the Weimar Republic*, Könighausen & Neumann, Würzburg, 2006, p. 54. This text was translated by Sebastian Stumpf.

4 Ibid., p. 59.

5 Monika Stadler and Yael Aloni (eds), *Gunta Stölzl. Bauhaus master*, Hatje Cantz, Ostfildern, 2009, p. 71.

6 Ibid., p. 85.

7 Ibid., p. 13.

8 For more on this story of her leaving, see Anja Baumhoff, 'Behinderte Karrieren im Umbruch der Zeit: Gunta Stölzl', in Ingeborg Hansen-Schaberg (ed.), *Frauen und Exil*, Edition Text + Kritik, vol. 5, Richard Boorberg, Munich, 2012.

9 Eckhard Neumann (ed.), *Bauhaus and Bauhaus People. Personal Opinions and Recollections of Former Bauhaus Members and Their Contemporaries*, Van Nostrand-Reinhold, New York and London, 1970, p. 98.

10 Brandt also expressed herself through photomontages and photography. See Elisabeth Wynhoff (ed.), *Marianne Brandt: Fotografien im Bauhaus*, Hatje Cantz, Ostfildern-Ruit, 2003; Elizabeth Otto, *Tempo, Tempo! The Bauhaus Photomontages of Marianne Brandt*, Jovis, Berlin, 2005.

11 Magdalena Droste, 'The Bauhaus Object between Authorship and Anonymity', in Jeffrey Saletnik, Robin Schuldenfrei (eds), *Bauhaus Construct. Fashioning Identity, Discourse and Modernism*, Routledge, London and New York, 2009, pp. 220.

12 Ibid., p. 218.

13 Hajo Düchting (ed.), *Seemanns Bauhaus-Lexikon*, E.A. Seemann, Leipzig, 2009, p. 71.

14 She studied for three years at the Reimann School and for roughly two more at the Unterrichtsanstalt des Kunstgewerbemuseums, Berlin, before arriving at the Bauhaus in 1922. See Ulrike Müller, *Bauhaus Women,* Flammarion, S.A., Paris, 2009, p.113. Translated by Emer Lettow and Sarah Kane.

15 For the difficulties this switch entailed see Anja Baumhoff, 'Verhaltenslehren der Kälte? Implikationen moderner Diskursformen am Bauhaus Dessau am Beispiel der Geschichte von Alma Buscher', in Christoph Wagner (ed.), *Esoterik am Bauhaus: Eine Revision der Moderne? Internationales Wissenschaftliches Symposium*, Schnell+Steiner, Berlin, 2009, p.12.

16 The game was distributed by Pestalozzi-Froebel-Publisher in Leipzig from 1926–1933, and has been available from the Swiss toymaker Naef since 1977.

17 Christine Mehring, 'Alma Buscher. "Ship" building toy. 1923', in Barry Bergdoll, Leah Dickermann (eds), *Bauhaus 1919–1933. Workshops for Modernity*, Oxford U.P., New York, 2009, p.158.

18 Anja Baumhoff, '"... und sind doch alle auf das Bauhaus hin entworfen." Strategien im Umgang mit geschlechtsspezifisch geprägten Mustern in Kunst und Handwerk am Bauhaus Weimar', in Jennifer John, Sigrid Schade (eds), *Grenzgänge zwischen den Künsten. Interventionen in Gattungshierarchien und Geschlechterkonstruktionen*, Transcript, Bielefeld, 2008, p.20.

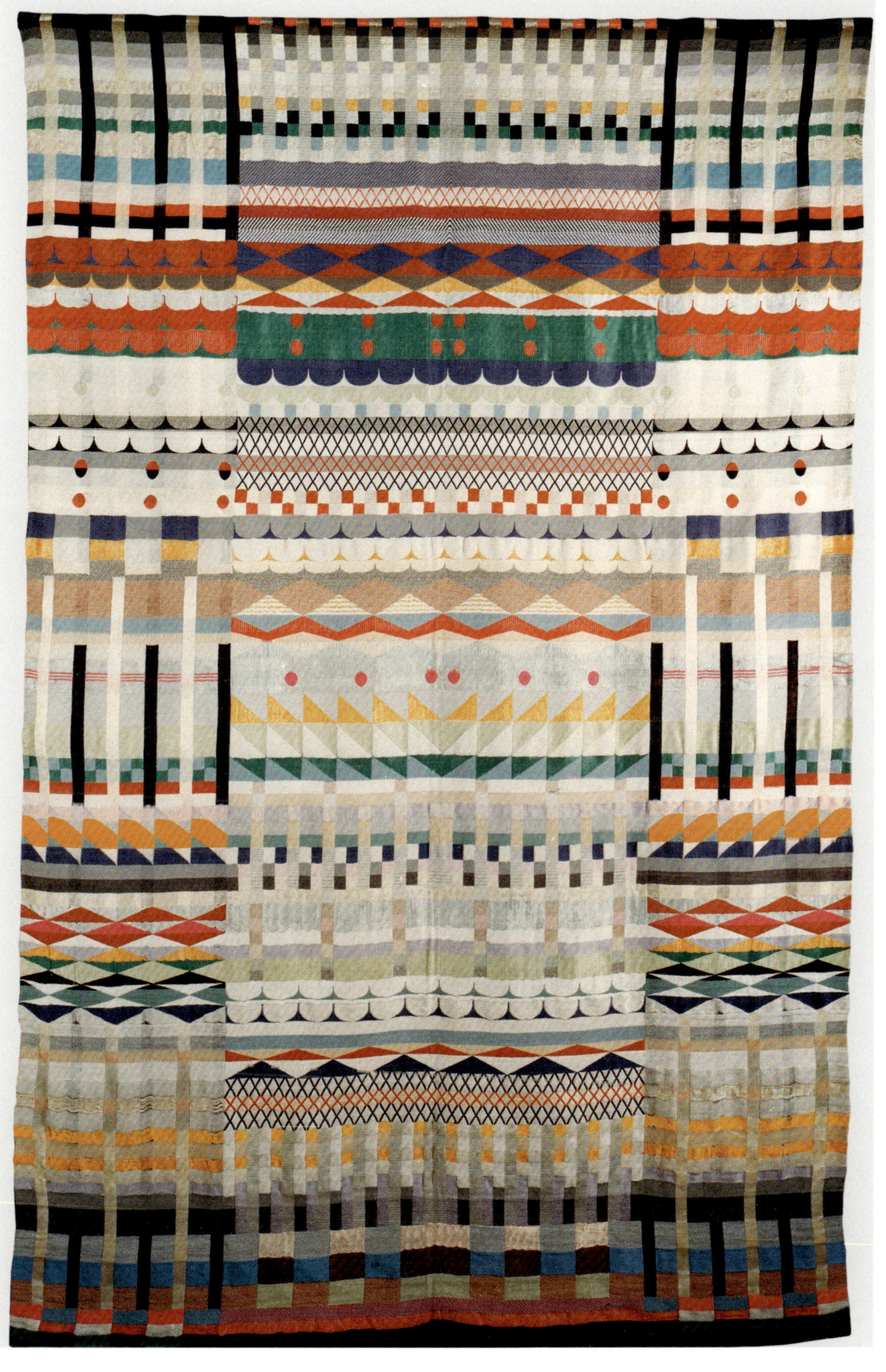

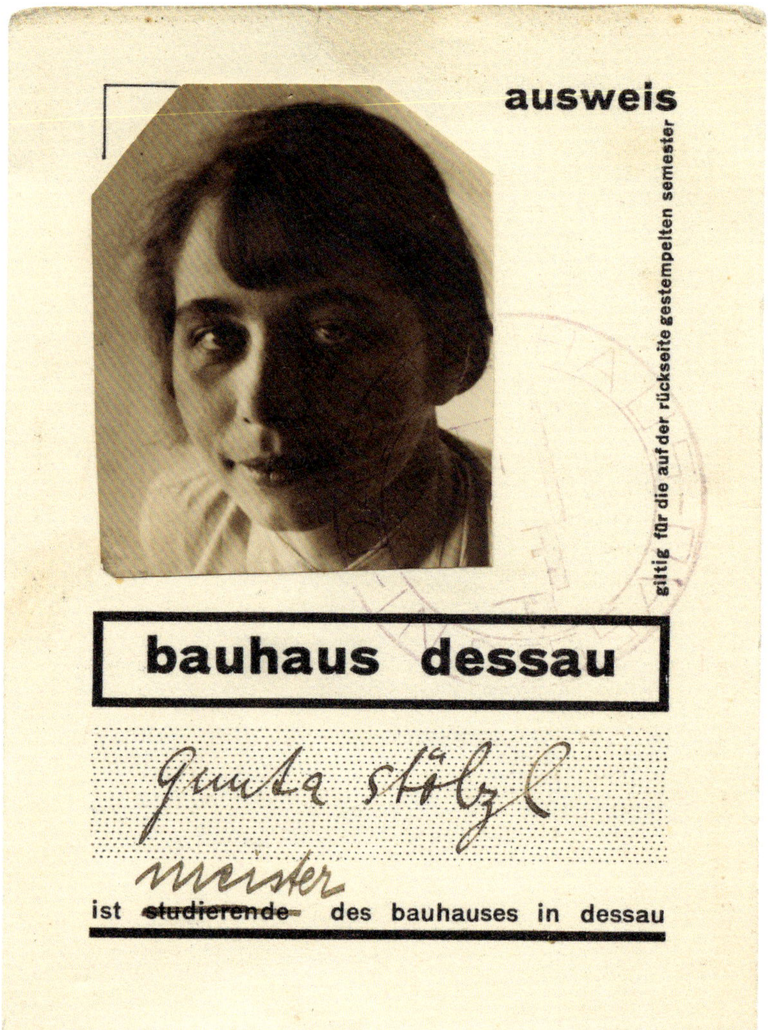

previous page
212
Gunta Stölzl
Fünf Chöre (*Five Choirs*), 1928
Jacquard weave in cotton, wool, rayon and silk
229 × 143 cm
Die Museen für Kunst und Kulturgeschichte der Hansestadt Lübeck

214
Gunta Stölzl's Bauhaus Dessau identity card, 1928
Letterpress, ink and gelatin silver print on card
12.2 × 8.9 cm
Bauhaus-Archiv Berlin

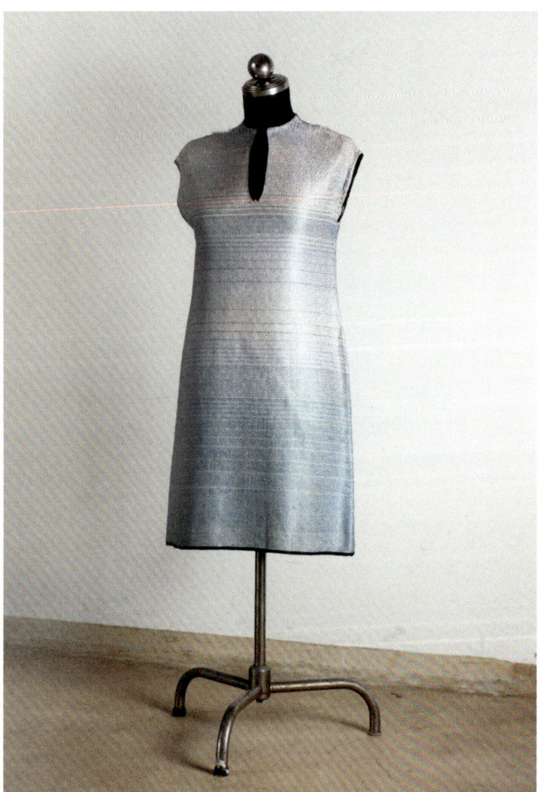

213
Lis Volger
Bauhaus dress, 1928
Cotton and synthetic silk
Length: 101 cm
Stiftung Bauhaus Dessau

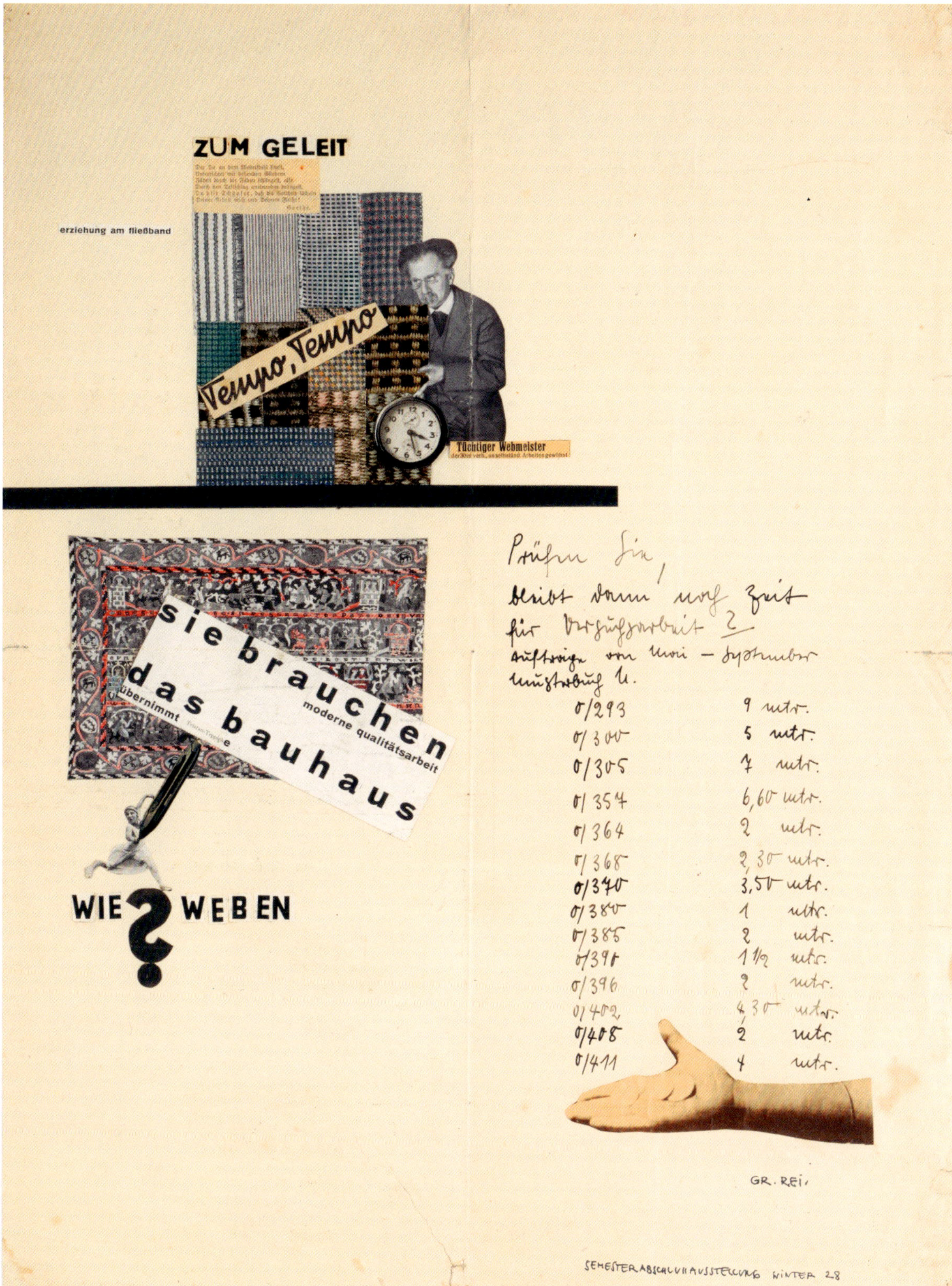

215
Grete Reichardt
you need the bauhaus, 1928
Collage
69.4 × 51.2 cm
Stiftung Bauhaus Dessau

the new vision

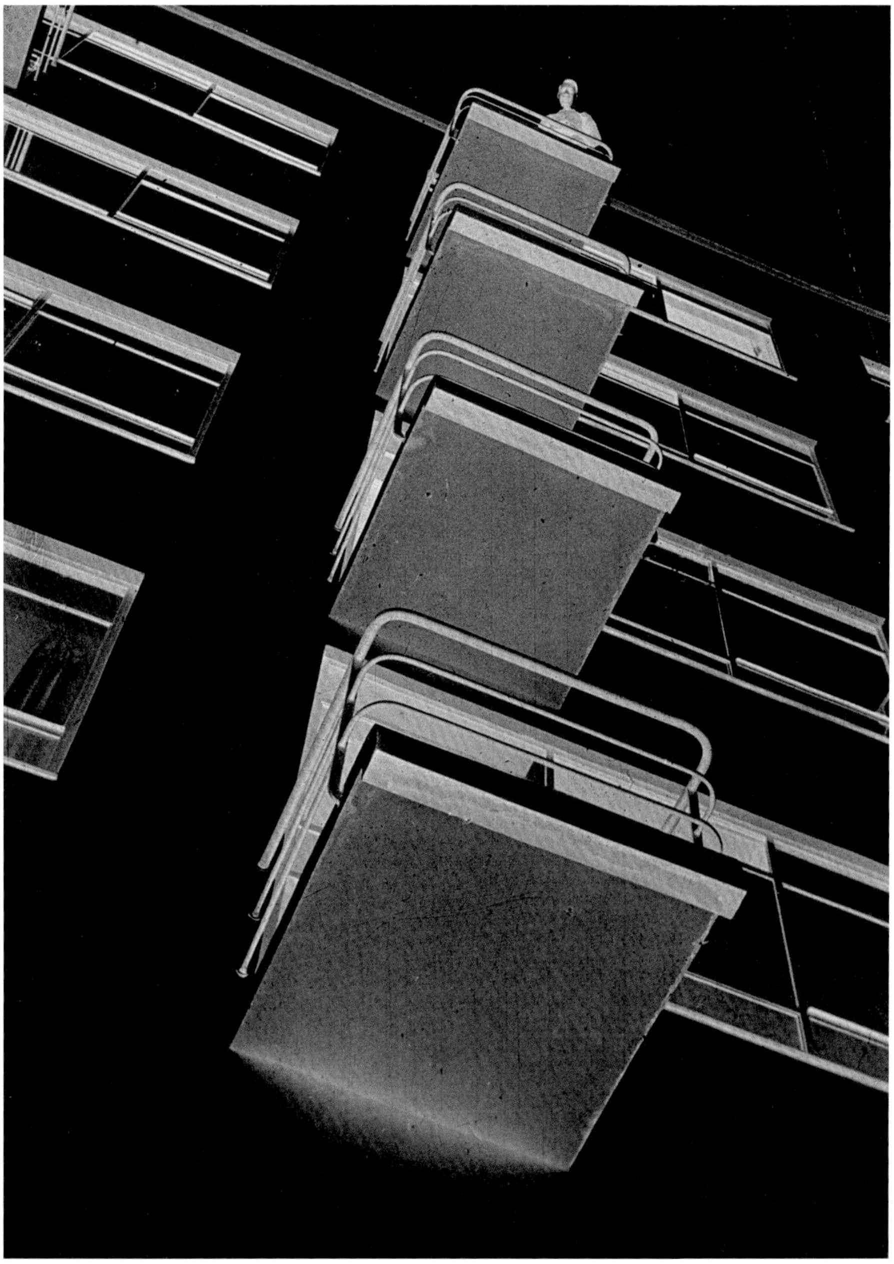

In spring 1929, Hannes Meyer appointed the Berlin-based professional photographer Walter Peterhans to lead the newly established photography workshop as part of the advertising department headed by Joost Schmidt. Meyer expected Schmidt's department to earn income through commissions for advertising and exhibition design, and he was impressed with Peterhans's emphasis on photography as a science rather than an art. Peterhans, whose father was director of the lens manufacturer Zeiss-Ikon, studied mathematics, philosophy, art history and photography. He brought a wealth of technical expertise and a rigorous approach to his teaching with exercises focusing on photography's optical and chemical processes. Peterhans also offered supplementary sessions in algebra so that his students could keep up with the mathematical calculations necessary for his photography course.

Although Peterhans's course was the first formal instruction in the medium, photography had been practised at the Bauhaus by enthusiasts and amateurs including László Moholy-Nagy, Georg Muche and Umbo (Otto Umbehr) in the Weimar period. Lucia Moholy, who studied photography and printing techniques in nearby Leipzig, was one of the most skilled in the medium at the time and took photographs of Bauhaus designs for promotional use. László Moholy's experimentation with the medium was a catalyst for others to try their hand. Once the school moved to Dessau, students and masters were afforded greater access to darkroom facilities and, with new advertising and publishing initiatives, including a series of Bauhaus books and the periodical *Bauhaus*, the demand for photographs increased significantly.

For students such as T. Lux Feininger and Erich Consemüller the medium was used to capture performances, social activities and group portraits. The informal snapshot quality of many of these photographs is underscored by the fact that most were only printed as small contact prints and therefore intended primarily as souvenirs for personal use.

The 1929 exhibition *Film und Foto* (Fifo) in Stuttgart, organised by the Deutscher Werkbund, served as a showcase for international developments in photography and film from the arenas of art, advertising, propaganda and reportage. Of the more than 100 participants in Fifo, twenty had affiliations with the Bauhaus, including Herbert Bayer, Irene Bayer, Marianne Brandt, Edmund Collein, Heinz Loew, Andreas Feininger, T. Lux Feininger, Werner Feist, Walter Funkat, Werner Graeff, Florence Henri, Lazsló Moholy-Nagy, Lucia Moholy, Hinnerk Scheper and Umbo (Otto Umbehr). This roster reflected the diverse spectrum of practices from commercial to avant-garde, attesting to the school's engagement with the broader photographic discourse of the late 1920s. The exhibition, moreover, situated their work in an international context, alongside other leading artists, filmmakers and photographers, including Berenice Abbott, Eugene Atget, André Kertész, El Lissitzky, Man Ray, Alexander Rodchenko, Kurt Schwitters, Edward Steichen and Edward Weston.

216
László Moholy-Nagy
Studio wing of the Bauhaus building, 1927
Gelatin silver print
24.6 × 17.9 cm
Galerie Berinson, Berlin

217
Paul Citroën
Metropolis, 1923
Cut-and-pasted photomechanical reproductions on paper
76.1 × 58.4 cm
Leiden University Library, Special Collections

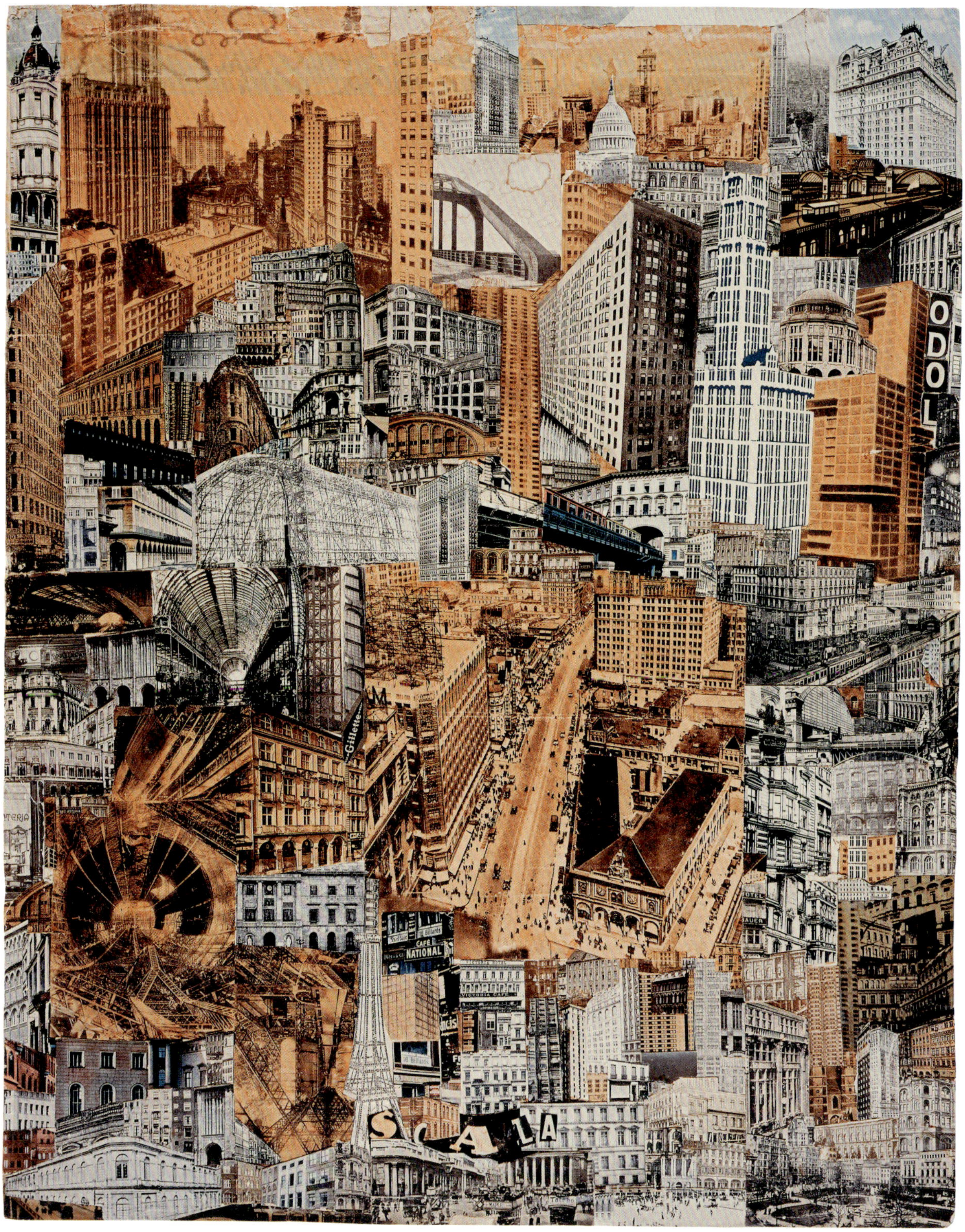

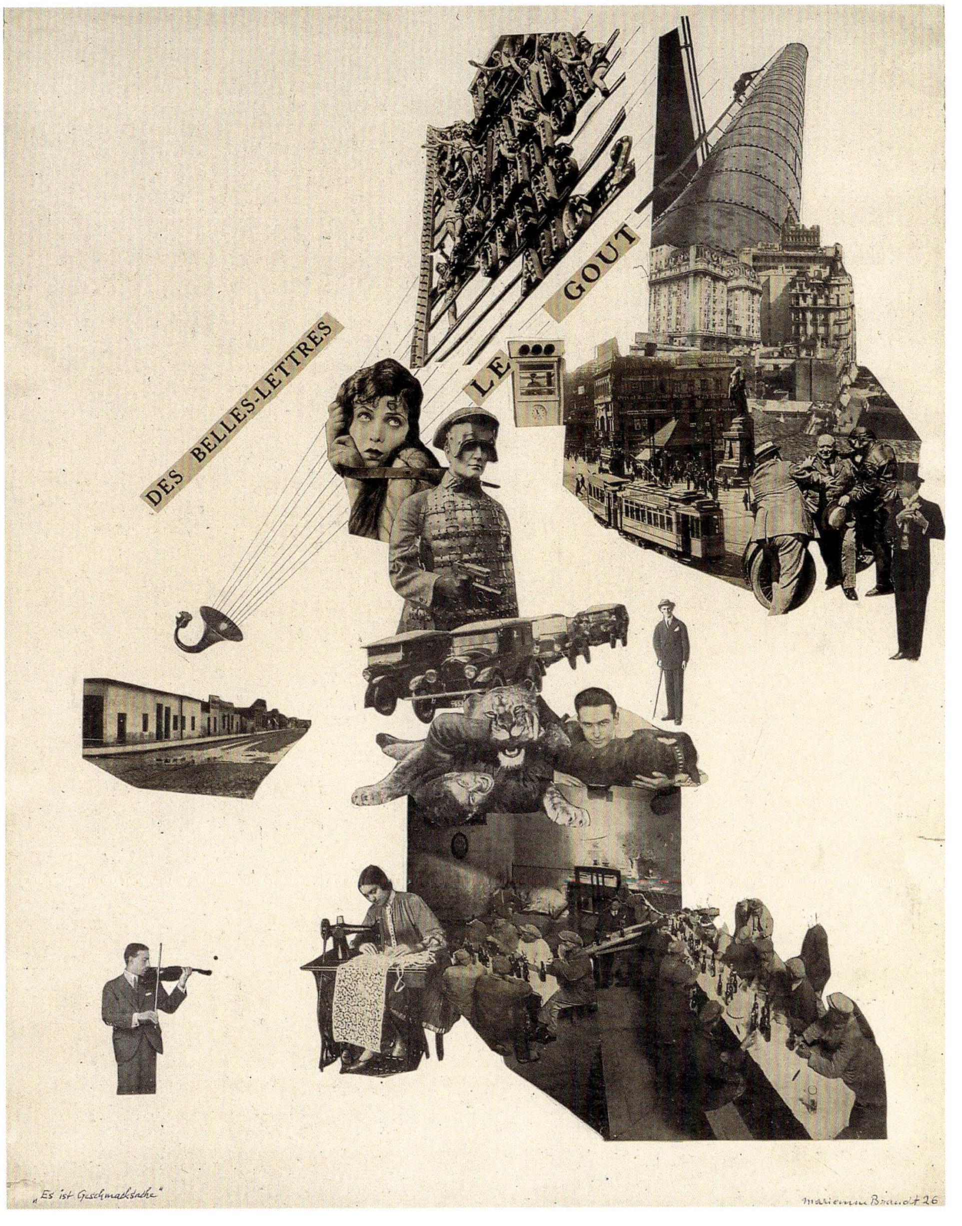

218
Marianne Brandt
It's a Matter of Taste, 1926
Collage and ink
65.1 × 50 cm
Galerie Berinson, Berlin

Brandt is primarily known for her work as a designer and metalworker. *It's a Matter of Taste* is an example of her experiments in montage, which she started around 1924 when other Bauhauslers were also working with the technique. Collaging found imagery from the illustrated press, Brandt's compositions offer a critical insight into the social, political and economic realities of the inter-war Weimar era. With its delight in visual pun, an aesthetic quality borrowed from the Dada movement, this work presents a satirical commentary on gender stereotypes and the changing role of women within a male-dominated society. Male ideals of femininity – a posing coquette and a group of scantily clad cabaret dancers – are juxtaposed with symbols of manhood: two heroic men battling a lion, a proud-standing soldier, smartly dressed businessmen and a phallic-shaped tower. Yet while the male workers indulge in beer and frivolity, a demure seamstress busily works at her needle. She is a symbol of the growing emancipation of women within the labour-force in the aftermath of World War I, and a figure that can be seen to represent Brandt herself.

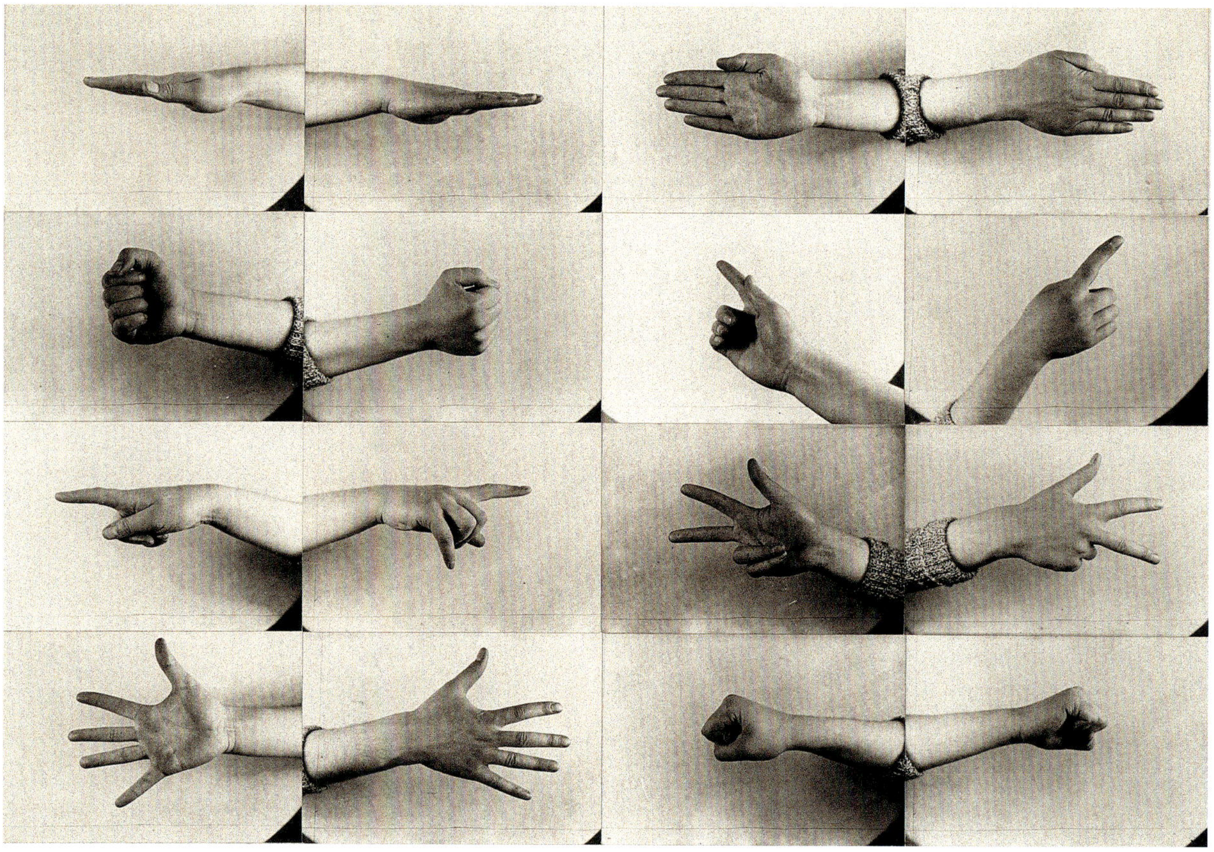

219
Kurt Kranz
Handgesten-Reihe
(*Hand Gestures Series*), 1931
(mounted 1981)
16 photographs mounted on board
85.5 × 70.6 cm
Kunsthalle Bremen – Kupferstichkabinett –
Der Kunstverein in Bremen

Created during the winter semester of 1930–31, during his time as a student at the Bauhaus photography workshop under Walter Peterhans, Kranz's *Hand Gestures Series* occupies a significant place within the history of photography at the Bauhaus. This series of images captured and assembled to create a sense of rhythm and movement testifies to the experimentation that took place at the school and can be linked to an interest in experimental film. While at the Bauhaus, Kranz had learned of the work of Hans Richter and wanted to make abstract films, but the school did not offer a film course.

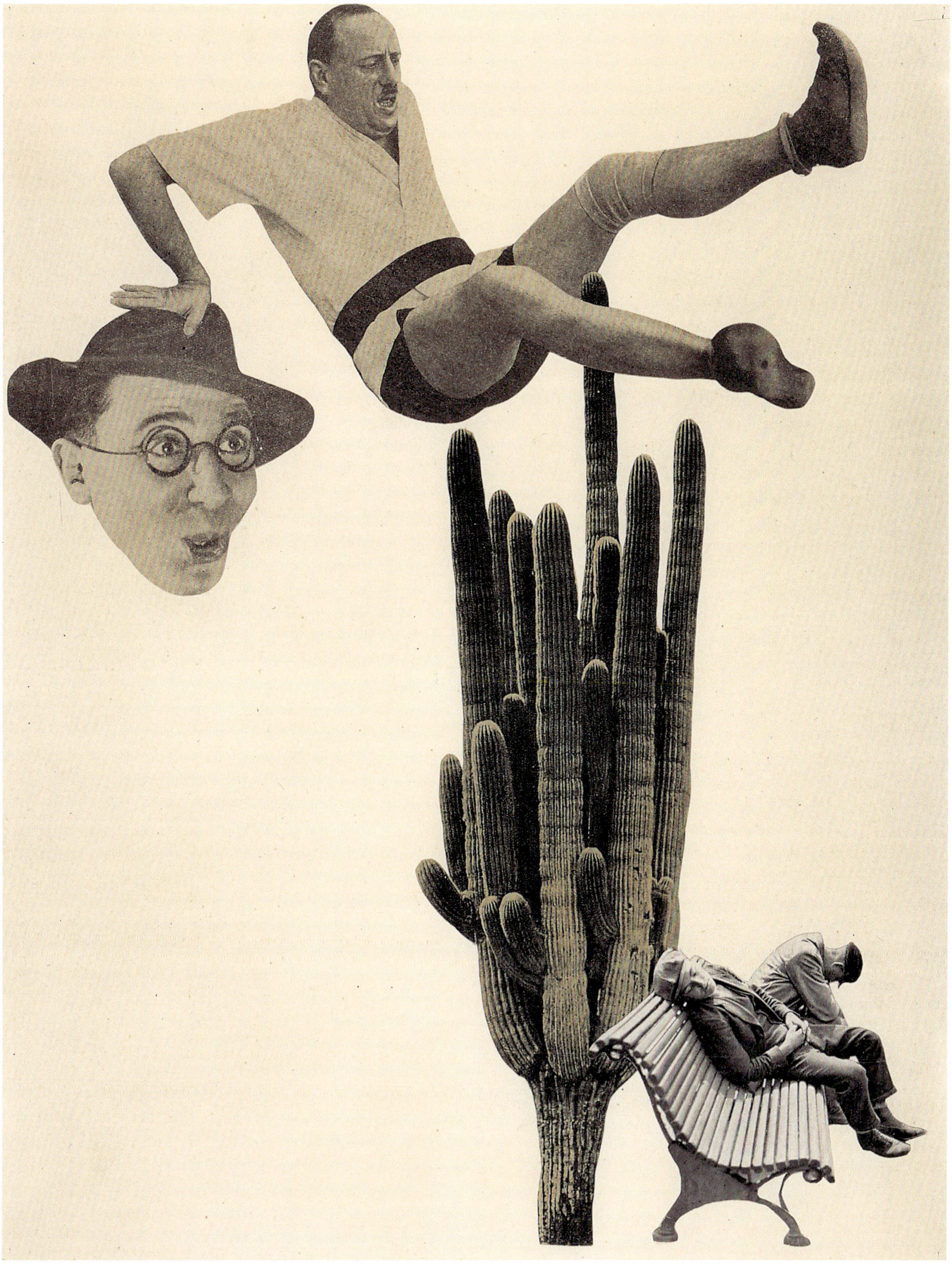

220
Günter Hirschel-Protsch
The Olympic Master Cactus, 1929
Collage
34.8 × 26.1 cm
Galerie Berinson, Berlin

lászló moholy-nagy
unprecedented photography

Until now, all the essays and commentaries about the paths and aims of photography have been following a false trail. Again and again, the question singled out from all the various possible approaches as the most essential has been that of the relationship between art and photography.

But the *fact* of photography does not grow or diminish in value according to whether it is classified as a method of recording reality or as a medium of scientific investigation or as a way of preserving vanished events, or as a basis for the process of reproduction, or as 'art.'

The photographic process has no precedent among the previously known visual media. And when photography relies on its own possibilities, its results, too, are without precedent. Just one of its features – the range of infinitely subtle gradations of light and dark that capture the phenomenon of light in what seems to be an almost immaterial radiance – would suffice to establish a new kind of seeing, a new kind of visual power.

But the subject of photography involves infinitely more. In today's photographic work, the first and foremost issue is to develop an integrally photographic approach that is derived purely from the means of photography itself; only after a more or less exact photographic language has been developed will a truly gifted photographer be able to elevate it to an 'artistic' level. The prerequisite for this is: no dependence on traditional forms of representation! Photography has no need for that. No ancient or contemporary painting can match the singular effectiveness available to photography. Why the 'painterly' comparisons? Why Rembrandt – or Picasso – imitations?

One can say without utopian extravagance that the near future will bring a great transvaluation in the goals photography sets itself. The investigation is already under way, although frequently along separate paths:

Conscious use of light-dark relationships. Activity of brightness, passivity of darkness. Inversions of the relationships between positive and negative values.

Introduction of greater contrasts.

Use of the texture and structure (facture) of various materials.

Unknown forms of representation.

The areas that have yet to be examined can be established in line with the new elements of photographic practice, as follows:

1 Unfamiliar views made by positioning the camera obliquely, or pointing it up or down.
2 Experiments with various lens systems, changing the relationships familiar to normal vision, occasionally distorting them to the point of unrecognisability. (Concave and convex mirrors, funhouse mirror shots, etc., were the first steps.) This gives rise to a paradox: the mechanical imagination.
3 Encircling the object (a further development of stereo photography on *one* plate).
4 New kinds of camera construction. Avoidance of the foreshortening effect of perspective.
5 Adapting experience with X-ray – aperspectivity and penetration – to the uses of photography.
6 Cameraless photographs, made by casting light on the sensitive surface.
7 True colour sensitivity.

Only a work that combines all possible interrelationships, the synthesis of these elements, will be recognised as true photography.

The development of photography is receiving a powerful impetus from the new culture of light, which is already highly cultivated in many places.

This century belongs to light. Photography is the first means of giving tangible shape to light, though in a transposed and – perhaps just for that reason – almost abstract form.

Film goes even further – generally one might say that photography culminates in film. The development of a new dimension in optical experience is achieved to a still greater degree by film.

But the spadework accomplished by still photography is indispensable for a developed cinema. A peculiar interrelationship: the master taking instruction from the apprentice. A reciprocal laboratory: photography as an investigatory field for film, and film as a stimulus for photography.

The issues raised by cinema provide lessons that serve as guiding principles for the practice of photography and can enrich the photographic results themselves: changing light intensities and light tempos, variations in spatial motion engendered by light, the extinguishing and flashing forth of the whole organism of motion, the triggering of latent functional charges in us, in our brain. Chiaroscuro. Light-palpability, light-movement. Light-distance and light-proximity. Penetrating and cumulative light rays. – The strongest visual experiences that can be granted to man.

László Moholy-Nagy, 'Die beispiellos Fotografie' in Das Deutsche Lichtbild*, Berlin, 1927*

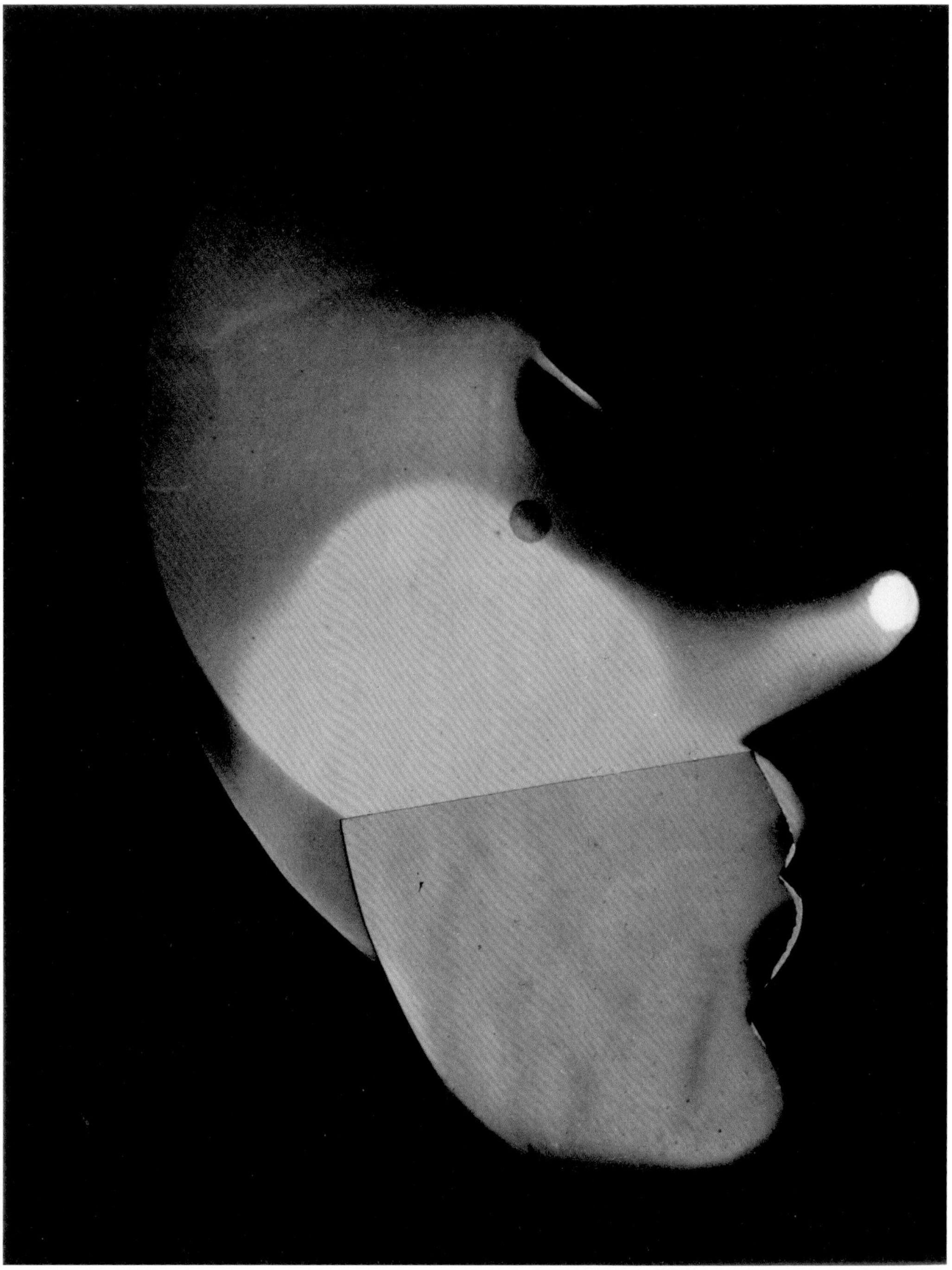

221
László Moholy-Nagy
Self-Portrait in Profile, 1926 (printed c.1928)
Gelatin silver print reproduced from the
artist's collaged photogram
30.2 × 23.6 cm
Bauhaus-Archiv Berlin

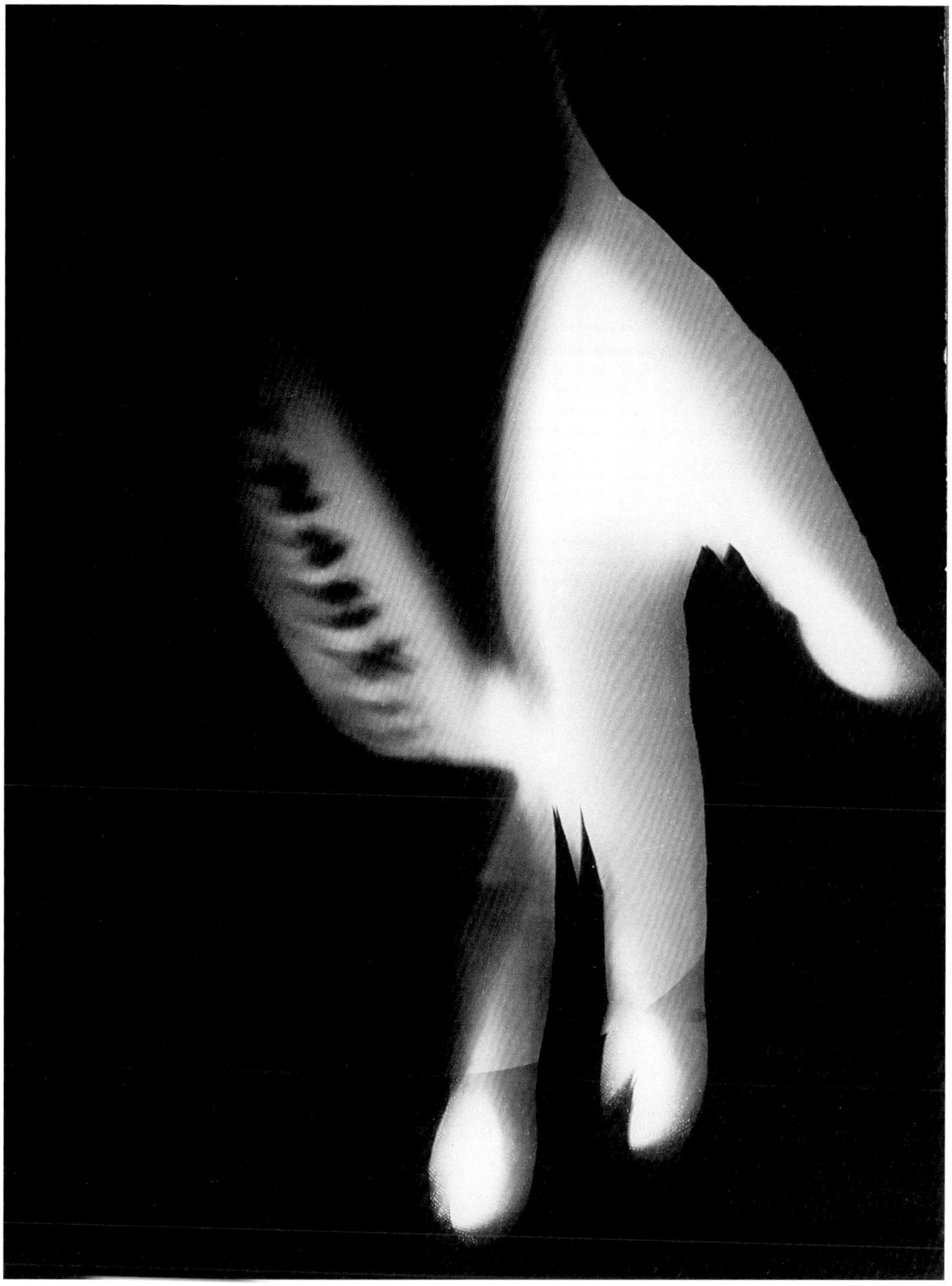

222
László Moholy-Nagy
Photogram–Hand, 1926
Gelatin silver print
29.3 × 22.4 cm
Galerie Berinson, Berlin

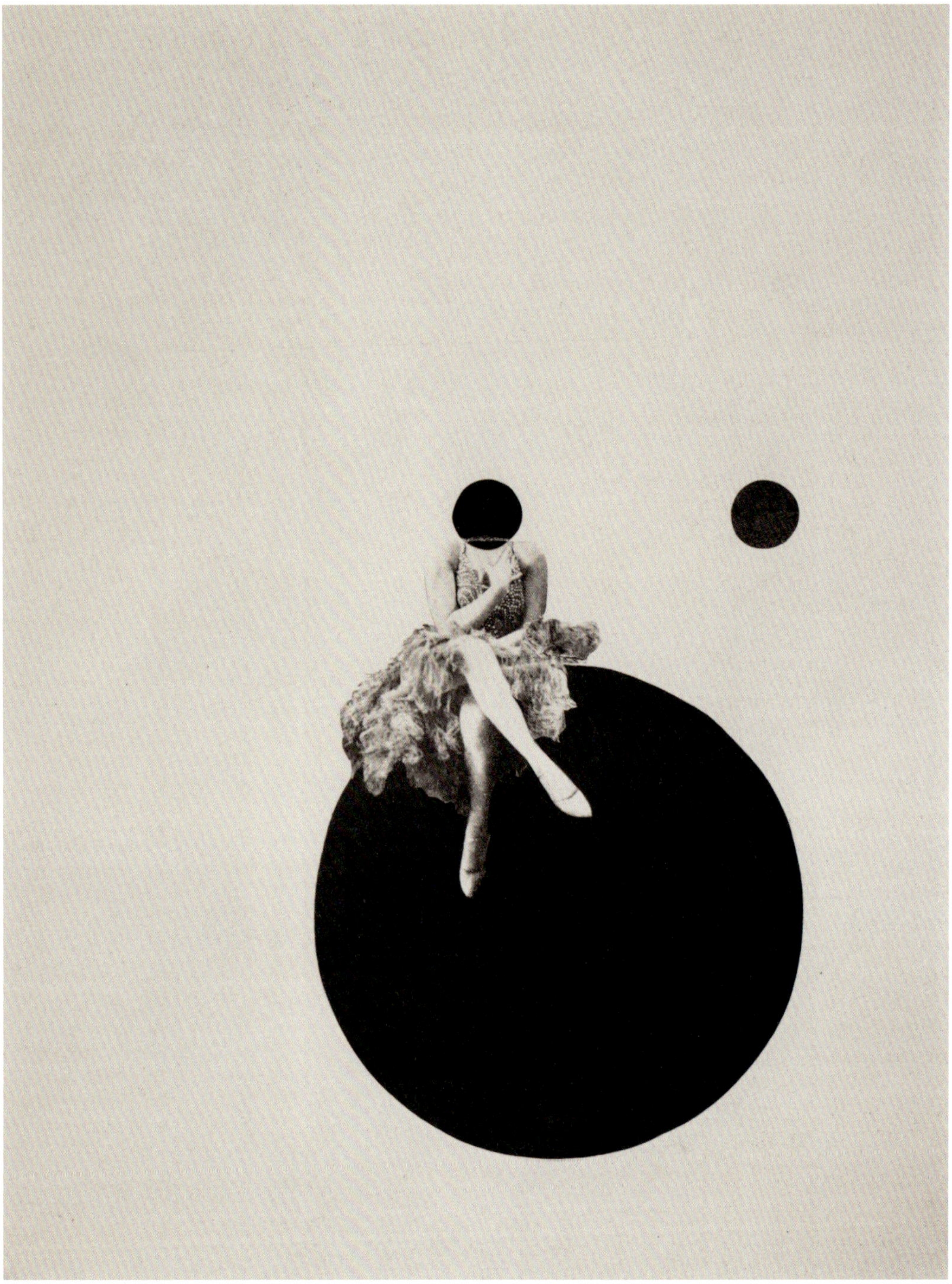

223
László Moholy-Nagy
The Dancing Sisters Olly and Dolly, 1925
Photomontage, gelatin silver print
16 × 11.7 cm
Centre Pompidou, Paris. Musée National d'Art Moderne/Centre de Création Industrielle. Purchased, 1994

224
Charlotte Voepel
Ja nur nivea, poster design for Nivea, 1928
Collage, newspaper clippings, ink, tempera and pencil on paper
50.3 × 65.1 cm
Bauhaus-Archiv Berlin

225
László Moholy-Nagy
Jealousy (Fotoplastiken; Jealousy), 1927 (printed 1973)
Gelatin silver print reproduced from the artist's collaged photogram
57.5 × 42.3 cm
Victoria and Albert Museum

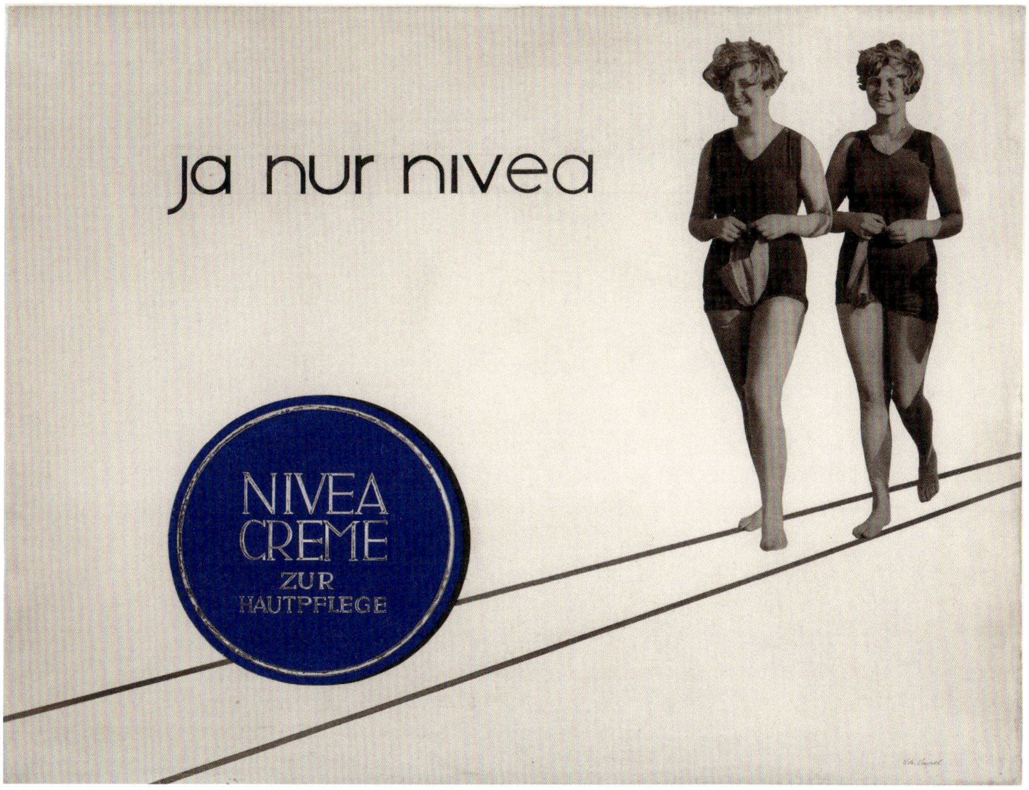
ja nur nivea
NIVEA
CREME
ZUR
HAUTPFLEGE

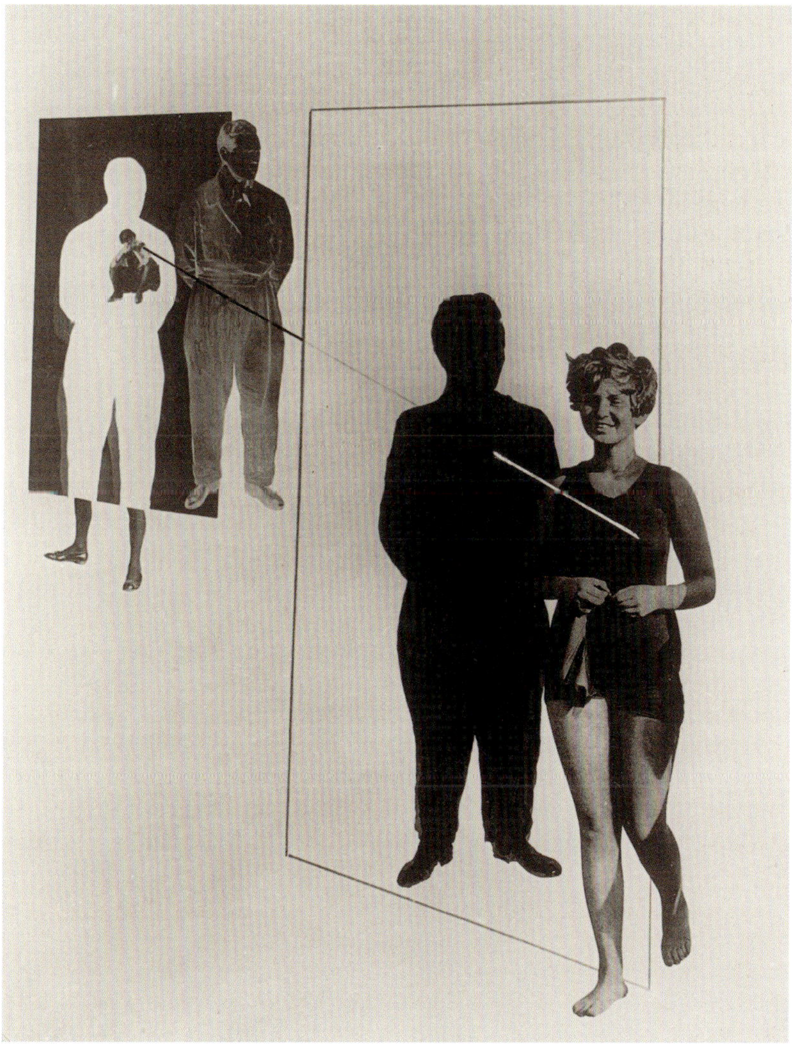

document, experiment, advertisement photography at the bauhaus

lydia yee

For the progressive young men and women of the Bauhaus, photography represented a modern medium unencumbered by the weight of history, reflecting the forward-looking aspirations of the new Weimar Republic. 'We weren't really photographers with the conscious aim of making art', explained Herbert Bayer, former Bauhaus student and later master of advertising and typography, 'We were simply interested in the possibilities of the camera. And we saw that there were more possibilities than those which already existed ... We simply took a camera and began to shoot'.[1]

Although photography had been around for a century, a number of new technical advances ushered in a period of experimentation in the arenas of art and commerce. In the late nineteenth and early twentieth centuries, practitioners of the dominant photographic aesthetic known as 'pictorialism' – characterised by soft focus, romantic subject matter and manipulated, painterly surfaces – sought to elevate photography by aligning it with the fine arts. By the end of World War I, this style of art photography was viewed as outmoded and bourgeois by a new generation of artists, who were proponents of a modern technological aesthetic in keeping with the times. In Germany, photographers associated with the post-war *Neue Sachlichkeit* (New Objectivity) movement favoured precision and clarity and were aided by optical innovations that improved the performance of photographic lenses. The introduction of portable cameras by the mid-1920s made it possible for photographers to shoot in a more spontaneous manner. In tandem with these developments, the 1920s also saw the rapid growth of illustrated newspapers and magazines, which created a demand for photographs to accompany both news stories and advertisements. Their widespread adoption of the halftone printing process facilitated the reproduction of photographs and gave publications a more modern look.

Photography was already an important tool for Walter Gropius when he established the school in 1919. He had his portrait taken by Louis Held, who ran a prominent local studio and had photographed the luminaries of Weimar, including the composer Franz Liszt, Elisabeth Förster-Nietzsche, the sister of the philosopher, and the architect Henry van de Velde. Presumably Gropius's portrait was for publicity purposes, to accompany press articles announcing his founding and directorship of the Bauhaus. From the beginning, Gropius understood the importance of public relations in his role as the new director of the fledgling institution that was entirely dependent on political support and funding from the local state government of Thuringia.

Gropius sent a notice to the Bauhaus workshop masters in April 1922: 'I have asked a photographer, Miss Stockmar, to photograph all the suitable works coming out of the workshops, in part for the archive that we are assembling in the secretary's office to provide an overview of everything that has been achieved so far, and in part for future publications'.[2] Although Gropius did not appear to have had any more specific use for the photographs at the time, he recognised the value of documenting the school's output from the early years in Weimar. These straightforward photographs provided a record of preliminary course studies, workshops and their production, as well as individual works of the masters, associates and apprentices. This archive would soon serve an important purpose.

As a young architect working with Adolf Meyer on his first major commission, the Fagus factory, Gropius realised the importance of photographs as documents. He collected images of industrial structures, primarily factories and silos in the United States, which he used in lectures and to illustrate his articles in *Der Industriebau*.[3] He also utlised these photographs to inform his designs for Fagus. Once the main building was completed, Gropius selected Edmund Lill to photograph the structure and these pictures accompanied his article on Fagus also published in *Der Industriebau*.[4]

With preparations for the 1923 Bauhaus exhibition underway in the autumn of 1922, the archive that Gropius established in the secretary's office now had a concrete purpose. It facilitated the selection of works for the exhibition and served as a source of images for the accompanying publication *Staatliches Bauhaus in Weimar 1919–1923*. Local studios including Hüttich-Oemler, Louis Held and Hermann Eckner and several from Berlin were hired to photograph works produced at the school and subsequently to document the 1923 exhibition. Lucia Moholy, who arrived at the Bauhaus with her husband László Moholy-Nagy in the spring of 1923, apprenticed at the Eckner studio and from 1923 to 1928 worked as a freelance photographer for the Bauhaus, documenting objects made in the workshops and later the new Dessau building and masters' houses, as well as taking portraits of Bauhauslers. Her photographs of teapots, glasses, lamps and other objects (figs.93, 95–96) from the school's workshops illustrated the *Katalog der Muster*. This catalogue of prototypes, designed by Herbert Bayer in 1925, was intended to market Bauhaus designs and ultimately improve the school's financial situation by generating sales and attention from German companies who could manufacture its products. Although these objects had the clean, streamlined look of industrially produced goods, many were exquisitely handcrafted objects and not suited for mass production.[5]

The arrival of the Hungarian-born Constructivist painter László Moholy-Nagy served as a major impetus for opening up new possibilities for photography at the Bauhaus. He joined the faculty as head of the metal workshop in March 1923, and he and Josef Albers took over the preliminary course from the departing Johannes Itten. One of his first tasks was to oversee the design and production of the book *Staatliches Bauhaus in Weimar 1919–1923*. Bayer, who was still a student at the time, designed the cover with heavy block capitals for the book's title and an inventive use of colour to divide words. Moholy did the interior layout, using type positioned vertically as well as horizontally, often in capitals and meeting at a right angle and with red bars to add emphasis. In contrast to the typography, the photographs were treated in a straightforward manner: each black-and-white reproduction had its own page, and select works were printed as colour lithographs. However, Moholy's essay in the book, titled 'The New Typography', proposed a more radical relationship between photograph and text. He identified the use of photographic reproductions 'placed in the text' as the most important aspect in contemporary typography.[6] When the school moved in to the new building in Dessau in 1926, the Bauhaus was finally able to realise more innovative typography in its printed materials.

Prior to Moholy's arrival, photography at the Bauhaus was primarily viewed as a reproductive medium. A newcomer to photography, Moholy had just started his photographic experiments with his wife Lucia, who was already versed in the medium. In his groundbreaking essay 'Production-Reproduction' published in the journal *De Stijl* in July 1922, Moholy asks if it is possible to open up reproductive media such as photography, film and sound recording to 'serve productive ends as well'. Regarding photography he writes: 'The camera captures light effects by means of a silver-bromide plate at the back. As yet we've only made use of this function of the camera in a secondary sense: to capture (reproduce) particular objects as they reflect or absorb light', and concludes that: 'A great deal of experimentation is needed here'.[7] Moholy does not mention photograms, but shortly after the publication of this text he and Lucia came across examples of cameraless photographs based on a process that had been around since the advent of photography. By placing objects on light-sensitive 'printing-out' paper and exposing them to the sun, they produced their first photograms without the aid of a darkroom.[8]

Recognising the potential of the photogram, Moholy began experimenting with the process, placing materials and objects of different degrees of density and translucency onto the paper to create 'light compositions' that initially resembled his paintings. Later, he positioned objects at varying distances from the paper to produce spatial effects, and used multiple exposures and light sources from different angles when he had access to a darkroom. These experiments yielded unique works that transcended photography's inherently reproductive quality. Moholy's *Self-Portrait in Profile* (1926; fig.221), for example, is evocative and mysterious even though its title suggests a conventional subject. What manner of objects passed between the light-sensitive paper and the light source to create the crescent-moon-shaped composition? It appears that the artist's profile was the initial basis of the image. Moholy then introduced other objects in subsequent exposures to shape the composition. A collaged element was probably added to a print and then rephotographed. The image, oscillating between man and moon, light and dark, is not fixed, and meaning not arrested.

While at the Bauhaus, Moholy was an enthusiastic exponent of other photo-based practices, most notably 'New Vision' photography and photomontage. He was connected to the Dadaist circles in Berlin where he had lived from 1920 until joining the faculty in Weimar – and familiar with the photomontage work of Raoul Hausmann and Hannah Höch. He did not, however, try his hand at photomontage until after he began teaching at the Bauhaus and creating typographical designs for the school, including the series *Bauhausbücher* and related promotional material. His interest in integrating type and photographs, which he termed 'typophoto', coincided with his first experiments with photomontage. In contrast to the Dadaists but in keeping with advertising techniques, Moholy photographed his montage works, calling them 'photoplastics', rather than presenting them as cut-and-paste collages. In *The Dancing Sisters Olly and Dolly* (1925; fig. 223), he makes use of elements appearing in his typographic designs, solid black circles at two different scales standing in for the dancers' heads and a larger sphere on which a single figure is perched. For Moholy, 'Photoplastics demonstrate quite clearly how to change the imitative photographic process into purposeful creativity'.[9]

Moholy's fervent embrace of new photographic techniques influenced fellow Bauhauslers to adopt them, including Paul Citroën and Marianne Brandt, who both produced complex photomontages. The montage technique chimed with a broad interest in collage – as exemplified by the material studies that emerged from Itten's preliminary course – and developed into the popular practice of creating handmade gifts that were exchanged among Bauhaus masters and students. Moholy also saw the potential for photomontage works to convey a directed message with commercial applications: 'My goal is to produce photo-plastics which – although composed of many photographs [copied, pasted, retouched] – create the controlled and coherent effect of a single picture equivalent to a photograph ... This method allows us to depict a seemingly organic super-reality. Its possible uses are infinite. Photosculpture can be especially effective in advertising.'[10]

In his groundbreaking *Malerie, Photographie, Film* (*Painting, Photography, Film*), published in 1925 as part of the series *Bauhausbücher*, Moholy collected together previously published and new articles alongside artistic and vernacular images to present his theoretical ideas on photography and film and their pedagogical potential. The book juxtaposes examples of photograms, photoplastics, photomontage works, double exposures, solarised images, mirror reflections and distortions, aerial and microscopic shots, X-rays, reflected light displays, animated films and advertisements by the Moholys and by fellow Bauhauslers Citröen, Georg Muche, Ludwig Hirschfield-Mack, Kurt Schwerdtfeger, as well as other avant-garde artists including Man Ray, Hannah Höch, Albert Renger-Patzsch and Viking Eggeling, plus images from the illustrated press and picture agencies. *Painting, Photography, Film* laid the framework for a technologically oriented 'New Vision', in which photography could extend the capacity of the eye and radically transform human perception. To this end, Moholy called for the application of photographic techniques from the field of science and for unconventional camera angles: 'the view from above, from below, the oblique view'.[11] It was his aim that 'we see the world with entirely different eyes' and that 'we create *new relationships*'.[12] His far-reaching vision resonated with a number of the young Bauhauslers, including Bayer, T. Lux Feininger and Florence Henri, in the period after the school's move in 1925 to the industrial city of Dessau, home to the Junkers airplane factory. As these and other aspiring young photographers explored the school's new purpose-built facilities from every angle, they fostered a vibrant new dynamic among their peers. The flat rooftops of the Dessau building and the balconies of the adjoining five-storey Prellerhaus – the studio accommodation for students and junior masters – afforded bird's eye and worm's eye views, as well as a stage for playful activity.

During the Dessau period, Gropius continued to commission photographs of the school's architecture, products, performances and other activities (most notably from Erich Consemüller), for documentation and promotional purposes, but he never established a workshop devoted to photography. This was due in part to the fact that Moholy did not view photography as a disciplinary medium, and that he was not technically adept in the darkroom.[13] It was only after Hannes Meyer became the school's director, following the departure of Gropius and Moholy, that a photography department was established as part of the advertising workshop: 'By expanding the advertising workshop (addition of a photographic studio under the direction of the well-known Berlin photographer, Walter Peterhans) ... the productive options open to the Bauhaus are to be further improved.'[14] Meyer reoriented the school in a scientific direction and appointed Peterhans, who had extensive photographic training and ran a commercial studio focusing on portraits and advertising, to head the workshop. He took up the position in summer 1929 and remained at the school until its closure four years later. Kurt Kranz recalls how Joost Schmidt's advertising workshop was organised: 'Peterhans, an avant-garde photography teacher; Mayer-Mark, a promotional expert, whose lecture series included the latest in advertising; and psychology of the gestalt kind, as part of general education under Karlfried, Count von Durkheim [visiting lecturer from Leipzig] – all that, combined and coordinated by Joost Schmidt with his own class and the advertising/printing workshop'.[15]

Peterhans, a consummate technician, took painstaking care in assembling his compositions, then lighting, exposing and printing them. In his still life *Portrait of the Beloved* (1929; fig. 231) he arranged pieces of fabric, a metal bowl and other material into an artful composition. The fastidious lighting draws attention to the materiality of the individual elements and transforms them into a surreal tableau. Ellen Auerbach, who trained in Peterhans's Berlin studio, recalled: 'I shall never forget being present for a still life of six small objects, wool, silk, chiffon, etc. which he set up and photographed. With the aid of two 500-watt bulbs and admirable stamina and sensitivity, he worked at it for hours'.[16] Former student Kranz later complained: 'Most students found Peterhans's course to be too technically mathematical, since he invested a great deal of theoretical interest in the chemical processes of photography.'[17]

Photography at the Bauhaus had been closely linked to advertising, particularly in the Dessau period. Moholy, who believed that photography was an effective tool for communication, designed posters and advertisements integrating photograms and photomontage. Bayer, Henri and other Bauhaus masters and students used striking photographs to create book and magazine covers and promotional materials for the Bauhaus and outside clients. Although photography became an integral part of the advertising workshop, Peterhans seemed to take a position at odds with the principles of advertising. He objected to modern photographers who 'make big and small posters, and produce graphic, not photographic effects'.[18] His essay 'On the Present State of Photography', published the year after he joined the Bauhaus, contains an implicit critique of Moholy's new vision: 'We fail to recognise the magic of its precision and detailing, thus allowing what we already possess to disappear – all in an attempt to make it the equal of the graphic arts, which rightly display other qualities arising from different technical means. Hence we have not even noticed that photography is capable of giving us its own new vision of things and people, a vision of upsetting forcefulness.'[19] Ultimately, it was Moholy's ideas that prevailed and made a lasting impact on both the fields of photography and advertising.

The reception of the Bauhaus has been indelibly shaped by photographs of all sorts. These images convey the richness and diversity of the school's activities and personalities, the range of its artistic expression, and how it wished to present itself to the outside world. Without this record we would not have such a full and complex picture of the Bauhaus today.

1 Cited in Frank Whitford (ed.), *The Bauhaus: Masters and Students by Themselves*, Conran Octopus, London, 1992, p.188.

2 Cited in Klaus-Jürgen Winkler (ed.), *Bauhaus-Alben 1*, Bauhaus-Universität Weimar, 2010, p.10.

3 See Annemarie Jaeggi, *Fagus: Industrial Culture from Werkbund to Bauhaus*, Princeton Architectural Press, New York, 2000, pp.44–45, 49–50.

4 Ibid., pp.106–7.

5 See Robin Schuldenfrei, 'The Irreproducibility of the Bauhaus Object', in Jeffrey Saletnik and Robin Schuldenfrei (eds), *Bauhaus Construct: Fashioning Identity, Discourse, and Modernism*, Routledge, London, 2009, pp.37–60.

6 The essay was originally published in *Staatliches Bauhaus in Weimar 1919–1923*, Munich, *1923*. An English translation appears in Richard Kostelanetz (ed.), *Moholy-Nagy*, Allen Lane, The Penguin Press, London, 1971, pp.75–76.

7 László Moholy-Nagy, 'Produktion-Reproduktion', *De Stijl* 5, no.7 (July 1922). Eng. trans. in Christopher Phillips (ed.), *Photography in the Modern Era: European Documents and Critical Writings, 1913–1940*, The Metropolitan Museum of Art/Aperture, New York, 1989, pp.80–81.

8 Christian Schad and Man Ray had used this technique to make photograms in an artistic context just prior to Moholy-Nagy, who claimed no knowledge of these precedents. See Herbert Molderings, 'Light Years of a Life: The Photogram Aesthetic of László Moholy-Nagy', in Renate Heyne and Floris M. Neusüss (eds), *Moholy-Nagy: The Photograms: Catalogue Raisonné*, Hatje Cantz, Ostfildern, 2009, pp.17–18.

9 Moholy-Nagy, 'Fotographie ist Lightgestaltung', *Bauhaus* 2, no.1 (1928). Eng. trans. in Krisztina Passuth (ed.), *Moholy-Nagy*, Thames & Hudson, London, 1985, p.303.

10 Moholy-Nagy, 'Die Photographie in der Reklame', *Photographische Korrespondenz*, no.9 (September 1927). Engl. trans., 'Photography in Advertising', in Phillips, op. cit., p.92.

11 Moholy-Nagy, *Painting, Photography, Film*, trans. Janet Seligman, Lund Humphries, London, 1969, p.28.

12 Ibid., p.29.

13 Andreas Haus, 'Laszlo Moholy-Nagy' in *Photography at the Bauhaus*, The MIT Press, Cambridge, MA, 1990, p.18.

14 Hannes Meyer quoted in Magdalena Droste, *Bauhaus 1919–1933*, Taschen, Cologne, 2006, p.172.

15 Kurt Kranz in Eckhard Neumann (ed.), *Bauhaus and Bauhaus People*, Chapman Hall, London, 1993, p.274.

16 Cited in Whitford, op. cit., p.276.

17 Kranz, op. cit, p.275.

18 Walter Peterhans, 'On the Present State of Photography', *Photography in the Modern Era: European Documents and Critical Writings, 1913–1940*, pp.124–25.

19 Ibid., p.124.

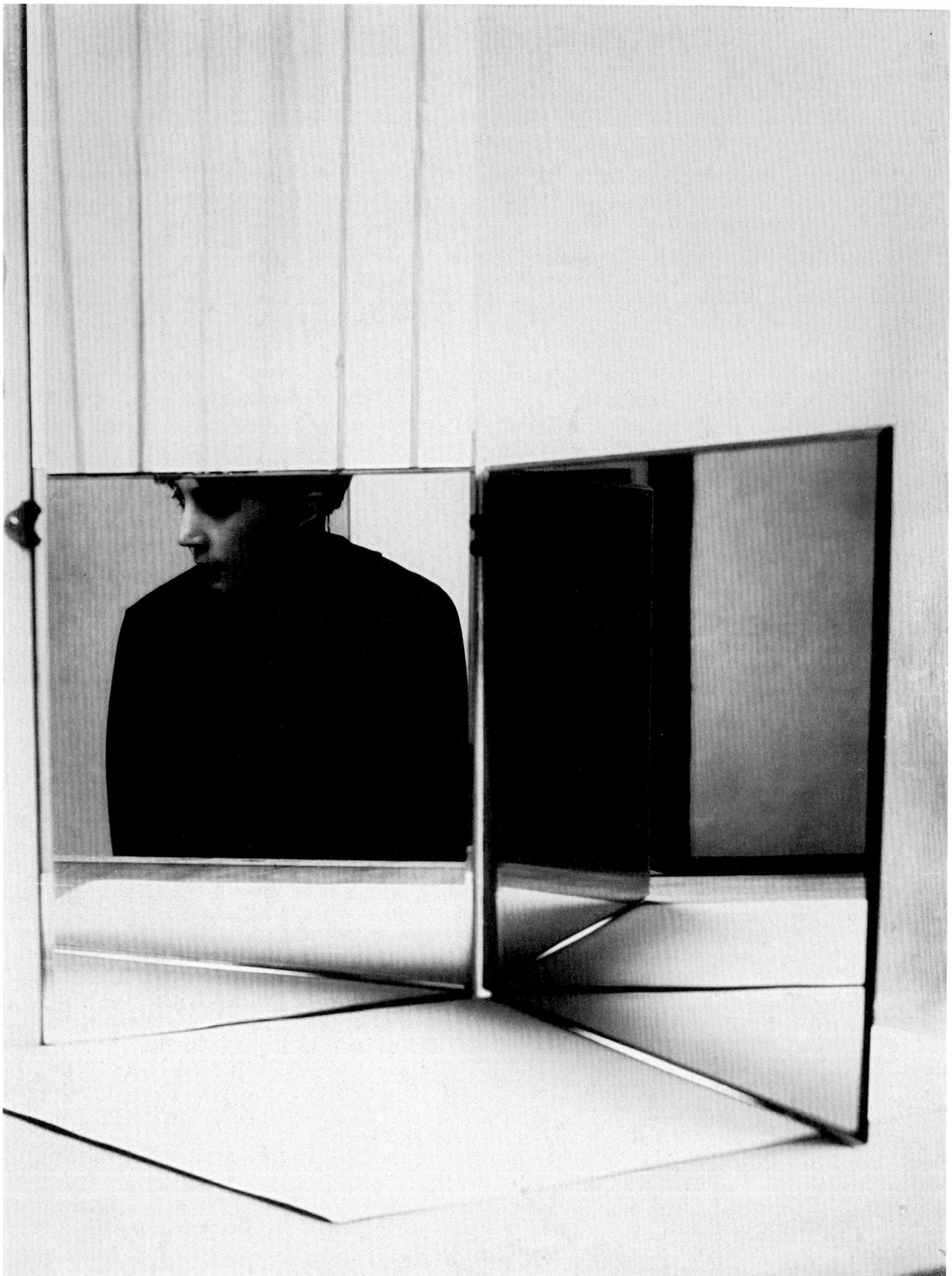

226
Florence Henri
Portrait Composition (Margaret Schall), 1928
Gelatin silver print
16.8 × 12.5 cm
Centre Pompidou, Paris. Musée National d'Art Moderne/Centre de Création Industrielle. Purchase 1987

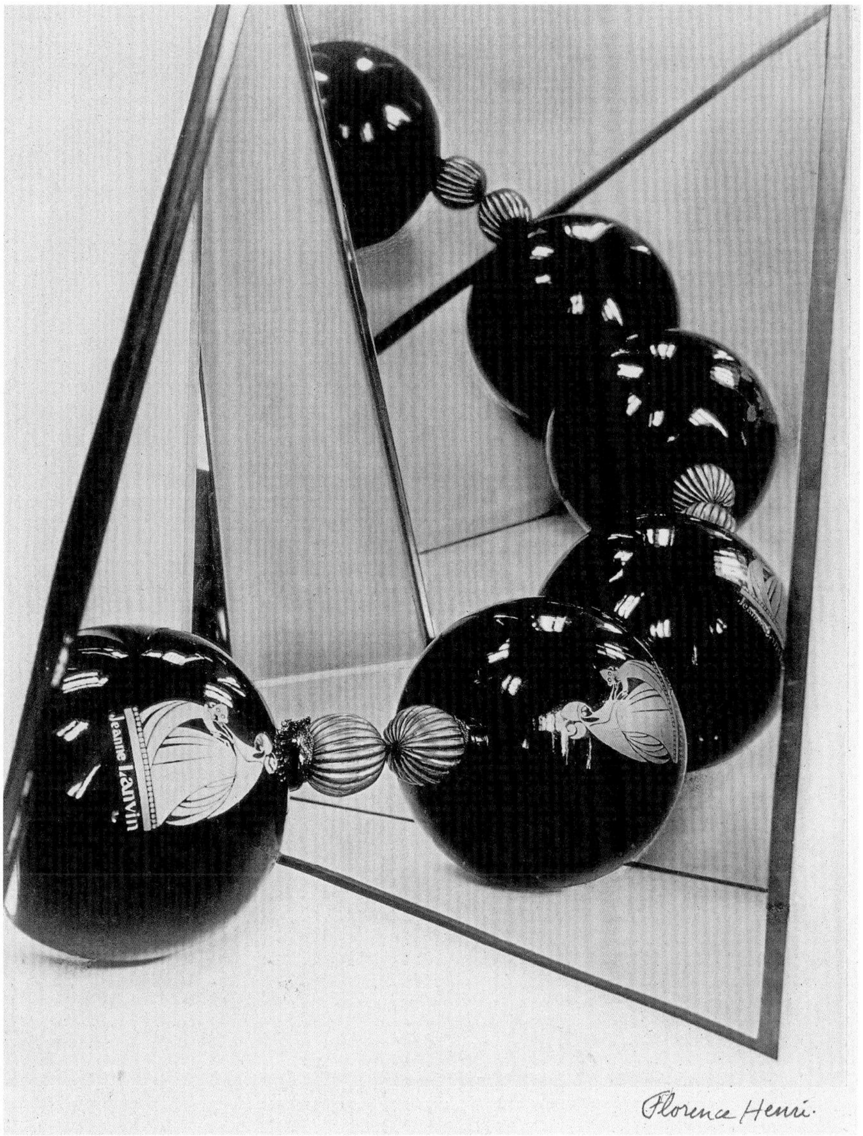

227
Florence Henri
Jeanne Lanvin, 1929
Gelatin silver print
57.5 × 42.3 cm
Victoria and Albert Museum

After studying painting with Fernand Léger in Paris, Henri enrolled at the Bauhaus for the summer session in 1927 and under the influence of Lázsló and Lucia Moholy began experimenting with photography. The Bauhaus also provided Henri with a model of artists who had both an individual studio and a commercial practice. Her portraits and still lifes featuring mirror reflections were composed in a similar manner to her subsequent advertising imagery. In a photograph for Jeanne Lanvin perfume, she multiplies the image of a single scent bottle with the aid of two mirrors to form a string of beads, emphasising both the product's uniqueness and its reproducibility.

228
Marianne Brandt
Self-portrait reflected in a sphere,
1928–29 (printed 1990)
Gelatin silver print,
reproduced from the original
23.8 × 17.7 cm
Bauhaus-Archiv Berlin

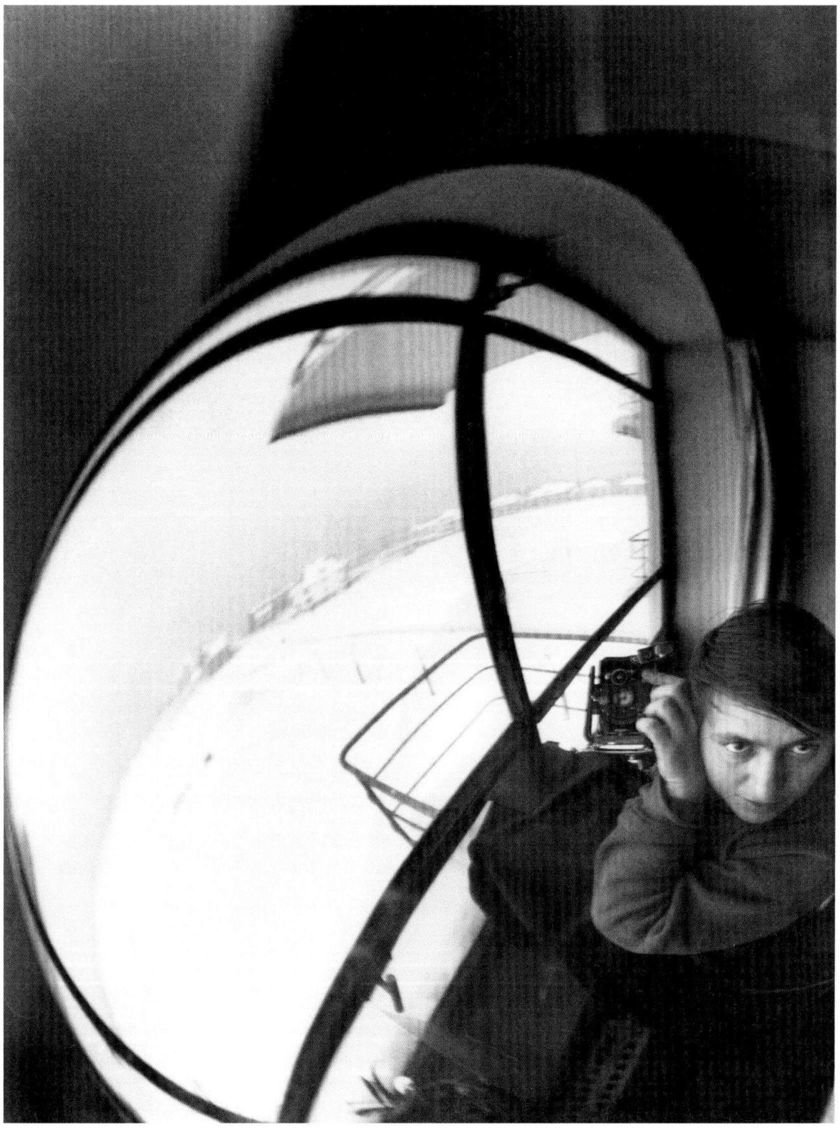

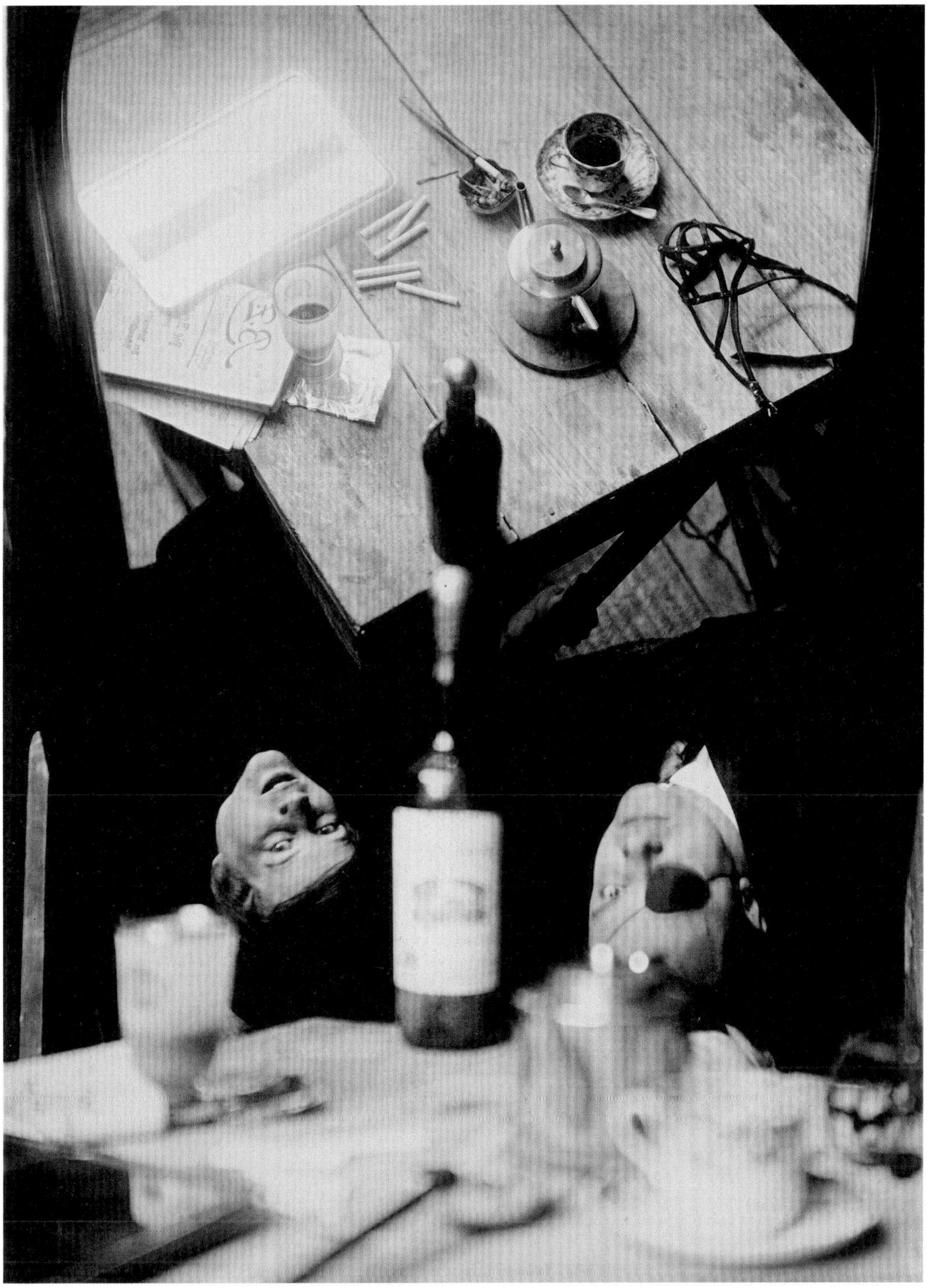

229
Umbo (Otto Umbehr)
Double portrait of Ilse Fehling and Nicolai Wassilieff, 1926
Gelatin silver print
17.9 × 12.9 cm
Bauhaus-Archiv Berlin

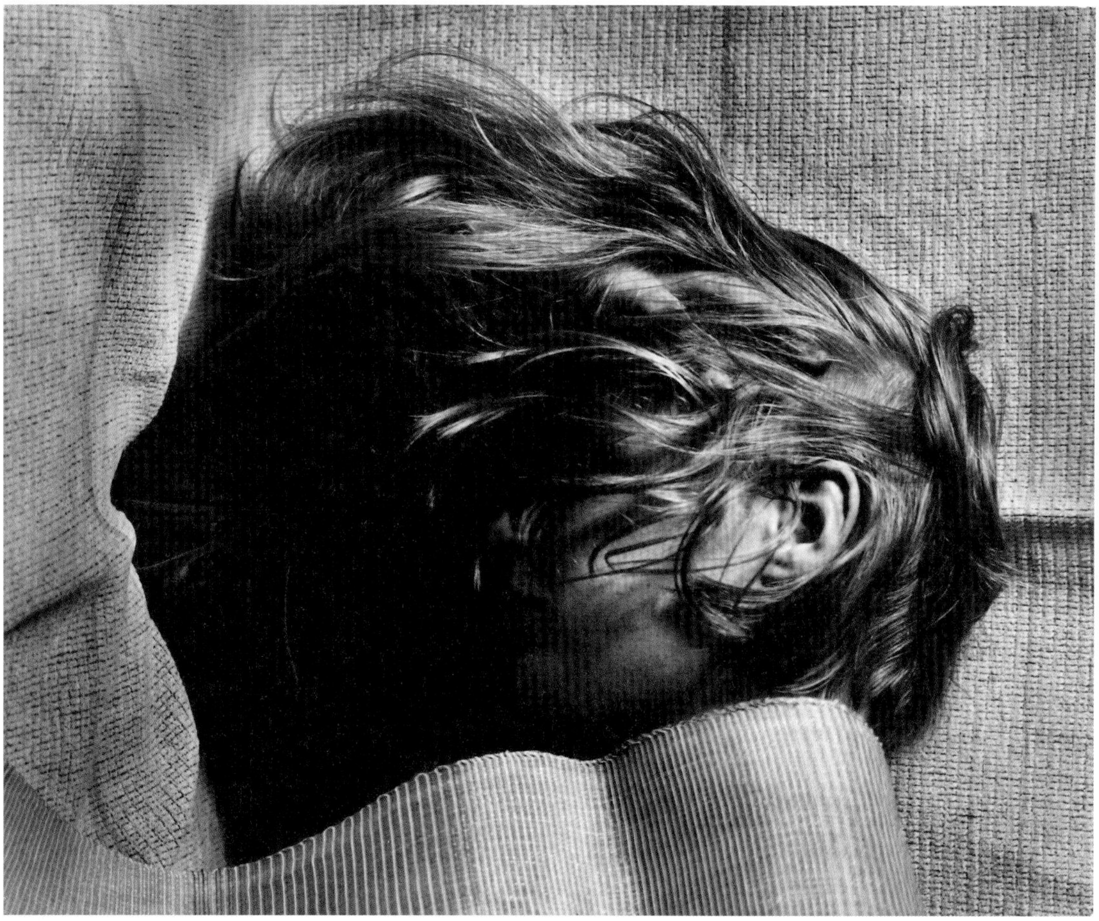

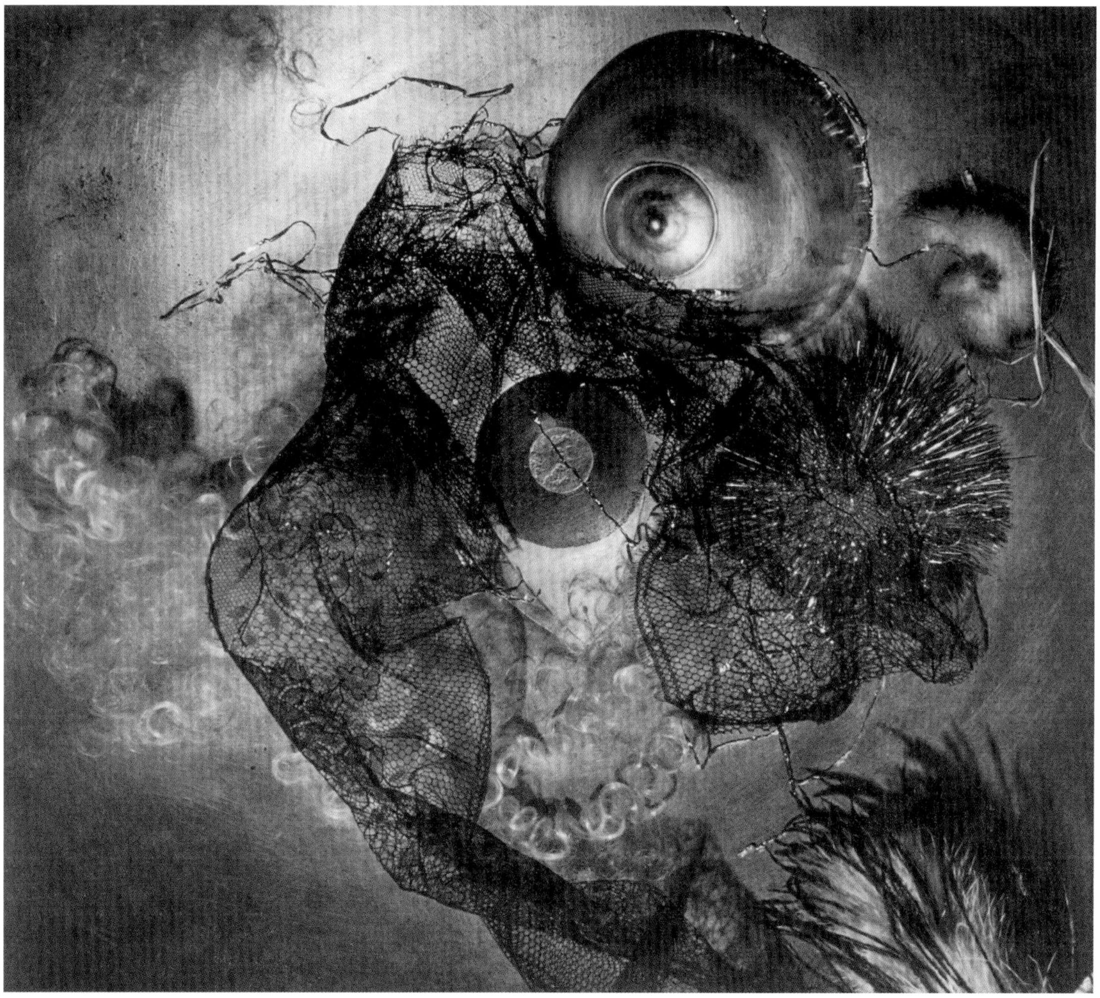

230
Walter Peterhans
Telly, 1928–32
Gelatin silver print
29.2 × 34 cm
Bauhaus-Archiv Berlin

231
Walter Peterhans
Portrait of the Beloved, 1929
Gelatin silver print
32.8 × 35.8 cm
Bauhaus-Archiv Berlin

232
Theo Ballmer
Study of materials from Walter Peterhans's class, c.1929
5 gelatin silver prints
38,8 × 29.6 cm
Gallery Kicken, Berlin

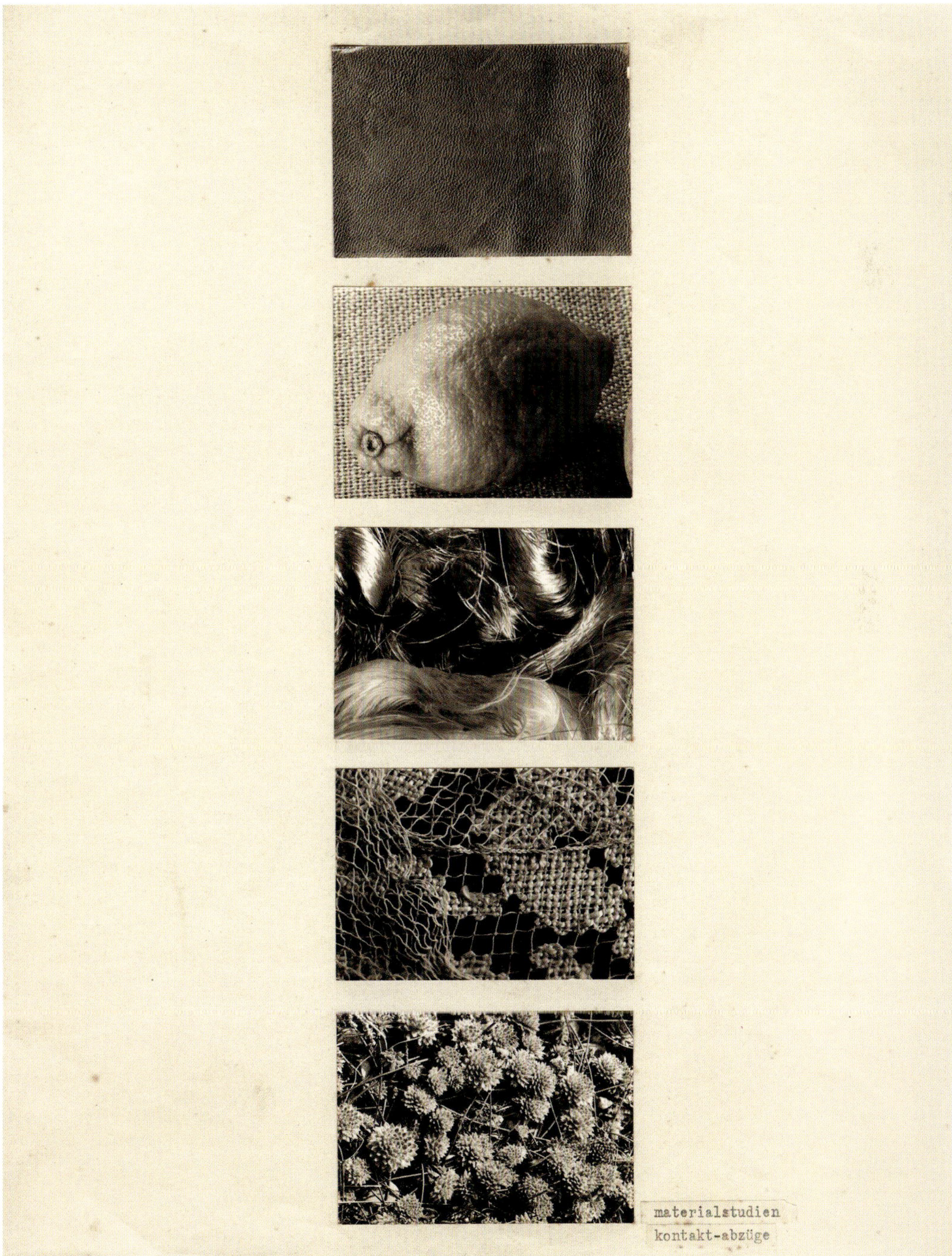

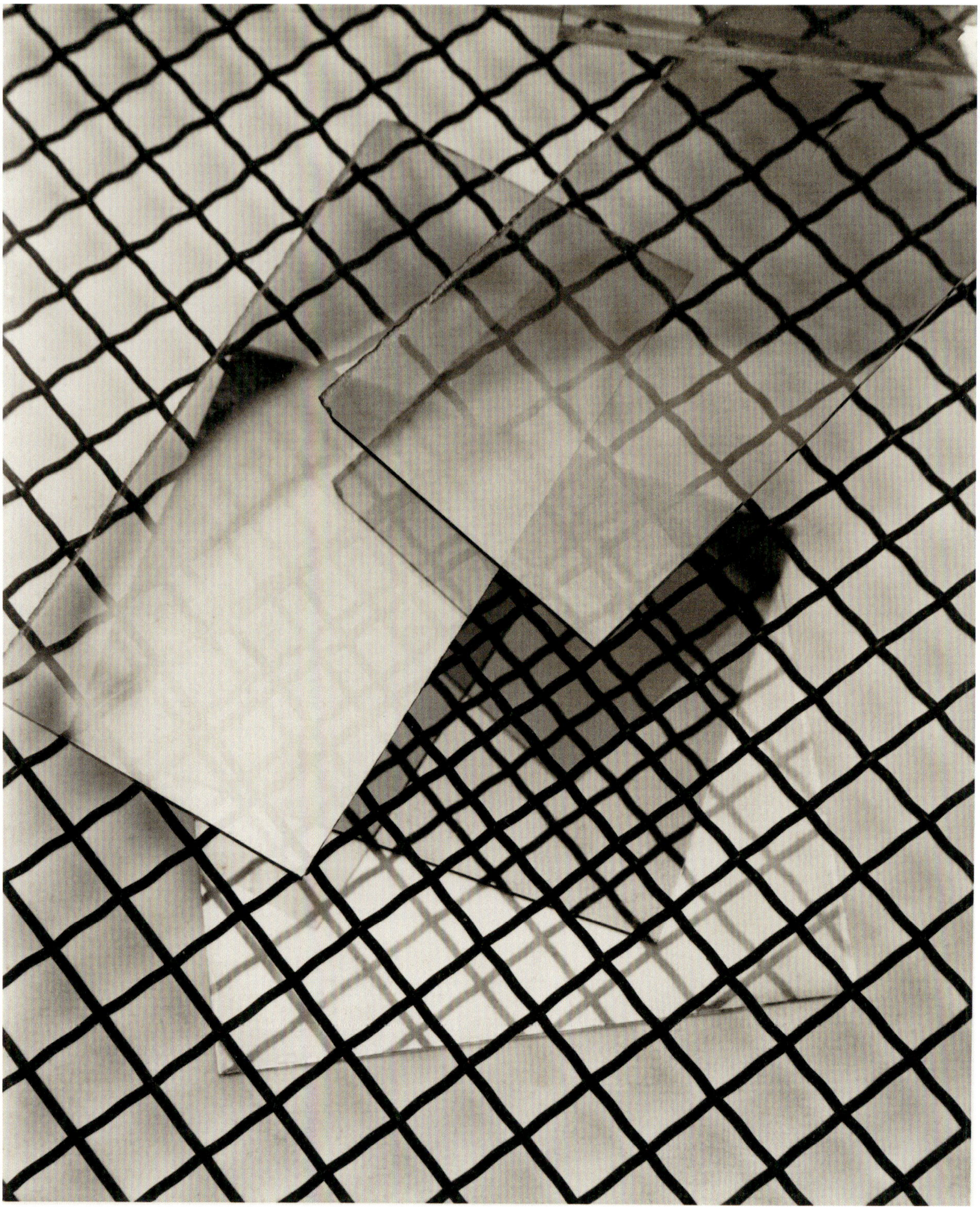

233
Herbert Schürmann
Untitled (composition with glass and fencing wire), 1933
Gelatin silver print
21.7 × 17.4 cm
Bauhaus-Archiv Berlin

234
Iwao Yamawaki
Untitled, 1932
Vintage print
22.9 × 16.5 cm
Galerie Berinson, Berlin

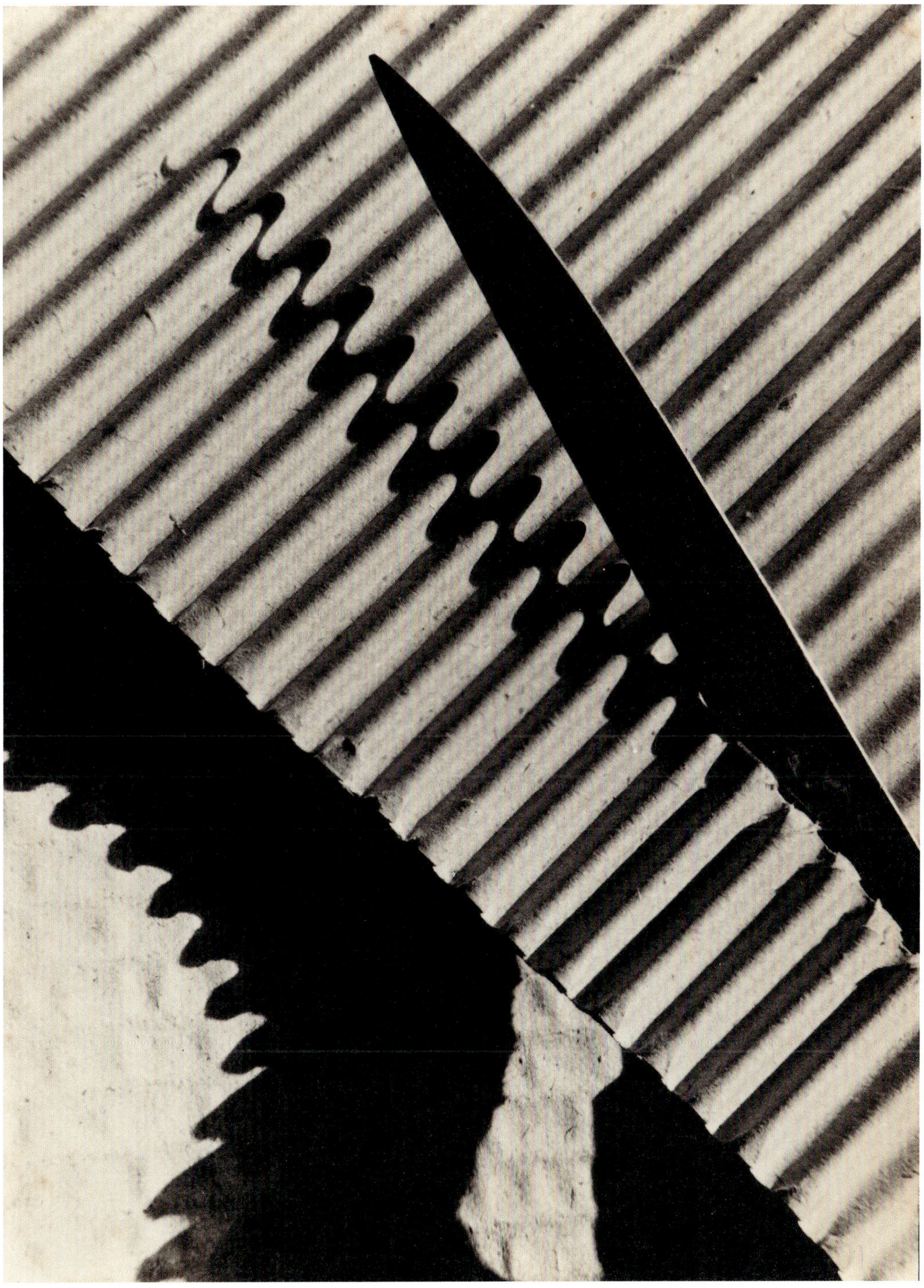

the final months of the bauhaus

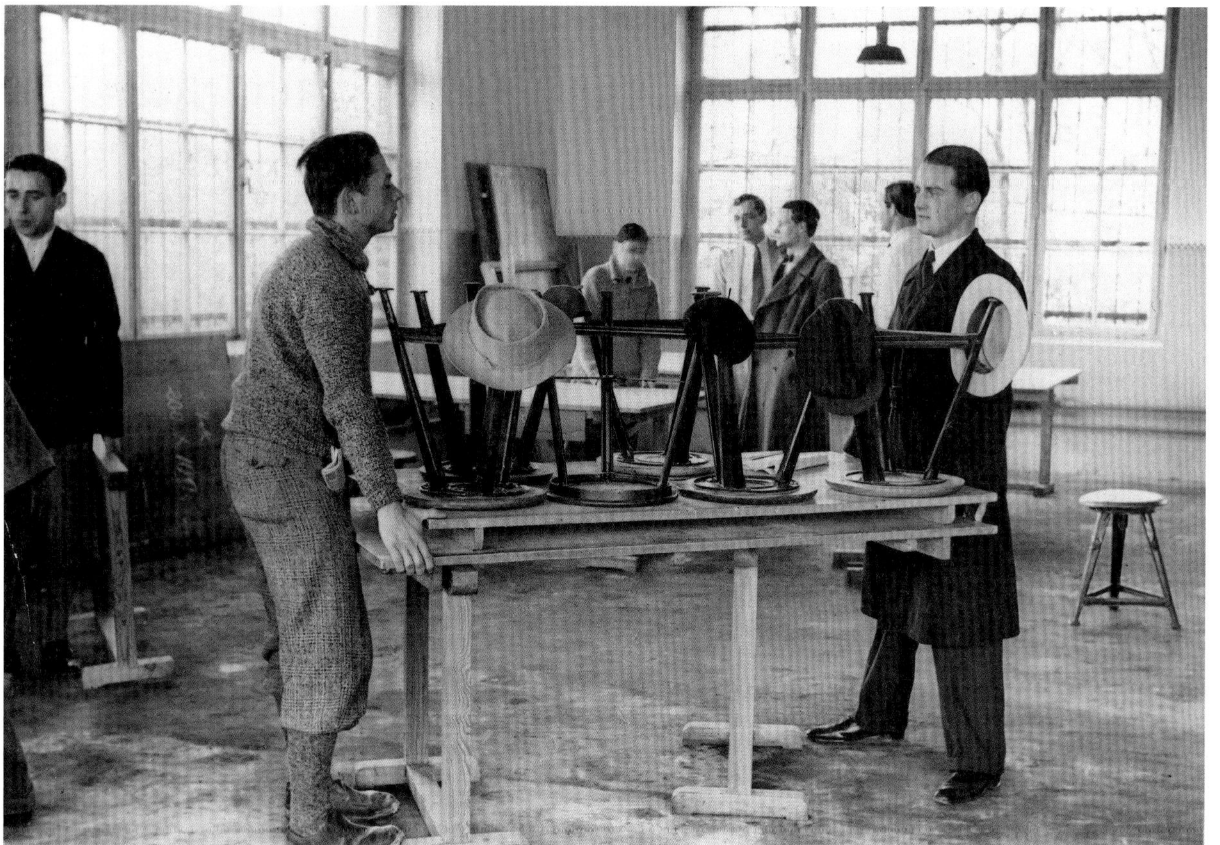

With the onset of the Great Depression in 1929 and the rise of the National Socialists (Nazi Party), funding for the Bauhaus in Dessau diminished and antagonism towards the school grew. In 1930, Hannes Meyer was dismissed by Mayor Fritz Hesse, who viewed his Communist leanings as unsupportable. At Gropius's suggestion, Ludwig Mies van der Rohe was appointed third director of the school.

By privileging professional vocational training in architecture and design, it was Mies, and not Meyer, who was responsible for the greatest break with Gropius's pedagogical model. The Bauhaus became something approaching a school of architecture. The director taught final-year students and appointed his collaborator Lilly Reich to lead the interior-design course.

Despite Mies's attempts to neutralise the school with an emphatically non-political approach to leadership, as well as exhibitions displaying the school's productivity, the Dessau state cancelled Bauhaus funding on 22 August 1932. In October, the Bauhaus moved to a former telephone company building in Berlin-Steglitz, with the aim of running the school independently on profits from its products, such as wallpaper manufactured by Gebr. Rasch. A small teaching staff accompanied the move to Berlin, including Albers, Hilberseimer, Kandinsky, Peterhans and Scheper, alongside a few former students. A party was held to raise funds, with a raffle for artworks by teachers – both present and former – as well as leading artists such as Emil Nolde and Pablo Picasso.

Growing hostility from the Nationalist Socialists resulted in a building search that closed the school for three months in the summer of 1933. Mies attempted to meet with the head of the Gestapo without success and on 20 July the faculty unanimously decided to dissolve the Bauhaus.

Many prominent Bauhaus teachers emigrated over the course of the following year, mainly to the US, as well as to France, Russia and Tel Aviv. Their dispersal disseminated the spirit of the school and its pedagogic principles, creating a lasting legacy for the Bauhaus. Gropius and Mies left Germany in 1934 and 1938 respectively. Gropius taught at the Harvard Graduate School of Design, after a brief sojourn in the UK, while Mies was appointed dean of architecture at the Armour Institute in Chicago. Albers worked as a respected teacher at Black Mountain College in North Carolina and later Yale University, and Moholy-Nagy founded the New Bauhaus in 1937, which evolved into the Chicago Institute of Design. While some Bauhaus students remained in Germany and taught at art schools, others emigrated or returned to their home countries.

The legendary status of the Bauhaus as a symbol of progressive attitudes to architecture and design was cultivated and propagated by Gropius. The Museum of Modern Art's exhibition *Bauhaus 1919–1921* in 1938, with his involvement, led to a popularisation of the school in the US and internationally. Although the Bauhaus's goal of reconciling man and technology in the aftermath of the World War I was groundbreaking, its pedagogical methods of workshop training already existed in a rudimentary fashion in Germany's art and craft schools. Moreover, the contradiction between the school's programme and the achievements of its practitioners were not wholly reconciled; handmade designs rarely went beyond the prototype stage or were too expensive for their intended consumer. Despite these inherent contradictions and the school's changing profile throughout its fourteen-year history, the Bauhaus acquired worldwide influence and its model of fine- and applied-art practice and teaching can still be seen today.

235
Students moving into the Bauhaus Berlin, October 1932
Bauhaus-Archiv Berlin
Photographer unknown

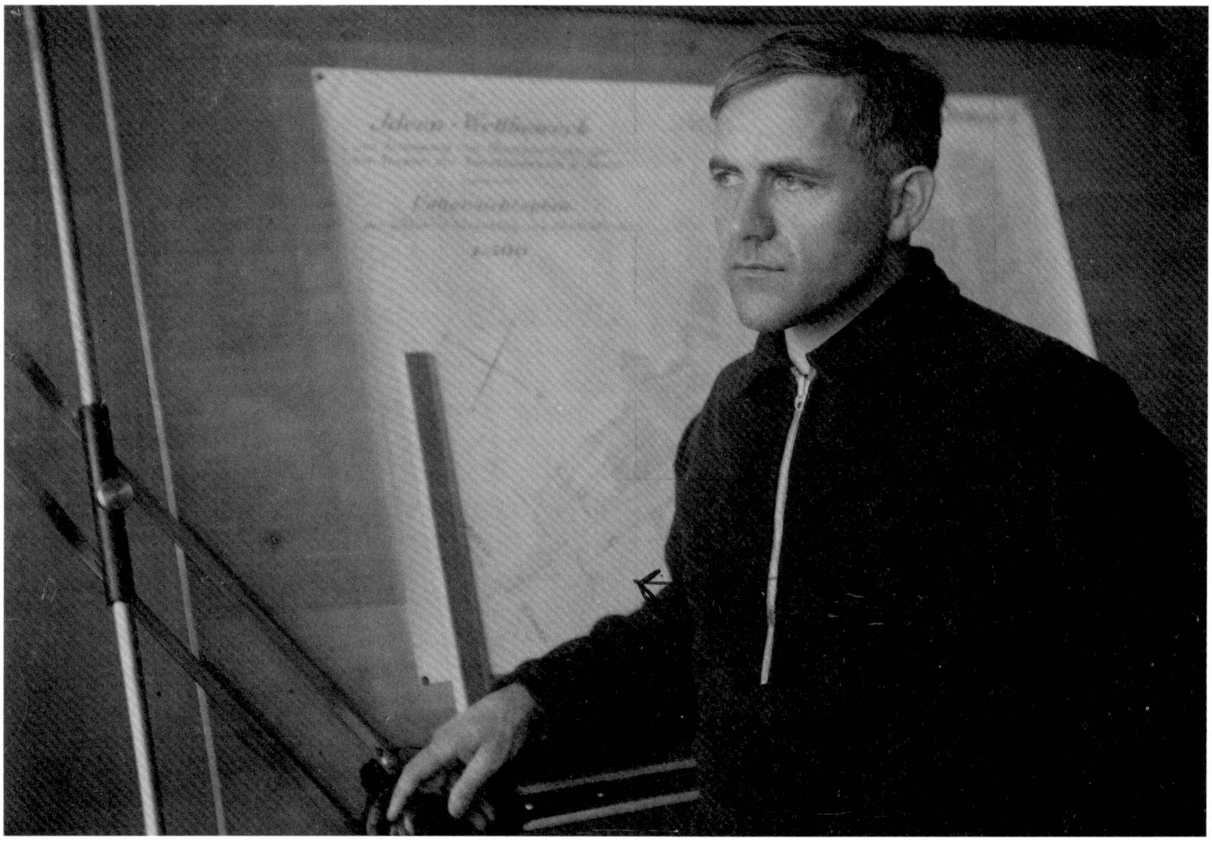

236
Umbo (Otto Umbehr)
Portrait of Hannes Meyer, 1928
Bauhaus-Archiv Berlin

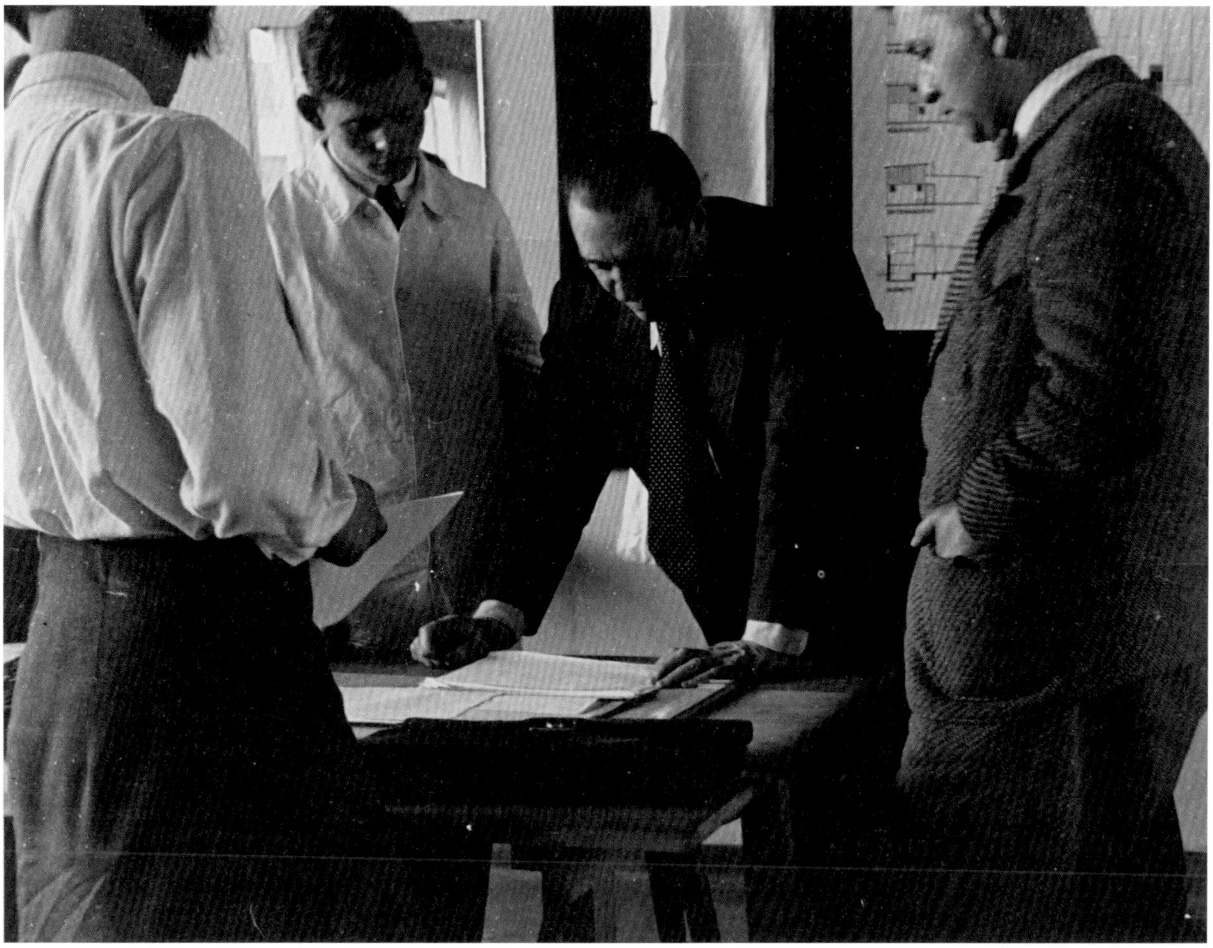

237
Portrait of Ludwig Mies van der Rohe correcting papers, c.1932
From left, Annemarie Wilke, Heinrich Neuy, Mies and Werner Klumpp
Bauhaus-Archiv Berlin
Photographer unknown

three paths of bauhaus modernism walter gropius, hannes meyer and ludwig mies van der rohe

wolfgang thöner

The Bauhaus directors Walter Gropius, Hannes Meyer and Ludwig Mies van der Rohe became radical modernisers of design education in the first half of the twentieth century. All three were architects, and assigned the discipline a major role at the school. Though they shared many principles, their concepts of architecture and its teaching were very different. Subsequent to 1933, even years later, it was Gropius and Mies in particular who fundamentally contributed to the shaping of modern architecture, as well as the debates around it. As a result, the name Bauhaus, regardless of whether it is understood as a style or, more complexly, as a method, is now synonymous with an entire era in the development of modernism. It was only at the end of the 1950s that criticism was voiced by some modernists, followed by the even harsher criticism of the postmodernists after 1970.

Gropius, Meyer and Mies were all born in the second half of the 1880s, a time of tremendous social and economic change. Culturally, these upheavals triggered a blossoming of new styles. Perceiving this eclecticism as chaotic, young architects and intellectuals embarked on a search for a new, uniform style that would not rely on quotations from the past. They sought an essential architecture through clear and sparse means abstracted from the field of technology or from basic geometric forms. They anticipated a new kind of man who trusted in progress. Urban planning, architecture and design thus took on a special educational and cultural function. The Bauhaus architects, in particular Gropius and Meyer, were among those who assigned architecture a social responsibility, focusing on its mission to provide design for society as a whole. Each of them would arrive at a different definition of the extent and way in which the Bauhaus should function as a place of experimentation and debate in the search for the social aspects of design.

Gropius grew up in Berlin, at the time the German city with the greatest number of factories and tenement houses. He was convinced that only the power of industry would be able to solve these and other problems of modernisation. In 1910, he began working at the office of Peter Behrens, who like him, was a member of the Deutscher Werkbund. Founded in 1907, this federation was not only intended to bring together industrialists, artists, architects, engineers, artisans and pedagogues to share in a common project that would have a broad effect and shape tastes, but also aimed to make products stamped 'Made in Germany' more appealing to the world market. It was with the uncompromisingly modern design of the Fagus shoe last factory, built in Alfeld from 1911 to 1914, that the young architect Gropius first attracted attention to his work. Like Le Corbusier, Gropius had studied America's silos and Frank Lloyd Wright's buildings and was interested in the new industrial methods of rationalisation.

For Gropius, as indeed for many other modern artists, the outbreak of World War I at first had a liberating effect. But the experience of the horrors of this industrialised war plunged Gropius into a crisis, inciting a fundamental turnaround. When he founded the Bauhaus in Weimar in 1919, he no longer connected the concept of industry with the urban environment. Instead, the emphatically expressionistic tone of his Bauhaus programme displayed a new, more radical orientation. The end of the war that had spelt a deep depression for industry, the collapse of the Hohenzollern monarchy, and a politically open situation was fertile ground for far-reaching change. Striving for social commitment, the Bauhaus confronted the traditional art school with a project that was a component of the Thuringian state government's school reform efforts, supported above all by Social Democratic politicians. Its objective was one school for all, with an emphasis on teamwork closely connecting theoretical education with practice. To achieve such teamwork, Gropius demanded that all artistic disciplines be gathered together. However, the basis was not to be industry, but craft, and the team did not dream up a new city, but a settlement that would create a new way of life based on handcraft methods. A cooperative was founded in 1921 in order to realise this idea, but it failed to get past the planning stages.

From 1922, Gropius pursued a new utopian ideal: 'Art and Technology: A New Unity.' The Bauhaus workshops began to gear themselves to industrial production. Once again, Gropius's experiments went in the direction of industrialised building and modular house types. The concept of the 'machine for living', borrowed from Le Corbusier, was now in the air and with it, questions concerning the standardisation of living functions and the industrial prefabrication of houses. In 1924, Gropius built his first private home with a flat roof in Jena, the Auerbach House, which with its cubes for various intersecting living functions, was the immediate precursor to the masters' houses in Dessau. In the Bauhaus building itself, erected immediately after the school moved to Dessau in 1925, many of these endeavours coalesced into a visionary form – a college campus with industrial workshops structured to coexist in one building. The Bauhaus buildings erected in Dessau between 1925 and 1932 may be interpreted as the cells of the modern city.

The analytical process that Gropius designated as 'ontological research'[1] (later referred to by others as 'functionalism') sought to determine the design of an object or a house not just through the materials, but also through social and psychological factors. Gropius was concerned with longevity, hygiene and opening up space, as well as with the vision of a better life that would be freed 'from unnecessary ballast', and based on a goal of social equality. [2] These new objects would visually convey their use, discreetly integrating themselves into a space of equally valued, non-hierarchical elements. With this refusal to submit to the notion of 'comfortableness' and other cultural norms, a claim was made that was intended as pedagogical: the ideal of a democratic development that presupposed the successful linkage of technical and social progress.

With the Törten estate (1926–28), industrial methods were tried out in the building of more than 300 single-family houses. In his urban planning, Gropius always took as a point of departure the notion of the basic dwelling unit, both in his attempts to establish norms and types as well as in his stipulation that the factory was the best place for producing housing. Houses were to be assembled through accurate and precisely fitting parts, just like automobiles. But it was not only the work in the construction office and on the building site that would take on a new shape; the spatial qualities of the rooms, from the floor plan to the last technical detail, were intended to improve the lives of the occupants of these houses. With more light, air and sun and by means of 'efficient, meaningful functioning', their existence would be healthier, more spirited, economic and rational.[3] For Gropius, the types and standards demanded and produced by industry were also key to urban development. In 1928 he left the Bauhaus and went on to build large housing developments in Karlsruhe-Dammerstock and elsewhere.

In recent years, the focus on Gropius as architect has been somewhat muted. Unlike with Mies, for instance, there have been no major exhibitions of his work. In part, this is due to Gropius's style of working, since, not a skilled draughtsman himself, he relied more than other architects on collaboration with colleagues. Adolf Meyer was his most important partner until 1925, then Richard Paulick, one of the managers of Gropius's private construction office, and others took on this role. On moving to England in the 1930s he entered into partnerships with Maxwell Fry and the Isokon firm in London; in 1938, he emigrated to the US becoming the first foreign director of the school of architecture at Harvard University, and entered into partnerships with Konrad Wachsmann, and former Bauhaus colleague Marcel Breuer. In the mid-1940s, Gropius founded TAC: The Architects Collaborative. Interesting buildings resulted, but after his time at the Bauhaus, Gropius's architectural work would never again reach the level of stringency and significance attained by Mies or Le Corbusier.

The somewhat hesitant praise for Gropius as an architect can also be put down to the fact that he had written theoretical texts to accompany his creations, which branded him a functionalist in the eyes of his professional admirers and critics alike. Although Gropius initially structured a house to reflect processes inside, their mutual coordination was not ultimately determined by technical or economic issues. For Gropius, building was always an aesthetic matter too. As late as 1964, he spoke out against any one-sided 'superfunctionalism'.[4] But the reality of the large housing developments built during those years – even Gropius constructed some in the western part of Berlin from 1960 – attracted widespread criticism. In the initial phase of the postmodern debate, Gropius and the Bauhaus became representatives of a functional modernism that a new generation of architects felt needed to be fought against.[5] If we look closely at the Bauhaus building in Dessau, finished in 1926, we discover that its design was certainly not derived solely from its construction, or from practical use only. The models for the serial structuring of the façade can be traced back to Karl Friedrich Schinkel's Bauakademie (1832–36), for example.

Many today regard Gropius's most outstanding achievement was to create a stimulating atmosphere for individual artists and designers at the Bauhaus. He himself contributed heavily to his identification as 'Mister Bauhaus'. The Bauhaus exhibition of 1938 at The Museum of Modern Art in New York, which he set up together with former masters from the school (the title already limiting the scope to the years during which he was director, 1919 to 1928), marked the beginning of a unique series of publications and further exhibitions that made the Bauhaus the mythical centre of classical modernism.

Meyer, born in Basel, was active in Swiss and German land reform and cooperative movements in 1909. The idea of the cooperative was to guide him throughout his life. Meyer studied the English garden city and worked, among other places, in the building administration at Krupp in Essen. In 1919 he opened his own architecture office in Basel and the first project he realised was the Freidorf cooperative settlement in Muttenz (1919–21), commissioned by the Verband Schweizer Konsumvereine (Union of Swiss Consumer Societies). Actively involved in product design, photography, graphic arts and agit-prop theatre, Meyer became a member of the ABC architects' association based in Basel, to which Mart Stam (whom Meyer subsequently brought to the Bauhaus in Dessau in 1929) and Hans Schmidt, among others, also belonged. Together with his partner Hans Wittwer, who followed him to the Bauhaus in 1926, Meyer submitted constructivist designs to the competitions for the Peterschule School in Basel and the Palace of Nations in Geneva. When Gropius appointed him as director of the newly established department of architecture in 1927, he introduced both projects in the Bauhaus magazine.

A professed Marxist, Meyer addressed social issues more radically than Gropius. He was already known as a functionalist, who separated art from an architecture above all defined by the material characteristics of its use. Gropius, too, felt that architecture was the 'organisation of life processes',[6] situated between technical and biological factors, and also strove to find economic solutions for abolishing poor living conditions. But Meyer went further and called for the participation of architects and designers in bringing about fundamental changes in social, economic and political structures. During his years at the Bauhaus in Dessau, and as its director from 1928 to 1930, he shifted the emphases in his theoretical statements, though one of the premises that remained was his rejection of the notion that architecture was art. Although his designs owed much to constructivist aesthetics, nevertheless in 1926 he wholeheartedly embraced new technologies. 'Purpose is function', he stated, and 'Building is a technical, not an aesthetic process.' The artistic form would contradict 'the practical function of a house'.[7] He brought the debate that this had unleashed internally in the Bauhaus to a head in 1928 by publishing it in the school's magazine.

Meyer had absorbed the work of Louis Sullivan and Frank Lloyd Wright, but also the principles and theories of Henry Ford, Konrad von Meyenburg, Raoul Francé and Bess M. Mensendieck. For him, the Neopositivist circle around the political economist Otto Neurath also played a crucial role.[8] Meyer invited specialists in this field – an analytical philosophy that combined empiricism with rationalism – to hold guest lectures at the Bauhaus. In 1928, he shifted the emphasis of his theories from the technical to the socio-biological: 'We are researching the relationships between the house and its occupants'.[9] For him, building was first and foremost a 'biological process'.[10] In matter-of-fact terms he stated: 'All things in this world are the product of the formula: (Function multiplied by economics).'[11] Meyer now rejected constructivist architecture even more decidedly. He wanted 'no geometric or stereometric structures, unsuitable to life and detrimental to function', while at the same time spoke of *Lebensraum* (living space) and the 'praise of harmony'.[12] No longer was the architect to be the isolated, creative genius, but a participant in a complex process involving all of society. Meyer expanded the concept of design to include the entire scope of the human environment, determined by the polarity between artist and engineer, and changed the Bauhaus curriculum accordingly.

By calling in teachers and guest lecturers with practical experience – among them, the architects Stam, Anton Brenner and Edward Heiberg – a sound curriculum had been established with direct links to Bauhaus construction sites, which became a staple of the school's pedagogical concept. During the construction of the school for the ADGB (German Trade Union Federation) in Bernau, students learned 'all working processes from unskilled labour to working with concrete, carpentry and bricklaying'[13] The 1928 competition brief emphasised balancing basic geometric and rounded natural forms. However, once the project got underway the sociological idiosyncrasies of the users of the school became more important and students were to be given the opportunity to experience collective action: 'We consciously organise within the "great circle" of the 120 students at the school the 12 small circles that will be the carriers of the community', wrote Meyer.[14]

That Meyer ultimately failed as Bauhaus director was mostly due to the fact that he did not maintain the great openness of internal discourse on political and social issues, or display enough diplomatic restraint to protect the image of the institution. He was the most controversial of the Bauhaus directors, considered a 'fanatic of purpose' as early as 1927 by architectural critics in Switzerland[15] and referred to as an 'anti-aesthetic functionalist' in 1932.[16] After 1933, he was largely ignored by historians, and the 1938 Bauhaus exhibition at The Museum of Modern Art, New York only mentioned him briefly. After 1945 he was criticised in both East and West Germany. However, in the West, many of the designers at the Ulm School of Design regarded Meyer as a model and stimulus and the structuring of space at the school – designed by its co-founder Max Bill in 1955 – bore reference to the Bernau trade union school. For Ulm co-founder, Otl Aicher, he was, three decades later, still the most important of the Bauhaus architects.[17]

In the East, Meyer was accused of having an anti-art attitude until well into the 1960s. During the so-called formalism debate, leading Communist politicians viewed the Bauhaus as being representative of the modern architecture to which they were opposed, branding it an affront to 'national traditions'. The most vehement criticism was directed toward the Bernau building, which was now being used as a school for the East German unified trade union. Communist politician Walter Ulbricht made express mention of the building in a speech of 1951, citing it as a 'bad example' and as an 'expression of cosmopolitan building'.[18] This school may 'as well stand in America or Africa', he said, since it was typical of the 'Bauhaus style' that 'exerted a powerful influence even after 1945'. It was imperative, he said, 'to clearly recognise the Bauhaus style as being hostile to the people', since it disavowed 'the need for a creative application of the most progressive elements of the national architectural heritage'.[19] Even subsequent to the re-appraisal of the Bauhaus in the 1960s, in East Germany Meyer continued to be accused of being 'latently anti-art',[20] while Gropius and, above all, Mies earned the highest recognition. Only after the mid-1970s, when the Bauhaus became part of the official culture of the East German state, similar to the way in which it had been assimilated in West Germany following the major Bauhaus exhibition in Stuttgart in 1968, was there appreciation of what was considered progressive in the Bauhaus. By 1976 and in the ensuing decade, Meyer's work and concepts were regarded as the most important 'Bauhaus legacy', apparently due to the fact that it seemed to be the best justification for the German Democratic Republic's housing programme. The detailed examination of Meyer's life and work began in 1965 with a monograph written by Claude Schnaidt,[21] while 1989 witnessed extensive publications in East and West Germany.[22]

In 1905 Mies left his hometown of Aachen for Berlin and two years later realised the first of his own projects, the Riehl House in Potsdam. He went on to work for Bruno Paul and Peter Behrens, among other architectural practices, and one year after the end of the Great War, he opened his own office in Berlin. Until the mid-1920s, his rather conventional-looking buildings (which were realised) ran parallel to his first radically modern designs (which remained on paper). One progressive design that did become reality, in 1926, was the monument to Karl Liebknecht and Rosa Luxemburg commissioned by the Communist Party. A year later, he oversaw the Deutscher Werkbund housing development in Stuttgart-Weissenhof, selecting leading proponents of modern architecture, including Hans Scharoun, Le Corbusier and Gropius to design the twenty-one buildings intended as prototype contemporary homes. In 1928, two villas were built in Krefeld, quickly followed by his pavilion for the German Reich erected at the World's Fair in Barcelona in 1929. The following year the Tugendhat House in Brno was completed and Mies was appointed the third Bauhaus director, at Gropius's recommendation.

Mies concentrated his Bauhaus activity entirely on the education and training of architects. He returned to established principles of architectural education: attention to detail, a command of drawing and an attitude of 'show them first, then let them copy'. The major thrust of his instruction was devoted to courtyard houses, single-storey buildings that closely connected living and garden space. In 1931, Philip Johnson wrote of Mies in the *New York Times*: 'Mies has long since passed the stage when the house is regarded by the architect as the cheapest, best-planned expression of the needs of the family.'[23] Students were also to refrain from taking part in political activities. In a letter of 1934, he stated emphatically: 'My entire time in Dessau was an ongoing struggle against the legacy left by Hannes Meyer! ... The Bauhaus under Gropius was not the same Bauhaus as under Hannes Meyer, and the Bauhaus I directed, was in turn different.'[24]

For many architectural historians, Mies's architecture was exemplary of its time, especially with respect to what was termed the 'International Style' from 1932 on. He created a new paradigm for architecture, a new type of office and residential high-rise building that spread throughout the world, particularly after 1945. It was referred to as 'skin-and-bones' architecture, because it was realised with a skeleton of steel and a curtain-wall façade, with the principle of flowing space and a language of forms developed from industrial construction techniques and materials. Mies's architecture stood for an aesthetic of making visible the construction and for a cool rationality, even as it maintained a subtle reference to tradition.

A few years after the closure of the Bauhaus in 1933, Mies went to the US, becoming its most influential architect, but he would continue to build in Germany. In West Berlin, he executed the Neue Nationalgalerie from 1962 to 1968. Even in East Germany, Mies was a role model at this time. Although in the 1950s for ideological reasons there had been a strict rejection of the purportedly simple boxes erected in the spirit of capitalism, Mies came to be greatly admired after 1965, at times being more highly regarded than Gropius, and especially Meyer. His acceptance among East German architects was due to his enduring understanding of architecture as art.

With the advent of postmodernism in the mid-1970s, Mies – as well as Gropius and Meyer – received considerable criticism due to their supposed break with tradition, the perceived coldness and uniformity of modern architecture and its destruction of the pre-modern city. In 1981, author Tom Wolfe, likened Mies's American skyscrapers to stacks of German workers' housing.[25] But even Charles Jencks, one of the leading postmodern theorists, pointed as early as 1973 to the 'ambiguity or multivalence of determining meanings' in Mies's buildings, in which one 'can intuit this complexity of factors rather than explain it away in a single answer'.[26] A flood of literature questioned Mies's works anew. On the 100th anniversary of his birthday in 1986, he was heralded by several historians as a precursor of postmodern double coding, which united objective rationality and classical legacy.[27]

However, it was Mies's concept of liberating interior space for a programme increasingly dominated by materials – referred to as the 'externalisation of the infrastructure' by Nikolaus Kuhnert and Angelika Schnell in 1998[28] – that has turned out to be of more lasting relevance and importance. Through concepts such as the 'glass house' and 'curtain wall', connections were established between Mies's buildings and projects by such contemporary architects as Rem Koolhaas and Peter Zumthor.[29] In 1994, Beatriz Colomina pointed to the material features of Mies's buildings, and to the image strategies that went hand in hand with them.[30] In 2002 an entire issue of the German version of *arch+* magazine was devoted to the contemporary reception of Mies's ideas, with Koolhaas asserting that – in a contradiction to postmodern criticism – Mies's buildings were to be understood as part of an urban context.[31] In 2011 the architect's 125th birthday anniversary provided impetus for a renewed, intense study of his work.

All three Bauhaus directors continue to be of importance today. Their theories, their work and the values they communicated at the Bauhaus offer us a great deal for the future and remain vitally relevant in our increasingly complex world.

1 Walter Gropius, 'Grundsätze der Bauhausproduktion', in *Neue Arbeiten der Bauhauswerkstätten*, Langen, Munich, 1925, p.5.
2 Walter Gropius, *Bauhausbauten Dessau*, Langen, Munich, 1930, p.92.
3 Ibid., p.101.
4 Walter Gropius, *Apollo in der Demokratie*, Kupferberg, Mainz, 1967, p.55.
5 See for example Robert Venturi, Denise Scott Brown and Steven Izenour, *Learning from Las Vegas*, MIT Press, Cambridge, MA, 1978, p.160.
6 Gropius, *Bauhausbauten Dessau*, op. cit., p.160.
7 Hannes Meyer, 'Die neue Welt', in *Werk*, vol.13, 1926, no.7, p.222
8 See Ute Poerschke, *Funktion als Gestaltungsbegriff. Eine Untersuchung des Funktionsbegriffs in Architekturtheoretischen Texten*, Dissertation, Brandenburgisch Technische Universität Cottbus, 2005, pp.188–224.
9 Hannes Meyer, 'Bauen', in *Bauhaus. Zeitschrift für Gestaltung, Dessau*, no.4, 1928, p.12.
10 Ibid.
11 Ibid.
12 Hannes Meyer, 'Bauhaus und Gesellschaft', in *Bauhaus. Zeitschrift für Gestaltung, Dessau*, 1929, no.1, p.2.
13 Konrad Püschel, *Wege eines Bauhäuslers. Erinnerungen und Ansichten*, Anhaltische Verlagsgesellschaft, Dessau, 1997, p.50.
14 Meyer, 'Bauen', op. cit., p.14
15 Peter Meyer, 'Zum Ereignis des Wettbewerbs für das Völkerbundgebäude in Genf', in *Schweizerische Bauzeitung*, 1927, no.8, p.105.
16 Henry-Russell Hitchcock and Philip Johnson, quoted in Poerschke, *Funktion als Gestaltungsbegriff*, op. cit., p.141.
17 Otl Aicher, 'Bauhaus und Ulm', in Herbert Lindinger (ed.) *Die Moral der Geganstande*, exhibition catalogue, Hochschule fur Gestaltung Ulm, Berlin, 1987, p.124–29.
18 Walter Ulbricht, Speech addressed to the Volkskammer (East German parliament) on 31 October 1951, quoted in Andreas Schätzke, *Zwischen Bauhaus und Stalinallee: Architekturdiskussion im östlichen Deutschland 1945–1955*, Braunschweig, Wiesbaden, 1991, p.145.
19 Ibid.
20 Diether Schmidt, *Bauhaus. Weimar 1919 bis 1925, Dessau 1925 bis 1932, Berlin 1932 bis 1933*, Verlag der Kunst, Dresden 1966, p.47.
21 Claude Schnaidt, *Hannes Meyer. Bauten, Projekte und Schriften, Buildings, projects and writings*, Niggli, Teufen, 1965.
22 Bauhaus-Archiv Berlin, Deutsches Architekturmuseum, Frankfurt am Main, Institut für Geschichte u. Theorie d. Architektur an d. ETH Zürich. u.a. (eds), *Hannes Meyer. Architekt Urbanist Lehrer 1889–1954*, Berlin, 1989.
23 Philip Johnson, 'In Berlin; Comment on Building Exposition', *The New York Times*, 9 August 1931.
24 Ludwig Mies van der Rohe, letter to the politician Alfred Freyberg, 1934, Stiftung Bauhaus Dessau, Archive, I 10806 D.
25 Tom Wolfe, *From Bauhaus to Our House*, Farrar Straus Giroux, New York, 1981, pp.74–5.
26 Charles Jencks, *Modern Movements in Architecture*, Penguin Books, London, 1973, p.104.
27 As, for example, via David Dunster. See Angelika Schnell, 1986, in *arch+*, no.616, June 2002, pp.75–7.
28 Nikolaus Kuhnert und Angelika Schnell, 'Die Moderne der Moderne', in *arch+*, no.143, October 1998, p.17.
29 Ibid.
30 Beatriz Colomina, 'Mies not', in Detlef Mertins (ed.), *The Presence of Mies*, Princeton Architectural Press, New York, 1994, pp.193–221.
31 Rem Koolhaas, 'Miesverständnisse', in *arch+*, no.161, June 2002, p.79.

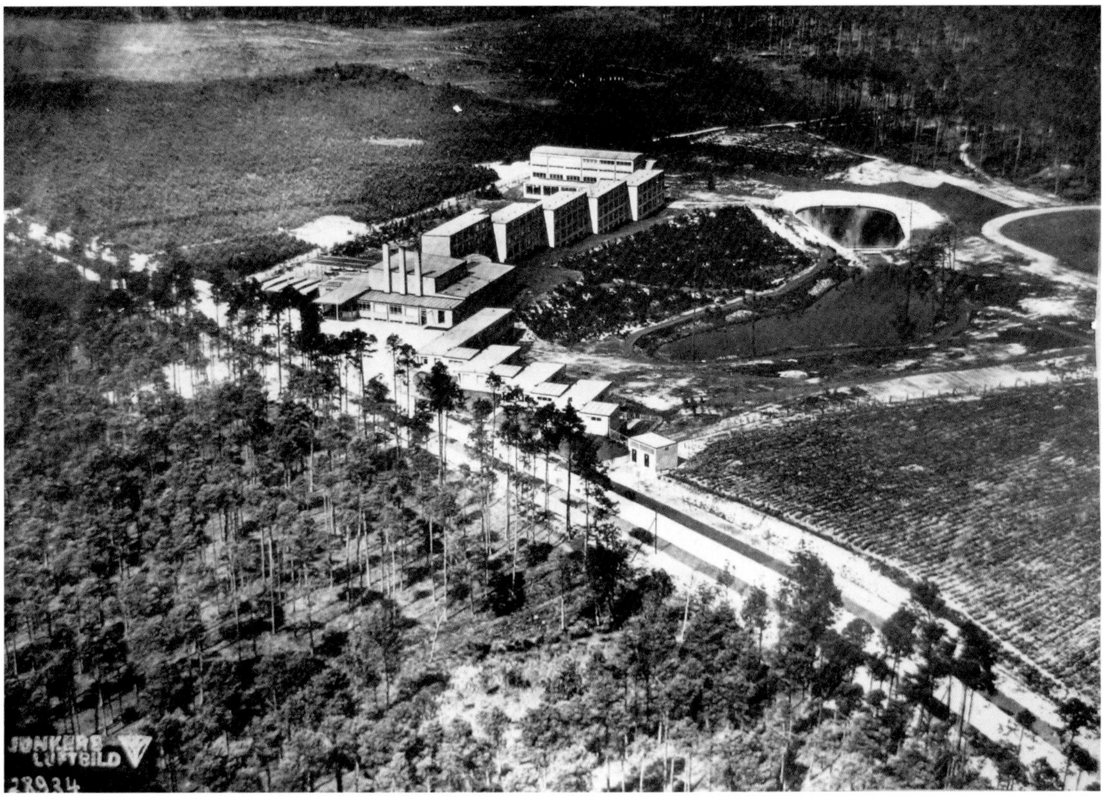

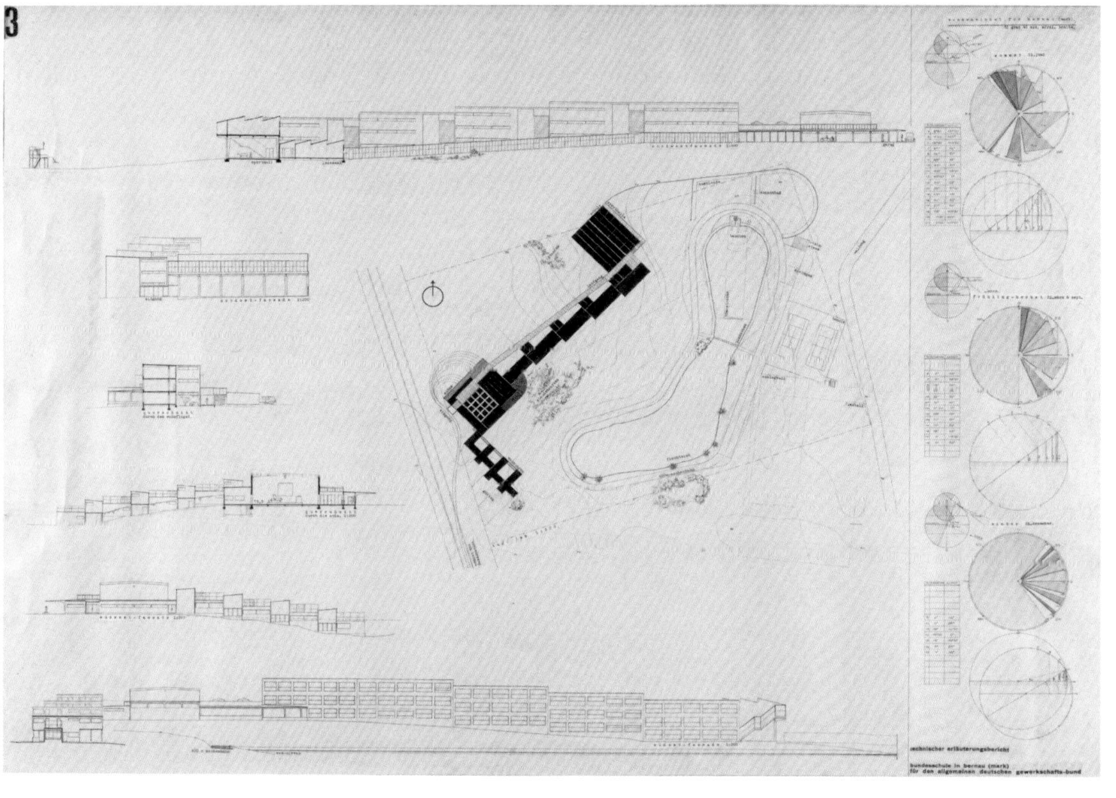

238
Hannes Meyer and Hans Wittwer
School for the ADGB (German Trade Union Federation), Bernau, 1930
Vintage print, mounted on card
11.9 × 17.2 cm
Photographer: Junkers Luftbild
Stiftung Bauhaus Dessau

239
Hannes Meyer and Hans Wittwer
School for the ADGB (German Trade Union Federation), Bernau, Page 3 of the competition application, 1928
Type and pencil on card
86 × 122 cm
Stiftung Bauhaus Dessau

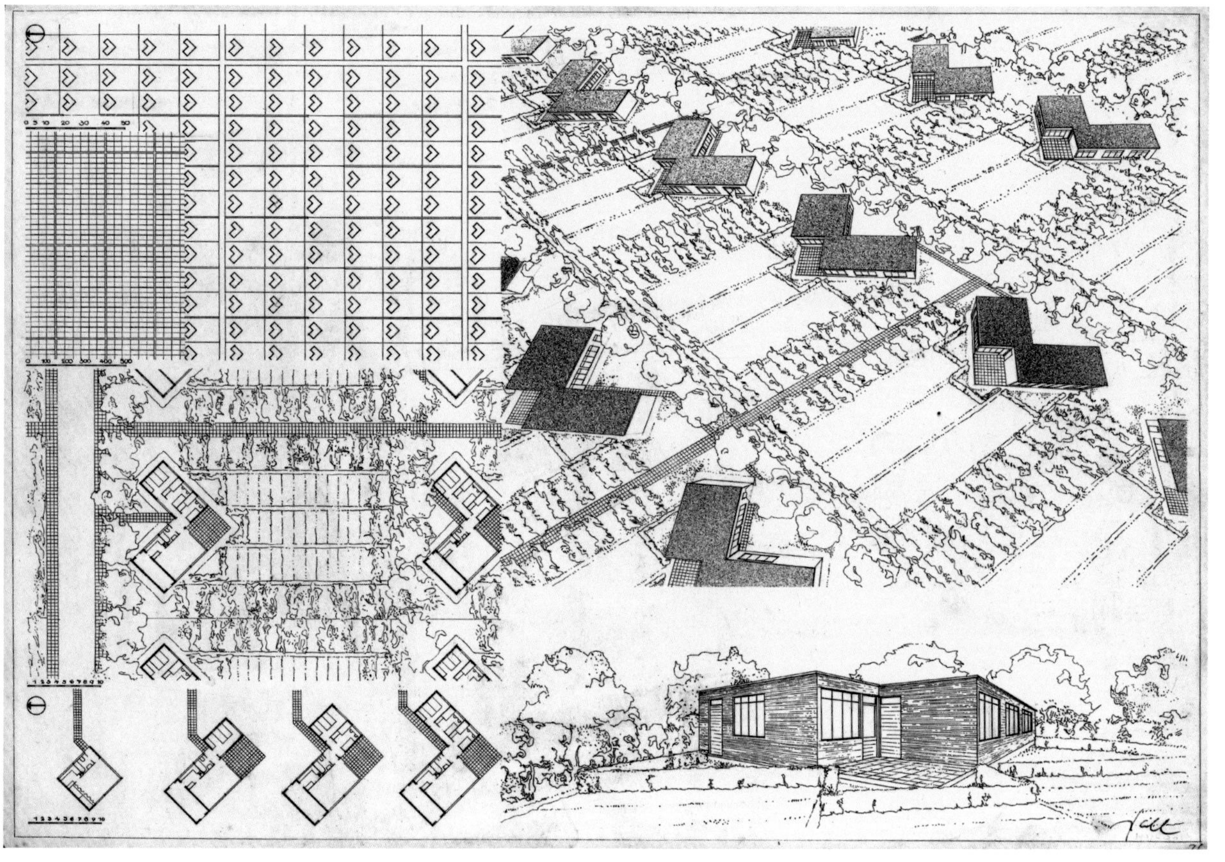

240
Pius Pahl
Low-rise building estate with L-shaped detached family homes, construction plan, floor plans and façades, 1931–32
India ink on tracing paper
43.7 × 61.4 cm
Bauhaus-Archiv Berlin

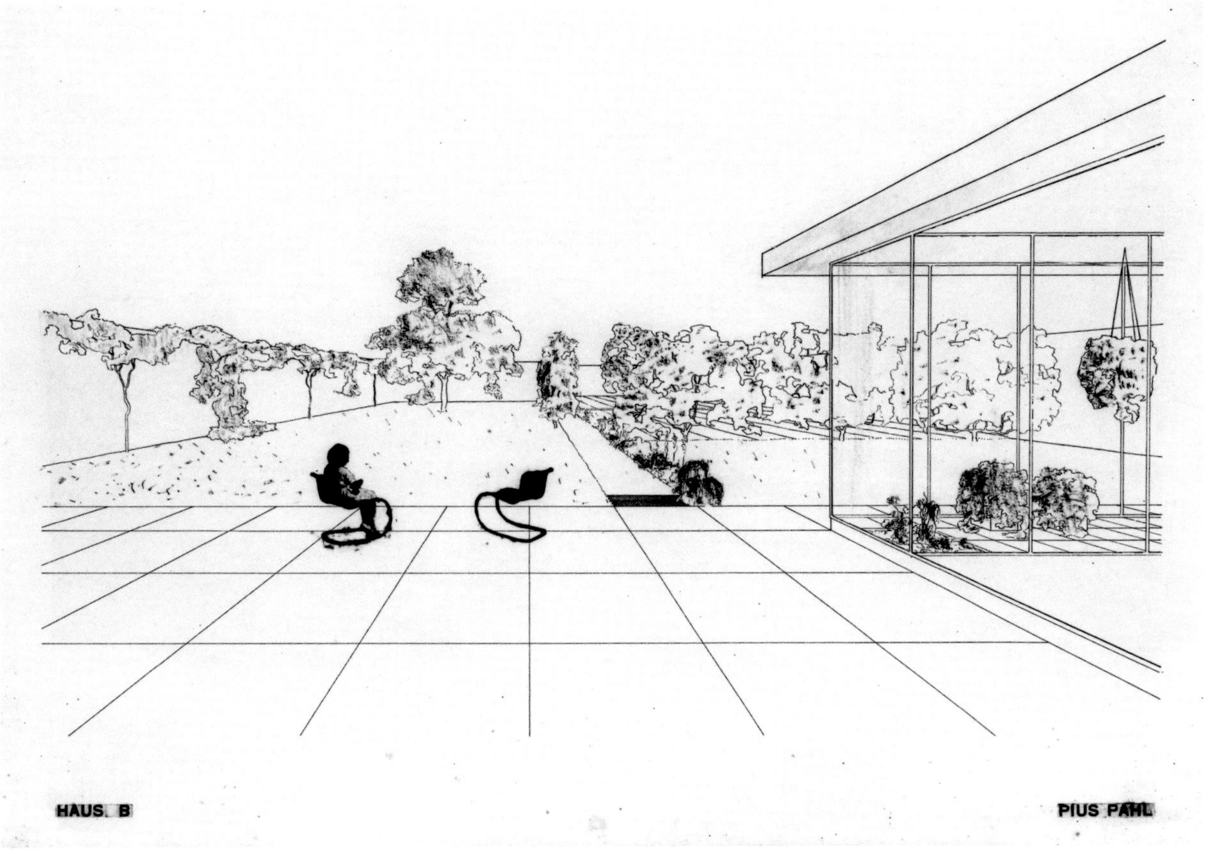

241
Pius Pahl
House B, perspective of the terrace looking on to the garden with cantilever chairs designed by Ludwig Mies van der Rohe, 1931
Ink, photocollage and printed label on tracing paper
45 × 69.8 cm
Bauhaus-Archiv Berlin

Mies van der Rohe's students experienced more academic architectural training than had been offered under Meyer or Gropius. In his pursuit of a purer approach to teaching, Mies placed less emphasis on the preliminary course and workshop training and introduced architectural drawing. Students in their final stage of architectural training would focus on the design of private houses under his personal instruction. The courtyard house was a building type on which Mies's own practice typically worked, and was the ideal model for testing spatial ideas and the fluid relationship between interior and exterior. Student exercises progressed from the simple to complex: from one-bedroom house to large bungalow. Pahl's perspective of the enclosed terrace of house-type 'B' – a two-storey detached house – incorporates collaged elements of Mies's cantilevered furniture and epitomises the homage that students often paid to the director's own architecture and design in their course work.

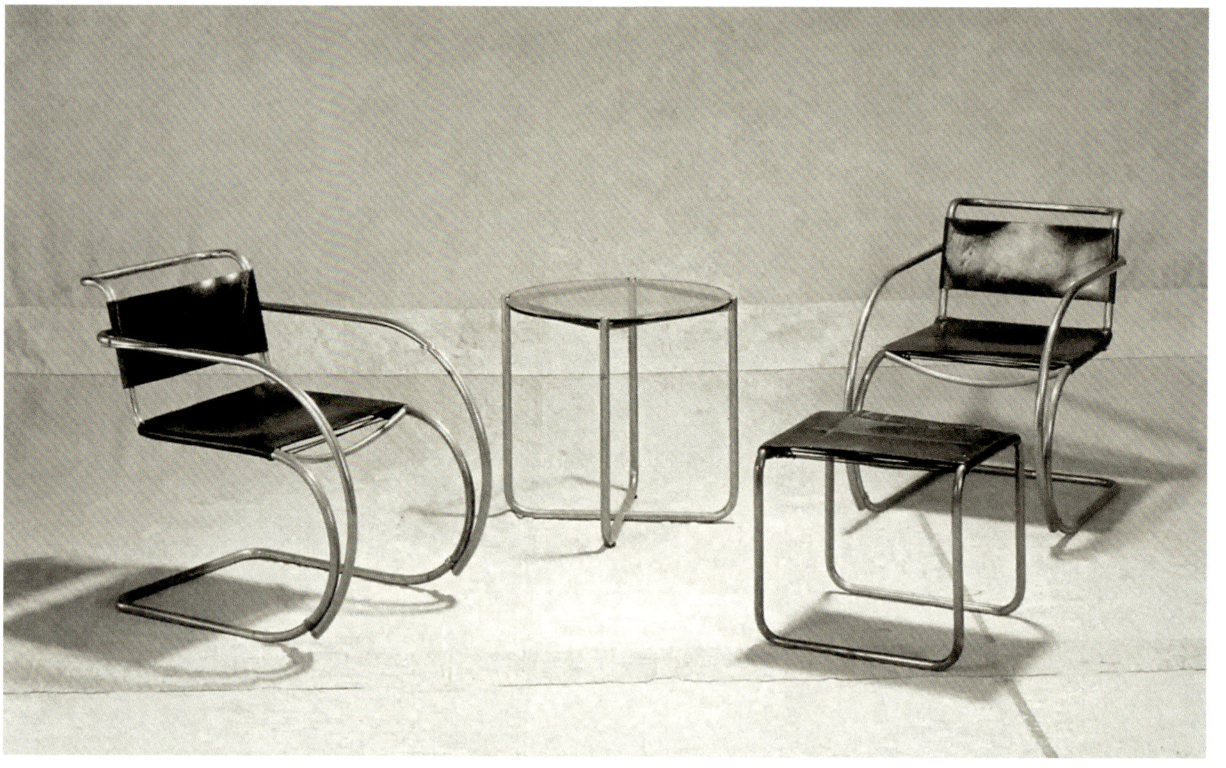

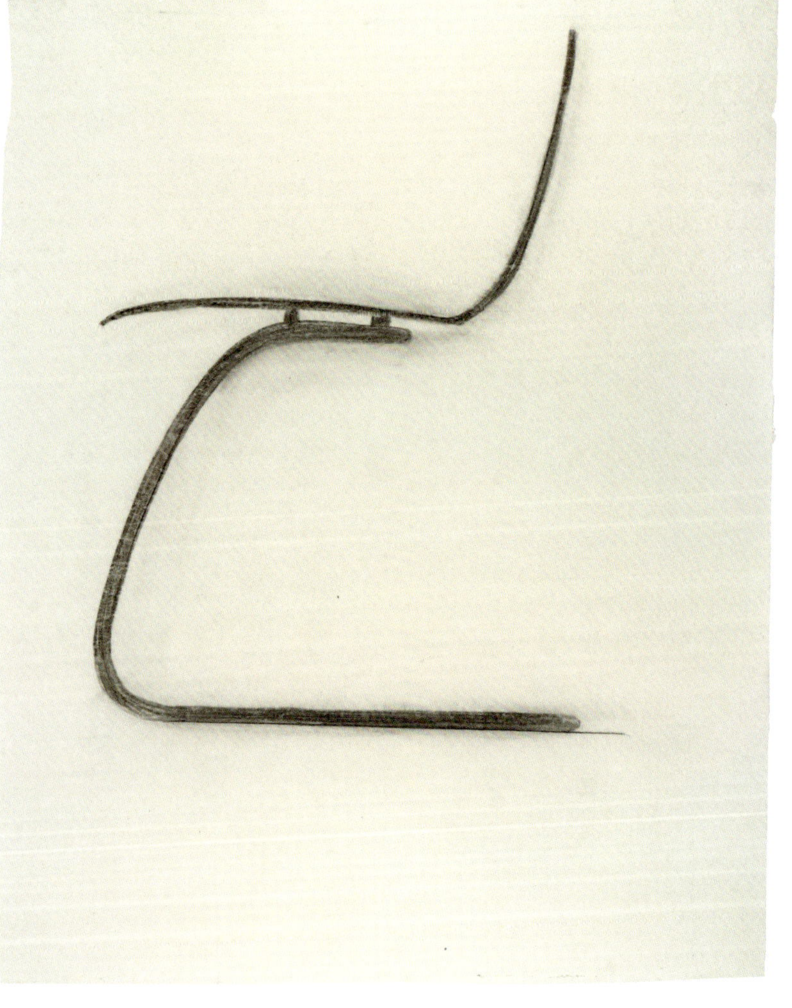

242
Ludwig Mies van der Rohe
Armchair (MR 20), table (MR 130) and stool, (MR1), 1927
Chair: nickel-plated steel and leather
Table: nickel-plated steel and glass
Stool: nickel-plated steel and leather
Stiftung Bauhaus Dessau

243
Lilly Reich
Design for a chair without arms, LR 120, c.1931
Charcoal on tracing paper
104.8 × 81.3 cm
The Museum of Modern Art, New York Lilly Reich Collection, Mies van der Rohe Archive

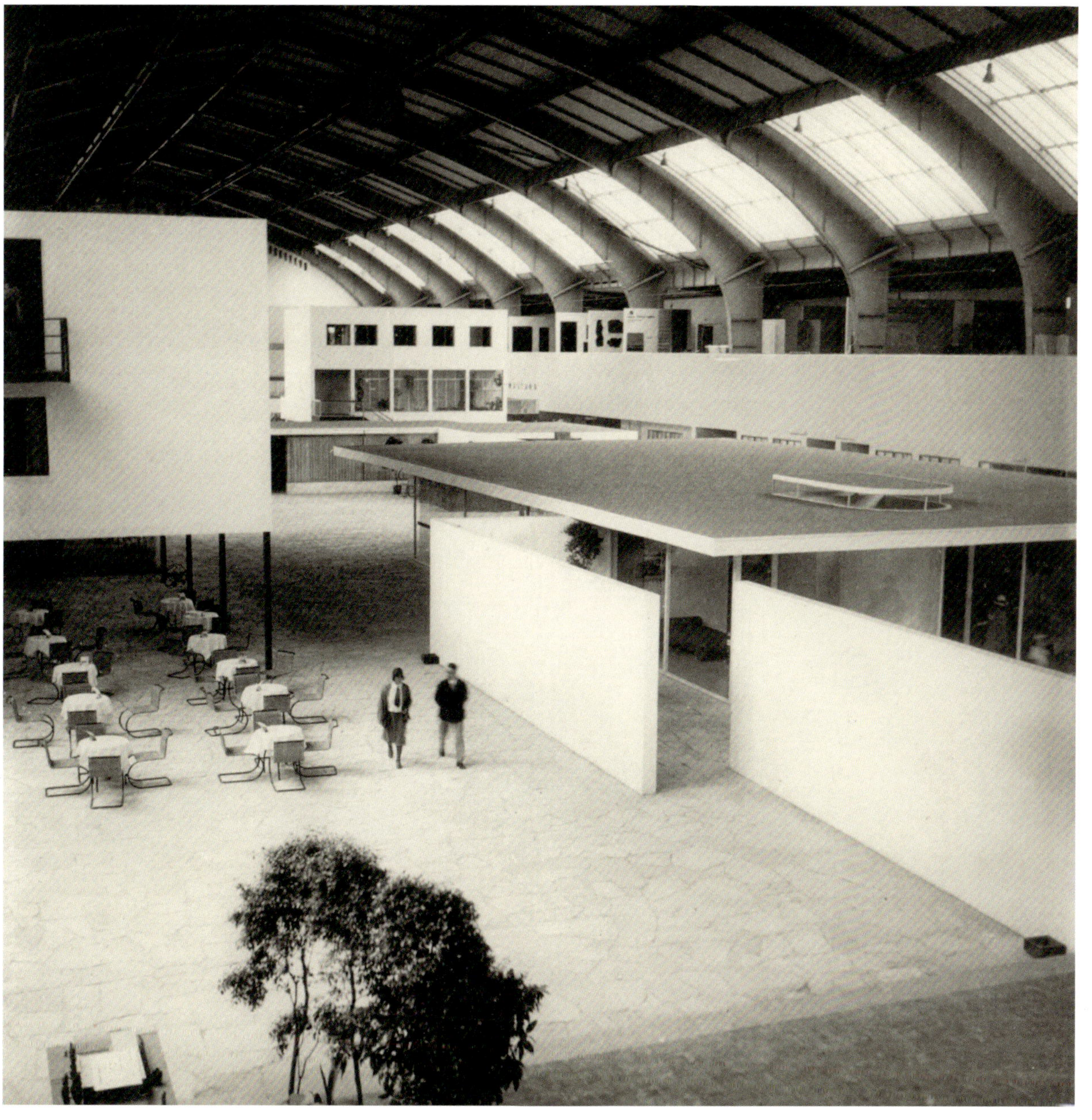

244
Display of *The Dwelling of our Time*
from the Deutsche Bauausstellung
Berlin, designed by Ludwig Mies van
der Rohe and Lily Reich at the Funkturm
Werkbund exhibition halls, 1931
22.8 × 21 cm
Gelatin silver print
Photographer: Berliner Bildbericht
On long-term loan from IRS – Instituts
für Photonenfotografie to Stiftung
Bauhaus Dessau

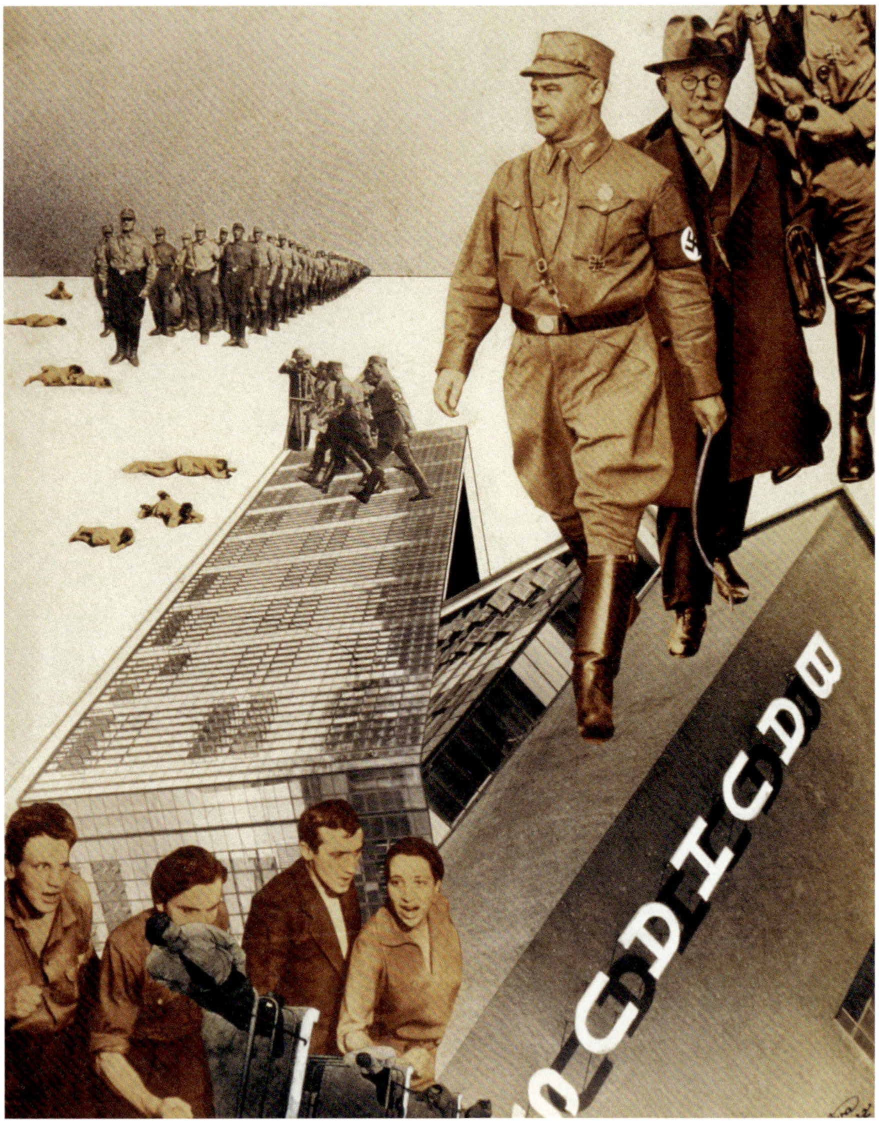

245
Iwao Yamawaki
Reproduction of the photocollage
Der Schlag gegen das Bauhaus
(*The Attack on the Bauhaus*),
from the magazine *Kokusai-Kenchiku*,
Tokyo, vol. 8, no. 12
December 1932
Letterpress
26 × 19.2 cm
Bauhaus-Archiv Berlin

In August 1932 the National Socialist German Workers' Party put forward a motion to close the Bauhaus, which passed with a majority vote and subsequently led to the closure of the school in Dessau. Although the director at the time, Mies van der Rohe attempted to run the school as a private institution in a disused telephone factory in Berlin, it was officially disbanded in July 1933. Yamawaki's bold photocollage foreshadows the demise of the school. The collaged figures of Nazi officials marching on Gropius's Dessau Bauhaus building is carefully constructed in a diagonal line to stress the urgent state in which the school found itself. The work also reflects Yamawaki's move towards photography, under the tutelage of Walter Peterhans and Kurt Kranz.

246
Wassily Kandinsky
Development in Brown, 1933
Oil on canvas
101 × 120.5 cm
Centre Pompidou, Paris.
Musée National d'Art Moderne/
Centre de Création Industrielle.
Purchased 1959
On long-term loan to
Musée Cantini, Marseille

Painted in the late stages of Kandinsky's tenure at the Bauhaus, this painting signals the end of the pioneering school and was completed in August 1933, a month after it was shut. The use of dark, sombre colours evokes the dire political circumstances that resulted in its closure. The central white opening, with the upward spiral of balanced triangles, however, can be seen as an allegory of hope and future direction. By the mid-1930s, many leading Bauhaus figures had departed Germany, setting the stage for the international dissemination of Bauhaus ideals. The formal aspects of the painting, moreover, reveal the influence of photography during that time. Here, Kandinsky transposes the effects of Moholy-Nagy's photograms by masking sections of the composition and airbrushing the surface of the canvas.

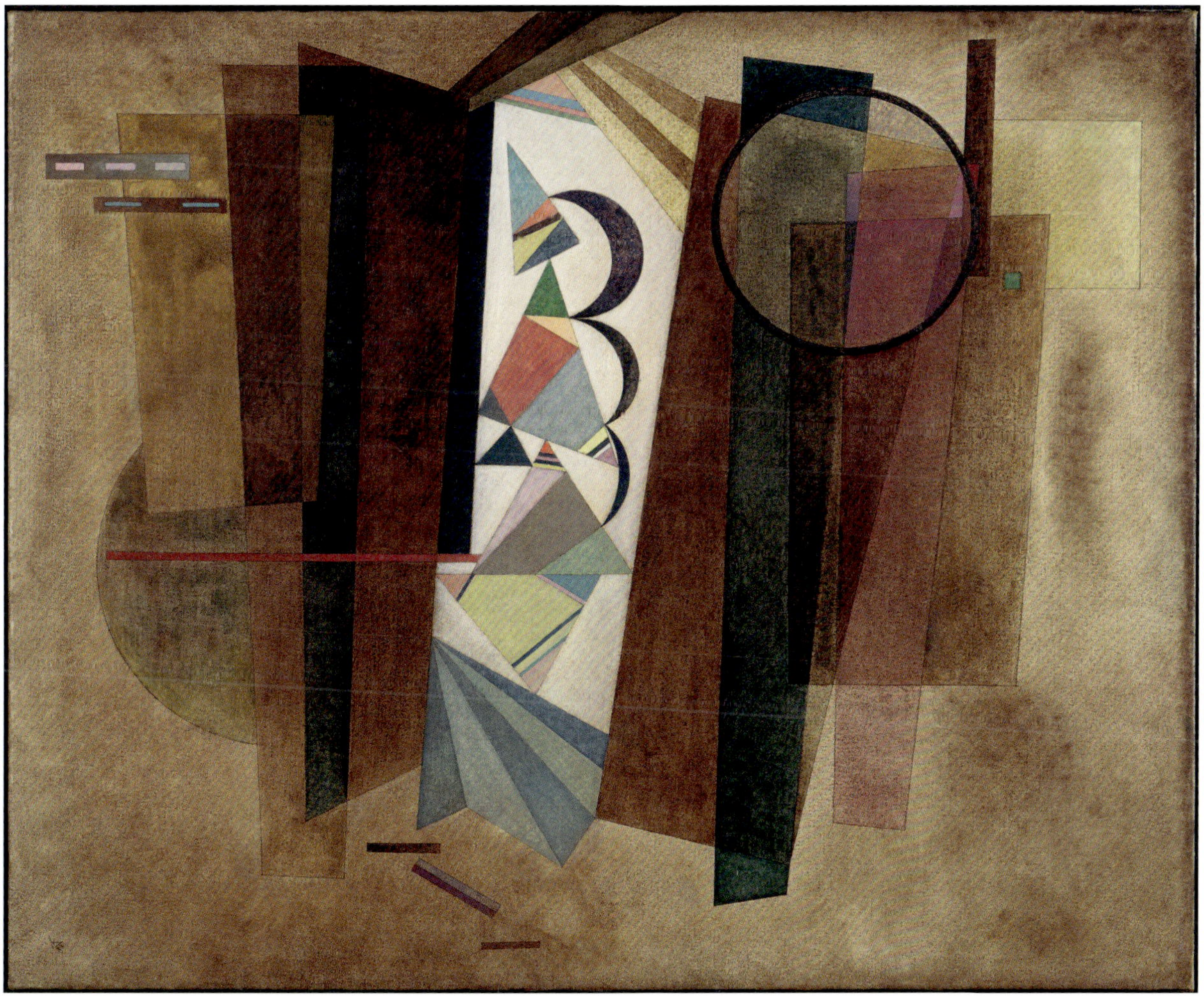

ludwig mies van der rohe
announcement to the students of the dissolution of the bauhaus

To the students of the Bauhaus. 10 August, 1933

At its last meeting, the faculty resolved to dissolve the Bauhaus. The reason for this decision was the difficult economic situation of the institute.

The Office of the State Secret Police, the Prussian Ministry for Science, Art, and Education, and the school administration have been informed of this decision.

This announcement has crossed with a notification by the Office of the State Secret Police in which we are told that 'in agreement with the Prussian Minister for Science, Art, and Education, the reopening of the Bauhaus is made dependent upon the removal of some objections.'

We would have agreed to these conditions, but the economic situation does not allow for a continuation of the Institute.

The members of the faculty are of course available to the students for advice at any time.

Grade records for all students will be issued by the secretariat.

From now on please address all letters to Professor Mies van der Rohe, Berlin W 35, Am Karlsbad 24.

Last leaflet distributed to Bauhaus students, 10 August, 1933

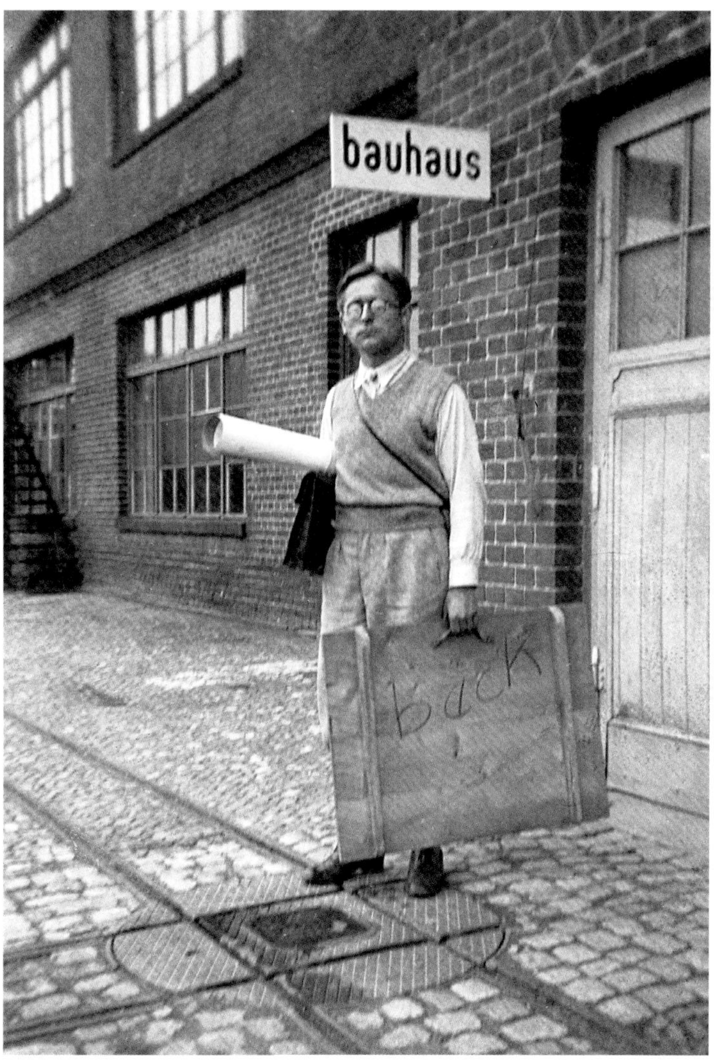

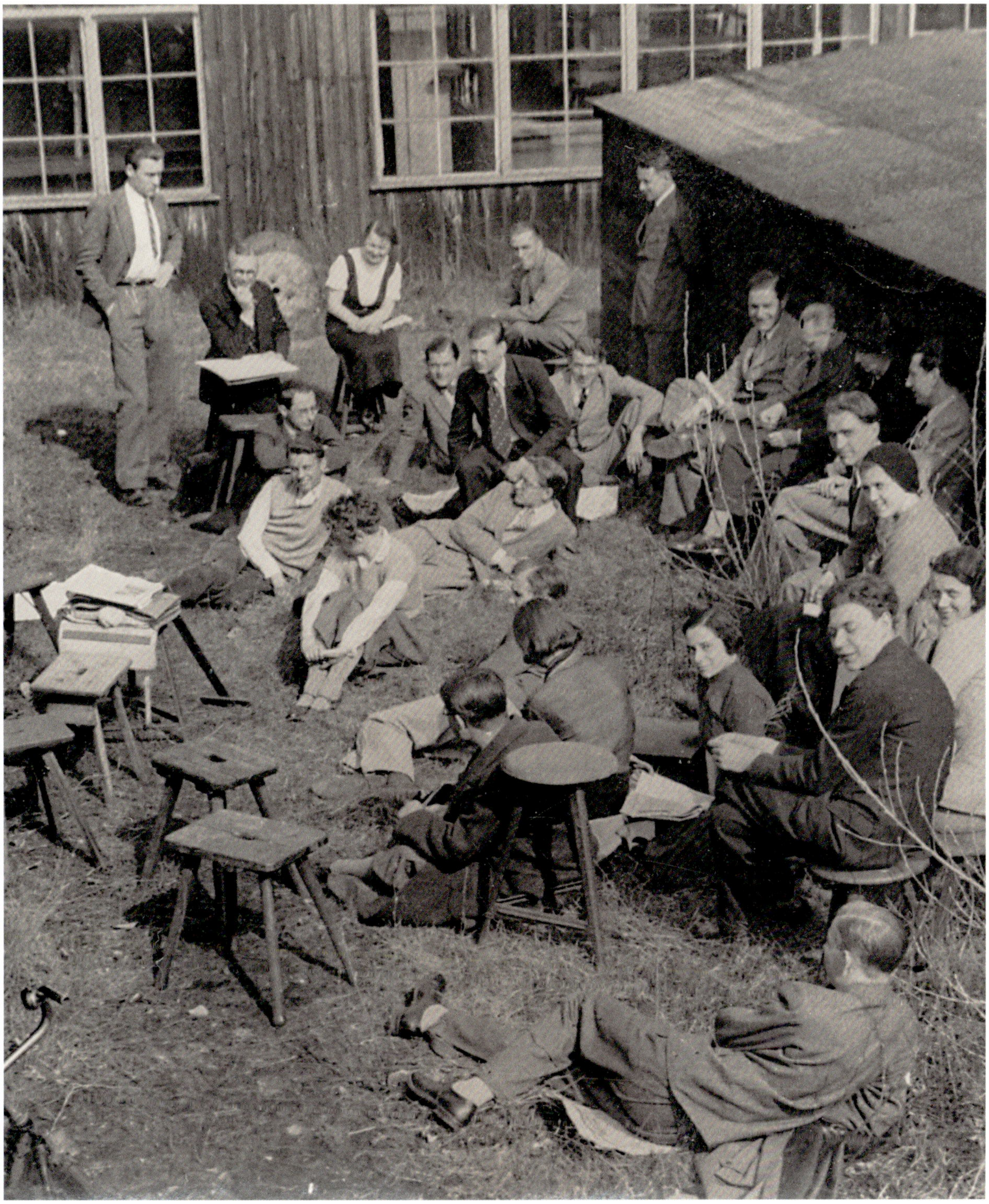

247
Ernst Louis Beck at the entrance of
the Bauhaus building in Berlin, 1932–33
Bauhaus-Archiv Berlin
Photographer unknown

248
Pius Pahl
Conference held following the
temporary closure
of the Bauhaus in April 1933
Bauhaus-Archiv Berlin

credits

Every effort has been made to trace copyright holders and to obtain their permission for the use of copyright material. The following list is ordered by source and copyright holder.

Courtesy Bauhaus-Archiv Berlin: pp. 11 (Estate Hannes Meyer), 12, 14 (Photographer Atelier Schneider, © DACS 2012), 21, 22 (© Gerhard-Marcks-Stiftung, Bremen, 2012), 26 (top: Estate Rudolf Baschant, bottom: © DACS 2012), 27, 28 (© DACS 2012), 29, 30 (© DACS 2012), 32 (© DACS 2012), 38 (bottom), 40 (bottom: Photographer Markus Hawlik, Estate Otto Werner), 42, 44, 45 (top and bottom), 46 (top), 50 (top), 52, 55 (top: Photographer Gunter Lepkowski, Estate Naum Slutzky), 56 (bottom: Photographer Markus Hawlik, Estate Anni Wottitz), 57 (Estate Marcel Breuer), 60, 62 (top: Estate Lena Meyer-Bergner, bottom: Photographer Markus Hawlik), 63 (© DACS 2012), 67 (Estate Xanti Schawinsky), 71 (top: Photographer Markus Hawlik), 74 (© DACS 2012), 76 (Estate Fritz Schleifer), 84 (Estate Kurt Schmidt), 85 (Photographer Markus Hawlik, © DACS 2012), 86 (© DACS 2012), 92 (Photographer Gunter Lepkowski, Estate Lothar Schreyer), 94 (top, bottom: Estate Kurt Schmidt), 98 (Photographer Gunter Lepkowski, Estate Eberhard Schrammen), 103 (top: © DACS 2012), 104 (both: © DACS 2012), 110 (© Hattula Moholy-Nagy/DACS 2012), 111 (© DACS 2012), 116 (© DACS 2012), 119 (bottom: © DACS 2012), 130–31 (Estate Hinnerk Scheper), 136-37 (© Société Kandinsky), 139 (top: © DACS, 2012, bottom: Estate Erich Consemüller), 140 (© DACS 2012), 141 (bottom), 142 (top), 142 (bottom: © DACS 2012), 147, 151–53 (© Estate T. Lux Feininger) 157, 158–59 (© DACS 2012), 160 (© Hattula Moholy-Nagy/DACS 2012), 161 (© DACS 2012), 167 (Photographer Markus Hawlik, © DACS 2012), 168–69 (© DACS 2012), 170–71 (Photographer Markus Hawlik, © DACS 2012), 172 (Photographer Markus Hawlik, Estate Edmund Collein), 174 (Photothek Berlin, © bpk Berlin), 175–76 (© DACS 2012), 178 (bottom: © DACS 2012), 179, 180, 182, 183 (© DACS 2012), 188 (© DACS 2012), 189, 190 (© DACS 2012), 194 (top), 207, 212 (Estate Marcel Breuer), 215 (top), 216, 217 (bottom), 218 (bottom: Estate Erich Consemüller), 219, 225 (Estate Marcel Breuer), 226 (top), 227 (© Robert Schürmann), 229 (© The Josef and Anni Albers Foundation/VG Bild-Kunst, Bonn and DACS, London 2012), 232–34 (© DACS 2012), 236 (© ARS, NY and DACS, London, 2012), 242 (bottom), 255 (top: Estate Charlotte Voepel), 262 (© DACS 2012), 263 (©Phyllis Umbehr/Galerie Kicken Berlin/DACS 2012), 264 (both: Estate Walter Peterhans, Museum Folkwang Essen), 266 (© Estate Robert Schürmann), 268, 269, 270 (©Phyllis Umbehr/Galerie Kicken Berlin/DACS 2012), 271, 278–79 (Estate Pius Pahl), 282 (Estate Iwao Yamawaki), 284, 285 (Estate Pius Pahl);

Courtesy Klassik Stiftung Weimar, Bestand Museen: pp. 38 (top left: Estate Theodor Bogler, top right: Estate Otto Lindig), 39 (Estate Otto Lindig), 40 (top), 43, 48, 53, 54 (bottom: © DACS 2012, Estate Wolfgang Rössger), 70 (Estate Peter Keler), 102 (top and bottom: © Benediktinerabtei Maria Laach), 103 (bottom: © Benediktinerabtei Maria Laach), 106, 107 (© DACS 2012), 117 (top: © DACS 2012) 154, 193 and 226 (bottom: Estate Erich Consemüller);

Courtesy Stiftung Bauhaus Dessau: pp. 87 (Photographer Kelly Kellerhoff, 1994, © DACS 2012), 96 (© DACS 2012), 108 (© Hattula Moholy-Nagy/DACS 2012), 117 (bottom: © DACS 2012), 119 (top: © DACS 2012), 120 (© Hattula Moholy-Nagy/DACS 2012), 122 (© DACS 2012), 123 (both: Estate Hannes Meyer), 128 (Kelly Kellerhoff 1993, © DACS 2012), 141 (top: © DACS 2012), 144–145 (Estate Hannes Meyer), 146 (Estate Fritz Schreiber), 242 (top), 243 (© Gisela Kaiser), 277 (both: Estate Hannes Meyer), 280 (top: © DACS 2012), 281 (© DACS, 2012, © Ingeborg Reich);

© 2012 Oskar Schlemmer, Bühnen Archiv Oskar Schlemmer, The Oskar Schlemmer Theatre Estate and Archive. Secretariat: IT–28824 Oggebbio, Italy, www.schlemmer.org. Photo Archive C. Raman Schlemmer, IT–28824 Oggebbio (VB), Italy: pp. 41 (top), 77, 93, 177, 192 (bottom), 193 (bottom), 194 (bottom), 195, 199, 205 (top), 206 (both); © 2012 C. Raman Schlemmer: pp. 194 and 207 (texts);

reprinted texts

© Gerhard-Marcks-Stiftung, Bremen, 2012: p.23;
Karl Peter Röhl Stiftung, Weimar: p.24;
Photographer Bernd Kirtz: pp.25 (© DACS 2012), 197 (© Schlemmer Family Estate);
© 2012. Digital image, The Museum of Modern Art, New York/Scala, Florence: pp.58–59 (© DACS 2012), 71, 125 (bottom), 173, 192 (top), 280 (bottom: © Ingeborg Reich);
Photographer Frank Höhler: p.66 (top: Estate Kurt Schmidt);
© Die Neue Sammlung: pp.66 (bottom: Photographer A. Laurenzo, © DACS 2012), 99 (© DACS 2012), 100 (Photographer A. Laurenzo, Estate Ludwig Hirschfeld-Mack), 101 (Photographer: A. Laurenzo, © DACS 2012);
© Hattula Moholy-Nagy/DACS 2012: pp.73, 75, 211, 244, 252–53;
Imaging Department © President and Fellows of Harvard College: pp.90 (© DACS 2012), 124 (© DACS 2012), 195, 204 (Photographer Allan Macintyre, © DACS 2012), 218 (top: © DACS 2012);
Estate Kurt Schwerdtfeger: p.95;
© Collection Centre Pompidou, Dist. RMN/ Jacques Faujour: pp.97 (© DACS 2012), 254 (© Hattula Moholy-Nagy/DACS 2012),
© DACS 2012: pp.72, 105 (both), 108 (bottom), 205 (bottom), 209 (both), 210, 241, 246–47;
Private collection. Courtesy Neue Galerie, New York: p.121;
© The Josef and Anni Albers Foundation/VG Bild-Kunst, Bonn and DACS, London 2012: pp.125 (top), 135, 162–163, 220, 237;
Estate Iwao Yamawaki: pp.138, 267;
© Tate, London, 2012: p.156 (Estate Iwao Yamawaki);
© Weininger Foundation, Inc. / DACS, London/VAGA, New York, 2012: p.208;
© Phyllis Umbehr/Galerie Kicken Berlin/DACS 2012: p.214;
© Victoria and Albert Museum, London: pp.224 (Estate Marcel Breuer), 255 (bottom: © Hattula Moholy-Nagy/DACS 2012), 261 (© Galleria Martini & Ronchetti, Genoa, Italy);
© Estate Kurt Kranz: p.248;
© Collection Centre Pompidou, Dist. RMN/Philippe Migeat: p.260 (© Galleria Martini & Ronchetti, Genoa, Italy);
© Estate Theo Ballmer: p.265;
© Collection Centre Pompidou, Dist. RMN/ Jean-Claude Planchet: p.283 (© DACS 2012).

Pages: 15–17, 61, 77, 85, 118, 126–27, 181, 196, 230–31, 284
Hans M. Wingler (ed.), *Bauhaus Weimar, Dessau, Berlin, Chicago*, 1969: pp.31, 57, 74, 76, 78, 89, 157, 161, and 189
© 1969 Massachusetts Institute of Technology, with permission of The MIT Press.
Page 196: with kind permission of Bühnen Archive Oskar Schlemmer/The Oskar Schlemmer Theatre Estate, C. Raman Schlemmer

Page 51: Moniker Stadler and Yael Aloni (ed.), *Gunta Stölzl: A Bauhaus Master*, 2009: p.45, With permission of Hatje Cantz Verlag and Estate Gunta Stölzl.

Pages 144–45: Bauhaus Dessau 'Komm ans Bauhaus Dessau'. With permission of Stiftung Bauhaus Dessau and Estate Hannes Meyer.

Page 224: Edward Dimendberg, Martin Jay and Anton Kaes (eds), *The Weimar Republic Sourcebook*, 1994: p.453
© University California Press and Estate Marcel Breuer.

Pages 250–51: Christopher Phillips (ed.), *Photography in the Modern Era: European Documents and Critical Writings, 1913–1940*, 1989: pp.83–85. With permission of The Metropolitan Museum of Art/Aperture, New York and Hattula Moholy-Nagy.

First published in May 2012 by Koenig Books London, in association with Barbican Art Gallery on the occasion of the exhibition *Bauhaus: Art as Life*, curated by Catherine Ince and Lydia Yee, 3 May – 12 August, 2012.

Barbican Art Gallery
Barbican Centre
Silk Street
London EC2Y 8DS
barbican.org.uk

Koenig Books Ltd
at the Serpentine Gallery
Kensington Gardens
London W2 3XA
koenigbooks.co.uk

exhibition

Head of Art Galleries
Kate Bush
Curators
Catherine Ince
Lydia Yee
Assistant Curators
Leila Hasham
Corinna Gardner
Exhibition Assistant
Juliette Desorgues

A Barbican Art Gallery exhibition in co-operation with Bauhaus-Archiv Berlin /Museum für Gestaltung, Stiftung Bauhaus Dessau and Klassik Stiftung Weimar.

Exhibition design
Carmody Groarke
Exhibition graphic design
A Practice for Everyday Life

catalogue

Catalogue texts
Juliette Desorgues, Corinna Gardner, Leila Hasham, Catherine Ince and Lydia Yee
Copy editor
Melissa Larner
Translator
Elizabeth Volk
Design
A Practice for Everyday Life
Produced, printed and bound
DZA Druckerei zu Altenburg GmbH, Germany

Front cover
Erich Consemüller, Lis Beyer or Ise Gropius sitting on the B3 club chair by Marcel Breuer and wearing a mask by Oskar Schlemmer and a dress fabric designed by Beyer, c.1927
Herzogenrath, Berlin
© Estate Erich Consemüller

Back cover
T. Lux Feininger
The jump over the Bauhaus/ Sport at the Bauhaus, c.1927
Bauhaus-Archiv Berlin
© Estate T. Lux Feininger

Title page
Bauhauslers inside and in front of the Prellerhaus, 1927
Bauhaus-Archiv Berlin
Photographer unknown

distribution

Buchhandlung
Walther König, Köln
Ehrenstr. 4, 50672 Köln
T. +49 (0) 221 20 59 653
F. +49 (0) 221 20 59 660
verlag@buchhandlung-walther-koenig.de

Distribution outside the United States and Canada, Germany, Austria and Switzerland by Thames and Hudson Ltd, London
www.thamesandhudson.com

US and Canada
D.A.P./Distributed Art Publishers, Inc.
155 6th Avenue, 2nd Floor
New York, NY 10013
T. +1 212 627 1999
F. +1 212 627 9484
eleshowitz@dapinc.com

British Library Cataloguing-in-Publication Data: a catalogue record for this book is available from the British Library.

ISBN 978-3-86335-163-2

catalogue supported by

EvS
ERNST VON SIEMENS KUNSTSTIFTUNG

exhibition supported by

tp bennett
swiss arts council prohelvetia
The Henry Moore Foundation
STANLEY THOMAS JOHNSON FOUNDATION

media partner

Wallpaper*